Enoch O. Aboh, Eric Haeberli, Genoveva Puskás, Manuela Schönenberger (Eds.)
Elements of Comparative Syntax

Studies in Generative Grammar

Editors
Norbert Corver
Harry van der Hulst
Roumyana Pancheva

Founding editors
Jan Koster
Henk van Riemsdijk

Volume 127

Elements of Comparative Syntax

—

Theory and Description

Edited by
Enoch O. Aboh
Eric Haeberli
Genoveva Puskás
Manuela Schönenberger

DE GRUYTER
MOUTON

ISBN 978-1-5015-1893-5
e-ISBN (PDF) 978-1-5015-0403-7
e-ISBN (EPUB) 978-1-5015-0397-9
ISSN 0167-4331

Library of Congress Cataloging-in-Publication Data
A CIP catalog record for this book has been applied for at the Library of Congress.

Bibliographic information published by the Deutsche Nationalbibliothek
The Deutsche Nationalbibliothek lists this publication in the Deutsche Nationalbibliografie;
detailed bibliographic data are available on the Internet at http://dnb.dnb.de.

© 2019 Walter de Gruyter Inc., Boston/Berlin
This volume is text- and page-identical with the hardback published in 2017.
Typesetting: Compuscript Ltd., Shannon, Ireland
Printing and binding: CPI books GmbH, Leck
♾ Printed on acid-free paper
Printed in Germany

www.degruyter.com

This book is dedicated to Liliane Haegeman, a colleague, friend, and mentor, in appreciation of her extensive contribution to the field of comparative syntax.

Contents

Enoch O. Aboh, Eric Haeberli, Genoveva Puskás, Manuela Schönenberger
1　Introduction —— 1

Part I: Comparative syntax: Focus on one language

Adriana Belletti
2　Labeling (Romance) causatives —— 13

Marcel den Dikken
3　Quantifier float and predicate inversion —— 47

Jacqueline Guéron
4　Beyond narrative: On the syntax and semantics of ly-Adverbs —— 57

Jim McCloskey
5　Ellipsis, polarity, and the cartography of verb-initial orders in Irish —— 99

Genoveva Puskás
6　Negation and modality: On negative purposive and "avertive" complementizers —— 153

Manuela Schönenberger
7　Are doubly-filled COMPs governed by prosody in Swiss German? The chameleonic nature of *dass* 'that' —— 185

Raffaella Zanuttini
8　Presentatives and the syntactic encoding of contextual information —— 221

Part II: Comparative syntax: Cross-linguistic studies

Enoch O. Aboh and Thom Westveer
9　On reflexives with an object in French, German, and Gungbe —— 259

Virginia Hill
10　A micro-parameter for allocutive agreement —— 283

Kathleen M. O'Connor
11 Apposition in English and French —— 299

Luigi Rizzi
12 Locality and the functional sequence in the left periphery —— 319

Ur Shlonsky
13 Wh in situ and criterial freezing —— 349

Sten Vikner
14 Germanic verb particle variation —— 371

Part III: Comparative syntax: Language acquisition and change

Lieven Danckaert
15 The loss of Latin OV: Steps towards an analysis —— 401

Eric Haeberli
16 Medial NP-adjuncts in English: A diachronic perspective —— 447

Eric Lander
17 Gothic *sai* and the Proto-Germanic verb-based discourse particle **se* —— 477

Terje Lohndal and Rosalind Thornton
18 The 3SGS morpheme in child and adult English: A formal analysis —— 499

Index —— 529

Enoch O. Aboh, Eric Haeberli, Genoveva Puskás,
Manuela Schönenberger

Introduction

The starting point of this volume was the intention of the editors to publish a collection of articles in honour of Liliane Haegeman for her contribution to the field of comparative syntax. A small number of friends and colleagues were invited to contribute to this volume, and the outcome of this selection process, which, from a scientific point of view, was fairly random, provides an excellent testimony of the way in which the field of comparative generative syntax has developed from the beginning of Liliane Haegeman's academic career in the late 1970s to today. These developments are reflected in the empirical basis of generative theorizing as well as the theoretical issues that are addressed in current work, and they illustrate how "[i]n this new comparative syntax, careful study of empirical data takes a central position with a stimulating two-way interaction between theoretical developments and empirical study" (Haegeman 1997a: 1).

Since the emergence of generative grammar in the middle of the 20th century, its aim has been to provide an explanatory model of grammatical competence and thereby to gain a deeper understanding of the nature of the human language faculty. Initially, this aim was pursued by examining evidence from a very limited number of languages, with standard English playing the most prominent role. This empirical bias is shown for example in the contributions to the first two volumes of *Linguistic Inquiry* (1970, 1971). Leaving aside work focussing on phonology and morphology, we observe that nearly three fourths of all research papers dealing with transformational grammar contain data that are exclusively drawn from English. Similarly, among over 70 squibs published, only 9 contain data from a language other than English. This empirical focus on a single language can be justified by the complexity of the task of providing a complete account of a speaker's knowledge of that language, but also in view of identifying the properties of Universal Grammar (UG), the genetic endowment for language hypothesized within the generative framework. According to the 'poverty of the stimulus' argument, aspects of linguistic competence that cannot be derived from the language learner's input must be attributed to properties of UG. To identify such properties, evidence from a single language is arguably sufficient.

However, since the mid-70s, generative work has considerably expanded its empirical scope. Increasing attention has been paid to other languages not only to test earlier theoretical proposals made on the basis of English but also to gain a better understanding of what is common to all languages and what the dimensions are along which they may vary. The present volume illustrates how rich and diversified the empirical basis of generative theorizing has become. Although English has maintained a prominent role (cf. e.g. the contributions by den Dikken, Guéron, O'Connor), other languages have been studied in depth by now, in particular members of the Germanic and Romance families (Vikner; Belletti, Rizzi, Shlonsky, Zanuttini). But generative studies now also cover such typologically diverse languages as Albanian (Hill), Gungbe (Aboh and Westveer), Hungarian (Puskás) or Irish (McCloskey). The last 40 years have also seen an increasing interest in empirical evidence from non-standard varieties (Schönenberger), language acquisition (Lohndal and Thornton), and language change (Danckaert, Haeberli, Lander). Finally, more recently, a certain diversification also emerged with respect to data collection. While the traditional generative method of collecting grammaticality judgments from a few native speakers may remain predominant, increasing numbers of studies also turn to various types of experimental evidence (illustrated in this volume in the acquisition context of Lohndal and Thornton's paper), naturally occurring examples (O'Connor, McCloskey) and corpus data (Schönenberger, and, by necessity, studies with a diachronic dimension [Danckaert, Haeberli, Hill, Lander]). Overall, whatever one's theoretical persuasion, there can be little argument that comparative generative syntax over the last 40 years has unearthed a wealth of empirical insights that is unparalleled in its breadth and depth.

Liliane Haegeman's early career coincides with the publication of Chomsky (1981), which gave rise to what is now generally referred to as the Principles and Parameters approach. Principles capture the syntactic properties common to all languages whereas parameters define areas of variation. The increasing interest in comparative syntax observed above has been closely linked to the goal of identifying the nature of syntactic parametrization. To pursue this goal, it has turned out to be useful not only to compare typologically diverse languages but also to analyze small-scale variation in very closely related languages or dialects (microcomparative syntax), the idea being that new insights can be gained into the mechanisms of variation if minor contrasts in otherwise very similar grammars are examined (see, for instance, Richard Kayne's seminal work since the 1970s).

Even though the basic theoretical tenets outlined in Chomsky (1981) still guide current work in generative syntax, the overall model of the grammar has undergone considerable changes (cf. e.g. Chomsky 1995). The studies included in this volume provide a good overview of the major areas in which the Principles and Parameters framework has developed over the last few decades. One important domain of research has focused on determining the exact shape of the clause structure (McCloskey, O'Connor, Rizzi). Furthermore, the concept of movement, which has been central within the generative framework since its beginnings, has been re-evaluated in much recent research, with new hypotheses emerging as to what triggers, constrains and undergoes movement (Belletti, Danckaert, Rizzi, Shlonsky). Generative work since the 1980s has also been characterized by increased attention to interface issues. Various studies have been exploring the interface between syntax and semantics/discourse (Hill, Zanuttini) and the interface between syntax and phonology (Lohndal and Thornton, Schönenberger). Finally, our understanding of a wide range of syntactic issues has been improved through detailed investigations presenting new evidence on long-standing topics such as reflexives (Aboh and Westveer), floating quantifiers (den Dikken), adjuncts (Guéron, Haeberli), grammaticalization (Lander), negation (Puskás), or particles (Vikner).

Like many researchers working within the field of comparative generative syntax, Liliane Haegeman has been pursuing, as one of our contributors succinctly puts it, the goal of "meld[ing] the descriptive care and attention to detail to be found in the best philological work with the intellectual daring and rigor to be found in the best generative work".[1] A highly successful linguist in this enterprise, Liliane Haegeman has made important contributions to many of the empirical and theoretical domains mentioned above. On the empirical side, she was one of the first generative researchers exploring the syntax of a non-standard variety, West Flemish, in depth (Haegeman 1984, 1992[2]). But many other languages are covered in her work as well, with English featuring most prominently (Haegeman 2012). Liliane Haegeman has also extended her research to domains such as first language acquisition (Haegeman 1995a), second language acquisition (Haegeman 1985) or register variation (Haegeman 1987, 1997). Having started her career with corpus-based descriptive work (Haegeman 1983, which draws on material from the *Survey of English Usage*), she has always been aware of the value of naturally occurring data and has used them extensively in her work.

Liliane Haegeman has played an important role in several of the theoretical debates that have marked the development of generative syntax over the last few decades. Topics addressed in her research include the properties of movement in the contexts of negation (Haegeman 1995b) or the left periphery (Haegeman 2012), the structural analysis of verb-final word order (Haegeman 2001), and aspects of the syntax-discourse interface (Haegeman 2014). Furthermore, Liliane Haegeman's work has provided new insights into a wide range of phenomena such as cliticization (Haegeman 1993), complementizer agreement (Haegeman 1992),

---

[1] https://people.ucsc.edu/~mcclosk/work.html
[2] Here and below only selected references are mentioned.

double object constructions (Haegeman 1986), and Verb (Projection) Raising (Haegeman and van Riemsdijk 1986, Haegeman 1994).

It is not possible, within a few paragraphs, to do justice to the full scope and impact of Liliane Haegeman's research as presented in her approximately 200 single- and co-authored publications. Even a brief overview of Liliane Haegeman's work should not omit the substantial pedagogical contribution that she has made to the field of comparative syntax. Her unique ability to make theoretical concepts accessible to the beginning student and to transmit her enthusiasm for the subject have made her not only an inspiring teacher but also a successful author of textbooks (Haegeman 1991, Haegeman and Guéron 1999, Haegeman 2006). A considerable number of today's researchers were first exposed to the excitement of doing comparative generative syntax in courses based on Liliane Haegeman's textbooks. As for the editors of this volume, who also had the privilege of being her students, it is quite likely that they would not be doing what they have the pleasure of doing today had it not been for Liliane's pedagogical skills and her enthusiasm for comparative syntax.

The contributions in this volume are divided into three major parts, the divisions being based on the empirical material covered by the studies. Part I includes papers treating aspects of the syntax of a specific language. Although the focus of these studies is primarily on one language, the analyses proposed also integrate, to a greater or lesser extent, comparative considerations. **Adriana Belletti** (Chapter 2 – *Labeling (Romance) causatives*) discusses causatives with a focus on Italian and observes that causatives in different languages typically involve displacement of constituents of different kinds: a verbal constituent in Romance/Italian-type languages and a DP in English-type languages. She takes the fundamental labeling requirement to be the driving force behind the derivation of causatives and suggests that the movement-triggering property of the causative head is parametrized. In languages like Italian a chunk of the verb phrase is attracted by the criterial causative voice head and undergoes movement of the *smuggling* type. The constituent remaining after movement is labeled as DP. In English-type languages the constituent that is attracted is the DP external argument of the lexical verb rather than a vP-chunk, which yields labeling of the remaining constituent as vP.

Marcel den Dikken (Chapter 3 – *Quantifier float and predicate inversion*) explores the internal structure of the floating quantifier *all*. He takes as a starting point the observation that a quantifier can float off a nominal subject of predication, while, in very similar conditions, quantifier float is blocked with predicate nominals. He argues that this contrast derives from the internal composition of the quantified expression. Adopting Doetjes' analysis, which essentially argues that floating quantifiers contain a silent (pro)nominal element, den Dikken proposes that the null nominal element is a PRO, which stands in a control relation with the nominal the quantifier is associated with.

Jacqueline Guéron (Chapter 4 – *Beyond narrative: On the syntax and semantics of ly-Adverbs*) discusses the interpretation and syntactic distribution of adverbials, focusing on the set of adverbs formed with *-ly* in English. She shows that many of these adverbials exhibit various construal possibilities and may occupy various syntactic positions. Rather than assuming a unique position/interpretation for each of the possible occurrences of adverbials, she proposes that they adjoin to different functional projections. The adverbials contribute aspectual as well as descriptive content to the maximal projection to which they adjoin, and may modify the truth conditions of the sentence. The *-ly* suffix of these adverbials is argued to carry a formal Tense feature which needs to be checked via adjunction of the adverbial to a maximal projection bearing the same formal feature. Any maximal projection which is marked with this feature within what Guéron calls the sentential T(-ense) chain is a potential host. As opposed to a Cinquean hierarchy for adverbials, she thus defends an adjunction approach based on semantic contribution.

Jim McCloskey (Chapter 5 – *Ellipsis, polarity, and the cartography of verb-initial orders in Irish*) offers a new analysis of word order in Irish according to which basic VSO order involves verb movement to a high functional head right below C, labeled Pol(arity)P. This proposal is supported by several empirical observations related to ellipsis in responses to yes-no questions (Responsive Ellipsis), the distribution of negation in finite and non-finite clauses, the licensing of NPIs, or Verum Focus interpretations of the verb. In addition, McCloskey postulates two tense heads, one below PolP and one above, with the higher head hosting copular-like elements and preverbal tense particles. This enriched structure enables him to account for various seemingly disjoint phenomena such as the lack of subject agreement in copular constructions or the requirement of strict verbal identity in ellipsis. McCloskey argues that his account of the verbal syntax in Irish provides support for the hypothesis that at least some instances of head movement are post-syntactic.

Genoveva Puskás (Chapter 6 – *Negation and modality: On negative purposive and "avertive" complementizers*) proposes a new account of a phenomenon at the crossroads between complementation and negation in Hungarian. Arguing against the standard view that the (purposive) complementizer + sentential negation constructions can freely alternate with a complementizer which incorporates the negation, she shows that they have to be treated as two distinct phenomena. While the "comp + neg" indeed realizes purposive clauses with sentential negation, the "incorporated" version is a different complementizer. It heads "avertive" clauses, which express a negative bouletic modality (of not wishing). Puskás proposes that the two "complementizers" share common features, but that the avertive COMP is morphologically more complex and crucially does not involve sentential negation. Therefore, it blocks selection from a higher predicate, does not license n-words and does not trigger verb-particle inversion typical of sentential negation.

Manuela Schönenberger (Chapter 7 – *Are doubly-filled COMPs governed by prosody in Swiss German? The chameleonic nature of* dass *'that'*) examines the distribution of doubly-filled COMPs in wh-complement clauses in spontaneous production data from a variety of Swiss German. In these data, clauses introduced by a monosyllabic wh-constituent generally occur without *dass*, while those with non-monosyllabic wh-constituents mostly occur with *dass*. She tries to show that a purely syntactic approach cannot account for the data and suggests that prosody plays a decisive role in determining the presence/absence of *dass* in wh-complement clauses. In particular, she argues against a syntactic analysis proposed elsewhere in the literature, in which short wh-constituents such as *was* 'what' are assumed to be complementizers in C, and defends the traditional view according to which these short wh-constituents are phrasal.

Raffaella Zanuttini (Chapter 8 – *Presentatives and the left periphery*) examines utterances referred to as 'presentatives', such as *Ecco Liliane* 'Here's Liliane', that are attested in various languages, and addresses the question whether information regarding the time and the location of the speaker could ever be encoded in the syntax. Information necessary to interpret indexicals such as 'I' and 'here' is usually assumed to be provided by the context of utterance rather than by the syntax itself. Zanuttini argues that presentatives, which generally have the interpretation of 'here and now', have clausal structure, and that Italian *ecco* spells out features that provide information about time and place of the utterance. By highlighting subtle differences in interpretation between presentatives with *ecco* and a certain locative construction in Italian, so-called *ci*-sentences, which seem to differ minimally, she arrives at a refinement of the structure underlying presentatives.

The papers included in Part II of this volume focus on cross-linguistic evidence in order to shed light on various syntactic phenomena and their theoretical analysis. **Enoch O. Aboh and Thom Westveer** (Chapter 9 – *On reflexives with an object in French, German and Gungbe*) argue that reflexives with an internal argument involve dative constructions in which the verb has a benefactive thematic role to discharge, but the relevant argument is missing. As a result, this thematic role is bundled together with the Agent role, while the dative case is absorbed in syntax by the so-called reflexive pronoun merged in Voice (*se* in French), or in [Spec VoiceP] (*sich* in German). The analysis extends to Gungbe (Kwa) bare reflexive constructions, even though this language involves a single bare internal argument only and no reflexive pronoun is overtly realized in the sentence. This, the authors argue, results from the fact that Gungbe exhibits a null pronoun that merges in Voice, similarly to French *se*.

Virginia Hill (Chapter 10 – *A micro-parameter for allocutive agreement*) discusses morpheme ordering variations involving clitic pronouns and inflectional endings in Romanian imperative constructions (V-infl-clitic vs. V-clitic-infl). Previous studies assume these patterns to be in free variation and attribute it to metathesis in morphophonology. Such analyses, however, fail to account for similar phenomena in Albanian, since the two languages exhibit different morphological rules. Moving away from such morphological analyses, Hill proposes a syntactic account in which the Romanian left periphery involves a specific functional projection that expresses speech act. In terms of this cartographic approach, Romanian imperative clauses involve a functional projection that denotes direct address (SAP) whose licensing triggers allocutive agreement. The latter is responsible for the observed morpheme alternation: each morpheme pattern therefore relates to a specific interpretation. This syntactic approach has broader implications for the typology of the Balkan Sprachbund and beyond.

Kathleen M. O'Connor (Chapter 11 – *The internal syntax of appositives in English and French*) examines what is generally referred to as appositives, i.e. structures in which a non-restrictive non-finite element follows and modifies a DP (e.g. *John, in hospital with flu, isn't coming to the meeting*). The aim of O'Connor's study is to determine the internal structure of appositives. Adopting a cartographic approach to clause structure, she shows that there is evidence for a CP-layer in appositives, albeit a truncated one. Furthermore, on the basis of evidence related to the licensing of adverbs and to quantifiers associated with DP positions, O'Connor argues that appositives also contain an extensive IP structure. The comparative evidence provided shows that English and French have striking similarities in the way appositives are structured.

Luigi Rizzi (Chapter 12 – *Locality and the functional sequence in the left periphery*) addresses some fundamental questions that are raised by work within the cartographic tradition. Cartographic studies have focused on identifying which functional projections cluster together to form a phrasal or clausal domain (e.g., C, I, D, and P), what interpretive properties these functional projections bring about and how they are hierarchically organized. While most cartographic studies focus on such hierarchies, not much is known with regard to why some hierarchies are found and not others, and how these structural hierarchies are constrained. Focusing on the syntax of the left periphery primarily in English and Italian, Rizzi addresses these issues, and he shows that requirements of the interface systems as well as formal principles constraining syntactic computations, such as locality, are likely to play important roles in constraining functional sequences.

Ur Shlonsky (Chapter 13 – *Wh in-situ and criterial freezing*) discusses subject wh in situ. Focusing initially on data from French, he shows that, despite the apparent absence of movement, subject wh-phrases are actually moved. Cross-linguistic evidence from Bantu languages, Portuguese and French embedded contexts confirms that wh subjects cannot appear in situ. Shlonsky's analysis, developed within the criterial approach, is based on the observation that a wh subject is caught between two contradictory requirements: satisfy the Subject Criterion and therefore undergo criterial freezing on the one hand, and satisfy the wh criterion on the other hand. Shlonsky argues that these conflicting requirements can be reconciled due to an alternative way of satisfying the Subject Criterion, which allows the wh subject to move directly to the focus/wh position. A consequence of the proposed account is that the Subject Criterion must be considered relevant also for covert movement.

Sten Vikner (Chapter 14 – *Germanic verb particle variation*) presents an overview of the variation affecting the position of verbal particles in the Germanic languages. Prepositions and (separable) particles are assumed to have the same syntactic structure, but the former can assign case while the latter cannot. Therefore the particle has to either incorporate into the verb to assign case or the object itself has to move to a position to which the verb can assign case. Variation between SVO languages and SOV languages is shown to affect the order of a separable particle and the verb, but not that between a non-separable particle and a verb. Crucially, in Yiddish those particles that do not incorporate, as shown by their not moving with the finite verb in V2 constructions, occur pre-verbally in non-V2 constructions. This is taken as evidence that Yiddish is an SOV language like German rather than an SVO language like Danish.

Part III of this volume includes articles focusing on aspects of language acquisition and language change. Research in these domains is inevitably of a comparative type. Child language phenomena can only be interpreted fruitfully by comparing them to the adult target language, whereas studies of language change require comparisons of two or more stages of a given language. The two fields of study are also closely related in that in generative accounts acquisition plays a central role in the explanation of change, and, on a methodological level, they crucially depend on corpus data as an empirical basis. **Lieven Danckaert** (Chapter 15 – *The loss of Latin OV: Steps towards an analysis*) discusses the alternation between OV and VO word orders in Latin and the possible reasons for the decline of the former option. Danckaert explores the hypothesis that the loss of OV can be related to an independent change in the grammar of Latin, namely a resetting of the parameter governing the way in which the EPP requirement was satisfied. Assuming a variational acquisition approach to language change, he shows that although the overall frequency of the VO order remains constant over time, in the Late Latin period the VO grammar is more robustly cued than the OV grammar. Given this result, the fact that the VO order ultimately ousts the competing OV pattern is expected.

Eric Haeberli (Chapter 16 – *Medial NP-adjuncts in English: A diachronic perspective*) offers an overview of the history of medial NP-adjuncts from Old English to Present-Day English. In Present-Day English, adverbs are perfectly grammatical in a position between the subject and the main verb (*He recently left for London*) whereas NP-adjuncts are at best stylistically marked in this position ((*)*He tomorrow leaves for London*). Haeberli shows that while medial placement of NP-adjuncts has been considerably less frequent as compared to adverbs ever since around 1500, the contrast was initially much stronger in clauses with finite main verbs than in clauses with finite auxiliaries. It is only in the 19th century that medial placement becomes equally marked in both contexts. Haeberli accounts for these developments in terms of processing constraints disfavouring the use of medial NP-adjuncts and a structural reanalysis of NP-medial adjuncts in Late Modern English.

Eric Lander (Chapter 17 – *Gothic* sai *and the Proto-Germanic verb-based discourse particle* *se) examines the etymology of the Northwest Germanic reinforcer particle *-*si*, which was appended to a neutral demonstrative to form the so-called reinforced demonstrative 'this' in early Northwest Germanic. A detailed study of the potentially cognate particle *sai* in East Germanic (Gothic) leads Lander to conclude that a verb-based etymology of this item as well as of NWGmc *-*si* is superior to alternative proposals and that we can securely reconstruct a Proto-Germanic discourse particle *se, derived from the full form *seh^w 'see! look!'. Using supporting comparative evidence from other languages, Lander then sketches a possible grammaticalization path from Proto-Germanic imperative 'see! look!' to the Gothic discourse particle *sai* and the Northwest Germanic reinforcer particle *-*si*.

Terje Lohndal and Rosalind Thornton (Chapter 18 – *The 3SGS morpheme in child and adult English: A formal analysis*) revisit a well-known property of English child language, namely the optional use of the 3SGS morpheme prior to linguistic maturation during the so-called Optional Infinitive stage. After a review of the evidence discussed in the earlier literature and some more recent experimental findings, Lohndal and Thornton develop a PF analysis of verbal morphology that aims to capture the distribution of the 3SGS morpheme both in child and in adult English. Their account suggests that there is a Pronunciation Rule in the morphophonological component that specifies which member of a chain to pronounce, while respecting the requirement that the 3SGS affix needs a host. Lohndal and Thornton argue that their findings underline the importance of incorporating data from acquisition when investigating questions concerning grammatical architecture.

Acknowledgement: We would like to thank our anonymous reviewers for their invaluable help in the preparation of this volume.

References

Chomsky, Noam. 1981. *Lectures on government and binding* (Studies in Generative Grammar). Berlin: Mouton de Gruyter.
Chomsky, Noam. 1995. *The Minimalist Program*. Cambridge, MA: MIT Press.
Haegeman, Liliane. 1983. *The semantics of will in present-day English: A unified account*. Brussels: Royal Academy of Sciences, Letters and Arts of Belgium.
Haegeman, Liliane. 1984. *Die* and *dat* in West Flemish relative clauses. In Hans Bennis & Wus Van Lessen Kloeke (eds.), *Linguistics in the Netherlands*, 83–91. Dordrecht. Foris.
Haegeman, Liliane. 1985. Scope phenomena in English and Dutch L2 acquisition. *Second Language Research* 1. 118–150.
Haegeman, Liliane. 1986. The double object construction in West Flemish. *The Linguistic Review* 5. 281–300.
Haegeman, Liliane. 1987. Register variation in English. Some theoretical observations. *Journal of English Linguistics* 20(2). 230–248.
Haegeman, Liliane. 1991. *Introduction to Government and Binding*. Oxford: Blackwell.
Haegeman, Liliane. 1992. *Theory and description in generative grammar. A case study in West Flemish*. Cambridge: Cambridge University Press.
Haegeman, Liliane. 1993. The morphology and distribution of object clitics in West Flemish. *Studia Linguistica* 47. 57–94.
Haegeman, Liliane. 1994. Verb Raising as Verb Projection Raising. Some empirical problems. *Linguistic Inquiry* 25(3). 509–522.
Haegeman, Liliane. 1995a. Dutch child root infinitives and truncated structures. *Language Acquisition* 3. 205–255.
Haegeman, Liliane. 1995b. *The syntax of negation*. Cambridge: Cambridge University Press.
Haegeman, Liliane. 1997. Register variation, truncation, and subject omission in English and in French. *English Language and Linguistics* 1. 233–270.
Haegeman, Liliane. 2001. Antisymmetry and verb-final order in West Flemish. *The Journal of Comparative Germanic Linguistics* 3. 207–232.
Haegeman, Liliane. 2006. *Thinking syntactically: A guide to argumentation and analysis*. Malden, MA, Oxford & Victoria: Blackwell.
Haegeman, Liliane. 2012. *Adverbial clauses, main clause phenomena and the composition of the left periphery: The cartography of syntactic structures*. Oxford: Oxford University Press.
Haegeman, Liliane. 2014. West Flemish verb-based discourse markers and the articulation of the Speech Act layer. *Studia Linguistica* 68. 116–139.
Haegeman, Liliane & Jacqueline Guéron. 1999. *English grammar: A generative perspective*. Oxford: Blackwell.
Haegeman, Liliane & Henk van Riemsdijk. 1986. Verb Projection Raising, scope, and the typology of rules affecting verbs. *Linguistic Inquiry* 17. 417–466.

Part I: Comparative syntax: Focus on one language

Adriana Belletti
Labeling (Romance) causatives

1 Introduction

Classical analyses of Romance causatives of the Italian/French type illustrated in examples like (2) and (3) below for Italian, proposed that an overt process of VP-preposing occurs in the derivation of these structures (in particular Kayne 1975; Rouveret and Vergnaud 1980; Zubizarreta 1985; Burzio 1986). Phrasing the proposal in current terms, this process can be identified with and reduced to an instance of a family of syntactic processes moving chunks of a verb phrase, often referred to as *smuggling*, following Collins' (2005) terminology. The main proposal of this article is that the crucial engine triggering this type of derivation of Romance causatives is the fundamental labeling requirement. The requirement is satisfied through a *smuggling*-type movement of a chunk of the verb phrase, probed by a criterial causative voice head. The remaining constituent is labeled DP. In a comparative perspective, the movement attracting property of the causative head is parametrized so that in English-type languages the attracted constituent is not a vP-chunk, but rather the DP-external argument of the lexical verb. This yields labeling of the remaining constituent as vP. The special yet well recognizable status of causatives in language after language, characteristically involves displacement of constituents of different kinds, a verbal constituent in Romance/Italian-type languages, a DP in English-type languages; this is consistent with the idea defended here that these are the only types of displacements possible, and in fact required given shared properties of the clausal functional structure containing the causative voice combined with the requirement of labeling of syntactic structures. Further differences such as e.g. the (im)possibility of passivization of the causative verb follow from the assumed criterial status of the causative voice in compliance with intervention locality within a syntactic architecture which is fundamentally homogeneous.

The presentation and the development of these ideas is organized as follows: In section 2 I will spell out the background analysis I will be assuming for Romance causatives of the Italian type, crucially involving *smuggling*. Section 3 introduces and develops the issue concerning the status of the process moving a chunk of the verb phrase and what its ultimate generator should be. The fundamental labeling requirement is identified as the generator of this movement, which is triggered by a causative voice, active in the clausal functional structure (3.1). This movement is parametrized yielding different types of causatives of the Romance/Italian type on the one side and of the English type on the other.

DOI 10.1515/9781501504037-002

The criterial status of the causative head is then assumed (3.1.2) as the fundamental source of differences in the possibility of passivization in the two types of causatives. Some comparative considerations on French conclude the analysis (3.1.2.1). Section 4 addresses the comparison between the *smuggling* process of causatives with the one currently assumed for passive (4.1). Some relevant considerations inspired by recent results in acquisition are finally discussed (4.2). Section 5 concludes the article.

2 Causatives and movement of a chunk of the verb phrase. Background assumptions.

Processes moving a chunk of the verb phrase yield different types of structures. Among them a core case is represented by passive following Collins' (2005) influential approach in terms of *smuggling*. According to this approach, passive is derived along the lines in (1) (only main aspects of the derivation are indicated). Another core case may precisely be Romance causatives of the type in (2) and (3) as will be proposed here (Belletti and Rizzi 2012 for a first discussion).[1]

(1) Main general steps of the analysis of passive with movement of a chunk of the verb phrase:

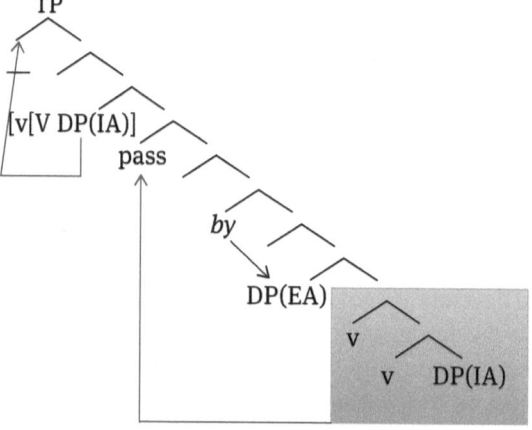

Movement of chunk of verb phrase/*smuggling*

---

[1] I will limit the use of the term *smuggling* somewhat to avoid the look-ahead flavor that this term may produce. See section 4.1 for some discussion of this point.

According to the schema of the analysis in (1), a chunk of the verb phrase containing (at least) the verb(/past participle) and its internal argument is attracted by (a component of) the passive voice into its specifier (indicated as pass in [1]).[2] Lack of accusative is a property of the passive voice, hence in the passive structure the internal argument is then moved into the nominative subject position.

Consider now the *fare-a* and *fare-da* causatives of Italian, illustrated in (2) and (3).

(2) *Maria   farà   [mangiare   il   gelato]   al   bambino*
    Maria   will make   eat   the   ice cream   to the child
    'Maria will make the child eat the ice cream'

(3) *Maria   farà   [mangiare   il   gelato]   dal   bambino*
    Maria   will make   eat   the   ice cream   by the child
    'Maria will make the child eat the ice cream'

Let us assume that the core ingredients of the derivation of a *fare-a* causative like (2), in which the external argument of the embedded infinitival verb phrase is marked with the preposition *a (dative)*, can be schematized as in (4); we may furthermore assume that a similar derivation is at play for the derivation of *fare-da* type causatives as illustrated in (6) (details aside); in (6) the external argument of the embedded infinitival verb phrase is marked with preposition *da(by)*, the same preposition present in passive.[3] When the infinitival verb phrase has no direct object, i.e. its verb is intransitive/unergative, its external argument is marked with accusative case as illustrated in (10). Assignment of accusative can be assumed to first involve an Agree relation with the relevant functional head in the matrix clause containing the (semi-) functional verb *fare* (indicated as *Acc* in the structures below, for convenience), as is indicated in all the following derivations (see

---

[2] The preposition *by* is responsible for Case marking of the DP/External Argument; in (1) only the Agree relation between the preposition and the DP is indicated. Presumably, DP/EA is attracted into the Spec of *by* which further moves into the higher (Case) head. This may be the mechanism always at work implementing Case marking into a clause structure in which prepositions are part of the functional spine, as in Kayne (2004), following a suggestion by Ur Shlonsky. More generally, Agree + movement into the Specifier of the relevant Case marking head may be considered the mechanism typically involved for assignment of structural Cases, including Accusative Case. To simplify the illustration of the proposed derivations, in the representations in the text only the Agree part of the process will be indicated.

[3] On the various differences between the two types of causatives, see Kayne (1975), and, in particular, Guasti (1993). Here we will focus on what the two may have in common.

footnote 2). In all cases a chunk of the verb phrase is attracted into the Specifier of a causative voice, indicated as *caus*.

(4) Main derivational ingredients of *fare-a* type causatives:
Maria farà [mangiare il gelato] al bambino
Maria will make eat the ice cream to the child
'Maria will make the child eat the ice cream'

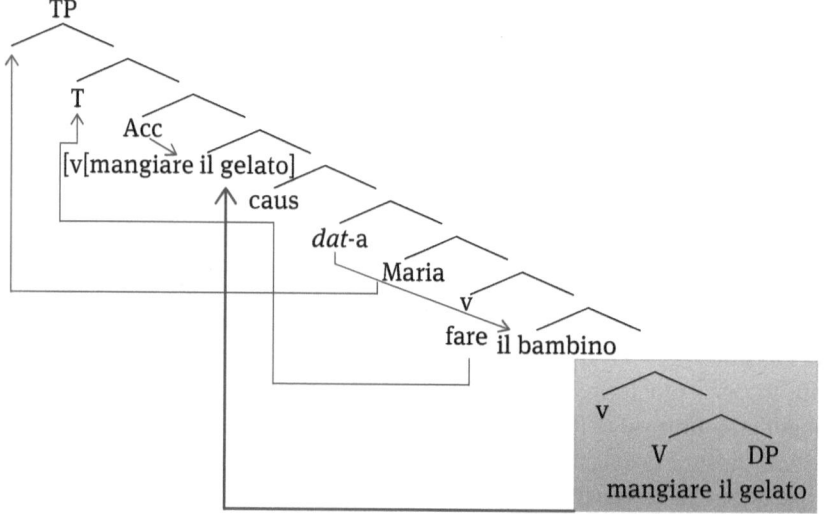

Movement of chunk of verb phrase/*smuggling*

Let us spell out in some more detail the main derivational steps assumed. In (4) the semi-functional verb *fare* is merged as the complement of a causative voice head, the head ultimately responsible for the causative meaning associated with *fare* in the causative constructions.[4] In the implementation in (4) the causative voice is incorporated by *fare*, on its way to the inflectional head(s) labeled T for convenience, as in current practice. The verb *fare* is considered here semi-functional (and not just functional) since it has, by hypothesis, an impoverished argument structure just containing an external argument, as the Initiator (Ramchand 2008) of the caused event, whose descriptive content is expressed in the lexical verb phrase. In (4) it is also hypothesized that a rich functional

---

[4] For similar assumptions on the causative voice and related structural analyses, see Folli and Harley (2007), Legate (2014), and Alexiadou, Anagnostopoulou, and Schäfer (2015).

structure dominates the semi-functional verb *fare*, with a small v-Case head responsible for the assignment of dative Case through Agree to the external argument of the infinitival verb phrase.

The causative voice head has the property of attracting the relevant chunk of the infinitival verb phrase into its specifier, in the same way as the passive voice illustrated in (1). This property and the induced process of movement of a chunk of the verb phrase is what passive and causatives have in common. In the causative construction, in contrast with passive, the moved chunk is overtly visible; it corresponds to the part in brackets of the example in (4) (*mangiare il gelato*). Differently from what happens in passive, in causatives the internal argument of the embedded infinitival verb phrase can remain in the position of direct object where it is accessible to assignment of accusative Case by entering an Agree relation with the relevant functional head in the clausal functional structure, labeled Acc in (4).[5] A crucial effect of the passive voice is that of blocking assignment of accusative Case. No such effect is induced by the presence of the causative voice.[6] Availability of accusative for the internal argument of the infinitival verb phrase is witnessed by the well-known possibility for this argument to be realized as an accusative clitic illustrated by examples like (5a); the ungrammaticality of (5b) is a clear indication that accusative is a property of the matrix clause since the clitic can only be cliticized on the matrix *fare*

---

5 Possibly the object vacates the position of internal argument of V where it is merged reaching some higher position in the moved verbal chunk. We will not go into these subtler details of the implementation. What is important here is the assumption that some functional head external to the verb phrase is ultimately responsible for the assignment of structural accusative Case, as in the traditional AgrO hypothesis. The object may then be attracted to the specifier of this Case head. See also footnote 2 for discussion of this point.

The same analysis would work for cases in which the moved verbal constituent contains an unaccusative verb and its internal argument (no external argument is present in these cases), which is marked with accusative Case, as is visible in (ib) (similarly to [5a], containing a transitive verb):

(i) a. Ho   fatto   partire   Gianni   per   Roma
       (I) have   made   leave   Gianni   to   Rome
    b. *L'ho*   fatto   partire   per   Roma
       (I) himcl have   made   leave   to   Rome

6 As far as Case is concerned, the different property should be due in part to the different status and to the different structural position of (the relevant heads of) the passive and causative voices respectively. The *pass* voice may in fact be in complementary distribution with the Acc head, whereas the *caus* voice should be lower. This is in essence the hypothesis adopted in the representations in the text. I will not attempt to offer a more detailed proposal in this respect here.

and cannot be (en-)cliticized on the infinitival verb, of which it is its internal argument:[7]

(5) a. *Il gelato, Maria lo farà mangiare al bambino*
the ice cream Maria it-CL will make eat to the child
'The ice cream Maria will make the child eat (it)'
b. **Il gelato, Maria farà mangiarlo al bambino*
the ice cream Maria will make eat- it-CL to the child
'The ice cream Maria will make the child eat (it)'

Consider now *fare-da* causatives of the type in (3), illustrated in (6):

(6) Main derivational ingredients of *fare-da* type causatives:
Maria farà [mangiare il gelato] dal bambino
Maria will make eat the ice cream by the child
'Maria will make the child eat the ice cream'

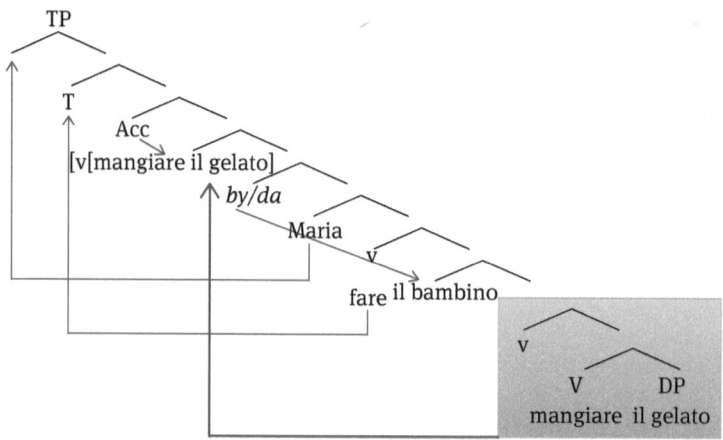

Movement of chunk of verb phrase/*smuggling*

---

7 This is an important difference between causatives and restructuring contexts, in which the clitic is allowed to be cliticized (as a pro-clitic) either onto the restructuring verb, a modal verb in the example (ia), or onto the infinitival verb (as an en-clitic), (ib):
(i) a. *(Questo libro) lo voglio leggere*
(this book) (I) it-CL want to read
b. *(Questo libro) voglio leggerlo*
(this book) (I) want to read- it-CL
'(This book) I want to read it'
See Burzio (1986) and Rizzi (1978) for a classical discussion of these differences, which also crucially point to some important structural distinctions to be assumed between causatives and restructuring structures, a discussion that is beyond the scope of this article.

The crucial hypothesis in (6) is that the causative voice in *fare*-da causatives is expressed by the preposition *by(da)*, possibly by incorporating it. The preposition *by(da)* is the same preposition which participates in the composition of the passive voice. There is a crucial difference between the preposition *by* in passive and the same preposition *by* in causatives though: whereas in passive sentences the nominal complement of the preposition *by* is interpreted as carrying exactly the same Th-role as the subject of the clause in a sentence containing the same verb in the active voice – i.e. as the external argument in the verb argument structure –, with the preposition *by* thus having the status of an expletive type preposition, in *fare*-da causatives the complement of the preposition *by* is necessarily agentive or anyway it is directly involved in the caused event. Hence, typically it cannot count as a simple experiencer of a psychological state. This is in sharp contrast with the *by*-phrase of passive sentences, as illustrated in (7):

(7) a. *Tutti   temono   il   terremoto*
    Everybody   fears   the   earthquake
   b. *Il   terremoto   è   temuto   da   tutti*
      The   eathquake   is   feared   by   everybody
   c. **Le   vittime   fanno   temere   il   terremoto   da   tutti*
      the   victims   make   fear   the   earthquake by   everybody
      'The victims make everybody fear the earthquake'

The impossibility of (7c) contrasts with the well-formed status of (8) containing a *fare-a* causative: the dative external argument is compatible with the experiencer interpretation. According to the analysis above this is expressed through the hypothesis that in *fare-a* causatives the causative voice is an independent head distinct from the dative preposition *a*:[8]

---

[8] Beside, there could be a privileged link between the dative preposition *a* and the experiencer role. This may not be surprising given the existence of dative-experiencer psych-verbs as those of the *piacere* class in Italian (Belletti and Rizzi 1988). This would suggest that the dative of *fare a* causatives has the same status as an experiencer dative. See Belluci's (2015) proposal according to which the dative of causatives behaves like a quirky subject. The relation of dative Case with the experiencer role would amount to saying that the *a*-DP of causatives is typically also associated with an experiencer role, possibly as an adjunct role which combines with the role carried by the nominal expression as the external argument of the infinitival verb phrase. The notion of adjunct theta-role is borrowed from Zubizarreta's (1982) proposal, where precisely this term is used. Furthermore, the hypothesis just hinted at here may also express the "affected" status of the external argument in these types of causatives as the experiencer of the caused event (beside being e.g. its agent as the external argument of the infinitival verb), often reported and discussed in the literature (see Guasti 1993 and references cited there on this point).

(8) *Le   vittime   fanno   temere   il   terremoto   a   tutti*
    the   victims   make   fear   the   earthquake   to   everybody
    'The victims make everybody fear the earthquake'

Assuming an approach along these lines, which hints at a possible route to differentiate in part the two types of causatives – as required by the literature on this issue (footnote 3) – the derivation in (6) highlights one crucial feature that both causatives have in common: the fact that they both involve movement of a chunk of the infinitival verb phrase, attracted by a head expressing the causative voice into its specifier. Much as in the *fare-a* causative, also in the *fare-da* causative the internal argument is assigned accusative Case, through Agree with the functional head generally responsible for structural accusative, labeled Acc in the structure. As the example in (9) shows, that this is an accusative object is explicitly indicated by the possibility of expressing it with an accusative clitic:

(9) *(Il   gelato)   Maria   lo   farà   mangiare   dal   bambino*
    (the   ice cream)   Maria   it-CL   will make   eat   by the   child
    'The ice cream Maria will make the child eat (it)'

We are now left with the last type of causative, the one containing no direct object of the verb in the infinitival verb phrase. The same derivational mechanisms can be assumed to be at work also in this case, with the chunk of the infinitival verb phrase attracted by the causative voice head into its specifier, as illustrated in (10). By assumption, the head responsible for dative in (4) is inactive/absent in this structure; accusative is not discharged onto the object of the moved chunk since there is no object in this case; thus, accusative is assigned to the external argument of the infinitival verb phrase through the establishment of Agree from the Acc head. That this argument is marked with accusative Case is once again shown by the familiar possibility of pronominalizing it with an accusative clitic (11).

(10) *Maria   farà   ridere   il   bambino*
     Maria   will make   laugh   the   child
     'Maria will make the child laugh'

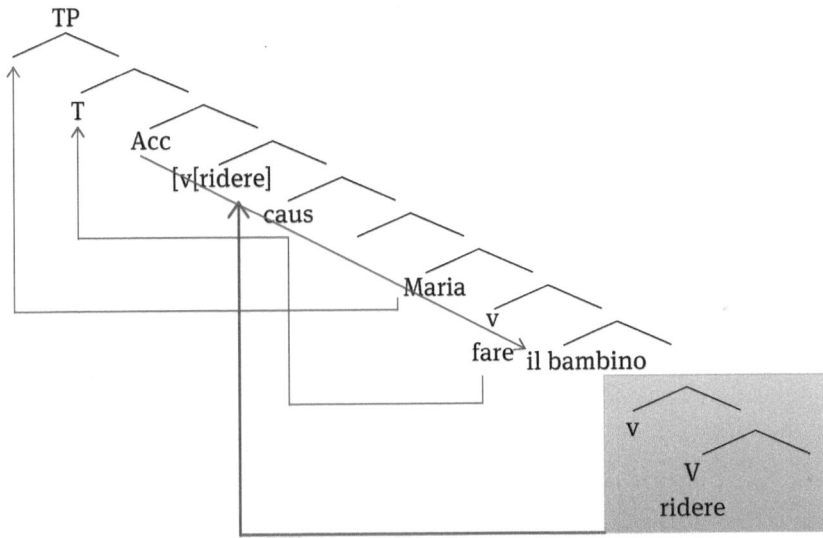

Movement of chunk of verb phrase/*smuggling*

(11) *(Il bambino) Maria   lo   farà   ridere*
     (the child)   Maria   him-CL   will make   laugh
     '(The child) Maria will make him laugh'

One last question must be addressed concerning the computations assumed to hold in causatives: in all of the assumed derivations the implicit hypothesis has been made that the Initiator external argument of *fare* which is raised into the matrix subject position does not count as an intervener in blocking the Agree relation between the relevant Case marking head and the external argument of the lexical vP. The assumption has been made despite the fact that the Initiator DP c-commands the DP/external argument of the lexical vP. How could this be possible in compliance with intervention locality/Relativized Minimality (Rizzi 1990, 2004)? Let us make the implicit assumption explicit: precisely because the Initiator external argument of *fare* raises into the matrix subject position, I assume that it does not count as an intervener. In the final representation of the derivation, it is only its copy that intervenes with respect to the lower external argument of the lexical vP. Thus, whereas derivationally it would count as an intervener (closest DP, Chomsky 2001), in the final representation it does not under the assumption that for an element to count as an intervener all of its occurrences must be in an intervention configuration, i.e. the whole chain of the element in question (Krapova and Cinque 2008 for the first detailed formulation of the proposal). Hence, just a copy of it would not destroy the relevant local relation. See section 3.1 below for more on this type of interpretation of intervention locality in these (causative) structures.

Let us assume that the analyses sketched out in (4), (6) and (10) above, which make crucial reference to the movement of a chunk of the verb phrase are empirically adequate in their essential respects and capture some fundamental descriptive properties of causatives, much as the analysis of passive does involving the same type of movement, following Collins' (2005) original *smuggling* proposal. Granted that a number of details may (and will have to) be further spelled out, I will consider this type of analysis as being on the right track and assume it.

One fundamental question is raised by this analysis, which I want to highlight here: if passives and Romance causatives of the type considered have one crucial derivational mechanism in common, i.e. movement of a chunk of the verb phrase, the following question arises: what is the status of this type of movement? We now turn to this question.

3 Movement of a chunk of the verb phrase: The issue

In minimalist terms the question above amounts to asking what the effect of such movement would be at the interface with the interpreting systems (Chomsky 1995 and much subsequent related literature), or, put differently, what movement of a chunk of the verb phrase contributes to the interpretation of the output structure.

We may ask the question in a straightforward way: What kind of syntactic operation is the movement of a chunk of the verb phrase? Typically, syntactic movement operations target nominal arguments (or clausal arguments or also adverbials, Haegeman 2012) and have an interpretive effect on their outcome: this is prototypically the case for A'-movements targeting different positions in the cartography of the left periphery of the clause, yielding e.g. wh-questions, (corrective/contrastive) focalizations (Rizzi 1997; Belletti 2009; Bianchi, Bocci, and Cruschina 2014), types of topicalizations (Benincà and Poletto 2004; Bianchi and Frascarelli 2010; Frascarelli and Hinterhölzl 2007). But this is also the case for the A-movement of the internal argument into the preverbal subject position of the clause as in passives or in sentences containing an unaccusative verb or in raising structures.[9] And this is more generally also the case whenever the external argument of a transitive or an intransitive verb raises from its merge position within the vP: movement of a DP into the preverbal subject position

---

9 Raising to subject or to object (see Chomsky 2015 for recent discussion on the latter).

has the interpretive effect of creating a predication/aboutness relation whereby the sentence is interpreted as being about the DP subject in a criterial type configuration expressed through a Subject criterion (Cardinaletti 2004; Rizzi 2005; Rizzi and Shlonsky 2007). The question raised above then becomes: What is the interpretive effect of movement of a verbal chunk? Has this movement a comparable effect to that of A or A' movement of e.g. a nominal/clausal constituent? Beside it being overtly visible and thus producing a clear effect on word order, as is clearly the case in the Romance causatives illustrated in (2), (3), and (10), why should such movement occur to start with? What is the ultimate generator for it?

3.1 Labeling causatives

I would like to put forth the proposal that this type of movement has in fact a deep motivation: it is a direct consequence of the so-called labeling algorithm (Chomsky 2013, 2015; Rizzi 2015a, 2015b; Cecchetto and Donati 2014; Boskovic 2008, 2015). This movement comes from the necessity to label a phrase that would otherwise remain unlabeled, thus leaving the structure uninterpretable at the interfaces. If this hypothesis is correct, the generator of this movement is in fact grounded within a crucial mechanism of syntactic computations and, as expected, has a fundamental effect on the outcome: the readability of the structure. According to the proposal developed in detail below, attraction by the causative voice head of the verbal chunk, as illustrated in section 2, creates the possibility for the external argument of the infinitival verb phrase, sometimes referred to as the causee, to transfer its DP label to the remaining phrase, which thus becomes visible for syntactic operations. It can be Case marked with accusative with intransitive verbs, as in (10), or by either the preposition *a* or *da*, as in (4) and (6).

Let us put the system into work. As is discussed in Chomsky (2013, 2015) and Rizzi (2015a, 2015b), the labeling algorithm requires that movement occurs in a situation as the one illustrated in (12), which results from having externally merged a phrase with another already constituted phrase:

(12)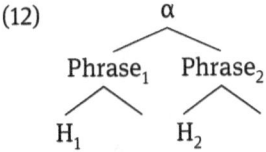

As Rizzi (2015a, 2015b) discusses in detail, the situation in (12) is the one that typically arises when an external argument is merged with the phrase containing a verb and its arguments. Hence, in the spirit of the dynamic approach à la Moro

(2000), movement of the external argument – Phrase$_1$ in (12) – takes place thus making it possible to attribute the label vP to the remaining category – α in (12) [10], a process that is illustrated in (13).

(13)

The external argument is attracted to the relevant subject position providing the criterial aboutness interpretation mentioned above. Thus, the overall structure can be interpreted at the interface, since all its constituents are labeled and all criterial features are attributed.

Assume now that the other option is taken in a structure of type (12), so that the phrase undergoing movement is Phrase$_2$. If Phrase$_2$ corresponds to the verb and its internal argument and the higher structure contains a causative head with the described attracting property, this movement corresponds precisely to movement of a chunk of the verb phrase, as discussed in section 2 for causatives. Compared to the schematic representation in (13), the result of movement of the vP chunk would correspond to (14):

(14)

Let us reconsider the derivation in (4), repeated in (15) illustrating with a *fare a* structure. For the sake of clarity only the relevant movement of the verbal chunk is illustrated in (15):

---

10 The reason why copies of moved phrases cannot provide a label is discussed in detail in Rizzi (2015a: 326). Essentially, all occurrences of a given element should be contained within the phrase in need of a label for it to be labeled with the category of that element. In this article I will assume that copies are not a possible labeling source without further discussion, along the lines of Chomsky's and Rizzi's approaches.

(15)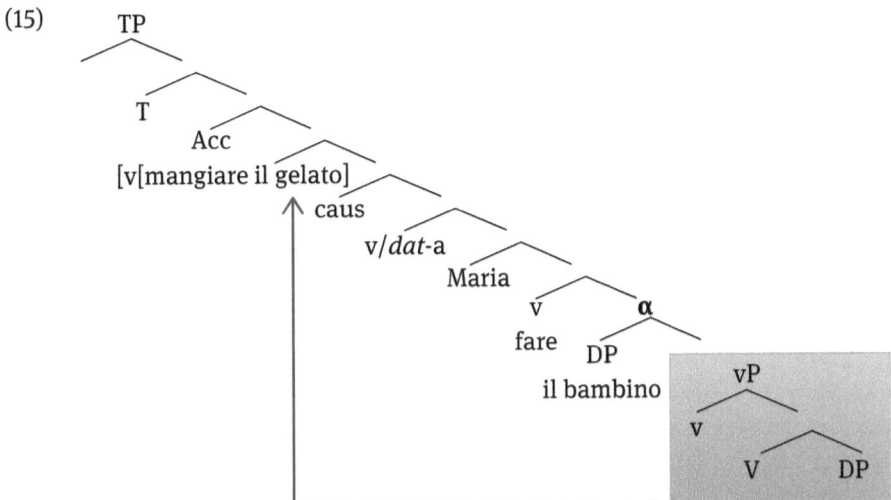

α is the phrase that needs to be labeled in (15), since it is generated by merging two phrases: the external argument (DP) and the verb with its internal argument (a vP chunk). By moving the verbal chunk to a higher position, the remaining phrase is the DP *il bambino*/the child. We can therefore assume that α is also labeled DP, through the same mechanism by which it is labeled vP when it is the external argument which moves, illustrated in (13). (15) instantiates the option available in principle, as illustrated in (14b). By hypothesis, in causatives the moving vP chunk is attracted by the causative voice head. It thus ends up filling the specifier of the phrase headed by the causative voice.[11]

The productive and rather pervasive presence of causatives in Romance and the rather widespread existence of causative structures with similar

---

[11] And labeled with the relevant voice label, e.g. CausP or just vP again. I leave this question open for now, which may ultimately be quite relevant depending on the role of morphological voices at the interpretive interface. See section 2.1.2 for some further proposal on the criterial status of the causative voice.

In a sentence like (i) the realization of the external argument of the lexical verb as a dative clitic indicates that movement of the chunk of the verb phrase must have occurred, thus making accusative accessible to the internal argument *il gelato*/the ice cream. These structures do not instantiate the English-type causative to be discussed in connection with (16).

(i) Maria   gli   farà   mangiare   il   gelato
    Maria   to him$_{cl}$ will make   eat   the   ice cream

properties across languages makes it natural to assume that some core computational mechanisms should be at the origin of these structures. One such core mechanism may originate from the labeling requirement of the syntactic structure.

How about moving the DP external argument of the verb also in a causative structure? Note that such movement would be permitted on locality grounds also in causative-type structures, should a landing site be present for the DP such that the higher Initiator external argument does not count as an intervener (under Krapova and Cinque's 2008 interpretation assumed above). It can be speculated that such a possibility is indeed instantiated by a different type of causative construction: the one that exists in English and various other languages (among which are also some Romance languages, e.g. EPortuguese Santos, Gonçalves, and Hyams 2015; Belletti and Costa 2015, French *laisser* etc.). Consider (16), and also the translations of the Italian examples above:

(16) a. *Mary made/let [the child eat the ice cream/run]*
b. *Mary made/let him eat the ice cream/run*

(16a) shares properties of the so-called ECM/Raising to object construction (Chomksy 1981), in which the causative verb *make* would take a small clause complement, from where the external argument would raise into some position in the matrix clause. As shown in (16b), the external argument of the embedded verb is marked with accusative Case, a property of the functional structure of the matrix clause. Let us assume here that the functional structure of examples like (16) is essentially the same as that of causative *fare*, as e.g. in (15) above.[12] We can then assume that the fundamental difference between causatives of the Italian type and causatives of the English type should concern the nature of the causative voice in one of the following two ways: the causative voice of English type languages could either be assumed not to have any movement attracting property at all, in contrast to the causative voice of Italian type languages or it could have a different movement attracting property. In the latter case, it should attract the DP/External Argument and not the vP-chunk.

---

12 With the proviso that the causative voice does not select any v/dative, nor is it ever incorporated into the expletive preposition *by*. For the time being we state this as an independent property, which should ultimately be derived from some more primitive (morphological) parameter, differentiating the Italian type from the English type causative verbal spine.

Let us consider the two options in turn. If the former option is taken, one should conclude that causative structures of the English type are ECM/Raising to object structures of the same type as classical ECM structures, as shown in (17) (Kayne 1981):

(17) *I believed [John to have solved the problem]*

In both (16) and (17) the External argument of the embedded complement would move into the matrix Case position. Movement of the DP in (16) would thus be independent of the presence of the causative voice in English, and it would only occur for Case requirements, as in (17). There are reasons to believe, however, that the causative case in (16) cannot be reduced to standard ECM/Raising to object constructions of the type in (17). Therefore the second option seems preferable: the moving engine in the case of causatives should be the causative voice in English as well, much as we have proposed for Romance Italian type causatives. The difference between the two types of causatives would only concern the element which is attracted: the vP chunk in the Italian type and the DP/external argument in the English type.

Let us now consider the potential weakness of reducing movement of the DP/External Argument in (16) to a regular ECM/Raising to object movement of the type in (17), triggered by pure Case requirements.[13] There is a well-known crucial difference between (16a) and (17): the nature of the embedded complement is not the same in the two cases, since it contains more functional structure in (17) than in (16a), as indicated by the presence of the infinitival marker *to* in the former and its absence in the latter. Indeed, the reduced complement of causative *make* is clearly identified in English by its impoverished functional structure (comparable to the complement of perception verbs). In current terms, we can say that the verbal complement of these verbs corresponds to the vP projection plus some functional structure containing it. However, this functional structure does not contain up to certain relatively high clausal functional heads, such as the head hosting the infinitival marker *to*. Thus, even if the complement in (17) is likely to be more reduced than a complete CP with a full-fledged left periphery,[14] it still has more clausal-type functional structure than the small clause complement of causative *make* (and of perception verbs). The external argument of the

---

[13] The relevance of the contrasts to be discussed momentarily in (18)–(20) has been brought to my attention by Luigi Rizzi in class discussion.
[14] As is assumed in literature on ECM (Chomsky 1980, 1981, Kayne 1981).

clausal complement of (17) is marked accusative, instantiating a typical ECM/ Raising to object, schematically illustrated in (18) for its essential steps, i.e. Agree and raising:

(18) *I believed... [him [Acc]... [<__> to have solved the problem]*
         Agree

Note that if the accusative head is not active, as in the presence of passive morphology, the DP is allowed to pursue its movement and become the subject of the matrix clause, as indicated by the possibility of passivizing the matrix verb, illustrated in (19):

(19) *John/He is believed <__> [__ to have solved the problem]*[15]

In (19) the position indicated as <__> is the position to which we assume that the DP has first moved from the embedded clause (see footnote 15). Consider now the fact that what may look like the same movement cannot take place if the matrix verb is causative *make*, as is indicated by the ungrammaticality of the following sentence in (20), the passive version of (16a):

(20) **The child was made/let <__> [__ eat the ice cream] (by Mary)*

All things being equal, the ungrammaticality of (20) strongly suggests that the position <__> is not the same in (20) and in (19). This conclusion may have consequences for the proper analysis of (16), in particular the question raised above whether the position to which the DP/External Argument raises could be the same position as that to which it raises in active ECM/raising to object structures (cf. [18]). If it were, it would not be obvious why the two structures should not

---

[15] Note that in (19) the passive voice in the matrix clause attracts the DP/External Argument of the complement clause directly (no violation of locality produced here as no intervention configuration is met since the moved DP is an external argument). In a more detailed analysis it should attract a vP chunk as is always the case in passive sentences (when the DP to be promoted to the subject position is an internal argument; see section 2). The chunk to move in this case is the vP headed by *believe*, containing the complement (reduced) clause, say TP for concreteness. Hence the DP moving from the *smuggled* position can only be the TP subject *John*, for familiar locality reasons. The schematic representation in (19) assumes direct movement of DP from the <__> position for the sake of clarity.

behave alike in the case of passive, as the ungrammaticality of (20) indicates, in contrast with the possibility of (19).[16]

Let us then assume that the position to which the DP/External Argument raises is in fact not the same in the two cases. If in ECM/Raising to object structures it corresponds to the specifier position in which accusative Case is assigned, in the causative *make* structure it could correspond to the specifier of the causative voice instead. Going back to our central question above, we can then propose that the crucial difference between Romance causatives of the Italian type and causatives of the English type is to be found in the different movement attracting property of the same causative voice head, which can be schematized in the following parametric difference:

(21) a. Romance Italian type: *caus* voice attracts vP chunk
 b. English type: *caus* voice attracts DP/External Argument

Hence, no movement of a verbal chunk is triggered in causatives like English (16).

Consider now the consequence that this has from the point of view of labeling. By labeling requirements, in English type causatives the phrase that moves so that α can be labeled is the DP external argument, according to the proposal just made. The relevant aspects of the proposed derivation are illustrated in (22):

(22)
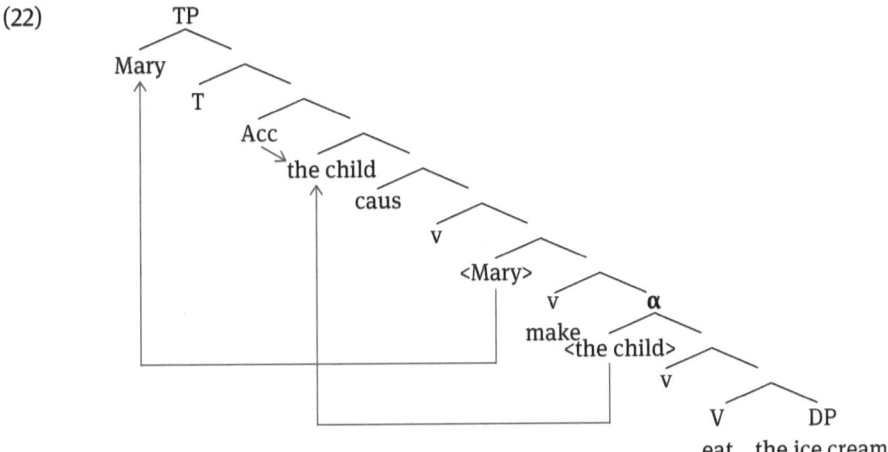

---

16 Speakers tend to marginally accept passivization with "causative *make*" by possibly treating it as a *believe*-type verb, as witnessed by the presence of the marker *to* in the infinitival complement of examples like the following:
(i) a. ?(?) *The child was made to eat the ice cream (by Mary)*
 b. ?(?) *He was made to feel special*
The possibility of a *believe*-type analysis, however, never extends to active causative structures, which is possibly due to the fact that ECM structures may be disfavored if alternatives are available such as the causative analysis of *make*.

Note that since the position to which the DP causee external argument moves is lower than the subject position to which the Initiator external argument of *make* moves (Spec/TP in [22]), the derivation satisfies locality. As proposed earlier, this is so under the natural assumption that a constituent of the same relevant type as the moved constituent counts as an intervener if all of its occurrences (structurally) intervene in the dependency created by movement. This is not the case in (22). Specifically, in (22) the two relevant constituents are both (lexically restricted) DPs. However, whereas the first occurrence of the DP/*Mary*, i.e. its copy, does intervene in the movement of the DP/*the child*, the occurrence of the head of the chain of the DP/*Mary* does not: the head of the chain of the moved DP/*the child* is hierarchically lower, as clearly indicated by the crossing of the two chains in (22). Hence, intervention locality is satisfied in this derivation under our assumptions.

In conclusion, in a language in which the causative voice has the movement attracting property of probing the DP external argument (EA) of the embedded verb phrase, the causee, the labeling procedure will attribute the vP label to the remaining constituent: α is thus labeled vP in (22). Unsurprisingly given the verbal nature of the small clause complement of the causative verb, in this type of causatives labeling works in the same way as in simple (non causative) clauses modulo the different landing site of the moved external argument, Spec/TP in simple clauses and Spec/*caus* in causatives. In contrast, if the causative voice has the movement attracting property of probing the vP phrase, movement affects a verbal chunk of the embedded verb phrase. The remaining constituent α is thus labeled DP. The former case corresponds to English type causatives, the latter to Italian type causatives. Both types of causatives are derived in compliance with the very fundamental labeling requirement. Zooming in on the relevant part of the structure, the two labeling operations look like (23a) for English type and (23b) for Italian type causatives respectively:

(23) a.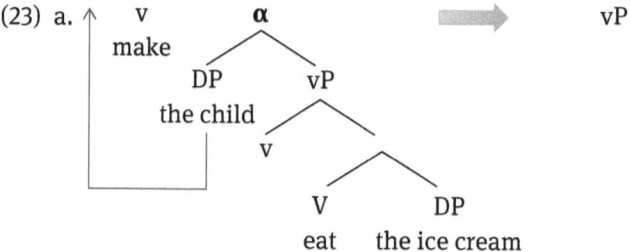

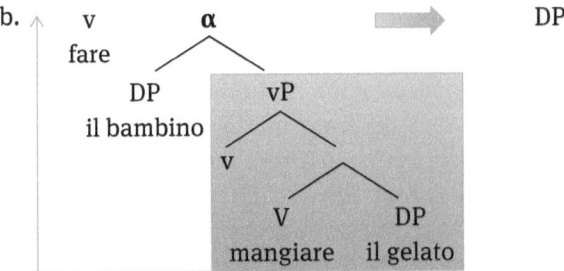

Thus, according to our proposal, the seemingly very different syntax of these two types of causatives shares in fact the same fundamental (structural) ingredients, and instantiates the two possible (movement) options allowed and in fact required by the structure generated by Merge:

- movement of DP (/EA)
- movement of vP(-chunk)

The ultimate impulse to movement in both cases is the labeling requirement in compliance with different properties of the causative voice head.

3.1.1 Speculations on the nature of the causative head at the interface: caus as a criterial head

In the preceding section we have highlighted the impossibility for the raised DP/external argument of the vP small clause complement of the causative verb *make* to be raised into the subject position of the clause in a passivized structure containing *make* (as in [20]). As a shortcut we can say that the causative cannot be passivized in English. It would be interesting to see whether the proposal developed in the preceding section could shed some light on this fact.

I would like to speculate that the proposal can in fact shed some light if it is assumed that the causative voice is a criterial head in the sense of Rizzi (2006) and subsequent work. From an interpretive point of view this assumption is fairly natural: the causative interpretation crucially involves the presence of this head in the clause functional structure. Hence, it should be expected that filling the specifier position of this head would create a criterial configuration such that the phrase in Spec and the head share the relevant cause feature and the phrase is interpreted as directly involved in the caused event. In English type causatives such a phrase is the DP/external argument, often referred to as the causee. If the *caus* head is a criterial head, this has the consequence that the element in its specifier is "frozen in place" under the principle of *Criterial Freezing* (Rizzi 2006, 2010; Boskovic 2008). In other words, the phrase cannot further move from this position. If the causative voice head is a criterial head, there is then a direct explanation as to why the DP/external argument cannot move from the position to which it has raised in the matrix clause. Whence passive of causative *make* is predicted to be impossible, as was illustrated in (20) above. Notice that there is no ban on passivizing *make* per se, as shown by possible sentences like the following and many similar ones containing non-causative *make*:

(24) *The cake has been made by Mary*

The ban is on passivizing *make* in the causative construction, but this should be expected if the causative voice head is a criterial head. This hypothesis has also the advantage of reducing the effect of the movement process of causatives to the general outcome of movement triggered by labeling requirements, as proposed in Rizzi (2015a): the output satisfies an interpretive criterion.

An obvious question to ask now is: What about Italian type causatives? Let us first of all establish the empirical minimal difference with English type causatives in the domain of passivization: causative *fare* can be passivized, resulting in structures in which the internal argument of the moved vP chunk is raised into the subject position, as illustrated in the active-passive pair in (25a, 25b) (the moved chunk within square brackets in [25]), with both *fare a* and *fare da* causatives:

(25) a. *Maria   ha fatto   [mangiare   il   gelato]   al/dal   bambino*
       Maria   has made   (to) eat   the   ice cream   to the/by the   child
     b. *Il   gelato   è   stato   fatto   [mangiare <___>   al/dal*
       the   ice cream (is) has been   made   (to) eat   to the/by the
       bambino   da   Maria
       child   by   Maria

Let us concentrate on the position from which movement of the DP/internal argument takes place in (25b): as in a regular passive derivation, movement should take place from the position where the vP chunk has been *smuggled*. Given the proposed analysis, it seems reasonable to assume that in the case of (25b) the vP chunk is first attracted into the specifier of the causative voice, in contrast to passive structures that do not contain the causative voice. Hence, the <___> position is contained within the phrase occupying the specifier of the criterial *caus* head voice. The natural question to ask then is: Is this extraction compatible with the criterial nature of this head assumed above? Specifically: Is it compatible with criterial freezing? I would like to suggest that it is, under Rizzi's (2010) interpretation of the freezing constraint: whereas the freezing constraint blocks movement of the whole constituent satisfying the relevant criterion, subparts of it can undergo movement in view of satisfaction of another criterion.[17] This is precisely what happens in (25b). The vP chunk satisfies a causative criterion, thus being interpreted as the caused event, and then the internal argument is moved into the subject position where the Subject criterion is thus satisfied in turn. The major relevant steps of the derivation are illustrated in (26), which highlights the movement of the vP chunk into the specifier of the causative voice and the subsequent extraction of the internal argument:[18]

---

17 This means that the only frozen constituent is the probed one, satisfying the criterion. In this way it can be explained why movement of part of a phrase into the R(elative) head position in the higher CP is possible, as in the example in (i). The constituent is extracted from a bigger focused phrase filling the left peripheral focus position of the lower CP, in which the Focus criterion is satisfied:
(i)   *L'autore di cui hanno detto [che [IL LIBRO <___>] hanno censurato (non il disco)]*
       the author of whom they said that the book they have consored (not the record)
18 To highlight the core of the proposal, a number of other major processes are not illustrated in (26), such as the Agree relation between the dative *a* and the caus-*by* head, here collapsed to simplify the structure, and the external argument of the vP, "il bambino", and movement into Spec of passive *by* of the Initiator external argument of *fare* and subsequent movement of *by* into the *pass* head. The *pass* voice, as is always the case, should attract a verbal chunk into its specifier. The chunk would consist (at least) of the verbal phrase labeled *causP* in (26). All these movements in the complete derivation do not affect the main point illustrated in (26): the internal argument of the lexical verb, i.e. *il gelato*, can undergo movement as it is an instance of sub-extraction from the criterial *Spec/causP*.

(26)

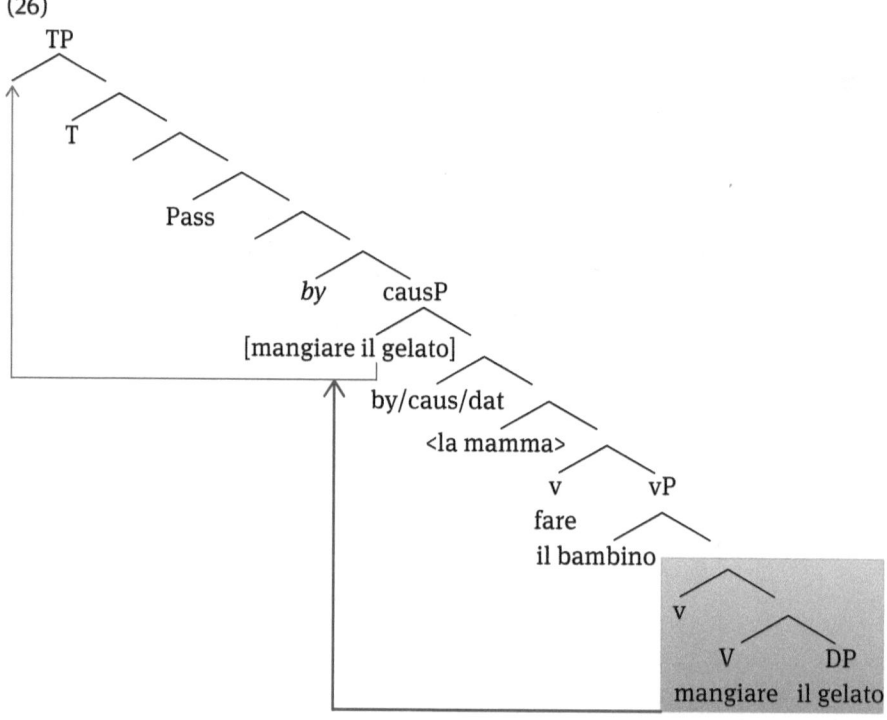

Notice incidentally that since the phrase satisfying the criterion induced by the *caus* head is, in this case, the verbal constituent, an immediate prediction of this analysis is that the whole verbal chunk satisfying the causative criterion could not itself be moved thus vacating the criterial position. This is indeed the case as shown by the ungrammaticality of (27a), in which the infinitival complement of *fare* has been pre-posed under clefting. (27a) minimally contrasts with the well-formedness of (27b), in which the pre-posed constituent is an ordinary infinitival complement clause:[19]

(27) a. *È   [prendere   la   medicina]   che   ho   fatto___   a
      (it) is   to take   the   medicine   that   (I) have   made   to
      Maria
      Maria

---

19 Thanks to Luigi Rizzi for pointing out these examples.

b. È   di prendere   la   medicina   che   ho   ordinato___
   (it) is to take   the   medicine   that   (I) have ordered
   a   Maria
   to   Maria

3.1.1.1 Some related considerations on French

In as far as the possibility of passivizing causatives is concerned, all things being equal, one would expect that French should behave like Italian, since the two languages have the same type of causative construction(s). However, this is not the case and this is in fact a well-known area in which the two languages differ: whereas passive of causative *fare* is possible in Italian, the equivalent passive of causative *faire* appears to be excluded in French (Ruwet 1972; Kayne 1975; Guasti 1993). There are reasons to believe, however, that the main reason for this exclusion does not mainly concern the causative construction *per se*, but rather the interaction between properties of past participle agreement and causative *faire* (Kayne 1989, 2008; Bouvier 2000). We now sketch the main features of what looks to us like a reasonable line to interpret the unexpected behavior of French.

Interestingly, Kayne (2008) points out that in his first illustration of the impossibility of passivizing causative *faire*, Ruwet (1972) offered an example like (28a), with no past participle agreement of passivized *faire*, and not one like (28b), in which the past participle of passivized *faire* agrees with the (feminine, plural) internal argument, which has moved into the subject position:

(28) a. * *Les   pommes   de   terre   ont   été   fait   manger*
        the   potatoes   have   been   made   to eat
     b.*(*) *Les   pommes de terre   ont   été   faites   manger*
        the   potatoes$_{FEM.PL}$ have   been   made$_{FEM.PL}$ to eat

Kayne comments on the exemplification provided by Ruwet in the following terms: "... presumably indicating that for Ruwet, (our, AB) 28b with agreement would have been even worse than (our, AB) 28a". In other words, past participle agreement is completely impossible, say inconceivable, with causative *faire*. Note that the past participle of the lexical verb normally agrees with the moved internal argument in French passives:[20]

(29) *Les   pommes de terre   ont   été   mangées/   cuites*[20]
     the   potatoes$_{FEM.PL}$ have   been   eaten$_{FEM.PL}$/   cooked$_{FEM.PL}$

---

[20] Agreement is audible in the past participle *cuites* 'cooked'.

Hence the fact of somehow preferring lack of past participle agreement in (28a) is all the more intuitively surprising. Causatives are surprising in the domain of past participle agreement also in another respect, again, as has been described since Kayne (1975) (but see also Kayne 2008 for re-discussion). Whereas past participle agreement is possible and for some speakers quasi-obligatory under cliticization of third person clitics (30a), the same does not hold at all in causatives. Here, once again, past participle agreement is impossible (30b) vs (30c). In contrast, when *faire* is used in its non-causative value, past participle agreement is regularly available (30d).

(30) a. *(La pomme),   Marie l'a   cuite*
       (the apple$_{FEM.SING}$) Marie it-CL$_{FEM.SING}$ has cooked$_{FEM.SING}$

   b.*(La pomme),   Marie l'a   faite   cuire*
       (the apple$_{FEM}$) Marie it-CL$_{FEM}$ has made$_{FEM}$ (to) cook

   c. *(La pomme),   Marie l'a   fait   cuire*
       (the apple$_{FEM}$) Marie it-CL$_{FEM}$ has made   (to) cook

   d. *(La tarte),   Marie l'a   faite   avec amour*
       (the cake$_{FEM}$)   Marie it-CL$_{FEM}$ has made$_{FEM}$ with love

All the Italian equivalents of the French examples are perfectly grammatical, with past participle agreement in all cases: under passive, as in French; under cliticization, as in French; but, differently from French, also in causatives, both in the active causative (possible in French with no past past participle agreement under cliticization), and in the passive causative (impossible in French, with or without past participle agreement, as in [28]):

(31) a. *Le patate   sono state   mangiate*[21]
       the potatoes$_{FEM.PL}$ have been$_{FEM.PL}$ eaten$_{FEM.PL}$

   b. *(La mela)   Maria l'ha   cotta*
       (the apple$_{FEM.SING}$) Maria it-CL$_{FEM.SING}$ has cooked$_{FEM.SING}$

   c. *(La mela)   Maria l'ha   fatta   cuocere*
       (the apple$_{FEM.SING}$) Maria it-CL$_{FEM.SING}$ has made$_{FEM.SING}$ (to) cook

---

[21] With the further well-known difference between Italian and French: in Italian past participle agreement also occurs with the (passive) past participle auxiliary, differently from French. See Belletti (2006/and forthcoming update) for an overview of past participle agreement phenomena; Kayne (1989) for the influential view that past participle agreement be implemented under a Spec-head relation, in a way that does not differ from other more familiar forms of agreement (e.g. subject-verb agreement in finite clauses), a fundamental insight assumed in the text.

d. *La mela è stata fatta cuocere da Maria*
the apple has been_FEM.SING made_FEM.SING (to) cook by Maria

It thus seems that the crucial difference between Italian and French in the domain of causatives is to be recognized in the unavailability of past participle agreement with causative *faire*, be it in the active or in the passive voice. We speculate that the impossibility of passivizing the causative in French is related to the impossibility of this agreement (in a spirit similar to Kayne's 2008 discussion). More specifically, following the insight of Bouvier (2000), I assume that *faire* in the causative voice has a somewhat reduced past participial structure, such that it does not contain the relevant agreement type projection which is crucially involved in past participle agreement: passing through the specifier of this agreement head (Belletti 2001, 2006; Friedemann and Siloni 1997) the moving DP internal argument in the passive causative or the clitic in the active causative should trigger past participle agreement. If there is no such position in French then agreement is not and cannot be activated. This may be the reason why DP movement in the causative seems degraded since past participle agreement is normally required in the passive in French.

Interpreting the relevant contrasts in French in this way may have interesting consequences as far as the comparison between French and Italian is concerned in the domain of passivization in the causative construction.

Recall that the proposal we made in the preceding section, which considers the *caus* voice as a criterial head yielding criterial freezing effects, allowed for the possibility that the internal argument be (sub-)extractable from the *smuggled* verbal chunk without the relevant causative criterion being violated. This is what we have assumed to be at work in Italian in the domain of passive, thus allowing passivization of causative *fare*, with extraction of the internal argument from the *smuggled* verbal chunk (cf. [26]). All things being equal, we would expect that this possibility should also be available in French, due to the similarity of the causative construction in the two languages. This is a more specific way of formulating the question from which the present section started. We can now conclude that there should be no ban in principle for the internal argument to be extracted from the moved verbal chunk in French as well. The problem in French causatives leading to the impossibility of passive should stem from the impossibility of performing past participle agreement in this language, due to the reduced structure of causative *faire*. If a non-agreeing past participle of causative *faire* were tolerated, passivization of the causative should also be available in French, i.e. the internal argument should be (sub-)extractable in French just like in Italian. This is precisely what Bouvier (2000) describes: whereas an agreeing feminine past participle is totally inconceivable in French causative *faire* as in (28b) and (30b) above, and in (32b) below, due to the lack of the relevant structural position for agreement, a non-agreeing past participle as in (32a) is much better. Since the non-agreeing (unmarked) form of the past participle corresponds to a masculine singular ending, the lack of obligatory agreement is in some sense less visible/aubible.[22] With this in mind, consider the contrast between (32a) and (32b), noted by Bouvier (2000):

(32) a. *Un pantalon   a   été   fait   faire   (par Marie)*
       a   pant_{MASC.SING} has been made_{MASC.SING} (to) make (by Marie)
     b. **Une jupe   a   été   fait(e)   faire   (par Marie)*
       a   skirt_{FEM.SING} has been made_{(FEM.SING)} (to) make (by Marie)

This amounts to claiming that the non-agreeing form of the past participle of causative *faire* in examples like (32a) is somehow reanalyzed *a posteriori*, as a masculine singular past participle, thus giving a "feeling" of agreement. Be it as it may, the crucial point for our discussion here is that passive of causatives should be considered ungrammatical in French due to the impossibility of performing past participle agreement, which itself, by hypothesis, is due to the structural reduction of causative *faire*.[23] Italian causative *fare*, on the other hand, is assumed to be contained within a fully specified past participial structure, whence the possibility and obligatoriness of past participle agreement in the passive of causatives, as is standardly the case in Italian. In as far as the prediction made by our analysis in section 3.1.2 is concerned, which makes crucial reference to the criterial nature of the causative voice and the consequent operation of criterial freezing, French seems indeed to behave like Italian, allowing for sub-extraction of the internal argument from the criterial

---

[22] Other instances of passivizing the causative are provided by impersonal passives, not involving movement of the internal argument, hence not needing past participle agreement on causative *faire* anyway. See Kayne (2008) and, again, Bouvier (2000) for the following sentence in (i), minimally contrasting with the ungrammatical (32b) in the text:

(i) *Il   a   été   fait   faire   une jupe*
    it has been made (to) make a   skirt

[23] I suspect that some normative pressure may also be at play in this domain: past participle agreement in passive is required as a reflex of the DP internal argument moving through the specifier of the (passive) past participial agreement head. Hence, if it cannot be realized, due to the structural reduction of the past participle (as in the case of causative *faire*), the non-agreeing form is still not "allowed". However, we should conclude that it is allowed to some extent, as shown by the possibility of sentences like (32a) (where agreement can plausibly be rescued *a posteriori*, as suggested in the text). The normative pressure is strong enough as not to allow that the non-agreeing form also occurs with a feminine subject, whence the ungrammaticality of sentences like (28a).

spec position of the causative voice, as indicated by the (marginal) possibility of examples like (32a). Note that the equivalent of (32a) in English type causatives is completely ungrammatical for all speakers, as discussed in relation with (20) in section 3.1. We have interpreted this impossibility as a consequence of the operation of criterial freezing, whereby no variation is expected with this type of causatives. This seems a reasonable idealization of the relevant distinctions and properties of the morphosyntax of the different types of causatives, analyzed in a comparative perspective.

4 Remarks on the comparison between passive and causatives and some related considerations from acquisition

4.1 Passive

We have pointed out in section 2 that movement of a verbal chunk is operative in passive, following Collins' (2005) analysis in terms of *smuggling*. The trigger for movement of the chunk is, in the case of passive, (some component of) the passive voice. Movement of the verbal chunk in this case has an important side effect: it eliminates the potential intervention-locality violation, which would inevitably arise in the application of one crucial step in the standard derivation of passive. This step is the movement of the object internal argument across the external argument, which is merged in a higher position in the verb phrase. This consequence has sometimes led some linguists to manifest a certain amount of skepticism about the *smuggling* operation, as if it had a "look-ahead" flavor, which is incompatible with minimalist assumptions, and more generally, with a purely formal view of syntactic computations. The look-ahead flavor would stem from the impression that movement of the chunk of the verb phrase is implemented in order to allow movement of the internal argument, thus avoiding the potential intervention locality violation. We want to submit here the idea that no such flavor is to be associated with the *smuggling* operation. As mentioned above, the fact that a potential locality violation is directly overcome through this movement operation is in fact a side effect. The crucial factor is presence of (a component of) the passive voice with the property of attracting movement of a chunk of the verb phrase. If the analysis for Romance causatives of the Italian type proposed in the previous sections is on the right track, it clearly indicates that operations moving chunks of verb phrases are widespread in grammar independently of any locality issue. Properties of different voices are at stake as well as properties of the verbal spine and the overall functional structure, which give rise to derivations that are necessarily in compliance with the locality principle and satisfy the basic labeling requirement. In passive, much as in Romance causatives of the Italian type, the moved constituent is a chunk of the verb phrase. However, it is only in passive that movement of the internal argument takes place from the *smuggled* landing site position of the moved verbal constituent, due to the Case properties of structures with passive morphology. No such movement occurs in causatives, as Case properties are different in these structures. Hence, there is no direct link between movement of a chunk of the verb phrase and the need to save the structure from a violation of locality provoked by movement of an internal argument across an external argument. There is no movement of the internal argument in causatives, but there is movement of a chunk of the verb phrase containing (at least) the verb and the internal argument. Hence, movement of a portion of the verb phrase may be independent of the occurrence of subsequent movement of the internal argument, so that the criticism of a look-ahead flavor in *smuggling* is not justified. If the line of analysis proposed in the previous sections is really sustainable, it shows that this type of derivation is fairly widespread, which, according to the proposal developed here, is in turn partly the consequence of the labeling requirement.[24]

4.2 Related considerations from acquisition

A recent interesting result from acquisition has indicated that Italian-speaking children seem to show an early access, possibly a preference, for a type of passive including the causative construction from their earliest stages of development. The structure at issue is illustrated by examples like the following:

(33) Il   bambino   si   fa   pettinare   dalla   mamma
      the   child   SI-cl   make   (to) comb   by the   mum
      'The child makes himself comb by the mum'

For reasons of space neither a detailed description of this construction nor a discussion of the relevant acquisition data can be provided here (see Belletti and Guasti 2015, chapter 4; Manetti and Belletti 2015; Belletti 2016, Belletti

---

24 Thus, depending on the active or passive voice, in simple sentences either the external argument DP moves (to Spec-TP, active) or the vP-chunk moves (to Spec of the relevant component of the passive voice).

2017; Belletti and Costa 2015 for detailed presentation). I wish to focus on one aspect of these results instead, the earliness and possibly the preference for a type of passive, which looks intuitively and pre-theoretically rather complex. It looks more complex than e.g. a copular passive for at least the following intuitive reasons: it includes a causative construction, and an anaphor binding dependency between the (derived) subject and reflexive clitic *si*, combined with the characteristic dependencies of passives, i.e. the A-dependency between the raised internal argument and its copy and, finally, the realization of the external argument as a *by*-phrase. As has already been mentioned, the latter dependencies are also present in the periphrastic passive with the auxiliaries *essere* (be) or *venire* (come), which are both possible in Italian (with eventive verbs), as illustrated in (34):

(34) a. *Il   bambino   è   pettinato   dalla   mamma*
        the   child   is   combed   by the   mum
     b. *Il   bambino   viene   pettinato   dalla   mamma*
        the   child   comes   combed   by the   mum
     'The child is combed by the mum'

Hence the crucial role in the early access to the seemingly more complex passive in (33) must be played by the presence of the reflexive binding relation and by the presence of the causative construction. Whereas it is known that children from relatively early ages (3;5) do have good mastery of Principle A, hence of anaphor binding, early access to the Romance causative construction of the Italian type is not known and it is intuitively somehow less expected. Although we cannot disentangle the respective role of anaphor binding and of the causative construction at the stage of our present knowledge[25], the fact that the presence of the causative construction does not make the structure more complex, but, if anything, it seems to make it less complex, is an important indication that the mechanisms involved in the derivation of causatives must be very basic mechanisms, and as such must be available early to the child. In the spirit of the discussion and analysis proposed here, some very basic computational mechanism has indeed been identified as being at play in the derivation of Romance causatives of the Italian type: *smuggling*, moving a chunk of the verb phrase. The ultimate generator of such computational

---

25 See the references quoted for some speculation based on experimental results from development; see also Belletti (2017) for a proposal on the further possible role of the reflexive in privileging causative passive as well, and for discussion that children's causative passive should indeed involve the *smuggling* operation along the lines discussed here.

mechanisms is the fundamental labeling requirement, which is an essential requirement to interpret structures at the interface.[26]

5 Conclusion

The main proposal of this article has been that the crucial engine triggering the derivation of Romance causatives of the Italian type may lie in the fundamental labeling requirement: the requirement is satisfied through movement of a chunk of the verb phrase of the *smuggling* type, probed by a criterial causative voice head. As a consequence, the remaining constituent is labeled DP. Furthermore, it has been proposed that the movement attracting property of the causative head may be parametrized, so that in some languages the attracted constituent is not a vP-chunk but rather a DP that is the external argument of the lexical verb phrase. This is the case of English type causatives and yields a structure in which compliance with the labeling requirement is obtained in a way closer, in that respect, to the situation of non-causative simple (active) clauses.

That the ultimate generator of the movement processes occurring in causatives of the Romance/Italian type is a fundamental requirement such as labeling, which is essential for the interpretation of syntactic structures at the interfaces, is consistent with the robust fact that indicates that, language after language, causatives are typically described as having a somewhat special yet well recognizable status, often involving displacement of constituents of different kinds, such as verbal constituents as in Romance and a DP as in English-type languages.

---

26 English-speaking children are known to have their earliest access to passive through the *get*-type passive (Crain 1991; Crain, Thornton, and Murasugi 2009), for which a similar analysis as the one developed in section 2 can be proposed. For a movement analysis of *get* passive see Haegeman (1985). For reasons of space this point cannot be developed here.

We are not yet in a position to conclude that access to active Romance causatives of the Italian type is in general rather early in development, as no reliable experimental evidence is available yet. The natural expectation is that it should be, and new experiments are under construction. We can also not yet say whether access to English type causatives should be equally early, provided that in Romance/Italian it indeed is. Some recent results (Santos, Gonçalves, and Hyams 2015) suggest that this is not the case, as English type causatives are present in EPortuguese and are acquired relatively late and dis-preferred by EPortuguese-speaking children. This suggests a possible intrinsic complexity in the raising operation that occurs from a reduced type of clausal complement (cf. structure [22]). See Belletti and Costa (2015) for some speculations along these lines in the context of a comparison between EPortuguese and Italian in the access to *si*-causative passive by young children.

According to the proposal developed here, these are the only types of displacements possible, and in fact required, given properties of the clause structure embedded under the causative voice and the requirement of labeling of syntactic structures. Causative is a fundamental voice, which yields a central interpretation that can be expressed in criterial terms, as in the proposal developed here. Minimal parametric differences in the attracting property of the causative voice yield the different types of causatives discussed, whose structural syntactic architecture is fundamentally homogeneous as is their resulting interpretive routine.

Acknowledgments: The research presented here was funded in part by the European Research Council/ERC Advanced Grant 340297 SynCart – "Syntactic cartography and locality in adult grammars and language acquisition". I also wish to thank Guglielmo Cinque, Luigi Rizzi, and all the participants in the class I held at the Department of Linguistics of the University of Geneva in the fall 2015 for their inspiring comments.

References

Alexiadou, Artemis, Elena Anagnostopoulou & Florian Schäfer. 2015. *External arguments in transitivity alternations*. Oxford & New York: Oxford University Press.

Belletti, Adriana. 2001. Agreement projections. In Mark Baltin & Chris Collins (eds.), *A Handbook of contemporary syntactic theory*, 483–510. Oxford: Blackwell.

Belletti, Adriana. 2006. (PAST) participle agreement: A case study. In Martin Everaert & Henk van Riemsdijk (eds.), *The Blackwell companion to syntax*. vol. 3, 493–521. Oxford: Blackwell; updated version forthcoming.

Belletti, Adriana. 2009. *Structures and strategies*. New York: Routledge.

Belletti, Adriana. 2016. (Reflexive) *Si* as a route to passive in Italian. In Ludovico Franco & Paolo Lorusso (eds.), *Linguistic variation: Structure and interpretation*. Boston & Berlin: De Gruyter Mouton.

Belletti, Adriana. 2017. On the acquisition of complex derivations with related considerations on poverty of the stimulus and frequency. In Elisa Di Domenico (ed.), *Syntactic complexity from a language acquisition perspective*, 28–48. Newcastle: Cambridge Scholars Publishing.

Belletti, Adriana & Luigi Rizzi. 1988. Psych-verbs and Th-Theory. *Natural Language and Linguistic Theory* 6. 291–352.

Belletti, Adriana & Luigi Rizzi. 2012. Moving verbal chunks in the Low Functional Field. In Laura Brugè, Anna Cardinaletti, Giuliana Giusti, Nicola Munaro & Cecilia Poletto (eds.), *Functional heads. The cartography of syntactic structures*, vol. 7, 129–137. New York: Oxford University Press.

Belletti, Adriana & Maria Teresa Guasti. 2015. *The acquisition of Italian. Morphosyntax and its interfaces in different modes of acquisition* (Language Acquisition and Language Disorders series). Amsterdam & Philadelphia: John Benjamins Publishing Company.

Belletti, Adriana & Joao Costa. 2015. Passive object relatives in Italian and Portuguese: *Smuggling* and intervention. Presented at Romance Turn 7, October 2015, University of Venice.

Bellucci, Giulia. The Romance *causee* as an oblique subject. Poster presented at the 41st IGG, Università per stranieri di Perugia, February 2015.

Benincà, Paola & Cecilia Poletto. 2004. Topic, Focus and V2: Defining the CP sublayers. In Luigi Rizzi (ed.), *The structure of CP and IP*, 52–75. New York: Oxford University Press.

Bianchi, Valentina & Mara Frascarelli. 2010. Is Topic a root phenomenon? *Iberia*, 2. 43–48.

Bianchi, Valentina, Giuliano Bocci & Silvio Cruschina. 2014. Focus and its implicatures. In Enoch Aboh, Afke Hulk, Jeannette Schaeffer & Petra Sleeman (eds.), *Romance languages and linguistic theory: Selected papers from Going Romance 2013*. Amsterdam: John Benjamins.

Bošković, Želiko. 2008. On the operator freezing effect. *Natural Language & Linguistic Theory* 26. 249–287.

Bošković, Želiko. 2015. If you are moving, it's important when you label. Talk at Séminaire de recherche, Université de Genève

Bouvier, Yves-Ferdinand. 2000. How to passivize French causatives. *Snippets*, 2, http://www.lededizioni.it/ledonline/snippets.html

Burzio, Luigi. 1986. *Italian syntax. A government-binding approach*. Dordrecht: Reidel.

Cardinaletti, Anna. 2004. Towards a cartography of subject positions. In Luigi Rizzi (ed.), *The structure of IP and CP. The cartography of syntactic structures*, vol. 2, 115–165. New York: Oxford University Press.

Cecchetto, Carlo & Caterina Donati. 2014. *(Re)Labeling*. Cambridge, MA: The MIT Press.

Chomsky, Noam. 1980. On binding. *Linguistic Inquiry* 11. 1–46

Chomksy, Noam. 1981. *Lectures on Government and Binding*. Dordrecht: Foris Publications.

Chomsky, Noam. 1995. *The Minimalist Program*. Cambridge, MA: MIT Press.

Chomsky, Noam. 2001. Derivation by Phase. In Michael Kenstowicz (ed.), *Ken Hale: A life in Language*, 1–52. Cambridge, MA: The MIT Press.

Chomsky, Noam. 2013. Problems of projection. *Lingua* 130. 33–49.

Chomsky, Noam. 2015. Problems of projection: Extensions. In Elisa Di Domenico, Cornelia Hamann & Simona Matteini (eds.), *Structures, strategies and beyond. Studies in honour of Adriana Belletti*, 3–16. Amsterdam & Philadelphia: John Benjamins.

Collins, Chris. 2005. A smuggling approach to the passive in English. *Syntax* 8.2. 81–120.

Crain, Stephen. 1991. Language acquisition in the absence of experience. *Behavioral and Brain Sciences* 14. 597–650.

Crain, Stephen, Rosalind Thornton & Keiko Murasugi. 2009. Capturing the evasive passive. *Language Acquisition* 16(2). 123–133.

Frascarelli, Mara & Roland Hinterhölzl. 2007. Types of topics in German and Italian. In Susanne Winkler & Kerstin Schwabe (eds.), *On information structure, meaning and form*, 87–116. Amsterdam: John Benjamins.

Friedemann, Marc Ariel & Tali Siloni. 1997. Agr$_{obj}$ is not Agr$_{participle}$. *The Linguistic Review* 14. 69–96.

Folli, Raffaella & Heidi Harley. 2007. Causation, obligation, and argument structure: On the nature of little *v*. *Linguistic Inquiry* 38. 197–238.

Guasti, Maria Teresa. 1993. *Causative and perception verbs. A comparative study*. Torino: Rosenberg & Sellier.

Haegeman, Liliane. 1985. The *get*-passive and Burzio's generalization. *Lingua* 66. 53–77.

Hagemann, Liliane. 2012. *Adverbial clauses, main clause phenomena, and composition of the left periphery: Cartography of syntactic structure*, vol. 8. New York: Oxford University Press.
Kayne, Richard. 1975. *French syntax*. Cambridge, MA: The MIT Press.
Kayne, Richard. 1981. On certain differences between French and English. *Linguistic Inquiry* 12. 349–371.
Kayne, Richard. 1989. Facets of Romance past participle agreement. In Paola Benincà (ed.), *Dialect variation on the theory of grammar*, 85–104. Dordrecht: Foris.
Kayne, Richard. 2004. Prepositions as probes. In *Structures and beyond. The cartography of syntactic structure*, vol. 3, 192–212. New York: Oxford University Press.
Kayne, Richard. 2009. A note on auxiliary alternation and silent causation. In Luc V. Baronian & France Martineau (eds.), *Le français d'un continent à l'autre. Mélanges offerts à Yves Charles Morin*, 211–235. Québec: Presse de l'Université de Laval.
Krapova, Iliana & Gugliemo Cinque. 2008. On the order of wh-phrases in Bulgarian multiple wh-fronting. In Gerhild Zybatow, Luka Szucsich, Uwe Junghanns & Roland Meyer (eds.), *Formal description of Slavic languages: The fifth conference, Leipzig 2003*, 328–336. Frankfurt am Main: Peter Lang.
Legate, Julie Anne. 2014. *Voice and v. lessons from Acehnese*. Cambridge, MA: The MIT Press
Manetti, Claudia & Aadriana Belletti. 2015. Causatives and the acquisition of the Italian passive. In Cornelia Hamann & Esther Ruigendijk (eds.), *Language acquisition and development. Proceedings of GALA-2013*, 282–298. Newcastle: Cambridge Scholars Publishing.
Moro, Andrea. 2000. *Dynamic antisymmetry*. Cambridge, MA: The MIT Press.
Ramchand, Gillian. 2008. *Verb meaning and the lexicon: A first phase syntax*. Cambridge, MA: The MIT Press
Rizzi, Luigi. 1978. A restructuring rule in Italian syntax. In Samul Jay Keyser (ed.), *Recent transformational studies in European languages*, 113–158. Cambridge, MA: The MIT Press.
Rizzi, Luigi. 1990. *Relativized minimality*. Cambridge, MA: The MIT Press.
Rizzi, Luigi. 1997. The fine structure of the left periphery. In Liliane Haegeman (ed.), *Elements of grammar*, 281–337. Dordrecht: Kluwer.
Rizzi, Luigi. 2004. Locality and left periphery. In Adriana Belletti (ed.), *Structures and beyond. The cartography of syntactic structures*, vol. 3, 223–251. New York: Oxford University Press.
Rizzi, Luigi. 2005. On some properties of subjects and topics. In Laura Brugé, Giuliana Giusti, Nicola Munaro, Walter Schweikert & Giuseppina Turano (eds.), *Proceedings of the XXX Incontro di Grammatica Generativa*, 203–224. Venezia: Cafoscarina.
Rizzi, Luigi. 2006. On the form of chains: Criterial positions and ECP effects. In Lisa Lai-Shen Cheng & Norbert Corver (eds.), *Wh-movement: Moving on*, 97–134. Cambridge, MA: The MIT Press.
Rizzi, Luigi. 2010. On some properties of criterial freezing. In E. Phoevos Panagiotidis (ed.), *The complementizer phase: Subjects and operators*, 1: 17–32. New York & Oxford: Oxford University Press.
Rizzi, Luigi. 2015a. Cartography, criteria, and labeling, in Ur Shlonsky (ed.), *Beyond functional sequence – The cartography of syntactic structures*, vol. 10, 314–338. New York & Oxford: Oxford University Press
Rizzi, Luigi. 2015b. Notes on labeling and subject positions. In Elisa Di Domenico, Cornelia Hamann & Simona Matteini (eds.), *Structures, strategies and beyond. Studies in honour of Adriana Belletti*, 17–46. Amsterdam & Philadelphia: John Benjamins.
Rizzi, Luigi & Ur Shlonsky. 2007. Strategies of subject extraction. In Hans-Martin Gärtner & Uli Sauerland (eds), *Interfaces + recursion = language? Chomsky's Minimalism and the view from syntax-semantics*, 115–160. Berlin: Mouton de Gruyter.

Rouveret, Alain & Jean Roger Vergnaud. 1980. Specifying Reference to the subject: French causatives and conditions on representations. *Linguistic Inquiry* 11. 97–202.

Ruwet, Nicolas. 1972. *Théorie syntaxique et syntaxe du français*. Paris: Editions du Seuil.

Santos, Ana Lúcia, Anabela Gonçalves & Nina Hyams. 2015. Aspects of the acquisition of object control and ECM-Type verbs in European Portuguese. *Language Acquisition*. DOI: 10.1080/10489223.2915.1067320.

Zubizarreta, Maria Luisa. 1982. *On the relationship of the lexicon to syntax*. Cambridge, MA: The MIT Press.

Zubizarreta, Maria Luisa. 1985. The relation between morphophonology and morphosyntax: the case of Romance causatives. *Linguistic Inquiry* 16. 247–289.

Marcel den Dikken
Quantifier float and predicate inversion

1 The baseline: Quantifier float

The distribution of floating quantifiers is standardly taken to be a good indicator of the distribution of intermediate traces: floating quantifiers are typically licit only in positions immediately local to intermediate traces of moved constituents.[1] From this, it is customary to conclude that *the problems one can have with this computer* in (2) and (4) binds an intermediate trace in between the occupant of T (*could* and *to*, resp.) and *be* (see (11) for a sketch of the standard derivation). Let us take this to be correct, and use it as our baseline for the present investigation.

(1) *All the problems one can have with this computer could be insurmountable.*
(2) *The problems one can have with this computer could all be insurmountable.*
(3) *They consider all the problems one can have with this computer to be insurmountable.*
(4) *They consider the problems one can have with this computer to all be insurmountable.*

2 The puzzle: Predicate inversion and quantifier float do not mix

Predicate nominals can host the quantifier *all*, as in (5) and (6), where the noun phrases introduced by *all* as a whole serve as predicate of the copular or small clause.

---

[1] From "stranding" approaches to quantifier float, such as Sportiche (1988), this follows straightforwardly (though such approaches have a hard time restricting the distribution of FQs to traces in specifier positions and excluding them from positions next to traces in complement positions). From "adverbial" approaches, it can be made to follow as well: see Doetjes (1992). For an overview of Q-float analyses, see Bobaljik (2003).

(5) a. *These three issues should be <u>all</u> the problems one can have with this computer.*
 b. *These shirts should be <u>all</u> the clothes I will need.*
 c. *This/The following is <u>all</u> the advice they could give me.*

(6) a. *They consider these three issues (to be) <u>all</u> the problems one can have with it.*
 b. *My wife considers these shirts (to be) <u>all</u> the clothes I will need.*
 c. *They consider this/the following (to be) <u>all</u> the advice they can/could give me.*

As is well known, nominal predicates of copular sentences can often change places with their subjects.[2] For the particular predicate nominal in the examples above, this possibility presents itself as well: (5) and (6) alternate grammatically with (7)[3] and (8).[4]

(7) a. *<u>All</u> the problems one can have with this computer should be these three issues.*
 b. *<u>All</u> the clothes I will need should be these shirts.*
 c. *<u>All</u> the advice they could give me is this/the following.*

(8) a. *They consider <u>all</u> the problems one can have with it to be these three issues.*
 b. *My wife considers <u>all</u> the clothes I will need to be these shirts.*
 c. *They consider <u>all</u> the advice they could give me to be this/the following.*

Interestingly, however, (9) and (10) are ungrammatical, in stark contrast to (2) and (4). The associate of *all* is exactly the same noun phrase in (2), (4), (9a) and (10a). The difference lies in the function served by this noun phrase: it is the subject of predication in (2) and (4) but the predicate in (9) and (10). Whereas *all* can float off of the subject of predication, it cannot float off of the predicate nominal.

---

[2] This is not, of course, a case of subject–predicate metathesis: the predicate moves around the subject's base position, into a higher A-position. See (13), and Moro (1997), Den Dikken (2006) for the syntactic derivation's details.

[3] Note also (i), inverse copular sentences with a quantified predicate from song lyrics, analogous to (7). Unfortunately, since *all* in (i) is itself the head of the relative clause, it cannot float, for independent reasons. So examples of the type in (i) cannot be mobilised to help undergird the main empirical point discussed in this paper.

(i) a. *<u>All</u> you need is love.*
 b. *<u>All</u> I ever need is you.*
 c. *<u>All</u> I ever needed was the music, and the mirror, and the chance to dance for you.*

[4] Predicate inversion gives rise to the obligatory presence of a copula (see Den Dikken 2006 for detailed discussion and relevant references), which is responsible for the fact that (8) must include *to be* while (6) need not.

(9) a. *The problems one can have with this computer should <u>all</u> be these three issues.
 b. *The clothes I will need should <u>all</u> be these shirts.
 c. *The advice they could give me <u>all</u> is this/the following.

(10) a. *They consider the problems one can have with it to <u>all</u> be these three issues.
 b. *My wife considers the clothes I will need to <u>all</u> be these shirts.
 c. *They consider the advice they could give me to <u>all</u> be this/the following.

The central question that this paper seeks to answer is why (9) and (10) should be ungrammatical.

3 It is not about successive cyclicity

One way to interpret the fact that a raised predicate cannot be associated with a floating quantifier in an intermediate position is to conclude from it that while NP-movement of the subject of predication proceeds via a succession of local steps ('successive-cyclically'), raising of the predicate nominal takes place in one fell swoop, without any intermediate stopovers. If there are no intermediate traces along the way between the base position of the predicate and its spell-out site, the fact that *all* cannot be floated in between the occupant of T and *be* in (9) and (10) will follow as a matter of course from one's favourite analysis of Q-float. (11) and (12) summarise this kind of approach to the problem. ('SC' is a shorthand for 'small clause'.)

(11) [$_{TP}$ [the problems]$_i$ [T=could/should/to [<✓<u>all</u>> t$_i$ [be [$_{SC}$ t$_i$ insurmountable]]]]]

(12) [$_{TP}$ [the problems]$_i$ [T=could/should/to [<*<u>all</u>> [be [$_{SC}$ these three issues t$_i$]]]]]

There is strong reason to believe, however, that the raising of predicates is very severely constrained by locality restrictions (see Den Dikken 2006 and references cited there for details). If *the problems* qua external argument of *insurmountable* is to raise via an intermediate position between the occupant of T and *be* in (11), then *the problems* qua predicate nominal should certainly do so as well. A predicate can only raise to an A-position crossing its subject if it lands in the specifier position of the copula outside the small clause: as Den Dikken (2006) demonstrates, the copula averts an imminent minimality violation by enclosing its own specifier position (serving as the landing-site of the predicate) and the base position of the subject in the same local domain ('phase') and rendering them equidistant. Since the predicate's first move must land it in the specifier position of the copula, (12) cannot be accurate. Instead, the derivation should proceed as in (13).

(13) [$_{TP}$ [the problems]$_j$ [T=could/should/to [<*all> t$_j$ [be [$_{SC}$ these three issues t$_j$]]]]]

The derivation in (13) is analogous in all relevant respects to that in (11). So if indeed there is an intermediate trace between T and *be* in the derivations of both (2)/(4) and (9)/(10), the difference between these examples with regard to the legitimacy of quantifier float cannot be attributed to (lack of) successive cyclicity. What then does explain this difference? The answer, as I will argue in the remainder of this paper, lies in the internal structure of the constituent harbouring the floating quantifier – in particular, in the nature of what the quantifier attaches to.

4 It is about the internal structure of floating quantifiers

Floating quantifiers tend to have the external syntactic distribution of adverbial elements, yet they often show morphological agreement with the constituent they seem to quantify over: see, for instance, the alternation in French (14) between *tous* and *toutes* 'all.MASC/FEM'.

(14) a. Les   garçons   ont   tous   fait   leurs   devoirs
        the   boys   have   all.MASC   done   their   homework
        'The boys have all done their homework.'

   b. Les   filles   ont   toutes   fait   leurs   devoirs
        the   girls   have   all.FEM   done   their   homework
        'The girls have all done their homework.'

A way to capture both the agreement properties and the external distribution of floating quantifiers at the same time is to say that the quantifier locally combines with a silent nominal element coindexed with the noun phrase that Q semantically associates with, and that the constituent made up of Q and the silent element occupies an adverbial position in the clause. Such an approach was proposed by Doetjes (1992).[5]

---

[5] Shlonsky (1991) presents an approach to the agreement and distribution facts in which DP moves through the specifier of the QP, triggering agreement. This approach could only throw light on the contrast between (2)/(4), on the one hand, and (9)/(10), on the other, if movement through the specifier of the QP could be argued – on principled grounds – to be the privilege of *argumental* DPs. If the Moro/Den Dikken line on predicate inversion is correct, predicative noun phrases can move to and through derived specifier positions. It is unclear, in that light, what principle of the grammar could block movement of predicate nominals through the specifier of the floating QP.

If we choose this approach, the next question we need to address is what the nature of the silent element is that the quantifier locally combines with in the structure in (15).

(15) [$_{QP}$ all/tous/toutes [$_{DP}$ Ø]]

Is 'Ø' (the projection of) an empty noun (à la Panagiotidis 2003, or perhaps of the type that Kayne has talked about in a series of works in recent years; see e.g. Kayne 2003, 2005), or is it some sort of pronoun? If the former, what is the identity of the silent noun? If the latter, what kind of pronoun is it? Is it *pro* or PRO (assuming that both exist)?

Doetjes (1992) takes Ø to be a pronoun — more specifically, *pro*. I would like to argue that this gets it half right: the quantifier float facts under discussion in this paper indicate that floating quantifiers of the *all*-type do indeed combine with a silent pronoun, but that this pronoun should be identified as PRO, not as *pro*.[6] The PRO in (16) is in a control relation with the noun phrase that the quantifier semantically associates with.

(16) [$_{QP}$ all/tous/toutes [$_{DP}$ PRO]]

Identifying Ø in (15) as PRO holds the key to a simple explanation for the facts reviewed above.

5 The predicate/argument distinction in anaphora and control

Predicate nominals raised to the structural subject position in predicate inversion constructions can antecede pronouns, with the number feature of the pronoun co-varying with the number feature of the raised predicate nominal. We see this in (17).

(17) a. *She considers the biggest problem we are facing today to be poverty and disease; he considers <u>it</u> to be terrorism and migration.*
b. *She considers the biggest problems we are facing today to be poverty and disease; he considers <u>them</u> to be terrorism and migration.*

---

[6] Both *pro* and PRO will serve to explain the fact that the floating quantifier has the same form as a corresponding pronominal quantifier that can be used in argument positions: the quantifier has a pronominal host throughout; the exact identity of the pronoun (*pro* or PRO) does not matter for this. The pronoun's identity does, however, make a vital difference in the account of the contrast between (2)/(4) and (9)/(10), as I show below.

But predicate nominals cannot serve as controllers for PRO, regardless of whether this PRO itself serves as a raised predicate nominal, as in (18b), or as an argument, as in (19b). The a–examples are added as controls to demonstrate that regular pronouns can be anteceded by *the problem with this computer* qua raised predicate; and of course *the problem with this computer* qua argumental expression (rather than raised predicate) can also control PRO without any difficulty, as shown in (20).[7]

(18) a. *The problem with this computer was the cooling system; it wasn't the keyboard.*
 b. **The problem with this computer was the cooling system before PRO being the keyboard.*

(19) a. *The problem with this computer was the keyboard; it proved insurmountable.*
 b. **The problem with this computer was the keyboard, despite PRO not at first appearing insurmountable.*

(20) *The problem with this computer was minor before PRO becoming insurmountable.*

We know independently that expletives cannot control PRO: (21) is ungrammatical.

(21) **There were chickens before PRO being eggs.*

From this, the conclusion emerges that PRO can only be referential. A predicate nominal is not a referential expression; it remains non-referential when raised into the structural subject position of the clause. The ungrammaticality of the b–examples in (18) and (19) can now be explained from the fact that PRO needs a referential controller and does not have one here.

6 The nature of the silent element associated with the floating quantifier resolved

With this in mind, a solution presents itself for the central puzzle of this paper: the fact that while the quantifier *all* can readily float off of an argument, as in (2) and (4), it cannot be associated with a raised predicate nominal, as in (9) and (10).

---

[7] See also the example in (i) (a simplified version of a sentence constructed by a reviewer), which is a grammatical canonical copular sentence with *the problem* and *the solution* serving as the predicate nominals of their respective clauses, and *the cooling system* as the subject of the matrix copular clause and the controller of PRO.
(i) *The cooling system was the problem before PRO becoming the solution.*

An approach to the internal structure of floating quantifiers along the lines of (16) helps us understand this contrast. As (18b) and (19b) have demonstrated, a raised predicate nominal cannot control PRO. So if, as (16) has it, the floating quantifier is locally combined with a PRO that is itself to be controlled by the semantic associate of the floating quantifier, the ill-formedness of (9) and (10) falls out immediately from the failure of the requisite control relation.

Identifying the silent element 'Ø' in (15) as *pro* would not throw light on the ungrammaticality of (9) and (10). This is because, as (17) and the a–examples in (18) and (19) showed, pronouns can readily be bound by raised predicate nominals. It is even possible for a pronoun anteceded by a raised predicate nominal to be explicitly quantified, as in (22):

(22) *Some of the trouble with this computer is its cooling system; but {most/ almost all} of it is its keyboard.*

Pronoun binding cannot be the problem, therefore.[8]

Identifying 'Ø' in (15) as a silent noun, whether à la Panagiotidis (2003) or as in Kayne (2003, 2005), is not expected to be beneficial in our quest for a solution to the puzzle at hand either – although this may depend at least to a certain degree on the silent noun's precise identity. It is certainly unlikely that this silent noun could be a null 'light noun' THING. In (23), the overt noun phrase *these things* is anaphoric to the raised predicate nominal *the problems with this computer* – the plausible reading for (23) is that it was the problems, not the screen and the keyboard, that emerged shortly before the computer was revealed to the general public.

(23) *The problems with this computer are the screen and the keyboard; these things emerged shortly before the computer was revealed to the general public.*

If the empty element in (15) is to be a silent noun, the properties of this noun must be different (in as yet mysterious ways) from its blandest audible congener, *thing*. To account for (9) and (10) based on the silent-noun approach, one would have to attribute to the silent noun the restriction that it cannot be anaphoric to predicate nominals. While certainly a logical possibility, doing so would be tantamount to the postulation of a custom-made, highly specific lexical entity — one that, moreover, never shows up on the surface. That would make the endeavour to predict the ungrammaticality of (9) and (10) on this basis a self-fulfilling prophecy.

---

8 This is binding, not coreference. There is no requirement that the binder of a pronoun be referential.

It appears, then, that the ungrammaticality of quantifier float off of a raised predicate nominal, the central explanandum of this paper, can be successfully derived from an approach to the internal structure of floating quantifiers that identifies 'Ø' in (15) as PRO, as depicted in (16), and not from either of the two alternative choices of 'Ø'. It is likely that the reason why *pro* and a silent noun are excluded has to do with Case: the QP in (15) finds itself in a Caseless adverbial position in the structure of quantifier-float constructions; of the three logical candidates for 'Ø' in (15), only PRO is known to survive in Caseless environments.⁹

7 Conclusion

In this short paper, I have discussed a hitherto unnoticed restriction on quantifier float: the fact that floating quantifiers cannot be associated with a raised predicate nominal, even when they can associate perfectly well with the same noun phrase when it serves as a subject of predication. I have shown that this empirical pattern cannot be explained with an appeal to successive cyclicity or lack thereof, but that a simple solution for the problem is forthcoming if we treat floating quantifiers as internally complex elements containing a silent associate of the noun phrase that the quantifier semantically associates with.

More specifically, I have argued that of the three logically possible candidates for this silent associate, only PRO (controlled by the noun phrase in subject position) explains the central contrast between (2)/(4), on the one hand, and (9)/(10), on the other. If correct, this vindicates a particular version of Doetjes' (1992) approach to floating quantification, and also stresses the importance of the distinction between *pro* and PRO.

Acknowledgements: It is with tremendous pleasure that I offer this paper to Liliane Haegeman as a token of my deep admiration for her as an outstanding educator and researcher, and of our enduring friendship. I would like to gratefully acknowledge the very useful comments of two anonymous reviewers.

---

9 The fact that PRO is itself in a Caseless environment in (15) does not preclude Case concord between it and its controller. It is through such concord that floating quantifiers can match the Case of the noun phrase to which they are associated (see Jaeggli 1982:29 for French *à* in *ces femmes, à qui j'ai parlé à toutes* 'the women to whom I have talked to all', and Bobaljik 2003 for some examples from German). I thank a reviewer for raising the case concord facts in this context. Note also that the observation that PRO, *qua* identifier of 'Ø', is in a Caseless environment in (15) does not necessarily entail that PRO can never be in a Cased position. The relationship between PRO and Case remains complex (see Sigurðsson 1991 and much work in its wake).

References

Bobaljik, Jonathan. 2003. Floating quantifiers: Handle with care. (Revision of 1998 article in GLOT International.) In Lisa Cheng and Rint Sybesma (eds), *The second GlOT International state-of-the-article book*, 107–148. Berlin: Mouton de Gruyter.
Dikken, Marcel den. 2006. Relators and linkers. *The syntax of predication, predicate inversion, and copulas*. Cambridge, MA: The MIT Press.
Doetjes, Jenny. 1992. Leftward floating quantifiers float to the right. *The Linguistic Review 9*. 313–332.
Jaeggli, Osvaldo. 1982. *Topics in Romance syntax*. Dordrecht: Foris.
Kayne, Richard. 2003. Silent years, silent hours. In Lars-Olof Delsing, Cecilia Falk, Günlog Josefsson & Halldór Á. Sigurðsson (eds), *Grammar in focus. Festschrift for Christer Platzack*. Volume 2. 209–226. Lund: Wallin & Dalholm. (reprinted in Kayne 2005).
Kayne, Richard. 2005. *Movement and silence*. New York: Oxford University Press.
Moro, Andrea. 1997. *The raising of predicates: Predicative noun phrases and the theory of clause structure*. Cambridge: Cambridge University Press.
Panagiotidis, Phoevos. 2003. Empty nouns. *Natural Language & Linguistic Theory* 21. 381–432.
Shlonsky, Ur. 1991. Quantifiers as functional heads: A study of quantifier float in Hebrew. *Lingua* 84. 159–180.
Sigurðsson, Hálldor Ármann. 1991. Icelandic case-marked PRO and the licensing of lexical arguments. *Natural Language & Linguistic Theory* 9. 327–363.
Sportiche, Dominique. 1988. A theory of floating quantifiers and its corollaries for constituent structure. *Linguistic Inquiry* 19. 425–450.

Jacqueline Guéron
Beyond narrative: On the syntax and semantics of ly-Adverbs

1 Introduction

Haegeman (2007, 2009) argues that the semantic function of adverbial clauses introduced by a subordinating conjunction such as *while* or *if* depends on their syntactic level of adjunction. Here, we analyze adverbs bearing the suffix *-ly* along the same lines. We claim that in syntax, *ly*-adverbs are not generated in the Specifier position of F-projections (cf. Cinque 1999) but, rather, *adjoined* to such projections (cf. Ernst 2000a). More precisely, the *-ly* suffix bears a formal T(ense)-feature which is checked via adjunction of the adverbial to any maximal projection marked with the same formal feature within the sentential T(-ense) chain. The T-chain consists of CP, TP, vP, and other projections such as NegP, AspP or ModalP (Guéron and Hoekstra 1988).

The semantics of adverbial adjunction involves *conflation* of the adverbial and its host at the syntax-semantics interface. The adverb adds both descriptive and aspectual information to the XP to which it adjoins. As adverbial adjunction is iterative, each adverbial contributes to the creation of a new domain for further descriptive modification. The content of the added material is constrained by the lexical content of the host XP: Material adjoined to a T-linked XP must specify aspects of the event description which are *already implicit* in XP. However, since descriptive modifications cannot be limited in number, we propose that the burden of avoiding infinite recursion of adverbial adjunction falls upon tense construal. The merger of the aspectual information contributed by the adverb with the tense value of the sentence defines a series of time spans within which the enriched descriptions of the event must fit. The relevant time spans correspond to well-defined syntactic domains.

2 The problem

2.1 Variation in the construal of Adverb Phrases

Haegeman (2007, 2009) shows that adverbial clauses are construed differently in different syntactic positions. In particular, *central* adverbial clauses headed by a subordinating conjunction as in (1a,b) differ both semantically and syntactically from *peripheral* adverbial clauses headed by the same subordinating conjunction as in (2a,b).

(1) a. *Nero fiddled **while** Rome burned.*
    b. *If he is smart, he will get a good mark in the exam.*

(2) a. ***While** Max is intelligent, Harry gets along better with people.*
    b. *If he's so smart, why didn't he get a better mark in the exam?*

Haegeman provides a mass of evidence supporting the hypothesis that the central adverbial is integrated into the matrix proposition, while the peripheral adverbial is a root clause licensed by a Force Phrase in the Complementizer domain signaling the point of the view of the speaker (cf. Rizzi 1997).

Thus, central adverbials do not allow epistemic modals but peripherals do.

(3) a. *?? John works best while his children are **probably** asleep.* (Central)
    b. *The ferry will be cheap while the plane will **probably** be too expensive.* (Periph.)

Central adverbials do not allow argument fronting while peripherals do.

(4) a. * *If these exams you don't pass, you won't get the degree.* (Central)
    b. *If some precautions they did take, many other possibilities were neglected.* (Periph.)

Here we apply Haegeman's syntax-based approach to the analysis of the morphosyntactic class of *ly*-adverbs. Although the *ly* morpheme selects an Adjective Phrase rather than a TP complement, it is, like *while* and *if*, a functional head whose projection is associated with different construals in different syntactic contexts. Below we propose an account of the grammatical mechanisms which license the syntactic and semantic flexibility of *ly*-adverbs.

We consider the homophony hypothesis which assigns distinct syntactic-semantic occurrences of an adverb to distinct lexical classes as the worst possible solution in terms of economy and explicative adequacy. Adverbs do define classes, but not, we claim, before the syntax-semantic interface.

Thomason and Stalnaker (1973) classified adverbs in terms of the syntactic domain they modify as "vP adverbs" or "S-adverbs". Jackendoff (1972) matched construal rules to surface structures, distinguishing manner, subject, and speaker adverbs. Alexiadou (1997) and Cinque (1999) argue for a fixed universal hierarchy of clausal functional projections. Each (class of) Adverb Phrase (AdvP) is located in the *Specifier* position of a specific F-projection, rather than, as previously claimed, *adjoined* to such a projection. Each adverb checks a lexical-semantic Formal Feature (FF) with a syntactic head containing the same FF. Cinque's demonstration that the order of different classes of AdvPs is in fact the same over unrelated languages leads him to define a universal hierarchy of F-projections and matching adverbs within the sentence skeleton.

However, given the multiple syntactic positions and construals available to many adverbs, and even assuming that there exists a finite number of adverbial classes, it would be necessary to cross-classify all adverbs manifesting flexibility. For it is not possible, in fact, to classify a particular instantiation of an adverb in terms of either its position as e.g., a vP adverb, or its semantics as e.g., an adverb of manner. Thus, *clearly* is a manner adverb in "John spoke clearly" but an evidential adverb in "John is clearly drunk".

We propose an adjunction hypothesis for adverbs, one form of which was elaborated in Ernst (1998, 2000a, 2000b). In our version of the hypothesis, the *-ly* head of a ly-adverb bears a single Formal Feature, T, which it checks via adjunction to any maximal functional phrase whose head also bears a T feature. Adjunction of an adverb to XP derives a two-tiered XP, in the same way that a syllable bearing a stress feature is a two-tiered syllable. A stressed syllable is significant on the level of interpretation as well as on that of intonation: it may in context be construed as marking the informational or contrastive focus of the sentence. In fact, as discussed further on, so does an adverb.

We propose that Adverb Phrases are adjoined to XP rather than being situated in the Specifier position of XP, as in the cartographic hypothesis of Cinque (1999). We assume that the Agree relation which holds between an X head and its specifier is blocked by the ly-head of the adverb phrase which lacks Formal agreement Features such as person, number, gender or case. Moreover, under Spec-Head Agreement, matching of a probe and a goal results in the *deletion* of an uninterpretable FF. Under Adjunction, on the contrary, the merging of the T-feature of the adverb and that of its XP host results in the *addition* of the semantic content of the adverb to that of its host. And while Spec-head relations are obligatory – non-deletion of an uninterpretable formal Feature participating in an Agree relation causes the derivation to crash –, adjunct-host relations, barring idiomatic selection, are optional. For the T-feature of the functional projection to which an adverb adjoins is saturated independently of the adverb by its relation to other projections bearing a T-feature.

Once adjoined, however, the non-selected adverb becomes an integral part of sentence construal. It may influence the truth conditions of its syntactic host. Thus, "Manner" adverbs like *carefully* and "Evaluative" adverbs like *fortunately* presuppose the truth of the event description in vP, while "Evidential" adverbs like *purportedly* and "Modal" adverbs like *probably* do not.[1] Adverbs also introduce a point of view (POV). While *carefully* is construed in the semantic scope of the overt or covert agent of an event, *fortunately* is construed in the scope of a subject of consciousness internal or external to the core TP. This is shown by the point-of-view ambiguity of "John fortunately won the race" with either the speaker or the subject as POV, or that of "Mary said that John fortunately won the race" with either the matrix or the embedded subject as POV, as compared with the non-ambiguous speaker POV in "Fortunately, John won the race". While an adjunct always adds semantic content to the host XP, the content varies with the level of adjunction. Consequently, the contribution of any given adverb cannot be determined in the lexicon but only after adjunction to a host in syntax.

We claim, moreover, that it is not necessary to define an adverbial hierarchy in the sentence grammar. For the sentence already possesses a universal functional skeleton independent of adverbs. This skeleton is composed of VP, which defines a core eventuality, vP, which adds a subject when the content of VP motivates one, TP, which places the eventuality in time, deriving a proposition, and CP, which places the proposition in a discourse-related time and world. The ordering of F-nodes has an internal logic: an event cannot be placed in a time and a world before it is defined. Other F-nodes depend on the existence of a governing Tense node. Negation, and Auxiliary, Aspect, Modal, and Causative verbs identify a domain of tense interpretation. Since any of these tense-dependent projections may host an adverb, the order of adverbs already follows from independently motivated obligatory and optional F-projections in the sentence structure.

We propose, further, that T-nodes may iterate and that any iterated node may host an adverb. The hypothesis of free adjunction of any adverb to any projection node involved in Tense construal accounts for the fact that many adverbs, such as *frankly, happily, quickly, clearly,* etc. appear in a number of positions both internal and external to vP or TP as well as in the form of parentheticals inserted almost anywhere in the sentence (cf. Godard and Bonami 2004). This part of our proposal raises the problem of how to avoid infinite recursion of T-nodes along with the adverbs they host. In the following discussion we will gradually

---

[1] I use the traditional names of Adverb classes although, being based on only one of a number of possible adverbial adjunction sites, they are not reliable. Nor are classes easily specified. For example is *easily* a manner adverb in either "The bag opens easily" or "John can easily run ten miles"? How does one distinguish a manner adverb from a result adverb as in "John was fatally wounded"? How does the degree adverb in "John read the letter (in)completely" turn into an emphatic measure phrase in "John has (*in)completely lost his mind"?

introduce a semantic constraint, formulated specifically in Appendix 1, that we claim can solve this problem on the syntax-semantics interface.

2.2 The T(ense)-chain

We argue that except for a few idiomatic combinations, like "John worded the letter *(carefully)", -ly adverbs are not selected by the lexical vP, but are freely adjoined to any member of an "extended VP" (Grimshaw 1990). Guéron and Hoekstra (1988) analyse this "extended VP" as a referential T(ense)-chain. All the F-projections composing the sentence skeleton bear a T-feature and contribute to tense and aspect construal at the interface.

The T-chains consist of the series of X° T-links in (5) (where the asterisk on v indicated the possibility of recursion in Guéron and Hoekstra 1988).

(5) T-chain: C–   T–   v*–   V–   (P)
              | | | | |
              +T   +T   +T   +T   +T

The T-heads in (5) are in a government relation in syntax and interact semantically via morpho-syntactic merger or a binding relation. Following Partee (1973), Guéron and Hoekstra assimilated tenses to pronominals. They proposed that the relation between C and T is either anaphoric, marking identity of time reference, or pronominal, marking non-identity of time reference (with Future having the all-new status of a Name). I assume that "little v" also bears a formal T-feature. The lexical V in a finite sentence bears a valued T-feature which must be checked by the closest governing Tense-node. The need for checking its T-feature triggers V-raising in syntax, as in Romance, or agreement of V and T in Logical Form, as in English. Particles must and Prepositions may be merged with or incorporate into a governing V, in which case they acquire a T-feature in syntax in addition to their lexical spatial FF and join the T-chain as well.

In (6) below, C_i denotes the present Speech Time (ST) and T_j, counter-indexed with C_j, denotes the past Event time (ET). As T nodes are referential and time is construed as linear, the pronominal ET denotes the realis past time rather than the *irrealis* or all-new future time. At the interface, temporal construal linearizes (6a) as (6b), with a temporal gap separating the past ET from the present ST.

(6) C_i John T_j read a book.
                        | |
    a.   ST   ET
    b.   ET   ST

A participle phrase is a defective TP. It belongs to the T-chain but differs from a finite TP in that its head bears an aspectual value, like English perfective *-ed* or non-perfective *-ing*, but no Tense value. In order to participate in tense construal, a participial T-chain must merge with a link of a finite T-chain headed by C.[2] In (7) below, $T1_i$ coindexed with C_i denotes the present time. The participial $T2_j$ head, ED, is counter-indexed with the governing $T1_i$-node and thus construed as past with respect to $T1_i$.

(7) *John has read a book*

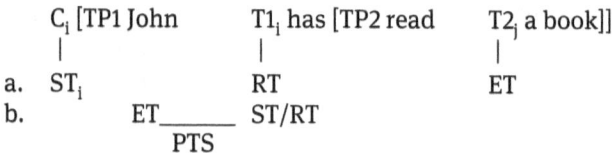

    a. ST_i RT   ET
    b.   ET_____ST/RT
                     PTS

The semantic difference between (6b) and (7b) is due to the role of Aspect. I define aspect as a verbal Number feature which merges with a Tense-feature to define the shape of the time T denotes. A [+plural]/imperfective verb defines an open time interval while a [–plural]/perfective verb defines a closed time interval if VP has an extended aktionsart and a point of time if VP lacks an extended acktionsart. In a finite sentence, an overt perfective or imperfective verbal affix merges with Tense in syntax or LF in order to determine the unbound, bound, or punctual shape of the time the Tense morpheme refers to. Aspect merges with Tense in syntax in ancient Greek. The merger occurs in the lexicon in Romance; in French, past imperfective *parlait* contrasts with past perfective *parla*. The aspect morpheme may also target the non-finite T-feature of a participle, as in English *spoken* vs *speaking*. In Russian, finite, infinitival and participial tenses all merge with aspect either lexically or in morphosyntax.

According to Guéron (2004), the English auxiliary verb *have* bears a [+pl]/imperfective aspect F. In (7) above, the [+pl] Aspect-feature of *have* merges in syntax with the [-pl] Tense-feature of T1, thus multiplying the point of ST and deriving the Perfect Time Span (PTS) of Iatridou et al (2001) into which the past ET is inserted.

When temporal construal is linearized at the interface, as in (7b), a continuous time span links the past ET at the left boundary of the PTS to the present ST

---

[2] A participle is headed by a non-finite T-node, say T2, which must combine in syntax with a finite T-node, T1. It may do this via *government*, as in the Perfect "John has written a letter" (perfective TP2 included in the time span defined by the higher imperfective TP1) or Progressive "John is writing a letter" (TP1 included in TP2); or else by *adjunction* as in "Une fois les enfants couchés, nous sommes partis" (Once the children put to bed, we left) (TP1 abuts TP2) or "Walking down the street, John met Mary" (Stative TP2 simultaneous with punctual TP1).

at its right boundary. This temporal continuity allows a past event to have what is called "present relevance", thus differentiating (6b) from (7b).

In (8) below, ST merges with RT1 and ET merges with RT2 at one point of the past event time interval (marked in (8b) by a bold **e**).

(8) *John has been reading a book.*
    a. C [TP1 John   T1$_i$ has   [TP2 T2+en$_j$ [VP be   [TP3 T3+ing$_j$
         | | | |
         ST   RT1   RT2   ET

        [vP John [VP read a book]]]]

    b. RT2/ET ST/RT1
                      | | | | | | | |
                      e **e** e e e e e e

If we assume that the T-feature of a syntactic head percolates to its maximal projection, we may state the syntactic constraint on the adjunction of a *ly*-adverbial to a host XP as in (9i–ii) and its semantic consequence roughly as in (9iii) (to be refined).

(9) (i) A *ly*-adverbial may adjoin to any XP bearing a T-feature.[3]
     (ii) Adjunction to XP$_i$ creates an additional tier of XP$_i$.
     (iii) The content of the adverbial adjunct expands the interpretation of its host XP by further specification of its descriptive content.

We propose that the T-feature borne by a ly-adverb is not precisely a Tense-feature but a Tense-dependent feature, Aspect. The lexical *aktionsart* of the adjectival base of the adverb is construed as grammatical *aspect* when a *ly*-head adjoins to it in the lexicon. If its newly-acquired aspectual value implies a span of time, then it adds a time period to the event description. For example, because a manner adverb like *carelessly* can only refer to an event which implies a time span, it changes the internal structure of an event construed as punctual in (10a) to one which includes a short time period during which John manifested the property of carelessness in the transition from before to the onset of the drop-the-vase event.

(10) a. *John (instantly) dropped the vase.*
       b. *John (# instantly) carelessly dropped the vase.*

---

3 Thus, the *-ing* head of the gerundive in (i) is part of a T-chain while that of the nominalisation in (ii) is not.
(i) *I don't like John's carelessly dropping the vase.*
(ii) * *I don't like John's carelessly dropping of the vase.*

An aspect morpheme obligatorily merges with a tense morpheme. The hypothesis that *-ly* bears an Aspect-feature thus accounts for the fact that a -ly adverb must adjoin to a link of the sentential T-chain. The assumption that Aspect and Tense FFs are in a one-to-one relation predicts that if a verb bears two aspectual affixes, these are integrated into the T-chain at two different syntactic levels, like the perfective prefix adjoined to V and the secondary imperfective affix adjoined to VP in Russian, for example. Under compositional construal, two syntactic levels define two semantic levels. The sentence "Clearly John intentionally served the tea carelessly" thus involves several T-links, TP and two vPs, each of which adds time-related information. Each link of the T-chain admits only one adverb of its "class", not because adverbs belong to different lexical classes, but because each adjunction site defines a different adverbial class at the interface.

3 From syntax to construal

3.1 Construal is determined by the level of adjunction in syntax

We claim that adjunction of an AdvP to a link of the T-chain adds a segment to that projection which triggers a finer-grained construal of its syntactic domain. More specifically, a ly-adverb adds aspectual information. A vP-adjoined adverb looks inside the event, as in Smith's (1977) definition of imperfectivity. It may target the whole running time internal to the event or else the transition from the end of the event to its result state. Infl-level adverbs target the transition from the time immediately previous to the event to the initiation of the event. TP-adjoined Topic adverbs introduce a time interval which covers the transition between a previous event in the discourse world and the current asserted event.

The adverb *cleverly*, for example, is construed as a VP modifier in (11a), an Infl modifier in (11b) and a TP adjunct or Topic in (11c).

(11) a. *John answered the question cleverly (*and stupidly).*
  b. *John cleverly answered the question (stupidly).*
  c. *Cleverly, John answered the question (stupidly).*

The syntactic structure of the adverb is shown in (12), where the Adjective complement raises to Spec ADVP to support the affixal *-ly* head. (In Romance languages the corresponding affixal head is *ment/mente*.)

(12)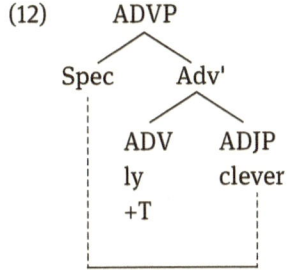

The ly-adverb in (12) contributes imperfective aspect after merger with an adjective implying a time span. The predicate *clever* denotes a property of a +human "subject of predication" which an individual can manifest only by controlling an event which unrolls in time. Consequently, while a punctual/perfective time adverb like *promptly* is acceptable with all the sentences of (13) and (14), *cleverly* is not.

(13) a. *John wrote the letter promptly/cleverly.*
b. *John promptly/cleverly convinced John to leave.*

(14) a. *John left/arrived promptly/*cleverly.*
b. *John spied Mary in the market place promptly/*cleverly.*

Following Travis (1988), Ernst (2000), and others, we may say that *cleverly* implies two theta-roles which must both be saturated in syntax.[4] It implies an event role saturated by the vP event description and an external role saturated via binding by a c-commanding argument. The external theta-role is saturated by the trace in Spec vP of the raised subject in (11a), by the matrix subject in (11b), and by a discourse antecedent identified with the subject in (11c).

If we assume, with Kayne (1994), that syntactic adjunction is always to the left (but maintaining the difference between adjunct and specifier), then adjunction of the adverb to the vP domain in (11) derives the structure in (15).

---

4 We assume, however, that "theta-roles", although based on the lexical content of V and its arguments, are not assigned solely within vP, but continue to be defined throughout the derivation. Thus the verb *sink* acquires an external theta-role only if an external argument appears in Spec vP. Adjectives like *clever, happy,* or *careless* imply an external theta-role identified with a governing [+hu] argument. If we assume that both vP and -ly adverbs imply an event argument, the construal of the sentence would be via theta-role identification and gradual expansion of an event description within the T-chain.

(15)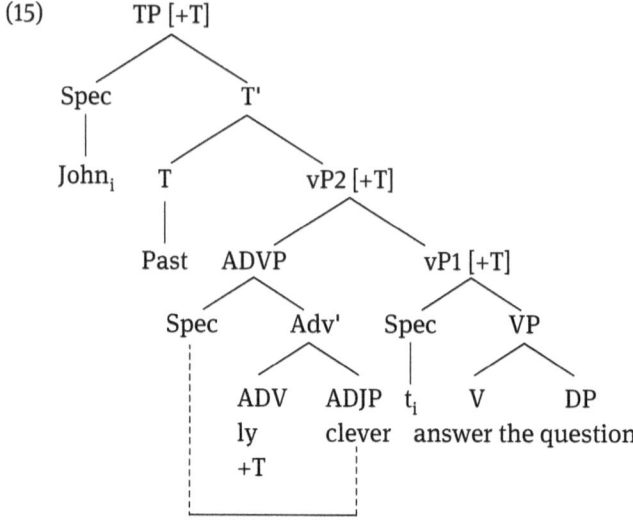

(15) has the interpretation (11b), not (11a), however. For here the external theta-role of *clever* is identified by the c-commanding matrix subject, not by the trace of the subject in Spec vP. Consequently, *cleverly* is construed as an Infl Adverb: its imperfective aspect merges with the past tense F of T to project an interval of time *external* albeit contiguous to the event. John manifested cleverness starting with his intention to answer the question and up to the initial boundary of the event. But as the possibility of adding the manner adverbial *stupidly* in (11b) shows, he was not necessarily clever throughout the event.

To derive the construal in (11a), vP1 must scramble to the left of the Adverb and adjoin to a still higher vP node, as in (16).

(16)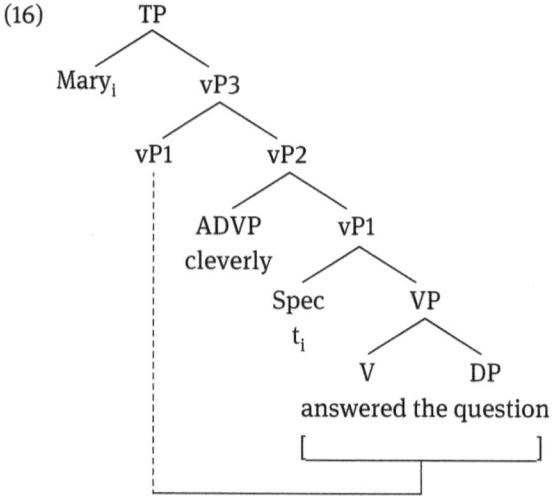

Movement of vP1 to the left of the Adverbial and its adjunction to vP2, creating vP3, derives (17), where the external theta-role of the adverb is now saturated by the trace of the raised subject within the vP3 projection.[5]

(17) Mary$_i$ [vP3 [vP1 t$_i$ answered the question [vP2 cleverly [t $_{vP1}$]]]] (= (11a))

Leftward movement of vP also accounts straightforwardly for the difference in construal between (18a) and (18b) (from Andrews 1983, discussed in Larson 2004). In (18a) John's intention was to knock on the door and he did it twice. In (18b) his intention was right from the beginning to knock on the door twice.

(18) a. *John knocked on the door **intentionally twice**.*
      b. *John knocked on the door **twice intentionally**.*

Larson (2004) suggests that *intentionally* is ambiguous between a simple (VP-final) event predicate and an (adjoined) scopal operator (while *twice* is a quantifier). We claim that ly-adverbs cannot be classified before they adjoin to a level of the T-chain to which they add a specific type of time-related information to the event description. Adverbs like *intentionally, inadvertently*, etc., contribute a span of psychological time which starts before the agent's action and goes up to the action but specifies nothing with respect to the internal structure of the event. Consequently, these adverbs must adjoin to a higher vP or Infl level; only on these syntactic levels can they introduce a time span which begins before the event.

The surface structures (18a-b) may both be derived from the underlying structure (19a). In (19b), vP1 adjoins to vP3, deriving (18a). In (19c), vP1 first adjoins to vP2 (movement A) and then the entire enlarged vP3 adjoins to vP4, creating vP5 (movement B) which derives (18b).

---

[5] Haider (2000) proposes that adverbs are *adjoined* to their embedding head if they precede it but are *embedded* under the containing head if they follow it. The construal mechanism we propose requires adjunction for vP as well as Infl and Topic adverbs. Note, however, that (16) derives an embedded position for vP Adverbs (also defended by McConnell-Ginet, 1982; Larson, 1988, 2004; and Stroik, 1990) since the adverb is embedded in the maximal vP3 after leftward movement of vP1 in syntax.

(19) a. John$_i$ [vP3 intentionally [vP2 twice [vP1 t$_i$ knocked on the door]]]
    b. John$_i$ [vP4 [vP3 intentionally [vP2 twice [vP1 t$_i$ knocked on the door]]

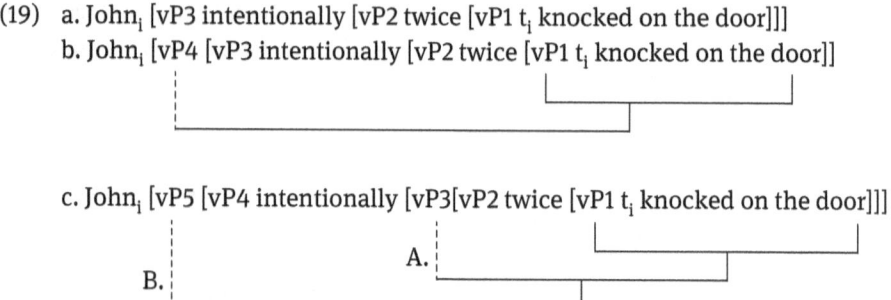

    c. John$_i$ [vP5 [vP4 intentionally [vP3[vP2 twice [vP1 t$_i$ knocked on the door]]]

Leftward movement of vP is independently attested in the grammar. In (20), under so-called "VP-fronting", the vP subject *Mary* raises in syntax to Spec TP and *did* realizes the T-node. The trace of the external argument t$_i$ must be included in the fronted vP or else the raised subject could not access the agent theta-role assigned in vP1 via Reconstruction or Agree.

(20) *John requested that Mary answer the question.*
    a. *and answer the question she did.*
    b. and [$_{VP}$ t$_i$ answer the question] she$_i$ did t$_{vP}$.

3.2 On the syntactic determination of adverbial classes

3.2.1 Speaker-oriented adverbs

Any adverb in a peripheral position is speaker-oriented. For example, adverbs such as *frankly* and *briefly* typically describe the subject's manner of conducting an event when adjoined to vP as in (21a), the attitude of the subject with respect to the event when adjoined to Infl as in (21b), and the attitude of the speaker with respect to the content of her speech act as directed to a hearer, when adjoined to TP as in (21c). Similarly in (22a–c).

(21) a. *Mary spoke to Bob frankly.*
    b. *Mary frankly criticized Bob's behavior.*
    c. *Frankly, this book is not as good as your last one.*

(22) a. *Mary spoke briefly (but to the point).*
    b. *Mary briefly had an affair with Bill this year.*
    c. *Briefly, Mary spoke too long.*

Other adverbs have an evidential meaning in a high syntactic position and denote manner -or become ungrammatical- in the vP-adjoined position.

(23) a. *Clearly/evidently, Mary spoke to the point.*
b. *Mary spoke to the point clearly/*evidently.*

Adverbs like *fortunately* and *sadly* presuppose the truth of the propositional complement. As they do not see the internal structure of the event, they cannot modify it via adjunction to vP.

(24) a. *John is fortunately eighteen years old.*
b. ** John is eighteen years old fortunately.*

Note, however, that, as mentioned earlier, the entire sentence is in the scope of the CP domain associated with the speaker. In addition to the insertion of adverbs in the right and left periphery, the speaker can intervene, with or without phonological pauses, between any two XP domains. Thus, a modal adverb associated with a subject of consciousness external to the event can intervene within the event description itself to focus one of its segments. Cinque (1999) points out that although the modal adverb *probabilmente* 'probably' precedes *già* 'already' in the syntactic hierarchy, *probabilmente* follows *già* when it focalizes an object argument.

(25) *Lo avra gia detto probabilmente a tutto.*
It (s/he) will have already told probably to everyone
's/he will have already told it probably to everyone'

We suggest that not only does the *mente*-adverb in (25) specify the focus of the sentence in (25), but that *mente/ly*-adverbs always focus the material in their syntactic domain. Information focusing is a speaker-oriented grammatical mechanism. An Infl-level adverb which focuses the whole event description in vP will exclude a focus on a sub-part of the event which is incompatible with the speaker's more global evaluation.

(26) a. *Mary enthusiastically/confidently/happily sent her article to John.*
b. *Mary sent her article only to John.*
c. ?? *Mary enthusiastically/confidently/happily sent her article only to John.*

(27) a. *Marie a généreusement prêté de l'argent à Jean.*
Marie has generously lent money to Jean
b. *Marie n'a prêté de l'argent qu'à Jean.*
Marie neg has lent money only to Jean
c. ?? *Marie n'a généreusement prêté de l'argent qu'à Jean.*
Marie neg has generously lent money only to Jean

Focusing by both an Infl adverb and a vP adverb embedded in an event description is, on the other hand, acceptable, if, as in (28) it helps to answer a question implied by the Infl adverb.

(28) a. *Mary secretly lent money to John.*
   b. *Mary lent money only to John.*
   c. *Mary secretly lent money only to John.*

3.2.2 Subject-oriented adverbs

The adverb *fortunately* is ambiguous between speaker-oriented POV and subject orientated POV in (29a,b) and between root subject-orientation and embedded subject orientation in (29c), as indicated by the material in parentheses.

(29) a. *Fortunately (for him/for us) John fully recovered from the accident.*
   b. *John fortunately fully recovered from the accident.*
      (i) Now he can vote for my candidate.
      (ii) Now he can vote for his candidate.
   c. *Mary said that John fortunately recovered from the accident (luckily for her/luckily for him).*

It is important not to confuse *evaluation* with *orientation/POV*. While the speaker always evaluates the adverbial content added to an event description, the party concerned by the evaluated material changes with the level of adjunction, the event description and the discourse context. Thus, in a high syntactic position, the adverb *cleverly* describes a property of the subject manifested by his behavior, while in final vP position, it denotes the manner in which the action is carried out and is integrated into the event description itself.

(30) a. *John cleverly answered the question and so did Bill (answer the question)*
   b. *John answered the question cleverly and so did Bill (answer the question cleverly)*

In all positions, however, this adverb adds aspectual information implying a time span.

(31) a. * *John cleverly saw a coin on the ground.*
   b. *John cleverly saw a solution to the problem.*

3.2.3 vP-adverbs

A vP-adverb targets the internal time of an event description and adds information concerning either the manner in which the event is carried out or the result of the event. It may look inside an event to define how it unrolls. It may extend the event to the point at which it describes the changed state of an object. vP-adverbs satisfy an implicit aspectual variable in an event description which corresponds to questions such as "What kind of force controls the event?", "How did the event unroll?" or "How did the event culminate?".

Barring idiomatic selection, a vP-adverb is filtered at the interface by its appropriateness to the lexical content of the event description it is adjoined to. We say "John spoke clearly" but not "*John left clearly": since speaking in a certain manner is a subevent of the event type of speaking, but not of the event-type of leaving. One can execute a concert – but, normally, not a criminal – *beautifully*. The adverb adds the information that the musician or orchestra was engaged in creating a beautiful (abstract) object. This shirt *washes easily* but the Eiffel Tower doesn't *see easily*. The information added to the event-type of shirt washing is that the agent implied by the VP can realize the washing activity without excessive effort. One can load a truck -yet not eat a dinner- *heavily*, even if the dinner consists solely of hamburger and French fries. Here the adverb extends the event time to include its result state: the loading event creates a heavily loaded truck but the dinner is not heavy, rather it has disappeared.

If the adjectival base of the adverb implies an external argument exercising force, mobility, or a psychological state, then the adverb must adjoin to a vP implying a force, a mobile individual or a subject of conscience, respectively.

(32) *The water boiled slowly/violently/*clumsily/*sadly*.

States which imply human will or force persisting over time accept adverbs while "Kimian" states (Maienborn 2008), which lack an internal time span, do not.

(33) a. *John sat on the chair silently/patiently.*
     b. * *John owns a car /carefully/intelligently/seriously/clumsily/slowly*.

Crucially, we claim that an AdvP whose content is not *already implied* by the lexical content of the vP cannot modify the event description, as illustrated in (34a-b).

(34) a. *John fixed the radio expertly/carefully/quickly/*loudly/*clearly/*heavily*.
     b. *They sang loudly/clearly/*fatally/*heavily*.

Like time and place expressions, "vP adverbs" answer questions already implied by the event description. While time and place are implied by all event descriptions, vP adverbs vary with the lexical content of vP. But both types of optional elements may be integrated into the event description, and fronted or deleted in syntax along with V. The examples in (35) and (36) suggest that manner adverbs and time-place phrases adjoin to two different levels of vP, each of which can undergo a syntactic process targeting vP.

(35) *John said he was working feverishly lately and*
     (i) working feverishly lately he is.
     (ii) working feverishly he is lately.

(36) *John sang beautifully on Friday.*
    (i) *and Mary did too.*
    (ii) *and Mary did on Saturday.*

An adverb which contributes a time span limited to the process itself or to its result cannot be placed in the TP domain, which includes a time span beginning before the event. The mismatched adverb either changes its meaning, as in (37b), or condemns the sentence, as in (38b–c) and (39b–c).

(37) a. *John changed the light-bulbs slowly.*
    b. *John slowly changed the light-bulbs.*

(38) a. *They loaded the truck heavily.*[6]
    b. ??*They heavily loaded the truck.*
    c. * *Heavily, they loaded the truck.*

(39) a. *Mary danced beautifully.*
    b. * *Mary beautifully danced.*
    c. * *Beautifully, Mary danced.*

3.2.4 Temporal adverbs

A temporal adverb contributes either imperfective or perfective aspect to the event description as determined by its lexical base. Any event may be placed either at a point or in an interval of time. However, "perfective" point adverbs are incompatible with "imperfective" manner adverbs. Thus a "serve the tea" event may be placed at a point of time corresponding to its inception as in (40a) or be spread over its whole running time as in (40b). However, the adverb *clumsily*, which contributes a time span internal to the event, while compatible with the imperfective time adverbial *all afternoon*, is incompatible with punctual *promptly* in (41).

(40) a. *John served the tea promptly at four.*
    b. *John served the tea all afternoon.*
    c. *John served the tea clumsily.*
    d. *John served the tea clumsily all afternoon.*

(41) a. * *John served the tea clumsily promptly at four.*
    b. * *John clumsily served the tea promptly at four.*
    c. * *Clumsily, John served the tea promptly at four.*[7]

---

6 For discussion of "result adverbs", cf. Geuder (2000), Chapter 3.
7 (40c) is ok if *clumsily* refers to John's lack of social grace but not if it refers to his lack of physical agility.

Formerly and *currently* are inherently punctual temporal adverbs which situate a state at a point of the time line while rejecting events, which have internal temporal structure.⁸

(42) a. *John was formerly married to Sue/a police officer.*
 b. * *John formerly hit Bill.*

(43) a. *John said that he was currently writing a book.*
 b. * *John said he currently wrote a book.*

3.2.5 Modal adverbs

Modal adverbs like *probably* or *possibly* are based on unaccusative speaker-oriented predicates. Unlike evaluative adverbs like *fortunately,* they do not presuppose the truth of the situation the sentence describes. Rather, they function as time-world operators which identify an event as accessible in the discourse world albeit not located in that world at the discourse time. While adjunction is free, any position lower than the Infl domain will not satisfy this semantic requirement.⁹

3.2.6 Degree adverbs

Degree adverbs such as *merely, hardly, scarcely, totally* or *completely,* must be included in the event domain. This is not because they lack aspectual content, for if aspect is a number feature, one may assimilate imperfective aspect, which multiplies points of time, to degrees on a scale. But rather than merging with tense to describe the shape of time, the degree adverb is integrated into vP where it specifies the degree to which the predicate holds of the subject, as illustrated in (44a–c).¹⁰

(44) a. *John is **merely** five years old.*
 b. *John **barely** survived the attack.*
 c. *John **completely** lost his nerve.*

---

8 For discussion of temporally locating adverbs and *currently* in particular, see Altshuler (2014).
9 See Bellert (1977) for discussion of modal adverbs, expecially in combination with negation.
10 See Geuder (2000), (2006), Gehrke (2015) for extended discussion of manner vs degree.

4 On the semantic contribution of ly-adverbs

4.1 Why adverbs?

One may ask why optional adjuncts such as adverbs exist. Many researchers have noted that adverbs add information to the sentence. For Jackendoff (1972), a manner adverb adds something to the verb it modifies whereas an S-adverb translates as a predicate. For McConnell-Ginet (1982), vP adverbs are integrated into vP where they "augment" verbal meaning. In " Louisa departed rudely", the adverb adds a manner of action while in a higher position, as in "Louisa rudely departed", it functions as a predicate operator related to a higher verb ACT. Revising McConnell-Ginet's analysis, Piñón (2009) proposes that some "alternating" adverbs like *rudely*, *cleverly*, or *clumsily*, function either as manner adverbs modifying the lower vP-event, or as agent-oriented adverbs modifying a higher *relation*, "decide to". The agent-oriented vs manner contrast depends on which event argument is modified, that of the "higher relation", or that of the verb.

With respect to agent-oriented adverbs, Piñón's proposal recognizes what is for us the principal contribution of all adverbs adjoined to T in the Infl domain: they include a time before the event began. On this level, as Pinon notes, the "decide to" relation is not always present, however. We claim that in fact the "decide to" relation is present only when it is *redundant*, that is, when an agentive vP already implies an agent's decision to act, as in "Louisa rudely departed" or "John brutally rejected the offer". The relation is not present when the adverb reflects the judgment of the speaker concerning the behavior of the agent, as in "John rudely yawned during my talk" or "John was rudely awakened by the noise"; or when it anticipates a future result of a helpless subject's behavior as in "Alexander fatally fell under Cleopatra's spell"; or when the subject is a natural force as in "the rain gently covered the ground". We claim, paradoxically perhaps, that an adverb cannot add information which is not already suggested by the event description. What all the above sentences have in common is not a decide-to relation, but the fact that they imply a time span which begins before the action and covers at least the initial phase of the action itself. Such a time span is placed in the scope of either subject or speaker depending on the context.

4.2 On conflation of meaning

The grammar contains various combinatorial mechanisms. A T-chain is built bottom-up starting with VP and ending with CP via iterated merger of syntactic phrases. The sentence is linearized in view of its temporal construal beginning with Comp, the first element of the T-chain, with each lower finite or non-finite T-head calculated as either before, after, or simultaneous with the link which governs it.[11] Another combinatorial mechanism is available which is already well documented for Formal Features and morphemes, but less well documented for theta-roles and partial structures. This mechanism is *conflation*, the merger of two syntactic phrases into one semantic unit.[12]

We earlier proposed conflation at the interface with respect to inalienable possession structures (Guéron 1983, 1985, 2003, 2006). The sentence "Jean lui a pincé la joue" ('John to her pinched the cheek' – 'John pinched her cheek') contains two levels of interpretation. It describes a physical event in vP where a hand pinches a cheek, and a psychological event in TP where a human Agent psychologically affects another human, a Benefactive argument. The two levels merge into one via the grammatical mechanism of anaphoric binding (the [+hu] dative *lui* in TP binds the [–hu] determiner *la* in the direct object in VP) and by temporal construal. As the sentence contains only one tense node, the physical event and the psychological event are necessarily construed as simultaneous.

We propose now that at the interface level of construal, the content of the adverb conflates with that of its host T-link, adding time-related information to the event-description. An imperfective adverb adds a time span which is simultaneous with or overlaps that of the event description. In (44), it is the simultaneous reading of the adverb and the event-description which accounts for the failure of a (simplified) Davidsonian-type representation like (45b) or (45c) to represent the meaning of (45a).

---

11 A reviewer notes that top-down construal violates the Phase Impenetrability Condition of Chomsky (2000). Plausibly, top-down construal, which is clearly necessary for the linearization of temporal interpretation and the formation of phonological words, is limited to the interface components of the grammar, meaning and sound.

12 Earlier proposals focused on the integration of a partial and a complete sentence structure. Lakoff (1974) posits syntactic *amalgams* in such a situation. Van Riemsdijk (1998) proposes multidimensional structures in which an incomplete sentence is *grafted* onto a complete one. With respect to adverbs, Bobaljik (1999) adopts both the multidimensionality favored by van Riemsdijk and the adverb order hierarchy of Cinque (1999). Bobaljlk proposes interleaved "multiple hierarchies". An intrinsically-ordered adverbial tier would collapse with a separate intrinsically-ordered argument/head tier by a form of *conflation*. Our own framework is simpler: there exists a single syntactic structure, the T-chain, into which additional information strongly implied by the event description is integrated into vP in syntax while weakly-implied additional material is adjoined to a T-link higher than vP and conflated with the event description at the interface.

(45) a. *John served the tea carefully.*
   b. LF: There was an event E (E=John served the tea) & The event was careful.
   c. LF: There was an event E (E=John served the tea) & John was careful.

(45a) is inadequate because events are not careful, careless, or rude, only people are, and only when involved in an action. Neither LF represents the fact that John's carefulness is manifested only during the time in which he is serving tea.[13] He may be a careless person in general.

Note that both linearization and overlap of points and/or intervals of time are already available for tense construal. Two events are placed at successive points of time in (46a–b), overlap partially in (47a) and are simultaneous in (47b).

(46) a. *John left **before** Mary entered.*
   b. *John played the piano **after** Mary finished her phone call.*

(47) a. *John was crossing the street **when** a bus hit him.*
   b. *Nero fiddled **while** Rome burned.*

(45b-c) also ignore the fact that the addition of vP adverb changes the information structure of the sentence and may affect its truth value. Given VP-final focus construal (cf. Guéron 1980) vP movement to the left shifts the information focus to the manner adverb. The event itself is no longer the Question under Discussion. As is often noted, if John served the tea carefully, then he served the tea.

Ernst (1987) attempts to improve on the LF in (48c) below, which fails to represent the meaning difference between (48a) and (48b).

(48) a. *APPROPRIATELY, Carl handled Jay's lawsuit.*
   b. *Carl handled Jay's lawsuit APPROPRIATELY.*
   c. Exist e (e, handle (c,l) and APPROPRIATE (e)

Ernst replaces (48c) by the Predicate Modification Rule (49) which applies to both (48a) and (48b).

(49) For any Adverb α modifying predicate β, there is an entity γ which is a property/aspect of "something about" the eventuality of β-ing (by the subject) such that Adverb γ.

---

[13] Stowell (1991) makes this same claim with respect to "mental attitude" Adjective Phrases like (i) or (ii). We discuss such sentences below.
(i) *John was clever/mean to punish the dog.*
(ii) *It was clever/mean of John to punish the dog.*

(50) HANDLE (c,l) and Exist γ, APPROPRIATE (γ)

We agree with the intuition formulated in (49) and (50). However, these schema are unnecessarily vague concerning what the "something about" relation between the adverb and the eventuality is. We claim that an adjoined adverb makes a specific aspectual contribution to temporal construal and adds information which is largely predictable on the basis of temporal construal, syntactic position, and the lexical content of the adverb and its host.

4.3 Adverb Phrase vs Adjective Phrase

As mentioned in note 13, Stowell (1991) points out that the property of the subject defined by "mental attitude" adverbs like *clever* or *mean* lasts only as long as the event lasts.

(51) a. *John was clever/mean to punish the dog.*
 b. *It was clever/mean of John to punish the dog.*
 c. *Punishing the dog was clever of John.*
 d. *That was clever of John.*

Such complex adjectival phrases correspond, not to a vP manner adverb – they don't mean that John punished the dog in a clever/mean manner – but rather to the Infl adverbial in (52). (52) is in fact often given as the meaning of (51a-d).

(52) *John cleverly/unkindly punished the dog.*

In (51) and (52), the adjectival base of the adverb implies the existence of an event which motivates the speaker's judgement that a certain property of the agent is revealed by his behavior. However, the sentences have different temporal construals. In (51a-d), the speaker judges that John showed cleverness in the period just before he started punishing the dog, when the event was still just an intention, as Piñón (2009) observes for such cases. In (52), however, the property of cleverness or meanness is asserted following the event, as indicated by the presence of the anaphoric deictic *that* in (51d).

The contrast in (53) shows that the event and the speaker's evaluation of the agent's property are established simultaneously in a sentence with an adverb but not in one with a complex Adjective Phrase.

(53) a. *I realize now that it was generous of John to have lent you his car last summer.*
 b. *I realize now that John generously lent you his car last summer.*

(54a) below expresses the speaker's judgement of John's previous action. (54b) can mean the same as (54a), if it is construed as speaker-oriented or else that John mistakenly married Linda instead of Louise if it is construed as subject-oriented. Under either reading of (54b), the speaker judges the subject during a time which overlaps the action, not a time after the action.

(54) a. *John was wrong to marry Linda instead of Louise.*
    b. *John wrongly married Linda instead of Louise.*

Bellert (1977) points out that while a complex Adjective Phrase may be focused under interrogation, the adverbial structure may not be.

(55) a. *It was clever of John to drop his coffee.*
    b. *John cleverly dropped his coffee.*

(56) a. *Was it clever of John to drop his coffee?*
    b. * *Did John cleverly drop his coffee?*

Bellert rules out (56b) by a semantic rule: one may not ask a question and assert a proposition in the same sentence; (56a) is good because one can ask a question and *imply* a proposition. We attribute the contrast to the temporal construal of the two sentences. It is possible to ask how someone behaved during an event he already participated in, as in (55a), but not to question his behavior during a period which includes a time before the event began.[14]

5 Stories

How can we know the dancer from the dance ?
(W.B.Yeats « Among School Children »)

5.1 From narrative to story

I propose that the addition of aspectual and other time-related information that an adverb contributes via the conflation of its semantic content with that of its

---

14 There is a similar contrast between (i) and (ii).
(i) *John sang (superbly) yesterday.*
(ii) *John sings (* superbly) tomorrow.*

syntactic host changes the mode of discourse of the sentence itself: it transforms a *narrative* into a *story*.

Benveniste (1966) distinguished "discours" which contains deictic items like *today* and *I* from "histoire" which contains no deictic items. The French passé simple is used in "histoire", not "discours". *You* and *I* are paired in "discours", not "histoire". But there are modes of discourse which need contain neither deictic items, like direct address, or the passé simple, like narrative. One of these is the *story*. In addition to asserting the existence of a succession of events, a story describes how events come about, how they unfold, and, in particular, how individuals reveal their character through their participation in events.

A story usually consists of a sequence of clauses or sentences. E. M. Forster (1927/1985) contrasts (57a), a narrative, with (57b), which illustrates what he calls a *plot* (and we call a *story*). To the narration of events in (57a), (57b) adds causality.

(57) a. *The king died and then the queen died.*
b. *The king died and then the queen died of grief.*

Asher and Lascarides (2003) represent a discourse by a logic based on rhetorical links between the logical forms of sentences. While (58a) below preserves the canonical narrative order of events, in (58b), which reverses the order of events, S2 is linked to S1 by the rhetorical device of Explanation.

(58) a. *John pushed Bill and he fell.*
b. S1 Bill fell. S2 John pushed him.

In (57b) and (58b), the second clause or sentence adds both a temporal and a psychological dimension to the narrative. Temporally, the second clause incites the reader to go back to the previous statement in order to grasp the relation between the two events. Psychologically, the second clause reveals the character of the main participant in the subsequent event. (57b) implies that the queen loved the king so much that she could not survive his death. (58b) leads us to wonder what earlier encounter between the two participants caused John to push Bill. Forster points out that with a purely narrative passage, the question we ask is "what then?". But if the narrated event is part of a plot, we ask "why?". Van de Velde (2010) demonstrated that within the sentence, manner adverbs answer the question "comment/how?". We interpret "comment" as implying time-related questions like "How did the event come about", "How did it unfold" and "How did it terminate"?

In a multi-sentence discourse, we often need to backtrack to a previous sentence in order to understand *why* something happened. But in a single sentence containing one or more adverbs, we are not obliged to backtrack to answer *how*? When the hierarchical structure of the sentence is flattened at the interface for temporal construal, the adverbial modifier and its domain are semantically integrated. The addition of adverbial aspect to sentential tense either provides a temporal profile of the event itself or else places the event within a time span overlapping its run time. The lexical content of the adverb evaluates the way the character of a protagonist is revealed by his behavior during the event. While the stative adjective *clever* describes an individual-level property in "John is clever" or "a clever man", the dynamic ly-adverb in "John cleverly answered the question", describes a stage-level property of the participant manifested during the period just before the event time and going up to event time. Conflation of the ly-adverb and its syntactic domain illustrates character-event interaction in time, which may be considered as a miniature or condensed version of the character - event interaction found in a novel, a play, or even an epic poem.[15]

5.2 On the role of secondary participants in a story

Theta-roles are notoriously difficult to define precisely. Perhaps precise definition is not necessary. Is it worth debating whether "the storm" is an Agent in "The storm destroyed the building" or the "pot" an Agent in "The pot whistled"? Who is the Patient in a sentence like "Jean lui a volé sa poupée" translatable as "John stole her doll on her". Such uncertainty suggests that theta-roles are not part of the lexical entry of a predicate. Rather, we propose, the need for an argument with certain properties is strongly or weakly implied by construal at every syntactic level. The existence of a Patient argument in VP is strongly implied by a verb which denotes a change of state of an object such as *destroy* or the creation of an object like *write*. Verbs which merely denote a change of place, such as *arrive*, do not imply a Patient argument, but rather, a Figure moving on a Ground.[16] The Instrument in "John hit Bill *with a stick*" are not selected but, rather, implied by agentive verbs of change of state. Time and Place arguments are implied by all sentences, for they are necessary to derive a proposition with a truth value at the

---

[15] For the novel think of *Madame Bovary*, whose romanticism and basic mediocrity, as revealed by her love affairs, lead to her downfall and death; for the play, think of *Hamlet*, whose inability to avenge his father's murder without introspection leads to tragedy; for the epic, recall how in *Beowulf*, immediately after listing the deeds of a famous Danish king, the bard adds "That was a good king!"

[16] The Figure-Ground relation is defined in Talmy (1975) as the expression of "one physical object moving or located with respect to another". The moving object is the Figure; the stable object is the Ground.

Reference Time. Time, Place and Instrument, which are all included in the core event proposed by Davidson (1967), exist, we claim, solely by implication.

(59) *Brutus   Caesar   [with a   [in the   [on the Ides of*
    killed   dagger]   forum]   March].
    Ag   Pat   Instr   Place   Time

Another argument appears in sentence structures which is not included in Davidson's core event. We claim that the presence of this argument in a transitive structure suffices to turn a sentence which otherwise qualifies as a Narrative into a Story. This argument adds human interest, that is, a personal relationship between event participants. Although it is basically a locative expression endowed with a person F, the name of the argument, Benefactive/Malefactive, already implies the type of content it adds to a sentence.

In a novel or short story, secondary characters are introduced essentially to motivate the behavior and thus reveal the psychology of the principal protagonist. Madame Bovary's lovers are in themselves uninteresting – they embody ordinary social types typical of the mid-nineteenth century. Their function in the story is to reveal the combination of romanticism and mediocrity which characterize the heroine and lead to her downfall and death. Rosencrantz and Guildenstern are indistinguishable; their purpose in the play's story is to reveal the perfidy of Claudius, who sends them to have Hamlet killed. In general, any transitive VP which contains an agent and denotes a change of state of the direct object may select a benefactive argument adjoined to vP whose role is to profit or suffer from the event. The presence of this argument extends the time and action implied by the event so as to include a relation with the agent. It reveals that in addition to the physical goal of affecting some inanimate object, the agent is motivated by a psychological goal involving another human being.

(60) a. *I baked **Susie** a cake.*
    b. *Je **lui** ai cassé sa tirelire (à **Marie**).*
       (I broke her her piggybank (to Marie)

A benefactive argument adjoined to the base vP may even cumulate the benefactive function with a core event function. In (61), the benefactive NP *Jean* identifies the implicit agent of *laver* in VP, thereby acquiring both the Benefactive and the Agent argument functions.[17]

---

[17] Kayne (1975) notes the difference between (61) with an "à DP" Benefactive and sentences like (i) with "par DP": in the first case, the referent of the DP must be *alive* at the Reference Time. In other words, it must be a participant in the Story told by the speaker.
(i) *Jean fera réparer la voiture par Georges.*

(61) *Marie a fait **laver** la vaisselle à **Jean**.*
     (AG)   (AG)   BEN
     Marie made wash the dishes (to Jean)   (Marie made Jean wash the dishes)

As noted earlier, in Inalienable Possession structures, a Benefactive nominal merged with a Patient body-part nominal is construed as both the physical and the psychological target of the agent's action.

(62) *Je   lui   ai pincé   la joue.*
     AG   BEN   PATIENT
     I to him/her pinched the cheek.   (I pinched his/her cheek)

A Benefactive argument is licensed by an agent with an eventive goal. While the epistemic modal in (63) does not satisfy this condition, the deontic modal in (64a) and (65) does. In (64a) the subject cumulates the roles of the Agent of the embedded event and the Benefactive argument licensed by the goal- or outcome-oriented VP. This is made explicit by the (somewhat stilted) paraphrase in (64b). In (65) an extra (malefactive) argument is implied. Here, the conversational context does not require the Benefactive to be explicitly identified: the hearer can guess that it is incumbent upon him to somehow supply the chairs.

(63) *John must have left.*

(64) a. *John must replace the vase he broke.*
     b. *It is incumbent upon John to vP.*

(65) *There must be 50 chairs in this room by tomorrow.*

The adverb *easily* is ubiquitous in middle sentences. Such sentences oscillate between the description of an unrealized generic event type and the predication of a property of an inanimate subject. The adverb *easily* reconciles the distinct functions of such a structure: the adverb contributes the deontic modal content denoting the possibility of realizing the described event while implying the existence of a benefactive argument to bring the event about. Its scalar content implies that the VP event type can become a reality without the expense of excessive energy by the implied agent of the event. Incorporation of the modal adverb in VP triggers acquisition by a sole covert participant of both the implied benefactive argument of the deontic modal and the implied agent argument of the eventive VP.

In English, the middle structure favors the property rather than the agentive interpretation.

(66) a. *That dress washes/sells/alters easily.*
     b. * *That dress sees/buys/admires easily.*

(67) a. *That apple digests easily.*
    b. * *That apple eats easily.*

Some sentences excluded in English are acceptable in French.

(68) a. *Cette robe s'achète facilement.*   (cf. (66b))
       This dress refl buys easily
    b. *Cette pomme se mange facilement.* (cf. (67b))
       This apple refl eats easily

Differences between languages plausibly reduce to differences in morpho-syntax. In a French middle sentence, the strongly implicit external theta-role of the verb is saturated in TP by the *se* morpheme adjoined to V+T, but it is only implied in vP in English, where V does not raise to T. We take the level of construal of the external argument to be responsible for the fact that the adverb can take scope only over an event property of the inanimate subject in the vP domain in English, while it takes scope over the entire event including its initiation by an external argument in the Infl domain in French.

Theta-role conflation between an Agent or Patient argument and a Benefactive in inalienable possession and modal structures violates the theta-criterion which requires a one-to-one relation between a syntactic argument and a lexical theta-role. This is no problem if, as suggested earlier, there are no lexical theta roles. Rather, argument roles are built up during a derivation on the basis of a gradually enriched syntactic structure. A theta-role is only partly defined by the lexical content of vP. When the Agent is construed in context as a human being endowed with both physical force and psychological intention, these agentive properties can be distributed onto two sentential participants. This occurs not only in inalienable possession and middle structures, but also in causative structures ("John made Bill fix the sink") and control structures "I promised Mary [PRO to fix the sink]". If, as we claim, the Benefactive argument is basically a locative DP or PP promoted to argument status by bearing a [+person] F, then this function has no independent lexical source.[18] Like all other arguments, the Benefactive is defined in context.

---

[18] Just as its locative cousin may be iterated in vP, taking different spatial scopes ("John was seated in the living room on the sofa"), in popular oral speech in French, a dative benefactive may be iteratively adjoined to T and construed as an "ethical dative" followed by a "dative of interest". The sentence "Je vais *te me* lui régler son compte" is roughly translatable as "I (*je*-subject) engage myself (*me*-ethical), with you as witness (*te*-interested party), to handle him (*lui*-indirect argument)". Such sentences are found only in familiar oral speech and only when licensed by a positively – or negatively – oriented event description attributed to the speaker (cf. Deschamps 2016).

The shortest story told via conflation which I know of constitutes an even more radical violation of the theta-criterion, since it involves the assignment of both the Agent and the Theme theta-roles to a single argument.

The verbs *wash*, *dress*, and *shave* strongly imply two theta-roles, Agent and Theme. Since VP is generated before merging with v, (69a) must have the structure in (69b): the direct object assigned the theta-role Theme of the event in VP moves into Specifier of vP where it obtains the additional role of Agent of the event. Few verbs allow this pattern (cf. * John killed/pinched/admired, etc.). The condition for the structure is temporal simultaneity of implied subevents: every movement of the Agent defines a phrase during which the "incremental theme" undergoes a partial change. The sentence describes a moving "Figure" within a stable Ground, both elements identified with the sole participant.

(69) a. *John washed/dressed/shaved.*
    b. John$_i$ washed t$_i$.
        AG   THEME

The inalienable possession structure (70a-b) merges a Possessor part and an Agent whole, creating a Figure which consists of a single Gesture within the same physical Ground as in (69) but over a shorter span of time.

(70) a. *John lève [**la main**].*
        AG   POSS
    b. *John raised [**his** hand].*
        AG   POSS

The existence of such sentences supports the hypothesis that while adverb-host conflation depends on temporal overlap, theta-role conflation depends on temporal simultaneity.

The sentences of (71), discussed among others, by Wyner (1998), tell a story involving two participants.

(71) a. *Kim reluctantly/ intentionally/ deliberately hit Sandy.*
    b. *Sandy was reluctantly/ intentionally/ deliberately hit by Kim.*

The problem here is how to account for the fact that in (71b) but not in (71a), *reluctantly, etc.* may denote an event-based property either of the Agent Kim or, alternatively, of the Theme subject Sandy.

Wyner tackles this problem by dividing the lexical entry of auxiliary BE into volitional and non-volitional auxiliaries, and by adding the notion of "volitional event" to the logical form of a sentence containing such adverbs. The adverb *reluctantly* would be associated with a logical form in which it selects both an Experiencer and a volitional event.

Such stipulations are unnecessary, however, if, as we propose, any eventive vP which selects an agent and a theme also licenses a benefactive argument. As co-participant in the event along with the Agent and Theme, the benefactive functions as the psychological goal of the event triggered by the Agent. (71a-b) each condense two sentences, (72a) and (72b), respectively, which qualify as discourses in the sense of Forster or Asher and Lascarides. While (72a-b) involve back-tracking in discourse, (71a-b) simultaneously assert two distinct facets of the same event.

(72) a. *Kim hit Sandy. He was reluctant to do it.*
b. *Sandy was hit by Kim. Sandy let Kim do it, in spite of his reluctance.*

6 Differences between languages

Presumably, the sentence structure of every language includes a vP denoting an eventuality, a TP placing the eventuality in time and denoting a proposition, and a CP node or nodes linking the proposition to the discourse world. If the language has adverbs, the adverbial system should work everywhere in the same way as in English, with free adjunction of the adverb to a link of the T-chain, consequently contributing aspect to tense construal and creating a more complex event description. The resulting structure is filtered on each level of the T-chain by lexically-inspired semantic dependencies between the adverb and the event description. Differences between language would depend on lexical variation and differences in the morpho-syntactic organization of the T-chain.[19]

7 Conclusion

I have proposed that ly-adverbs freely adjoin to any link of the sentential T-chain to check their aspectual T-F against the tense F of that link. The aspectual value of the adverb varies with its adjectival content: while *clever* and *careful* contribute a [+pl]/imperfective value to the event, temporal adjectives like *prompt* or *current* project a [-pl]/punctual-perfective time. An imperfective adverb merged with

---

[19] Above we accounted in this way for differences in the construal of middle structures in French versus English. For differences between English and German in the positioning of adverbs, see e.g., Haider (2000), Frey (2000), and Laenzlinger (2002).

a T-link extends the point of time T denotes at one level of temporal construal. Adverbs which adjoin to vP target the internal structure of the event either totally or else overlapping with its result state. Infl adverbs introduce a span of time which leads from before to the beginning of the event. Topic adverbs link the new event to the discourse situation and suppose previous acquaintance with the subject, some other event participant, or the previous discourse setting (as in "Slowly the snow covered the ground" which presupposes that it previously started to snow).

I have claimed that adverbs not only contribute a more finely grained temporal structure to an event-description, but also, that by evaluating the behavior of participants during an event, they tap into one of the basic devices of storytelling, which is how events reveal character. While a simple narrative need manifest no sign of the speaker, in sentences with ly-adverbs the speaker story-teller is omnipresent via the evaluative content of the adverb and the focusing effect of adjuncts on the information structure of the sentence. If, as we propose, conflation of the adverb and the event description produces (a fragment of) a story, then conflation is one more mechanism to add to the list of already documented mechanisms such as anaphora, ellipsis and causal structures (cf. Halliday and Hassan, 1976) which show that sentence and discourse have more in common than was previously thought.[20]

Appendix 1: On the cartographic hypothesis

A.1 On the order of adverbs

Cinque (1999) presents the impressive results of an empirical experiment and offers a theoretical explanation of these results. Comparing the order of adverbs and semantically matching functional heads two by two, Cinque finds that the same order occurs over a number of unrelated languages. He concludes that the sentence structure contains a universal ordered hierarchy of some 40 adverbs in specifier position of related functional heads. If adverb order is built into the sentence skeleton, it poses no problem for memory or acquisition.

Cinque's results constitute a challenge for any scopal account of adverb order. We have not attempted to account for all empirical data presented in Cinque (1999), in part because we suspect that the conditions of construal differ for different morpho-syntactic types of adverbial modifiers. Here, we offer a scopal account of *ly*-marked adverbs based on their free adjunction to any F-node

---

[20] This is the theme of the volume we edited, *Sentence and Discourse* (2015).

bearing a T F. We noted that a small number of basic T-links are independently necessary in the grammar in order to transform the description of an eventuality *type* into an event *token* possessing a truth value by placing the event description in a discourse-related time and world (cf. Gehrke, 2015). In addition to the obligatory T-links V, v, T, and C, a T-link with a Tense F licenses additional T-links like Negation (cf. Zanuttini, 1991), Auxiliary, Modality and Aspect. The T head also identifies arguments via agreement between a FF of T with one or more FFs borne by a nominal, such as Person, number, or gender. The order of T-nodes is determined by the semantic function of a T-chain. An event must be described before it is placed in a time and in a world. Aspect must merge with tense to define the shape of time as an open or closed time span or as a temporal point. The projection of an event in the discourse time and world depends on the presence or absence of Negation and Modality modifiers of the event description.

We have claimed that not only are T-links inherently ordered, but that they may recur. One T-head can merge with another in the lexicon, like Future and Past in modal/temporal *would* (to which Cinque, 1999, assigns two ordered T-nodes in the syntactic skeleton). T-nodes iterate when the finite root T combines with a non-finite participial T to define, for example, a past time located in the present time span as in the Perfect structure, or a present state of an event with an internal time span as in the Progressive, or a succession of these as in "Mary T1 has [T2 been [T3 being naughty]]". Modal nodes reiterate. The lower modal may be bare as in "Mary should can come" in some dialects (cf. di Paolo, 1989), or infinitival as in "Marie doit pouvoir réparer le lavabo" ('Mary should can fix the sink'). vPs iterate when a finite verb governs a 'causative or perception verb as in "John [vP t made [vP Mary let [vP Sue see the fireworks]]]". Bare VPs merge in serial verb languages (cf. Haspelmath, 2016). We conclude that any link of a T-chain may iterate. If so, the iteration of an XP hosting an adverbial and creating a two-level XP is not a grammatical innovation.

A.2 A problem with the cartographic account

It seems to us that a major problem with the sentence structure proposed in Cinque (1999) is what we might call a lack of *punctuation*. The sentence structure is not divided into smaller articulated segments independent of adverbs. I assume, however, that it is not possible to interpret any complex syntactic structure, perhaps any syntactic structure, without segmenting it into smaller constituents which define its construal compositionally.

I claim that the grammar contains a number of elements which, among other functions, segment the sentence into syntactic-semantic groupings for construal.

I propose that adverbs are sensitive to these elements rather than to any fixed ordering based on lexical FFs.

(i) In the phonological component, pauses divide a sentence into intonational groups. Phonological groups invariably coincide with maximal (XP) syntactic boundaries. If we assume that syntactic boundaries define a segment for construal, then each phonologically defined segment also constitutes a syntactic and a semantic segment to which an adverb may be adjoined.

For example, an intonational pause after the first or last element of the sentence core sets off an adverb from the rest of the sentence: on the left periphery, these include domain adverbs like *politically*, speech act adverbs like *frankly*, evaluative adverbs like *fortunately*, modal adverbs like *probably*, and even subject-oriented and manner adverbs like *joyously* or *slowly*. Once separated from the rest of the sentence phonetically, these adverbs acquire a semantic property in common: they represent the point of view of the speaker at speech time with respect to a propositional domain which may be situated at a different time ("Frankly, John was wrong to fire Bill yesterday"). "vP adverbs" on the contrary, even when identical in form to an Infl or Topic adverb, are never set off by a comma intonation: in final position in vP they define the information focus of an event description. Thus, a vP-adverb can be the focus of a question while the same adverb is outside of the event focus in a speaker-oriented domain.

(1) a. *Did John answer the question frankly?*
    b. *Frankly, did John answer the question?*

(ii) Just as phonological pauses create a speaker-oriented domain of adverbial construal, the presence of an agentive subject in TP defines a subject-oriented domain. However, since, as mentioned earlier, the speaker controls the entire sentence, ambiguity may arise with respect to attributing an adverb to speaker or subject point of view. In (2a-b), is John's winning the race fortunate for him or for the speaker? In (3a-c) does the speaker simply report or does she judge that the nurse's movement was gentle?

(2) a. *Fortunately, John won the race.*
    b. *John fortunately won the race.*

(3) a. *Gently, the nurse moved the patient's pillow.*
    b. *The nurse gently moved the patient's pillow.*
    c. *The nurse moved the patient's pillow gently.*

Such examples show not only that an adverb cannot be construed until its domain of interpretation is defined in syntax, but also, given the embedding of lower syntactic domains in higher domains, that it may not be decidable even then.

(iii) Auxiliary verbs and other tense dependent nodes introduce segments for temporal construal.

Cinque (1999) analyses auxiliary verbs like *have* and *be* as semantically empty fillers which appear when an F-head such as *-ed* or *-ing* blocks verb raising to tense. However, auxiliaries have specific aspectual lexical meaning and are not mutually substitutable: in English active sentences, *have* selects *-ed* while *be* selects *-ing*, as shown in (4). Aspectual auxiliaries merge with a T head and select a TP complement, dividing the sentence into independent segments which combine for tense interpretation.

(4) a. *John has seen/*seeing Mary.*
    b. *John is seeing/*seen Mary.*

Neg, Modality, Aspect and agreement cluster obligatorily on or in the scope of a finite or non-finite TP. While Cinque (1999) assumes that Perfect and Progressive define VPs, the existence of more than one T-dependent node in a sentence, such as agreement in (5a) or negation in (5b) illustrates iteration of TP not VP.

(5) a. [TP1 Les filles   sont [TP2 ti   venues ti]]
         |_____| |_____|
              agr   agr

    b. [TP1 John is   not/no longer [TP2   not speaking to Mary]]
                        NEG   NEG

(iv) Syntactic Movement/Merge in syntax marks a syntactic phrase as an independent segment for interpretation.

Perfect and progressive participles define a TP which may move in syntax as in (6a-b) or merge with the root TP as in (7a-b).

(6) a. *John said he has seen Mary/ is seeing Mary.*
    b. *And seen Mary he has/seeing Mary he is.*

(7) a. *Seeing Mary, John blushed.*
    b. *Conosciuta-mi, Gianni è cambiato.* (Belletti, 1981),
       knowing me, Gianni changed

A participle can adjoin to a finite TP to define a point of time which intersects with or abuts the time of the matrix event description, while a vP, which lacks temporal construal in isolation, cannot.

(8) a. *Walking/*walk down the street, John met Mary.*
    b. *Une fois les enfants couchés/*coucher, nous partirons.*

(v) Pronominal clitics are also T-dependent and identify segments for interpretation. Borer and Grodsinsky (1986) illustrated this phenomenon with the dative clitic in Hebrew. Beninca and Tortora (2009), analyzing data in Burzio (1986), illustrate it for *si* in Italian and Borgomanerese.

(9) a. *Si mangia bene qui.*   Impersonal si.
        One eats well here.
     b. *Maria si vede.*   Reflexive si.
        Maria sees herself.
     c. *Il vetro si rompe.*   Ergative si.
        The glass pane breaks.
     d. *Maria si sbaglia.*   Inherent si.
        Maria is wrong (Maria self deceives).

These authors conclude that each instance of the dative or the *si* clitic is located in a different position in the sentence structure. The interpretation of each instantiation of the same lexical element being distinct, one must infer that each identifies the position to which it adjoins as a distinct domain of interpretation.

We conclude this part of the discussion by claiming that (i) the sentence structure is made up of obligatory and optional syntatic segments which combine in different ways, independent of adverbial adjuncts, (ii) tense construal is the major factor determining the order and manner of composition of its segments to form a T(ense)-Chain, and (iii) ly-adverbs are construed on the level of the T-chain to which they adjoin and to which they contribute information.

A.3 The problem of productivity

A.3.1 Adverb order and F-node iteration

Cinque (1999) lists "only" forty-some F-projections which agree in some syntax-semantic FF with a class of adverbs and whose order is specified in syntax. We claim that the order of F-projections reflects the order of the links of the sentential T-chain as determined by the necessity of defining an event and placing it in a time and a world. The independently necessary order of T-links defines both the order and the construal of the adverbs which adjoin to them.

We also claimed that T-links can be iterated. When an adverb is adjoined to a T-link, the interpretation of the sentence at the point of adjunction is enriched by the conflation of the content of the adverb with that of its XP host. Consequently, each adjunction of an adverb to an XP may imply and thereby motivate a further adverbial adjunction, leading to successively higher levels of structure and adjunction. Like phonological pauses and Tense-dependent F-projections, ly-adverbs are grammatical mechanisms which define segments for construal. Consequently, there are at least as many interpretable segments in a sentence as there are T-links plus ly-adverbs adjoined to them.

In this framework, the prevention of infinite iteration of T-links and adverbs depends solely on semantic construal at each level of interpretation and conditions on construal.

For example, sometimes two adjuncts contradict each other. In (10), the modal adverb *probably*, which assumes non-realization of the event in its scope, is incompatible with factive *fortunately*, which presupposes its realization.

(10) a. # *Fortunately, probably, John will leave soon.*
     b. # *Probably, fortunately, John will leave soon.*

Subject-oriented adverbs introduce a period of time controlled by the subject which precedes the event itself. Such adverbs can iterate if they take scope over overlapping or successive points of time external and internal to the event description as in (11).

(11) a. *John joyously, quickly, cautiously opened the package.*
     b. *John quickly joyously, cautiously opened the package.*
     c. *John cautiously, quickly, joyously opened the package.*

These same adverbs cannot cumulate VP-finally, because being construed in this context as manner adverbs, they exhaustively modify the running time of the event but not any time span previous to the event.

(12) a. *How did John open the package?*
     b.   (i) *He opened it joyously*
         (ii) *He opened it quickly*
        (iii) *He opened it cautiously*
     c. * *He opened it joyously quickly cautiously*

As the intention to initiate an event occupies a time span which precedes the act, it cannot follow an adverb which includes a manner component.

(13) a. *John intentionally quickly left the room.*
     b. ?? *John quickly intentionally left the room.*

Nor, of course, can an adverb introducing an intention to engage in an action follow an adverb which modifies the action plus its result.

(14) a. *John purposely fatally shot his enemy.*
     b. * *John fatally purposely shot his enemy.*

Expanding on our former remark concerning redundancy, we propose (15) as an overarching constraint on adverb iteration.

(15) Material adjoined to a T-linked XP must specify aspects of the sentential event description which are already implicit in XP.

Thus, Activities invite imperfective adverbs like *slowly*, while Achievements change their meaning with such an adverb or else exclude it altogether.

(16) a. *John walked down the street slowly.*
   b. * *John found a coin/blinked/ spied Mary slowly.*

Each level of the sentence structure contains *qualia* in the sense of Pustejovsky (1995). Some of the event participants connoted by a predicate, such as, in general, Agent and Patient, are obligatorily realized as arguments because they are necessary to construct an event description. Other implicit modifiers are optionally realized, like time and place expression or Instruments. The mutation of a locative expression into a Benefactive participant, while not being strictly necessary in a proposition, is, like adverbs themselves, based on qualia which offer a means of extending the core event description. Similarly, while an AdvP is freely adjoined to any link of the T-chain, it must be construed at the interface as introducing a semantic extension of the event which was already lurking as a connotation or open question in the event description at the point of adjunction.

Any attempt to define an order of adverbs prior to the syntax-semantics interface inevitably introduces ordering paradoxes, as discussed in Bobaljik (1999). Some paradoxes may be resolved on the vP aktionsart level. While *completely* precedes the particle in (17), it follows it in (18).

(17) a. *John has completely lost his head.*
   b. # *John has lost his head completely.*

(18) a. * *John has completely read the book.*
   b. *John has read the book completely.*

Completely is a degree adverb whose position depends on the aktionsart of the vP. In (18b) *completely* measures the extent of a book-reading event, whereas in (17a) it modifies a property of the subject, as in "He is completely mad". Although limited to the domain of the event description, *completely* and other degree adverbs do not occupy a sole position within that domain.

The syntactic position of a VP or vP adverb depends on whether it denotes only manner or result as well. A manner adverb may be fronted, but not one whose scope includes the result of the event.

(19) a. *John held Mary to him tightly.*
    b. *John screwed the cap on the bottle tightly.*

(20) a. *Tightly, John held Mary to him.*
    b. * *Tightly, John screwed the cap on the bottle.*

Cinque (1999) points out that *sempre/already* precedes *già/always* in the adverb hierarchy. Consequently, (21a) is expected while (21b) is not.

(21) a. *lui sa **già sempre** come fare.*
        (He already always knows how to behave.)
    b. *Hanno **sempre già** mangiato.*
        (They have always already eaten.)

The adverbs are not in the same syntactic domain, however. In the simple sentence (21a), *gia/already* is construed with respect to the speaker's time: at this point in time, on all occasions, « they » know how to behave. (21b) is a complex sentence with two tense/aspect domains. Here, while *sempre* still refers to the speaker's time, *già* refers to the subject's time: on all occasions in the past, (they tell me) they have already eaten.

A.3.2 On the meaning of adverbs

Cinque (1999) cites the contrast in (22) to argue against ordering adverbs on the basis of their semantics. While *probably* cannot precede *evidently* in (22b), it can in (22c). The deciding factor which determines the meaning of the adverb must thus be its syntactic position, not its inherent meaning.

(22) a. *Evidently, John will probably give up.*
    b. * *Probably John will evidently give up.*
    c. *It is probable that it is evident that John will give up.*

However, the very fact that an adverb may occupy a variety of positions in the sentence, with each position determining a distinct construal, suggests that adverbs have no meaning in isolation, or at least that their inherent semantic content is not sufficient to classify them outside of a syntactic context.

While a ly-adverb bears a T-feature which determines a possible point of adjunction in syntax, the content of its adjectival base is lexically underdetermined. When there are two CPs, each T-chain orders, classifies, and filters its adverbs independently. In (22a), the speaker is a subject of conscience who refers to an external source of information or else a preparatory process of reasoning before giving his own opinion as to the truth of the proposition in TP. Thus, in

(22b) the judgement which relies on evidence cannot precede allusion to the existence of evidence. But (22c) contains two subjects of consciousness. Here, *probably* bears on the existence of evidence, not on that of an event. The sentence means that it is probable for the speaker now that evidence was submitted before now that the proposition holds. Such examples say nothing about the semantic relation between two adverbs in isolation, which, we hold, is impossible to calculate.

Appendix 2: On adverbial clauses

Returning to Haegeman's account of sentential adverbs, we see that central adverbial sentences in TP relate the times of two events as either a before b, a after b, or a simultaneous to b. But peripheral adverbs belong to the speaker's cognitive domain in which a reasoning process allows two propositions to be true simultaneously. In the framework suggested here, central adverbs belong to narration, which need not contain a speaker point of view, while peripheral adverbs set off by pauses are speaker-oriented adverbs which turn a narration into a story told directly by a speaker.[21]

Acknowledgements: I am grateful to two anonymous readers for a careful critical reading of an earlier version of this work which led to a number of improvements.

References

Alexiadou, Artemis. 1997. *Adverb placement: A case study in antisymmetric syntax*. Amsterdam: John Benjamins.
Altshuler Daniel 2014. Discourse transparency and the meaning of temporal locating adverbs. *Natural Language Semantics* 22. 55–88.
Andrews, Avery. 1983. A note on the constituent structure of modifiers. *Linguistic Inquiry* 14. 695–697.
Asher, Nicholas. & Alex Lascarides. 2003. *Logics of conversation*. Cambridge: Cambridge University Press.

---

[21] As a reviewer reminds us, there are various kinds of stories. Here we have analyzed stories in which the speaker expands an underlying narrative by adding time-related information. The peripheral adverbs in example (2) of the main text illustrate the speaker's contribution to rational conversation with the hearer. Note 18 refers to strictly familiar narratives with iterated benefactives involving relations between speaker, hearer, and event participants. Other kinds of stories are discussed in Smith (2002) under the label Modes of Discourse.

Bellert, Irena. 1977. On semantic and distibutional properties of sentential adverbs. *Linguistic Inquiry* 8. 337–351.
Belletti, Adriana. 1981. Frasi ridotte assolute. *Rivista di Grammatica Generativa* 6. 3–32.
Benincà, Paola & Cristina Tortora. 2009. Toward a finer-grained theory of Italian participial clause architecture. *University of Pennsylvania Working Papers in Linguistics* 15(1). 17–26.
Benveniste, Emile. 1966. *Problèmes de linguistique générale*. Paris: Gallimard.
Bobaljik, Jonathan D. 1999. Adverbs: The hierarchy paradox. *Glot International* 4(9/10). 27–28.
Bonami, Olivier, Danièle Godard & B. Kamers-Manhe. 2004. Adverb classification. In Francis Corblin & Henriëtte de Swart (eds), *Handbook of French semantics*. Stanford: CSLI Publications.
Borer, Hagit & Yosef Grodzinsky.1986. Syntactic cliticization and lexical cliticization: The case of Hebrew dative clitics. In Hagit Borer (ed.), *The syntax of pronominal clitics* [Syntax and Semantics 19], 175–215. New York: Academic Press.
Burzio, Luigi. 1986. *Italian syntax: A government-binding approach*. Dordrecht: Reidel.
Chomsky, Noam. 1995. *The minimalist program*. Cambridge, MA: The MIT Press.
Chomsky, Noam. 2000. Minimalist inquiries: The framework. In Roger Martin, David Michaels, Juan Uriagereka & Samuel Jay Keyser (eds.), *Step by step. Essays on minimalist syntax of honor of Howard Lasnik,* 89–155. Cambridge, MA: The MIT Press.
Cinque, Guglielmo. 1999. *Adverbs and functional heads: A cross-linguistic perspective*. Oxford: Oxford University Press.
Davidson, Donald. 1967[1980]. The logical form of action sentences. In Nicholas Rescher (ed.), *The logic of decision and action*. Pittsburgh: University of Pittsburgh Press. [reprinted in Davidson, Donald. 1980. *Essays on actions and events*, 105–148.]
Deschamps, Alain. To appear. Je vais te me lui régler son compte: les limites de la syntaxe. In Audrey Roig & Laurence Rosier (eds.), *Actes du colloque de Bruxelles, Linguistique des formes exclues* (2013).
di Paolo, Marianna. 1989. Double modals as single lexical items. *American Speech* 64(3). 195–224.
Ernst, Thomas. 1987. Why epistemic and manner modification are exceptional. *Proceedings of the thirteenth annual meeting of the Berkeley Linguistics Society.* 77–87.
Ernst, Thomas. 1998. Scope-based adjunct licensing. In Pius Tamanji & Kiyomi Kusumoto (eds.), *Proceedings of NELS*, 127–142. Amherst: University of Massachusetts, GLSA.
Ernst, Thomas. 2000a. *The syntax of adjuncts*. Cambridge: Cambridge University Press.
Ernst, Thomas. 2000b. Semantic features and the distribution of adverbs. *ZAS Papers in Linguistics* 17. 79–97.
Forster, E.M. 1927/1985. *Aspects of the novel*. New York City: Harcourt.
Frey, Werner. 2000. Syntactic requirements on adverbs. In Catherine Fabricius-Hansen, Ewald Lang & Claudia Maienborn (eds.), *Approaching the grammar of adjuncts* [ZAS Working papers in linguistics 17], 107–134, ZAS, Berlin.
Gehrke, Berit. 2015. Adjectival participles, event kind modification, and pseudo-incorporation. *Natural Language and Linguistic Theory* 33(3). 897–938.
Gehrke, Berit and Elena Castroviejo. 2015. Manner and degree: An introduction. *Natural Language and Linguistic Theory* 33(3). 745–790.
Geuder, Wilhelm. 2000. *Oriented adverbs*. Tübingen: Universität of Tübingen dissertation.
Geuder, Wilhelm. 2006. Manner modification of states. In Christian Ebert & Cornelia Endriss (eds.), *Proceedings of Sinn and Bedeutung* 10, 111–124. Berlin: ZAS. https://www.deutsche-digitale-bibliothek:de/binary/...full/1.pdf.

Grimshaw, Jane. 1990. *Argument structure*. Cambridge, MA: The MIT Press.
Guéron, Jacqueline. 1980. On the syntax and semantics of PP extraposition. *Linguistic Inquiry* 11. 637–678.
Guéron, Jacqueline. 1983. L'emploi 'possessif' de l'article défini en français. *Langue Française* 58. 23–35.
Guéron, Jacqueline. 1985. Inalienable possession, PRO-inclusion and lexical chains. In Jacqueline Guéron, Hans-G. Obenauer & Jean-Yves Pollock (eds.), *Grammatical representation* 43–86. Dordrecht: Foris.
Guéron, Jacqueline. 2003. Inalienable possession and the interpretation of determiners. In Martine Coene & Yves D'hulst (eds.), *From NP to DP*, 189–220. Amsterdam: John Benjamins.
Guéron, Jacqueline. 2004. Tense interpretation and the argument structure of auxiliaries. In Jacqueline Guéron & Jean Lecarme (eds.), *The syntax of time*, 299–328. Cambridge MA: The MIT Press.
Guéron, Jacqueline. 2006. Inalienable possession. In Henk van Riemsdijk & Martin Everaert (eds.), *The syntax companion*, 589–638. Oxford: Blackwell.
Guéron, Jacqueline. 2015. *Sentence and discourse*. Oxford: Oxford University Press.
Guéron, Jacqueline & Toen Hoekstra. 1988. T-Chains and the constituent structure of auxiliaries. In Anna Cardinaletti, Giuliana Giusti & Guglielmo Cinque (eds.), *Constituent Structure: Proceedings of the GLOW conference in Venice*, 35–99. Dordrecht: Foris.
Haegeman, Liliane. 2007. Operator movement and topicalisation in adverbial clauses. *Folia Linguistica* 41. 279–325.
Haegeman, Liliane. 2009. Main clause phenomena and the derivation of adverbial clauses. In Anastasios Tsangalidis (ed.), *Selected papers from the 18th International Symposium on theoretical and applied Linguistics*, 1–18. Thessaloniki: Monochromia.
Haider, Huber. 2000. Adverb placement – convergence of structure and licensing. *Theoretical Linguistics* 26. 95–134.
Halliday, M.A.K. & Ruqaiya Hasan. 1976. *Cohesion in English*. London: Longman.
Haspelmath, Martin. 2016. The serial verb construction: Comparative concept and cross-linguistic generalizations. *Language and Linguistics* 17(3). 291–319.
Higginbotham, James. 2009. *Tense, aspect, and indexicality*. Oxford: Oxford University Press.
Iatridou, Sabine, Elena Anagnostopoulou & Roumyana Izvorski. 2001. Observations about the form and meaning of the perfect. In Michael Kenstowicz (ed.), *Ken Hale, a life in language*, 189–238. Cambridge, MA: The MIT Press.
Jackendoff, Ray. 1972. *Semantic interpretation in generative grammar*. Cambridge, MA: The MIT Press.
Kayne, Richard. 1975. *French syntax*. Cambridge, MA: MIT Press.
Kayne, Richard. 1994. *The antisymmetry of syntax*. Cambridge, MA: The MIT Press.
Laenzlinger, Christopher. 2002. A Feature-based theory of adverb syntax. *Generative Grammar in Geneva* 3. 67–105.
Lakoff, George. 1974. Syntactic amalgams. *Papers from the tenth regional meeting, Chicago Linguistic Society*. 321–344.
Larson, Richard. 1988. Events and modification in nominals. In Devon Strolovitch & Aaron Lawson (eds.), *SALT* VIII, 145–168. Ithaca, NY: Cornell University Press.
Larson, Richard. 2004. Sentence-final adverbs and scope. In Keir Moulton & Mathew Wolf (eds.), *Proceedings of NELS 34*, 127–142. Amherst: University of Massachusetts, GLSA.
Maienborn, Claudia. 2008. On davidsonian and kimian states. In Ileana Comorovski & Klaus von Heusinger (eds.), *Existence: semantics and syntax*, 107–130. Heidelberg: Springer.

McConnell-Ginet, Sally. 1982. Adverbs and logical form. A linguistically realistic theory. *Language* 58.144–184.
Partee, Barbara. 1973. Some structural analogies between tenses and pronouns in English. *The Journal of Philosophy* LXX(18). 601–609.
Piñón, Christopher. 2009. Agent-oriented adverbs as manner adverbs. Ereignissemantik-Workshop, Humbold-Universitat.
Pustejovsky, James. 1995. *The generative lexicon*. Cambridge, MA: The MIT Press.
Van Riemsdijk, Henk. 1998. On the expansion of the multidimensional universe. Fest-Web-Page for Noam Chomsky. URL http://cognet.mit.edu/library/books/chomsky/celebration/essays/riemsdyk.html.
Rizzi, Luigi. 1997. The fine structure of the left periphery. In Liliane Haegeman (ed.), *Elements of grammar*, 281–337. Amsterdam: Kluwer.
Smith, Carlota. 1991/1997. *The parameter of aspect*. Dordrecht: Kluwer.
Stowell, Timothy. 1991. The alignment of arguments in adjective phrases. In Susan Rothstein (ed.), *Syntax and semantics 2. Perspectives on phrase structure: Heads and licensing*, 105–135. New York: Academic Press.
Stroik, Thomas. 1990. Adverbs as V-sisters. *Linguistic Inquiry* 21. 654–661.
Talmy, Lenord. 1975. Figure and ground in complex sentences. *Proceedings of the first annual meeting of the Berkeley Linguistics Society*. 419–430.
Thomason, Richmond & Robert Stalnaker. 1973. A semantic theory of adverbs. *Linguistic Inquiry* 4. 195–220.
Travis, Lisa. 1985. The syntax of adverbs. *McGill Working Papers in Linguistics*, 280–310.
Van de Velde, Danièle. 2010. Le rôle "instrument" en question. *Travaux de Linguistique* 61. 7–30.
Wyner, Adam Z. 1998. Subject-oriented adverbs are thematically dependent. In Susan Rothstein (ed.), *Events and grammar*, 333–348. Dordrecht: Kluwer.
Zanuttini, Raffaella. 1991. *Syntactic properties of sentential negation: a comparative study of Romance languages*. Philadelphia: University of Pennsylvania dissertation.

Jim McCloskey
Ellipsis, polarity, and the cartography of verb-initial orders in Irish

1 Clause structure and ellipsis

Probably the single best-known fact about Irish is that it is a VSO language. And indeed finite clauses of every type conform, for the most part, to the informal schema shown in (1) and exemplified in (2):

(1) VERB < SUBJECT < OBJECT < OBLIQUE ARGUMENTS < ADVERBIALS

(2) a. *Sciob   an   cat   an   t-eireaball   den   luch.*
       cut.PAST   the   cat   the   tail   off-the   mouse
       'The cat cut the tail off the mouse.'
    b. *Má   bhriseann   tú   an   fhaocha,   tifidh   tú   na*
       if   open.PRES   you   the   periwinkle   see.FUT   you   the
       castái   atá   ina   leath   deiridh.
       twists   C-be.PRES   in-its   half   rear.GEN
       'If you break open a periwinkle, you will see the twists that are in its hind parts.'

Needless to say, deviations from the pattern in (2) are not unknown. For now, however, our focus will not be on those but on the more fundamental question of what the syntax is which yields as outcome the pattern in (1) and the examples in (2).

What has been most clearly established about such structures is that their constituency is as in (3), which shows a skeletal structure for (2a):

(3)
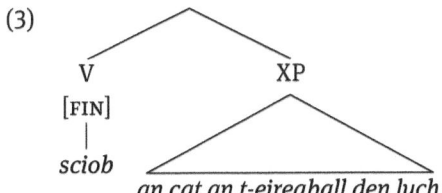

That is, there is a large postverbal constituent which subsumes virtually all of the material of the clause to the exclusion of the finite verb. The evidence for this somewhat surprising conclusion is substantial; every way that I know of to detect constituency in Irish suggests that the pattern shown in (3) is real (McCloskey (1991, 2011b), Elfner (2012, 2015), Bennett et al. (2013)). I will not review that evidence here, but I will focus on one of its strands – partly by way of illustration, partly because the phenomenon in question will be important for the discussion that follows.

Consider the question-answer pair in (4):

(4) a. *A-r   sciob   an   cat   an   t-eireaball   den   luch?*
       Q.PAST   cut.PAST   the   cat   the   tail   off-the mouse
       'Did the cat cut the tail off the mouse?'
    b. (i)   *Sciob.*
             cut.PAST
             'Yes'
       (ii) *Ní-or   sciob.*
             NEG-PAST   cut.PAST
             'No.'
       (iii) *Creidim   gu-r   sciob.*
             believe.PRES.S1   C.PAST   cut.PAST
             'I believe it did.'

It seems clear that the isolated verbs in the three possible responses of (4b) emerge from elision of the large postverbal constituent (XP) of structures like (3). The task of understanding such ellipses, therefore, is inextricable from the task of understanding what XP of (3) is and what the syntactic mechanisms are which determine its existence and form. We will focus on those questions here, then – in the first place for what they reveal about the nature of XP of (3), and in the second place for what they reveal about ellipsis, head movement, and their interaction.

1.1 Responsive ellipsis

The apparently isolated verbs of (4b) are known as 'responsive' forms in traditional descriptions. I will therefore use the term Responsive Ellipsis for the process which is at work in licensing them. Although a term is needed, and this one is convenient, it is undeniably inaccurate, since such fragments have many uses which do not involve answering questions. They appear freely, for instance, in coordinate structures (as in (5a)), in tag questions (as in (5b)), in adverbial clauses (as in (5c)) and in relative clauses (as in (5d)):

(5) a. Dúirt   siad go dtiocfadh   siad, ach ní   tháinig   ariamh.
       say.PAST they C   come.COND   they   but NEG-FIN   come.PAST   ever
       'They said that they would come but they never did.'
    b. Beidh   muid   connáilte,   nach   mbeidh?
       be.FUT   we   frozen   NEGQ   be.FUT
       'We'll be frozen, won't we?'
    c. le   heagla   go   gceapfá   go   bhfuil, ...   níl   aon
       for   fear   C   think.COND.S2   C   be.PRES   is-not   any
       cheann   de   leabhra   móra   an   Oileáin   san
       one   of   books   great   the   island   DEMON
       léite   agam   fós
       read.PERF-PASS   by-me   yet
       'Lest you think that I have, I have not yet read any one of the great books
       of that Island.'   GLL 61
    d. tráth   a   raibh   an   Contae   sin   daonmhar   ar   chaoi
       time   C   be.PAST   the   county   DEMON   populous   on   way
       nach   bhfuil   inniu
       NEG-C   be.PRES   today
       'at a time when that County was populous, in a way that it is
       not today'   CE 183

The possibilities of (5) suggest a kinship with VP Ellipsis in English and in fact the presence of (4) in the grammar of Irish has had an effect on varieties of English spoken in Ireland – namely that responsive patterns like that in (6) are much more common in those varieties than in other forms of English.

(6) a. *Did you apply for the job?*
    b. *I did.*

The pattern in (6) has been much discussed in the dialectological literature (and much mocked on social media); it seems indisputable that its ubiquity in Irish English reflects substratal influence from Irish. In his comprehensive overview, for instance, Filppula (1999: 166) reports the results of a corpus study showing that responsive patterns like (6) are most frequent in the English of those parts of Ireland (e.g. County Clare) from which Irish has most recently disappeared. What this means is that in the language contact situations in which Irish dialects of English are forged, speakers identify Responsive Ellipsis in Irish with VP Ellipsis in English. This identification (though remarkable, given the extensive surface dissimilarities between the two processes) is surely correct. Responsive Ellipsis in Irish in fact mirrors point for point the distribution and formal characteristics of VP Ellipsis in English and it seems clear that each is a fairly exact functional and formal analog of the other. The relevant evidence is developed in detail in McCloskey (1991, 2011b), and I will therefore not review it here.

Accepting the conclusion, though, the analytic challenges seem clear. In trying to understand Responsive Ellipsis, what we seek is an analysis which is in the first place in harmony with what is independently established about the syntax of Irish clauses and which in the second place makes the needed typological link with VP Ellipsis in English. In trying to meet those challenges, I will begin with the issue of VSO order.

2 The syntax of verb initial order

Understanding VSO order, as we have seen, is a matter of understanding what the syntactic mechanisms are which give rise to the structure in (3), representable more generally as in (7):

(7)
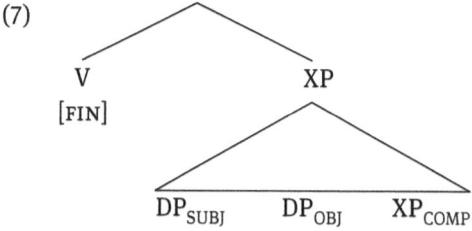

The large postverbal constituent XP excludes the inflected verb but includes its subject (if there is one), its object (if there is one), any other complements, and some, but not all, kinds of adjuncts.[1] An initial question, then, is how the finite

---

[1] Witness the adverbial survivors of what we take to be ellipsis of XP in (5a), and (5d) for example. This phenomenon deserves a paper in its own right, but the empirical generalizations seem clear enough. The adverbials which escape elision in such cases are high temporals (in this, the examples of (5a) and (5d) are completely typical) which, in the absence of ellipsis, may appear either at the left edge of the TP-layer (to the left of the finite verb) or at the absolute right edge of the clause. Given that they appear to the right of the stranded verb under Responsive Ellipsis, it is presumably this second option that underlies the stranding possibilities exemplified by (5a) and (5d). How one understands this empirical generalization will depend to a great extent on larger commitments concerning the syntax of adverbs, the status of adjunction structures, and whether or not one adopts the antisymmetry stance originating in Kayne (1994). However the core point (for present purposes) seems clear enough – adverbials of this type may appear outside XP of (7). See McCloskey (1996a,b) for some relevant observations.

verb comes to occupy initial position. There is in fact good reason to believe that both the form and the position of the finite verb reflect head-movement from a clause-internal to a left-peripheral position. When the verb is uninflected (in non-finite clauses and in small clauses), it appears in medial position, following the subject and preceding (most) complements:

(8) a. *Níor mhaith liom* [*í   a rá   liom   gur   loic   mé*].
       I-wouldn't-like her   say.NON-FIN with-me   C.PAST   failed   I
       'I wouldn't like her to say to me that I had failed.'
    b. *Ba   mhinic   [iad   ag troid   liom   ]*.
       PAST   often   them   PROG-fight   with-me
       'They often fought with me.'

On every analysis, therefore, some link must be made, in one way or another, between the initial position of verbs and the mechanisms by which they come to have the various morphemes that define them as 'finite verbs'. The hypothesis of head-movement through the various heads of the extended projection makes exactly this link. But there is extensive evidence, in addition, that the inflected verb does not appear in C (Carnie (1995), Duffield (1995), McCloskey (1996a), Ostrove (2016) among others). It must therefore raise to a position beyond the verbal domain but within the inflectional layer.

The simplest version of an analysis along these lines is probably that schematized in (9), in which there is no raising of the subject (perhaps because EPP is inactive on T) and in which the V/v amalgam raises to fuse with a Tense head, creating an inflected verb:

(9)
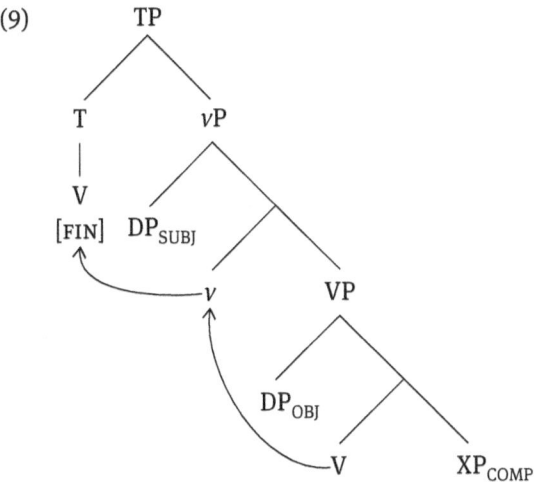

In the context of this very simple proposal, Responsive Ellipsis in Irish and VP Ellipsis in English emerge as the same process; both represent elision of the *v*P-complement of T, the subject raising and surviving in English, but remaining within *v*P and being elided in Irish, the verb raising and surviving in Irish, but remaining within *v*P and being elided in English. The fact that these parallels emerge in the context of (9) is a very welcome result indeed, since, as we have seen, the many properties that the two ellipsis processes share virtually demand some commonality in analysis.

Welcome as this result is, however, it is clear that the analysis sketched in (9) cannot be correct. Its central feature is that the subject remains inside *v*P (within the thematic domain). However, evidence has steadily accumulated that the subject in fact raises out of *v*P (McCloskey (1996b, 2001a, 2011b, 2014)). There is, for example, a lower subject position available in familiar contexts. In the examples of (10), the indefinite subject appears to the right of *v*P-peripheral adverbs, though subjects in general must appear to the left of the same class of adverbs:

(10) a. *ní   raibh   riamh   díospóireacht   fá   na   nithe   seo*
       NEG-FIN be.PAST   ever   debate   about   the   things   DEMON
       'there was never any debate about these things'   PNG 187

   b. *Bhí   chomh   maith   mórchuid   daoine   ann   ná*
      be.PAST   as   well   many   people   in-it   NEG-C
      faca   riamh   cheana.
      see.PAST.S1   ever   before
      'There were also many people there that I had never seen before.' FI 236

There must then be at least two distinct postverbal subject-positions in finite clauses – a conclusion very much in line with much recent work on clause structure across languages (for a review, see for instance Cardinaletti (1997)). For Irish we must distinguish at least one low position, reserved for indefinites and typical of existential constructions, and one high position (see McCloskey (2014) for more detailed discussion and argumentation). The semantic and discourse-properties of the higher position, furthermore, closely parallel those of the relatively high English subject position (see McCloskey (2001a)). Given all of this, the region of syntactic space below C in Irish (the inflectional layer) must be at least as complex as suggested in (11):

(11)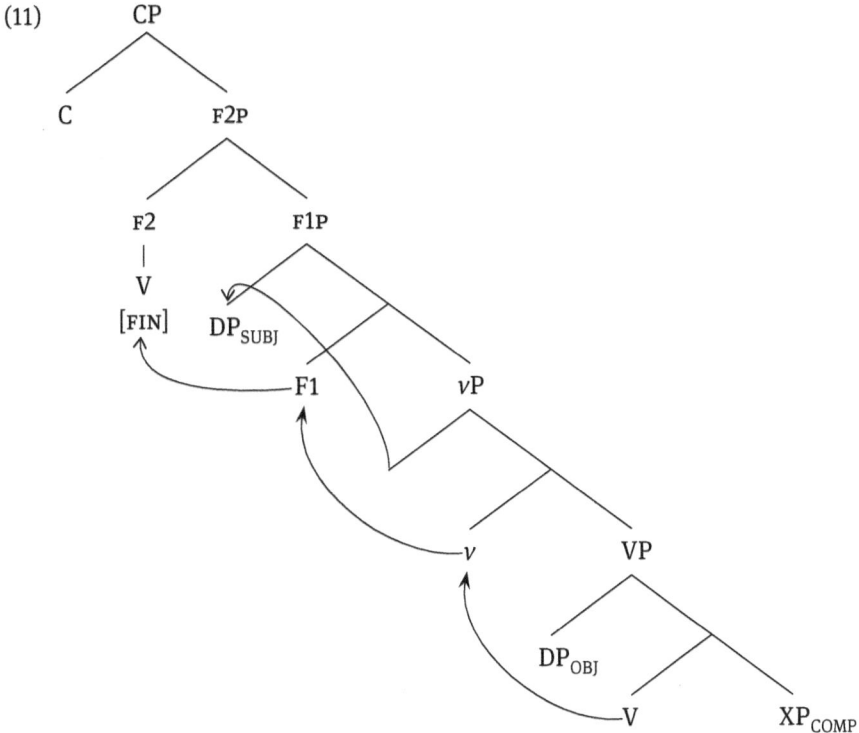

Given (11), the 'inflected verb' simultaneously lexicalizes four syntactic atoms – a verbal stem, a voice head *v*, and the content of F1 and of F2 respectively. The most prominent case-less nominal in *v*P, meanwhile, must (in the general case) raise to the specifier position of F1; the evidence for distinct high and low subject positions is thereby accommodated. VSO order emerges in turn because the verbal complex ultimately raises to F2 – higher than the subject. But since F2 is itself below C, the evidence that the verb does not appear in C is also accommodated. The constituency pattern of (3) falls out as before, except that XP of (3) and (7) is now identified as the larger F1P rather than as *v*P.

If the skeletal proposals of (11) are to have real substance, however, we must now ask if a believable account can be provided of what F1 and F2 of (11) are; and the answer to that question should have some grounding within the language and within some reasonable typological landscape. We must also ask if (11) provides a way of understanding the kinship between Irish Responsive Ellipsis and English VP Ellipsis. Responsive Ellipsis is now elision of F1P – the complement of the position to which the verb raises. Well and good, but it remains unclear how that configuration might relate to the configuration in which English VP Ellipsis does its work.

3 The syntax of negation

We will try to address these issues by embarking on what may feel like an extensive detour, examining the syntax of clausal negation. We will begin that investigation in turn by looking first at nonfinite clauses (so-called 'verbal noun clauses'). Since the nonfinite verb is morphologically simple and is in medial position, we do not have to deal in nonfinite clauses with the obscuring complexities of head movement, or not at least to the same extent as in finite clauses. The elements that constitute the extended projection therefore emerge with somewhat greater clarity in nonfinite clauses than in finite clauses.

3.1 Negation in nonfinite clauses

If finite clauses show the rough pattern of (1), we can similarly characterize nonfinite clauses as in (12), a schema which is exemplified by (13).[2]

(12) [(NEG) DP   DP   V   XP ADJUNCTS]
              [SUBJ] [OBJ]   [−FIN]

(13) i ndiaidh   é   an   teach   a dhíol   le   n-a   dheartháir
     after   him   the   house   sell.NON-FIN   with   his   brother
     'after he had sold the house to his brother'

---

[2] The full range of possibilities schematized in (12) is instantiated only in some dialects (northern). The pattern of cross-dialect differences is important and interesting but will not affect the argument to be developed here. We set it aside for now.

Subjects (which are accusative when overt) are preverbal. Direct objects are also accusative and preverbal, while complements of all other syntactic types are postverbal; for extended discussion, see McCloskey (1980, 1986a), Chung & McCloskey (1987), McCloskey & Sells (1988), Guilfoyle (1990), Noonan (1992), Guilfoyle (1994), Noonan (1994), Duffield (1995), McCloskey (1996b), Carnie & Harley (1998), McCloskey (2001a), Doyle (2012).

As indicated in (12) and as illustrated in (14), negation is expressed at the left edge of the clause, to the left of the (accusative) subject. It is realized by the element *gan*, which is homophonous with, but distinct from, the preposition meaning 'without'.

(14) B'fhearr liom   gan   iad   mé a fheiceáil   ag   caoineadh.
     I-would-prefer NEG-NON-FIN them   me see.NON-FIN   PROG   cry
     'I'd prefer that they not see me crying.'

How, then, should we understand the syntax of *gan*? Two positions have been advocated in earlier work. One (which I have consistently adopted) takes the left-peripheral position of *gan* to indicate that it is a negative complementizer (a member of the class C, endowed with the feature NEG). Others (see especially Duffield (1995)) have argued that *gan* is within a negative projection, lower than C. It now seems clear that that second position is correct and that *gan* is never in C. The crucial evidence comes from examples such as (15):

(15) Má chailleann   tú   agus   gan   eisean do   mharbhadh ...
     if lose.PRES   you   and   NEG-NON-FIN him   you   kill.NON-FIN
     'if you lose and he doesn't kill you'   ACO 473

(15) is an instance of a very common coordination pattern in Irish – in which a finite clause is coordinated with a nonfinite clause. This much is routine, as is the fact that the finite clause, in such cases, comes first in the coordinate series. The crucial observations about cases such as (15) are first that the marker of negation *gan* appears at the left edge of the rightmost conjunct, and second that the coordinate constituent itself is, in turn, the complement of *má*, the (realis) conditional marker. But all the evidence suggests that *má* is itself a complementizer – that is, it is in C (for the detailed evidence, see McCloskey (2001b)). It follows in turn that the marker of negation in nonfinite clauses is at the left edge of a constituent which is not CP but which is rather the complement of C. That is, what is needed for (15) is the schematic structure in (16a), a structure already suggested by considerations of compositionality. But, since word-like elements at the left edge of a constituent are almost always heads in this heavily head-initial language, the interpretation in (16b) for nonfinite clauses in general seems warranted.

(16) a.
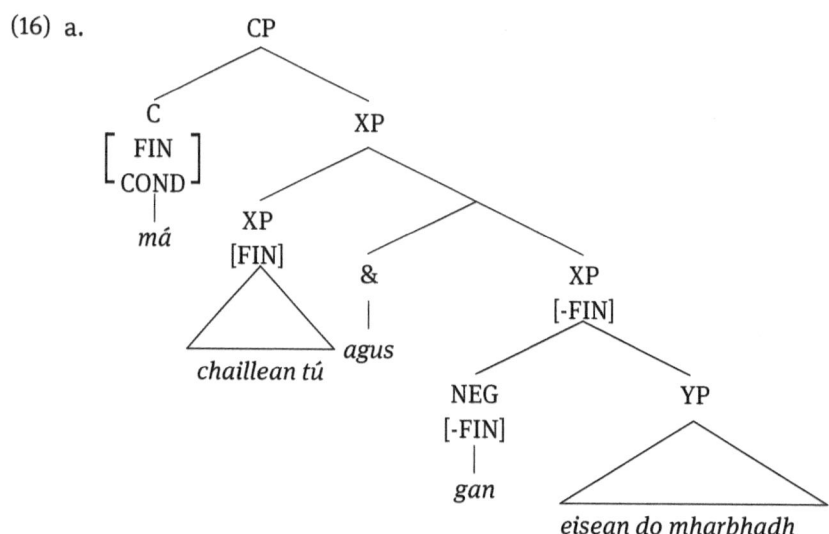

b.
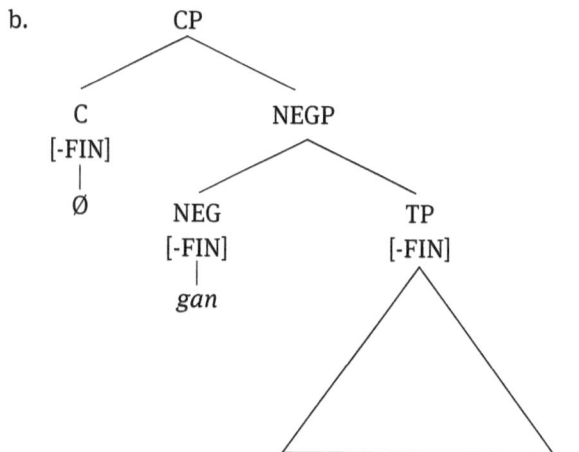

That is, we will assume that negation is a head relatively high in the clausal projection (just below c) and takes TP as its complement. Coordination in (15) is at the level of NEGP and its properties are as expected.[3] This conclusion is in harmony with the typological proposals of Zanuttini (1997) and is further supported by the evidence that there is an A-position to the left of negation, but to the right of the C-projection – a position in which dative subjects are licensed under certain circumstances (see McCloskey

---

[3] We will generalize the proposal in the obvious way shortly, so that (15) involves coordination at the level of a polarity projection which is itself the complement of c.

(2001a:180–189) and Doyle (2012) for the details). In the example of (17), the dative subject appears to the right of a fronted WH-phrase, suggesting that it is below C, but to the left of the negative head, suggesting again that *gan* is below C.[4]

(17) *Conas   d'   aonaránach   gan   a bheith   ag*
     how   to   solitary-person   NEG-C.NON-FIN   be.NON-FIN   PROG
     braistint   aonarach?
     feel   solitary
     'How could a solitary person not feel solitary?'   AGMTS 102

Finally, *gan* appears freely at the left edge of clauses out of which Raising has applied:

(18) a. *n'   fhéadfadh   a   cuid   feola   gan*
        NEG-FIN can.COND   his   share   blood.GEN   NEG-NON-FIN
        a bheith   righin
        be.NON-FIN   stiff
        'His blood couldn't not be thick.'   NAOT 77
     b. *Ní   fhéadfadh   sé   gan   a bheith   go maith.*
        NEG-FIN can.COND   he.NOM   NEG-NON-FIN   be.NON-FIN   well
        'He couldn't not be well.'   T 15

If *gan* is taken to be in C, then examples such as (18) raise severe difficulties for the standard, and successful, analysis of Raising as involving the selection of

---

4 Duffield (1995) also demonstrates that for some (but not all) speakers of northern varieties, accusative subjects of nonfinite clauses may appear to the left of the negative marker. It seems likely that such accusative subjects occupy the same position as the dative subjects of examples such as (17). It is likely in turn, I think, that that position is the (unique) specifier-position of the polarity projection. Making that case here, however, would take us too far from our principal purposes. It is in part to allow for this possibility, though, that I do not assume, as Duffield (1995) does, that gan is itself a specifier of NEG.

A reviewer raises the interesting possibility that the head which attracts the dative subject of (17) and the accusative subjects observed by Duffield could be taken to be a Topic head in a framework such as that of Rizzi (1997). I know of no study of the pragmatic properties of the relevant elements (whether they are topics in one of the senses of that term). One thing that is clear, however, is that the locality constraints on the movements which raise such subjects to their high position are the constraints characteristic of case-driven A-movement (McCloskey (2001a:180–189)). So if the attracting head is in some sense topic-defining, it must also be endowed with whatever features drive such raisings – it must act as a ϕ-probe.

All of these issues have to do with the role of the polarity head in the A-system, an important question that we return to briefly in the concluding section.

defective (sub-phasal) clausal complements. If *gan* is taken to be an element of the 'inflectional layer', as we are arguing here, the difficulty disappears.

We will return to all of these questions in a slightly changed and elaborated context. For now, the principal conclusion we take away is that the marker of sentential negation in nonfinite clauses (*gan*) is a head, that it occupies a high position in the extended projection, but crucially that it is below C.

3.2 Negation in finite clauses

If it is now clear that negation in nonfinite clauses cannot be in C, it is just as clear that in finite clauses, negation is always expressed in the C-position. Each complementizer in the language has a 'negative' variant, which may never co-occur with any other complementizer, and which may never co-occur with any other expression of sentential negation. Negative C takes the form of *ní* or *cha* in root finite clauses, *nach* or *ná-* in embedded finite clauses.[5]

The relevant observations are gathered in the examples of (19)–(26), the first two illustrating the root case, each subsequent pair of examples illustrating one of the finite complementizers alongside its negative counterpart. Finite complementizers are traditionally said to have non-past and past variants as well, many of which are illustrated in (19)–(26). How such forms are best analyzed is a question that we will return to. For discussion of all of these observations and patterns, see McCloskey (2001b) and references cited there. For more up to date discussion, see Acquaviva (2014), Oda (2012), and Ostrove (2016).

(19) ROOT NEGATIVE COMPLEMENTIZER, NON-PAST
    a. *Ní   chuireann   sé   isteach   ar   phostanna.*
       NEG-FIN   put.PRES   he   in   on   jobs
       'He doesn't apply for jobs.'
    b. *Cha   gcuireann   sé   isteach   ar   phostanna.*
       NEG-FIN   put.PRES   he   in   on   jobs
       'He doesn't apply for jobs.'

(20) ROOT NEGATIVE COMPLEMENTIZER, PAST
    a. *Ní-or   chuir   sé   isteach   ar   phost   ar bith.*
       NEG-PAST   put.PAST   he   in   on   job   any
       'He didn't apply for any job.'

---

5 *Cha* is found only in Ulster varieties.

b. *Cha-r   chuir   sé   isteach   ar phost   ar bith.*
   NEG-PAST put.PAST he   in   on job   any
   'He didn't apply for any job.'

(21) DEFAULT DECLARATIVE COMPLEMENTIZER, NON-PAST
   a. *Creidim   go   gcuirfidh   sí   isteach   ar   an   phost.*
      I-believe C   put.FUT   she   in   on   the   job
      'I believe that she'll apply for the job.'
   b. *Creidim   nach   gcuirfidh   sí   isteach   ar   an   phost.*
      I-believe NEG-C   put.FUT   she   in   on   the   job
      'I believe that she won't apply for the job.'

(22) DEFAULT DECLARATIVE COMPLEMENTIZER, PAST
   a. *Creidim   gu-r   chuir   sí   isteach   ar   an   phost.*
      I-believe C.PAST   put   she   in   on   the   job
      'I believe that she applied for the job.'
   b. *Creidim   ná-r   chuir   sí   isteach   ar   an   phost.*
      I-believe C-NEG-PAST   put   she   in   on   the   job
      'I believe that she didn't apply for the job.'

(23) POLAR INTERROGATIVE COMPLEMENTIZER
   a. *An   gcuirfidh   sí   isteach   ar   an   phost?*
      Q   put.FUT   she   in   on   the   job
      'Will she apply for the job?'
   b. *Nach   gcuirfidh   sí   isteach   ar   an   phost?*
      NEGQ   put.FUT   she   in   on   the   job
      'Won't she apply for the job?'

(24) WH-COMPLEMENTIZER
   a. *an   rud   a   iarann   tú –*
      the   thing   C   ask.PRES   you
      'the thing that you ask for'
   b. *an   rud   nach   n-iarann   tú –*
      the   thing   NEG-C   ask.PRES   you
      'the thing that you don't ask for'

(25) RESUMPTIVE COMPLEMENTIZER
   a. *an   post   a-r   chuir   tú   isteach   air*
      the   job   C.PAST   put   you   in   on-it
      'the job that you applied for'
   b. *an   post   ná-r   chuir   tú   isteach   air*
      the   job   C-NEG-PAST   put   you   in   on-it
      'the job that you didn't apply for'

(26) CONDITIONAL COMPLEMENTIZER
    a. *Má   chuireann   sí   isteach   ar   an   phost ...*
       if   put.PRES   she   in   on   the   job
       'if she applies for the job, ... '
    b. *Muna   gcuireann   sí   isteach   ar   an   phost ...*
       if-not   put.PRES   she   in   on   the   job
       'if she doesn't apply for the job'

Given these observations, Irish must have a set of realization rules roughly along the lines of those in (27a–c):

(27) a. $\begin{bmatrix} \text{C} \\ \text{FIN} \\ \text{NEG} \\ \text{ROOT} \end{bmatrix} \longrightarrow$ /niː/, /xa/

    b. $\begin{bmatrix} \text{C} \\ \text{FIN} \\ \text{NEG} \\ \text{COND} \end{bmatrix} \longrightarrow$ /munə/, /murə/

    c. $\begin{bmatrix} \text{C} \\ \text{FIN} \\ \text{NEG} \end{bmatrix} \longrightarrow$ /nax/, /naː/

The realization rules of (27) presuppose, first, that the embedded form in (27c) is the elsewhere case (root and conditional complementizers having more specific licensing environments) and, second, that the 'past tense forms' of the complementizers should be dealt with by way of some different mechanism. We return to this second issue presently.

    The question now arises of how C acquires the negative feature referred to in (27). An obvious possibility is that the feature is there simply as an inherent lexical specification – that Irish expresses sentential negation in the C-position, and that no other expression of negation is necessary or possible in the clause. This was the view adopted in McCloskey (1979) and other earlier work. It is true to the patterns of realization just discussed but, given the discussions of the previous section, leaves us with an unexplained asymmetry between finite and nonfinite clauses. An alternative (developed, for instance, in Guilfoyle (1990), Duffield (1995)) is that the negative complementizers are derived heads, which have the surface form that they do as a consequence of raising of a lower independent negative head to the C-position.

    Neither of these views can be entirely correct. There is indeed evidence that, as Guilfoyle and Duffield argued, there is a negative head lower than the C-position.

But there is also evidence that the relation between that lower negative head and the c-position is not one of movement. Consider (28), which constitutes, in a certain sense, the mirror image of examples such as (15).

(28) *Mur' dtéighinn agus iad cailleadh, mhuirbhfeadh siad mé.*
 if-not go.COND.S1 and them lose.NON-FIN kill.COND they me
 'If I were not to go and they were to lose, they would kill me.' SHS 132

Like (15), such examples involve coordination of finite and nonfinite clauses within the scope of a conditional complementizer. Also as in (15), there is just one expression of negation. However (28) differs from (15) in that negation is overtly expressed only on the conditional complementizer (see (27b) and (26b)) – a position from which it should take scope over both conjuncts (finite and nonfinite). But it is not interpreted in that high position; the scope of negation in examples such as (28) is restricted to the left conjunct of the complement of c. That is, the logical form of (28) is as in (29):

(29) [[¬p] & [q]] → [r]

in which negation associates only with the leftmost propositional variable of the protasis. There is in the form of (28), then, a curious misalignment between the position in which negation receives its morphophonological expression and the position in which it makes its semantic contribution. The logical form in (29) suggests the syntactic representation in (30):

(30)
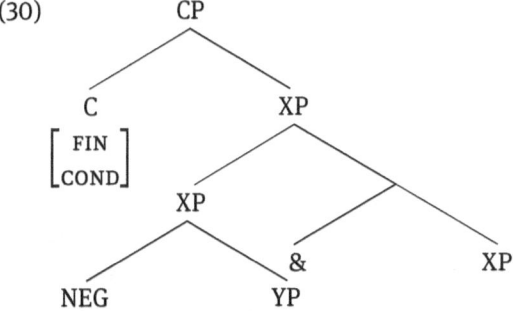

with coordination at the level of the complement of c (finite clause with nonfinite clause as before) and crucially negation only in the left conjunct. The representation in (30), which accurately reflects compositional properties, must now be squared with the morphophonological facts of (21)–(26). We can bridge that gap by way of the following general analysis of negation in finite clauses: From our discussion of negation in nonfinite clauses (see (15) above), we take the idea that there is a semantically potent expression of negation just below c. We are thereby relieved of an otherwise surprising asymmetry between the two clause-types while at the same time bringing the Irish facts into alignment with typological expectation (see Laka (1990), Zanuttini (1997), Cheng et al. (1996), Ladusaw (1992), Martins (1994), Potts (2002) among many others).

But we must now reconcile this conclusion with the observation that in morphophonological terms negation in finite clauses is clearly in C. We do this by way of the general analysis schematized in (31). This analysis in the first place follows Laka (1990) and a great deal of subsequent work in assuming that there is a a functional category POLARITY of which the various expressions of negative polarity (finite and non-finite) are members; in the second place it assumes that the semantically active finite polarity head is null and enters into an agreement relation with the (uninterpretable) negative feature in C – the feature which is crucial for the realization rules of (21)–(26).

(31)

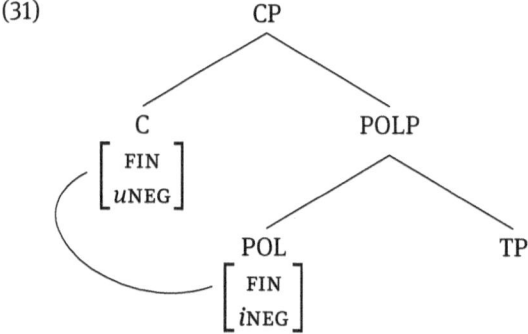

Landau (2002) develops an intriguingly parallel proposal for certain instances of negation in Hebrew as does Gribanova (2016a) for Russian.

In this changed context, the relation between C and the negative POL head in examples like (28) and structures like (30) emerges as an instance of left-conjunct agreement. The polarity head in such cases cannot be linked with C by way of head movement, because that would entail a head movement which violates the Coordinate Structure Constraint (CSC). But it is well established that head movement is subject to the CSC, as shown, for example, by the English examples in (32), the first illustrating the violation, the second illustrating the grammatical counterpart involving Across the Board head movement:

(32) a. *Which car will Freddie choose and his parents will pay for?
     b. Which car will Freddie choose and his parents pay for?

Head movement seems wrong, then, as an analysis of the link between C and the polarity head. However it has been long established that left conjunct agreement is a pervasive feature of Irish morphosyntax (see McCloskey & Hale (1984), McCloskey (1986b), Munn (1999), McCloskey (2011a)). That being so, the otherwise puzzling status of examples like (28) falls into place relatively smoothly, as long as it is agreement which links finite C with the polarity head that it most immediately commands.

Nor do the assumptions about coordination that are required by these proposals seem unreasonable. We will assume an asymmetric theory of coordination in which the coordinator is a head and all conjuncts but the last are specifiers of that head (the final conjunct is its complement). The requirement of identity across conjuncts is a requirement of semantic type (which ensures that there will be a close approximation to a requirement of syntactic identity across conjuncts, given that semantic type and syntactic category are at least loosely correlated). The selectional requirements of a complementizer like *má* or its negative counterpart *muna* are satisfied on the highest (closest) conjunct (because it provides its label as the label of the coordinate phrase) and this is why finite clauses precede nonfinite clauses in coordinations such as those in (15) and (28) (see Munn (1993), Johannessen (1993, 1998), Kayne (1994), Chomsky (2013)). These positions on coordination seem reasonably well supported and they permit a straightforward understanding of the relationship between finite C and the finite polarity head:

(33) COMPLEMENTIZER POLARITY AGREEMENT
The label of C agrees, with respect to the values of the features [NEG] and [FIN], with the label of the most prominent element in its domain which contains the same features.

(33) is presumably one instance of the operation AGREE (Chomsky (2000, 2001)).

This seems reasonable enough overall and marks, I think, at least a descriptive advance over previous treatments. It remains embarrassing, no doubt, that a core property of the system does not emerge right away – namely that negation on C is incompatible with any independent expression of sentential negation. To prevent such 'polarity doubling' we have at present only the stipulation that the polarity head (in finite contexts) is null. But Irish is very strongly a head-marking language, in the sense defined first by Johanna Nichols (1986) and prominent in much subsequent typological work. That is (in our terms) in probe-goal interactions, the morphological effects of the interaction are realized on the probe and the phrase whose label provides the goal is characteristically null (McCloskey & Hale (1984), McCloskey (1986b), Andrews (1990), Legate (1999), Ackema & Neeleman (2003), Doyle (2002), McCloskey (2011a)). Given that we have analyzed the relation between finite C and finite polarity as a probe-goal relation, the fact that the finite polarity head is always null might be properly seen as one aspect of that larger pattern. It must be recognized, though, that in the absence of a real understanding of those patterns, this is little more than a promissory note at present.

It might also be regarded as embarrassing (as a reviewer suggests) that, although we have argued for a fundamental symmetry between finite and nonfinite clauses in the expression of negation (in both, the semantically relevant expression of negation is below C), an asymmetry remains – in nonfinite clauses the overt expression of negation is in the lower position and C is at least in this case null. This too, though, is one aspect of a larger pattern (explored in ongoing work). In nonfinite clauses, as noted earlier, the sequence of heads which defines the inflectional projection is surface-visible in a way that it is not in finite clauses. The reasons for this are almost certainly diachronic. Nonfinite clauses are recent innovations in the language, emerging only in the seventeenth century by way of re-analysis of earlier nominal structures (Stüber (2015)). The morphological fusions and accretions which provide evidence for grammars which include head movement and other exotic externalization devices have therefore not yet had time to accumulate and the sequence of functional heads can be seen in what seems to be their pristine arrangement.

Many other questions also now arise – about patterns of coordination that go beyond those displayed in (15) and (28) and about how these proposals interact with the post-syntactic lowering of complementizers proposed by McCloskey (1996a) and further investigated by Ostrove (2016). These issues are closely related and they are important and interesting; but they are not crucial for our immediate concerns. For the discussion that follows what we principally need is the conclusion that an initial map of the topmost region of the clausal projection in Irish should look like (34) and the proposals so far developed can be summarized as in (35):

(34)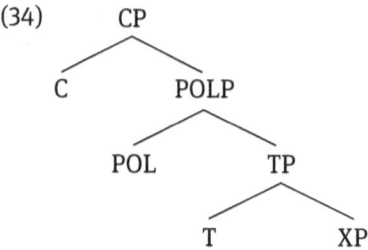

(35) – The semantically potent expression of polarity is in a head below C but above T. This is the result that will really matter for the discussion that is to follow.
– In nonfinite clauses, NEG (realized as *gan*) appears in the polarity position of (34).
– In finite clauses the polarity head is null.
– In finite clauses, C may bear an uninterpretable NEG feature which enters into an agreement relation with the semantically active NEG head immediately below it (see also Kramer & Rawlins (2009, 2012)).

We will return to and elaborate these proposals in various ways in what follows. First, though, we must make the obvious move.

4 Polarity and verb raising

Our discussion of how VSO order is derived in Irish ended with the skeletal proposal in (11) above and with a series of challenges that it provokes. In particular, we were left with the challenge of identifying believable candidates for the two crucial heads of (11) – F1, to which the finite verb raises, and F2 which attracts the 'subject' into its specifier (below F1 and therefore below and to the right of the ultimate position of the verb). We were also left with the challenge of saying how that structure could provide the basis for a reasonable understanding of Responsive Ellipsis – both how it functions internal to Irish and how it relates to apparently similar ellipsis processes in other languages (especially VP Ellipsis in English). Our discussion of the syntax of polarity suggests some answers to these questions: F1 is the polarity head of (34), F2 is T of (34); verb raising is raising to the head which expresses polarity, and we interpret (11) as in (36):

(36)

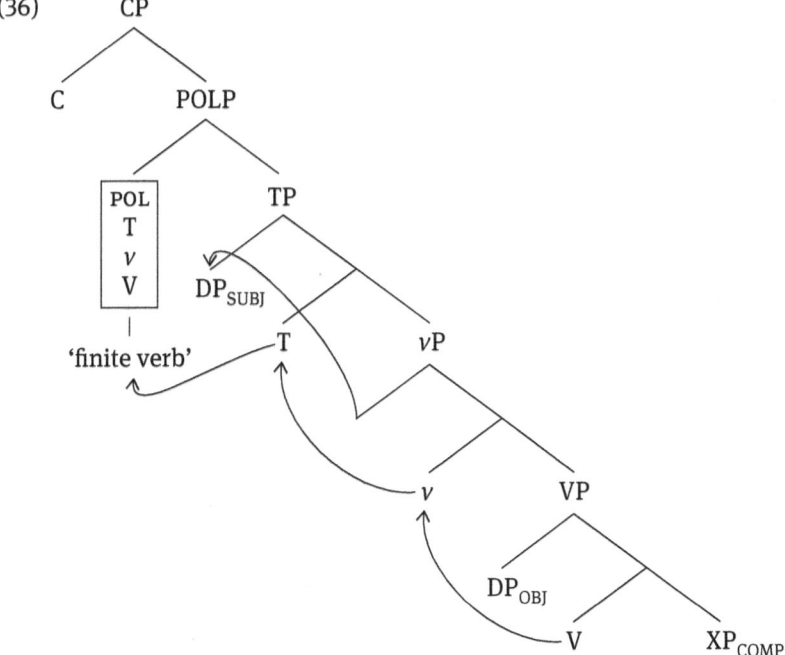

I want to argue that in this case the obvious move is the right move. The section which follows traces some consequences and entailments of the proposal in (36) and argues that it makes possible an understanding of certain patterns and observations which would remain surprising in the absence of the core commitments of (36).

5 Consequences and entailments

5.1 Basics

The core results we want to secure – the observations about constituency which suggest that finite VSO clauses have the general shape in (3) and (7) above – are captured, of course, as before. The inflected verb has a phrasal sister which includes the subject, and the object, along with complements and other dependents of v. Given (36), that large postverbal constituent is TP and it is, further, TP which is elided under Responsive Ellipsis, stranding the finite verb to its left but taking the subject with it.[6]

Certain scope facts are also captured as before (see McCloskey (1996a, 2001a, 2014). Given (36) the finite verb occupies the polarity position, positive or negative; thus any element to its right will be in the scope of that polarity expression. We correctly expect, then, that Negative Polarity items will be licensed in the subject position of negative clauses:

(37) a. *Níor   ith   éinne   riamh   a   dhotháin   le   haon*
       NEG-PAST   eat.PAST   anyone   ever   his   fill   with   one
       anlann   amháin.
       meal   one
       'Nobody ever ate their fill at one sitting.'   CFOC 11
   b. *Níor   thaibhsigh   gáire   éinne   acu   neirbhíseach.*
       NEG-PAST   appear.PAST laugh   anyone.GEN   of-them   nervous
       'None of them's laugh seemed nervous.'   LG 138

We also expect the contrast between English (38), which is ambiguous, and Irish (39), which is not:

(38) *Every player didn't get a goal.*

---

[6] As pointed out by a reviewer, the class of 'large' ellipses (that is, TP-sized) which show the properties of English VP Ellipsis is probably large in crosslinguistic terms. For some intriguing parallels in Hungarian, see Bánréti (2001).

(39) Ní   bhfuair   achan   imreoir   cúl.
    NEG-FIN   get.PAST   every   player   goal
    'Not every player got a goal.'

The two readings of English (38) depend on whether the expression of negation or the universal quantifier in subject position takes wider scope. In the Irish example of (39), by contrast, only one reading is available and on that reading negation has wider scope than the universal quantifier in subject position. This is an expected contrast, if we attribute the English ambiguity to the availability of scope reconstruction under A-movement. In raising from its thematic position to the specifier position of T, the subject of (38) crosses the negative head. If it is interpreted in its higher position, we get the reading on which the universal quantifier out-scopes negation. If it reconstructs to its thematic position, then negation out-scopes the universal quantifier. In undergoing an exactly parallel raising, however, the Irish subject can never escape the scope (the command-domain) of the polarity-head, whose scopally relevant position, according to (36), is that of the finite verb.

These are not new results. On earlier interpretations they would be guaranteed by the assumption that negation on C is the semantically relevant polarity position and the reasoning otherwise would be entirely parallel. However, in arguing, as we will shortly, that the analysis in (36) yields an improved understanding of certain phenomena, it will be important to also establish that there is no analytic slippage in other areas.

5.2 Verum focus

If the proposal currently on the table is correct, every finite verb in Irish contains within itself an element which expresses polarity, negative or positive. Although this element has no phonological exponent, its presence within the verb ought to be detectable in some way. In this section I argue that it is, briefly summarizing a longer and more detailed discussion which can be found in Bennett et al. (2015).

Finite verbs, if this proposal is to be believed, are constructed by combining a sub-sequence of the functional heads of (36) into a single morphological word, one that can be represented roughly as in (40):

(40) { V v T POL }

The verb *thosnaíodar*, for example (the 3rd person plural past tense form of 'begin'), will have the internal representation in (41), in which the order of morphemes (when they can be heard) is a faithful mirror image of the syntactic sequence we have argued for in (36):[7]

(41) { [$_V$ thosn-] [$_v$ -aí] [$_T$ -odar] [$_{POL}$ ∅] }

How might the presence of the null polarity item of (40) or (41) be detected? The answer is that its presence is indirectly but palpably detectable when it is F(ocus)-marked.

Consider the exchange in (42), extracted from a radio interview broadcast on November 3rd 2016. (42a) is the interviewer's question; (42b) is the interviewee's response.

(42) a. Siud   é   an   chéad   chuid   den   fheachtas   seo   – an
       DEMON   it   the   first   piece   of-the   campaign   DEMON   the
       agóidíocht   seo   a   tá   sibh   ag   dul   a dhéanamh.
       protest   DEMON C   be.PRES   you.PL   PROG   go   do.NON-FIN
       Ar   oibrigh   sé?
       Q   work.PAST   it?
       'This was the first phase of this campaign – this protest that you are mounting. Did it work?'

   b. D'oibrigh.   D'oibrigh   sé.
      work.PAST   work.PAST   it
      'It did. It absolutely did.'   RNG 03112016

In (42b), we use small caps to indicate the fact that the simple pronoun *sé* ('it') in the second part of the interviewee's response bears a strong focal accent (and its vocalic nucleus is long). In this it contrasts sharply with the corresponding pronoun in the interviewer's question, which is unaccented, has a short and centralized vocalic nucleus and forms a prosodic word with the preceding finite verb. Both pronouns are of course given. In fact both are anchored to the same discourse referent – the campaign of protest referred to in the interviewer's opening statement. Despite the fundamental similarity in the discourse relations that the two pronouns enter into, however, they are treated phonologically in profoundly different ways. The phonological form of the first is exactly as one would expect for a pronoun which is given – it is deaccented (and it's vocalic nucleus is therefore shortened and centralized). The second pronoun, by contrast, bears a very distinctive focal accent.

But of course in cases such as (42), in semantic terms, focus is not on the pronoun at all. As argued in Bennett et al. (2015), what we have in the second

---

[7] On identifying the stem suffix *-aí* with the voice head *v*, see Ó Sé (1991), Acquaviva (2014), Ostrove (2016).

clause of (42b) is an instance of Verum Focus in the sense originally identified by Tilman Höhle (1992) for German – appropriate in a context in which the truth or falsity of a proposition *p* is a salient discourse issue and in which the truth of *p* is asserted with some force. With Samko (2014, 2016), Bennett et al. (2015) argue that Verum Focus is best understood in terms of F(ocus)-marking (in the sense of Jackendoff (1972), Rochemont (1986), Selkirk (1996, 2008) and much related work) on the polarity head, positive or negative. That is, the syntax will present to the interpretive system a structure like the schematic (43a), which will in turn yield the complex morphological word (43b) in the position of the polarity expression:

(43) a. SYNTAX:

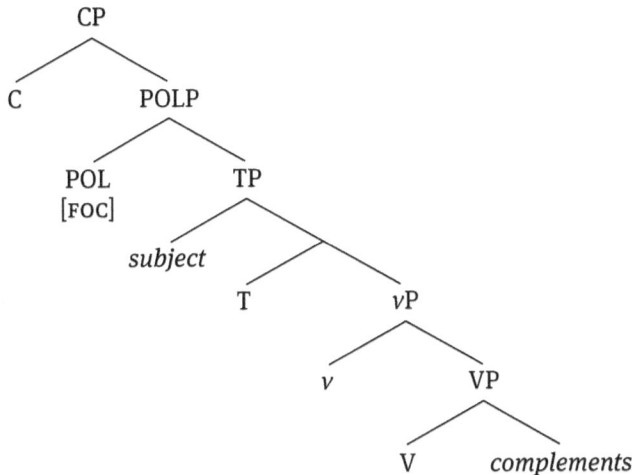

b. MORPHOLOGY:
 { V v T POL }
            [FOC]

If we now assume for Verum Focus the kind of alternative semantics proposed by Samko (2014, 2016), building on Rooth (1985, 1992a), the focus semantic value of a clause containing an F-marked polarity head (as in (43a)) will be an alternative set consisting of positive and negative variants of the same propositional core (in effect, a polar question), while its ordinary semantic value will be the propositional core – which is what is asserted in a use of (43). In the exchange of (42), for example, what we expect is that the second clause of the interviewee's response should be appropriate only in a discourse context in which the truth of *p* (*that the protest worked*) is a salient issue and in which the interviewee wishes to assert the truth of *p*. This seems correct; that is, assuming the representation in (43a) for (42b) seems to yield the right interpretive results. Furthermore, the availability of

(43) as a possible and appropriate response is more or less inevitable, given the framework we have gradually been assembling.[8]

The question that remains, of course, is how the syntax of (43) might relate to the actual phonological outcome in (42b), why, in particular, an accent should appear on a subject pronoun in the context of Verum Focus. The crucial link, though, is provided by a very old and well established generalization: in Irish finite clauses, simple subject pronouns incorporate into the verbal complex to their left as phonological clitics (Quiggin (1906: p. 155, § 486), de Bhaldraithe (1966: p. 65, § 339), Greene (1973), Lucas (1979: p. 120, § 461), Chung & McCloskey (1987: 226–228), Doherty (1996: 23–25), Ó Baoill (1996: 88–89), Bennett et al. (2015)). The example in (44a), for instance, has the prosodic structure indicated in (44b) and a phonemic realization as in (44c) (in Ulster varieties):

(44) a. *Chonaic   mé   fear   mór   ar   an   bhealach   mhór.*
       saw   I   man   big   on   the   way   great
       'I saw a large man in the roadway.'
   b. (chonaic mé)   (fear mór)   (ar an bhealach mhór)
   c. (xanɨkʲ mə)   (fʲar moːr)   (erʲ ə valax woːr)

If we interpret this cliticization in terms of right-adjunction (though that interpretation is by no means crucial), then the actual output structure we expect for the finite verb is not in fact (43b), but rather (45), in which the mono-morphemic pronoun (D) right adjoins to the complex created by head movement through the extended projection:

(45) {{ V v T POL } D }
              [FOC]

The generalization that then emerges, as Bennett et al. (2015) make clear, is a fundamentally phonological one – focal accents are realized at the right edge of the phonological constituent which most immediately contains them. The mismatch between (43a) and (42b) is then another instance of the kind of approximate and imperfect matching that is the hallmark of syntax phonology interactions.[9]

---

[8] This account of the semantics and pragmatics of Verum Focus seems reasonable as far as it goes, but it can hardly be complete. What is missing is an account of the very mysterious notion of 'emphasis' or 'forcefulness'.

[9] In the absence of a subject pronoun, Verum Focus may be realized either on a verbal agreement suffix (one that has sufficient prosodic substance) or on certain otherwise semantically empty post-verbal particles. What is common to all cases, however, is that the accent appears at the right edge of the verbal complex. See (Bennett et al., 2015: 27, 29) for discussion.

Much work remains to be done to flesh out this account in a serious way, particularly with respect to the phonological mechanisms involved (on which see Bennett et al. (2015)); but this has already been something of a detour and the core point can be fairly quickly recapped. It is this: we were led to claim that verb-raising in Irish finite clauses targets a high polarity head (below C but above T and therefore above the position of the subject). We therefore predict that every finite verb in the language has within it a semantically active expression of polarity. The initially very strange Verum Focus effects described here are ultimately, we have argued, phonological manifestations of the presence of that polarity element within the fronted verb.

Before leaving the topic, though, it is worth adding a final observation. The discussion so far has been concerned with the expression of Verum Focus in the context of positive polarity. But the mechanisms are exactly the same in the context of negative polarity, as we can see from an example like (46), which is again taken from a radio interview):

(46) a. *A-r   shíl   tú   ariamh   go   mbeadh   sé   i*
       Q.PAST   think.PAST you   ever   C   be.COND   he   in
       nDáil   Éireann?
       Parliament   Ireland.GEN
       'Did you ever think that he'd be in the Irish Parliament?'
    b. *Nío-r   shíl   MÉ.*
       NEG-FIN.PAST   thought   I
       'I certainly did NOT.'   RNG 29112010

Here too, we see the focal accent displaced on to the incorporated pronoun to express Verum Focus, just as in (42b), and the mechanisms that are at work are evidently the same in the two kinds of cases. Here, however, we have a negative complementizer and further there is no phonological reason why that element should be unable to support a focal accent (consisting as it does of a closed syllable with a long vocalic nucleus). If the negative complementizer were the actual expression of negative polarity, then, we should expect the focal accent to appear on that element. On the analysis so far developed, however, the negative feature on C is uninterpretable and agrees with the semantically relevant expression of negative polarity which, in (46b) as in (42b), is actually within the inflected verb. The facts of (46), then, and their parallel with cases like (42b) are as expected. Also expected, given our proposal about the syntax of polarity, is the observation that it is utterly impossible to place the focal accent on the apparent expression of negative polarity, that is, on the negative complementizer:

(47) **NÍOR shíl mé.*

5.3 Responsive ellipsis and the typology of ellipsis

On the analysis of (36), what we have called 'Responsive Ellipsis' in Irish emerges as elision of the phrasal complement of the polarity head.[10] This way of understanding Responsive Ellipsis has several consequences.

The first is that the parallel between Responsive Ellipsis in Irish and VP Ellipsis in English is restored. The English ellipsis type is at least sometimes, and perhaps generally, also to be analyzed as elision of the complement of the polarity head. This is clearest for cases like (48), on which see Lobeck (1995) and especially Potsdam (1997):

(48) *You CAN smoke in these rooms, but we suggest that you not.*

As Potsdam shows, such cases are best analyzed along the lines shown in (49), with the polarity head being the licenser of the ellipsis and the constituent elided being its complement:

(49) ENGLISH:

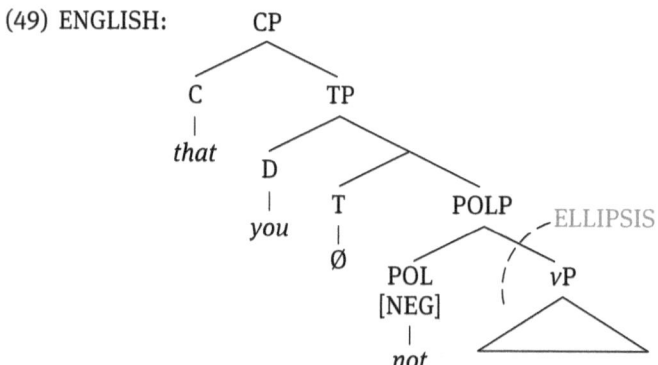

Given the proposals developed so far, our Irish cases are entirely parallel, a result that, as we saw in section 2 above, is one that we need to secure. The parallels between English and Irish become clear if we compare the English structure in (49) with that in (51), which is the structure that our proposals, as so far developed, assign to the Irish example in (50).

(50) *D'iarr   mé   air   a theacht   ach deir sé nach   dtiocfaidh.*
     ask.PAST I   on-him   come.NON-FIN   but say he NEG-C   come.FUT
     'I asked him to come but he says that he won't.'

---

10 For parallels in Finnish, Hungarian and Russian respectively, see Holmberg (2001), Liptak (2013), and Gribanova (2016a).

(51)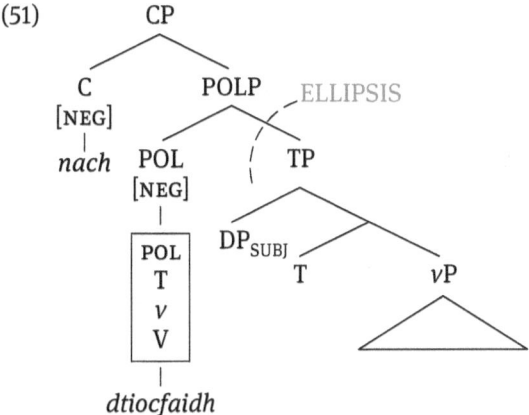

The differences between the ellipsis processes of the two languages now emerge as reflections of an independent and more fundamental difference – where the polarity head occurs in the inflectional projection. Because polarity is higher in Irish than it is in English, Responsive Ellipsis in Irish is elision of a larger constituent – one, crucially, that subsumes even the high subject position (specifier of T) but of course excludes the finite verb. The kinship between the ellipsis constructions of the two languages is therefore restored and both emerge as instances of the larger class of polarity ellipses – on which see especially Gribanova (2016a).

We also now perhaps better understand why both Responsive Ellipsis in Irish and VP Ellipsis in English occur so naturally in the responsive function (although, as we have seen, neither is restricted to that function). The discourse context in which a Yes or No answer is appropriate is one in which two propositions have been made salient by previous moves in the discourse game: p and $\neg p$. This is exactly the discourse context in which, in a response, there would be FOCUS-marking on the expression of polarity (signaling that the alternatives p and $\neg p$ are salient) and in which the semantic content of its complement (that is: p) is therefore given. But these are in turn exactly the conditions in which ellipsis is licensed and favoured. Given-ness (in the sense of Rooth (1985, 1992a,b), Tancredi (1992), Schwarzschild (1999), Merchant (2001)) is the key component in many theories of the semantic licensing of ellipsis, but focus just outside the ellipsis-site is often a crucial additional requirement (Rooth (1992a), Heim (1997), Merchant (2001), Romero (1988), Takahashi & Fox (2005) and much subsequent work). Therefore we need no additional theoretical apparatus to understand why Responsive Ellipsis (like VP Ellipsis) should be so frequently deployed in the answering of polar questions.

Finally there is also a distributional expectation internal to the language which should be considered. We have seen that in nonfinite clauses there is little or no head movement (this is probably the principal language-internal difference within the language between the two clause-types). We have also seen that in nonfinite clauses the marker of negation (*gan*) appears below C and in the polarity head position (see the discussion of Section 3.1 above). If Responsive Ellipsis is elision of the complement of a polarity head, we now have an expectation – *gan* too should be a licenser of the same kind of ellipsis. This possibility is in fact fairly well attested in the language as we see, for example, in (52):

(52) B'fhéidir   nár dhóite   dhuit   é   siúd   a tharrac
     perhaps   it-would-not-be-good   to-you   him   DEMON   draw.NON-FIN
     ort;   b'   fhearra   dhuit   gan.
     on-you   COP-COND   better   to-you   NEG-NON-FIN
     'Maybe it would do you no good to bring that guy down on you.
     You'd better not.'   CFOC 90

In the second clause of (52), all but the negative polarity marker has been elided from the infinitival complement of the modal *b'fhearra dhuit* ('you had better'). This is the expected possibility.

The hedge 'fairly well attested' is used here because the pattern in (52) is not accepted by all speakers or in all varieties. This variability is probably attributable to whether or not the speaker or variety in question has an accented version of *gan*. It is well known that phonologically dependent elements may not appear at the left edge of ellipsis-sites. This restriction (behind which there is a long history of investigation[11]) is the basis for the humour in Richard Armour's celebrated poem in (53):

(53) *Shake and shake the catsup bottle*
     First none will come and then a lot'll.

Given this requirement, (52) should be possible in Irish only if *gan* appears in a fully accented form. However it is characteristically unaccented and proclitic, as is typical for functional heads in Irish (see Bennett et al. (2013: pp. 221–224) for relevant discussion). Therefore our expectation will be that examples like (52) will be available only in idiolects and dialects which have innovated or inherited an accented version of *gan* to co-exist with its unaccented version. If this set of

---

11 See, among many others, Zwicky (1970), Kaisse (1983), Selkirk (1984), Anderson (2008), Ito & Mester (2016).

ideas is tenable, we will have an understanding not only of the possibility in principle of (52), but also of the vagaries of its distribution. We will also have some further reason for confidence in our general approach to what should really be termed 'polarity ellipsis' in Irish.

6 Ellipsis and identity

Our starting point was the body of evidence which suggests that in Irish VSO structures there is a large postverbal constituent – one which seems to exclude the verb but to include all of the other major clausal constituents (as in (7) above). The analysis proposed is a standard one, according to which the verb originates inside that postverbal constituent and raises to its high initial position. An important commitment of the proposal, then, is that every VSO structure in the language includes two occurrences of the verb – one high and peripheral, one low and medial (the position in which the verb appears in nonfinite clauses). The goal of this section is to argue that the lower occurrence of the verb is in fact detectable – by way of a particular restriction on Responsive Ellipsis, one which is by now fairly familiar, but which is nonetheless surprising. Making this argument will force us to engage certain ongoing controversies about the nature of head movement – the process that gathers the independent syntactic atoms of the extended projection into a single morphological word.

Responsive Ellipsis in Irish is one instance of a phenomenon that has come to be known as 'Verb Stranding VP Ellipsis' (perhaps better now 'Verb Stranding Ellipsis' or VSE), a term which originates with Goldberg's (2002, 2005) extensive and careful discussion of the phenomenon in Modern Hebrew. First identified independently for Irish and for Hebrew in the very early 1990's, VSE has since been identified in an impressively broad range of languages and language-families.[12] VSE is the reduction to silence of some constituent XP out of which a verb has raised via head movement to a position outside XP. Having raised, the verb survives the mechanisms of elision, which target only elements exclusively dominated by XP.

---

[12] See McCloskey (1991, 2005, 2011b), Doron (1991, 1999), Sherman (Ussishkin) (1998), Goldberg (2002, 2005), Ngonyani (1996), Martins (1994, 2000), Holmberg (2001), Matos (1992), Cyrino & Matos (2002, 2005), Santos (2009), Schoorlemmer & Temmerman (2011), Rouveret (2011), Liptak (2013), Gribanova (2010, 2013b, 2016a,b), Cyrino & Lopes (2016).

For many of the languages in which the phenomenon has been most closely studied, there is a confound which makes it hard to identify VSE. In those languages, VSE co-exists with a process of object drop and it is not always easy to tell for a given expression whether it should be taken to involve VSE or object drop. However investigators like Goldberg (2005) for Hebrew and Gribanova for Russian (2010, 2013a, 2016a) have developed arguments that object drop cannot be responsible for the full range of observations and that appeal to something like VSE is also required (see also Matos (1992) and Cyrino & Lopes (2016) for European and Brazilian Portuguese). For Irish the view is somewhat clearer, since the potential confound does not arise; there is no process of object drop in the language which might provide an alternative way of understanding examples such as those in (4b) above.

The phenomenon is real then, and well-attested. And it is hardly surprising that this should be so. If verb-raising is real, it would be very strange if those XP's out of which a verb happens to have raised were somehow excluded from the purview of the normal ellipsis operations of a language (though it has occasionally been suggested that they should be). But if the existence of VSE is unsurprising, what is genuinely surprising is the fact that VSE in every case so far studied closely also shows a 'Verbal Identity Condition'. Responsive Ellipsis in Irish shows this effect in a particularly strong and clear way, as we now show.

6.1 The verbal identity condition

Pedagogical grammars of Irish invariably introduce the phenomenon we have called here Responsive Ellipsis with the dictum that to answer a polar question 'one repeats the verb of the question'. And that is an accurate prescription, since, as it turns out, the stranded verb in Responsive Ellipsis must be identical to the verb of its antecedent. This prescription is violated in the examples of (54), all of which are ill-formed:

(54) a. *Níor   cheannaigh   mé   teach   ariamh,   ach   dhíol.
       nior   buy   I   house   ever   but   sold
       'I never bought a house, but I sold one.'

   b. *Cé   gur   mhol   an   bainisteoir   na   himreoirí
       although   C.PAST   praise   the   manager   the   players
       inné,   cháin,   inniu.
       yesterday, criticized   today.
       'Although the manager praised the players yesterday, he criticized them today.'

c. *Níor   éist   sí   le-n-a   cuid   daltái   ach   labhair.
   NEG-PAST   listen she   with-her   portion   pupils   but   spoke
   'She didn't listen to her pupils but she spoke to them'

d. *Cháin   sé   é   féin,   ach   ag   an   am   chéanna
   criticized he   him REFLEX   but   at   the   time same
   chosain.
   defended
   'He criticized himself, but at the same time he defended himself.'

The ill-formedness of the examples in (54) was re-confirmed by six native speaker consultants without disagreement (summer 2011). In addition, examination of 294 examples of Responsive Ellipsis chosen at random from various texts and audio sources revealed 100% compliance with the verbal identity condition. Speakers have no difficulty in composing meanings for examples such as (54) – the relevant inferential steps are straightforward and salient; they are, nevertheless, systematically unacceptable. Similar observations hold for Hebrew (Goldberg (2002, 2005)).[13]

The Verbal Identity Condition, however, does not require complete identity of form between the two verbs:

---

[13] VSE can seem similar to the much-studied 'Argument Ellipsis' of many East Asian languages (see Xu (1986), Huang (1987), Otani & Whitman (1991), Hoji (1998), Oku (1998), Kim (1999), Saito (2004, 2007), Takahashi (2006, 2008a,b, 2009)), as illustrated for Japanese in (i).

(i) a. Taroo-wa   zibun-no   hahaooya-no   sonkeisiteiru.
       Taroo-TOP   self-GEN   mother-ACC   respect
       'Taroo respects self's mother.'
    b. Ken-mo [ ]   sonkeisiteiru
       Ken-also   respect-PRES
       'Ken also respects (self's mother).'

The Japanese pattern in fact is similar enough (on the surface) to the Irish and Hebrew patterns that it was originally analyzed as another case of VSE (see Otani & Whitman (1991)). Subsequent work, however, beginning with Hoji (1998), has shown that the ellipsis at work in (i) targets a much smaller constituent than vp or VP (it is elision of an argument of the verb). Crucially there seems to be no Verbal Identity Condition for Argument Ellipsis; the Japanese example in (ii), for example, is unlike the superficially similar Irish example in (54d) in being fully well-formed:

(ii) Taroo-wa   zibun-o   semete-ga   Ken-wa   [ ]   kabatta.
     Taroo-TOP   self-ACC   blamed-while   Ken-TOP   defend-PAST
     'While Taroo blamed self, Ken defended (self).'

This contrast suggests strongly that the identity condition holds in Irish and in Hebrew because the constituent targetted for ellipsis is large enough to have contained the original occurrence of the verb.

(55) a. *Chuireadh   sé   as   do Bhreandán   dul   ar   cuairt*
     put.PAST.HABIT it   out   to   go.NON-FIN   on   visit
     chuici   agus   is   annamh   a   théadh.
     to-her   and   COP-PRES   rare   C   go.PAST.HABIT
     'It bothered Breandán to go to visit her and he would seldom go.'   IA 333
  b. *Ní   theastaíonn   sin   uaim.   Cén   fáth   a   dteastódh?*
     NEG-FIN   want.PRES   that   from-me   what   reason   C   want.COND
     'I won't want that. Why would I?'   FF 7
  c. *Ní   labharfaidh   mé   focal   amháin   agus   má   labhrann,*
     NEG-FIN   speak.FUT   I   word   one   and   if   speak.PRES
     is   orm   féin   a   bheas   an   locht
     COP-PRES   on-me   REFLEX   C   be.FUT   the   fault
     'I won't speak a word, and if I do, the fault is my own.'   OTA 159
  d. *Gabh   ar   mo   dhroim   anseo.   Chuaigh.*
     go.IMPERV   on   my   back   here   go.PAST
     'Get up here on my back. He did.'   CD 242
  e. *Suigh   síos.   ... Ní   shuífidh.*
     sit.IMPERV   down   NEG-FIN   sit.FUT
     'Sit down. ... I won't.'   LAD 29

Nonfinite forms may antecede finite forms (in (55a), the nonfinite (and suppletive) *dul* matches the finite past habitual form *théadh*). Present tense forms may antecede conditional forms, as in (55b). Verbs in the future tense may antecede verbs in the present tense, as in (55c). And imperatives may antecede finite verbs in various tenses – in (55d) the imperative (and again suppletive) form *gabh* matches the simple past form *chuaigh*, while in (55e) the imperative form of 'sit' matches a finite future form of the same verb. And so on. As long as the requirement is observed that the two stems be identical (*modulo* suppletive allomorphy), the ellipsis site and the antecedent may vary in any way with respect to tense, mood, force and finiteness. Again, similar observations hold for Hebrew.[14]

What one makes of these observations will obviously depend on what one's commitments are about how ellipsis works in general or about how ellipses of this type work in general. But there is surely a pre-theoretical sense in which such observations are very surprising: the isolated finite verbs of (54) and (55) seem to be entirely outside the elided constituent; why, then, should they be required to be identical to anything? And the contrast with Japanese argument ellipsis (see

---

14 On the implications of the observations about apparent root allomorphy, see Gribanova (2015). On the mechanisms which determine the allomorphy see Acquaviva (2014), Ostrove (2016).

footnote 13), in which the ellipsis site clearly does not include the verb and in which there is no Verbal Identity Condition, reinforces this sense of surprise.

Surprising or not, though, if we take on some theoretical commitments, we may begin to understand why such patterns should hold. For example, if there is a requirement of lexical and syntactic parallelism between the form of the antecedent and the form of the ellipsis-site,[15] then the Verbal Identity Condition can immediately be understood as reflecting that more general requirement, as long as there is a bare (that is uninflected) verb inside the elided constituent in cases like (54) and (55). But the presence of such a bare verb in that position is exactly the core commitment of the verb-raising analysis schematized in (36). On this view, then, the Verbal Identity Condition holds because for all relevant (syntactic and semantic) purposes, the uninflected verb is inside the ellipsis site. It is no more surprising, then, that verbal identity should be enforced under Responsive Ellipsis in Irish than that it should be enforced under VP Ellipsis in English.

This is a simple and in many ways attractive proposal, but it is subject to at least two serious objections.

6.2 Objection one

If head movement is a syntactic movement like any other, it should leave a 'trace' (a lower occurrence) like any other. When inside an ellipsis-site, the trace of phrasal movement can, under certain conditions, be 're-bound' by a phrase distinct from its binder in the antecedent. We see this for A-movement in (56) and for Ā-movement in (57) (Rooth (1992a), Heim (1997), Schuyler (2001), Takahashi & Fox (2005), Hartman (2011)).

(56) a. *Sandy gets on well with her advisor, but Christina doesn't.*
 b. *John's coach thinks he'll do well, and Bill's coach does as well.* (Rooth (1992a))
 c. *Aubergines seem to do well here, but carrots don't.*

(57) a. *There are things which big data science CAN explain and things which it CAN'T.*
 b. *The BLUE one, I like; the BLACK one, I don't.*

---

[15] On this issue, see among others Rooth (1992a), Fiengo & May (1994), Heim (1997), Takahashi & Fox (2005), Merchant (2015), Chung (2013), Rudin (2016), Kroll & Rudin (2016). For comprehensive overviews of the state of the discussion, see Merchant (2005), Craenenbroeck & Merchant (2013:710–714) and Merchant (2016).

That is: no identity condition is imposed on phrases that undergo movement out of an ellipsis-site. In which case, unless head movement is different in some important way from phrasal movement, there should be no Verbal Identity Condition.

6.3 Objection two

The logic that 'explains' the Verbal Identity Condition leads us to expect that the inflectional material expressed on the finite verb should also be required to be identical to corresponding material within the antecedent. We have argued above that the Tense head, in particular, is lower than the position of the subject and is therefore within the constituent (TP) which is targeted for ellipsis. If the Verbal Identity Condition follows from a requirement of lexical and syntactic parallelism between ellipsis site and antecedent, it is hard to see why that same requirement would not impose a similar parallelism requirement on all of the heads within the ellipsis site, including the Tense head. It follows then that there should be a requirement of strict inflectional identity between the antecedent verb and the verb in the Responsive Ellipsis clause and all of the well-formed examples in (55) should be impossible.

In the section which follows we will address the narrower empirical concern (OBJECTION TWO). We will then turn in the final section to OBJECTION ONE, which has to do, at bottom, with the status of head movement in linguistic theory and therefore demands a larger context.

7 The syntax of tense in Irish

The discussion so far has taken a fairly simple view of the syntax of verbal inflection in Irish, assuming as it does that all relevant distinctions are expressed on the single head T of (36). But this view takes no account of one of the most distinctive aspects of the Irish system – the curious double marking of certain tenses and moods.[16]

---

[16] Discussions with Paolo Acquaviva, Kenji Oda and Jason Ostrove over several years were very helpful with the material of this section. See Sells (1984:127–131), Chung & McCloskey (1987), Duffield (1995), Cottell (1995), McCloskey (2001b), Acquaviva (2014), Oda (2012), Ostrove (2016) for further discussion and alternatives. The papers of Acquaviva, Oda, and Ostrove all draw on earlier presentations of much of the material of the present paper and the four jointly define a more or less harmonious framework of analysis, though with a number of important differences of (what one might regard as) detail.

This double marking is exemplified for the past tense in the examples of (59), all of which have the general form in (58):

(58) C–PTC–V+AFFIX

That is, certain tenses and moods (including past) have a double exponence – one component in the form of a preverbal 'particle' and one component as a verbal suffix.

(59) a. *gu–r   ól+adar   an   deoch*
       C–PAST drink-PST-P3 the drink
       'that they drank the drink'
   b. *an fear a–r   labhr+adar   leis*
       the man C–PAST speak-PST-P3   with-MS3
       'the man that they spoke to'
   c. *a–r   ól+adar   an   deoch?*
       INTERR–PAST drink-PST.P3   the drink
       'Did they drink the drink?'
   d. *ní–r   ól+adar   an   deoch*
       NEG–PAST   drink-PST.P3   the drink
       'They didn't drink the drink.'

(60) a. *má d'   ól+adar   an   t-uisce*
       if   PAST drink-PST.P3 the water
       'if they drank the water'
   b. *an   t-uisce a   d'   ól+adar*
       the water   C-WH   PAST drink-PST.P3
       'the water that they drank'
   c. *D'   ól+adar   an   t-uisce.*
       PAST drink-PAST.P3 the water
       'They drank the water.'

The preverbal particle *do* is proclitic on the finite verb which follows it;[17] the particle *-r* is enclitic on the complementizer to its left. Which 'past tense particle' is used depends on the selecting complementizer. Most members of the class C demand the preverbal past tense marker *-r*, but a smaller group forces appearance of *do-*. In the absence of a complementizer (in root clauses), *do-* appears (see

---

[17] In most contemporary varieties, *do* appears only before vowel-initial verbs and its vowel is elided. In many of the dialects of Munster, however, especially in conservative varieties, it appears quite generally. See Ó Buachalla (1962, 1964, 2003) and the editors' Introduction to Ó Buachalla (2016) for discussion.

(60c)). I want to argue here that the double morphological exponence of tense in VSO clauses in fact reflects the presence of two independent inflectional heads and their projections. So for (59a) we will have the structure in (61):

(61)
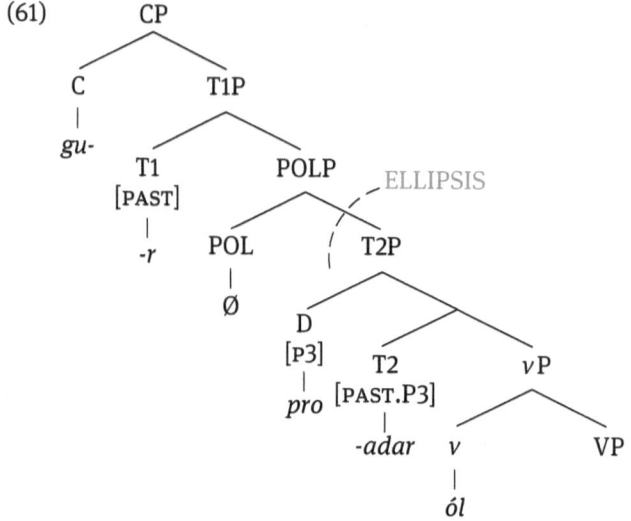

T1 is the position in which the 'past tense particles' *do-* and *-r* appear (along with certain other elements which we will consider shortly). T2 is the position through which the finite verb raises, and the various tense affixes (present, past, future and so on) are its exponents. T2 is also the locus of ϕ-agreement with the subject. T2, that is, acting as a probe, drives the array of morphosyntactic interactions which define subjecthood in verbal clauses (position, case, and agreement). Subjects are therefore in the specifier of T2 and agreement with the subject is expressed on the tense affixes (the exponents of T2). The higher tense (T1) never interacts with the subject and therefore has no agreeing forms. Verb-raising, as before, targets the position just below T1 (the polarity head) resulting in the observed orders of (59) and (60).

The innovation in (61) that matters most here is the postulation of an additional high projection (T1 of (61)) which is implicated in the expression of tense, broadly construed. One might instead view the appearance of the preverbal particles in fundamentally morphological terms (Cottell (1995), Oda (2012), Acquaviva (2014)). But there is evidence that the high T-position of (61) has an independent syntactic, semantic, and selectional function – as host to a class of elements whose status as independent syntactic heads is not in question. I have in mind here the various realizations of the 'copula' – the high functional element which introduces verb-less predications of various types – nominal, adjectival, and prepositional. The copula shows a range of positional, interpretive, and morphological commonalities with the preverbal tense particles that we can begin to understand if they are members of the same (functional) category. The basic facts for copula clauses are illustrated in (62), using the case of AP-predicates, and the general form of such clauses is schematized in (63).

(62) a. *Is   cosúil   le   taibhse   é.*
       PRES   similar with   ghost   he.ACC
       'He's like a ghost.'
    b. *Ba   chosúil le   taibhse   é.*
       PAST similar with   ghost   he.ACC
       'He was like a ghost.'
    c. *Ba   chosúil le   taibhse   é.*
       COND similar with   ghost   he.ACC
       'He would be like a ghost.'

(63) [T   XP   DP   ]   (where XP can be NP, AP, or PP)
           [PRED]   [ACC]

In semantic terms, the property expressed by XP of (63) is predicated of the referent of the (accusative) subject. The T-element of such clauses, however, can express only a very restricted range of tense or tense-like distinctions. In semantic terms, T can be gnomic (as in (62a)), past (as in (62b)), or conditional (as in (62c)). In terms of their realization, however, the past and the conditional/irrealis forms are not distinguished (see especially Ó Sé (1987, 1990) for documentation and discussion of this pattern, which is fully systematic).

Such verb-less predicational structures are much investigated (Ahlqvist (1972), Stenson (1981), Doherty (1996, 1997), Carnie (1995, 1997, 2000, 2006), Legate (1997, 1998), DeGraff (1997), Adger & Ramchand (2003), McCloskey (2005, 2014), Lash (2011)) and while disagreements of course remain, there are also clear areas of consensus. It is agreed, I think, that the copula itself is not a lexical verb but is rather a functional element, an expression of tense, in some sense. It is also agreed that the copula must be relatively high in the inflectional projection but below C.

If the copula is an expression of tense, however, its various realizations must crucially be distinct from the element (T2 in the analysis sketched in (61)) which is implicated in the morphosyntax of subjecthood in verbal clauses. There are two reasons for insisting on this distinction. The first is that the verbal affixes (exponents of T2) express a much broader range of tense distinctions (present, past, future, past habitual, present habitual and so forth) than are expressible in copula clauses, which are restricted to the limited range of options illustrated in (62) above – two forms, three possible interpretations. The second reason for insisting on a distinction between the copula and T2 is that the morphosyntax of subjecthood in copula clauses is entirely different from the morphosyntax of subjecthood in verbal clauses – the subjects of copula clauses are accusative, they never enter into agreement relations and they are not subject to the Highest Subject Restriction on resumption (McCloskey (1990/2011) and much subsequent work). The case and agreement properties have already been illustrated; the final contrast (regarding the Highest Subject Restriction on the distribution of resumptive pronouns) is illustrated in (64):

(64) a. *Fear   a   raibh   sé   breoite.
        man   C   be.PAST   he.NOM   ill
        'a man that (he) was ill'
     b. Fear   a-r   chosúil   le   taibhse   é.
        man   C-.PAST   similar   with   ghost   him
        'a man that was like a ghost'/'a man that would be like a ghost'

The contrast between the ill-formed (64a) and the routinely well-formed (64b) suggests strongly that subjects of copula clauses appear in positions that are lower, and therefore more distant from their potential binders in Ā-positions, than subjects of verbal clauses. In the terms that we are now considering, T2 is the pivotal element for all of the relevant interactions in verbal clauses (case, agreement, and raising). The natural conclusion would seem to be that T2 is absent from the extended projection of copula clauses. This being so, subjects of such clauses do not raise; they are not nominative; and they do not agree. And only the limited range of semantic distinctions expressible on T1 is expressible in copula clauses. These facts are now linked – they are all reflections of a single difference between the inflectional projection of a copula clause and the inflectional projection of a verbal clause. The absence of T2 may well be the defining feature of the distinctive syntax and semantics of copula clauses.[18]

In a striking parallel, however, the tense, or tense-like, distinctions that can be made in copula clauses correspond exactly to the distinctions that can be expressed within the small class of preverbal particles. We have noted that the T1-particle *do-* appears in past tense contexts (simple past and habitual past), but it is also an obligatory presence in conditional forms:

---

18 Copula clauses have their subjects in post-predicate position, as is clear from the examples in (62). There are two traditions for the analysis of this fact. One holds that the predicate fronts around the subject, which appears in a leftward specifier position. The other holds that the subject appears in a rightward specifier position and is sceptical of the appeal to predicate-fronting. See Lash (2011) for a comprehensive overview and extensive commentary. As far as I can tell, it does not matter for the issues that we are concerned with in the present paper which of these options is closer to the truth.

(65) D'	ól-fainn	deoch	uisce.
    PAST/COND	drink.COND.S1	drink	water
    'I'd drink a drink of water.'

This mirrors closely the pattern that we see all through the many forms of the copula in different dialects: there is an under-specified form and alongside the under-specified form there is a form which can in different contexts be either past or conditional in interpretation (see (62) above). Diarmaid Ó Sé (1987) makes this point and also documents a series of intricate and pervasive morphological parallels between forms of the copula and forms of the preverbal particles. In certain Munster varieties, for example, the past/conditional form of the copula may be realized as *do* – exactly like the past/conditional preverb in the same dialect and overt in exactly the same circumstances as that preverb (in conservative registers and as a mark of emphasis):

(66) a. *do*   *bhreá* *leat*   *bheith*   *ag*   *éisteacht* *leis*
        PAST/COND fine   with-you   be.NON-FIN PROG listen   with-him
        'You'd love to be listening to him.'
   b. *do*   *mhaith* *liom*   *dul*   *ann*
        PAST/COND good   with-me   go.NON-FIN there
        'I'd like to go there.'   Ó Sé (1987: 103)

The *-r* enclitic form which appears as one of the markers of past tense in verbal clauses (see (59) above) also appears in copula clauses and is selected by the same set of complementizers as in verbal clauses:

(67) a. *rud*   *a–r*   *chosúil* *le*   *míorúilt* *é*
        thing   C–PAST/COND   like   with   miracle   it.ACC
        'a thing that would be/was like a miracle'
   b. *A–r*   *mhaith* *leat*   *a bheith*   *ag*   *éisteacht*
        INTERR–PAST/COND good   with-you   be.NON-FIN   PROG listen
      leis?
      with-him
      'Would you like to be listening to him?'

In this use, *-r* permits both a past and a conditional interpretation, as seen in (67). There is clear evidence that this parallelism is not an instance of accidental homophony but rather that both the copula form and the preverb form reflect the same morpheme. In a very recent diachronic shift affecting many of the dialects of West Kerry, the enclitic *-r* preverb is disappearing (being replaced by a zero-realization). This is illustrated in the examples of (68), in which other dialects (and indeed the same West Kerry dialects 60 years ago) would have had *gu-r* and *níor* respectively:

(68) a. go   dteastaigh   uaidh   cúpla   punt   a thuilleamh
       C   want.PAST   from-him   couple   pound   earn.NON-FIN
       'that he wanted to earn a few pounds'   MOD 210
    b. Ní   fhágais   id dhiaidh   é?
       NEG-FIN leave.PAST.S2   after-you   it
       'You didn't leave it behind you?'   MOD 38

As stressed in the detailed discussion in Ó Sé (1987), this ongoing shift applies equally not just to the preverbs (as in (68)), but also to the relevant forms of the copula, as seen in the examples of (69), where again other dialects would have *ní–r* (in (69a)) and *cá–r* (in (69b)).

(69) a. Ní   mhaith   liom   mo mhéar   a chur   eatarthu
       NEG-FIN good   with-me   my finger   put.NON-FIN   between-them
       'I didn't want to put my finger between them.'   MOD 33
    b. cá   gceart   dúinn   a bheith?
       where   proper   to-us   be.NON-FIN
       'Where should we be?'   MOD 186

These and the many other parallels and parallel shifts documented by Ó Sé (1987) suggest that the past preverbs *do-* and *-r* are not simply alternative, or additional, morphological exponents of past tense, but rather belong to the same grammatical category as the various forms of the copula. But if the extensive literature on copula constructions is correct in concluding that the copula is a functional head in the extended clausal projection, it follows that we should reach a similar conclusion about the preverbal particles.

More specifically, the various patterns we have considered begin to fall into place once it is assumed (i) that there is a functional category T1 (ii) that all forms of the 'copula' belong to that category, (iii) that the preverbal particles *do-* and *-r* belong to that category and (iv) that there is a distinct category T2 which expresses a broader range of distinctions than are expressible on T1 alone. The higher head T1 is present in all finite clauses (verbal and copular); the lower tense head T2 is present only in verbal clauses. We are left, then, with the syntax of (61) for verb-initial clauses.[19] And for the more particular purposes of the present discussion, what is most crucial is that, given the more elaborated structure in

---

19 One might consider an alternative – close to the system tentatively advocated by Acquaviva (2014) – in which there is no independent polarity head below T1, but in which polarity, positive or negative, is a sub-feature of what we are calling here T1. Such a system would capture most of the results that are of concern to us here, as far as I can tell, and distinguishing it empirically from the proposal in (61) will be, I think, a delicate matter.

(61), only T2 is 'trapped' within the ellipsis site when Responsive Ellipsis applies. T1 is outside the elided constituent (which is now taken to be T2P).

7.1 Identity redux

In a series of papers over many years, but most comprehensively in Stowell (2007), Tim Stowell has argued for a view of the syntax of tense which closely parallels the claims made here on the basis of the very particular facts of Irish. Specifically, he argues, on grounds that are entirely independent of our concerns here, for a syntactic decomposition of each tense into two interacting but independent functional heads, one high in the inflectional projection and one low, very close to the verbal domain. In semantic terms, the high tense head introduces a Reference Time (RT) argument and the low tense head, in a way that is related to its appearance just above the verbal domain, introduces an Eventuality Time (ET) argument. In a root clause, Reference Time is (usually) the Utterance Time. The semantics of the higher head imposes an ordering relation on the value of the RT variable and the value of the ET variable (so for instance, past tense orders RT after ET). Crucially for our concerns here, the relation between the higher head and the lower is taken to be a binding relation, analogous in important ways to the relation of Control. The parallels between Stowell's general findings and the findings of the present paper, based as they are on very particular syntactic and morphological facts of Irish, seem striking.

If we adopt something like Stowell's proposals, we would identify our T1 with his higher tense head and we would identify our T2 with his lower tense head, the head which introduces a temporal variable corresponding to the time of the eventuality of which its *v*P complement provides a description.

An important claim of the discussion just completed is that copula clauses in Irish lack that lower tense head (T2 for us). The evidence presented for that conclusion was fundamentally morphosyntactic. But if we take from Stowell's framework the idea that the lower tense head is the element which introduces a temporal variable (the event time), it must follow that copula clauses allow no such temporal variable and that they express no event time. It is a well-established property of the predications that are expressed by copula clauses that (as Ó Sé (1990: 65) puts it) they express 'inherent qualities' as opposed to 'transient states' and he describes such predications as 'timeless' (1990: 66). Doherty (1996, 1997) interprets such 'timelessness' in terms of individual-level predication, in the sense of Carlson (1977). His claim is that copula clauses express only individual-level and never stage-level predications. But if individual-level predicates are understood in the way proposed by Angelika Kratzer (1995) and developed in much subsequent work, their central semantic property is that they have no spatio-temporal event argument. If this proposal proves tenable, we will have established a link between the very distinctive morphosyntactic profile of copular clauses (which have their source in the absence of T2) and one of their most striking semantic properties (which also has its source in the absence of T2). We have not previously had such a link.

But we were led into this elaborate investigation originally by way of a very particular puzzle – why there should be mismatches in tense and finiteness between antecedent and elided clause under Responsive Ellipsis (see the examples of (55) above). Returning now to that puzzle, we have a possible resolution. A central element in Stowell's proposals, as we have seen, is that the semantic material introduced by T1 enters into a binding relation with the semantic content of T2. As a consequence, the lower temporal variable would be as open to rebinding as any bound anaphoric element inside an ellipsis site – a reflexive as in (70a), controlled PRO as in (70b), or an A-bound trace as in (70c):

(70) a. *Fred criticized himself and Jack did as well.*
    b. *Sally decided to apply for the position and Greta did as well.*
    c. *The protesters were arrested and the photographers were as well.*

In the context of the theory of ellipsis resolution developed in Heim (1997), (see also Rooth (1992a), Takahashi & Fox (2005)) the temporal variable introduced by the lower expression of tense (T2) would be ripe for re-binding because it would be un-bound within the ellipsis-site, but bound within the larger parallelism domain forced by its presence. This should yield the effects of (55) if the higher head, T1, is focused.

7.2 Interim conclusion

These tentative remarks amount to little more than a promissory note. The actual work of designing and testing a system along the lines suggested here remains to be done.[20] The prospects, though, do not seem unreasonable, especially if one could manage to incorporate into it the insights of Ó Sé (1990) concerning the semantics of what we have called here T1, the head which hosts both the preverbal particles and the copula. Ó Sé argues that the core semantic distinction

---

20 In particular, to capture the kinds of mismatches documented in (55) the variable which is free in the ellipsis site would have to be a variable over relations between reference time and event time. This does not seem unthinkable, but the hard work remains to be done.

encoded there is the distinction between realis and irrealis mood (past tense must be taken to be at least possibly irrealis in this system, as he discusses). Melding this insight with a system like that proposed by Stowell would make for a challenging and interesting project. But for our narrower present purposes what matters is that there seems to be a way of understanding the coexistence of the Verbal Identity Condition with the tense-related mismatches seen in (55).[21]

8 Identity and head movement

We return finally to our original puzzle – why the Verbal Identity Condition should hold in the relation between an instance of Responsive Ellipsis and its antecedent clause. It is of course as true of the more articulated structure proposed in (61) as it is of its ancestor proposals, that inside every phrase elided by Responsive Ellipsis there is a bare verb – a verb dissociated from the inflectional bric-à-brac that it comes to have in virtue of its clause-initial position. It seems unlikely that it is an accident that this is exactly the unit of identity that the Verbal Identity Condition cares about (compare (54) above with (55)).

If the discussion of the previous section survives scrutiny, then the simple and intuitive proposal entertained in section 6.1 above is viable: the Verbal Identity Condition holds because for all relevant purposes (syntactic and semantic) the bare verb is within the ellipsis-site and representations such as (61) are the only representations that the ellipsis-licensing mechanisms are ever exposed to. This result is delivered immediately if the operations which build inflected verbs are post-syntactic, part of the process by which morphological exponents are found for the atomic elements of syntax. There have been a number of influential proposals along these lines, especially since Chomsky (2000) argued that head-movement, as classically conceived, was not easily integrated into otherwise plausible and attractive minimalist architectures (Boeckx & Stjepanović (2001), Harley (2004), Platzack (2013), Merchant (2013) and,

---

21 There is an alternative path which one might follow in thinking about the problem posed by the legal mismatches illustrated in (55). In some very recent work on sluicing, Rudin (2016) and Kroll & Rudin (2016) discuss some fairly dramatic possible mismatches between antecedent and ellipsis-site with respect to sluicing in English and German and from that starting point argue for a syntactic licensing condition on sluicing which inspects only elements appearing within the 'eventive core' of the clause (in syntactic terms, the *v*p-phase), a domain much smaller than the constituent targeted for elision. If extended to the case of Responsive Ellipsis in Irish, the approach would lead us to expect identity of heads within *v*p, but possible mismatches in the syntactic space above *v*p. In this way we would derive the Verbal Identity Condition but allow the mismatches of (55). In the context of such proposals, of course, our conclusions about the syntactic expression of tense in Irish stand.

in a very different theoretical context Wescoat (2002)). The identity condition on vse has already played a role in these discussions (McCloskey (2011b), Schoorlemmer & Temmerman (2011)).

The post-syntactic view of head-movement yields the Irish facts (and probably also the relevant Hebrew facts) immediately and correctly, and as far as the principal goals of the present paper are concerned, the discussion could end here. It would be wrong to end, however, without recognizing that the theoretical and typological landscape is both more varied and more interesting than this over-brief discussion would suggest. As work on Verb-Stranding Ellipsis has proceeded, it has become clear that two types at least must be distinguished, determined in part by the form that the Verbal Identity Condition takes. There is a sub-type (which includes Irish and Hebrew) in which the requirement seems to be strict and invariant (as we have seen here) and a second group (which includes at least Russian, Hungarian, varieties of Portuguese and Ndendeule) in which the facts are more complex. In these languages verbal identity largely holds, but verbal mismatches are possible under a particular circumstance – if the verbs are themselves focus-marked (Ngonyani (1996), Santos (2009), Liptak (2013), Cyrino & Lopes (2016), Gribanova (2016a)).

As part of an ongoing program to re-map the theoretical landscape for head-movement, Boris Harizanov and Vera Gribanova (2017) have argued that when cases of successful empirical appeal to the device of head-movement are examined carefully, two rather different classes of phenomenon emerge. There are cases of true head-movement, in which already fully-formed morphological words displace to higher positions – often to positions associated with the expression of focus or with the expression of clausal force. But there are also cases in which head movement seems to be principally driven by the needs of morphological composition – the building of morphologically complex words. The two classes exhibit very different clusters of properties and the contrasts, they argue, fall into place if one assumes that the first type reflects syntactic movement of a more or less familiar kind, while the second reflects the work of a set of post-syntactic word-building operations. The typology they thus elaborate marks, in an important sense, the restoration of an earlier typology for head-movement proposed by Luigi Rizzi and Ian Roberts (1989)[22] and the framework developed by Gribanova and Harizanov seems very promising as a way of resolving the many difficulties that have marked the attempt to integrate head movement into the architecture of mature minimalist theory.

---

22 The typology proposed by Rizzi and Roberts turned on the difference between substitution and adjunction; their results were lost sight of when it came to be widely believed in the 1990's that head movement always proceeds by adjunction. See also Riemsdijk (1998).

These proposals also have implications for the question of how we should understand the Verbal Identity Condition, since it seems more than possible that when we see the Verbal Identity Condition in its strong form (as in Irish and Hebrew) we are dealing with the post-syntactic word-building type of head movement, but that when focus-related exceptions to the Verbal Identity Condition are tolerated, the head-movement in question is of the second type – true syntactic movement to a focus-position. The Irish head movements we have been concerned with in this paper – which result in the construction of morphologically complex verbs in a relatively high region of the extended projection – are clearly of the post-syntactic type and it is therefore expected, within the framework under development, that Irish should show a strong form of the identity condition.

Much empirical and theoretical work remains to be done to flesh out and explore these possibilities (see Gribanova (2016b) for an initial laying out of the territory) but the prospects seem promising.

9 Conclusion

We have seen that the proposals of (61) provide a basis for understanding a broad range of observations about Irish clause-structure – some of them very basic (verbs come first ...), some of them more esoteric. The final part of the discussion provides both an independent piece of evidence for the basic thrust of the proposal (there is evidence for the presence of a bare verb inside the postverbal constituent of (7)) and an argument for the postsyntactic status of at least some instances of what has been called 'head movement'.

Achieving some new understanding in this area will have important consequences for the larger goal of understanding in crosslinguistic perspective how clauses are built. With respect to that question, I think it is fair to say that the general program of focusing on combinatorial properties of functional heads has yielded both a better understanding of the various clause-types in Irish and a better understanding of their inter-relatedness, than has previously been available. More fundamental questions – where those atomic elements come from, what the combinatorial possibilities are, what the limits of variation are in how they express themselves in particular languages (the cartographic questions in effect) – remain mysterious.

The discussion has also exposed a central role for the polarity projection as a morphosyntactic actor in defining the crucial clause-internal relationships. Given that the polarity head is the head of the complement of the phase-defining head c, this is not so surprising if one accepts the general framework of Chomsky (2008).

Acknowledgements: This paper began life far too long ago as a presentation at a GIST workshop in Gent. I have very happy memories of the event and of the liveliness and supportiveness of the research community that I encountered there. For that and for many other reasons it is an honour and a pleasure to dedicate this paper to Liliane Haegeman – my colleague and friend of many years. Subsequent presentations at CSSP 23 (2011), UCLA (2011), Nanzan University (2012), the University of California, Berkeley (2013), and at the University of Groningen (2015) led to numerous improvements. I owe a special debt to Vera Gribanova and Boris Harizanov at Stanford, whose ongoing work on head movement and on ellipsis has informed the discussion here throughout. Comments by two reviewers were also very helpful in improving and sharpening the final version. The research reported on here was supported by the National Science Foundation, by way of Award No. 1451819 (*The Implicit Content of Sluicing*).

References

Ackema, Peter & Ad Neeleman. 2003. Context-sensitive spell-out. *Natural Language and Linguistic Theory* 21. 681–735.
Acquaviva, Paolo. 2014. The categories of Modern Irish verbal inflection. *Journal of Linguistics* 50. 537–586.
Adger, David & Gillian Ramchand. 2003. Predication and equation. *Linguistic Inquiry* 34. 325–359.
Ahlqvist, Anders. 1972. Some aspects of the copula in Irish. *Éigse* xiv. 269–274.
Anderson, Stephen. 2008. English reduced auxiliaries really are simple clitics. *Lingue e Linguaggio* VII. 1–18.
Andrews, Avery. 1990. Unification and morphological blocking. *Natural Language and Linguistic Theory* 8. 507–557.
Bántréti, Zoltán. 2001. Multiple lexical selection and parallelism in Hungarian VP Ellipsis. *Acta Linguistica Hungarica* 48. 25–58.
Bennett, Ryan, Emily Elfer & James McCloskey. 2013. Lightest to the right: An apparently anomalous displacement in Irish. *Linguistic Inquiry* 47. 169–234.
Bennett, Ryan, Emily Elfer & James McCloskey. 2015. Prosody, focus, and ellipsis in Irish. Manuscript, Yale University, University of British Columbia and University of California Santa Cruz. Available at http://ohlone.ucsc.edu/~jim/Papers/.
de Bhaldraithe, Tomás. 1966. *The Irish of Cois Fhairrge, County Galway*. Dublin: Dublin Institute for Advanced Studies.
Boeckx, Cedric & Sandra Stjepanović. 2001. Headings towards PF. *Linguistic Inquiry* 32. 345–355.
Cardinaletti, Anna. 1997. Subjects and clause structure. In Liliane Haegeman (ed.), *The new comparative syntax*, 33–63. London: Longman.
Carlson, Gregory. 1977. Reference to kinds in English. Doctoral dissertation, University of Massachusetts Amherst.
Carnie, Andrew. 1995. Non-verbal predication and head-movement. Doctoral dissertation, MIT, Cambridge, Massachusetts.
Carnie, Andrew. 1997. Two types of non-verbal predication in Modern Irish. *Canadian Journal of Linguistics/Revue Canadienne de Linguistique* 42. 57–73.

Carnie, Andrew. 2000. On the notions XP and X⁰. *Syntax* 3. 59–106.
Carnie, Andrew. 2006. Flat structure, phrasal variability and non-verbal predication in Irish. *Journal of Celtic Linguistics* 9. 13–31.
Carnie, Andrew & Heidi Harley. 1998. Clausal architecture: the licensing of major constituents in a verb initial language.
Cheng, Lisa, James Huang & Jane Tang. 1996. Negative particle questions: A dialectal comparison. In J. R. Black & Virginia Motapanyane (eds.), *Microparametric syntax: Dialectal variation in syntax*, 41–78. Amsterdam and Philadelphia: John Benjamins.
Chomsky, Noam. 2000. Minimalist inquiries, the framework. In Roger Martin, David Michaels & Juan Uriagereka (eds.), *Step by step: Essays on minimalist syntax in honor of Howard Lasnik*, 89–156. Cambridge, Massachusetts: MIT Press.
Chomsky, Noam. 2001. Derivation by phase. In Michael Kenstowicz (ed.), *Ken Hale: A life in language*, 1–52. Cambridge, Massachusetts: MIT Press.
Chomsky, Noam. 2008. On phases. In Robert Freidin, Carlos Otero & Maria Luisa Zubizaretta (eds.), *Foundational issues in linguistic theory: Essays in honor of Jean-Roger Vergnaud*, 133–166. Cambridge, Mass.: MIT Press.
Chomsky, Noam. 2013. Problems of projection. *Lingua* 130. 33–49.
Chung, Sandra. 2013. Syntactic identity in sluicing: How much and why? *Linguistic Inquiry* 44. 1–44.
Chung, Sandra & James McCloskey. 1987. Government, barriers and small clauses in modern Irish. *Linguistic Inquiry* 18. 173–237.
Cottell, Siobhan. 1995. The representation of tense in Modern Irish. *GenGenP* 3. 105–124.
Craenenbroeck, Jeroen van & Jason Merchant. 2013. Ellipsis phenomena. In Marcel den Dikken (ed.), *The Cambridge handbook of generative syntax*, 701–745. Cambridge, United Kingdom: Cambridge University Press.
Cyrino, Sonia & Ruth Lopes. 2016. Null objects are ellipsis in Brazilian Portuguese. *The Linguistic Review* 33. 483–502.
Cyrino, Sonia & Gabriela Matos. 2002. vp ellipsis in European and Brazilian Portuguese: A comparative analysis. *Journal of Portuguese Linguistics* 1. 177–214.
Cyrino, Sonia & Gabriela Matos. 2005. Local licensers and recovering in VP Ellipsis in European and Brazilian Portuguese. *Journal of Portuguese Linguistics* 4. 79–112.
DeGraff, Michel. 1997. Nominal predication in Haitian and Irish. In Emily Curtis, James Lyle & Gabe Webster (eds.), *WCCFL 16: Proceedings of the sixteenth west coast conference on formal linguistics*, 113–128. Stanford, California: CSLI Publications.
Doherty, Cathal. 1996. Clausal structure and the Modern Irish copula. *Natural Language and Linguistic Theory* 14. 1–48.
Doherty, Cathal. 1997. Predicate initial constructions in Irish. In Brian Agbayani & Sze-Wing Tang (eds.), *WCCFL 15: Proceedings of the Fifteenth West Coast Conference on Formal Linguistics*, 81–95. Stanford, California: CSLI Publications.
Doron, Edit. 1991. v-movement and vp-ellipsis. Manuscript, The Hebrew University of Jerusalem.
Doron, Edit. 1999. v-movement and vp ellipsis. In Shalom Lappin & Elabbas Benmamoun (eds.), *Fragments: Studies in ellipsis and gapping*, 124–140. New York and Oxford: Oxford University Press.
Doyle, Aidan. 2002. *Covert and overt pronominals in Irish*. Lublin, Poland: Wydawnictwo Folium.
Doyle, Aidan. 2012. The flying subject: Dative case-marking in Irish. Presented to the Conference on Non-Canonically Case-Marked Subjects, University of Iceland.
Duffield, Nigel. 1995. *Particles and projections in Irish syntax*. Boston, MA: Kluwer.

Elfner, Emily. 2012. Syntax-prosody interactions in Irish. Doctoral dissertation, University of Massachusetts, Amherst.

Elfner, Emily. 2015. Recursion in prosodic phrasing: Evidence from Connemara Irish. *Natural Language and Linguistic Theory* 33. 1169–1208.

Fiengo, Robert & Robert May. 1994. *Indices and identity*. Cambridge, Massachusetts: MIT Press.

Filppula, Markku. 1999. *The grammar of Irish English:Language in Hibernian style*. London and New York: Routledge. Routledge Studies in Germanic Linguistics 5.

Goldberg, Lotus. 2002. An elucidation of null direct object structures in Modern Hebrew. In Line Mikkelsen & Christopher Potts (eds.), *WCCFL 21: Proceedings of the Twenty-First West Coast Conference on Formal Linguistics*, 99–112. Cascadilla Press.

Goldberg, Lotus. 2005. *Verb-stranding vp ellipsis: A cross-linguistic study*: McGill University, Montreal, Canada dissertation.

Greene, David. 1973. Synthetic and analytic: A reconsideration. *Ériu* 24. 121–133.

Gribanova, Vera. 2010. Composition and locality: The morphosyntax and phonoloy of the Russian verbal complex. Doctoral dissertation, University of California, Santa Cruz.

Gribanova, Vera. 2013a. A new argument for verb-stranding verb phrase ellipsis. *Linguistic Inquiry* 44. 145–157.

Gribanova, Vera. 2013b. Verb stranding verb phrase ellipsis and the structure of the Russian verbal complex. *Natural Language and Linguistic Theory* 31. 91–136.

Gribanova, Vera. 2015. Roots in ellipsis and multidominance. Paper presented to the Roots IV Conference, nyu, June 30th 2015.

Gribanova, Vera. 2016a. Head movement and ellipsis in the expression of Russian polarity focus. Manuscript, Stanford University. To appear in *Natural Language and Linguistic Theory*.

Gribanova, Vera. 2016b. On head movement and the verbal identity condition in ellipsis. Presented to the Comparative Syntax Meeting, Universiteit Leiden, December 14th 2016.

Guilfoyle, Eithne. 1990. *Functional categories and phrase structure parameters*. Montreal, Canada: McGill University dissertation.

Guilfoyle, Eithne. 1994. VNP's, finiteness and external arguments. In M. Gonzalez (ed.), *NELS 24, Proceedings of the Twenty-fourth Annual Meeting of the North East Linguistic Society*, 141–155. Amherst, Massachusetts: GLSA, Graduate Linguistics Student Association, University of Massachusetts, Amherst.

Harizanov, Boris & Vera Gribanova. 2017. Whither head movement? Manuscript, Stanford University. Presented at the Workshop on the Status of Head Movement in Linguistic Theory, Stanford University, September 17, 2016.

Harley, Heidi. 2004. Merge, conflation, and head movement. In Keir Moulton & Matthew Wolf (eds.), *NELS 34, Proceedings of the Thirty Fourth Annual Meeting of the North East Linguistic Society*, 239–254. Amherst, Massachusetts: GLSA, Graduate Linguistics Student Association, University of Massachusetts, Amherst.

Hartman, Jeremy. 2011. The semantic uniformity of traces: Evidence from ellipsis parallelism. *Linguistic Inquiry* 42. 367–388.

Heim, Irene. 1997. Predicates or formulas? evidence from ellipsis. In Aaron Lawson (ed.), *SALT VII, Proceedings from Semantics and Linguistic Theory VII*, 197–221. Ithaca, New York: Cornell University, CLC Publications.

Höhle, Tilman. 1992. Über Verum-Fokus im Deutschen. In Joachim Jacobs (ed.), *Informationsstruktur und Grammatik*, 112–141. Westdeutcher Verlag.

Hoji, Hajime. 1998. Null objects and sloppy identity in Japanese. *Linguistic Inquiry* 28. 127–152.

Holmberg, Anders. 2001. The syntax of yes and no in Finnish. *Studia Linguistica* 55. 141–175.

Huang, James. 1987. Remarks on empty categories in Chinese. *Linguistic Inquiry* 18. 321–337.
Ito, Junko & Armin Mester. 2016. Matching light elements. Presented to the workshop on *The Effects of Constituency on Sentence Phonology*, University of Massachusetts Amherst, July 29–31 2016.
Jackendoff, Ray S. 1972. *Semantic interpretation in generative grammar*, vol. Two Current Studies in Linguistics. Cambridge, Massachusetts: MIT Press.
Johannessen, Janne Bondi. 1993. *Coordination: A minimalist approach*. Doctoral dissertation, University of Oslo.
Johannessen, Janne Bondi. 1998. *Coordination*. Oxford, United Kingdom: Oxford University Press.
Kaisse, Ellen. 1983. The syntax of auxiliary reduction in English. *Language* 59. 93–122.
Kayne, Richard S. 1994. *The antisymmetry of syntax*. Cambridge, Massachusetts: MIT Press.
Kim, Soowon. 1999. Sloppy/strict identity, empty objects, and NP ellipsis. *Journal of East Asian Linguistics* 8. 255–284.
Kramer, Ruth & Kyle Rawlins. 2009. Polarity particles: An ellipsis account. In *NELS 39, Papers from the Thirty-Ninth Annual Meeting of the North Eastern Linguistics Society*, Amherst, Massachusetts: GLSA.
Kramer, Ruth & Kyle Rawlins. 2012. An ellipsis approach to polarity particles across languages. Paper presented to the Workshop on the Syntax of 'Yes' and 'No', University of Newcastle, June 8th 2012.
Kratzer, Angelika. 1995. Stage-level and individual level predicates. In Gregory N. Carlson & Francis J. Pelletier (eds.), *The generic book*, 125–175. Chicago, Illinois: University of Chicago Press.
Kroll, Margaret & Deniz Rudin. 2016. Licensing and interpretation: A comprehensive theory of sluicing. In *NELS 47: Proceedings of the Forty-Seventh Annual Meeting of the North East Linguistic Society*, Amherst, Massachusetts: GLSA, Graduate Linguistics Student Association, University of Massachusetts, Amherst. To appear.
Ladusaw, William A. 1992. Expressing negation. In Chris Barker & David Dowty (eds.), *Proceedings of SALT II, OSU Working Papers in Linguistics*, 237–259. Columbus, Ohio: Ohio State University.
Laka, Itziar. 1990. *Negation in syntax: On the nature of functional projections in syntax*: MIT dissertation.
Landau, Idan. 2002. (Un)interpretable Neg in Comp. *Linguistic Inquiry* 33. 465–492.
Lash, Elliott. 2011. A synchronic and diachronic analysis of Old Irish copular clauses. Doctoral dissertation, Cambridge Univesity.
Legate, Julie. 1997. Irish predication: A minimalist analysis. Masters Thesis, University of Toronto.
Legate, Julie. 1998. Reconstruction and the Irish nonverbal predicate construction. Unpublished MS, MIT.
Legate, Julie. 1999. The morphosyntax of Irish agreement. In Karlos Arregi, Benjamin Bruening, Cornelia Krause & Vivian Lin (eds.), *MITWPL 33: Papers on morphology and syntax, cycle one*, 219–240. Cambridge, MA: Department of Linguistics, MIT.
Liptak, Anikó. 2013. The syntax of emphatic positive polarity in Hungarian: Evidence from ellipsis. *Lingua* 128. 1247–1271.
Lobeck, Anne. 1995. *Ellipsis: Functional heads, licensing, and identification*. New York and Oxford: Oxford University Press.
Lucas, Leslie W. 1979. *Grammar of Ros Goill Irish, County Donegal*. Queen's University Belfast: Institute of Irish Studies.
Martins, Ana-Maria. 1994. Enclisis, vp-deletion and the nature of Sigma. *Probus* 6. 173–205.

Martins, Ana-Maria. 2000. A minimalist approach to clitic climbing. In Jo ao Costa (ed.), *Portuguese syntax, new comparative studies*, 169–190. Oxford University Press.

Matos, Gabriela. 1992. Construções de elipse do predicado em Português – sv nulo e despojamento. Doctoral dissertation, University of Lisbon.

McCloskey, James. 1979. *Transformational syntax and model theoretic semantics: A case-study in Modern Irish*. Dordrecht: Reidel.

McCloskey, James. 1980. Is there raising in Modern Irish? *Ériu* 31. 59–99.

McCloskey, James. 1986a. Case, movement and raising in Modern Irish. In S. MacKaye J. Goldberg & M. Wescoat (eds.), *WCCFL IV: Proceedings of the Fourth West Coast Conference on Formal Linguistics*, 190–205. Stanford, CA: Stanford Linguistics Association.

McCloskey, James. 1986b. Inflection and conjunction in Modern Irish. *Natural Language and Linguistic Theory* 4. 245–281.

McCloskey, James. 1990/2011. Resumptive pronouns, Ā-binding and levels of representation in Irish. In Randall Hendrick (ed.), *Syntax of the modern Celtic languages*, vol. 23 Syntax and Semantics, 199–248. New York and San Diego: Academic Press. Republished in Rouveret (2011), pp 65–119.

McCloskey, James. 1991. Clause structure, ellipsis and proper government in Irish. *Lingua* 85. 259–302.

McCloskey, James. 1996a. On the scope of verb raising in Irish. *Natural Language and Linguistic Theory* 14. 47–104.

McCloskey, James. 1996b. Subjects and subject-positions in Irish. In Robert Borsley & Ian Roberts (eds.), *The syntax of the Celtic languages: A comparative perspective*, 241–283. Cambridge, England: Cambridge University Press.

McCloskey, James. 2001a. The distribution of subject properties in Irish. In William Davies & Stanley Dubinsky (eds.), *Objects and other subjects: Grammatical functions, functional categories, and configurationality*, 1–39. Dordrecht: Kluwer Academic Publishers.

McCloskey, James. 2001b. The morphosyntax of Wh-extraction in Irish. *Journal of Linguistics* 37. 67–100.

McCloskey, James. 2005. A note on predicates and heads in Irish clausal syntax. In Andrew Carnie, Heidi Harley & Sheila Ann Dooley (eds.), *Verb first: On the syntax of verb-initial languages*, 155–174. Amsterdam and Philadelhphia: John Benjamins.

McCloskey, James. 2011a. Inflection and silent arguments in Irish. Handout for a talk at CASTL, University of Tromso, September 2011. Available at: http://ohlone.ucsc.edu/ jim/papers.html.

McCloskey, James. 2011b. The shape of Irish clauses. In Andrew Carnie (ed.), *Formal approaches to Celtic linguistics*, 143–178. Newcastle: Cambridge Scholars Publishing. Available at http://ohlone.ucsc.edu/~jim/papers.html

McCloskey, James. 2014. Irish existentials in context. *Syntax* 17. 343–384.

McCloskey, James & Kenneth Hale. 1984. On the syntax of person number marking in Modern Irish. *Natural Language and Linguistic Theory* 1. 487–533.

McCloskey, James & Peter Sells. 1988. Control and A-chains in Modern Irish. *Natural Language and Linguistic Theory* 6. 143–189.

Merchant, Jason. 2001. *The syntax of silence: sluicing, islands, and the theory of ellipsis*. Oxford: Oxford University Press.

Merchant, Jason. 2005. Sluicing. In Martin Everaert & Henk van Riemsdijk (eds.), *The Blackwell companion to syntax*, Oxford: Blackwell.

Merchant, Jason. 2013. How much context is enough? Two cases of span-conditioned stem allomorphy. *Linguistic Inquiry*. 46. 273–303.

Merchant, Jason. 2015. Voice and ellipsis. *Linguistic Inquiry* 44. 77–108.
Merchant, Jason. 2016. Ellipsis: A survey of analytical approaches. Manuscript, University of Chicago.
Munn, Alan. 1993. Topics in the syntax and semantics of coordinate structures. Doctoral dissertation, University of Maryland, College Park.
Munn, Alan. 1999. First conjunct agreement: against a clausal analysis. *Linguistic Inquiry* 30. 643–668.
Ngonyani, Deo. 1996. VP ellipsis in Ndendeule and Swahili applicatives. In Edward Garrett & Felicia Lee (eds.), *Syntax at Sunset, UCLA Working Papers in Syntax and Semantics, Number 1*, 109–128. Department of Linguistics, UCLA.
Nichols, Johanna. 1986. Head-marking and dependent-marking grammar. *Language* 62. 56–119.
Noonan, Máire. 1992. *Case and syntactic geometry*. Montreal, Canada: McGill University dissertation.
Noonan, Máire. 1994. vp internal and vp external agrop: evidence from Irish. In WCCFL 13, *Proceedings of the Thirteenth Annual Meeting of the West Coast Conference on Formal Linguistics*, Stanford, CA: Stanford Linguistics Association.
Ó Baoill, Dónall P. 1996. *An Teanga Bheo: Gaeilge Uladh*. Dublin: Institiúid Teangeolaíochta Éireann.
Ó Buachalla, Breandán. 1962. Phonetic texts from Oileán Cléire. *Lochlann* II. 103–121.
Ó Buachalla, Breandán. 1964. The relative particle *do*. *Zeitschrift für Celtische Philologie* 29. 106–113.
Ó Buachalla, Breandán. 2003. *An Teanga Bheo: Gaeilge Chléire*. Dublin: Institiúid Teangeolaíochta Éireann.
Ó Buachalla, Breandán. 2016. *Cnuasach Chléire*. To appear. Edited by James McCloskey and Cathal Goan.
Oda, Kenji. 2012. Issues in the left periphery of Modern Irish. Doctoral Dissertation, University of Toronto.
Oku, Satoshi. 1998. A theory of selection and reconstruction in the minimalist perspective. Doctoral dissertation, University of Connecticut.
Ó Sé, Diarmaid. 1987. The copula and preverbal particles in West Kerry Irish. *Celtica* xix. 98–110.
Ó Sé, Diarmaid. 1990. Tense and mood in Irish copula sentences. *Ériu* XLI. 61–75.
Ó Sé, Diarmuid. 1991. Verbal inflection in Modern Irish. *Ériu* 42. 61–81.
Ostrove, Jason. 2016. On the role of linear order in portmanteaux. Manuscript, University of California Santa Cruz. Available at http://people.ucsc.edu/~jostrove.
Otani, Kazuto & John Whitman. 1991. v-raising and vp elllipsis. *Linguistic Inquiry* 22. 345–358.
Platzack, Christer. 2013. Head movement as a phonological operation. In Lisa Lai-Shen Cheng & Norbert Corver (eds.), *Diagnosing syntax*, 21–43. Oxford and New York: Oxford University Press.
Potsdam, Eric. 1997. NegP and subjunctive complements in English. *Linguistic Inquiry* 28. 533–541.
Potts, Christopher. 2002. The syntax and some of the semantics of *as*-parentheticals. *Natural Language and Linguistic Theory* 20. 623–689.
Quiggin, E. C. 1906. *A dialect of Donegal*. Cambridge and London: Cambridge University Press.
Riemsdijk, Henk van. 1998. Head movement and adjacency. *Natural Language and Linguistic Theory* 16. 633–678.
Rizzi, Luigi. 1997. The fine structure of the left periphery. In Liliane Haegeman (ed.), *Elements of grammar*, 281–337. Dordrecht: Kluwer Academic Publishers.

Rizzi, Luigi & Ian Roberts. 1989. Complex inversion in French. *Probus* 1. 1–30.
Rochemont, Michael. 1986. *Focus in generative grammar*. Amsterdam and Philadelphi: John Benjamins Publishing Company.
Romero, Maribel. 1988. Focus and reconstruction effects in wh-phrases. Doctoral dissertation, University of Massachusetts Amherst.
Rooth, Mats. 1985. Association with focus. Doctoral dissertation, University of Massachusetts Amherst.
Rooth, Mats. 1992a. Ellipsis redundancy and reduction redundancy. In Steve Berman & Arild Hestvik (eds.), *Proceedings from the Stuttgart Ellipsis Workshop*, vol. 340 (Arbeitspapiere des Sonderforschungsbereichs 9), 1–26. Heidelberg: Universität Stuttgart.
Rooth, Mats. 1992b. A theory of focus interpretation. *Natural Language Semantics* 1. 75–116.
Rouveret, Alain. 2011. VP ellipsis, phases, and the syntax of morphology. *Natural Language and Linguistic Theory* 30. 897–963.
Rudin, Deniz. 2016. Head-based syntactic identity in sluicing. Manuscript, University of California Santa Cruz.
Saito, Mamoru. 2004. Ellipsis and pronominal reference in Japanese clefts. *Studies in Modern Grammar* 36. 1–44.
Saito, Mamoru. 2007. Notes on East Asian argument ellipsis. *Language Research* 43. 203–227.
Samko, Bern. 2014. Verum focus in alternative semantics. Paper presented at CUSP 7: California Universities Semantics and Pragmatics, UCLA November 7th 2014.
Samko, Bern. 2016. Syntax and information structure: The grammar of English inversions. Doctoral dissertation, University of California Santa Cruz.
Santos, Ana Lúcia. 2009. *Minimal answers: Ellipsis, syntax and discourse in the acquisition of European Portuguese*. Amsterdam and Philadelphia: John Benjamins.
Schoorlemmer, Erik & Tanja Temmerman. 2011. Head movement as a PF-phenomenon: evidence from identity under ellipsis. Presented at WCCFL 29: Proceedings of the Twenty-Ninth West Coast Conference on Formal Linguistics, University of Arizona, Tucson, April 23rd 2010.
Schuyler, Tamara. 2001. *Wh*-movement out of the site of VP ellipsis. In Séamas Mac Bhloscaidh (ed.), *Syntax and Semantics at Santa Cruz*, vol. 3, 1–20. Santa Cruz, California: Linguistics Research Center, University of California Santa Cruz.
Schwarzschild, Roger. 1999. Givenness, AvoidF and other constraints on the placement of accent. *Natural Language Semantics* 7. 141–177.
Selkirk, Elisabeth. 1984. *Phonology and syntax: The relation between sound and structure*. Cambridge, Massachusetts: MIT Press.
Selkirk, Elisabeth. 1996. Sentence-prosody: intonation, stress, and phrasing. In John A. Goldsmith (ed.), *The handbook of phonological theory*, 550–569. London and Cambridge, Massachusetts: Basil Blackwell Publishers.
Selkirk, Elisabeth. 2008. Contrastive focus, givenness and the unmarked status of "discourse-new". *Acta Linguistica Hungarica* 55. 1–16.
Sells, Peter. 1984. Syntax and semantics of resumptive pronouns. Doctoral dissertation, University of Massachusetts, Amherst.
Sherman (Ussishkin), Adam. 1998. VP ellipsis and subject positions in Modern Hebrew. In Adam Zachary Wyne (ed.), *Proceedings of the 13th annual meeting of the Israel Association of Theoretical Linguistics, Bar-Ilan University, Tel-Aviv, Israel*, 211–229. Jerusalem: Akademon.
Stenson, Nancy. 1981. *Studies in Irish syntax*. Tübingen: Max Niemeyer Verlag.
Stowell, Tim. 2007. The syntactic expression of tense. *Lingua* 117. 437–463.
Stüber, Karin. 2015. *Die Verbalabstrakta des Altirischen*, vol. 15, Münchner Forschungen zur historischen Sprachwissenschaft. Bremen: Hempen Verlag.

Takahashi, Daiko. 2006. Apparent parasitic gaps and null objects in Japanese. *Journal of East Asian Linguistics* 15. 1–35.
Takahashi, Daiko. 2008a. Noun phrase ellipsis. In Shigeru Miyagawa & Mamoru Saito (eds.), *The Oxford handbook of Japanese linguistics*, Oxford: Oxford University Press.
Takahashi, Daiko. 2008b. Quantificational null objects and argument ellipsis. *Linguistic Inquiry* 39. 307–326.
Takahashi, Daiko. 2009. Argument ellipsis, anti-agreement, and scrambling. Unpublished, Tohoku University.
Takahashi, Shoichi & Danny Fox. 2005. MaxElide and the re-binding problem. In Aaron Lawson (ed.), *SALT XV, Proceedings from Semantics and Linguistic Theory XV*, 223–240. Ithaca, New York: Cornell University, CLC Publications.
Tancredi, Christopher. 1992. Deletion, deaccenting, and presupposition. Doctoral dissertation, MIT, Cambridge, Massachusetts.
Wescoat, Michael. 2002. On lexical sharing. Doctoral dissertation, Stanford University.
Xu, L. 1986. Free empty category. *Linguistic Inquiry* 17. 75–53.
Zanuttini, Raffaella. 1997. *Negation and clausal structure*. New York and Oxford: Oxford University Press.
Zwicky, Arnold. 1970. Auxiliary reduction in English. *Linguistic Inquiry* 1. 323–336.

Appendix: Sources of examples

ACO:	*An Chloch Órtha*, Walter Scott, trans. Niall Ó Domhnaill
AGMTS:	*Ar Gach Maoilinn Tá Síocháin*, Pádraig Ó Cíobháin
CD:	*Cith is Dealán*, Séamus Ó Grianna
CE:	*Caithfear Éisteacht, Aistí Mháirtín Uí Chadhain in Comhar*, ed. Liam Prút
CFOC:	*Cnuasach Chléire*, Breandán Ó Buachalla
FF:	*Fonn na Fola*, Beairtle Ó Conaire
FI:	*Fan Inti*, Domhnall Mac Síthigh
GLL:	*An Gealas i Lár na Léithe*, Pádraig Ó Cíobháin
IA:	*Iomramh Aonair*, Liam Mac Con Iomaire
LAD:	*Lár an Domhain*, Beairtle Ó Conaire
LG:	*Le Gealaigh*, Pádraig Ó Cíobháin
MOD:	*An Mám Ó Dheas*, Muiris Mossie Ó Scanláin
NAOT:	*Na hAird Ó Thuaidh*, Pádraig Ua Maoleoin
OTA:	*Ón tSeanam Anall, Scéalta Mhicí Bháin Uí Bheirn*, ed. Mícheál Mac Giolla Easbuic
PNG:	*Pobal na Gaeltachta*, ed. Gearóid Ó Tuathaigh, Liam Lillis Ó Laoire, Seán Ua Súillebháin
RNG:	*Raidió na Gaeltachta*
SHS:	*Scéal Hiúdaí Sheáinín*, Eoghan Ó Domhnaill
T:	*Taidhgín*, Tomás Ó Duinnshléibhe

Genoveva Puskás
Negation and modality: On negative purposive and "avertive" complementizers

1 Introduction

Complementizers have been argued to have two functions, that of subordinators and of clause-type indicators (see Bhatt and Yoon 1992, Szabolcsi 1992). Given this distinction, pure subordinators are not expected to appear in matrix clauses; neither do those "complementizers" which conflate subordinator and clause-typing. Only pure clause-type indicators will be able to occur in matrix clauses. In many languages, these two components are realized as two different morphemes. This is the case in Hungarian, as illustrated in (1) below:

(1) a. *János   megkérdezte   a fiától,   hogy   mit*
       Janos   PART-ask-PAS-3S   the son-POSS-ABL   that   what-ACC
       akar   tanúlni.
       want-PRES-3S   study-inf
       'János asked his son what he wanted to study.'
    b. *János   megkérdezte   a fiától,   hogy   gondolt-e*
       Janos   PART-ask-PAS-3S   the son-POSS-ABL   that   think-PAS-3S-Q
       a jövőre.
       the future-SUBL
       'János asked his son if he had thought about the future'.

In both of these sentences, the complementizer *hogy* signals subordination while the *wh*-phrase *mit* (1a) and the bound Q-morpheme *-e* (1b) encode clause-type, namely interrogative.

The Hungarian complementizer *hogy* ('that') has been argued to belong to the class of pure subordinators. It can be omitted in certain circumstances (see Kenesei 1985, Tóth 2009, Turi 2010), and does not occur on its own in matrix clauses. On the other hand, it is the all-round complementizer which, along with *ha* ('if') (as well as the compound form *hogyha*), introduces embedded clauses. Both *hogy* and *ha* have been analyzed as heads of a C projection.[1] Strikingly,

---

[1] Note that concessive clauses are introduced by the conjunction *bár* (optionally *habár*), which may also appear (optionally with *ha*, as *bárha*) in optatives. The optionality of the *ha*, a 'pure subordinator' seems to confirm the status of *bár* as a (pure?) clause-typing element.

so-called "complex complementizers" (see Kenesei 1992) are also made up of a *wh*-element and *hogy* as in *mert hogy* ('because (that)'), *mivel hogy* ('since (that)'), etc.

While it is clear that *hogy* may appear in morphologically complex forms, suggesting that its sole contribution is subordination, a more detailed analysis of various embedded clauses reveals that this is a rough approximation, and that even what appears to be a pure subordinator is a bundle of features which encode more than sheer subordination. In this paper, I will approach the question of the components of the complementizer from the perspective of a "negative complementizer" which has attracted little attention, mainly because of its apparently transparent morphological make-up. It will, hopefully, bring some new light on (i) the featural composition of complementizers and (ii) the way negation and modality may be realized at the clausal level, in the guise of a "complementizer".

The paper is organized as follows: section 2 gives the data and states the problem. It will be shown that the target complementizer *nehogy* is only seemingly related to *hogy+negation*. Section 3 gives a detailed description of the specific features of this complementizer; section 4 proposes an analysis, arguing in favor of a complex complementizer, which encodes negative modality. Section 5 accounts for the various properties of *nehogy*, in the light of the proposed analysis; section 6 briefly discusses an alternative analysis and section 7 concludes the paper.

2 The problem

The Hungarian complementizer *hogy*, which has been argued to be a pure subordinator (see Bhatt and Yoon 1992, Szabolcsi 1992) introduces indicative embedded clauses (2a). Negative embedded clauses are predictably built up with the same complementizer *hogy*, followed by the sentential negative marker *nem:*

(2) a. *János fia   azt mondta,   hogy   popsztár   lesz.*
       Janos son-POSS that said-3S that   popstar   be-FUT-3S
       'János' son said that he will be a popstar'.
    b. *János fia   azt mondta,   hogy   nem   lesz   futballista.*
       János son-POSS that said-3S that   NEG   be-FUT-3S   football player
       'János' son said that he will not be a football player'.

The same complementizer *hogy* also introduces embedded subjunctive clauses (3a). The sentential negative marker is *ne*. It occurs, as in indicative clauses, after the complementizer (3b):

(3) a. *János   azt akarja,   hogy   híres   legyen   a fia.*
       Janos   that want-3s   that   famous   be-SUBJ-3s   the son-POSS
       'János wants his son to be famous'.
       (lit:János wants that his son be famous)
   b. *János   csak   azt   kívánja,   hogy   ne   költözzön   el*
      Janos   only   that   wish-3s   that   MOD.NEG   move-SUBJ-3s   PART
      a fia.
      the son-POSS
      'János only wishes that his son would not move away'.

É.Kiss (2011) claims that *ne* is the realization of negation in a modal environment and may appear in optative and imperative clauses:

(4) a. *Bárcsak   ne   kapná   meg   Péter   a díjat.*
       If.only   MOD.NEG   get.COND.3s   PRT   Peter   the prize.ACC
       'If only Peter wouldn't get the prize!'
   b. *Ne   csak   Pétert   hívd   meg.*
      MOD.NEG   only   Péter.ACC   invite-imp.2s   PRT
      'Don't invite only Peter!'
      [É.Kiss 2011]

I assume, following É.Kiss (2011), that the negative marker *ne* is the realization of [neg]+[modal] features, and is licensed in a clause which has a mood specification (see below for details). That *ne* is a modal negator is confirmed by its occurrence, always below the complementizer *hogy*, in various environments associated with subjunctive mood, such as directives (5a), desideratives (5b) and purposives (5c):

(5) a. *(Azt)   parancsolta,   hogy   ne   menjünk   el   otthonról.*
       (that)   order-PAS-3s   that   MOD.NEG   go-SUBJ1PL   PART   home-DELAT
       'He ordered us not to leave home'.
       [lit: he ordered that we not leave home]
   b. *(Azt)   óhajtotta,   hogy   ne   menjünk   el   otthonról*
      (that)   wish-PAS-3s   that   MOD.NEG   go-SUBJ-1PL   part   home-DELAT
      'He wished that we not leave home'.
   c. *(Arra)   törekszik,   hogy   ne   veszítsen   pénzt*
      (that)   strive-PRES-3s   that   MOD.NEG   lose-SUBJ-3s   money-ACC
      ebben   az üzletben.
      this-INESS   The business-INESS
      'He strives not to lose money in this business'.
      [lit: he strives that he not lose money in this business]

The examples above confirm that the complementizer *hogy* is disjoint from the modal marking of the sentence.

It has been claimed in the literature that *hogy...ne* can (freely) alternate with *nehogy*, as in (6):

(6) *Nehogy   korán   haza   gyere!*
    MOD.NEG-that   early   home   come
    'Don't come home early!'
    [É.Kiss 2011:(34)]

It is indeed noted that "If the subjunctive clause of purpose is negated, it may begin with *hogy...ne* or *nehogy*" (Rounds 2001: 43). Similarly, the author of Hunlang blog recommends to "Use whichever you want to. One is heard as often as the other" (Hunlang blog).

(7) a. *Vigyázz,   hogy   ne essél el !*
       'Watch out   that   you don't fall'!
    b. *Vigyázz,   nehogy elessél!*
       'Watch out   that   you don't' fall'!
       [Rounds 2001:43]

(8) a. *Vigyél   kabátot,   nehogy   megfázz!*
       'Take   your jacket   lest   you catch a cold.
    b. *Vigyél   kabátot,   hogy   meg ne fázz!*
       'Take   your jacket   so that   you don't catch a cold'.
       [Hunlang blog]

According to É.Kiss, "the structure in [6] involving a covert [imperative] particle in spec CP can be negated without verb movement, if *ne*, the modal negative particle, is fused with the complementizer *hogy* 'that'" (2011: 102).

However, the alternation described above is not systematic. For example, the *nehogy* variant is totally excluded from clauses embedded under directives and desideratives:

(9) a. **Azt   parancsolta,   nehogy   elmenjenek.*
          That   order-PAS-3S   MOD.NEG-that   PART-go-SUBJ-3PL
    b. **Azt   óhajtotta,   nehogy   elmenjenek.*
          That   wish-PAS-3S   MOD.NEG-that   PART-go-SUBJ-3PL

Actually, the only case of subjunctive embedded clauses which can occur with *nehogy* is that of clauses embedded under purposives:

(10) *Arra   törekedett,   nehogy   veszítsen   pénzt*
     that-SUBL   strive-PAS-3S   MOD.NEG-that   lose-SUBJ-3S   money-ACC
     az üzletben.
     the business-INESS
     [lit: he strived that he do not lose money in this business]

The claim of this paper is that *hogy...ne* and *nehogy* are not equivalent, as *nehogy* exhibits properties which are very different from those of *hogy...ne*. I will argue that the two variants are (parts of) different complementizers and that the apparent morphological transparency hides a complex complementizer where mood and negation interact. Although the major part of the discussion will focus on purposive clauses, it will also be shown that the analysis extends to other instances of *nehogy*.

3 What differences do we observe?

A first important point is the fact that when there is alternation between *hogy...ne* and *nehogy*, the two versions have a different meaning:

(i) the *hogy...ne* examples can be analyzed as "pure" purposives. In other words, the event described in the matrix clause has a goal, which is explicated in the embedded clause. (7b), repeated here as (11a) can be paraphrased as (11b):

(11) a. *Vigyél   kabátot,   hogy   meg   ne   fázz!*
        take-IM   jacket-ACC that   PART   MOD.NEG   catch-a-cold-SUBJ-3S
        'Take your jacket so that you don't catch a cold'.
     b. *Take your jacket, with the purpose that you do not catch a cold*

Similarly, (12a) can be paraphrased as (12b):

(12) a. *Hallottnak   tetettem   magam,   hogy   ne*
        dead-DAT   put-CAUS-PAS-3S   self-ACC   that   MOD.NEG
        üssenek   tovább.
        hit-SUBJ-3PL   further
        'I pretended to be dead so they would not beat me further'.
        [http://tenyek.hu/belfold/200730_megvert-uber-sofor-halottnak-tettettem-magam-hogy-ne-ussenek-tovabb.html]
     b. *I pretended to be dead, with the goal that they don't beat me further*

This is equivalent to English *in order to ..not, so that ..not*, or French *afin que(...) ne (...) pas, pour que (...) ne (...) pas.*

(ii) the *nehogy* examples, on the other hand, are not pure purposives. Rather, they express the *fear that p* might happen. Again, (7a), repeated as (13a) can be paraphrased as (13b), and (14a) as (14b):

(13) a. *Vigyél   kabátot,   nehogy   megfázz!*
        Take-IMP.   jacket-ACC   MOD.NEG-that   PART-catch-a-cold-SUBJ-2S
        'Take your jacket lest you catch a cold'.
     b. *Take your jacket, because x (the speaker) is afraid that you will catch a cold.*

(14) a. *Hallottnak tetettem   magam,   nehogy   üssenek*
       Dead-DAT   put-CAUS-PAS-3S self-ACC MOD.NEG-that   hit-SUBJ-3PL
       tovább.
       further
       'I pretended to be dead for fear that they would not beat me further'.
   b. I pretended to be dead, because I was afraid they would go on beating me.

This version is actually equivalent to English *lest*, French *de peur que*.
   A second difference concerns the structure of the embedded clause. As repeatedly pointed out, both in Hungarian grammars and recent linguistic studies (see e.g. É.Kiss 2011), whereas *hogy...ne* clauses exhibit verb-particle inversion (15a), clauses with *nehogy* do not (15b):[2]

(15) a. *Taxival   ment,   hogy   ne   késse   **le***
       Taxi-INSTR go-PAS-3S   that   MOD.NEG   miss-SUBJ-3S   PART
       a vonatot.
       the train-ACC
       'She took a taxi, in order not to miss the train'.
       [litt: she went by taxi that she not miss the train]
   b. *Taxival   ment,   nehogy   **le**késse   a vonatot.*
       taxi-INSTR go-PAS-3S   MOD.NEG-that   PART-miss.SUBJ   the train-ACC
       'She took a taxi, lest she miss the train'.

A third difference is the interesting, but to my knowledge unnoticed fact that the *hogy...ne* clause licenses n-words, while the *nehogy* clause does not:

(16) a. *Korán   kelt   fel,   hogy   ne   kelljen   senkivel (sem)*
       early   get-PAS-3S   up   that   MOD.NEG   must-SUBJ   n-body-INSTR sem
       beszélnie.
       speak-INF-3S
       'She got up early, in order not to have to speak to anyone'.
       (lit: that she need not speak to anyone)
   b. *Korán   kelt   fel,   nehogy   *senkivel sem/ valakivel is*
       early   get-PAS-3S   up   MOD.NEG-that   n-body sem/ somebody- INSTR
       beszélnie   kelljen
       speak-INF3S   must-SUBJ
       'She got up early, so that she would not have to speak to someone'.

---

2 See below for discussion.

Hungarian n-words, morphologically identifiable as "*se*-words", are licensed by the (sentential) negative marker in a clause-mate configuration (see Puskás 1998), and behave like strong NPIs (Surányi 2002).³ In (16a), the negative (modal) marker *ne* licenses the n-word *senkivel* ('with no one'). On the other hand, *nehogy* (16b) does not. Only *valakivel is* ('with anyone'), an existentially interpreted weak NPI (see Surányi 2006) is legitimate in *nehogy* clauses.⁴

Finally, that the negative morpheme *ne* in *nehogy* is syntactically independent from the negative (modal) marker *ne* is also attested by the observation that *nehogy* may co-occur with the negative marker:⁵

(17) *Péter   ímélezett   Jánosnak,   nehogy   ne*
Péter-NOM   emailed-2SG   János-DAT   MOD.NEG-that   MOD.NEG
jöjjön   el.
come.SUBJ.3SG   part
'Peter emailed John so that he shouldn't not come along'.

The observations given here appear as compelling evidence for the fact that *nehogy* cannot be the equivalent of *hogy* and *ne*, even in an "incorporated" form. I will propose that it is a complementizer which has its own semantics and which occurs in specific syntactic environments.

4 The analysis

Although there have been claims that *hogy* is a pure subordinator, the complementizer actually assumes several functions, that is, it may realize several features. Thus, following work by Baunaz and Puskás (2014), Baunaz and Lander (2015), I assume that complementizers are complex elements which may encode at least subordination, mood specification and possibly some form of clause typing. In this respect, since different indicative and subjunctive embedded clauses in Hungarian are all headed by *hogy*, I conclude that *hogy*, like other complementizers, exhibits syncretisms, in that different sets of complementizer-related features are spelled out as *hogy*.⁶

---

3 The particle *sem* is a negative reinforcer which may optionally appear in negative sentences with an n-word.
4 See Tóth 1999, Szabolcsi 2004 for a proposal that the *valaki* is type elements are PPIs.
5 Many thanks to a Reviewer who pointed this out to me and provided the example.
6 On the question of syncretisms in complementizers, see Baunaz and Lander (2015).

4.1 Hogy...ne

4.1.1 *Hogy* as a subordinator

Baunaz and Lander (2015) assume that complementizers consist in (at least) a Base (a nominal core/THING) and an operator-like element. I will assume that Hungarian *ho* is a nominal-like base (see Baunaz and Lander 2015, Szabolcsi et al. 2014), and that it combines with *-gy*, a manner affix which occurs in several elements, (such as *így* 'this way', *úgy* 'that way'). This functions as the core. The operator-like element may be either a subordinating operator or an interrogative operator. In Hungarian, the complementizer *hogy* is syncretic with the (manner) wh-word *how*. I will therefore assume that *hogy* may realize either the basic subordinator [sub] or the interrogative element:[7]

(18)

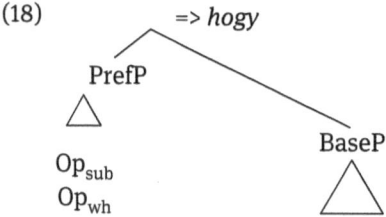

PrefP

Op$_{sub}$
Op$_{wh}$

=> *hogy*

BaseP

4.1.2 Bouletic operator

As is also mentioned in the previous sections, the complementizer *hogy* appears both in indicative and subjunctive contexts. This means that the [sub] operator may itself alternate between a modal value and a "realis" one. The notion of operator should be taken here as referring to an element operating over propositions (see Manzini & Savoia 2003, 2011, Roussou 2010). In other words, complementizers (subordinators) range over sets of propositions. The "realis" operator will range over a set of realistic propositions, while modal operators will range over propositions which express possible/nonrealistic situations (see e.g. Farkas 1992 on the notion of non-realistic modal base). I follow Puskás (2015), Baunaz and Puskás (2016) and assume that subjunctive, as occurring in clauses selected by certain classes of predicates, is the expression of modality related to some emotion. This means that subjunctive mood is licensed in the environment of a subordinating

---

[7] Actually, it is claimed that *hogy* was (only) an operator in Old Hungarian, which got then reanalyzed as a complementizer (see Bacskai and Dékány 2014).

operator which has a bouletic value, as expression of some emotion or desire (see Blochowiak 2014) and which ranges over propositions expressing desirable situations.

Hungarian does not offer overt evidence for this split, in that both the realis subordinating operator and the modal/emotive subordinating operator, associated with the base, spell out as *hogy*. However, such evidence can be found crosslinguistically, as discussed in Baunaz and Puskás (2016). I will therefore consider that *hogy* is the exponent of the Op$_{boul/real}$ and the Base, as in (19):[8]

(19)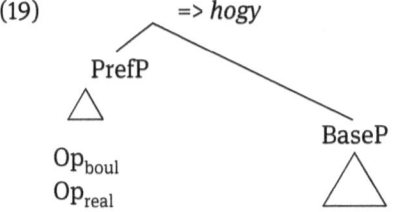

4.1.3 The structure of *hogy* as a "subordinator" in the case of purposives

Purposive *hogy*, as discussed in section 2 above, occurs with an embedded subjunctive clause. The complementizer, selected by the matrix purposive predicate, is the exponent of the structure discussed above which contains an operator bearing the bouletic modal value. I take this to mean that such an operator licenses a Modal projection within the embedded clause. When the embedded clause contains a negative marker, the latter occurs in its modal form, and the embedded clause will therefore have the partial structure as follows:[9]

(20) [$_{CP}$ hogy$_{boul}$ [$_{ModP}$ ...ne ....]]

In these contexts, the embedded purposive clause exhibits the properties of selected complements. Indeed, as discussed elsewhere (see Puskás 2015), Puskás and Baunaz 2016), predicates selecting a purposive complement contain a (bouletic) little *v* head which licenses an "emotive" external argument and

---

[8] Whether PrefP is itself sub-tree with hierarchically organized components remains to be investigated.
[9] I am not, at this point, committed to the exact relation between negation and ModP. E.Kiss suggests that negation occurs in (raises to?) the Mod head, an analysis which is compatible with the present proposal.

participates in the selection of the complementizer containing a bouletic subordinating operator.[10]

4.2 Nehogy

Recall that section 3 led us to the conclusion that *nehogy* cannot be analyzed as the standard subordinator *hogy* with an incorporated *ne*. Indeed, as opposed to *hogy...ne*, it does not occur in selected contexts; moreover, the scope patterns with respect to negation are different. I will propose a decomposition of this "complementizer" along the following lines.

4.2.1 Subordinator component and bouletic operator

Since *nehogy* occurs in embedded contexts, it must contain a [sub] component, very much like *hogy*. The base we identified in section 4.1.1. also combines with a Prefix.

As also discussed above, *nehogy* heads subjunctive clauses which express (non-)desirable situations, just like "bouletic" *hogy*. I will propose that the Prefix contains a subordinating operator of the bouletic type.

4.2.2 Type feature

As opposed to *hogy*, though, *nehogy* can appear in matrix clauses. Consider the pair in (21):

(21) a. *Nehogy   csak Pétert   hívd   meg.*
          MOD.NEG-that   only Peter-ACC   invite. IMP 2SG   PRT
      b. *Ne   csak Pétert   hívd   meg.*
          MOD.NEG   only Péter-ACC   invite.IMP.2SG   PRT
      'Don't invite only Peter.'
      [Adapted from É.Kiss 2011: (36)]

---

10 In a nutshell, the analysis relies on a Ramchandian decomposition of predicates and associates the sentient emotive external argument of "emotive" predicates with a little v which is not a "cause" but a "desire". Embedded subjunctive clauses are licensed by the bouletic (desire) component of these predicates. See Baunaz and Puskás (2016) for a detailed analysis.

(21a) is a case of negative imperative. It can be compared with (21b), a standard negative imperative. In the latter case, the verb in the imperative form occurs in the left periphery (as attested by particle-verb inversion). It occurs in the scope of the modal negative marker *ne*, but need not be adjacent to it (in (21b), the focused constituent *csak* Pétert ('only Peter') sits between the verb and the negative marker). However, the negative marker itself does not occupy the complementizer position where clause-typing is encoded. Indeed, topicalized material can precede *ne*:

(22) *Pétert   ne   hívd meg.*
     Péter-ACC   MOD.NEG   invite.2.IMP.SG PART
     'Péter, don't invite (him)'

This contrasts with the behavior of imperative *nehogy*. In addition to the fact that, according to E.Kiss (2011), (21a) bears some additional flavor of "warning", it also appears that it occupies the actual C(omplementizer) position, since it cannot be preceded by topicalized material:

(23) **Pétert   nehogy   hívd meg/   meghívd*
     Péter-ACC   MOD.NEG-that   invite.IMP.2SG PART/   PART-invite.IMP.2SG

This speaks in favor of an additional component *nehogy* can spell out, a clause-typing feature. That *hogy* may combine with some clause-typing property is also attested by the following:

(24) a. *Hogy   mennyien   eljöttek!*
       COMP   how.many   came
       'What a lot of people have come'
       [Kenesei and Ortiz de Urbina 1994]
   b. *(Hogy)   milyen   rohadt   hideg   van!*
       COMP   how   rotten   cold   is
       'How awfully cold it is!'
       [Lipták 2005]

It appears that in the cases illustrated in (24), *hogy* also contains a clause-typing (exclamative) component. Given the observations above, I will propose that the *hogy* involved in the composition of *nehogy* is not only a [sub] but also a [type]. A discussion of the detailed organization of the functional sequence [fseq] involved is left for future research.[11]

---

[11] Obvioulsy, one might suggest that the clause-typing element is null, and may co-occur with *hogy*. The difference with the proposal that *hogy* realizes a clause-typing feature (on top of other features) boils down to what one considers as a possible set of features.

4.2.3 The structure of nehogy as a "complementizer"

Given this, we can now express the difference between *hogy...ne* and *nehogy* not only in terms of a surface morphological difference, but, more crucially, in terms of a different featural composition. Indeed, *nehogy* will have the following representation:

(25) a.

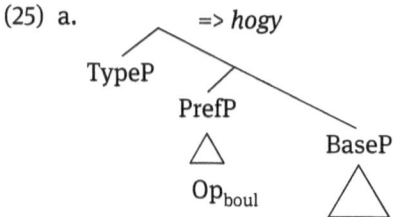

The merging of BaseP and PrefP lexicalizes as *hogy*, as discussed above. Further merging of Type(P) requires spell-out of this component. However, Hungarian has no lexical item which corresponds to [type] alone. *Hogy* is therefore the only possible exponent of the sequence, hence the syncretism observed.[12]

The negative component is then merged, giving (25b), a complex complementizer:

(25) b.

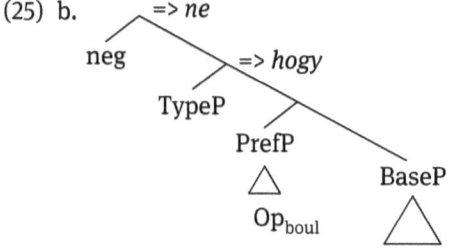

I will propose that *ne* can only merge above the clause-typing *hogy*. In other words, there can be no pure subordinator with a negative component. *Nehogy* thus appears as a complex complementizer.

---

[12] This may be expressed formally in terms of the Superset Principle (see Starke 2009, Caha 2012):
(i)   Assumption 2: The Superset Principle (cf. Starke 2009):
     A lexically stored tree matches a syntactic node iff
       a. the lexically stored tree contains the syntactic node including the material dominated by that node OR
       b. the lexically stored tree matches all daughter nodes (ignoring traces)
     [Caha 2012: 23]

5 Consequences

5.1 Scope of the modal

We have seen above that the version of *hogy* which is relevant for the present study is purposive *hogy*, that is, a subordinator which, along with other features, contains a bouletic modal operator. In this perspective, the *hogy...ne* sequence must be interpreted as a purposive subordinator, which co-occurs with sentential negation. The modal component introduced by the bouletic operator licenses the modal negator *ne*. In other words, *ne* contributes sentential negation, and the bouletic operator scopes over it.[13]

We have also seen that, just like purposive *hogy...(ne)*, *nehogy* triggers the subjunctive. This suggests that, very much like in the previous case, the complementizer includes the bouletic operator which licenses the modal head. However, the scope relations are not identical. Indeed, *nehogy* contributes a content which is very different from the one provided by the combination of the subordinator and sentential negation, as made explicit in examples (15) repeated here:

(15) a. *Taxival   ment,   hogy ne   késse   le   a vonatot.*
     Taxi-INSTR go-PAS-3S that MOD.NEG miss-SUBJ PART the train-ACC
     'She took a taxi, in order not to miss the train'.
     [subject does x, with a wish that p is not the case]
  b. *Taxival   ment,   nehogy   lekésse   a vonatot.*
     taxi-INSTR go-PAS-3S MOD.NEG-that PART-miss.SUBJ the train-ACC
     'She took a taxi, lest she miss the train'.
     [subject does x, with a negative wish that p is the case]

Clauses which contain the purposive subordinator *hogy* and sentential (modal) negation give rise to an interpretation where the bouletic modality of the clause is positive, but the propositional content of the clause is negative. In (15a), the subject has an attitude of (positive) wish that she does not miss the train. As opposed to this, *nehogy* appears as a complementizer which realizes a negative bouletic attitude of the subject, a "negative wish". In (15b), the subject has an attitude of negative wish (i.e. a fear) that she would miss the train. In other words, (15a) expresses

---

[13] The fact that the sentential negative marker is realized as *ne* (rather than the *nem* of indicative clauses) indeed relates to its association with non-indicative mood. I will not discuss modal negation here, I only assume that the bouletic operator licenses a modal head which c-commands negation and requires a "modal" version of the negative marker (see e.g. É.Kiss 2011 for further discussion). The exact nature of such modal negators remains to be explored.

a situation where the modal scopes over negation, and the interpretation is that the subject of the matrix clause expresses a wish that the event would not be the case; (15b), on the other hand, expresses a situation where negation scopes over the bouletic operator, giving rise to negative wishing. The contrast is given in (26).

(26) a. wish [¬ p]
　　 b. [¬ wish] p

It is well known (see a.o. Horn 1989, de Haan 1997, Iatridou and Zeijlstra 2013 and references therein) that modals exhibit different scopal properties with respect to negation. Iatridou and Zeijlstra argue that while some modals behave as PPIs and others as NPIs, there are also what they call "neutral" modals in the sense that they may occur under negation but do not have to. I will propose that the (covert) bouletic modal marker belongs to this latter category. The negative marker which combines with the complementizer can thus take the modal feature in its scope.

As it appears now clearly, the semantic contribution of *nehogy* is not that of a negative subordinator. Rather, it associates the subordinator properties of embedding particles with the bouletic modal operator and a clause typing component. I will propose that the modal operator WISH and the clause typing contribute to some "optative" reading. Negation of the "optative" reading is equivalent to *not wish*. M. Brody (p.c.) suggests that this negative purposive, where negation scopes over the bouletic component, can be rephrased as *to avoid that*. Other languages lexicalize the sequence as *lest* (English) or *de peur que* (French), a semantically transparent form. I will call such negative optative clauses *avertive* clauses.[14]

5.2 Selection

It must first be noted that in the cases where alternation is usually taken to be free (as in 7, 8 above), the embedded clauses are not selected clausal complements. Typically, (27) contains an unaccusative matrix verb, érkezik ('arrive'), which does not select the embedded clause:

(27) a. *Korán   érkezett,   nehogy   panaszkodjon   az elnök.*
　　　 early   arrive-PAS-3S MOD.NEG-that   complain-SUBJ-3S the boss
　　　 'He arrived early, for fear that the boss would complain.'

---

[14] Many thanks to a Reviewer for suggesting this label to me. My first analysis did not explicitly give an account of "negative optative", but it turns out that the term *avertive* is exactly what it corresponds to.

b. *Korán   érkezett,   hogy   ne   panaszkodjon   az elnök.*
   early   arrive-PAS-3S   that   MOD.NEG   complain-SUBJ-3S the boss
   'He arrived early, so that the boss wouldn't complain.'

They appear as adjoined clauses, in that they do not bear any argumental relation to the matrix predicate. In this respect, their interpretation is close to that of causal clauses, in that they can answer a *why* question. However, they correspond to the particular flavor, which answers the *what-for*, rather than the *what-cause* question, hence the *purposive* interpretation:

(28) Q. *Miért   érkezett   korán?*
         Why   arrive-PAS-3S early
         'Why did he arrive early?'
   Aa. *Hogy   ne   panaszkodjon   az elnök.*
         that   MOD.NEG   complain-SUBJ.3S   the boss
   Ab. *?Nehogy   panaszkodjon   az elnök.*
         MOD.NEG-that   complain-SUBJ.3S   the boss

However, a closer look at these apparently parallel cases reveals a clear distinction. Hungarian subordinate clauses may appear with a demonstrative expletive-like element.[15] The demonstrative expletive bears the case-feature associated with the semantic role the co-indexed subordinate clause assumes.[16] The demonstrative expletive is perfectly fine with the *hogy...ne* clause, both when the latter occurs after the matrix clause and when it occurs adjacent to the demonstrative (29). On the other hand, the *nehogy* clause is sharply degraded in these contexts (30):

(29) a. *Azért   érkezett   korán, hogy   ne   panaszkodjon*
        that-for   arrive-PAS-3S   early, that   NEG.MOD   complain-SUBJ-3S
        az elnök.
        the boss
        'He arrived early, so that his boss would not complain.'
        [litt: For that he arrived early, that his boss would not complain]
    b. *Azért,   hogy   ne   panaszkodjon   az elnök, korán érkezett.*
        That-for that   MOD.NEG   complain-SUBJ-3S   the boss, early arrive-PAS-3S
        [litt: for that, that his boss would not complain, he arrived early]

---

15 On the analysis of the demonstrative *azt* occurring with embedded clauses in Hungarian, see e.g. Horváth 1997, E.Kiss 2002.
16 Clearly, the notion of "semantic role" has to be taken is a wider sense than that of "thematic role", since causal and temporal relation are also expressed by case marking.

(30) a. ?? *Azért érkezett korán, nehogy panaszkodjon az elnök.*
     That-for arrive-PAS-3S early MOD.NEG-that complain-SUBJ-3S the boss
   b. **Azért, nehogy panaszkodjon az elnök, korán érkezett*
     That-for MOD.NEG-that complain-SUBJ-3S the boss early arrive-PAS-3S

Whereas *hogy...ne* clauses bear some semantic relation to be matrix predicate, *nehogy* clauses are "freely adjoined". Similarly, while *hogy...ne* clauses can be selected by the matrix predicate, *nehogy* clause cannot. A purposive verb like *gondoskodik* ('take care'), may take a nominal complement, introduced by the delative case marked suffix *-ról, -ről*:

(31) *Lényegében a gyerekekről gondoskodott.*
   Essentially the children-DELAT take-care-PAS-3S
   'She took primarily care of the children.'

The same verb can select a (purposive) embedded clause:[17]

(32) *Arról$_i$ gondoskodik [hogy a gyerekek ne maradjanak*
   that-DELAT care-PRES.3S that the children-NOM MOD.NEG stay-SUBJ-3PL
   iskola nélkül.]$_i$
   school without
   'She is doing her best for the children not to remain without a school.'
   [lit: she takes care of that, that children do not remain without a school]

In (32), the demonstrative expletive *arról*, bears the delative case corresponding to the internal argument of the verb. The complement clause, introduced by *hogy*, may be analyzed as a "co-argument" of the demonstrative. It provides the content associated with the demonstrative expletive.[18] Compare now with (33) below:

(33) *[Arról]$_i$ gondoskodik, [**nehogy** iskola nélkül*
   that-DELAT care-PRES.3S MOD.NEG-that school without
   maradjanak a gyerekek]$_{*i}$
   stay-SUBJ.3PL the children-NOM
   'She takes care of that, lest the children remain without a school'

---

17 Purposive predicates include *rászánja magát* 'make up one's mind', *törekszik* 'strive', *igyekszik* 'endeavour', *vállalkozik* 'undertake', *tesz róla* 'take care/see', *hajlandó* 'willing', *elszánja magát* 'make up one's mind', *az a célja* 'his aim is', *az a szándéka* 'his intention is', *azon van* 'be after', and all require an embedded subjunctive clause (Tóth 2014).
18 Obviously, the whole question of the role of a complement clause should be examined, as even "bridge verbs" may occur with the demonstrative associated with the complement clause in Hungarian. On the issue of the nominal status of embedded clauses, see Haegeman and Urögdi (2010), Aboh (2005) and also Baunaz (2015).

The *nehogy* clause is possible, but it cannot be interpreted as explicating the content of the demonstrative argument. It can only appear as an adjoined clause, which gives *the reasons* of the care. Thus, while the *hogy (..ne)* clause does function as the complement of purposive verbs, *nehogy* clauses do not. We can conclude that while *hogy* is a *bona fide* subordinator, *nehogy* cannot function as such.

Why would this be the case? I see two components to the answer. First, I have proposed above that while the (embedding) *hogy* which occurs in the *hogy...ne* construction is a pure subordinator, *nehogy* can only be constructed as a clause-typer. As such, it may not appear in the complement position of a predicate.[19] The absence of selection is then due to the fact that the PrefP, which contains, among others, the bouletic component of the complementizer is no longer in a local relation with the matrix predicate. Indeed, when *hogy* functions as a clause-typer (in e.g. exclamative contexts, see 24 above), it cannot be embedded:

(34) *Azt   mondta,   hogy$_{excl}$ mennyien   eljöttek!*
     That-ACC   say-PAS.3S   that   how-many   came

A second component may be the presence of the negative marker taking the clause-typer in its scope. Negation, as we will see below, plays a role in some syntactic mechanisms, and may also contribute to the intervention effect.

The ban on the selection of the avertive clause accounts for the contrast below. While a *hogy...(ne)* clause can occur jointly with a *nehogy* clause, only the order given in (35a) is possible. (35b) is ungrammatical, at least with a regular intonational pattern.[20]

(35) a. *Arról   gondoskodik,* **hogy** *a pénz   ne   fogyjon*
      that-DELAT   care-PRES.3S   that   the money-NOM   MOD.NEG   run-SUBJ.3S
     el, **nehogy**   *iskola   nélkül   maradjanak   a gyerekek.*
     PRT   NEG.MOD-that   school   without   stay-SUBJ.3PL   the children-NOM
     'She takes care that the money does not run out lest the children remain without a school.'

---

[19] Actually, it might even be related to the fact that there is no possible construal ("semantic role" sharing) with a demonstrative. While this seems to be a very promising question, the scope of this paper does not allow to go beyond this basic proposal. However, the co-occurrence of the demonstrative in all cases where the subordinator *hogy* is legitimate seems to point towards a crucial distinction.

[20] Note that (35b) may be acceptable if the *nehogy* clause is uttered with long pauses on either side and a lower tone, signaling its parenthetical function.

b. *Arról   gondoskodik,   **nehogy**   iskola   nélkül
   that-DELAT   care-PRES.3S   MOD-NEG-that   school   without
   maradjanak   a gyerekek,   **hogy**   a pénz   **ne**
   stay-SUBJ-3PL.   the children-NOM   that   the money.NOM   MOD.NEG
   fogyjon   el.
   run-SUBJ-3S   PART

While the purposive subordinator *hogy* introduces the embedded clause and is co-indexed with the demonstrative *arról* (that-delat, 'about that'), the avertive clause functions as a freely adjoined clause. (35) can thus be ruled out under the assumption that locality constraints on selection are violated: the *hogy* clause is no more in a local selection relation with the purposive predicate.

Since *nehogy* clauses are not selected, we predict that they should co-exist with *hogy* clauses in a relatively productive way, modulo the constraint observed above. In addition to example (35a) discussed above, *nehogy* can indeed occur with a *hogy* clause in an unexpected way:

(36) McCain   azért$_i$ nem   ímélezik,   [$_i$**hogy**   [**nehogy**
     McCain   that-CAUS   NEG   email-PRES.3S   that   MOD.NEG-that
     mérgében   valami olyasmit   írjon   valakinek,
     his-anger-INESS   something similar-ACC   write-SUBJ-3S   someone-DAT
     amit   később   megbán.]]
     REL-ACC   later   regret-3S
     'McCain doesn't write e-mails, for fear that in his anger he write something to someone that he would later regret.'
     (litt: McCain doesn't write e-mails for that reason, that lest he write something ...)
     [http://444.hu/2015/03/05/mccain-azert-nem-imelezik-hogy-nehogy-mergeben-valami-olyasmit-irjon-valakinek-amit-kesobb-megban/]

The example in (36) illustrates a particular property of the *nehogy* clause. The purposive subordinator *hogy* heads a clause which is co-indexed with the demonstrative *azért* ('for that reason'). This is an authentic purposive interpretation, similar to that discussed in (29) above. The complementizer *nehogy* in turn introduces the avertive clause. Since *nehogy* was argued to head a CP, *hogy* and *nehogy* must head two distinct CPs, and belong to two clauses.

Such an analysis raises the question of the nature of the clause headed by *hogy*. Recall that a purposive clauses introduced by *hogy* may function as "associate" of the demonstrative expletive element *az*, even when the latter is not an argument of the matrix verb. In this case, the clause contributes as the explication of the purpose associated with the event described in the matrix clause. However, the demonstrative also has a discourse function: it occurs in a left-peripheral position, either in the Focus position, triggering verb-particle inversion, or in a Topic position. It can never appear in a post-verbal "neutral" position:[21]

(37) a. *Péter   AZT   mondta,   hogy   János   elfelejtette*
      Peter-NOM that-ACC   say-PAS.3S that   János-NOM   PRT-forget-pas.3S
      az előadást.
      the talk-ACC
      'Peter said, that János forgot the talk.'
      (litt: Peter that said, that János forgot the talk)
   b. *Azt   mindenki   tudja,   hogy   János.   elfelejtette*
      that-ACC everybody-NOM know-PRES.3S   that   János   PRT-forget.3S
      az előadást.
      the talk-ACC
      'Everybody knows that János forgot the talk.'
      (litt: everybody knows that, that János forgot the talk).
   c. #*Péter   mondta,   azt   hogy   János   elfelejtette*
      Peter-nom say-PAS.3S   that-ACC   that   János-NOM PRT-forget-PAS.3S
      az előadást.
      the talk-ACC

I will propose that the role of the *hogy* clause in (36) is exactly that: to be the associate of the demonstrative expletive, which indicates a focusing of the subordinate content. We saw above that *nehogy* clauses cannot function as the associate of the expletive (see 30). The *nehogy* clause can therefore not be focused (or, for that matter, topicalized), as there is no sentence-internal element which can function as a discourse-related place-holder. I propose that the solution to circumvent this ban on the use of a demonstrative expletive is to "embed" the *nehogy* clause in a *hogy* clause. Obviously, the *hogy*-clause itself does not seem to

---

[21] Since the demonstrative expletive seems to co-occur with all embedded *hogy* clauses which are semantically related to the matrix predicate, it should appear in all positions. (37c) is odd in neutral sentences. I assume that (i), its grammatical counterpart, contains a null version of the "demonstrative". The latter does not have to be realized in this position as it does not convey any discourse-related information.

(i)   *Péter mondta Ø, hogy János elfelejtette az előadást.*
      Péter say-pas-3s that János prt-forget-pas.3s the talk-acc
      'Peter said that János forgot the talk.'

provide any crucial semantic contribution. Indeed, (38) is, in terms of its semantic contribution, very similar to (36):

(38) *McCain   nem   ímélezik,*   **[nehogy**   *mérgében*
McCain   NEG   email-PRES.3S   MOD.NEG-that   his-anger-INESS
valami olyasmit   írjon   valakinek,   amit   később
something similar-ACC   write-SUBJ-3S   someone-DAT   rel-ACC   later
megbán.]]
regret-3S
'McCain doesn't write e-mails, lest in his anger he write something to someone that he would later regret.'

The fact that the *hogy* clause does not provide anything to the semantics of the sentence suggests that it is a dummy subordinate clause. Its only contribution is its association with the demonstrative expletive which signals the focus interpretation of the *nehogy* clause. I will follow Marcel den Dikken's suggestion, in the spirit if not the letter, and assume that the dummy *hogy* clause contains a null copular or equative (in the sense of an existential predicate) element (see section 6 below fo a discussion of M. den Dikken's original proposal). As such, it provides the demonstrative expletive, and enables the (content of the) *nehogy* clause to reach a left-peripheral focus related position in the matrix clause:

The data below may seem to challenge the by-clausal analysis of the sequence *hogy nehogy*. Indeed, the occurrence of topicalized material between the two complementizers may argue in favour of a split CP analysis:[22]

(39) *Péter   azért$_i$ ímélezett,   [$_i$**hogy**   János   **[nehogy***
Peter-NOM   that-CAUS   email-PAS.3S   that   János-NOM   MOD.MOD-that
elfelejtsen   eljönni.]]
PRT-forget-SUBJ.3S   PRT-come.INF
'Peter e-mailed lest János forget to come.'
[litt: Peter for-that e-mailed, for fear that János forget to come]

Topicalized constituents like *János* typically occur in a left-peripheral position (see Puskás 2000, E. Kiss 2002 a.o.). A split-CP approach would account for the position of the (higher) *hogy* in the subordinator position, followed by topicalized material; this would also suggest that *nehogy* occurs in a lower left-peripheral position, maybe ModP itself. However, an analysis assigning to *nehogy* a lower

---

[22] Many thanks to the Reviewer who suggested the example and the analysis.

position in the clause also predicts that topicalized material may always precede the "complementizer", contrary to fact:

(40) *Péter   ímélezett,   János   **nehogy**   elfelejtsen
     Peter   e-mail.PAS.3S János-NOM MOD.neg-that forget.3S.SUBJ
     eljönni.
     PART-come.INF

Moreover, topics may appear after *nehogy:*

(41) Először   meg   kell   tisztítani   az erdőket,   **nehogy**
     First   PART   must-PRES   clean.INF   the forests.ACC NEG.MOD-that
     a fák   rothadásnak   induljanak.
     the trees.NOM   rotting.DAT   start.3PL.SUBJ
     'The first thing to do is clear the forest to prevent the timber rotting.'
     (litt: first one must clean the forrests, lest the trees start rotting.)
     [http://en.bab.la/dictionary/hungarian-english/nehogy, glosses mine]

I take this as evidence for the fact that *nehogy* occurs as the head of the highest projection of the clause, as is expected of clause-typing elements. In (39), the topic *János* raises from the *nehogy* clause to the left peripheral topic position of the *hogy* clause:²³

(42) Péter azért₁ ímélezett, [_CP hogy [_Top János [vP ∅ [_CP nehogy <János> elfelejtsen eljönni.]]]]

Finally, while *hogy...ne* clauses can never occur as matrix clauses, recall that negative imperatives, as well as negative hortatives, may alternate between a bare *ne* and a *nehogy* form:

(43) a. *Ne*   csak   Pétert   hívd   meg
         MOD.NEG   only   Peter-ACC   Invite-IMP.2SG   PART
      b. *Nehogy*   csak   Pétert   hívd   meg
         MOD.NEG-that   only   Peter-ACC   invite-IMP.2SG   PRT
         'Don't invite only Peter'
         [Adapted from É.Kiss 2011: (36)]

Despite the apparent optionality of the two forms, É.Kiss herself claims that the *nehogy* version has an additional flavour of "warning". This seems to suggest

---

[23] The question of extraction of a topicalized constituent from a non-selected CP remains to be investigated, especially in the light of the observation that the extraction of focused or quantified material is impossible, suggesting that *nehogy* clauses behave like weak islands.

that compared to *ne*, *nehogy* contains some additional information. Recall that we have analyzed *nehogy* as encoding *fear that* or, more plausibly, *avoid that*. As such, it indeed contains more information than a pure complementizer, since it encodes the type of the clause (imperative, and other associated sub-types)[24], with the additional information that the bouletic attitude of the subject or the speaker is negatively set (*not wish*). As such, a *nehogy* clause is expected to occur in embedded contexts, whenever the bouletic attitude of the *subject* of the matrix clause is explicated. But given this, the same may occur at the level of the matrix clause, in which the (negative) bouletic position is not that of the subject, but of the *speaker*. The "warning" flavor suggested by É.Kiss is a pragmatic inference of the speaker's modal position of "not wishing". If this is on the right track, we might expect other instances of matrix *nehogy* to occur, in situations in which the speaker expresses her "wish to avoid that" or her "fear that" *p*. And indeed, examples as in (44) below may be interpreted as expressing the speaker's wish to avoid the situation denoted by *p*.

(44) *Nehogy   az ördög   ülve   találjon.*
　　　MOD.NEG-that   the devil-NOM   sitting   find-SUBJ-3S
　　　'Lest the devil finds me/you/us sitting.'

5.3 Inversion

Another contrasting feature of the *nehogy* clause is the fact that it does not trigger verb-particle inversion. Verb-particle inversion has been taken as a diagnostic for verb movement (see Horváth 1981, 1986, É.Kiss 1987, Brody 1990 and subs. literature).[25] Typically, so-called neutral sentences, that is, sentences which are all-new, exhibit the (default) order particle-verb:

(45) *János   elolvasta   a levelet.*
　　　János-NOM   PART-read-PAS-3S   the letter-ACC
　　　'János read the letter.'

---

24 Along the line of Portner's (2004) analysis of imperatives, I assume that purposives, as well as desideratives, may be assimilated to imperative clause type, in that they express not a state of affairs in the world, but modify the speaker's or addressee's 'To-do List'.
25 Particles include the all-purpose completive particle *meg*, as well as a host of aspectual particles, path and location elements which contribute to the meaning of the predicate in a transparent or opaque way. On a recent analysis of verbal particles, see É.Kiss 2006.

The order particle-verb is modified in various situations, including sentential negation:[26]

(46) *János   nem   olvasta   el   a levelet.*
     Janos-NOM   NEG   read-PAS.3S PART   the letter-ACC
     'János didn't read the letter.'

Various analyses account for this inversion (see e.g. Puskás 2002, Surányi 2003, É.Kiss 2002) but they all include some assumption about the fact that the verb moves up past the particle, to a position which is adjacent to that of the sentential negation marker. This is also what happens when a *hogy* clause contains sentential negation:

(47) a. *Mari   azt   hiszi,   hogy   János   nem   olvasta*
        Mari   that-ACC   believe-PRES.3S that   János   NEG   read-PAS.3S
        el   a levelet.
        PRT   the letter-ACC
        'Mari thinks that János dit not read the letter.'
     b. *Mari   azon   volt,   hogy   János   ne   olvassa*
        Mari   that-SUPER be-PAS-3S   that   János   MOD.NEG   read-SUBJ.3S
        el   a levelet.
        PRT   the letter-ACC
        'Mari did her best so that János would not read the letter.'

In (47a), the embedded clause introduced by *hogy* is in the indicative mood, and the sentential negation marker *nem* triggers verb-particle inversion. In (47b), the clause embedded under the purposive *azon volt* ('do one's best') is also introduced by the complementizer *hogy*, and sentential negation, realized here as *ne*, also triggers verb-particle inversion. Moreover, negation may also take in its scope a focused constituent:[27]

(48) *Mari   azt   hiszi,   hogy   nem   János   olvasta*
     Mari   that-ACC   believe-PRES.3S that   NEG   Janos   read-PAS.3S
     el   a levelet.
     PRT   the letter-ACC
     'Mari believes that it is not János who read the letter.'

---

[26] The most common and most frequently discussed inversion triggering element is preverbal Focus.
[27] Actually, Surányi (2002, 2006) argues that this "pre-focus negation" takes not only the focused constituent, but the whole projection in its scope.

I assume that in this case, it is not negation *per se* which triggers inversion, but the fact that the constituent in the scope of negation is (contrastively) focused.

As is repeatedly underlined in the literature, *nehogy* clauses do not trigger inversion:

(49) Mari   bezárta   az irodáját,   nehogy   János
     Mari   lock-PAS.3S   the office-POSS-ACC   MOD.NEG-that   János
     ***el**olvassa*   *a levelet.*
     PART-read-SUBJ-3S   the letter-ACC
     'Mari locked her office, lest János read the letter.'

The analysis given here proposes that the negative element, morphologically realized as *ne*, is a component of the complementizer itself. As such, it does not occur in a focus-related position which triggers the inversion mechanism. Negation is to be interpreted locally and not at the clausal level. Obviously, when a *nehogy* clause contains a focused constituent, inversion occurs as expected:

(50) Mari   bezárta   az irodáját,   nehogy   *a LEVELET*
     Mari   lock-PAS.3S   the office-POSS-ACC   MOD.NEG-that   the letter-ACC
     olvassa   ***el***   *János.*
     PART-read-SUBJ-3S   PART   János-NOM
     'Mari locked her office, lest János read the LETTER.'

5.4 N-word licensing

Yet another contrasting property of the *hogy..ne/nehogy* pair pertains to the licensing of negative expressions (n-words). Hungarian n-words are licensed by the sentential negation marker *nem/ne* in a local (clausemate) relationship:

(51) a. *János   nem   talált   semmit.*
        János   NEG   find-PAS.3S   N-thing-ACC
        'János didn't find anything.'
    b. *Mari   azt   hiszi,   hogy   János   nem   talált*
        Mari   that-ACC   believe-PRES-3S   that   János   NEG   find-PAS.3S
        semmit.
        N-thing-ACC
        'Mari believes that János didn't find anything.'

c. Mari azt kívánja, hogy János ne találjon
Mari that-ACC wish-PRES-3S that János MOD.NEG find-SUBJ-3S
semmit.
N-thing-ACC
'Mari wishes that János would not find anything.'

As observed above, *nehogy* clauses do not license n-words:

(52) *Mari magával vitte a táskáját, nehogy János
Mari self-INSTR take.PAS.3S the bag.POSS.ACC MOD.NEG-that János
találjon semmit.
find-SUBJ-3S N-thing-ACC

In the light of what is proposed here, this is predictable: since the (morphologically) negative component *ne* only bears on the semantics and the syntax of the complementizer itself, it cannot count as a sentential negation element, and therefore cannot license an n-word. What is more intriguing, though, is that weak polarity items are licit. Tóth (1999) shows that polarity sensitive items in Hungarian include the n-words just discussed, but also a class of polarity elements which are licensed by non-local negation, while being incompatible with clause-mate negation:

(53) a. Mari nem hiszi, hogy talált valamit is.
Mari NEG believe-PRES.3S that find-PAS-3S vala-thing is
'Mari does not believe that he found anything.'
b. *János talált valamit is.
János find-PAS-3S vala-thing is
c. *János nem talált valamit is.
János NEG find-PAS-3S vala-thing is

These *vala*-type elements are banned from negative clauses, and thus predictably from *hogy...ne* clauses. They are nevertheless licit in *nehogy* clauses:

(54) a. *Mari magával vitte a táskásját, hogy ne
Mari self-INSTR take-PAS-3S the bag-POSS-ACC that MOD.NEG
találjon János valamit is.
find-SUBJ-3S János vala-thing-ACC is
b. Mari magával vitte a táskáját, nehogy János
Mari self-INSTR take-PAS-3S the bag-POSS-ACC NEG-MOD-that János
valamit is találjon.
vala-thing-ACC is find-SUBJ-3S
'Mari took her bag with her, for fear that János would find anything.'

Obviously, the complementizer plays a role in this licensing process. I have argued that the negative component of *nehogy* cannot be interpreted as sentential negation (as it does not license n-words, for example). However, the morphological make-up does contain an element that must contribute some negative meaning. Tóth (1999) shows that *vala-PIs* are also licensed in clauses embedded under various predicates which have some negative component. Typically, morphologically negative predicates, such as *lehetetlen* ('impossible') behave in this way:[28]

(55) Lehetetlen   valamit is   megtanítanunk   az embereknek
     impossible   vala-thing-ACC   PART-teach-INF.1PL the men-DAT
     'It is impossible for us to teach men anything.'
     [http://www.logosdictionary.org/index.php]

In (55), the matrix clause does not contain sentential negation. Indeed, n-words are not licensed in such an environment:

(56) *Lehetetlen   semmit   megtanítanunk   az embereknek.
      impossible   N-thing-ACC   PART-teach-INF.1PL the men-DAT

I have argued that *nehogy* also contains morphological negation, but is not involved in sentential negation. Its behavior in the licensing of weak polarity items and the anti-licensing of n-words falls out from this analysis.

The analysis of *nehogy* as a complex complementizer including clause-typing information and local negation and occurring as the head of the highest functional projection of the clause thus accounts for the contrasting behavior this elements exhibits with respect to the subordinator *hogy* in the negative purposive *hogy...ne* constructions.

6 Alternative proposal

An alternative analysis was proposed to me by Marcel den Dikken (p.c.). The essence of the approach is that *nehogy* itself is actually the realization of two clauses: a clause which includes sentential negation as given by *ne* and an abstract verb, which den Dikken suggests might be a silent *legyen* (be.subj'), and a second clause headed by *hogy*, the standard subordinator, dependent on the abstract verb. Crucially, the analysis relies on the fact that *ne* and *hogy* (and

---

[28] Toth shows that verbs like *kétli* 'doubt', where negation is not morphologically identifiable but semantically retrievable, also licensed these weak PIs.

hence everything in the *hogy* clause) are not clausemate. This would account in a straightforward way for the failure to license n-words, as well as verb-particle inversion since the material following *hogy* is crucially not in the same clause as the negator *ne*. In the same line, den Dikken suggests that matrix occurrences of *nehogy* reduce to negative imperatives with an abstract verb, similar to *ne legyen hogy* ('[may it] not be that').

While this analysis does give an account of the phenomena mentioned above and is compatible with the majority of the phenomena observed in this paper, it does not, *prima facie* at least, offer a clear explanation of some more complex facts. First, the proposal that matrix *nehogy* is an instance of negative imperative with an embedded *hogy* seems to be challenged by the data below:

(57) a. *Soha   ne   jöjjön   vissza!*
        never   MOD.NEG   come-SUBJ.3S   back
        'He must never come back!'
        (litt: he never come back)
    b. *Azt   ne   felejtsük   el,   hogy   még
        havazhat*
        that-ACC   MOD.NEG   forget-SUBJ.1PL   PART   that   still
        snow-poten-PRES.3S
        'let's not forget that it my still snow.'

These examples seem to show that *ne* in these negative imperatives can be preceded by temporal adverbials, as well as a topicalized demonstrative expletive. This is not possible with *nehogy*:

(58) a. **Soha   nehogy   visszajöjjön*
         never   MOD.NEG-that   back-come-SUBJ.3S
    b. *??azt   nehogy   elfelejtsük   hogy   még
         havazhat*
         that-ACC   NEG.MOD-that   part-forget-SUBJ.1PL   that   still
         snow-POT-PRES.3S

If indeed *nehogy* is the combination of (imperative) *ne* and *hogy*, one would expect a similar behavior with respect to high left-peripheral material. The analysis proposed in this paper, which attributes to *nehogy* clause-typing properties, gives a straightforward account of this asymmetry.

A second objection I can see bears on the selectional properties of the "complementizers" discussed here. It was argued that *nehogy* can never occur in selected environments because of its internal composition. If, as proposed by M. den Dikken, it is actually a combination of *ne* and another clause containing *hogy*, one should expect the combination to occur under verbs which select for (negative) imperative-like subjunctives, such as *követel* ('demand'). While this is indeed the case with the bare *ne* clause (59a), *nehogy* cannot occur in these contexts (59b):

(59) a. *János követelte, (hogy) ne hívjuk fel*
 János demand-PAS.3S that MOD.NEG call-SUBJ.1PL part
 'János demanded that we not call him up.'
 b. **János követelte, hogy nehogy felhívjuk*
 János demand-PAS.3S that MOD.NEG PART-call-SUBJ.1PL

It may well be that the current *nehogy* did emerge as a combination of the subjunctive/imperative *ne* and a subordinator *hogy* in a bi-clausal structure. Additional work, among others on the prosodic issues, might shed more light on the question.[29] However, the data presented in this section may prove to constitute convincing arguments in favour of an evolution toward an independent complementizer.

7 Conclusion

In this paper, I have taken a closer look at the complementizer *nehogy*, which is usually assumed to alternate freely with the subordinator *hogy* and sentential negation *ne*. I have argued that it cannot be a simple combination of sentential *ne* incorporated into *hogy*. On the basis of syntactic and semantic differences I have shown that *nehogy* is a different kind of "complementizer", which encodes negation, modal information and some clause-typing information. I have also argued its semantics has to be that of a modal in the scope of negation. While its semantics as a modal complementizer predicts that it can co-occur with other embedded clauses, and that it can occur in matrix clauses as well, its syntactic make-up accounts for the fact that it can never introduce a selected complement clause, that it cannot license n-words and particle-verb inversion. I have also suggested

---

[29] A first look at the prosodic patterns associated with different occurrences of *hogy, ne* and *nehogy* seem to reveal a distinction between the two "complementizers". A bi-clausal approach to *nehogy* would predict that both *ne* and *hogy* occur with some prosodic prominence. Indeed, in the sequence *hogy...nehogy* discussed in section 5.3 above the intonation pattern in which the first *hogy* occurs, a medium pitch, seems to be distinct (predictably) from the relatively high pitch the *nehogy* is pronounced. In a bi-clausal analysis of *nehogy*, one would expect a high pitch on *ne*, with a (relatively) medium pitch on the *hogy* somewhat on a par with the first *hogy*. However, *nehogy* rather appears to have one high pitch followed by a strong deaccenting, which could suggest that the *hogy* does not have an independent phonological status. However, these observations are very preliminary, and would clearly require an in-depth investigation.

that the semantic content provides the negative modal interpretation, but some of the possible additional interpretations, such as "warning", or "fear" may be attributed to pragmatic inferences triggered in the context of the subject/speaker.

Acknowledgements: This paper is dedicated to Liliane Haegeman. No doubt she will recognize her major influence, both in the choice of the topic (Negation, CP and the left periphery) and in the data-oriented approach. I am therefore indebted to her for all that might be convincing in the paper. For the shortcomings, on the other hand, she can in no way be held responsible. My gratitude also goes to Misi Brody, Gillian Ramchand, Tarald Taraldsen, Michal Starke, Andrea Márkus, António Fábregas, and the participants in the Tromsø workshop for valuable suggestions and comments. Many thanks as well to the two Reviewers for their extremely valuable and helpful comments.

References

Aboh, Enoch O. 2005. Deriving relative and factive constructions in Kwa. In Laura Brugè, Giuliana Giusti, Nicola Munaro, Walter Schweikert and Giuseppina Turano (eds.), *Contributions to the thirtieth Incontro di Grammatica Generativa*, 265–285. Venezia: Libreria Editrice Cafoscarina.

Bab.la dictionary:
http://en.bab.la/dictionary/hungarian-english/nehogy (accessed 14 January 2017).

Bácskai-Aktari, Judit & Eva Dékány. 2014. From non-finite to finite subordination. In Katalin E.Kiss (ed.), *The evolution of functional left peripheries in Hungarian*, 148–223. Oxford: Oxford University Press.

Baunaz, Lena 2015. On the various sizes of complementizers. *Probus* 27(2). 193–236.

Baunaz, Lena & Eric Lander. 2015. Syncretisms with nominal complementizers. University of Gent unpublished manuscript.

Baunaz, Lena & Genoveva Puskás. 2014. On subjunctives and islandhood. In Marie-Hélène Côté & Eric Mathieu (eds.), *Variation within and across Romance Languages. Selected papers from the 41st Linguistic Symposium on Romance Languages (LSRL), Ottawa, 5–7 May 2011, [CILT 333]*. Amsterdam: John Benjamins.

Baunaz, Lena & Genoveva Puskás. 2016. Selecting subjunctive clauses: Syncretic complementizer(s), different worlds. University of Geneva unpublished manuscript [under review].

Bhatt, Rakesh & James Yoon. 1992. On the composition of COMP and parameters of V2. *Proceedings of WCCFL*, Vol. 10. 41–52.

Blochowiak, Joanna. 2014. *A theoretical approach to the quest for understanding. Semantics and pragmatics of whys and becauses*. Geneva: University of Geneva dissertation.

Brody, Michael. 1990. Some remarks on the Focus field. *UCL Working Papers in Linguistics* 2. 201–225.

Caha, Pavel. 2012. Explaining the structure of case paradigms by the mechanisms of Nanosyntax. *Natural Language and Linguistic Theory* 31(4):1015–1066. [lingbuzz/001720]

É.Kiss, Katalin. 1987. *Configurationality in Hungarian*. Budapest: Akadémiai Kiadó.
É.Kiss, Katalin. 2002. *The syntax of Hungarian*. Cambridge: Cambridge University Press.
É.Kiss, Katalin. 2006. The function and the syntax of the verbal particle. In Katalin É.Kiss, (ed.), *Event structure and the left periphery*. [Studies in Natural Language and Linguistic Theory]. Dordrecht: Springer.
É.Kiss, Katalin. 2011. On a type of counterfactual construction. In Catherine O. Ringen and Tibor Lácsko (eds.), *Approaches to Hungarian, vol. 12: Papers from the 2009 Debrecen Conference,* 85–107. Budapest: Akademiai Kiadó.
Farkas, Donka. 1992. Mood choice in complement clauses. In István Kenesei & Csaba Pléh (eds.), *Approaches to Hungarian, vol. 4: The structure of Hungarian,* 207–225. Szeged: JATE.
de Haan, Ferdinand. 1997. *The interaction of modality and negation: A typological study*. New York: Garland Publishing.
Haegeman, Liliane & Barbara Ürögdi. 2010. Referential CPs and DPs: An operator movement account. *Theoretical Linguistics* 36(2–3). 111–152.
Horn, Laurence R. 1989. *A natural history of negation*. Chicago, IL: Chicago University Press.
Horváth, Julia. 1981. *Aspects of Hungarian syntax and the theory of grammar*. Los Angeles: University of California Los Angeles dissertation.
Horváth, Julia. 1986. *FOCUS in the theory of grammar and the syntax of Hungarian*. Dordrecht: Foris.
Horváth, Julia. 1997. The status of "wh-expletives" and the partial wh-movement construction of Hungarian. *Natural Language and Linguistic Theory* 15. 509–572.
Hunlang blog:
https://hunlang.wordpress.com/2010/06/02/word-order-negation-ne-se-sem-nehogy-soha/
Iatridou, Sabine & Hedde Zeijlstra. 2013. Negation, polarity and deontic modals. *Linguistic Inquiry* 44. 529–568.
Kenesei, István. 1985. Subordinate clauses: types and structures. In István Kenesei (ed.) *Approaches to Hungarian* 1. 141–165. Szeged: JATE.
Kenesei, István. 1992. On Hungarian complementizers. In István Kenesei and Csaba Pléh (eds), *Approaches to Hungarian* 4. 37–50. Szeged: József Attila University.
Kenesei, István & Jon Ortiz de Urbina. 1994. Functional categories in complementation. Unpublished manuscript.
Lipták, Anikó. 2005. The left periphery of Hungarian exclamatives, In Laura Brugè, Giuliana Giusti, Nicola Munaro, Walter Schweikert and Giuseppina Turano (eds.), *Contributions to the thirtieth Incontro di Grammatica Generativa,* 161–183. Venezia: Libreria Editrice Cafoscarina.
Manzini, Maria Rita & Leonardo Savoia. 2003. The nature of complementizers. *Rivista di Grammatica Generativa* 28. 87–110.
Manzini, Maria Rita & Leonardo Savoia. 2011. *Grammatical categories*. Cambridge: Cambridge University Press.
Puskás, Genoveva. 1998. On the Neg-criterion in Hungarian, *Acta Linguistica Hungarica*, 45(1–2). 167–213.
Puskás, Genoveva. 2000. *Word-order in Hungarian: the syntax of A-bar positions*. Amsterdam: John Benjamins.
Puskás, Genoveva. 2002. On negative licensing contexts and the role of n-words. In István, Kenesei, Katalin É.Kiss & Peter Siptár (eds), *Approaches to Hungarian* vol. 8. 81–106. Budapest: Akadémiai Kiadó.

Puskás, Genoveva. 2015. Embedded subjunctives: A family business. University of Geneva unpublished manuscript.
Portner, Paul. 2004. The semantics of imperatives within a theory of clause types. In Kazuha Watanabe & Robert Young (eds.), *Proceedings of Semantics and Linguistic Theory 14*. Ithaca, NY: CLC Publications.
Rounds, Carol. 2001. *Hungarian: An essential grammar*. Abingdon: Routledge.
Roussou, Anna. 2010. Selecting complementizers. *Lingua* 120(3). 582–603.
Starke, Michal. 2009. Nanosyntax. A short primer to a new approach to language. *Nordlyd* [Peter Svenonius. Gillian Ramchand, Michal Starke & Knut Tarald Taraldsen (eds.), special issue on Nanosyntax] 36(1). 1–6.
Surányi, Balázs. 2002. Negation and the negativitiy of n-words in Hungarian. In István Kenesei, Katalin É.Kiss & Péter Siptár (eds.), *Approaches to Hungarian 8*. 39–61. Budapest: Akadémiai.
Surányi, Balázs. 2003. *Multiple operator movements in Hungarian*. Utrecht: LOT Publications.
Surányi, Balázs. 2006. Quantification, focus and Negative Concord. *Lingua* 116. 272–313.
Szabolcsi, Anna. 1992. Subordinators: Articles and complementizers. In István Kenesei & Csaba Pléh (eds.), *Approaches to Hungarian 4*. 123–137. Szeged: József Attila University.
Szabolcsi, Anna. 2004. Positive polarity - negative polarity. *Natural Language and Linguistic Theory* 22/2. 409–452.
Szabolcsi Anna, James Doh Whang & Vera Zu. 2014. Quantifier words and their multi-functional(?) parts. *Language and Linguistics* 15(1). 115–155.
Tóth, Ildikó. 1999. Negative polarity item licensing in Hungarian. *Acta Linguistica Hungarica* 46. 119–142.
Tóth, Enikő. 2009. *Mood choice in complement clauses*. Frankfurt am Mein: Peter Lang.
Tóth, Enikő. 2014. The imperative and the subjunctive proper: Two distinct grammatical moods in Hungarian. *Argumentum* 10. 631–644.
Turi, Gergő. 2010. Kötőmód a mai magyar nyelvben [The subjunctive in modern Hungarian]. *Argumentum* 5. 25–38.

Manuela Schönenberger
Are doubly-filled COMPs governed by prosody in Swiss German? The chameleonic nature of *dass* 'that'

1 Introduction

Several decades ago, Chomsky and Lasnik (1977) stipulated the doubly-filled COMP filter according to which the co-occurrence of a wh-constituent and a complementizer is banned. In those days, COMP was a single position that could either contain a wh-constituent or a complementizer, but not both. Nowadays two positions, SpecCP, hosting maximal projections, and C, hosting heads, correspond to what was once labelled as COMP. There is thus no a priori reason why a wh-constituent in SpecCP could not co-occur with a complementizer in C, since these two elements do not compete for the same position. Indeed, many languages exist that violate the doubly-filled COMP filter. In some, doubly-filled COMPs (DFCs) are obligatory, e.g. West Flemish (see Haegeman 1992) and in others, DFCs are optional, at least to a certain extent, e.g. Bavarian and Alemannic (see Bayer and Brandner 2008a, 2008b; Bayer 2015; and Penner and Bader 1995; Penner 1986 for Bernese Swiss German; Schönenberger 2010 for Lucernese Swiss German) and Belfast English (Henry 1995). In yet others, they seem to be banned, e.g. Standard German and Standard English, but this may be due to normative pressure, since earlier stages of these languages allowed them. Zwicky (2002), for instance, lists various examples with DFCs produced by speakers of different varieties of modern English (see [1] and [2]).

(1) We asked **what sort of health care that** they rely on.
(2) **What a mine of useless information that** I am!

Based on acceptability judgement data, Bayer and Brandner advance a structural account for DFCs in Alemannic and Bavarian, in which wh-words are generally incompatible with *dass* 'that' while wh-phrases generally require the presence of *dass*. These authors embrace a non-split CP and assume that wh-words are complementizers in C, which straightforwardly accounts for why wh-words are incompatible with *dass*, since that would also occupy C. Based on spontaneous production data from another Alemannic dialect spoken in eastern Switzerland I argue against a purely structural account, and try to show that prosody is also relevant. As in the dialects described by Bayer and Brandner, monosyllabic wh-constituents ('wh-words') in this Swiss-German dialect are incompatible with

DOI 10.1515/9781501504037-007

dass, while non-monosyllabic wh-constituents (most of these corresponding to 'wh-phrases') generally require *dass*. There are several counter-examples to both generalizations, but in many of these the stress pattern seems unusual. This suggests that we are not dealing with a purely structural issue.

The paper is organized as follows: Section 2 summarizes previous findings from the Swiss-German dialect under investigation, and reports the generalizations derived from these data that rely on the number of syllables of the wh-constituent. Section 3 discusses the syntactic analysis proposed by Bayer and Brandner (2008a, 2008b) for Bavarian and Alemannic. Section 4 introduces more spontaneous production data from Swiss German, which show much more variation than the previous sample from the same dialect. In Section 5 the predictions made by the syllabic account and by the syntactic account are evaluated against these data. Neither can fully cover the variation found in these data. Both analyses concentrated on the type of wh-constituent itself, but DFCs crucially also involve *dass*, and its function has not been examined in depth until now. Here the possible function of *dass* is examined, and an analysis is outlined that attempts to show that *dass* plays an important part in the prosodic phrasing of a wh-complement clause. Section 6 contains my tentative conclusions.

2 Previous findings on Swiss German

Concentrating on Bernese Swiss German, Penner and Bader (1988: 10) pointed out that "Bernese German displays an unrestricted distribution of interrogative element [...] and *dass*". This observation was modified in Penner and Bader (1995: 118), who suggested that a DFC is "generally preferred" with simple wh-phrases and "strongly preferred" with complex wh-phrases. They provide the examples in (3) but no description of what they mean by "simple" and "complex". Penner (1996: 65) noted that DFCs are optional with light wh-phrases in Bernese and obligatory with heavy wh-phrases, but he does not clarify what "light" and "heavy" mean either.

(3) a. I   ha   ne   gfragt   wo   (dass)   er   wohnt.
       I   have him   asked   where   that   he   lives
       'I asked him where he lives.'
    b. I   ha   ne   gfragt   i   welem   Huus   ?*(dass)   er   wohnt.
       I   have him   asked   in   which   house   that   he   lives
       'I asked him in which house he lives.'
       (Penner and Bader 1995: 128)

Despite the vagueness in description, it is apparent that not all wh-constituents are equally compatible with *dass* in Bernese.

Based on spontaneous production data from speakers of another Swiss-German dialect, I maintained in Schönenberger (2010) that there is a clear contrast between monosyllabic and non-monosyllabic wh-constituents. Monosyllabic wh-constituents do not co-occur with *dass* in this dialect, while non-monosyllabic wh-constituents do. As can be seen from Tab. 1, the data seem to be clear-cut, but the amount of data is limited and comes from only a small number of speakers.

Tab. 1: Distribution of DFCs in wh-complement clauses in St. Galler German (classified according to the number of syllables of the wh-constituent)

Speaker	One syllable	Two syllables	> two syllables
AS	1/40	8/8	2/2
KS	0/20	1/1	1/1
MS	0/56	12/12	3/3
Total	1/116	21/21	6/6
(cf. Schönenberger 2010: 48)			

I also discussed spontaneous production data from another Swiss-German dialect, Lucernese Swiss German, collected for a longitudinal acquisition study, in which the input to a child was examined. These data, summarized in Tab. 2, look different from those from St. Galler German. DFCs did generally not occur in wh-complement clauses with monosyllabic wh-constituents, but they also often did not occur in those with non-monosyllabic wh-constituents. The data sample is larger but the number of speakers is again small.

Tab. 2: Distribution of DFCs in wh-complement clauses in Lucernese Swiss German (classified according to the number of syllables of the wh-constituent)

Speaker	One syllable	Two syllables	> two syllables
Mother	1/397	36/75	26/33
Father	1/17	0/0	2/2
Sister	0/27	4/4	2/2
Total	2/441	40/79	30/37
(cf. Schönenberger 2010: 48)			

Several shortcomings of this comparative study were pointed out (2010: 48):

> While the St. Galler German data are taken from a conversation between adults, the Lucernese data arise from adults interacting with a child. Moreover, most of the adult data in the Lucernese sample come from a single speaker, the mother, who speaks a mixed dialect. It is also noticeable that she often speaks particularly clearly when addressing the child, which might subtly distort the data. If prosody is indeed relevant to the occurrence of DFCs then clear speech might influence the overall prosodic structure.

In these two Swiss-German samples I also looked at the type of element selecting a wh-complement, as well as what kind of element immediately followed a wh-constituent with or without *dass*. I concluded that the type of selector does not play any role in whether a DFC is used, but that the type of element following the wh-constituent may play a role. I also considered D-linking as a potential influence on the production of DFCs, and concluded that the number of syllables of a wh-constituent is indeed relevant while D-linking is not.

Based on the difference between the two samples, the following tentative conclusions were reached (2010: 47):
- If the wh-phrase and the following constituent form a prosodic unit – a trochaic foot – DFCs are excluded.
- If the constituent following the wh-phrase is a clitic, which cannot be integrated into the prosodic structure of the wh-phrase, a DFC must be inserted. The clitic and *dass* form a trochaic foot.
- In all other contexts, DFC may be optional in Lucernese, while in St. Galler German they are obligatory with all non-monosyllabic wh-phrases.

This account in terms of the number of syllables of a wh-constituent is purely descriptive. While the predictions for the occurrence of DFCs in St. Galler German are clear, the relation between the occurrence of DFCs and prosody is not. In the face of new data from St. Galler German presented in Section 4, in which variation is also visible, in the sense that a given wh-constituent can occur with or without *dass*, this account is no longer tenable.

3 A syntactic account in terms of a latent C-feature

Bayer and Brandner (2008a, 2008b) investigated the distribution of DFCs in Middle Bavarian and Lake Constance Alemannic by carrying out a judgement study. Between 8 and 15 dialect speakers per dialect were asked to rate the acceptability of a sentence on a scale from 1 to 6, 1 being good and 6 being bad. There were 70 test items with wh-items that varied in length and in whether they were followed by *dass*. These sentences were read to the informants by a native speaker of the dialect.

Bayer and Brandner found that short wh-items (*wer* 'who.NOM', *wen* 'who. ACC', *was* 'what', *wie* 'how', *wo* 'where'), which they label as 'wh-words II', combined with *dass* were generally judged as bad, while phrasal wh-constituents (e.g. *womit* 'with what', *welcher Student* 'which student') combined with *dass* were judged as good. The word-sized wh-items *wem* 'who.DAT', *warum* 'why' and *wie viel* 'how much', which are labelled as 'wh-words I', occupied an intermediate status. The authors consider these three wh-items as morphologically more complex. Both *warum* and *wie viel* are bi-morphemic: *warum* contains the preposition *um*, and *wie viel* consists of *wie* 'how' and Q(P) *viel* 'much'. Following Bayer, Bader, and Meng (2001) they analyse dative *wem* as containing a Kase Phrase (KP) in contrast to nominative and accusative *wer* and *was*. Hence *wem* is structurally also more complex. Bayer and Brandner suggest that the co-occurrence of these three word-sized wh-items with *dass* may have been judged as quite acceptable because from a syntactic point of view they are phrasal. Since the authors discuss group data and not individual data, it is unclear whether any one informant's judgements were consistent across all three wh-items and whether some informants clearly accepted and others clearly rejected these. Their findings are summarized in Tab. 3.

Tab. 3: Hierarchy of wh-items with respect to DFC

X-bar status	Subtype	DFC restriction	
wh-phrase	wh-DP, wh-PP	best with overt C	
wh-word I	*warum, wie viel, wem*		↓
wh-word II	*wer, wen, was, wie, wo*	worst with overt C	
(from Bayer and Brandner 2008a: 89)			

Similar findings from two studies with Bavarian speakers are reported in Bayer (2015). These studies used the same test design but fewer items. The findings of the first study with 10 informants closely resemble those in Bayer and Brandner. The second study with 13 informants involved test items with various wh-words of type II, one kind of wh-word of type I (*wem*), and one kind of wh-phrase (P+wh-word). Test items containing a wh-word of type II and *dass* were judged as bad and test items with P+wh-word and *dass* were judged as good, replicating earlier findings. But, in a subgroup of the informants, no clear contrast in acceptability was found between wh-words of type II and *wem*.[1]

To account for the distribution of DFCs, these authors propose that wh-items contain a latent C-feature, as in (4), which can be activated when the wh-item undergoes movement to the left periphery.

---

[1] In the second study, results are reported separately for 3 informants, aged 25–35, with a university education and for 10 young informants (no age-range is given) with a mixed educational background. A difference in educational background or age might have led to a difference in judgement of test items with *wem* in these two (sub)groups.

(4) Latent C-feature
Wh-items may possess a latent C-feature αC. If α can be set to +, the wh-item is simultaneously C and will project a CP. If α is set to –, the C-feature will delete.
(Bayer 2015: 12)

In the case of wh-words of type II the C-feature is activated when the wh-word is merged with TP, a movement that is triggered by the requirement for embedded questions to be typed as <interrogative>, in the sense of Cheng's (1991) Clausal Typing Hypothesis. This is an instance of internal merge ('move') that is not feature-driven. By discharging the C-feature the wh-word projects a CP. Since a wh-word also contains a wh-feature, the projection of a wh-CP results from "self-attachment". The overt realization of a DFC with a wh-word is excluded for reasons of economy. Such a derivation would be more costly since it would involve external merge of *dass* and then internal merge of the wh-word. However, if the wh-word receives contrastive stress, *dass* insertion is possible, as shown in (5). Following Cardinaletti and Starke (1999), Bayer and Brandner assume that a focussed wh-word just like a strong pronoun has more syntactic structure than a weak or clitic pronoun and that therefore the focussed wh-word can no longer merge as a head.

(5) Ich woass WO dass er abfahrt aber noit WENN.
    I know where that he leaves but not.yet when
    'I know WHERE it (the train) will leave but not WHEN.'
    (Bayer and Brandner 2008a: 93, attributing this example to Noth 1993: 424)

In the case of wh-phrases, the C-feature is trapped in a branching structure, e.g. *für was* 'for what' [$_{PP}$ für [$_{NP}$ was]]. Therefore the wh-item will never be a sister of TP and the structural conditions for discharging the C-feature will not be met. The wh-phrase moves as a maximal projection (e.g. PP) to SpecCP and "the insertion of the complementizer *dass* is possible, resp. required" (Bayer and Brandner 2008: 90). Apparently, the latent C-feature in contrast to 'regular' features, e.g. a wh-feature, does not need to be discharged/valued, and unlike the wh-feature it does not percolate up. In root wh-questions, which typically show the Verb-Second pattern, the finite verb moves to C and therefore a wh-item with a latent C-feature can no longer merge as a head with TP. The wh-item merges as a maximal projection instead, ending up in SpecCP, and the C-feature is not discharged (see Bayer and Brandner 2008a: 93).

From a theoretical point of view this syntactic account of the distribution of DFCs is not unproblematic. For example, how can a wh-phrase merge with TP before C is filled with *dass* in an embedded clause? What prevents merging the wh-item with TP before the finite verb undergoes movement in a matrix clause? In other words, when merging with TP is to take place, what determines what kind of clause – embedded or matrix – is being derived? The authors address some of these problems, e.g. chain-uniformity, economy. (See also Bayer 2015 for a detailed discussion of how this account can be recast in modern theoretical terms and in particular, how the various features of a wh-item are discharged). I shall not dwell on these, but instead point out a potential problem regarding their assumptions about variation. Bayer and Brandner (2008b: 4) note that there may be an artefact in their data, because all their informants know Standard German as well, which does not have DFCs. This may in general have biased them towards rejecting rather than accepting a test item presented with a DFC. Bayer (2015) acknowledges that "*was* is the most underspecified wh-element of the German lexicon and as such the top candidate in adopting additional features [e.g. the C-feature: added by MS] without running into conflicts, and that there are other wh-lexemes which can do so to a higher or lower degree, and that this variation may be a matter of the individual mental lexicon" (2015: 19). Elsewhere he concedes that wh-PPs can be interpreted as syntactic heads (see my footnote 6). To tie variation to the lexicon is a perfectly natural assumption and to ascribe some remaining variation to the influence of German is defensible, but both of these notions need to be made precise.[2] There is also some redundancy. For example, is a test item with *wie viel* 'how much' and *dass* judged as bad because of the influence from German or because of the variation in the individual speaker's lexicon? Is the test item more likely to be rejected if the two conspire? Bayer's evaluation of *was* as the top candidate suggests that other wh-words of type II are less likely to be such candidates, i.e. are ultimately less likely to be heads. If this is so, why were test items with any wh-word of type II, and not just *was*, consistently

---

2 One reviewer observes that prepositional elements such as *bis* 'until' and *(so)bald* 'as soon as' co-occurred with *dass* up until Early New High German, and that in the modern languages they no longer do. This reviewer suggests that reanalysis of *bis* and *(so)bald* as heads could explain why this is. In our data, there are no examples of *bis dass* (0/121), but examples of *sobald dass* (5/33), *bevòr dass* 'before that' (1/53) and *nòchdäm dass* 'after that' (5/8) do occur. Penner and Bader (1995: 145) distinguish adverbial clauses with *dass* from wh-complement clauses with *dass*, and refer to the former as 'multiply-headed', involving two heads – a preposition and a complementizer. There is no reason to assume that *bis, sobald, bevòr* and *nòchdäm* are anything but heads in these constructions. The distribution of *dass* in these adverbial clauses is quite different from that in wh-complement clauses (see also Schönenberger 2010: 56–59 for child and adult data in Lucernese). For example, clitics can surface adjacent to bisyllabic *sobald* (*sobald mer* 'as soon as we.CL') and *bevòr* (*bevòr mer* 'before we.CL' – there are 33 examples with clitics – but there are no examples of *wiso mer* 'why we.CL' and *worum mer* 'why we.CL'.

judged as bad with a DFC? And if a wh-PP can be interpreted as a head, why were test items with wh-PPs consistently judged as good with a DFC?

I shall now consider the empirical evidence that is used by Bayer and Brandner to support the assumption that wh-words of type II are heads resembling interrogative complementizers. To support this assumption the authors observe that in several languages short wh-items, in particular the wh-item corresponding to *what*, have been grammaticalized as declarative complementizers (e.g. *que* 'what' in French and *che* 'what' in Italian). Similarly, *wo* 'where' can function as a relative complementizer in certain Alemannic dialects. They also note that *n*-intrusion – an instance of consonantal epenthesis – can occur in intervocalic contexts of adjacent words but not phrases, and that *n*-intrusion typically occurs when the word starting with a vowel is a pronominal clitic.[3] According to Ortmann (1998), *n*-intrusion is only possible if the host of the pronominal clitic is a functional word. Importantly, *n*-intrusion is possible in an embedded context, as in (6a), where *wa* is taken to occupy C, but *n*-intrusion is not possible in a root context where *wa* occupies SpecCP, as in (6b). *N*-intrusion is also excluded when the potential host is contained in a phrase, as in the examples in (7). Insertion of *dass* can render the latter grammatical, as shown in (8), since *dass* "establishes a proper context for cliticization to succeed" (Bayer and Brandner 2008a: 92).

---

3 The phenomenon of *n*-intrusion is quite complex and its domain of application seems to vary across dialects. In St. Galler German, for example, *n*-intrusion is also possible with emphatic pronouns (in capitals), as in (i), provided these are in the nominative. *N*-intrusion is not possible with emphatic pronouns in e.g. the dative (ii), or with possessive pronouns independent of whether they are stressed or not (iii). Furthermore, *n*-intrusion is possible even if the monosyllabic wh-word is stressed (see [iv]). However, if the vowel is long, i.e. WOO rather than WO, *n*-intrusion becomes unacceptable. (See Cooper 1994: 76–78 for *n*-intrusion in Zurich German). In Bayer and Brandner's analysis a stressed wh-item is phrasal and moves to SpecCP not C in an embedded clause. *N*-intrusion is therefore expected to be impossible, but in this dialect it is possible (see also Section 5.5).

(i) Ich waiss wo-n-ÄR woont aber ha kan Blasse wo SII woont.
   I know where-N-he lives but have no faint where she lives
   'I know where HE lives but do not have the faintest idea where SHE lives.'

(ii) Ich waiss wo-*n-EM de Josef über de Wääg glòffen isch aber...
    I know where-N-him the Josef on the path walked is but
    'I know where Josef came across HIM, but...'

(iii) I waiss au nöd wo-*n-eren Maa woont.
     I know also not where-N-her husband lives
     'I also don't know where her husband lives.'

(iv) Mi intressiert nöd WIE-n-er s flickt sòndern WO-n-er s flickt.
    me interest not how-N-he it repairs but where-N-he it repairs
    'I am not interested in HOW he repairs it but in WHERE he repairs it.'

(6) a. ... wa-n-er   tuet
          what-N-he   does
    '...what he does'
    b. *Wa-n-isch   denn   do   passiert?
        what-N-is   PART   there   happened
    'What has happened there?'
    (Bayer and Brandner 2008a: 92)

(7) a. *... vo   wo-n-er   herkommt?
            from   where-N-he   comes
       'where he is coming from'
    b. *... wieso-n-er   nümme   kunnt.
            why-N-he   no-longer   comes
       'why he doesn't show up any more'
       (Bayer and Brandner 2008a: 92)

(8) ... wieso   dass-er   nümme   kunnt.
         why   that-he   no.longer   comes
    'why he doesn't show up any more'
    (Bayer and Brandner 2008a: 93)

Bayer (2015) observes that, in general, "'Wackernagel-type' morpho-phonological processes – cliticization, consonantal epenthesis, comp inflection – uniformly apply to the C-position" (2015: 26) and that wh-words of type II show the same morpho-phonological properties as complementizers and verbs in the V2 position.

These observations, which are offered as evidence that wh-words can be syntactic heads, raise several questions. The first was raised by one of the reviewers. (i) The observation that wh-items corresponding to *what* have been grammaticalized as declarative complementizers does not mean that in those cases where grammaticalization has taken place there was a previous stage at which these wh-items (in their purely interrogative meaning) already occupied the C-head. Instead, they could have been reanalysed as heads, but only once their interrogative meaning had been bleached. (ii) Is the wh-item *wieso*, which is also bimorphemic and also means *why*, treated in the same way as *warum*, i.e. sometimes as a head? If *wieso* is treated as a head, the unacceptability of example (7b) is unexpected, because *n*-insertion is said to be possible with heads. Similarly, *n*-insertion is expected to be possible in (7a) if wh-PPs can be heads, as suggested by Bayer (2015: footnote 20). (iii) As concerns the difference in acceptability between the examples in (6), it may not be due to a difference in the syntactic status of *wa*. Consider the examples in (9) from St. Galler German, in which the relative complementizer *wo* is a head. Example (9b) is unacceptable although in both (9a) and (9b) *wo* is a head. Perhaps *isch*, as opposed to a pronominal clitic, is not the right kind of element to surface in *n*-insertion contexts.[4,5] If this is indeed the case then the observation that *n*-insertion is possible in (6a) but not in (6b) cannot be used as evidence that *wa* occupies different positions in the two examples.

(9) a. De   Maa   wo-n-i   gescht   gsee   ha   ...
       the   man   who-N-I   yesterday   seen   have
       'the man who I saw yesterday'
   b. De   Maa   wo-*n-isch   uf   Bern   go   singe   ...
       the   man   who-N-is   to   Berne   go   sing
       'the man who's gone to Berne to sing'

(iv) Although in Germanic pronominal clitics and reduced pronouns tend to 'migrate' to the C-position, they can surface in other positions. In Hessian, for example, a prominent object pronoun can intervene between a complementizer and a reduced subject pronoun, as in (10). In Dutch an object clitic must not be separated from the finite verb in a subject-initial sentence (11a), but it cannot occur on the finite verb in a non-subject-initial sentence (11b). In West Flemish an object clitic can be separated from the complementizer by intervening

---

4 One of the reviewers observes that (9b) may be degraded for independent reasons, referring to work by Salzmann et al. (2013). Based on detailed questionnaire studies, Salzmann et al. show that the sequence 'C-Vfin', i.e. COMP followed by a finite verb, is judged as degraded in Swiss German and German, as opposed to the sequence 'C-Adverbial-Vfin'. These authors assume a minimal tree-structure for these languages, with basically just one maximal projection (CP) above *v*P. To account for the difference in acceptability between 'C-Vfin' and 'C-Adverbial-Vfin', they propose a phonological EPP that requires that a projection referred to as FP, which occurs between CP and *v*P, be overtly filled at PF. Positioning 'uf Bern' between 'wo' and 'isch' in example (9b) would result in 'wo uf Bern isch...', which does indeed sound less marked than 'wo isch uf Bern...'. However, without the adverbial 'uf Bern', the sequence 'wo isch go singe' sounds perfectly fine while 'wo-n-isch go singe' does not.

5 Interestingly, contraction between *da* 'this' in SpecCP and *isch* 'is' in C is possible in rapid speech, as shown in (ii). Contrary to expectation, *isch* can lean on an element in SpecCP but not on an element in C (cf. example [9b]).

(i) *Da*   *isch*   *nöd*   *möglech.*
     this   is   not   possible
(ii) *Dasch*   *nöd*   *möglech.*

material, as shown in (12) (see also Cooper 1994 for Zurich Swiss German; Penner 1991 for Bernese Swiss German).

(10) weil /MIR se NET gfalle.
 because me.DAT they.NOM not please
 'because I don't like them'
 (Gärtner and Steinbach 2003: 480)

(11) a. *Jan heeft *gisteren 'r gekust.*
  John has yesterday her kissed
  'John has kissed her (yesterday)'
 b. **Heeft 'r Jan gekust?*
  has her John kissed
  'Has John kissed her?'
 b.' *Heeft Jan 'r gekust?*
  has John her kissed
  (Zwart 1997: 63)

(12) *da Valere verzkerst Marie t a/ no/ we gegeven eet*
  that Valere probably Marie it already still well given has
  'that Valere has probably already/still/well given it to Marie'
  (Haegeman 1993: 13)

These data, in which clitics and reduced pronouns are separated from the element in the C-position, clearly show that they cannot have moved to the C-position. And even if an enclitic leans onto the preceding word, we cannot conclude that the clitic has syntactically adjoined to it. To illustrate, if the enclitic *r* had adjoined to the finite verb *heeft* in (11a) it would have moved along with it, but (11b) is ruled out. To account for the distribution of clitics in West Flemish, Haegeman (1993) proposes that clitics, just like shifted objects in general, undergo A-movement before they adoin to empty Agr(eement)-heads or C, which is assumed to also have agreement features. In Gärtner and Steinbach's analysis reduced pronouns in German and Dutch and their dialects also undergo XP-movement, but they do not adjoin to heads in the syntax. These authors argue that reduced pronouns, because of their phonological deficiency, have to prosodically integrate into an adjacent phonological word (π-word). In contrast to Romance clitics, reduced pronouns can be integrated into different types of π-words: complementizers, finite verbs in root clauses, nouns, adverbials and prepositions. Müller (2001) argues that unstressed, weak and reduced pronouns in German move to the Wackernagel position, which he situates below TP, since these pronouns can follow the subject (in SpecTP). It seems that cliticization data in Germanic do not support the assumption that short wh-items are heads.[6]

To summarize, in contrast to the syllabic account, Bayer and Brandner's account is grounded in syntactic theory. However, their core assumption – the treatment of certain wh-elements as C-heads – is not unproblematic from a theoretical point of view, and there seems to be little empirical evidence to support it. Their ideas of why there is variation are plausible but have not yet been fully worked out.

4 Overview of the data from St. Galler German

The data reported here come from a larger project, the aim of which is to gain a better understanding of inter- and intra-speaker variation in syntax based on spontaneous speech data from a dialect of Swiss German. Swiss-German dialects are perfectly suited for dialect studies because they are used naturally in everyday life by members of all social classes. There is no normative pressure from a 'standardized dialect' and the various Swiss-German dialects seem to be relatively resistant to influences of the standard (i.e. German). Although native speakers of Swiss German also know German, which they learn at school from a very early age, it is learned as a second language (L2).

The specific dialect in question is that spoken in Wil, a town in the canton of St. Gallen in north-eastern Switzerland with about 24 000 inhabitants. The St. Galler German sample discussed in Schönenberger (2010) comes from the same area. The corpus we are compiling is steadily growing, and so far contains roughly 650 000 words produced by 35 adult speakers during informal interviews of about 90 minutes each. These speakers include 7 young (20–30), 17 middle-aged (45–55) and 11 elderly (75+) male and female informants. Many more interviews have been conducted, but have not yet been transcribed.

---

[6] Bayer (2015) shows that comp inflection is found on complementizers as well as on short wh-words in Bavarian. He notes that some speakers have comp inflection even on a short wh-word contained in a wh-PP, as in (i), which leads him to concede that wh-PPs can be heads ("I tend to say that PP is an extension of the category in its complement. If the complement is X°, P+X° is also an X°" [2015: footnote 20]). This is not a very natural assumption, and, as noted above, would not agree with the finding that test items with a wh-PP and a DFC were judged as good rather than bad by Bavarian informants.

(i) ... [an wo]-*st* du schon wieder denk-*st*
at what-2SG you already again think-2SG
'...what you already have thoughts about'

In contrast to Bavarian, comp inflection in St. Galler German is restricted to *t* (2SG) and is rare in our data (see Cooper 1994: 106–109 for *t* in Zurich German).

Ultimately we hope to have data from 20 speakers per age group (10 male and 10 female), and in total about 1 million words.

The wh-complements in the transcribed data were searched for by hand, as so far only a fraction of the data have been grammatically annotated and parsed.[7] There were 1066 wh-complements. Table 4 summarizes the occurrence of DFCs in these wh-complements, divided into monosyllabic and non-monosyllabic wh-constituents, and into age groups. The interviews were conducted by two middle-aged interviewers – Anna and Thea – who also speak the local dialect. Their data are not subsumed under those from the middle-aged group, but are listed separately, because there are much more data from these two speakers. As can be seen from this table, wh-complement clauses with monosyllabic wh-constituents occurred about 4 times more often than those with non-monosyllabic ones. Monosyllabic wh-constituents usually occurred without *dass* while non-monosyllabic ones usually occurred with *dass*. This is clearly visible in all three age groups.

Tab. 4: Distribution of DFCs in wh-complement clauses (with mono- and non-monosyllabic wh-constituents) in spontaneous production data (St. Galler German)

Age groups	mono +DFC	mono −DFC	non-mono +DFC	non-mono −DFC
G1: young (n = 7)	12 (7.2%)	154 (92.8%)	66 (92.9%)	5 (7.1%)
G2: middle-aged (n = 15)	7 (3.6%)	190 (96.4%)	63 (91.3%)	6 (8.7%)
Interviewers (n = 2)	4 (1.3%)	305 (98.7%)	66 (89.2%)	8 (10.8%)
G3: elderly (n = 11)	1 (0.7%)	152 (99.3%)	23 (85.2%)	4 (14.8%)
Total (n = 35)	24 (2.9%)	801 (97.1%)	218 (90.4%)	23 (9.6%)

All three age groups also produced some counter-examples. The production of DFCs in wh-complement clauses with monosyllabic wh-constituents by the young group differs significantly from that by the interviewers (p<0.002) according to Fisher's exact test. None of the other comparisons between groups reached significance, i.e. the p-values are all >0.05. Note, though, that the number of speakers per group is very different.

Table 5a lists the frequency of occurrence of the different monosyllabic wh-constituents with and without *dass*. Some of these received heavy stress (see Section 5). We found many examples with *wa* 'what' and *wie* 'how', fewer

---

[7] For the transcription EXMARaLDA ('Extensible markup language for Discourse Annotation') was used. EXMARaLDA is a program designed for the transcription of spoken language (see Schmidt and Wörner 2009), which is easy to use and which is free of charge and downloadable from the URL: www.exmaralda.org. A tool for extracting patterns (EXACT) is also available from this link. EXACT was used to search for wh-items.

with *wo* 'where' and very few with *wär* 'who' and *wenn* 'when'. Although *wäm* 'whom' is a possible word in this dialect, in these data it did not occur on its own but only as the complement of a preposition.

Tab. 5a: Distribution of DFCs in wh-complement clauses with monosyllabic wh-constituents

	+DFC	−DFC
wär 'who.NOM/ACC'	1	28
wa 'what'	2	320
wo 'where'	8	100
wie 'how'	10	328
wenn 'when'	3	25
Total	24	801

Table 5b lists the frequency of occurrence of the various non-monosyllabic wh-constituents with and without *dass*. *Worum* and *wiso*, both meaning 'why', *wie* Adj 'how ADJ' and *wi vil* (N) 'how much (N)/how many (N)' occurred quite often. Monosyllabic wh-items selected by a preposition occurred less often, and there were even fewer wh-items containing e.g. *wele* 'which' and *wa för* 'what kind of'.

Tab. 5b: Distribution of DFCs in wh-complement clauses with non-monosyllabic wh-constituents

	+DFC	−DFC
wär/wie au immer 'who ever/how ever'	2	0
P *wa* 'what'/*wo* 'where'/*wenn* 'when'/*wäm* 'whom'	27	6
wohär 'from where'/*wohi* 'where to'	14	0
P *wohär* 'from where'	1	0
worum/wiso 'why'	51	3
wie ADJ 'how ADJ'	39	8
wa för N 'what type of N'	19	2
P *wa för* N 'what type of N'	0	1
wele/weli/weles 'which one/ones'	7	0
wele/weli/weles N 'which N'	5	0
P *welne* N 'which N'	10	1
wi vil 'how much'	24	1
wi vil/wenig N 'how many, much/few N'	19	1
Total	218	23

The most frequently used predicate selecting a wh-complement was (Neg) *wüsse* 'know' (392×). Other predicates that were attested 20 or more times are: *luege* 'see, check' (72×), *fròòge* 'ask' (69×), *säge* 'say' (43×), *gsee* 'see' (43×), *intressiere* 'be interested' (28×), *druf aacho* 'depend on' (26×), and *ka Aanig* (ha) '(have) no idea'

(24×). These eight predicates make up almost 2/3 of the predicates selecting a wh-complement. The element that most often occurred after a DFC is an unstressed subject pronoun, an issue I shall return to in the next section.

5 How to account for the data from St. Galler German?

After applying the syllabic account and the syntactic account to the Swiss-German data, I shall try to show that the production of a DFC also depends on the prosodic phrasing a speaker uses in the wh-complement clause. Thus not only the stress pattern of the wh-item itself but also that of the words following it is relevant. I cannot offer a solution, but I argue that examination of the surrounding prosody is an avenue worth exploring. If the production of DFCs is indeed also influenced by prosody then reading out a given test item, as was done in the studies in Bayer and Brandner (2008a, 2008b) and Bayer (2015), may have influenced its acceptability.

5.1 The syllabic account

The generalizations derived from a much smaller sample of St. Galler German (see Section 2), in which monosyllabic wh-constituents never combined with *dass*, while all non-monosyllabic ones did, are no longer valid. There are counter-examples to both of those generalizations. In all 24 counter-examples with monosyllabic wh-constituents, the latter is stressed, as in the examples in (13).[8] In the examples, the age group a speaker belongs to is appended to their name: G1 = young speakers, G2 = middle-aged speakers, and G3 = elderly speakers.

---

8 In the examples, conventions for the transcription in EXMARaLDA are implemented, where one to three dots "•••" stand for short intonational breaks of varying length, a forward slash "/" signals a false start, and capital letters highlight syllables with heavy stress. For the broad transcription of Swiss German the rules proposed by Dieth (1986) were used. According to these rules, the 2SG clitic and the clitic article are both transcribed as *d*, although *t* would be more accurate, since neither the pronominal clitic nor the clitic article are voiced.

(13) a. *tüe mer   luege   WIE   dass mer   dòò*
     do we.CL look   how   that we.CL here
    löösigsorientiert   fürschimachet   (Arabella G2)
    solution.oriented   ahead.make
    'we'll see HOW, with a solution in mind, we can proceed'
  b. *Wüsset Si   nò   WOO   dass da   gsi   isch z   Gämf?*   (Anna)
    know   you   still   where   that this been is   in Geneva
    'Do you still know WHERE this was in Geneva?'

That a stressed monosyllabic wh-constituent can co-occur with *dass* is unexpected, since a clitic and the wh-constituent could form a trochaic foot, e.g. in (13a). And in contexts without a pronominal clitic, as in (13b), there would be no need for *dass*.

There are many more counter-examples with non-monosyllabic wh-constituents. These are expected to combine with *dass*, but 23 do not, as shown in (14).

(14) *Die   wüsset   immer   zu   welere   Zit   wäär   döt   ischt.* Anja (G2)
    they   know   always   at   what   time   who   there   is
    'They always know who is there and at what time.'

Even if it cannot be excluded that Swiss-German speakers are also influenced by their knowledge of Standard German, in which DFCs are ruled out, there seem to be too many examples that would have to be ascribed to this factor, i.e. almost 10%. If Standard German did have a major impact on a dialect speaker's production of DFCs then a dialect speaker with more extensive exposure to German might be expected to produce more examples without a DFC in wh-complement clauses with non-monosyllabic wh-constituents than a dialect speaker with less extensive exposure. This is not confirmed by the data from the interviewers. Anna spent over 15 years living and working in Germany, using German almost exclusively at work and in private, but she produced fewer examples without a DFC than did Thea, who has spent only 3 months living and working in Germany, and who generally uses Swiss German at work and in private. Only 5 of 61 (8%) of Anna's examples lack a DFC while 3 of 13 (23%) of Thea's examples do.

Note that my earlier conclusions that a monosyllabic wh-constituent and a clitic form a prosodic unit – a trochaic foot – and that *dass* and a pronominal clitic do so too, cannot be maintained. Neither the combination of *wa* and *s* 'they' in (15a) nor the combination of *dass* and *d* 'you.2SG' in (15b) form a trochaic foot.

(15) a. *si   higet   kai   Aanig   wa   s   machet*   (Anna)
    they   have.COND   no   idea   what   they   make
    'they have no idea what they are going to do'

b. *Egaal wi vil Chind dass d häsch...* (Leonard G2)
   irrelevant how many children that you have
   'It is irrelevant how many children you have...'

5.2 The syntactic account

The assumption is that wh-items that can function as heads discharge a C-feature when they merge with TP and therefore insertion of *dass* is prevented. The wh-items *wär* 'who. NOM/ACC', *wa* 'what', *wo* 'where', *wie* 'how, and *wenn* 'when', if they are unstressed (i.e. wh-words of type II), are assumed to be heads. If wh-words of type II are indeed heads that would account for all 801 examples that contain a monosyllabic wh-item and no DFC.[9] Furthermore, it is assumed that the C-feature is trapped inside a wh-item that is phrasal, and insertion of *dass* is possible and required. Some wh-items are assumed to vary in syntactic status, and therefore they are predicted to occur without *dass* if they are heads and with *dass* if they are not heads. According to Bayer and Brandner (2008a, 2008b) these are the wh-items of type I: *warum* 'why', *wie viel* 'how much', and *wäm* 'whom'. Presumably *wiso* 'why' is treated on a par with *warum*. *Wäm* does not occur in the data, but there are a number of examples with *wi vil* and with *warum/wiso*. These generally occur with a DFC: *wi vil* (24/25 examples), *warum* (29/32) and *wiso* (22/22). There is thus some variation, albeit little. According to Bayer (2015) a wh-PP may also behave like a head if the complement of P is a wh-word and therefore some variation is expected to occur with these as well. And indeed there is some variation: most wh-PPs co-occur with *dass* (27 examples) but there are also several without *dass* (6 examples), illustrated in (16).

(16) *Dä hät gnau gwüsst um wa s gòòt.* (Franz G3)
     this has exactly known about what it goes
     'He knew exactly what it was all about.'

All other wh-items are phrasal, including stressed wh-words of type II (and presumably also stressed *wäm*). Phrasal wh-items are predicted to combine with *dass*, which is not borne out by the data. There are several counter-examples with

---

[9] Bayer (2015) observes that "one can easily find examples of *wer dass* and even *was dass*, i.e. of the least favoured combinations" (2015: 18) and he does not mention contrastive stress on *wer* and *was*. We have over 300 examples with unstressed *wer* oder *was* in our data and in none is a DFC used.

wie ADJ 'how ADJ': 8 of 47 examples do not have a DFC, as shown in (17). There are 5 additional counter-examples with other wh-phrases (cf. [14]).

(17) *Mi intressiert da überhaupt nöd aso wie alt die Brugg isch.* (Anna)
me interests this totally not PART how old this bridge is
'I am not at all interested in how old this bridge is.'

When a wh-word of type II is stressed it often, but not always, occurs with *dass*. In their discussion of example (5), Bayer and Brandner (2008a) specifically mention contrastive focus, not stress. In the St. Galler German sample none of the examples with a stressed monosyllabic wh-item involves contrastive focus. There are 37 such examples: 24 examples contain a DFC and 13 do not, as shown in (18).[10] If Bayer and Brander mean that only monosyllabic wh-items with contrastive focus are syntactically complex, i.e. phrasal, then none of these 37 examples should contain a DFC, because the monosyllabic wh-item, although stressed is not contrastively focussed, and therefore it would be a head. If Bayer and Brandner mean that any stressed monosyllabic wh-item is syntactically more complex, then all 37 examples should contain a DFC, because a phrasal wh-item requires the presence of *dass*.

(18) a. *Denn händ s müese usefinde WOO daa isch.* (Zacharias G3)
then have they must out.find where this is
'Then they had to find out WHERE this is.'
b. *Gseesch immer ... WENN WOO irgendöppis loos isch.* (Nadine G1)
see.2SG always when where something on is
'You can always see WHEN something is on and WHERE.'

The 8 (of 47) counter-examples with *wie* ADJ and the 13 (of 37) examples with stressed wh-words of type II could be ascribed to influence from German, but as mentioned above, German influence seems minimal in Swiss German. Moreover, the number of counter-examples in these two contexts is unexpectedly large, particularly as compared to the number of counter-examples with wh-words of type I. These are expected to sometimes occur without a DFC, but only 1 (of 25) examples with *wie vil* 'how much' and 3 (of 32) examples with *warum* 'why' do.

---

10 In the data from the elderly group, 1 of 4 examples with a stressed monosyllabic wh-constituent contains a DFC, in the middle-aged group 11 of 20 examples do, and in the young group 12 of 13 examples do. The group of young speakers behaves significantly differently from both the elderly group (p<0.03) and the middle-aged group (p<0.05) according to Fisher's exact test, while there is no significant difference between the elderly and the middle-aged group.

5.3 Intermediate summary

My earlier generalizations that monosyllabic wh-constituents do not combine with *dass*, while non-monosyllabic ones do, are not supported by this larger data sample. Bayer and Brandner's syntactic account cannot cover these data either. The syllabic account would predict that DFCs never occur in wh-complement clauses with stressed monosyllabic wh-constituents, but in fact they sometimes do. The syntactic account would predict that stressed monosyllabic wh-constituents either always combine with *dass* or never combine with *dass*, depending on whether the authors mean 'stress' in general or 'contrastive focus' specifically. Neither prediction is supported. The syllabic account cannot account for any of the examples with a non-monosyllabic wh-constituent but without a DFC. The syntactic account can at least cover some of these examples, although not entirely convincingly. On one hand, some variation was found where none is expected to occur, and on the other, some variation was expected to occur but hardly any was found. Attributing any example in which a DFC does not occur, although it is expected to, solely to the influence of Standard German on Swiss German does not seem warranted. Some noise is expected in the data but not to this extent. Thus another explanation is called for to account for the lack of DFCs in certain wh-complement clauses.

5.4 Outline of a prosodic approach and the function of *dass* 'that'

5.4.1 *Dass* as a phonological host for prosodically weak elements

Both the syllabic account and the syntactic account imply that *dass* is relevant as a host for clitics. If this were its only function then in all the wh-complement clauses with a DFC *dass* should be followed by a clitic. This is not the case. There are two types of clitics in this dialect: clitic pronouns and clitic articles. Following Cardinaletti and Starke (1999), I classify pronouns as clitics if they cannot occur in the sentence-initial position of a V2 clause, and as weak pronouns if they can occur in the sentence-initial position but they cannot co-ordinate. Strong pronouns can also occur sentence-initially, but in contrast to weak pronouns they can also co-ordinate (or co-occur with a focus particle, e.g. *nur* 'only'). This is shown for the 3PL pronoun in (19).

(19) a. *Si/   *s   fräuet   sich   wenn   s   gwünet.*
       they.WEAKP   they.CL   please   self   if   they.CL   win
       'They'll be pleased if they win.'

b. Si:/   *si/   *s   und au mir säget da.
    they.STRONGP they.WEAKP they.CL and also we say this
    'They and also we are saying this.'

Only a few pronouns have distinctive clitic forms and weak forms in the nominative: 2SG: *d* vs. *du*; 1PL/3SG.impersonal *mer* vs. *me* (or *mir*); 3PL: *s* vs. *si*. The weak pronoun of the polite form (3PL) is *Si*, and the clitic form *S* only surfaces when it precedes another clitic with an initial vowel, as in (20). For all other pronouns the clitic form and the weak form seem to coincide in the nominative.

(20) Wenn S en gseend händ Si /*S Glück.
      if   you.CL him.CL see have you you.CL luck
      'If you see him you are in luck.'

Note that due to assimilation clitics can sometimes be inaudible or hard to discern. The clitic *d* is particularly audible in intervocalic contexts, as in (21a). In other contexts it can induce gemination and sometimes it cannot be heard at all, as in (21b) (see Werner 1999).

(21) a. Wo d en gsee häsch isch er überascht gsi.
        when you.CL him.CL seen have.2SG is he surprised been
        'When you saw him he was surprised.'
    b. Wenn ggòòsch isch guet dass au wider zruggchusch.
        if   you.CL.go.2SG is good that also again back.come.2SG
        'If you go it's good that you'll come back again.'

In our data, in 160 (of a total 242) wh-complement clauses with a DFC the element following *dass* is an unstressed pronoun, and in 158 cases this pronoun is in the nominative.[11] Besides many examples with a clitic (22a), there are many examples with a pronoun whose form is ambiguous between a clitic and a weak pronoun (22b) – I shall refer to these as 'clitic/weak pronoun' – and also a few examples with an unambiguous weak pronoun (22c).

(22) a. *dass* clitic (n = 74)
        18 × d (2SG); 36 × mer (1PL); 19 × s (3PL); 1 × em (3SG.IMPERS.DAT)
    b. *dass* clitic/weak pronoun (n = 81)
        16 × i; 6 × ich (1SG); 6 × er (3SG.M); 9 × si (3SG.F); 28 × s (3SG.N);
        15 × Si (3PL.polite form); 1 × sich 'REFL.ACC'
    c. *dass* weak pronoun (n = 5)
        4 × du (2SG); 1 × si (3PL)

---

11 In 14 of the 242 wh-complements with DFC the 'element' that immediately follows *dass* is a subject-trace. Because a trace is never audible, I considered the element that immediately follows it.

In an additional 10 examples the element following *dass* is an article, either a clitic (23a) or a non-clitic (23b). The clitic article *d* 'the.SG.FEM.NOM/ACC; the.PL.NOM/ACC', just like the 2SG clitic *d*, is sometimes inaudible (see Krähenmann 2009). The 2SG clitic is an enclitic, but the clitic article seems to be a proclitic, given the contrast between *dass d Ida...* (that.the.CL Ida...) and *dass *d/di iifrig Ida...* (that.the.CL/the busy Ida...). Despite this, Lahiri and Plank (2010: 390) say that they "do not want to rule out that even plain consonantal *t* [the clitic article *d*, added by MS] does lean left rather than right" in non-sentence initial position.

(23) a. *dass* clitic article (n = 4)
    4 × *d* 'the.F.CL'
 b. *dass* non-clitic article (n = 6)
    3 × *de* 'the.M'; 1 × *di* 'the.F'; 1 × *s* 'the.N'; 1 × *e* 'a'

In most of the remaining 72 examples with a DFC a light element – light in the sense of being monosyllabic – follows *dass*. Many of these elements bear word-stress (e.g. the proper name *Wiil*, the demonstrative pronoun *dä* 'this.M') or heavy stress (e.g. *äär* 'he.stressed'). Only in 11 examples does a non-monosyllabic element follow *dass*. I illustrate these three cases in (24). In example (24a) the element following *dass* is an unstressed monosyllabic element (a clitic/weak pronoun), while in example (24b) the element following *dass* is a stressed monosyllabic element (a strong pronoun). In example (24c) the element following *dass* is a non-monosyllabic word with word-stress. The audio characteristics of examples (24a) and (24b), visualized in Praat[12], are shown in Figs. 1 and 2.

(24) a. *Waiss   nüme   gnau   WOO   dass   er   reklamiert*
       know.1SG   no.longer   exactly   where   that   he   complained
       hät.   (Nora G3)
       has
       'I no longer know WHERE he complained.'
    b. *Wi   vil   Begaabige   dass   ÄÄR   ka   hät   da   chan*
       how   many   talents   that   he   had   has   this   can
       i   etz   nöd   säge.   (Nora G3)
       I   now   not   say
       'How many talents HE has had I cannot say now.'

---

[12] All the visual representations in the paper were created with Praat (www.praat.org), a free software package for the analysis of speech in phonetics, developed and actively maintained by Paul Boersma and David Weenink (2016). The continuous line in each figure shows the intensity contour, and the non-continuous line the pitch contour with units of semitones re 1Hz.

c. *I waiss nöd wi vil dass Hüròòte chòschtet.* (Arabella G2)
   I know not how much that marrying costs
   'I don't know how much it costs to get married.'

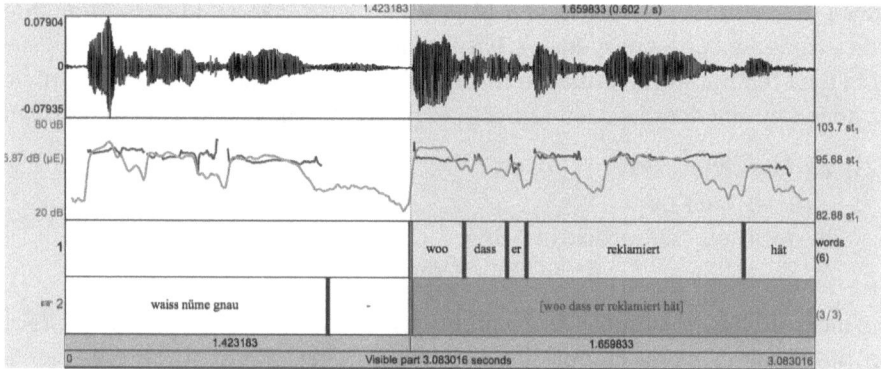

Fig. 1: Visualization of example (24a)

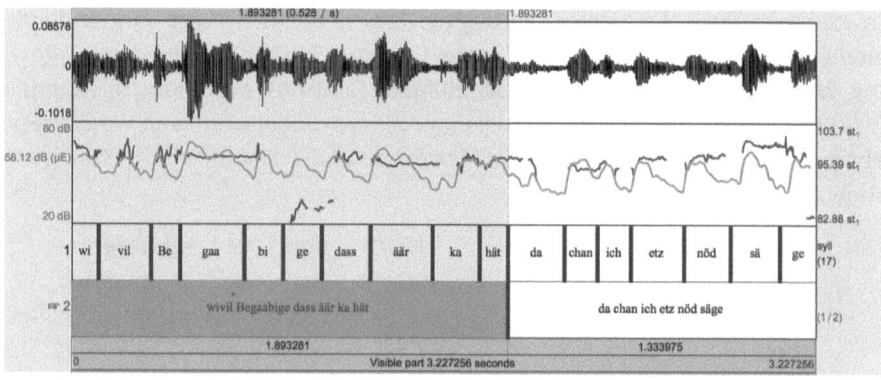

Fig. 2: Visualization of example (24b)

Note that *dass* and the weak monosyllabic element in (24a) form a prosodic unit, a trochaic foot: a stressed or long syllable is followed by a short or unstressed syllable. The trochee is the preferred stress pattern of Germanic dialects according to Kabak and Schiering (2006), who examined the combination of two function words. Korth (2014) suggests that the trochee is the preferred stress pattern even in larger prosodic entities in these dialects. In example (24b) the pattern is iambic: an unstressed syllable is followed by a stressed syllable.

Based on the fact that the element immediately following *dass* is often, but by no means always, weak, I conclude that the sole function of *dass* cannot be to provide prosodic support for clitics or, more generally, for an adjacent prosodically weak element.

5.4.2 *Dass* as a provider of an extra syllable

Besides surfacing in contexts where it functions as a phonological host for prosodically weak elements, *dass* can surface in others contexts to bring about a more natural rhythm in the wh-complement clause. On one hand, *dass* can add weight to a prosodic unit to make it more similar in length to that of an adjacent prosodic unit, and on the other, *dass* can provide an unstressed syllable between stressed syllables.

Let us first consider the case where *dass* adds weight to a prosodic unit. Both examples in (25) contain the same stressed wh-constituent, but in (25a) *woo* co-occurs with *dass* while in (25b) is does not.

(25) a. *i   däm   i   ... Merkmòòl   erarbaitet   ha   ... und*
      in   that I   features   explored   have   and
      au   Òòrt   WOO   dass   Komnikazioon • schtattfindet (Alisia G1)
      also places where that communication   place.takes
      'in that I explored features and also places WHERE communication happens'
   b. *Denn   händ   s   müesen   uesefinde   WOO   daa   isch.* (Zacharias G3)
      and   then   they   must   out.find   where this is
      'And then they had to find out WHERE this is.'

In (25a) the word *Komnikazioon* following *dass* is polysyllabic and lasts 0.87s, while *woo* by itself only lasts 0.26s, but the sequence *woo dass* of course lasts longer. Figure 3 suggests that *woo* and *dass* form a prosodic unit. Although the duration of *woo dass* is shorter than that of the following prosodic unit (0.45s vs. 0.87s), the two units are less unbalanced in duration.

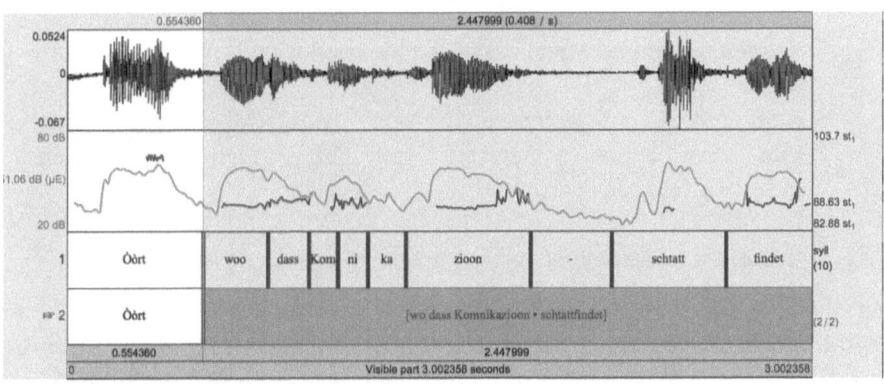

Fig. 3: Visualization of example (25a)

In example (25b) the words in the wh-complement clause are all pronounced individually and the vowel not only in *woo* but also in *daa* is long. As can be seen in Fig. 4, *woo, daa* und *isch* all have their own well-defined contour. Had *dass* been used, the prosodic phrasing would have been different: e.g. [woo] [dass da] [isch], and the vowel in *da* would be short.

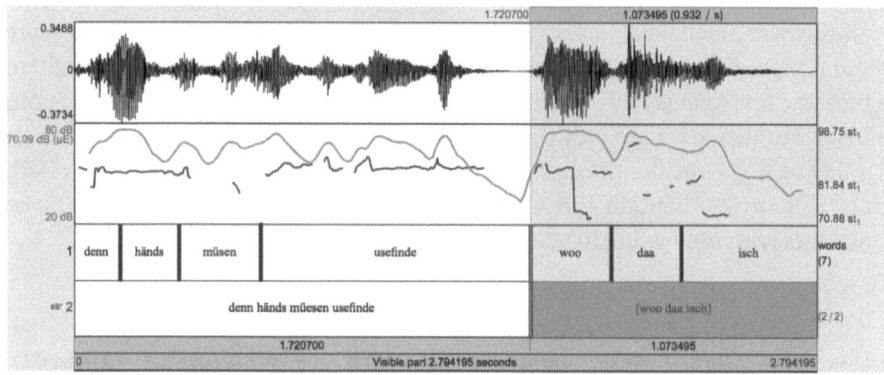

Fig. 4: Visualization of example (25b)

In the examples in (26) larger prosodic units in the wh-complement clauses can be discerned, which show similar intensity contours and are of roughly the same duration.

(26) a. *Mängmòl   lärnt   mer   sich   jò   au   ersch   im*
       sometimes   learns   one   self   PART   also   only   in.the
       Verlauf   vom   Läbe   käne   oder
       duration   of.the   life   know   part.
       • *WAS   am   würklech* • *WICHtig   isch.* (Thea)
         what   one.DAT   really   important   is
       'Sometimes one only realizes over a life span what is really important to one.'
    b. *Daa   hät   mi   intressiert   nöd   wie   hooch   die   Brugg*
       this   has   me   interested   not   how   high   this   bridge
       isch. (Anna)
       is
       'I found this interesting and not how high the bridge is.'

As shown in Fig. 5, the prosodic unit *WAS am würklech* is slightly longer than *WICHtig isch*. If *dass* were used it would further lengthen the duration of the first unit. Note in passing that both units are preceded by a short intonational break and start with a heavily stressed syllable, which enhances their 'rhythmic symmetry'.

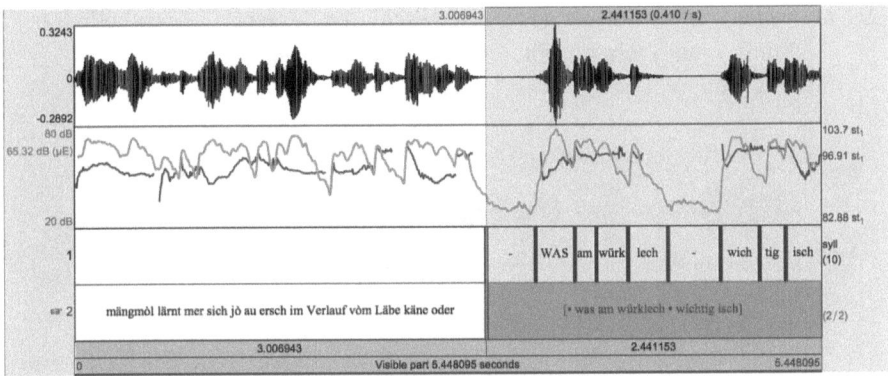

Fig. 5: Visualization of example (26a)

In Fig. 6 the prosodic units formed by *wie hooch* and *die Brugg* are both iambic and of roughly the same duration. Had the speaker used *dass* the prosodic phrasing would have been different: e.g. [wie hooch] [dass die] [Brugg] [isch].

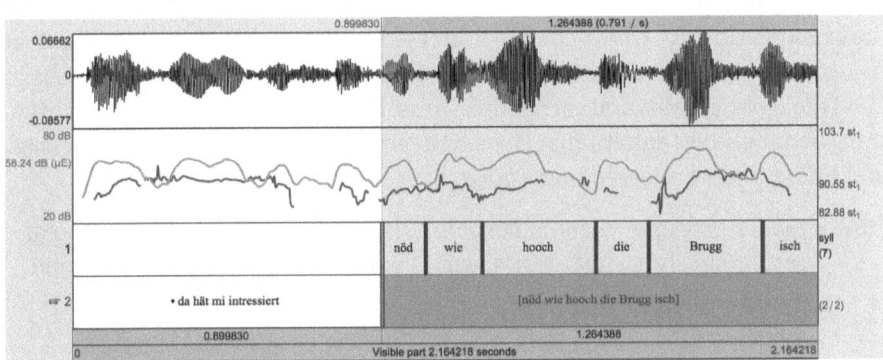

Fig. 6: Visualization of example (26b)

Example (27) is interesting because a pronominal clitic follows a non-monosyllabic wh-constituent (a wh-PP). I assume that the fact that the clitic's host is contained inside a PP is not relevant: as long as they are adjacent, the clitic (*d*) can prosodically integrate into the host (*wa*), in the spirit of Gärtner and Steinbach (2003). As shown in Fig. 7, 'uf wa d usewilsch' is of similar length to 'en Aier' (0.69s vs. 0.73s). Had *dass* been used it would have unnecessarily lengthened the duration of the prosodic unit. Moreover, *dass* is not required to host the clitic, since *wa* can apparently do so.

(27) I   waiss   uf   wa   d   usewilsch   en   Aier.[13]   (Isabelle G2)
     I   know   on   what you out.want   an   egg
     'I know what you have in mind, an EGG.'

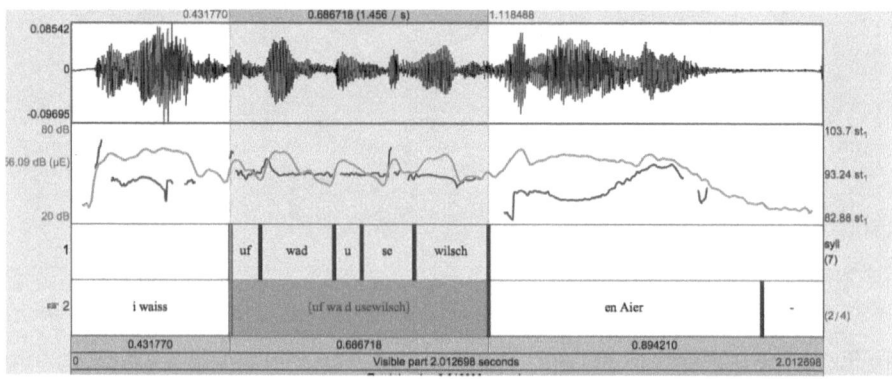

Fig. 7: Visualization of example (27)

Let us now turn to the case where *dass* provides an unstressed syllable. Consider the examples in (28), which contain a stressed monosyllabic wh-constituent that co-occurs with *dass* in (28a) but not in (28b). The three words following *dass* in (28a) are monosyllabic and carry word-stress. Figure 8 suggests that *dass* helps to bring about a stress pattern that is trochaic, since *waa* is more stressed than *dass*, and *Gründ* is more stressed than *chönd*.

(28) a. Sind   langsam achli bekannt WAA   dass Gründ   chönd
        are   slowly   bit   known   what that the.causes could
        si.   (Nadine G1)
        be
        'It has gradually become clear WHAT the causes may be.'

---

[13] A typical feature of this dialect is that a few words in the singular look like plural forms, e.g. *en Aier* 'an egg' (instead of *en Ai*) vs. *Aier* 'eggs'; *e Töchter* 'a daughter' (instead of *e Tochter*) vs. *Töchter* 'daughters'. These forms seem to be dying out.

Are doubly-filled COMPS governed by prosody in Swiss German? — 211

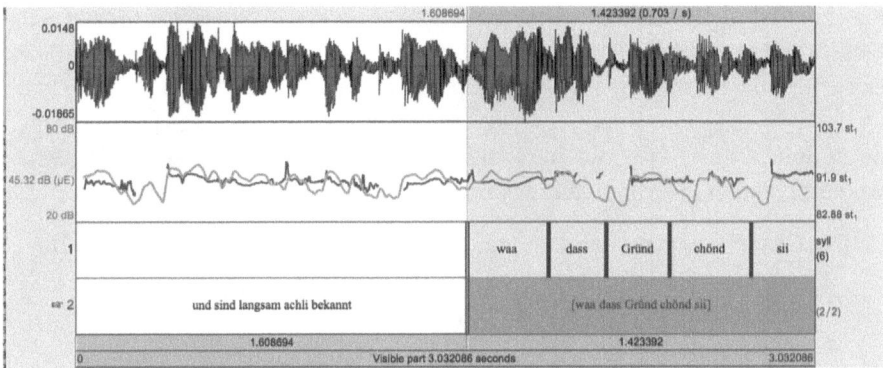

Fig. 8: Visualization of example (28a)

In (28b) *wa* is also stressed, but in contrast to (28a) its duration is shorter (*wa* 0.16s vs. *waa* 0.28s). Apparently it can 'host' the adjacent prosodically weak pronominal *s*. As can be seen in Fig. 9, the stress pattern in the wh-complement clause is again trochaic. Note that before Anna finishes pronouncing *isch*, her interlocutor starts to mumble *mmh*, thus there is a slight overlap between the two speakers.

(28) b. I   cha   der   etz   nöd   gnau   säge   WA   s   isch. (Anna)
     I   can   you.DAT   now   not   exactly   tell   what it   is
     'I cannot tell you exactly WHAT it is.'

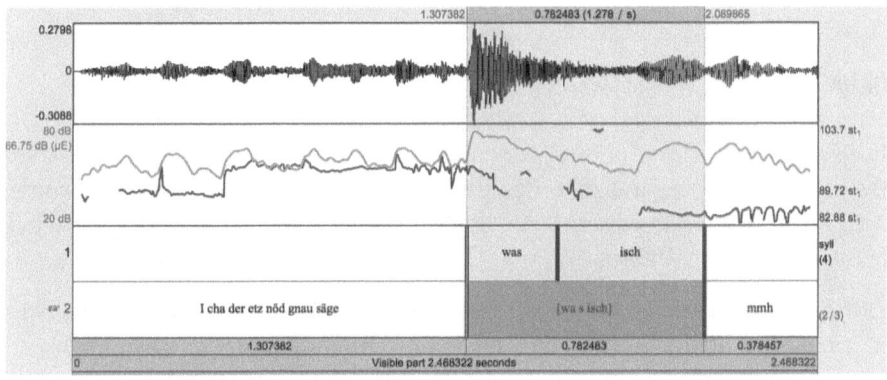

Fig. 9: Visualization of example (28b)

Examples of the type in (29) are interesting because they contain a finite verb in the 2SG but no 'audible' subject. Perhaps the 2SG clitic has assimilated to *dass* and that is why it cannot be heard. But there may be another explanation. *Dass* may be used to provide an unstressed syllable between two heavily stressed syllables. At the same time, using *dass* gives rise to a trochee, as shown in Fig. 10. For examples like these Cooper (1994) proposes that DFCs are used to mark a clause as clearly being subordinate. It seems to me that without *dass* the 2SG clitic would be audible in these examples, so that no ambiguity would arise as to whether the wh-complement is an embedded main clause or a subordinate clause.

(29) a. Chunt   immer   druf   aa   WOO   dass   BISCHT.   (Leo G2)
        comes   always   there   on   WHERE   that   are.2SG
        'It always depends on WHERE you ARE.'
    b. *Je nòchdäm   WIE   dass   SCHAFFSCH*   ...   (Nadine G1)
        depending   how   that   work.2SG
        'Depending on how you work...'

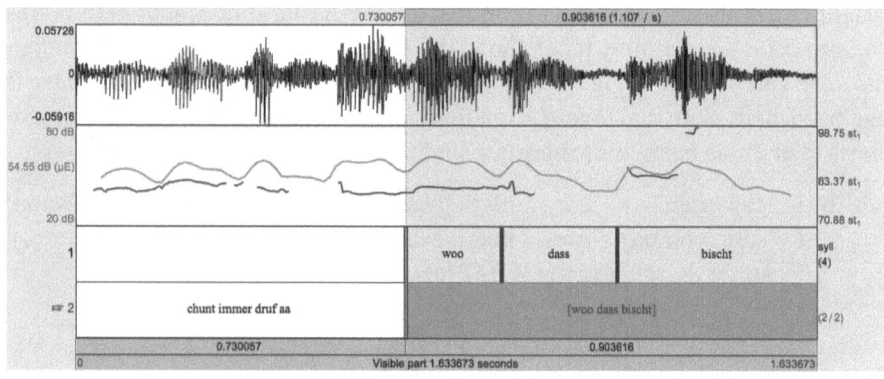

Fig. 10: Visualization of example (29a)

In example (30) *dass* follows *worum*, which is bisyllabic with word-stress on the second syllable, and precedes three heavily stressed monosyllabic words. Although the resulting pattern is not trochaic, *dass* provides an unstressed syllable between stressed syllables.

(30) *sòndern   würklech   au   eri   persönleche   Iidrück   vom   • Daavid*
     but   really   also   her   personal   impressions   of.the   David
     aso   worum   dass   SII   DÄÄ   SCHÖÖ   findet (Anna)
     so   why   that   she   him   beautiful finds
     'but also her personal impression of David, why SHE found HIM BEAUTIFUL'

The above examples show that *dass* can be used to add weight to a short prosodic unit in order to counter-balance the length of an adjacent longer prosodic unit, and *dass* can also be used to provide an unstressed syllable in a 'stressed' environment. In either case the use of *dass* has an impact on the prosody in the wh-complement clause and, by assumption, helps bring about a more natural rhythm, which is often more trochaic.

5.4.3 A note on prosodic 'disruption' in the wh-complement clause

I assume that any disfluency during the production of a wh-complement clause, or the use of a long pause or an unusual stress pattern may have an impact on prosodic phrasing and on the use of *dass*. The following examples illustrate these three cases. In (31a) the speaker first produces a monosyllabic wh-constituent, which he then replaces by a wh-PP. In (31b) the speaker pauses after the wh-constituent and then produces a heavily stressed pronoun. In (31c) WIE and GROOSS are stressed individually, which is rather unnatural, and a slight hesitation can be heard before GROOSS.

(31) a. *Ich waiss nöd wa denn die/ über wa die ales*
    I know not what then they about what they everything
    gredt händ. (Oskar G3)
    talked have
    'I don't know what they talked about.'
  b. *Dò gseet mer etz wider wie guet •• iich*
    here sees one now again how well I
    unterrichtet bi. (Anna)
    informed am.
    'Here one can see once more how well I am informed.'
  c. *Denn fallt s aim würklech uuf WIE GROOOSS de*
    then falls it one.DAT really up how big the
    Underschiid isch. (Thea)
    difference is
    'Then one realizes HOW BIG the differences are.'

5.5 Towards an explanation of the distribution of DFCs

As has been noted for Alemannic (on both sides of the lake of Constance) and Bavarian, DFCs rarely occur in wh-complement clauses with short wh-constituents, while they do in those with non-short wh-constituents. I would now like to address the question why *dass* is never found with monosyllabic wh-constituents that do not bear stress, while it is sometimes found with them when they do bear stress.

In our data, there are no examples in which an unstressed monosyllabic wh-constituent co-occurs with *dass*. Why is this? Consider the examples in (32). The wh-constituent is followed by a clitic/weak pronoun in (32a), a stressed pronoun in (32b), and a proper name with stress on the first syllable in (32c).

(32) a. *I   cha   mi   nüme   erinnere   wie-n-er   früener*
        I   can   me   no.longer remember   how-N-he   formerly
        gsi   isch. (Anna)
        been is
        'I can no longer remember what he was like in the past.'
   b. *Waisch   wie-n-II   da   mach?* (Nikolaus G1)
      know   how-N-I   this   do
      'Do you know how I do this?'
   c. *Ich   ha   dòch   nöd   emòl   gwüsst   wo   Frankriich*
      I   have   PART   not   even   known   where   France
      isch. (Lars G2)
      is
      'I didn't even know where France is.'

I take the occurrence of *n*-intrusion in (32a) and (32b) to signal that the wh-constituent and the following pronoun form a prosodic unit, resulting in a trochee in (32a) and in an iambus in (32b) (see Figs. 1 and 2 above for an illustration of these patterns). What would have happened if a DFC had been used in these examples? In (32a) *dass* would take over the function of phonological host from *wie*. Although *dass+er* would also form a trochee, *wie* would no longer be part of the trochaic foot and the resulting structure would be less optimal. In (32b) the insertion of *dass* would not result in a trochee, since *dass* cannot be stronger than the emphatic pronoun. Thus inserting *dass* would not result in a more optimal stress pattern in (32a) and it would not change an overall dispreferred pattern, the iambus in (32b), into a more preferable one, a trochee. If *dass* were inserted in (32c) and neither *wo* nor *dass* were stressed, they would not combine to form a prosodic foot, since they would be of the same prosodic strength. There are no examples with stressed *dass* in our data, but *dass* can be stressed in cases where it has verum focus and, in this case, *dass* is quite acceptable even in German (see [33]), which does not usually allow DFCs.

(33) *Ich   weiss   zwar   wer   es   NICHT   gelesen   hat   aber*
     I   know   indeed   who   it   not   read   has   but
     nicht   wer   DASS   es   gelesen   hat.
     not   who   that   it   read   has
     'I know, in fact, who has NOT read it, but not who HAS read it.'

There are 37 examples with a stressed monosyllabic wh-constituent, and 24 of these contain a DFC. The distribution of DFCs per wh-item is summarized in Tab. 6, and the type of element following *dass* (+) or the wh-constituent without *dass* (−) is classified into prosodically weak or non-weak.

Tab. 6: Distribution of DFCs in wh-complement clauses with a stressed monosyllabic wh-constituent, taking into account the following element

	wäär 'who(m)'		*wie* 'how'		*wenn* 'when'		*wa* 'what'		*wo* 'where'	
	+	−	+	−	+	−	+	−	+	−
weak	1	0	9	3	2	1	1	3	5	0
non-weak	0	3	1	0	1	0	1	1	3	2

These data seem puzzling for the following reason: if stressed monosyllabic wh-constituents can prosodically support the following weak element why do they ever co-occur with *dass*? The combination of the stressed monosyllabic wh-constituent and the adjacent weak element could result in a trochaic foot, as in WIE *mer* 'HOW we'. In footnote 3 I pointed out that *n*-insertion is possible with stressed *wo* (and *wa*) provided the vowel is short. Perhaps vowel length is relevant here as well. Interestingly, in all 8 examples in which *wo* co-occurs with *dass* the vowel is long (average length of *woo*: 0.25s, ranging from 0.21s–0.34s). The same is true of the two examples of *wa* combined with *dass* (length of *waa*: 0.26s and 0.28s). The vowel is also long in the two examples in which *wo* immediately precedes a non-weak element and in the example in which *wa* does (length of *woo*: 0.21s and 0.25s; length of *waa*: 0.26s). In total, there are 6 examples in which the stressed monosyllabic wh-constituent is immediately followed by a non-weak element, and in five of these this element is monosyllabic and its vowel is also long (cf. [25b] above), and in the remaining example the element is polysyllabic. In contrast, in the three examples in which stressed *wa* immediately precedes a prosodically weak element, it is pronounced twice with a short vowel (length of *wa*: 2× 0.16s, cf. [28b] above) and once as *was*, but again with a short vowel (cf. [26a] above). A similar effect can be found in wh-PPs that contain *wa*. There are five examples with and four without a DFC. In the five examples with a DFC the vowel in *wa* is relatively long (average length of *waa*: 0.17s, ranging from 0.14s–0.19s), while in three of the examples without a DFC the vowel in *wa* is relatively short (average length of *wa*: 0.1s, ranging from 0.09s–0.12s). In the fourth example *durch waa sich dää* 'by what self this' the vowel of *wa* is long (length of *waa*: 0.18s) as is the vowel in *dä* (length of *dää*: 0.23s). There is only one example of a wh-PP with *wo*, and it contains a DFC. The vowel in *wo* is long (length of *woo*: 0.16s).

These data suggest that vowel length may indeed be relevant. If the vowel in *wo* or *wa* is long and *wo* or *wa* would be followed by a prosodically weak element – a clitic or a clitic/weak pronoun – *dass* is used. Encliticization to the wh-constituent may be blocked in these cases because some phonotactic rule is violated (cf. Gärtner and Steinbach 2003: 482).[14] Moreover, *n*-intrusion is blocked just as with non-monosyllabic wh-constituents (e.g. *wiso* 'why', *wele* 'which').[15] And if *wo* or *wa* is followed by a non-weak monosyllabic element that element's vowel is also pronounced as long, presumably to make the two items more similar in length.

Let us now briefly consider DFCs in clauses with a non-monosyllabic wh-constituent. Whenever such a wh-constituent would be followed by a clitic, our data show *dass* is used. However, *dass* also often precedes a weak monosyllabic element that is not a clitic. Why is this? The word-stress in a bisyllabic wh-constituent can either be iambic or trochaic. Using *dass* either brings about a more trochaic rhythm or it helps maintain such a rhythm. This hypothesis can be extended to wh-constituents with more than two syllables, and using *dass* in these cases also helps to 'adjust' the weight of an adjacent prosodic unit. Thus the impression that *dass* seems to become more 'obligatory' with long wh-constituents could receive quite a natural explanation: not only does *dass* promote a trochaic rhythm but it also helps to counter-balance the weight of adjacent prosodic units.

To summarize, not only is the length of the wh-constituent relevant but so is the type of element following it. In contexts where a prosodically weak element can be hosted by the wh-constituent *dass* is never used. The only such contexts involve monosyllabic wh-constituents with short vowels, i.e. *wär, wo, wa, wenn* or with a diphthong moving to schwa (*wie*). Since other wh-constituents do not qualify as hosts, *dass* must be used to host the prosodically weak element, i.e. *dass* is obligatory. In other contexts *dass* seems to be used by native speakers for the purpose of prosody, to reinforce the natural rhythm of Swiss German. In these contexts *dass* seems to be more or less optional. A speaker can influence the prosodic phrasing in different ways, by a change in speech rate, by using an intonational break, by adding stress to a syllable, etc. Optionality seems to require different prosodic phrasing. How could this be tested? In an experiment one could remove *dass* from the original recorded utterances with DFCs and check how native speakers judge

---

14 In varieties of German that have deficient pronouns but no DFCs other strategies would be used in cases like these, e.g. using a strong pronoun instead of a deficient one.

15 In the visualization of some of the examples with *woo* or *waa* two intensity peaks can be seen, which suggests that the speaker may have pronounced *woo* or *waa* as bisyllabic, cf. (28a) and (29a).

these edited utterances. A different response would be expected depending on whether *dass* is optional or obligatory.

6 Concluding remarks

The phenomenon of DFCs seems to be very much alive in St. Galler German, as attested by the data described in this paper, which come from 35 speakers who were classified into different age groups. Young speakers are just as likely as older speakers to produce DFCs. Standard German, which is learned at school, does not seem to greatly influence the production of DFCs in these dialect speakers. Note that dialect speakers in Germany are typically exposed to Standard German considerably earlier than those in Switzerland, and thus the influence from Standard German could be larger.

In these spontaneous production data from Swiss German, DFCs never occurred in wh-complement clauses with unstressed monosyllabic wh-constituents, but they often occurred with stressed monosyllabic wh-constituents, and very often with non-monosyllabic wh-constituents. Some variation was found in these data that was not attested in a previous, smaller, sample from the same dialect. My previous account in terms of the number of syllables of the wh-constituent was based on this smaller sample, but is no longer tenable because of this variation.

Instead of concentrating on the wh-constituent itself, as in my previous syllabic account, I examined the role of *dass* more closely. In this approach, the influence that *dass* can have on the overall prosody of a wh-complement clause is seen as playing an important role in whether a DFC is used. By providing a stressed or unstressed syllable, *dass* can lead to a more trochaic pattern, and by adding an extra syllable it can increase the length of a prosodic unit which otherwise seems too short compared to an adjacent prosodic unit. In either case *dass* is somewhat optional. Whether a native speaker actually uses *dass* is largely dependent on the prosodic phrasing used during the production of the wh-complement clause. However, when a phonologically deficient pronoun needs to be prosodically integrated and the wh-constituent does not qualify as an appropriate host then using *dass* is obligatory. Almost two decades ago, Weiss (1998) proposed that DFCs should be dealt with at the level of Phonological Form and provided a rough outline of how this could be done. I do not wish to claim that DFCs are governed by prosody alone. Syntax also plays a role. In future work I intend to explore the interface between syntax and phonology to account for DFCs. Although I have said nothing about how DFCs are derived, I continue to assume that even short wh-constituents are maximal projections, because the empirical evidence used by Bayer and Brandner (2008a, 2008b) and Bayer (2015) to support their core idea that short wh-constituents are syntactic heads does not extend to St. Galler German. Finally, I outlined an approach to the occurrence of DFCs that may be worth pursuing. We continue to collect and analyse spontaneous production data from Swiss-German speakers which I hope will clarify the issues discussed above.

Acknowledgements: The research presented here was carried out in the project 'Studying variation in syntax: a parsed corpus of Swiss German', which is supported by a three-year grant (SNSF 146450) from the Swiss National Science Foundation. I am grateful to two anonymous reviewers for very detailed and constructive comments, and to Antoine Auchlin, Giuliano Bocci, Eric Haeberli, Christopher Laenzlinger, Peter Öhl and Ur Shlonsky for discussion of various aspects of this topic. I also wish to thank Liliane Haegeman for arousing my interest in linguistics and in dialect syntax in particular. Had it not been for her I would never have realized what treasures lie hidden in dialects. Liliane has always emphasized that a careful description of the data is a good thing because analyses may come and go but the data 'stay'. So I have tried to take her advice to heart. And although I know that my analysis of DFCs will not make the headlines – there are far too many loose ends – I hope to have succeeded in providing a reasonable description of the data.

References

Bader, Thomas & Zvi Penner. 1988. A government-binding account of the complementizer system in Bernese Swiss German. *Arbeitspapier 25*. Universität Bern. Institut für Sprachwissenschaft.

Bayer, Josef. 2015. Doubly-filled Comp, wh head-movement, and derivational economy. In Marc van Oostendorp & Henk van Riemsdijk (eds.), *Representing structure in phonology and syntax*, 7–39. Berlin & Boston: De Gruyter Mouton.

Bayer, Josef, Markus Bader & Michael Meng. 2001. Morphological underspecification meets oblique case: Syntactic and processing effects in German. *Lingua* 111. 465–514.

Bayer, Josef & Ellen Brandner. 2008a. On wh-head-movement and the doubly-filled-comp filter. In Charles B. Chang & Hannah J. Haynie (eds.), *Proceedings of the 26th West Coast Conference on Formal Linguistics*, 87–95. Somerville: Cascadilla Proceedings Project.

Bayer, Josef & Ellen Brandner. 2008b. Wie oberflächlich ist die syntaktische Variation zwischen Dialekten? Doubly-filled COMP revisited. In Franz Patocka & Guido Seiler (eds.), *Dialektale Morphologie, dialektale Syntax*, 9–26. Vienna: Praesens.

Boersma, Paul & David Weenink. 2016. Praat: doing phonetics by computer [Computer program]. Version 6.0.19, retrieved 19 October 2016 from http://www.praat.org/

Cardinaletti, Anna & Michal Starke. 1999. The typology of structural deficiency: A case study of the three classes of pronouns. In Henk van Riemsdijk (ed.), *Clitics in the languages of Europe*, 145–233. Berlin: Mouton de Gruyter.

Cheng, Lisa. 1991. *On the typology of wh-questions*. Cambridge, MA: MIT dissertation.

Chomsky, Noam & Howard Lasnik. 1977. Filters and control. *Linguistic Inquiry*. 425–504.
Cooper, Kathrin E. 1994. *Topics in Zurich German syntax*. Edinburgh: University of Edinburgh dissertation.
Dieth, Eugen. 1986. Schwyzertütschi Dialäktschrift. Dieth-Schreibung. In Christian Schmid-Cadalbert (ed.), *Lebendige Mundart*, vol. 1. Aarau & Frankurt: Verlag Sauerländer.
Gärtner, Hans-Martin & Markus Steinbach. 2003. What do reduced pronominals reveal about the syntax of Dutch and German? *Linguistische Berichte* 196. 459–490.
Haegeman, Liliane. 1992. *Theory and description in generative syntax. A case study in West Flemish*. Cambridge: Cambridge University Press.
Haegeman. Liliane. 1993. Object clitics in West Flemish and the identification of A/A'positions. *Geneva Generative Papers* 1. 1–30.
Henry, Alison. 1995. *Belfast English and Standard English: Dialect variation and parameter setting*. New York & Oxford: Oxford University Press.
Kabak, Baris & René Schiering. 2006. The phonology and morphology of function word contractions in German. *Journal of Comparative Germanic Linguistics* 9. 53–99.
Korth, Manuela. 2014. *Von der Syntax zur Prosodie. Über das strukturelle Verhältnis zweier Komponenten der Grammatik im Deutschen*. Stuttgart: University of Stuttgart dissertation.
Krähenmann, Astrid. 2009. The perception of the word-initial quantity contrast in voiceless Swiss German stops. PDF of presentation at the 17th Manchester Phonology Meeting May 28–30, 2009.
Lahiri, Aditi & Frans Plank. 2010. Phonological phrasing in Germanic: The judgement of history, confirmed through experiment. *Transactions of the Philological Society*, vol. 108(3). 370–398.
Müller, Gereon. 2001. Order preservation, parallel movement and the emergence of the unmarked. In Géraldine Legendre, Jane Grimshaw & Sten Vikner (eds.), *Optimality-theoretic syntax*, 279–313. Cambridge, MA: The MIT Press.
Noth, Harald. 1993. *Alemannisches Dialekthandbuch vom Kaiserstuhl und seiner Umgebung*. Freiburg: Schillinger.
Ortmann, Albert. 1998. Consonant epenthesis: its distribution and phonologial specification. In Wolfgang Kehrein & Richard Wiese (eds.), *Phonology and morphology of the Germanic languages*, 51–76. Tübingen: Niemeyer.
Penner, Zvi. 1991. Pronominal clitics in Bernese Swiss German and their structural position. Jakob Wackernagel and language acquisition. In Henk van Riemsdijk & Luigi Rizzi (eds.), *Clitics and their hosts*, 253–268. Proceedings of the ESF colloquium, University of Geneva.
Penner, Zvi. 1996. From empty to doubly-filled complementizers. A case study in the acquisition of subordination in Bernese Swiss German. *Arbeitspapier Nr. 77*, Fachgruppe Sprachwissenschaft der Universität Konstanz.
Penner, Zvi & Thomas Bader. 1995. Issues in the syntax of subordination: A comparative study of the complementizer system in Germanic, Romance and Semitic languages with special reference to Bernese Swiss German. In Zvi Penner (ed.), *Topics in Swiss German syntax*, 73–290. Bern: Lang.
Salzmann, Martin, Jana Häussler, Markus Bader & Josef Bayer. 2013. *That*-trace effects without traces. An experimental investigation. In Stefan Keine & Shayne Sloggett (eds.), *Proceedings of the 42nd Annual Meeting of the North East Linguistic Society*, vol. 2, 149–162. Amherst: GLSA.
Schmidt, Thomas & Kai Wörner. 2009. EXMARaLDA-Creating, analysing and sharing spoken language corpora for pragmatic research. *Pragmatics* 19.4. 565–582.

Schönenberger, Manuela. 2010. 'Optional' doubly-filled COMPs (DFCs) in wh-complements in child and adult Swiss German. In Merete Anderssen, Kristine Bentzen & Marit Westergaard (eds.), *Variation in the input. Studies in the acquisition of word order*, 33–64. Dordrecht: Springer.

Weiss, Helmut. 1998. *Syntax des Bairischen. Studien zur Grammatik einer natürlichen Sprache.* Tübingen: Niemeyer (Linguistische Arbeiten 391).

Werner, Ingegerd. 1999. *Die Personalpronomen im Zürichdeutschen.* Inauguraldissertation, Universität Lund. Stockholm: Almqvist & Wiksell International (= Lunder germanistische Forschungen, 63).

Zwart, C. Jan-Wouter. 1997. *Morphosyntax of verb movement. A Minimalist approach to the syntax of Dutch* (Studies in Natural Language and Linguistic Theory). Dordrecht, Boston & London: Kluwer.

Zwicky, Arnold M. 2002. I wonder what kind of construction that this example illustrates. In David Beaver, Luis D. Casillas Martínez, Brady Z. Clark & Stefan Kaufmann (eds.), *The construction of meaning*, 219–248. CSLI Publications.

Raffaella Zanuttini
Presentatives and the syntactic encoding of contextual information

1 Presentatives and the challenges they present

1.1 Is contextual information encoded in the syntax?

Linguists and philosophers have long noticed that there are linguistic elements whose interpretation is tightly related to the context of utterance. For example, the referents of pronouns like *I* and *you* can only be determined if we know who the speaker and addressee are; similarly, temporal elements like *now, today, tomorrow* and a locative like *here* are interpreted in relation to the time of the utterance and the location of the speaker, respectively. We label these elements *indexicals* and commonly assume that the information we need to interpret them comes from the semantics and pragmatics, and is not necessarily represented in the syntax. This raises the question of whether information regarding the context is ever encoded in the syntax. The possibility that it might be was prominently raised in Ross (1970), an article that proposed that all root clauses contain syntactic structure (sometimes overt, sometimes phonetically null) encoding information concerning the speaker, the addressee, and the illocutionary force of the clause – a hypothesis that proved problematic (cf. Fraser 1974; Gazdar 1979) and was later largely set aside. More recently, that possibility has been revived in works like Speas and Tenny (2003), Sigurðsson (2004, 2014), Bianchi (2006), Hill (2007a, 2007b, 2014), Baker (2008), Giorgi (2010), Miyagawa (2012), Haegeman and Hill (2013), Haegeman (2014), Heim et al. (2014) and Wiltschko (2017). For example, Haegeman's work undertakes a systematic study of discourse particles in West Flemish, focusing on their syntactic distribution and asking which of their properties (if any) is best analyzed by assuming that certain aspects of the discourse context are encoded in the syntax. Her work forcefully argues that their distribution supports a syntactic representation of speaker and addressee in the left-periphery of the clause, above the CP layer.[1]

---

[1] I am writing this article as a tribute to Liliane Haegeman, thanking her for her willingness to share her thoughts and ideas in person and in writing, for never being afraid to change her mind when new evidence requires it, for the time and effort she puts into making her work clear and accessible, and for setting a very high standard for her work. On a more personal level, I am also writing to thank her for taking me to a wonderful café in Geneva (Chocolaterie Micheli), when I was a student, and engaging in an interesting discussion that led to our two joint publications (Haegeman and Zanuttini 1991 and Haegeman and Zanuttini 1996), and to lifelong gratitude and admiration on my part.

I will be addressing a question that is related to but distinct from the one discussed by Haegeman, namely whether information concerning the time and the location of the speaker is encoded in the syntax. I will do so by investigating utterances of a type that has not yet received much scrutiny from syntacticians, exemplified in (1):

(1) a. *Voilà Liliane.* (French)
　　b. *Ecco Liliane.* (Italian)
　　c. *Evo Liliane.* (Serbian)
　　d. *İşte Liliane.* (Turkish)
　　e. *Here's Liliane.* (English)

I refer to utterances of this type as PRESENTATIVES.[2] They have several remarkable properties, as I will highlight throughout the paper. One is that, regardless of whether they contain an overt locative and/or temporal element, they have a 'here and now' interpretation: the examples in (1), for instance, convey that Liliane is here now (perhaps she was not here earlier, or perhaps she was here but we were not aware of it). How do they get such an interpretation? It is not usually the case that sentences (or sentence fragments) convey this kind of information about time and location in the absence of overt material expressing it.

In this article, I focus on presentatives in Italian that contain *ecco*.[3] They may exhibit *ecco* followed by a noun phrase; in (2a) we see a lexical noun phrase, in (2b) a clitic:

(2) a. *Ecco　Liliane.* (Italian)
　　　　ecco　Liliane
　　　　'Here's Liliane.'
　　b. *Ecco-la.*
　　　　ecco-her
　　　　'Here she is.'

---

[2] Grammatical descriptions often mention 'presentative particles' (cf. Petit 2010, 2011; Julia 2016; Porhiel 2012, a.o.), elements like French *voici, voilà*, Latin *ecce, em*, etc. Petit (2010, 2011) points out that this label was first applied to the Biblical Hebrew particle *hinneh* and then used to refer to French *voici, voilà*. Following Wood et al. (2015), I will use the term *presentative* to refer to the entire utterance, not to the particle.

[3] I will not discuss *ecco* used as a discourse marker (cf. Bazzanella 1995 and De Cesare 2011), as in (i):
(i)　*La verità, ecco, non so se posso dirtela.* (Bazzanella 1995: 227)
　　　'The truth, well, I don't know if I can tell you that.'
In such cases, *ecco* is separated from the rest of the clause by an intonational break, and can occur in different positions within the utterance, with different discourse functions, which are not obviously related to that of presentatives.

They may also consist of *ecco* followed by a clause:[4]

(3) a. *Ecco   che   Liliane   scrive   un   altro   articolo.*
        ecco   that   Liliane   writes   an   other   article
        'Here's Liliane writing another article.'
    b. *Ecco   Liliane   che   scrive   un   altro   articolo.*
        ecco   Liliane   that   writes   an   other   article
        'Here's Liliane writing another article.'

I will focus on the syntax of presentatives in which *ecco* co-occurs with a noun phrase as a first step toward a deeper understanding of presentatives more generally.[5] I will argue that presentatives like those in (2) have more structure than meets the eye; in particular, they have clausal structure. They consist of a functional head T and a small clause complement, which has the noun phrase as the subject and a null locative as the predicate. The null T and the null locative get their interpretation from functional elements in the left periphery that encode the time and the location of the speaker. I take *ecco* to be the overt realization of such features in the left-periphery.

1.2 On the inadequacy of a simple solution

One might wonder whether it is necessary to postulate the presence of a null locative element and a null temporal element. Why not analyze *ecco*[6] as a locative (or temporal) element that functions as the predicate? If so, Italian presentatives would involve small clauses with predicate inversion:

---

4 Example (3b) contains a so-called pseudo-relative; see Cinque (1995: Ch. 8) and Casalicchio (2013). Casalicchio (2013: 2.5.3) contains an interesting discussion of *ecco* and points out that it takes the same range of complements as a perception verb: a DP, a finite clause, a pseudo-relative and an infinitival clause (*Ecco arrivare Elisa*, 'Here comes Elisa').
5 As pointed out in De Cesare (2010), *ecco* is more common in speech than in writing in Italian. I will translate it into English using *here's*, which is appropriate in informal contexts. But *ecco* can also be used in formal contexts, and in such cases *behold* would be a more appropriate English translation. For example, the ritual prayer said in preparation for communion during mass contains *ecco* in Italian and *behold* in English, as we see in (i) and (ii) below. In the gospel of John (1:29), this sentence has *ecco* in Italian and *behold*, *look* or *here's* in different English versions.
(i)   *Ecco l'agnello di Dio che toglie i peccati del mondo.*
(ii) *Behold the lamb of God who takes away the sins of the world.*
6 Etymologycally, *ecco* stems from Vulgar Latin *eccum*, in turn derived from Latin *ecce* 'behold' and *eum* 'him' (Rohlfs 1969: paragraphs 910, 911, 702). The origin of *ecce* can be traced to two deictic particles (*ed+k̂e) (Petit 2010). For a detailed study of Latin *ecce* and the Romance forms derived from it, see Adams (2013: 465–480).

(4) ecco   Liliane   ~~ecco~~
    ↑_____|

We cannot analyze *ecco* as a run-of-the-mill locative element because it does not exhibit the same distributional properties as other locative elements in Italian. In particular:

- *Ecco* can never occur in post-verbal position, in contrast with other locative elements. We can see this with a ditransitive verb like *mettere* 'put' in (5a), an intransitive verb like *abitare* 'live' in (5b), an unaccusative like *venire* 'come' in (5c), and a copula construction with a locative predicate in (5d):

(5) a. Ho   messo   la   giacca   qui   / nell'armadio   / *ecco.
       have   put   the   jacket   here   / in.the.closet   / *ecco
       'I put the jacket here / in the closet.'
    b. Abitano   qui   / in   questa   casa   / *ecco.
       live   here   / in   this   house   / *ecco
       'They live here/ in this house.'
    c. Veniamo   qui   / in questo   ristorante   / *ecco tutti i giorni.
       come   here   / in this   restaurant   / *ecco all the days
       'We come here / to this restaurant every day.'
    d. Le   tue   chiavi   sono   qui   / sulla   sedia   / *ecco.
       the   your   keys   are   here / on.the   chair   / *ecco
       'Your keys are here / on the chair.'

It cannot occur in pre-verbal position, either, again in contrast to other locative elements:

(6) a. Qui   / *ecco   noi   avevamo   messo   le   scatole   di   cartone.
       here   / *ecco   we   had   put   the   boxes   of   cardboard
       'Here we had put the cardboard boxes.'
    b. In   casa   / qui   / *ecco troverai   tutto   quello   che
       in   house   / here   / *ecco will.find   all   that   which
       ti   serve.
       to.you   serves
       'In the house / here you'll find everything you need.'

- *Ecco* cannot be used in a copula construction, unlike other locative predicates:

(7) a. Le   chiavi   sono   qui.
       'The keys   are   here.'
    b. *Le   chiavi   sono   ecco.

In fact, *ecco* does not co-occur with an overt verb (unless the overt verb is in the complement clause, as in [3]).

- *Ecco* cannot be modified by the elements that can modify adverbs, like *proprio*:

(8) a. *Abito   proprio   qui.*
       live   right   here
      'I live right here'
   b. **Proprio   ecco   le   chiavi.*
       right   ecco   the   keys

- *Ecco* cannot be used as a fragment answer to a question about location, again in contrast to other locatives:

(9) a. *Dove   le   hai   messe?*
       where them have put
      'Where did you put them?'
   b. *Qui. / Sul tavolo. / *Ecco.*
      'Here.' / 'On the table.'

The same tests also show that *ecco* does not behave like other temporal adverbs in Italian (not even like *adesso* 'now'). First, it cannot be used as a modifier of a predicate, either in situ or preposed. Second, it cannot be modified by the elements that can modify temporal adverbs (e.g. *proprio adesso* 'right now'). Third, it cannot be used as an answer to a *when* question:

(10) a. *Quando si riuniscono?*
        'When are they going to meet?'
    b. **Ecco.*

We might wonder whether perhaps *ecco* expresses both time and location. As we see in (11), it cannot be used as an answer to a question concerning both time and location:

(11) a. *Dove si riuniscono, e quando?*
        'Where are they meeting, and when?'
    b. **Ecco.*

For these reasons, I will not analyze *ecco* as a locative or temporal adverb. The challenge, then, lies in understanding what the syntactic analysis of presentatives is, how they get the interpretation of 'here and now' that characterizes them, whether *ecco* contributes to it and, if it does, how.

1.3 Roadmap

The article is organized as follows. I begin by characterizing the semantic and pragmatic contribution of Italian presentatives and discussing the felicity conditions that govern their occurrence (section 2). We will see that the noun phrase must denote an entity, or quantify over a set of entities, that were not in the attention sphere of the interlocutors, but whose existence is presupposed or can be inferred from the context. Then I examine the syntactic structure of Italian presentatives with *ecco* followed by a noun phrase (section 3). I argue that they have clausal structure, and in particular that they contain a temporal element and a locative predicate whose interpretation is restricted to the time and place of the speaker. The null temporal and locative elements are licensed by *ecco*, which I take to be the spell-out of features that provide information about the time and place of the utterance (section 4). I also discuss similarities and differences between presentatives and locative sentences with which (in some cases) they form minimal pairs (section 5). Finally, I provide a summary and frame the discussion in a broader context.

2 Restrictions on the noun phrase

Before we discuss the syntax of presentatives with *ecco* and a noun phrase, let us discuss the felicity conditions on their use. This will help us characterize their semantic and pragmatic contribution, and understand the discourse properties of the noun phrase.

Consider the presentatives in (12). Informally speaking, they are used to convey that the entity denoted by the noun phrase is now saliently present in the context of utterance:

(12) a. *Ecco Liliane.*
 'Here is Liliane.'
 b. *Ecco le chiavi.*
 ecco the keys
 'Here are the keys.'
 c. *Ecco una giacca.*
 ecco a jacket
 'Here's a jacket.'

The entity or entities whose presence is being pointed out need not be visible. They can be perceived through other senses, as in the examples below:

(13) a. *Ecco il caffè.* (said upon smelling coffee)
'Here's the coffee.'
b. *Ecco i primi ospiti.* (said upon hearing knocks on the door)
'Here are the first guests.'

In fact, such entities do not have to be perceivable to one of the senses; they can also be in the space of mental possibilities being contemplated.[7] For instance, (14) is felicitous in a context where the interlocutors have been discussing a problem that needs a solution, and (15) in one where they have been considering a number of possible ideas or ways to tackle an issue:

(14) *Ecco una possibile soluzione:*
ecco a possible solution
'Here's a possible solution: ...'

(15) *Ecco un'idea che mi piace.*
ecco an.idea that me pleases
'Here's an idea I like.' or 'There's an idea I like.'

Hence the entities denoted by the noun phrase must become present either in the physical space of the interlocutors, or in the space of possibilities that they are contemplating.

There seem to be felicity conditions associated with these utterances: the entity (or entities) denoted by the noun phrase must be a member of a set that has been evoked in the previous discourse ('disourse-old' in the terms of Prince 1992), or is somehow salient in the context. For example, (12a) is felicitous if the speaker was expecting to see Liliane or hear from her, and she arrives or calls.[8]

---

[7] This seems to be true of biblical Hebrew *hinne* as well, according to Sadka (2001: 481).
[8] If the speaker was not expecting to see the entity that enters the context, a presentative with *ecco* can be used only if preceded by a marker like *Oh!*:
(i) *Oh, ecco Liliane!*
(ii) *Oh, ecco le chiavi!* 'Oh, here are the keys.'
Informally, that *oh* seems to evoke a context in which the speaker was expecting Liliane, or was looking for his or her keys. The context was not salient at the moment of utterance, but *oh* brings it into the picture, and makes it salient. (I thank Martina Wiltschko for asking me probing questions that helped me realize this.)

Similarly, (12b) is felicitous if the speaker or the addressee have misplaced the keys, and now find them. As Larry Horn pointed out to me (personal communication), this example is evidence that the noun phrase does not necessarily have to refer to an entity that has been explicitly mentioned in the discourse – the existence of such an entity must have either been previously mentioned, or be inferrable from the context. For example, speaker and addressee might both know that one of them has misplaced their keys, and might utter (12b) in a situation where they have not been recently mentioned. For the utterance to be felicitous, though, that shared knowledge is essential; if the speaker simply happens to find a pair of keys that are not somehow salient, (12b) would not be felicitous. This suggests that the notion of 'discourse-old' relevant for these presentatives is one that includes information that can be inferred, as in Birner (2006).

This salience requirement holds regardless of whether the noun phrase is indefinite or definite. For instance, *Ecco una giacca* (12c) is felicitous only if the speaker or the addressee have been looking for a jacket, or for some set of items of which a jacket is a member (for example, warm clothes, or clues of someone's presence). The same holds if we take a proper name like *Obama*. We can safely assume that, when this article is being written, everyone is aware of the existence of President Obama; yet the following example is infelicitous if uttered out of the blue:

(16) #*Guarda, ecco   Obama.* (infelicitous if uttered out of the blue)
     look   ecco   Obama
     'Look, here's Obama!'

The utterance in (16) is felicitous only if Obama, or the possibility of seeing him, is salient either because it has been previously mentioned in the conversation, or because the speaker has been waiting for him (as a reporter might). This is in contrast with other ways of calling attention to the same entity, which are felicitous when uttered out of the blue, as in (17):

(17) a. *Guarda, Obama!*
        'Look, Obama!'
     b. *Guarda,   c'è   Obama!*
        look   there.is   Obama
        'Look, Obama is there!'

I take the contrast between (16) and (17) to confirm that, in presentatives with *ecco*, the noun phrase must refer to an entity that is not discourse-new.

This conclusion helps us explain which noun phrases can and which cannot occur in presentatives. *Ecco* can co-occur with certain quantified noun phrases, as we see in (18):

(18) a. *Ecco   tutti   i   miei   amici.*
        ecco   all   the   my   friends
        'Here are all my friends.'
    b. *Ecco   molti   dei   miei   libri.*
        ecco   many   of.the   my   books
        'Here are many of my books.'

However, it cannot occur with certain bare quantifiers, or indefinites, like those in (19):

(19) a. #*Ecco   qualcuno.*
         ecco   someone
    b. #*Ecco   qualcosa.*
         ecco   something

The ungrammaticality of these examples is now expected: if the entity or set of entities introduced by the noun phrase must be discourse-old (cf. Birner 2006), then indefinites like 'someone' or 'something' are predicted to be impossible, at least when used to introduce new entities. Indeed, examples like those in (19) become acceptable if we manipulate the context. For example, if the speaker is expecting people to arrive, he or she can say *Ecco qualcuno!* 'Here's someone!' upon hearing some noise. In this case, *qualcuno* picks out an individual whose identity is not known, but who is a member of a set that is salient in the context, and the utterance is acceptable.

Because they share several properties, it is worth comparing presentatives with existential and locative sentences. I will devote section 5 to a comparison with the latter, so I will mention only the former here. As is well known, existential sentences can be used to assert the existence of an entity or set of entities. For instance, the sentences in (20) can be used to assert the existence of the entities denoted by the noun phrases that follow the copula *sono*:

(20) a. *Ci   sono   delle   persone   che   si   lamentano   sempre.*
        there   are   some   people   that   self   complain   always
        'There are people who complain all the time.'
    b. *Ci   sono   tanti   tipi   di   mele.*
        there   are   many   types   of   apples
        'There are many kinds of apples.'

c. Ci　　 sono　 degli　 angeli　 che　 ci　 proteggono.
　　　 there　 are　 some　 angels　 that　 us　 protect
　　　 'There are angels that protect us.'

Presentatives differ sharply from existential sentences in that they cannot be used to assert the existence of some entity or entities (either in general or in some unspecified location).[9] In contrast to the examples in (20), those in (21) do not convey that the entities denoted by the noun phrases exist, but rather that they are present at the time and place of the utterance:

(21) a. *Ecco　 delle　 persone　 che　 si　 lamentano　 sempre.*
　　　 ecco　 some　 people　 that　 self　 complain　 always
　　　 'Here are some people who complain all the time.'
　　b. *Ecco　 tanti　 tipi　 di　 mele.*
　　　 ecco　 many　 types　 of　 apples
　　　 'Here are many kinds of apples.'
　　c. *Ecco　 degli　 angeli　 che　 ci　 proteggono.*
　　　 ecco　 some　 angels　 that　 us　 protect
　　　 'Here are some angels that protect us.'

In sum, the pragmatic function of *ecco* followed by a noun phrase is that of bringing to the attention of the addressee the presence of an entity (or entities) in the context of utterance. Such entities can be introduced with a definite or indefinite noun phrase, or with a quantificational element, as long as they have been previously evoked or can be inferred from the context (they are "familiar topics" in the terms of Frascarelli and Hinterhölzl 2007; "referential topics" in the terms used in Cruschina 2012: 80–81, note 3, and references therein).

---

9 In addition to this stark difference in interpretation, presentatives and existential sentences also differ in that existentials can be negated (i) and embedded (ii), whereas presentatives cannot (as we see in (iii) and (iv)):
(i)　 *Non　 ci　 sono　 angeli　 che　 ci　 proteggono.* (existential, negated)
　　 neg　 there　 are　 angels　 that　 us　 protect
　　 'There are no angels who protect us.'
(ii)　 *Lui　 è　 convinto　 che　 ci　 siano　 angeli　 che　 ci　 proteggono.*
　　 (existential, embedded)
　　 he　 is　 convinced　 that　 there　 are　 angels　 who　 us　 protect
　　 'He's convinced that there are angels who protect us.'
(iii)　**Non　 ecco　 gli　 angeli　 che　 ci　 proteggono.* (presentative, negated)
　　 neg　 ecco　 the　 angels　 that　 us　 protect
(iv)　**Lui　 è　 convinto　 che　 ecco　 gli　 angeli　 che　 ci　 proteggono.*
　　 (presentative, embedded)
　　 he　 is　 convinced　 that　 ecco　 the　 angels　 who　 us　 protect
The impossibility of being negated and embedded sets presentatives apart not only from existentials, but also from other types of clauses (cf. Lakoff 1987), and makes them similar to imperatives.

3 The structure of presentatives with *ecco*

The presentatives under investigation exhibit *ecco* followed by a noun phrase (DP or QP). In this section, I will argue that they also contain a null functional head T and a null locative predicate, which provide the time and location of the speaker. I will propose that they have a restricted interpretation because they receive their value from a temporal and a locative feature syntactically encoded in the left periphery of the clause.

My proposal consists of several independent components that I will introduce one at a time, both to highlight their independence and to make the exposition clearer.

3.1 Evidence for the presence of T

Based on evidence from pronominal clitics, I will make the following proposal:

Proposal 1: The structure of presentatives contains the functional head T.

As is well known, Italian has both strong and clitic pronouns.[10] In presentatives, strong pronouns follow *ecco* as independent phonological words:

(22) *Ecco* **me** *quando avevo cinque anni.*
 ecco me.acc when had five years
 'Here's me when I was five years old.'

Clitic pronouns, in contrast, cliticize onto *ecco*:

(23) *Ecco-**mi**.* / *Ecco-**ti**.* / *Ecco-**la**.*
 ecco-me / ecco-you / ecco-her
 'Here I am.' / 'Here you are.' / 'Here she is.'

Since the seminal work of Kayne's (Kayne 1981, 1989, 1990, 1991), a widely accepted assumption about Italian clitics is that they are adjoined to a functional head in the inflectional domain of the clause.[11] Hence I propose that presentatives have a T head to which pronominal clitics are adjoined.[12]

---

10 See Kayne (1975) for an early, foundational study of the systematic differences between strong and clitic pronouns in French, and Cardinaletti and Starke (1999) for a more recent and broader investigation of the properties of different classes of pronouns in French, Italian, and a number of other languages.
11 The proclitic versus enclitic order is taken to result from different extents of verb movement (Kayne 1991), with non-finite verbal forms raising to a higher position than finite verbal forms.
12 Another possibility would be that clitics are adjoined to a functional head in the left periphery of the clause, like the heads proposed for phenomena that highlight the role of the speaker, such as the Speaker head in Giorgi (2010), or the Speech Act head in Haegeman and Hill (2013), Haegeman (2014), Hill (2014).

Assuming that the structure of the presentatives contains T makes the presence of clitics unremarkable. What is still puzzling is that clitics always lean on verbal elements in Italian,[13] but here they lean onto *ecco*, which does not look like a verb: it does not exhibit the morphological properties that characterize finite or non-finite verbs (like tense and agreement marking; infinitival, participial, or gerundival morphology).[14] Might *ecco* be a a verb despite the lack of verbal morphology? Two pieces of evidence (independent of the behavior of clitics) suggest that it might be. The first one, pointed out in Casalicchio (2013), is that *ecco* takes the same range of complements as perceptual verbs:

(24) a. *Ecco / vedo   / sento   Maria.*
     ecco   / see.1SG   / hear.1SG   Maria
     'Here's Maria', 'I see/hear Maria.'
   b. *Ecco / vedo   / sento   Maria   che   sale   le   scale.*
     ecco   / see.1SG   / hear.1SG   Maria   that   climbs   the   stairs
     'Here's Maria.', 'I see/hear Maria climbing the stairs.'
   c. *Ecco / vedo   / sento   Maria   ubriaca.*
     ecco   / see.1SG   / hear.1SG   Maria   drunk
     'Here's Maria drunk.', 'I see/hear Maria drunk.'

The second piece of evidence is that a strong pronoun following *ecco* bears accusative case, as we saw in (22).[15] In many approaches to Case, this suggests that the structure contains an element with verbal features. In light of these considerations, I propose that we see *ecco* as a defective verb that only has an invariant form.[16]

---

13 Though clitic pronouns always cliticize onto verbs in Italian and many other well-known Romance languages, there is at least one variety of Romance where they also cliticize onto the past participle and on certain prepositions: Borgomanerese, spoken in Northern Italy and described extensively in Tortora (2014).
14 So-called "true imperatives" also lack tense marking and infinitival, participial, or gerundival morphology. They consist of a verbal root and a thematic vowel, which can be -*a* or -*i*, hence they differ from *ecco* in their morphology.
15 Default case is nominative (and not accusative) in Italian.
16 Italian has other defective verbs, such as *bisogna* (cf. Benincá and Poletto 1994) and *fa* (cf. Benincà et al. to appear), so *ecco* would not be the only one. Morin (1985) views French *voici* and *voilà* as invariant forms of a finite verb – present indicative forms (cf. also Bouchard 1988 and Morin 1988). The -*o* ending of *ecco* could be analyzed by today's speakers as the first person singular morpheme of present tense indicative forms; but it could also be taken to be a default word marker, along the lines of Harris (1991). A wild speculation would be that *ecco* contains more than one morpheme: *e*-, a form of *essere* 'be', plus -*cco*, which could in turn consist of the locative morpheme -*c*- (as in the clitic locative form *ci*) plus the -*o* ending. I leave this as an unsupported speculation for now. Note that the Indoeuropeanist A. L. Prosdocimi studied Latin *ecce* and a colloquial imperative form (*cetto*) and proposed that *ecce* be viewed as an imperative with an incorporated locative (Paola Benincà, personal communication). Indeed, Casalicchio (2013) views Italian *ecco* as an imperative form.

3.2 Evidence for an indexical temporal element

The presentatives under discussion are interpreted as conveying that the entity denoted by the noun phrase is present at the time of the utterance. For example, if a speaker is on the phone and her children (somehow salient) arrive, she can utter (25) meaning that they entered the context where she is, at the time of the utterance:

(25) *Ecco   i   ragazzi.*
      ecco   the   kids
      'Here are the kids.'

In other words, presentatives are interpreted as if they contained an indexical element that is interpreted as simultaneous to the utterance time, like *adesso* 'now'.[17]

I propose that we capture the restricted temporal interpretation of presentatives as follows:[18]

Proposal 2: In presentatives, the functional head T is an indexical element.

The similarity between the temporal interpretation of presentatives and that of sentences containing an indexical temporal expression goes one step further. There is one case where indexicals are not interpreted in relation to the time of

---

17 Languages often exhibit both *indexical* and *anaphoric* temporal elements: the former can only get their interpretation from the context of utterance, while the latter can get it from the linguistic context. To exemplify this distinction, consider the contrast between an indexical like *domani* 'tomorrow' and an anaphoric temporal element like *il giorno dopo*, 'the day after' (Giorgi 2010):
(i) *Gianni disse   che   sarebbe   partito   il   giorno   dopo.*
     Gianni said   that   would.be   left   the   day   after
     'Gianni said that he would leave the next day.'
(ii) *Gianni disse   che   sarebbe   partito   domani.*
     Gianni said   that   would.be   left   tomorrow
     'Gianni said that he would leave tomorrow.'
The anaphoric temporal expression *il giorno dopo* is interpreted with respect to the time of Gianni's speaking (if he spoke on December 25, it picks out December 26, even though the speaker might utter the sentence on December 30). In contrast, the indexical temporal expression *domani* 'tomorrow' is interpreted with respect to the time of the speaker; so, if the speaker utters the sentence on December 30, the indexical *domani* picks out December 31.
18 One reviewer suggests that we should test whether presentatives are compatible with *adesso* 'now': assuming that a temporal adverb can only merge in the presence of a TP, that would be evidence for postulating a null T. Presentatives with *adesso* are natural if they can be interpreted as pointing to a contrast between now and another point in time; for example, looking at two pictures of Liliane, it would be possible to say:
(i) *Ecco Liliane adesso e quando era piccola.*
     'Here's Liliane now and when she was a child.'

the utterance: Free Indirect Discourse. This is a style in which the narrative takes the point of view of one of the characters in the story, as if that character had become the speaker/writer. As pointed out in the literature on this topic (Banfield 1982; Doron 1991; Schlenker 2004; Guéron 2006, 2007; Giorgi 2010; Eckardt 2015), in this style the verb is in the past tense, the character that is narrating is identified by means of a third person pronoun, and spatial and temporal indexicals are interpreted in relation to the coordinates of that character (and not in relation to the spatial and temporal coordinates of the writer of the sentence). We see this in the following examples, from Giorgi (2010: 183–185):

(26) a. *It was, **he** now realized, because of this other incident that he had suddenly decided to come home and begin the diary **today**.* (Orwell, *1984*, New York, Penguin, Ch.1)
b. ***Tomorrow** was Monday, Monday, the beginning of another school week.* (Lawrence, *Women in Love*, London, Heinemann, 1971: 185)

As discussed in Giorgi (2010), narratives in Free Indirect Discourse in Italian exhibit the same characteristics as they do in English, with the verb in the past tense (the imperfect), the main character referred to with a third person pronoun, and spatial and temporal indexicals interpreted in relation to the coordinates of that character (the 'internal source', in Giorgi's terms).

Interestingly, in Free Indirect Discourse presentatives with *ecco* behave like indexicals: their temporal interpretation is shifted to the time of the character that assumes the role of narrating:

(27) *Stava passeggiando in silenzio, da sola. **Ecco** un momento di pace.*
'She was strolling in silence, alone. Here was a moment of peace.'

In this case, the moment of peace is not at the time of the utterance, but rather at the time when the character was walking in silence. The proposal that presentatives contain a temporal indexical allows me to capture their restricted temporal interpretation and the fact that, in Free Indirect Discourse, their interpretation shifts.

The most straightforward way of expressing the interpretative restriction of a temporal indexical would be to invoke what is called a "context parameter", which can be thought of as an n-tuple, $< c_t, c_l, c_w >$, where c_t, c_l, c_w are, respectively, the time, the location, and the world of the context c.[19] The restriction on the interpretation of T in presentatives could then be stated as a semantic restriction

---

[19] Information concerning the speaker and addressee might also be included.

that does not have a syntactic representation: we can say that the temporal value of T must coincide with the temporal value provided by the context parameter.

Alternatively, the restriction on the temporal interpretation of presentatives could be seen as rooted in their syntactic representation. As mentioned in the introduction, a significant body of recent literature addresses the question of whether any of the coordinates of the context parameter (time, location, speaker and addressee) are represented in the syntax. Let me review briefly the proposals by Sigurðsson (2004, 2014) and Giorgi (2010), which concern time/tense (time's grammatical representation) and location.

Sigurðsson (2004, 2014) argues that all the elements of the context parameter are encoded in the syntax as features in the left periphery of the clause. In his view, there are features concerning the time of the utterance, T_s (S stands for 'speech event') and the location of the utterance or speech event, L_s, as well as features for the speaker and the addressee. Sigurðsson (2014: 178) proposes that T_s and L_s correspond to Fin, which, as the lowest category in the CP layer, appears above TP but below TopicP (Rizzi 1997).

Giorgi (2010) also proposes that the time of the utterance event is encoded in the syntax, in the CP layer. She discusses two cases. One is that of clauses (such as 'John said that Mary is pregnant') that exhibit a so-called 'double access reading', by which the eventuality denoted by the embedded clause (Mary's pregnancy) needs to hold both at the time of the utterance (when the speaker is uttering the sentence) and at the time of the reported speech event (when John is speaking). For her, the characteristic property of these sentences is that the CP layer encodes what she calls the 'coordinates of the speaker', that is, information about the speaker's time and location. The other case concerns Free Indirect Discourse, where indexicals are interpreted not with respect to the speaker or writer of the sentence, but to that of the character that is leading the narration, as we saw above. For these cases as well, she invokes a layer of structure that she calls the "informational layer", at the left of the C-layer, where the information concerning the speaker or writer is replaced with the information concerning the character doing the narration. In Giorgi's (2010) terms, in these cases the syntax encodes either the speaker's coordinates or, in the case of narratives in Free Indirect Discourse, the coordinates of the internal source.

Building on these proposals, I suggest that we view the T of presentatives as dependent on some element in the left periphery that encodes the time of the utterance (in Giorgi's terms, the time coordinates of the speaker). Both Sigurðsson and Giorgi envision such an element as a feature of one of the functional heads that make up CP, though they do not discuss empirical or theoretical evidence in support of associating this feature with a particular functional head. Because I also lack evidence to determine its exact structural position, I will leave this issue open: it might be a feature within CP, or a feature in a functional layer above CP, which brings in contextual information. I will represent it as c_T:

(28)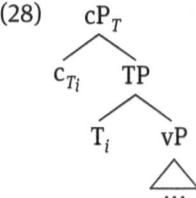

Note that I am postulating that Italian presentatives have a T head that never has phonetic content and is always dependent for its interpretation on the temporal value of the context parameter. In this respect, it is reminiscent of PRO, which also lacks phonetic content and is referentially dependent on its antecedent. Livitz (2014) proposes that the silent nature of PRO is not an intrinsic property of this element, but rather a result of its syntactic properties. She argues that pronouns that are referentially dependent on a sufficiently local antecedent are featurally and structurally deficient, consisting of only a bundle of unvalued ø-features, and that this structural deficiency forces them to enter an Agree relation to acquire their values, while also allowing them to be silent (because their features are a subset of the features of the probe). Along these lines, we can think of the T of presentatives as a structurally deficient T, which is forced to enter an Agree relation with a higher head that values its features and allows it to remain silent.

3.3 The locative component

In addition to a characteristic temporal interpretation, presentatives also have a characteristic locative interpretation, namely 'in the same context as the speaker'. I will argue that they contain a locative element, as follows:[20]

    Proposal 3: Presentatives contain the locative [DEM reinf/REINF PLACE].

When an overt locative phrase is present, it is separated from what precedes it by an intonational break, similar to the break that separates a right dislocated element from the rest of the clause:

(29) a. *Ecco le   chiavi, per terra.*
       ecco the keys   for ground
      'Here are the keys, on the ground.'

---

20 The notation follows the convention of using small caps to indicate a phonetically null element.

b. *Ecco   la   giacca   di   Gabriele,   sulla   sedia.*
   ecco the jacket   of   Gabriel   on.the   chair
   'There is Gabriel's jacket, on the chair.'

I take this as evidence that the overt locatives, when present, are adjuncts that provide additional information. Indeed the examples in (29) convey that the entity under discussion is in the same location as the speaker, with the overt locative specifying where exactly it is.

The postulation of a null locative element also finds indirect support in the fact that presentatives with *ecco* can exhibit an overt *qui* 'here' (also *qua, lì, là*, which indicate proximity to or distance from the speaker), as shown in (30):

(30) a. *Ecco **qui**   le   chiavi,   per   terra.*
        ecco here   the   keys   for   ground
        'Here are the keys, on the ground.'
     b. *Ecco **qui**   la   giacca   di   Gabriele,   sulla   sedia.*
        ecco here   the jacket   of   Gabriel   on-the   chair
        'Here is Gabriel's jacket, on the chair.'

Let me explain why. Outside of presentatives, in Italian, *qui* can occur alone with a locative interpretation, as in (31a), or with noun phrases introduced by demonstratives, as in (31b):

(31) a. *Abito   **qui**.*
        live   here
        'I live here.'
     b. *questo   libro   **qui***
        this   book   here
        'this here book'

I will adopt the proposal put forth in Kayne (2004) for the English counterparts of these elements, which takes them as being reinforcers of some (possibly null) noun. For Kayne, even when English *here* and *there* have a locative interpretation, as in (32), they are not to be analyzed as locatives themselves, but rather as reinforcers of an unpronounced noun. That is, they are the same kind of reinforcers as the ones that we find co-occurring with demonstratives in the nonstandard English constructions discussed in Bernstein (1997), given in (33):

(32) *I live **here** and she lives **there**.*

(33) a. *this **here** book, these **here** books*
     b. *that **there** book, those **there** books*

Kayne proposes that the English locatives *here* and *there* correspond to a more complex structure, with an unpronounced noun and an unpronounced demonstrative. Using PLACE to indicate the unpronounced noun and THIS, THAT to represent the unpronounced demonstrative, he proposes that locative *here* and *there* have the structure indicated in (34):[21]

(34) a. THIS *here* PLACE
    b. THAT *there* PLACE

Adopting this analysis, I propose that in Italian, too, locatives consist of a null demonstrative, a null noun corresponding to PLACE, and an overt reinforcer, which I represent as in (35a) or, more abstractly, as in (35b):[22]

(35) a. QUESTO   *qui*   POSTO
       THIS   here   PLACE
    b. DEM reinf PLACE

Hence a declarative like (31a) contains a complex locative element consisting of a null demonstrative, a null noun and a phonetically overt reinforcer, most likely introduced by a null P:[23]

(36) *Abito*   [P   DEM   *qui*   PLACE]
     live   [P   DEM   here PLACE]
     'I live here.'

Turning back to presentatives, I propose that they also contain a locative constituent that consists of a null demonstrative, a null noun corresponding to place, and a reinforcer. What is special is that, in presentatives, the reinforcer has the option of being null.

Moreover, I propose that the locative constituent and the noun phrase merge and form a small clause that has the noun phrase (DP or QP) as the subject and the locative as the predicate:[24]

(37) [$_{\text{Small Clause}}$ XP$_{\text{Subject}}$ YP$_{\text{Locative Predicate}}$]

---

21 Movement operations then alter the underlying order, but they are not strictly relevant to the present discussion and I will not describe them here.
22 Once again, I will omit discussion of further movements, as they are not strictly relevant.
23 The reinforcers in Italian are *qui, qua, lì* and *là*, corresponding to English 'here' and 'there'. I will continue to limit my examples to *qui* for simplicity.
24 In presentatives where *ecco* is followed by a clause, the clause will be the subject and the locative the predicate.

3.4 Restrictions on the locative interpretation

In presentatives, the location is always interpreted in relation to the speaker. If the subject refers to an entity, it is interpreted as being present in the context where the speaker is (38a); if the reinforcer is overt, it specifies whether the entity is close to (38b) or distant from the speaker (38c):

(38) a. *Ecco Liliane.*
    b. *Ecco qui   Liliane.*
       'Here's   Liliane.'
    c. *Ecco là   Liliane.*
       'There's Liliane.'

This interpretive restriction is not simply a subjective impression. Kandel (2015) devised and conducted a small but carefully designed experimental study and showed that, even when two locations are equally available from the context, the one near the speaker is favored. I will express this as the following component of my proposal:

> Proposal 4: The locative predicate in presentatives is an indexical element.

Indeed, the locative predicate in presentatives always has an indexical interpretation and cannot have an anaphoric one, unlike other locatives. This can be seen in the examples that follow:

(39) Speaker A to Speaker B, in a context that is not B's home:
    Ho sentito che hai ospiti a casa.
    'I heard that you have guests at home.'

Speaker B can follow up with a locative sentence like (40), providing further information concerning the guests who are at home. However, B could not felicitously use a presentative:

(40) *Ci   sono   i   miei   genitori   e   mia   sorella.* (locative sentence)
     there are   the   my   parents   and   my   sister
    'My parents and my sister are there.'

(41) #*Ecco   i   miei   genitori   e   mia   sorella.* (presentative)
     ecco   the   my   parents   and   my   sister
    'Here're my parents and my sister.'

This shows that the locative sentence in (40) can be interpreted with the location interpreted as corresponding to the one previously introduced in the discourse ('My parents and my sister are at home') – anaphorically. In contrast, the presentative in (41) cannot: even though the previous context explicitly mentioned a location, the presentative can only be interpreted as saying that the parents and sister are near the speaker (thus it is not an appropriate follow up to (39), as it does not provide information concerning the guests who are at home). In other words, while the location can be interpreted anaphorically in a locative sentence like (40), it can only be interpreted indexically in a presentative. This is encoded in Proposal 4.

Viewing the locative of presentatives as an indexical makes a prediction: since the interpretation of indexicals shifts in Free Indirect Discourse narratives, the locative interpretation of presentatives should also shift in those contexts. Indeed, it does: in narratives, the location is interpreted with respect to the place where the character leading the narration is, and not the place where the speaker is speaking or the writer is writing.

As we discussed in the case of T, there is more than one way to account for this restriction. It could be stated as a semantic restriction that does not necessarily have a syntactic representation: we can say that the value of the null locative predicate in presentatives must coincide with the locative value provided by the context parameter ($< c_t, c_l, c_w >$).

Alternatively, we might think that this locative predicate gets its reference from an element that encodes the location of the speaker in the syntactic structure. This could be a single functional head that brings in the speaker's coordinates for time and location, as in Giorgi (2010), or two independent heads, each of which brings in one piece of information, as in Sigurðsson (2014).

Building on these proposals (as I did in the case of T), I suggest that we view the null locative of presentatives as dependent for its interpretation on some element in the left periphery that encodes the location of the speaker. This element might be a feature in the articulated structure of CP or in a higher functional layer. I will represent it as c_L, and indicate its relation with the locative predicate as one of co-indexation:

(42) c_{Lj} [T_i [$_{Small\ Clause}$ XP$_{Subject}$ YP$_{Locative\ Prdicate\ j}$]]

The structure in (42) gives us the base position of the subject and the predicate of the small clause contained in a presentative, but does not say anything about *ecco*, or about how we derive the word order that we see in the data. For example, in (43) we see that the locative reinforcer precedes the subject of the small clause if it is lexical, but follows it if it is a clitic pronoun:

(43) a. *Ecco* **qui** *Liliane.*
    ecco here Liliane
    'Here's Liliane.'

b. *Ecco-la   qui.*
   ecco-her   here
   'Here she is.'

I will address the status of *ecco* in section 4 and the word order issues in section 5.

4 What is *ecco*?

Earlier I pointed out that *ecco* behaves like a verb in being able to host pronominal clitics and taking the same range of complements as perception verbs, but differs from a verb in that it is an invariant form lacking any marking for tense, aspect or agreement. Here I suggest that, in addition to having verbal features, *ecco* also spells out the temporal and locative feature of *c*. I view it as a defective verb that starts out in *v* and raises to *c*.

The features c_L and c_T bring in information concerning the time and place of the speaker and restrict the temporal and locative interpretation of the sentence. They may reside on two distinct functional heads[25] or on one, perhaps as a result of movement, as in the structure in (44):

(44)
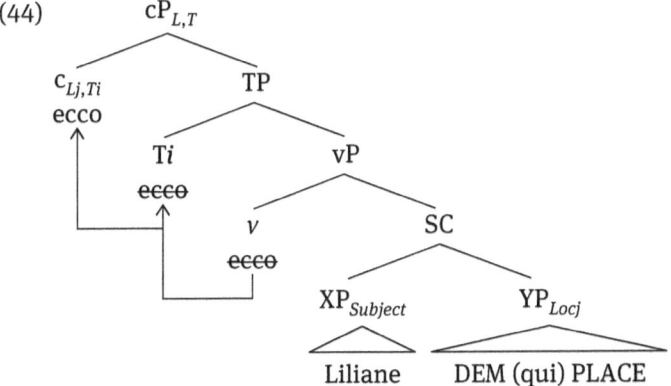

---

25 A single morpheme that spells out multiple adjacent heads would be an instance of "spanning" in the terms of Williams (2003), Svenonius (2012), Merchant (2015).

In this view, *ecco* takes as its complement a small clause, whose subject can be a noun phrase or a clause.[26] This way of thinking about *ecco* nicely captures the intuition that its semantic contribution comprises both a temporal and a locative component – 'here and now'. When it co-occurs with a noun phrase, even if it does not denote a concrete, tangible object, as in (45), the interpretation is that the entity denoted by the noun phrase is present in the context where the speaker is:

(45) a. *Ecco   il   fischio   dell'arbitro.*
         ecco   the   whistle   of.the.referee
         'Here's the referee's whistle.'
     b. *Ecco   il   canto   della   civetta.*
         ecco   the   singing   of.the   owl
         'Here's the owl's call.'

Similarly, when *ecco* takes a finite clause, both a locative and a temporal meaning are clearly present. The examples in (46) convey that a certain state of affairs holds here and now:[27]

(46) a. *Ecco   che   i   presidenti   si   stringono   la   mano.*
         ecco   that   the   presidents   self   squeeze   the   hand
         'The presidents are shaking hands here and now.'
     b. *Ecco   che   si   mette   a   piovere.*
         ecco   that   self   starts   to   rain. INF
         'It's starting to rain here and now.'

In section 6 I will return briefly to the status of *ecco*, and compare it to other elements that have been argued to occur in a layer of syntactic structure higher than CP.

---

26 Hill (2014: Ch.5) examines particles of direct address with injunctive and ostensive function in Romanian. She argues that, though they have verbal features, they do not originate in V or v but rather in the left-periphery of the clause: they are the spell-out of Speech Act heads. The Romanian particles *na* and *uite* seem particularly similar to Italian *ecco* because of their presentational function, though they differ in being able to take imperatives as their complement (*ecco* may co-occur with an imperative clause, but only with an intonational break separating the two). Hill (2014) analyzes *na* as selecting an imperative clause; when the imperative contains the verb for 'take', the verb can be deleted, and *na* can host a pronominal clitic; but *na* itself is said to have no argument structure and no TP field. Similarly, *uite* is analyzed as selecting an imperative with the verb for 'look'; when the verb is deleted, the particle is the host for the clitic.
27 In a narrative, the proposition is interpreted as holding at the time of the narrated event, as also noted in Casalicchio (2013). We see an example below, from the Gospel of Matthew:
(i) *E Gesù, emesso un alto grido, spirò. Ed ecco il velo del tempio si squarciò in due.* (Matteo, 27: 50-51) 'Then Jesus shouted out again, and released his spirit. And behold, the curtain of the temple was torn in two.'

5 Comparison with locative sentences

I will now further probe the syntax of presentatives by comparing them with locative sentences that in some respects form a minimal pair with them: "locative ci-sentences" (Cruschina 2012).

Italian has two types of locative sentences. One consists of a noun phrase, a form of the copula and a locative element:

(47) a. *Maria è   in   giardino.*
    Maria is in garden
    'Maria is in the garden.'
  b. *Mio papà è   in   cucina.*
    my   dad   is in kitchen
    'My dad is in the kitchen.'

The other consists of a noun phrase, a form of the copula, the clitic pronoun *ci* 'there' and an optional locative element:

(48) a. *C'è   Maria   (in giardino).*
    there.is   Maria   in garden
    'Maria is in the garden.'
  b. *C'è   mio   papà   (in cucina).*
    there.is   my   father in kitchen
    'My father is in the kitchen.'

Cruschina (2012) labels sentences like (48) locative *ci*-sentences. Though they resemble existential sentences, they differ from them in being able to have a definite noun phrase (Moro 1997a; Zucchi 1995; Zamparelli 2000), and having a clearly locative interpretation.

The presentatives we have been examining resemble locative *ci*-sentences in being able to have a definite noun phrase and having a locative interpretation. However, they also exhibit some interesting differences. I will devote this section to examining two of these differences:

1. Locative *ci*-sentences can introduce new entities:

(49) a. *Senti!   C'è   qualcuno   alla   porta. (locative ci-sentence)*
    listen   there.is   someone   at.the   door
    'Listen! There's someone at the door.'
  b. *Guarda!   C'è   una   volpe   in giardino!*
    loo   there.is   a   fox   in garden
    'Look! There's a fox in the yard.'

In contrast, as we discussed in section 2, presentatives cannot:

(50) a. *Senti!* **Ecco qualcuno alla porta.* (presentative)
  listen ecco someone at.the door
  b. *Guarda!* **Ecco una volpe in giardino!*
  look ecco a fox in garden

Sentences like those in (50) can be used felicitously only if the previous discourse context contains mention of someone being expected, or of an animal in the backyard, as in (51):

(51) a. *Gli ospiti dovrebbero cominciare ad arrivare. (...) Ecco qualcuno alla porta.*
  'The guests should be about to arrive. (...) Here's someone at the door.'
  b. *A volte degli animali arrivano fino a qui, e vengono in giardino a cercar da mangiare. (...) Ecco una volpe in giardino!*
  'Sometimes animals come all the way here and come inside our backyard looking for something to eat. (...) Here's a fox in our yard!'

The noun phrase that follows *ecco*, even when indefinite, must pick out an entity whose existence has been previously mentioned or can be inferred from the context.

2. Locative *ci*-sentences are appropriate answers to questions concerning the nominal element, while presentatives are not:

(52) a. *Chi c'è?*
  who there.is
  'Who's there?'
  b. *C'è Gianni (in cucina).* (locative *ci*-sentence)
  there.is Gianni (in kitchen).'
  'Gianni (in the kitchen).'
  c. **Ecco Gianni.* (presentative)

(53) a. *Cosa c'è in garage?*
  what there.is in garage
  'What's in the garage?'
  b. *Ci sono le macchine di Maria e Gianni.* (locative *ci*-sentence)
  there are the cars of Maria and Gianni
  'Maria's and Gianni's cars.'
  c. **Ecco le macchine di Maria e Gianni.* (presentative)
  ecco the cars of Mary and Gianni

Presentatives can answer questions concerning the location of an entity (or the time of an event), directly or indirectly, something that locative *ci*-sentences cannot do:

(54) a. *Dove   sono   le   chiavi?*
        where   are   the   keys
        'Where are the keys?'
   b. *Eccole.* 'Here they are.' (presentative)
   c. **Ci   sono   (qui / in cucina).* (locative *ci*-sentence)
       there   are   (here / in kitchen)

(55) a. *A   che   ora   arriva   Gianni?*
        at   what   time   arrives   Gianni
        'At what time will Gianni get here?'
   b. *Eccolo.* 'Here he is.' (presentative)
      **C'è   (qui   / in cucina).* (locative *ci*-sentence)
       there.is (here   / in kitchen)

In sum: the entity denoted by the noun phrase is new in locative *ci*-sentences, old in presentatives; the information concerning location is old in locative *ci*-sentences, new in presentatives.

Let us start from the analysis of locative sentences of the type exemplified in (47). Following Moro (1997b, 2000), we assume that they contain a small clause with *Maria* as the subject and *in giardino* as the predicate, and that the subject raises to a subject position higher than the copula. Next consider the locative *ci*-sentences in (48). Cruschina (2012) (building on Moro 2009) proposes a derivation in which the subject of the small clause movs to a clause-internal FocusP:

(56)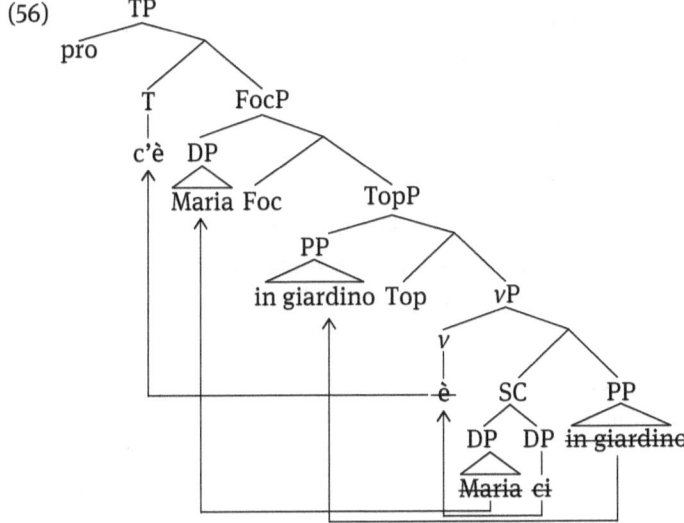

Now we turn to the presentatives under investigation. I propose a derivation that is similar to the one for a locative *ci*-sentence, but with one crucial difference: in the case of presentatives it is the locative predicate, not the subject, that moves to a clause-internal FocusP:

(57)

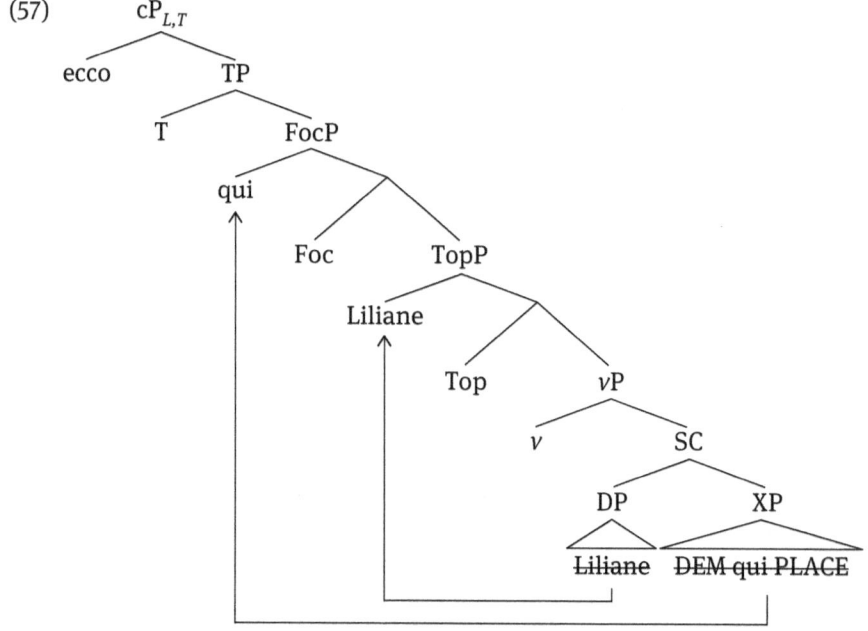

This derivation can account for the two properties of presentatives we highlighted earlier. (i) The fact that the noun phrase must be discourse-old is captured by viewing it structurally as a topic (it moves to the specifier of TopicP). (ii) The fact that the information concerning the location is new follows if the locative predicate is focused (it moves to the specifier of FocusP). This derivation also accounts for the fact that non-specific indefinites (like 'someone, something') are not possible, as we saw in (19): they could not possibly be topics.

Moreover, it accounts for the word order we see in presentatives, in particular the different position exhibited by the noun phrase when it is lexical and when it is a clitic pronoun. When the reinforcer *qui* is overt, a lexical noun phrase follows it (*ecco – qui –* lexical DP), as in (58):

(58) *Ecco* **qui** *Liliane.*
     ecco here Liliane
     'Here's Liliane.'

In contrast, a clitic precedes the reinforcer *qui* (*ecco* – clitic – *qui*), as in (59):

(59) a. *Ecco-**la** qui.*
　　　 ecco-her　here
　　　 'Here she is.'
　 b. *Ecco-**ne** qui tre.*
　　　 ecco-PART　here　three
　　　 'Here's three of them.'

This contrast in word order follows straightforwardly from the structure assigned to presentatives, in combination with independently established differences between lexical noun phrases and clitic pronouns: the former can stay low in the structure (in presentatives, they move to the specifier of the low TopicP projection); the latter are structurally higher, adjoined to T. If the reinforcer *qui* is in the specifier of the FocusP, it is in a position lower than a clitic but higher than a lexical noun phrase, hence it will follow a clitic but precede a lexical noun phrase in linear order:

(60)

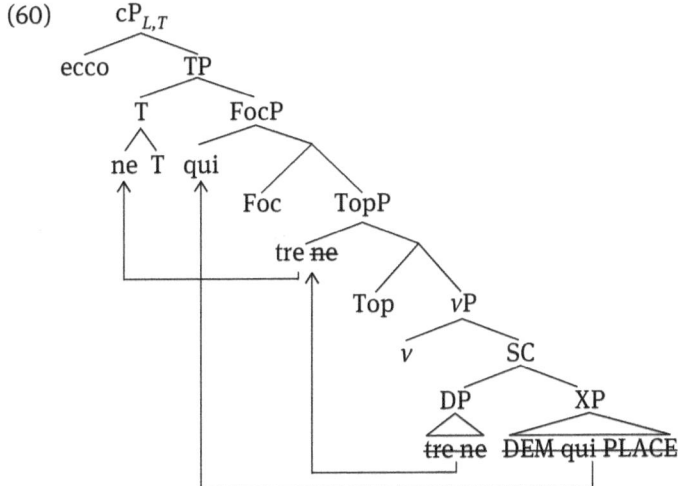

6 Summary and further issues

6.1 Summary

This work addresses the question of whether and when information concerning the speaker is encoded in the syntax. I focused on Italian presentatives like (61), which convey that the entity denoted by the noun phrase (already present in the discourse, or inferrable from the context) is salient at the time and place of the speaker:

(61) *Ecco (qui) Liliane.*
  'Here's Liliane.'

The 'here and now' interpretation seems to come from *ecco*, yet I showed that *ecco* does not have the distribution of a temporal or spatial adverb or PP. I argued that the syntactic structure of presentatives contains features that encode information usually thought to be supplied outside the syntax by the context parameter – in particular, features that express the time and the location of the speaker – and that these features, encoded in the left periphery, are spelled out as *ecco*.

In my analysis, *ecco* contributes to the locative and temporal meaning through two null elements that it c-commands: a null T, and a locative constituent headed by a null noun with locative meaning. The reasoning can be summarized as follows:

- Evidence for the presence of a phonetically null T comes from the fact that clitic pronouns can occur in presentatives (as in *Eccola!* 'Here she is'). Given the well-supported assumption that clitics adjoin to T in Italian, postulating the presence of a phonetically null T is less problematic than postulating that clitics have exceptional behavior in these clauses. This null T is similar to an indexical element like 'now' in that its interpretation is restricted to the time when the speaker is speaking (or, in Free Indirect Discourse, the time when the main character is speaking). I capture this by viewing the null T as dependent for its tense value on a feature in the left-periphery that expresses the time of the speaker (c_T).

- Evidence for the presence of a null locative element comes from the following observations: overt locative adverbs or PPs are separated from the presentative by a comma intonation, suggesting that they are adjuncts; only *qui* (*qua, lì, là*) can be part of the same intonational phrase as *ecco* and its complement. Following Kayne (2004), I analyze *qui* and its counterparts as reinforcers of a null noun denoting place. I take their presence within the same intonational phrase as *ecco* as evidence for the presence of a null locative constituent in presentatives. I further suggest that we view the null locative as dependent for its interpretation on a feature in the left-periphery that expresses the location of the speaker (c_L).

6.2 Further issues

There are several issues left open and worth mentioning. One concerns the exact nature of the relation that holds between the features in the left periphery (c_T, c_L) and the null T and null locative whose interpretation they restrict. A second issue concerns the cross-linguistic extension of my proposal: assuming that I have correctly identified the 'ingredients' of a presentative, we should expect to find them in other languages as well. Is there cross-linguistic evidence in support of the structure I proposed for Italian presentatives? In particular, do we find evidence for the components of the null locative that I postulated, or for T? I cannot provide a full answer to this question here, but I have reasons to think that the answer is positive. Petit (2010) points out that four strategies seem to exist for expressing presentatives across languages: (i) a locative element in co-occurrence with a form of *be*, such as English *here's* or German *hier ist*; (ii) a demonstrative, such as Polish *oto* or Serbo-Croatian *evo*; (iii) forms that can be traced back to imperatives meaning 'see' or 'look', such as English *lo* (from *look*) and *behold*, French *voici* and *voilà* (from *vois ci, vois là* 'look here, look there'); (iv) forms like Latin *ecce*, for which the etymological relation with a predicate is no longer transparent. The presence of locatives and demonstratives certainly supports the proposal put forth in this paper. Moreover, the fact that some presentatives are expressed using an overt form of the copula provides support for the presence of T in the structure of presentatives. Finally, the use of forms originally derived from verbs with the function of getting the addressee's attention supports the idea that presentatives involve a layer of syntactic structure higher than CP, where such elements have been argued to be (see Haegeman and Hill 2013, and Hill 2014).[28]

Going back to Italian presentatives, they have another interesting property: they cannot have a goal argument realized as a PP (62), but they may have a dative clitic (63). This dative clitic can only refer to the addressee: it can be 2nd person, singular or plural, or a formally 3rd person singular clitic that refers to the addressee (the so-called 'polite form', shown in [63c]). But it

---

[28] See also Kandel (2015) for a comparison between Italian *ecco* and the Romanian verb-based particles of address discussed in Hill (2014).

cannot be a form that refers to someone other than the addressee, as we see in (64):

(62) *Ecco le chiavi a te.
ecco the keys to you

(63) a. *Ecco-ti* le chiavi.
ecco-you.SG.FAMILIAR the keys
b. *Ecco-vi* le chiavi.
ecco-you.PL.FAMILIAR the keys
c. *Ecco-Le* le chiavi.
ecco-you.SG.POLITE the keys
'Here are the keys for you.'

(64) a. **Ecco-mi* le chiavi.
ecco-me the keys
b. **Ecco-gli* le chiavi.
ecco-him the keys

This dative clitic is not an argument, and shares some of the properties of ethical datives. Due to time and space restrictions, I will leave this as something to investigate at a later date.

The final issue that I want to mention is the following: I chose to analyze *ecco* as a morpheme that reflects the syntactic encoding of contextual information because I want to account for the 'here and now' interpretation of presentatives. One might object that this amounts to creating a new syntactic category just for *ecco*. But this is not the case. In my view *ecco* is a member of a class of elements that express syntactically encoded information about the context, and are in the left periphery of the clause (above CP). Evidence in support of the existence of such a class of elements comes from different empirical domains. I will briefly discuss two here:

(1) Haegeman and Hill (2013) examine verb-based discourse particles in West Flemish and Romanian that express the speaker's relation to the addressee and argue that they are part of the syntactic structure of the clause, as they exhibit strict ordering restrictions and can show agreement.[29] In particular, they view them as part of a layer of syntactic structure above the CP domain, which they represent building on (and modifying) the proposal in Speas and Tenny (2003).

---

[29] For example, the Romanian particles *hai* and *lasă* can bear 2nd person singular and plural agreement, as well as 1st person plural marking. They may co-occur, but only in a fixed order; when they co-occur, the agreement marker can only occur on the second particle.

(2) Oyharçabal (1993) discusses the presence of a special agreement marker in Basque that conveys whether the addressee is a peer of the speaker or has higher status, is male or female:[30]

(65) a. To a male friend:
  Pettek   lan   egin   **dik.** (Basque)
  Peter.ERG work.ABS do.PRF   aux-3.S.ABS.2.S.C.MSC.ALLOC-3.S.ERG
  'Peter worked.'
 b. To a female friend:
  Pettek   lan   egin   **din.**
  Peter.ERG work.ABS do.PRF   aux-3.S.ABS.2.S.C.FEM.ALLOC-3.S.ERG
  'Peter worked.'
 c. To someone older or higher in status:
  Pettek   lan   egin   **dizü.**
  Peter.ERG work.ABS do.PRF   aux-3.S.ABS.2.S.F.ALLOC-3.S.ERG
  'Peter worked.'

Miyagawa (2012) argues that allocutive agreement is truly syntactic on the basis of the observation that it competes with 2nd person subject and object agreement (i.e., if the auxiliary already marks agreement with a 2nd person subject or object, allocutive agreement cannot be expressed). Like Haegeman and Hill (2013), he also builds on Speas and Tenny (2003) and provides an analysis of allocutive agreement involving a syntactic layer above CP that encodes information about speaker and addressee traditionally relegated to the semantic and pragmatic component.

Ecco shares with the elements just mentioned the properties that it expresses information concerning the speaker and that it cannot be embedded:

(66) *Ti   dico   che   **ecco**   Maria.
     you   tell   that   ecco   Maria
     (intended meaning:) 'I'm telling you that Maria is here now.'

I see my proposal that Italian *ecco* is the realization of features expressing the time and location of the speaker as being in line with the observations and results of these other works: they all show that information concerning the context of utterance is sometimes encoded syntactically, in the left periphery of the clause.

---

[30] Umbundu, a Bantu language, is also said to have allocutive agreement; cf. Hill (2014) and references therein.

Acknowledgments: I would like to thank Paola Benincà, Ivano Caponigro, Jan Casalicchio, Guglielmo Cinque, Silvio Cruschina, Bob Frank, Alessandra Giorgi, Larry Horn, Beth Levin, Nicola Munaro, Nigel Vincent, Martina Wiltschko, Jim Wood and Jason Zentz for their helpful comments. This paper also benefitted from the insights of two anonymous reviewers.

References

Adams, J. N. 2013. *Social variation and the Latin language*. Cambridge, MA: Cambridge University Press.
Baker, Mark C. 2008. *The syntax of agreement and concord*. Cambridge, MA: Cambridge University Press.
Banfield, Ann. 1982. *Unspeakable sentences*. London: Routledge.
Bazzanella, Carla. 1995. I segnali discorsivi. In Lorenzo Renzi, Giampaolo Salvi & Anna Cardinaletti (eds.), *Grande grammatica italiana di consultazione*, vol. 3, 225–260. Bologna: Il Mulino.
Benincà, Paola, Mariachiara Berizzi & Laura Vanelli. to appear. L'espressione della distanza temporale di anteriorità in italiano e altre varietà romanze. Unpublished manuscript, University of Padua.
Benincà, Paola & Cecilia Poletto. 1994. Bisogna and its companions: The verbs of necessity. In Guglielmo Cinque, Jan Koster, Jean-Yves Pollock, Luigi Rizzi & Raffaella Zanuttini (eds.), *Paths towards Universal Grammar: Studies in honor of Richard S. Kayne*, 35–57. Washington, DC: Georgetown University Press.
Bernstein, Judy B. 1997. Demonstratives and reinforcers in Romance and Germanic languages. *Lingua* 102. 87–113.
Bianchi, Valentina. 2006. On the syntax of personal arguments. *Lingua* 116(12). 2023–2067.
Birner, Betty. 2006. Inferential relations and noncanonical word order. In Betty J. Birner & Gregory Ward (eds.), *Drawing the boundaries of meaning: Neo-Gricean studies in pragmatics and semantics in honor of Laurence H. Horn*, 31–51. Amsterdam & Philadelphia: John Benjamins Publishing Company.
Bouchard, Denis. 1988. French *voici/voilà* and the analysis of pro-drop. *Language* 64(1). 89–100.
Cardinaletti, Anna & Michal Starke. 1999. The typology of structural deficiency: On the three grammatical classes. In Henk van Riemsdijk (ed.), *Clitics in the languages of Europe*, vol. 8, 145–233. Berlin: Mouton de Gruyter.
Casalicchio, Jan. 2013. *Pseudorelative, gerundi e infiniti nelle varietà romanze: Affinità (solo) superficiali e differenze strutturali*: University of Padua dissertation.
Cinque, Guglielmo. 1995. *Italian syntax and Universal Grammar*. Cambridge: Cambridge University Press.
Cruschina, Silvio. 2012. Focus in existential sentences. In Valentina Bianchi & Cristiano Chesi (eds.), *Enjoy linguistics! Papers offered to Luigi Rizzi on the occasion of his 60th birthday*, 77–107. Siena: CISCL Press.
De Cesare, Anna-Maria. 2010. Gli impieghi di *ecco* nel parlato conversazionale e nello scritto giornalistico. In Angela Ferrari & Anna-Maria De Cesare (eds.), *Il parlato nella scrittura italiana odierna: riflessioni in prospettiva testuale*, 105–148. Bern: Peter Lang.

De Cesare, Anna-Maria. 2011. L'italien *ecco* et les français *voici, voilà*. Regards croisés sur leurs employs dans lex textes écrits. *Languages* 184. 51–67.

Doron, Edit. 1991. Point of view as a factor of content. In Steven K. Moore & Adam Zachary Wyner (eds.), *Proceedings from SALT I*, 51–64. Ithaca, NY: Cornell University Press.

Eckardt, Regine. 2015. *The semantics of Free Indirect Discourse: How texts allow us to mind-read and eavesdrop*. Leiden & Boston: Brill.

Frascarelli, Mara & Roland Hinterhölzl. 2007. Types of topics in German and Italian. In Kerstin Schwabe & Susanne Winkler (eds.), *On information structure, meaning and form: Generalizations across languages*, 87–116. Amsterdam & Philadelphia: John Benjamins Publishing Company.

Fraser, Bruce. 1974. An examination of the performative analysis. *Papers in Linguistics* 7. 1–40.

Gazdar, Gerald. 1979. *Pragmatics: Implicature, presupposition, and logical form*. New York: Academic Press.

Giorgi, Alessandra. 2010. *About the speaker: Towards a syntax of indexicality*. Oxford & New York: Oxford University Press.

Guéron, Jacqueline. 2006. Point of view in literary and non-literary text: On Free Indirect Discourse. Unpublished manuscript.

Guéron, Jacqueline. 2007. Remarks on the grammar of unspeakable sentences. Unpublished manuscript.

Haegeman, Liliane. 2014. West Flemish verb-based discourse markers and the articulation of the speech act layer. *Studia Linguistica* 68(1). 116–139.

Haegeman, Liliane & Virginia Hill. 2013. The syntacticization of discourse. In Raffaella Folli, Christina Sevdali & Robert Truswell (eds.), *Syntax and its limits*, vol. 48, 370–390. Oxford: Oxford University Press.

Haegeman, Liliane & Raffaella Zanuttini. 1991. Negative heads and the Neg Criterion. *The Linguistic Review* 8. 233–251.

Haegeman, Liliane & Raffaella Zanuttini. 1996. Negative concord in West Flemish. In Adriana Belletti & Luigi Rizzi (eds.), *Parameters and functional heads: Essays in comparative syntax*, 117–179. New York & Oxford: Oxford University Press.

Harris, James W. 1991. The exponence of gender in Spanish. *Linguistic Inquiry* 22(1). 27–62.

Heim, Johannes, Hermann Keupdjio, Zoe Wai-Man Lam, Adriana Osa Gómez & Martina Wiltschko. 2014. How to do things with particles. In Laura Teddiman (ed.), *Proceedings of the annual conference of the Canadian Linguistic Association*, http://cla-acl.ca/actes-2014-proceedings/.

Hill, Virginia. 2007a. Romanian adverbs and the pragmatic field. *The Linguistic Review* 24(1). 61–86.

Hill, Virginia. 2007b. Vocatives and the pragmatics-syntax interface. *Lingua* 117. 2077–2105.

Hill, Virginia. 2014. *Vocatives: How Syntax meets with Pragmatics*, vol. 5. Leiden & Boston: Brill.

Julia, Marie-Ange. 2016. Les présentatifs français *voici, voilà* et latins *ecce, em, en*: Essai d'étude comparative. In Eva Buchi, Jean-Paul Chauveau & Jean-Marie Pierrel (eds.), *Actes du XXVIIe Congrès international de linguistique et de philologie romanes (Nancy, 15-20 juillet 2013)*, Nancy, France: Editions de linguistique et de philologie. https://halshs.archives-ouvertes.fr/halshs-01340524.

Kandel, Margaret. 2015. *Ecco* location: The Italian presentative *ecco* and its spatial interpretation. Yale University senior thesis.

Kayne, Richard S. 1975. *French syntax*. Cambridge, MA: MIT Press.

Kayne, Richard S. 1981. Binding, quantifiers, clitics, and control. In Frank Heny (ed.), *Binding and filtering*, 191–211. London: Croom Helm.

Kayne, Richard S. 1989. Null subjects and clitic climbing. In Osvaldo Jaeggli & Kenneth J. Safir (eds.), *The null subject parameter*, 239–261. Dordrecht: Kluwer.
Kayne, Richard S. 1990. Romance clitics and PRO. In Juli Carter (ed.), *Proceedings of NELS XX*, vol. 2, 255–302. Amherst: GLSA, Univ. of Massachusetts.
Kayne, Richard S. 1991. Romance clitics, verb movement and PRO. *Linguistic Inquiry* 22(4). 647–686.
Kayne, Richard S. 2004. Here and there. In Christian Leclère, Éric Laporte, Mireille Piot & Max Silberztein (eds.), *Lexique syntaxe, et lexique-grammaire / Syntax, lexis & lexicon grammar: Papers in honour of Maurice Gross*, 253–275. Amsterdam & Philadelphia: John Benjamins Publishing Company. Reprinted in [Kayne 2005, Ch. 4].
Lakoff, George. 1987. *Women, fire and dangerous things: What categories reveal about the mind*. Chicago: University of Chicago Press.
Livitz, Inna G. 2014. *Deriving silence through dependent reference: Focus on pronouns*. New York: New York University (NYU) dissertation.
Merchant, Jason. 2015. How much context is enough? Two cases of span-conditioned stem allomorphy. *Linguistic Inquiry* 46(2). 273–303.
Miyagawa, Shigeru. 2012. Agreements that occur mainly in the main clause. In Lobke Aelbrecht, Liliane Haegeman & Rachel Nye (eds.), *Main clause phenomena: New horizons*, 79–112. Amsterdam & Philadelphia: John Benjamins.
Morin, Yves-Charles. 1985. On the two French subjectless verbs *voici* and *voilà*. *Language* 61(4). 777–820.
Morin, Yves-Charles. 1988. French *voici* and *voilà*: A reply to Bouchard. *Language* 64(1). 101–103.
Moro, Andrea. 1997a. Dynamic antisymmetry: Movement as a symmetry-breaking phenomenon. *Studia Linguistica* 51(1). 50–76.
Moro, Andrea. 1997b. *The raising of predicates: Predicative noun phrases and the theory of clause structure*. Cambridge: Cambridge University Press.
Moro, Andrea. 2000. *Dynamic antisymmetry*. Cambridge, MA: MIT Press.
Moro, Andrea. 2009. Rethinking symmetry: A note on labeling and the EPP. *Snippets* 19. 17–18.
Oyharçabal, Beñat. 1993. Verb agreement with non-arguments: On allocutive agreement. In José Ignacio Hualde & Jon Ortiz de Urbina (eds.), *Generative studies in Basque linguistics*, 89–114. Amsterdam: John Benjamins.
Petit, Daniel. 2010. On presentative particles in the Baltic languages. In Nicole Nau & Norbert Ostrowski (eds.), *Particles and connectives in Baltic, Acta Salensia*, vol. 2, 151–170. Vilnius: Vilniaus Universiteto Leidykla.
Petit, Daniel. 2011. Old Lithuanian añskat, šìskat, tàskat and cognates. *Acta Linguistica Lithuanica* LXII-LXIII. 11–25.
Porhiel, Sylvie. 2012. The presentative *voici/voilà* – towards a pragmatic definition. *Journal of Pragmatics* 44. 435–452.
Prince, Ellen. 1992. The ZPG letter: Subjects, definiteness, and information-status. In William C. Mann & Sandra A. Thompson (eds.), *Discourse description: Diverse analyses of a fundraising text*, 295–325. Amsterdam & Philadelphia: John Benjamins Publishing Company.
Rizzi, Luigi. 1997. The fine structure of the left periphery. In Liliane Haegeman (ed.), *Elements of grammar: Handbook of generative syntax*, 281–337. Dordrecht: Kluwer Academic Publishers.
Rohlfs, Gerhard. 1969. *Grammatica storica della lingua italiana e dei suoi dialetti – sintassi e formazione delle parole*, vol. 3. Torino: Einaudi. Translation (with author's updating) of Rohfls (1954).

Ross, John R. 1970. On declarative sentences. In Roderick Jacobs & Peter Rosenbaum (eds.), *Readings in English transformational grammar*, 222–272. Waltham, MA: Ginn.
Sadka, Yitshak. 2001. *Hinne* in Biblical Hebrew. *Ugarit-Forschungen* 33. 479–493.
Schlenker, Philippe. 2004. Context of thought and context of utterance: A note on Free Indirect Discourse and historical present. *Mind and Language* 19(3). 279–304.
Sigurðsson, Halldór Ármann. 2004. The syntax of Person, Tense and speech features. *Journal of Italian Linguistics/Rivista di Linguistica* 16(1). 219–251.
Sigurðsson, Halldór Ármann. 2014. Context-linked grammar. *Language Sciences* 46. 175–188.
Speas, Margaret & Carol L. Tenny. 2003. Configurational properties of point of view roles. In Anna Maria Di Sciullo (ed.), *Asymmetry in grammar*, 315–344. Amsterdam: John Benjamins.
Svenonius, Peter. 2012. Spanning. Unpublished manuscript, CASTL, University of Tromsø.
Tortora, Christina. 2014. *A comparative grammar of Borgomanerese*. Oxford & New York: Oxford University Press.
Williams, Edwin. 2003. *Representation theory*. Cambridge, MA: MIT Press.
Wiltschko, Martina. 2017. Ergative constellations in the structure of speech acts. In Jessica Coon, Diane Massam & Lisa deMena Travis (eds.), *The Oxford handbook of ergativity*, chap. 18. Oxford & New York: Oxford University Press.
Wood, Jim, Laurence Horn, Raffaella Zanuttini & Luke Lindemann. 2015. The Southern Dative Presentative meets Mechanical Turk. *American Speech* 90(3). 291–320.
Zamparelli, Roberto. 2000. *Layers in the Determiner Phrase*. New York: Garland Publishing, Inc.
Zucchi, Alessandro. 1995. The ingredients of definiteness and the definiteness effect. *Natural Language Semantics* 3(1). 33–78.

Part II: Comparative syntax: Cross-linguistic studies

Enoch O. Aboh and Thom Westveer
On reflexives with an object in French, German, and Gungbe

1 Introduction

A common property of human languages is to allow reflexive constructions in which an apparently transitive verb licenses two participants which refer to the same referent also functioning as subject of the clause, as illustrated here in (1a) and (1b) in French and German, respectively.[1]

(1) a. *Il   se   lave.*   [French]
       He   REFL.3SG   wash.3SG
    b. *Er   wäscht   sich.*   [German]
       He   wash.3SG   REFL.3SG.ACC
       'He washes himself.'

The apparent transitive nature of the verb in such constructions raises the question whether these reflexive sentences should be analyzed as involving transitive structures in which the reflexive pronoun represents an argument of the verb or rather as instances of intransitive structures, in which the reflexive pronoun is not an argument but serves a functional purpose (Reinhart and Siloni 2005).

At first sight, it seems reasonable to assume a transitive structure for these sentences, since the French example (1a) can be compared to example (2a) from which one can derive the clitic alternative in (2b). Notwithstanding language specificities, a comparable scenario could be imagined for German.

(2) a. *Jean   lave   la   voiture.*
       John   wash.3SG   DET   car
       'John washes/is washing the car.'

---

[1] In writing this paper, one thing was clear to us: comparison of typologically and genetically unrelated languages always leads to new observations. This rewarding feeling is one of the many things that Liliane Hageman made us discover (as her student for one of us and as the student of her student for the other). We are grateful to her for showing us the way. We are also grateful to two anonymous reviewers whose comments helped improve the paper significantly. All remaining errors are obviously ours.

b. *Jean la lave* ~~*la.*~~
   John 3SG wash.3SG 3SG
   'John washes/is washing it.'

If one were to maintain the comparison to transitive verbs, the next question to answer would be how to account for the reflexive meaning. How to analyze the French or German reflexive pronouns *se* and *sich*, respectively?

There have been various proposals in the literature, but the one we adopt in this paper is Reinhart and Siloni (2005). In their account for reflexives cross-linguistically, these authors argue that the reflexive pronoun (e.g., French *se* or German *sich* in (1a–b)) is not an argument of the verb, but a grammatical element that licenses case. Therefore, reflexivization allows manipulation of the argument structure of the verb such that the two thematic roles of a transitive verb are bound to one position only. This arity operation, they show, may take place in the lexicon or in syntax, hence the distinction between lexicon and syntax languages.

We refer the reader to Reinhart and Siloni (2005) for a detailed discussion and the theoretical and typological implications of the analysis. In this paper, we focus on a related construction which Reinhart and Siloni (2005) did not discuss specifically but which we account for by adapting their analysis. Beside the reflexive constructions in (1a–b), in which the reflexive pronoun bears accusative case, French and German also have a reflexive construction that contains an additional direct object marked with accusative case, while the reflexive pronoun takes dative case (3–4). The case shift is visible in German with first or second person pronouns, as in (4b):

(3) a. *Il se lave les mains.*
       He REFL.3SG wash.3SG the.PL hand.PL
    b. *Er wäscht sich die Hände.*
       He wash.3SG REFL.3SG the.PL hand.PL
       'He washes his hands.'

(4) a. *Je me lave les mains.*
       I REFL.1SG wash.1SG the.PL hand.PL
    b. *Ich wasche mir die Hände.*
       I wash.1SG REFL.1SG.DAT the.PL hand.PL
       'I wash my hands.'

This paper extends Reinhart and Siloni's (2005) theory to these examples. Building on our findings, we propose an analysis of Gungbe (Kwa) seemingly unrelated constructions (5) in which the constituent that represents the additional object in French and German is present, but there is no reflexive pronoun even though the sentence has a reflexive meaning only.

(5) Súrù   klɔ́   àlɔ̀.
    Suru wash hand
    'Suru washed his hand(s).'

We address the following questions (i) What licenses the presence of both a direct object and a reflexive pronoun in these reflexive sentences? (ii) How to account for case distribution in these reflexives? (iii) How to account for the Gungbe sentences?

The paper is structured as follows: Section 2 briefly presents Reinhart and Siloni's (2005) analysis of reflexive constructions. In section 3, we take a closer look at the reflexive construction with an additional argument in French and German, and motivate the analysis elaborated in section 4. Section 5 extends the analysis to the Gungbe data. We argue that this language involves a similar structure as German and French even though the reflexive element is silent. Section 6 concludes the paper.

2 Reinhart and Siloni's analysis of reflexives

Reinhart and Siloni's (2005) analysis is motivated by the observation that the reflexive pronoun does not behave like a typical internal argument. Some of the empirical facts that led to this conclusion are reproduced below. For the sake of the discussion we mainly use French data to illustrate the authors' line of argumentation, but the reader is referred to the paper for a detailed discussion on French, German and typologically different languages.

2.1 The reflexive pronoun is not an argument of the verb

Focusing on the distribution of the French reflexive clitic *se*, the authors show that this element does not exhibit typical properties of internal arguments but seems to be required in the reflexive construction to license Case. Building on Kayne (1975), who showed that French *se* differs from object clitics with regard to both its reflexive meaning and structural behavior, Reinhart and Siloni (2005) argue that French reflexive sentences pattern with intransitive rather than with transitive sentences.[2]

---

[2] Reinhart & Siloni (2005) also discuss expletive insertion in intransitives and reflexives as indication of the parallels between the two structures, but see Koeneman & Neeleman (2001) for an alternative on expletive insertion in German.

Causative constructions instantiate this behavior: In French, a *faire*-causative construction involving a transitive verb requires the preposition *à*, which introduces the external argument/Agent of the embedded verb as in (6a). Example (6b) is ungrammatical because the preposition is missing.

(6) a. *Je   ferai   laver   Max   à   Paul.*
       I   make.FUT   wash.INF   Max   to   Paul
   b. **Je   ferai   laver   Max   Paul.*
       I   make.FUT   wash.INF   Max   Paul
      'I will make Paul wash Max.'

With an intransitive verb, however, the pattern is reversed: the external argument/Agent must not be introduced by the preposition hence (7a) is ungrammatical unlike (7b).

(7) a. **Je   ferai   courir   à   Paul.*
       I   make.FUT   run.INF   to   Paul
   b. *Je   ferai   courir   Paul.*
       I   make.FUT   run.INF   Paul
      'I will make Paul run.'

Reflexive *faire*-causatives line up with intransitive sentences in precluding the preposition *à*.

(8) a. **Je   ferai   se   laver   à   Paul.*
       I   make.FUT   REFL   wash.INF   to   Paul
   b. *Je   ferai   se   laver   Paul.*
       I   make.FUT   REFL   wash.INF   Paul
      'I will make Paul wash himself.'

Finally, reflexive *faire*-causatives are different from transitive sentences with a clitic pronoun, since the latter occurs in a higher position than the reflexive, and the construction must involve the preposition *à* (9b).

(9) a. **Je   le   ferai   laver   Paul.*
       I   3SG   make.FUT   wash.INF   Paul
   b. *Je   le   ferai   laver   à   Paul.*
       I   3SG   make.FUT   wash.INF   to   Paul
      'I will make Paul wash him.'

That reflexives pattern with intransitives could be interpreted as indication that reflexive verbs are unaccusatives. The following section shows that this is not the case.

2.2 Reflexives are not unaccusatives

Reinhart and Siloni show convincingly that French reflexives should not be analyzed as unaccusatives, but rather as unergatives. If reflexives were unaccusatives, this would mean that the subject function is occupied by the internal argument. This predicts that reflexives and unaccusatives should pattern similarly with regard to defining properties of the internal argument. French *en*-cliticization represents an effective tool to test internal argumenthood. As the examples in (10) show, unaccusative verbs allow expletive insertion doubled with *en*-cliticization.

(10) a. *Il   est   arrivé   trois   filles.*
 There   is   arrived   three   girls.PL
 'There arrived three girls.'
 b. *Il   en   est   arrivé   trois.*
 There   of.them   is   arrived   three
 'There arrived three of them.'

Even if an unaccusative sentence contains the reflexive pronoun *se*, as for instance in middles, *en*-cliticization is still possible. This is illustrated in (11):

(11) a. *Il   s'   est   cassé   beaucoup   de   verres.*
 There   REFL   is   broken   many   of   glass.PL
 'There broke many glasses.'
 b. *Il   s'   en   est   cassé   beaucoup.*
 There   REFL   of.them   is   broken   many
 'There broke many of them.'

However, when the sentence expresses a genuine reflexive meaning, *en*-cliticization is disallowed, as indicated by (12b):

(12) a. *?Il   s'   est   lavé   beaucoup   de   touristes.*
 There   REFL   is   washed   many   of   tourist.PL
 'There washed themselves many tourists.'
 b. **Il   s'   en   est   lavé   beaucoup.*
 There   REFL   of.them   is   washed   many
 'There washed themselves many of them.'

The fact that *en*-cliticization is not possible with reflexives shows that the subject of a reflexive verb is the external argument. This led Reinhart and Siloni to conclude that French reflexives should be analyzed as unergatives rather than as unaccusatives.[3]

Summarizing therefore, French reflexives show distributive properties which distinguish them from transitive and unaccusative verbs formally. With this in mind, the next question to answer is how to account for the reflexive pronoun in such a construction.

2.3 Reflexivization as arity operation

A conclusion that arises from the discussion in the previous paragraphs is that the subject of reflexives is the external argument. The apparent reflexive pronoun is not an argument of the verb: it is a grammatical device. In terms of their analysis, Reinhart and Siloni (2005) argue that reflexivization consists of two operations:
(i) Bundling: this operation bundles any non-assigned thematic role to the external theta-role. The operation happens upon merger of the external theta-role.
(ii) Case reduction: absorbs the case of the argument whose theta-role is targeted by bundling.

In French, case reduction is achieved thanks to the reflexive pronoun *se*, taking place in syntax. In terms of Reinhart and Siloni (2005), reflexives instantiate reduction of the internal argument. Such an arity operation takes place in syntax or in the lexicon depending on the language, a cross-linguistic variation that the authors account for on the basis of the Lexicon-Syntax parameter. In languages like French and German, the operation occurs in syntax, and correlates with specific constructions which allow bundling and case reduction. Other syntax languages include Romance languages in general, Czech,

---

[3] This conclusion is not uncontroversial since reflexivization triggers a change of the auxiliary from *avoir* to *être*, a hallmark of unaccusative verbs.
(i) J' ai lavé ma main.
    I   have washed my hand
    'I washed my hand.'
(ii) Je me   suis   lavé   la   main.
     I   REFL be.1SG washed the hand
     'I washed my hand.'
In this regard, we refer the reader to de Alencar and Kelling (2005), Labelle (2008), Oya (2010), and references therein for arguing that reflexive constructions involve transitive verbs.

Serbo-Croatian, and Greek. In lexicon languages, however (e.g. Hebrew, Dutch, English, Hungarian, Russian) reflexive constructions generally exhibit specific morphologies that can be seen as evidence of the availability of arity operations within the lexicon. Reinhart and Siloni further show that cross-linguistic differences that distinguish syntax languages from lexicon languages are not limited to reflexive constructions only. We refer the reader to their paper for further discussion. The following section discusses French and German reflexives containing an additional argument.

3 Reflexives with an internal argument

If reflexives are unergatives, it is unexpected that they would involve an internal argument as in the examples under (3) repeated below for convenience.

(13) a. *Je   me   lave   les   mains.*
         I   REFL.1SG   wash   the.PL hand.PL
     b. *Ich   wasche   mir   die   Hände.*
         I   wash   REFL.1SG.DAT   the.PL hand.PL
        'I wash my hands.'

3.1 Distinguishing between two sentence types

Let us first take a closer look at these constructions. Beside the sentences in (13), French and German also display the possessive constructions in (14), which involve a transitive verb and a possessive noun phrase functioning as object.

(14) a. *Jean   lave   ses   cheveux.*
         John   wash.3SG   his.PL   hair.PL
     b. *Jan   wäscht   seine   Haare.*
         John   wash.3SG   his.PL.ACC   hair.PL
        'John washes his hair.'

These constructions, however, are ambiguous between the reflexive meaning in (13) (i.e., John is washing his own hair) and a situation in which *John* is washing someone else's hair. The ambiguity arises with the 3rd person pronoun only but it is sufficient to illustrate the difference between these possessive constructions and the reflexive ones under study in this paper. Compare, for instance, the following examples from French:

(15) a. *Jean   lave   les/ses   cheveux   à   lui.*[4]
       John   wash.3SG   the.PL/his.PL   hair.PL   to   him
       'John washes his hair.' (*à lui* > (i) *Jean* / (ii) someone else)
   b. *Jean   lave   ses   cheveux.*
       John   wash.3SG   his.PL   hair.PL
       'John washes his hair.' (*ses* > (i) *Jean* / (ii) someone else)
   c. *Jean   se   lave   les   cheveux.*
       John   REFL   wash.3SG   the.PL   hair.PL
       'John washes his hair.' (*se* > *Jean*)
   d. *Jean   lui   lave   les   cheveux.*
       John   to.him   wash.3SG   the.PL   hair.PL
       'John washes his hair.' (*lui* > someone else)

These examples show that the constructions involving a third person possessive argument are ambiguous (15a–b), unlike the reflexive sentence with additional object in (15c). Example (15d) indicates that constructions involving clitic pronouns should be treated differently (see also example 9).

These observations hold for the relevant German examples too:

(16) a. *Jan   wäscht   die/seine   Haare   für   ihn.*
       John   wash.3SG   the.PL/his.PL   hair.PL   for   him
       'John washes his hair.' (*ihn* > someone else)
   b. *Jan   wäscht   seine   Haare.*
       John   wash.3SG   his.PL   hair.PL
       'John washes his hair.' (*seine* > (i) *Jan* / (ii) someone else)
   c. *Jan   wäscht   sich   die   Haare.*
       John   wash.3SG   REFL   the.PL   hair.PL
       'John washes his hair.' (*sich* > *Jan*)
   d. *Jan   wäscht   ihm   die   Haare.*
       John   wash.3SG   to.him   the.PL   hair.PL
       'John washes his hair.' (*ihm* > someone else)

French and German largely overlap, as can be concluded from the comparison between examples (15) and (16). Though the German example (16a) is not ambiguous, unlike the French equivalent (15a), the sentences with a possessive phrase (i.e., 15b, 16b) are ambiguous in both languages.

---

[4] It is possible to add – *même* to the pronoun *lui* (creating *lui-même*) to disambiguate this sentence.

In German, case morphology distinguishes between simple reflexives and a reflexive with an additional object: a simple reflexive as in (17a) requires accusative case on the reflexive pronoun, while a reflexive construction with an additional object involves a reflexive pronoun with dative case (17b).

(17) a. *Ich wasche mich.*
 I wash.1SG REFL.1SG.ACC
 'I wash myself.'
 b. *Ich wasche mir die Hände.*
 I wash.1SG REFL.1SG.DAT the.PL hand.PL
 'I wash my hands.'

This contrast suggests that the additional argument is associated with a benefactive theta-role. This is compatible with the fact that German benefactives are usually marked with dative case.

(18) a. *Ich helfe ihm.*
 I help.1SG him.DAT
 'I help him.'
 b. *Er gibt ihr ein Buch.*
 He give.3SG her.DAT a.ACC book
 'He gives her a book.'

In French, the reflexive pronoun does not show case morphology and thus behaves like weak or clitic pronouns according to the typology of Cardinaletti and Starke (1996). We take this to be evidence that the reflexive pronoun is a clitic in French, and a full pronoun in German.

3.2 The structural make-up of the reflexive pronoun

Following the literature on clitic pronouns in Romance (e.g., Kayne 1975, Cardinaletti and Starke 1996, Déchaine and Wiltschko 2002), we assume that clitics, weak pronouns, and strong pronouns involve different structural properties: clitics are heads, weak pronouns are reduced (or deficient) DPs, while strong pronouns are full DPs. This would mean that the French reflexive pronoun is a head that realizes a functional head position within the spine of the clause. With regard to German *sich*, Cardinaletti & Starke (1996) argue that it is a strong pronoun expressing a full DP structure. Similarly to full DPs, it can be coordinated with the object pronoun *mich*, as in (19a). This is not possible with the French reflexive *se* (19b). As a full DP, *sich* must be licensed in a specifier position.

(19) a. Er   sieht   sich   und   mich.
       He   see.3SG REFL   and   me.ACC
    b. *Il   se   et   me   voit.
       He   REFL   and   me   see.3SG
       'He sees himself and me.'

Summarizing therefore, we assume *se* to be a clitic that spells out a head position within the clause, while *sich* realizes a specifier position. Under Reinhart and Siloni's (2005) approach, both elements fulfill the same function as case absorbers. In extending their analysis to these specific cases, we propose that *se* and *sich* are realizations of the same functional projection: French reflexive *se* spells out the head of the functional projection whose specifier hosts *sich* in German.

The question that now arises is the nature of this projection. Here, we adhere to Sportiche's (2014) approach to French *se*, in which he proposed a unified account for *se* in reflexives as well as in other constructions with no reflexive meaning, such as, middles and inchoatives. The examples in (20) are taken from (Sportiche 2014: 115).

(20) a. Ces   choses   se   savent.
       DEM.PL   thing.PL   REFL   know.3PL
       'People know these things.'
    b. Les   habits   se   sont   salis.
       The.PL   cloth.PL   REFL   be.3PL   dirtied
       'The clothes got dirty.'

These examples indicate that *se* can occur in a variety of constructions in French, which do not all require a reflexive reading. While these data further support Reinhart and Siloni's (2005) view that *se*, and also German *sich*, should not be analyzed as 'reflexivizing morphemes or pronouns', they are further evidence for Kayne (2000), as cited in Sportiche (2014: 115), that there is a unique *se* in French, which has the following properties:

(21) a. *se* is composed of a morpheme *s–* and an epenthetic *–e* (in front of consonants)
    b. the *s–* morpheme parallels first and second person morphemes *m–* and *t–* in combining with a variety of other endings yielding *moi/toi/soi, mien/tien/sien, mon/ton/son, mes/tes/ses*.
    c. *s–* is incompatible with gender, unmarked for number and unspecified for person (unlike third object person clitics *le/la/les/lui/leur*).
    d. *s–* is *not* intrinsically anaphoric in the *sense needed for reflexivity* (although its lack of person specification may be a precondition for anaphoricity) as shown by the nonanaphoric character of, for example, *sien/son*.

Given these characterizations of *se*, Sportiche (2014) argues that *se* spells out the head of a Voice phrase, and must be bound by the closest DP because of its lack of person specifications. This proposal is compatible with the fact that French *se* is excluded from passives in which Voice hosts a distinct passive morpheme. Combined with our view that French *se* and German *sich* realize the same functional projection as case absorbers, our interpretation of Sportiche's view can be partially represented as in (22).[5]

(22)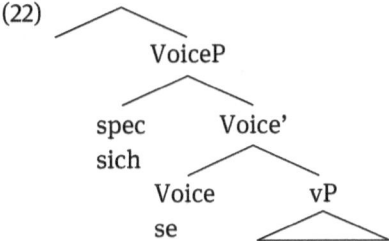

With these ingredients in place, let us now return to the main concern of this paper: how to account for reflexives with an apparent internal argument as illustrated again in (23).

(23) a. *Pierre   se   rase   la   barbe.*
        Peter   REFL   shave.3SG   the   beard
     b. *Peter   rasiert   sich   den   Bart.*
        Peter   shave.3SG REFL   the.ACC beard
        'Peter shaves his beard.'

4 The proposed analysis

Recall from Reinhart and Siloni's (2005) analysis that even though reflexive constructions do not involve an internal argument, the transitive verb does have a Theme role to assign. Accordingly, the authors propose that an example like *John washes*, in a lexicon language such as English, is described as follows (Reinhart and Siloni 2005: 401):

(24) a. Verb entry: wash$_{acc}$[Agent][Theme]
     b. Reflexivization output: wash[Agent-Theme]
     c. Syntactic output: Max$_{[Agent-Theme]}$ washed.

---

5 Unlike Sportiche (2014) we claim that *se* (as well as *sich*) are base-generated in Voice and [Spec VoiceP], respectively.

In a syntax language, the same operation happens in syntax with languages developing various strategies (e.g., *se* vs. *sich*) to absorb the accusative case. With this view in mind, we propose that reflexives with an internal argument are types of dative constructions in which the verb has three thematic roles to assign: agent, theme, and benefactive. The verb selects for both an external and internal argument to which it assigns the roles agent and theme, respectively. We further claim that such reflexives arise from the fact that there is no benefactive argument to receive the benefactive role. Bundling targets the agent and benefactive roles which are mapped onto the subject position. What appears to be the reflexive pronoun, on the other hand, absorbs the unlicensed dative case.[6] Adopting Reinhart and Siloni's (2005) conventions, reflexivization in this case results in bundling of the benefactive and agent roles as described in (25) for example (23a).

(25) a. VP: [SE rase$_{\theta i\text{-Agent}; \theta j\text{-Theme}; \theta k\text{-Benefactive}}$]
  b. IP: [Pierre$\langle_{\theta i\text{-Agent}; \theta k\text{-Benefactive}}\rangle$ se rase [VP ~~rase~~ la barbe$_{\theta j\text{-Theme}}$]]

This further implies that in syntax languages (e.g., French, German), the pronoun serves primarily to absorb dative case, but not to induce reflexivization, as partially represented below for this example.

(26)
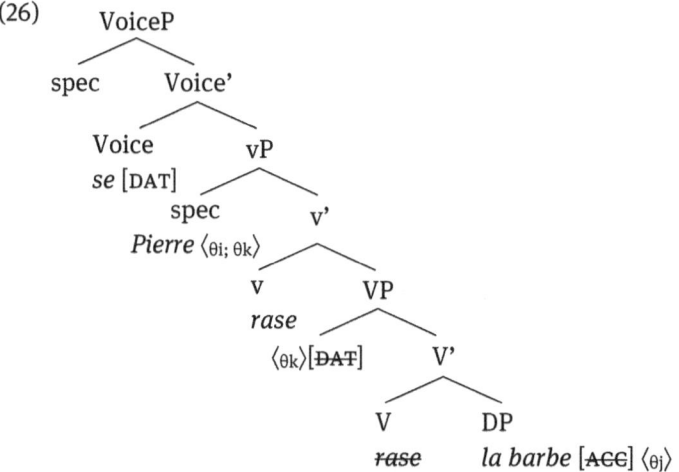

This structure builds on the analysis of simple reflexives, with the difference that the VP now contains an unlicensed benefactive theme that is bundled together with the Agent role mapped on the subject position. This analysis is compatible

---

6 Reinhart and Siloni (2005: 411) already mention the possibility for *se* to absorb dative case: "It is a general Case reducer, not selective regarding the Case."

with the fact that reflexive constructions with an object require the preposition *à* in *faire*-causatives, unlike simple reflexives. In the sentences under (9) repeated here as (27a–b) we showed that in *faire*-causatives, the agent cannot be introduced by the preposition, contrary to transitive verbs. The sentences in (27c–d) show a reverse pattern. The benefactive reflexive construction requires the preposition *à* in *faire*-causatives.

(27) a. *Je   ferai   se   laver   Paul.*
      I   make.FUT   REFL   wash.INF   Paul
   b. **Je   ferai   se   laver   à   Paul.*
      I   make.FUT   REFL   wash.INF to   Paul
      'I will make Paul wash himself.'
   c. **Je   ferai   se   raser   la   barbe   Paul.*
      I   make.FUT   REFL   shave.INF   the   beard   Paul
   d. *Je   ferai   se   raser   la   barbe   à   Paul.*
      I   make.FUT   REFL   shave.INF   the   beard   to   Paul
      'I will make Paul shave his beard.'

We extend this analysis to the German example in (23b), taking into account the fact that this language exhibits SOV order in surface form.

(28)
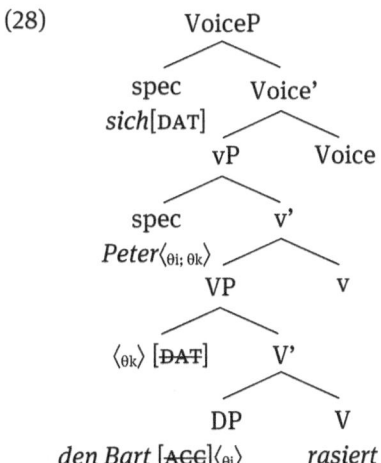

Given this analysis, one may wonder which class of verbs allows these constructions in these languages. In French, for instance, the construction is particularly productive with self-grooming verbs typically involving body parts (29).

(29) *Jean   se   brosse   les   dents.*
     John   REFL   brush   DET   tooth-PL
     'John brushes his teeth'

As discussed extensively by Junker and Martineau (1987) the English translation with a possessive phrase (*his teeth*) can make one think that these constructions are essentially possessive constructions, a view that has also been entertained for reflexive constructions (cf. Postma 1997). Junker and Martineau (1987), however, show that these constructions must be contrasted with the example in (30) which also translates into a possessive construction in English.

(30) *Jean   lève   la   tête.*
     John   REFL   DET   head
    'John raised his head.'

The two constructions show similar behavior with regard to various syntactic tests: they do not allow passivization (similarly to reflexives).

(31) a. **La   tête   a   été   levée.*
       DET   head   has   been   raised
   b. *Les   dents   ont   été   brossées   par   Jean.*
      DET   tooth-PL   have   been   brushed   by   John
    'The teeth (of somebody else)' have been brushed by John
    *'The teeth (of John) have been brushed by himself.'

The two constructions exclude qualification of the body part with descriptive adjectives, while restrictive adjectives further distinguishing body parts are allowed. Consider the following contrast.

(32) a. *Jean   lève   la   jolie   main.*
      Jean   raises   DET   nice   hand
     '*John raises his nice hand'
     'John raises the nice hand (of someone else).'
   b. *Jean   lève   la   main   droite.*
      Jean   raises   DET   hand   right
     'John raises his right hand.'
     ?'John raises the right hand (of someone else).'

In these examples, the reflexive meaning disappears with addition of a descriptive adjective, but not with restrictive adjectives. The same holds of reflexive constructions with an additional object.

(33) a. **Jean   se   lave   les   jolies   mains.*
      Jean   REFL   wash   DET   nice   hands
     '*John washes his nice hands'
   b. *Jean   se   lave   la   main   droite.*
      Jean   REFL   wash   DET   hand   right
     'John washes his right hand'

Despite these similarities, Junker and Martineau (1987) argue convincingly that the two constructions should be distinguished syntactically. Due to space limitation, we cannot reproduce all their arguments here but refer the interested reader to the paper. We only summarize their ideas that prove relevant for discussing the Gungbe facts below.

According to these authors, the two constructions in (29) and (30) involve two classes of verbs: the first class illustrated by (30) results from an inclusion relation between the external and internal arguments (e.g., the raised hand is part of the body of John) and the fact that the internal argument (i.e., the hand) has the property of being 'auto-V-able'.[7] Being 'auto-V-able' translates an intrinsic property of the internal argument, namely the body part, which is determined by the meaning of the verb. In this case, *John's* hand is perceived as capable of performing an action initiated by the external argument *John*, that is, the hand is capable of performing actions instructed by the mind of the agent. Junker and Martineau (1987: 203) conclude that even though such structures are transitive in their underlying structure, the interpretation of the whole sentence gives the impression that it contains an intransitive predicate. According to these authors, if the internal argument cannot be described as 'auto-V-able' the reflexive or inalienable interpretation is impossible.

(34) *Elle   bouge   les   yeux/   mains/   *cheveux.*
     she   moves   DET   eyes   hands   hair-PL
     'She moves her eyes/hands/*hair.'

Note that addition of the reflexive pronoun to constructions involving this class of verbs renders the sentence marginal. While most of our consultants (and one of the authors of this paper) find (35a) quite marginal, all judge (35b) as bad.

---

7 In absence of an inclusion relation the use of a reflexive pronoun with a self-grooming verb is ungrammatical:
(i)   **Il   se   lave   la   voiture.*
      He   REFL   wash.3SG   the   car
      'He washes his car.'
In a sentence without a self-grooming verb, the use of a reflexive pronoun is possible without an inclusion relation (iia). In such sentences, modification by means of a descriptive adjective is possible (iib), unlike in sentences with a self-grooming verb:
(ii) a. *Il   s'   achète   la   voiture.*
        He   REFL   buy.3SG   the   car
        'He buys himself the car.'
     b. *Il   s'   achète   la   voiture   rouge.*
        He   REFL   buy.3SG   the   car   red
        'He buys himself the red car.'

(35) a. ??*Jean se lève la main.*
　　　 Jean REFL raises DET hand
　　　 'John raises his hand himself.'
　　b. **Jean se lève le doigt.*
　　　 Jean REFL raises DET finger
　　　 'John raises his finger himself.'

We take this to mean that adding the reflexive pronoun to these constructions produces ungrammatical structures even though speakers can accommodate them pragmatically. Because of the inclusion relation between the external and internal arguments as well as the 'auto-V-able' property assigned to the internal argument, verbs of this class form a smaller set and typically involve self-grooming verbs or verbs denoting body-oriented actions.

This is different for verbs of the second class which occur in constructions involving the reflexive pronoun and an additional object. For Junker and Martineau (1987), there is no inclusion relation between the external argument and internal arguments of these verbs. The reflexive pronoun is therefore required in these contexts to establish a relation between the external argument and the internal one. This is compatible with the bundling hypothesis argued for by Reinhart and Siloni (2005). In terms of this description, John's teeth in (29) are not 'auto-brushable'. An external agent is therefore needed to perform the act of brushing. This boils down to saying that constructions involving verbs of the second class are datives in which the external argument and the unrealized dative argument are coreferential as a result of bundling, and the reflexive pronoun absorbs the dative case as we argue for in this paper. According to Junker and Martineau (1987: 204) this also explains why this class is larger: the construction involves a syntactic operation that relies on the usage of the clitic *se* to link the two arguments. In the next section, we account for Gungbe facts using the insight from our analysis based on Reinhart and Siloni (2005) and on Junker and Martineau's (1987) description.

5 Extending the analysis to Gungbe reflexives

Recall from the examples just discussed that French has the constructions in (36) both of which translate into a possessive construction in English.

(36) a. *Jean lève la tête.*
　　　 Jean raises DET head
　　　 'John raises his head'
　　b. *Jean se gratte la tête.*
　　　 Jean REFL scratch DET head
　　　 'John scratches his head.'

German is like French as indicated by the examples in (37) taken from Junker and Martineau (1987: 206).

(37) a. *Johan   schüttelt   den   Kopf.*
      Jean   shake.3SG DET head
      'John shakes his head'
   b. *Johan   wäscht   sich   die   Hände.*
      Jean   wash.3SG REFL DET hand
      'John washes his hands.'

The discussion of the French data further shows that these sentences have the same semantics but involve two classes of verbs that require two syntactic structures: (36a) is a transitive structure presumably including a possessive phrase, while (36b) is a dative construction in which *se* absorbs the dative case, and bundling merges the thematic role of the external argument and the missing benefactive argument. Given the contrast between French and German on one hand, and English on the other, one can conjecture that the two verb classes established by Junker and Martineau (1987) exist in English as well even though this does not translate into any specific surface structure or morphological specification on the verb and its arguments.

5.1 Gungbe reflexive constructions with a single internal argument

One can make the same conjecture about Gungbe. In this language, the French examples in (36) translate into an apparent transitive construction as in English (38). Unlike English, German, and French, however, the construction does not even involve a possessive or reflexive pronoun: the single internal argument is a bare noun. Based on their meaning, we refer to these constructions as *bare reflexive constructions*.

(38) a. *Dótù   zé   àlɔ̀.*
      Dotu raise hand
      'John raised his hand'
   b. *Dótù   klú   tà.*
      Dotu scratch head
      'John scratches his head'

In accounting for the reflexive meaning of these constructions, one could suggest that Gungbe displays body-oriented reflexives (cf. Osam 2002) in which the internal argument involves a hidden possessive phrase, whose possessor is bound by the subject, in a way superficially comparable to the English sentence *John$_i$ scratches his$_i$ head*.

Yet, we know from Junker and Martineau (1987) that such English examples could be misleading because the same 'construction' may hide two different structures. Indeed, Gungbe bare reflexives show similar properties as the French examples. The internal argument excludes a descriptive adjective, but not a restrictive one.

(39) a. *Dótù zé àlɔ̀ ɖàxó.*
Dotu raise hand big
*'Dotu raised his big hand.'
'Dotu raised someone else's big hand.'
b. *Dótù zé àlɔ̀ ɖùsí.*
Dotu raise hand right
'Dotu raised his right hand.'
*'Dotu raised someone else's right hand.'

The different interpretations in (39) indicate that addition of a descriptive adjective obliterates the reflexive meaning suggesting that we are dealing with a different structure. The same holds of internal arguments which cannot be characterized as 'auto-V-able' in terms of Junker and Martineau (1987).

(40) a. *Dótù gbò àlɔ̀ ɖàxó.*
Dotu cut hand big
'*Dotu cut his big hand.'
'Dotu cut someone else's big hand.'
b. *Dótù gbò àlɔ̀ ɖùsí.*
Dotu cut hand right
'Dotu cut his right hand.'
*'Dotu cut someone else's right hand.'

The examples in (39) and (40) show that the reflexive meaning arises non-ambiguously only when the internal argument is bare in the sense of Aboh and DeGraff (2014): it cannot involve the specificity and/or number markers which are associated with the D-layer (Aboh 2004). Adding these markers cancels the reflexive meaning.

(41) a. *Dótù zé àlɔ̀ lɔ́ lé.*
Dotu raise hand DET PL
'*Dotu raised his hands.'
'Dotu raised the hands in question.'
b. *Dótù gbò àlɔ̀ lɔ́ lé.*
Dotu cut hand DET PL
'*Dotu cut his hands.'
'Dotu cut the hands in question.'

The fact that these Gungbe bare reflexives exclude descriptive adjectives as well as markers that express the D-layer suggests to us that the internal argument does not involve the relevant structure to host these elements. Note, for instance, that adding a possessive pronoun to these constructions destroys the non-ambiguous reflexive meaning and blurs the contrast in (39) and (40).

(42) a. *Dótù   zé   àlɔ̀   ɖàxó/àɖùsí   étɔ́n.*
       Dotu   raise   hand   big/right   3SG-POSS
       'Dotu raised his big/right hand.'
       'Dotu raised someone else's big/right hand.'
    b. *Dótù   gbò   àlɔ̀   ɖàxó/àɖùsí   étɔ́n.*
       Dotu   cut   hand   big/right   3SG-POSS
       'Dotu cut his big/right hand.'
       'Dotu cut someone else's big/right hand.'

The examples in (42) are comparable to the French and German possessive examples in (15) and (16), respectively. As we showed in previous sections, such possessive constructions must be treated differently from the reflexive constructions with an additional object. Following the same line of argumentation, we argue that the Gungbe bare reflexive constructions must be distinguished from possessive constructions like those in (42) in which the internal argument involves a full DP including a possessive pronoun.

5.2 Distinguishing between possessives and bare reflexives

A property that distinguishes possessive constructions such as (42) from bare reflexives is that the former exclude an additional reflexive pronoun, while the latter do not, even though the resulting meaning is emphatic. Before getting on to this, however, let us first consider reflexive pronouns in Gungbe. These pronouns consist of a pronoun and a body part generally glossed as *self* or *body* in the literature (cf. Awóyalé 1986). Example (43) illustrates this.

(43) a. *Dótù   mɔ̀n   é-ɖé   tò   mɛ̀kpɔ́nú   mɛ̀.*
       Dotu   see   3SG-self PREP   mirror   IN
       'Dotu saw himself in the mirror.'
    b. *Dótù   hù   é-ɖé   ná   wányínyí   àsì   étɔ̀n   útù.*
       Dotu   kill   3SG-self PREP   love   wife   his   CAUSE
       'Dotu killed himself for the love of his wife.'

The following table lists reflexive pronouns in Gungbe.

Tab. 1: Gungbe personal pronouns (adapted from Aboh 2004: 129)

Pers/Numb	Strong forms	Weak forms		Possessives	Reflexives
		Nominative	Accusative		
1SG	nyɛ̀	ùn	mì	cé	nyɛ̀-ɖé
2SG	jɛ̀	à	wè	tòwè	jɛ̀-ɖé
3SG	éɔ́/úɔ́	é	e (ɛ - ì)	étɔ̀n	é-ɖé
1PL	mílɛ́	mí	mí	mítɔ̀n	mí-ɖé-lɛ́
2PL	mìlɛ́	mì	mì	mìtɔ̀n	mì-ɖé-lɛ́
3PL	yélɛ́	yé	yé	yétɔ̀n	yé-ɖé-lɛ́

As can be seen from this table, the reflexive pronouns derive from a combination of a strong pronoun and the morpheme -ɖé. As a result, strong pronouns and reflexive pronouns are bi- or tri-syllabic, unlike weak forms which are monosyllabic. We take these morphological properties to indicate that the reflexive pronouns are strong pronouns. This conclusion is compatible with the fact that these pronouns can be used as fragment answers (44a–b), or can be focused as indicated in example (44c) in which the reflexive pronoun is fronted to the left of the focus marker (cf. Aboh 2004).

(44) a. *Ménù   wɛ̀   à   xɔ̀   kèké   ná?*
         who   FOC   2SG   buy   bicycle   PREP
         'Who did you buy the bicycle for?'
   b. *Ná   nyɛ̀-ɖé.*
         who   1SG-sefl
         'To myself.'
   c. *Nyɛ̀-ɖé   wɛ̀   ùn   xɔ̀   kèké   ná.*
         1SG-sefl   FOC   1SG   buy   bicycle   PREP
         'I bought a bicycle to MYSELF.'

Putting these facts together, we propose that the Gungbe reflexive is, like the German pronoun, a strong pronoun that realizes a full DP.[8]

---

[8] These reflexive pronouns agree in person and number with the antecedent. Note, however, that the plural forms are ambiguous between the reflexive and reciprocal meaning, as shown below. Such an overlap between reflexives and reciprocals is found in many languages including French and German.

(i) *Mí   mɔ̀n   mí-ɖé-lɛ́   tò   mèkpɔ́nú   mè*
     1PL   see   1SG-self-PL   PREP   mirror   IN
     'We saw ourselves/each other in the mirror.'

Finally the following examples (46a–b) indicate that the reflexive pronoun is necessary to express the reflexive meaning, unlike bare reflexive constructions discussed in previous paragraphs.

(45) a. *Sésì nɔ̀ ɖɔ̀ xɔ́ gbígblé ɖó é-ɖé jí.*
   Sesi HAB say word bad PREP 3SG-self on
   'Sesi often says bad things about herself.'
 b. *Sésì nɔ̀ ɖɔ̀ xɔ́ gbígblé.*
   Sesi HAB say word bad
   'Sesi often says bad things.'

With this description of reflexive pronouns in mind, let us now consider the contrast in (46) in which we add a reflexive pronoun to a possessive construction (46a) as opposed to a bare reflexive construction (46b).

(46) a. **Dótù gbò àlɔ̀ étɔ́n ná é-ɖé.*
   Dotu cut hand 3SG-POSS PREP 3SG-self
   'Dotu cut his hand for himself/by himself.'
 b. *Dótù gbò àlɔ̀ ná é-ɖé*
   Dotu cut hand PREP 3SG-POSS
   'Dotu cut his hand by himself.'

It appears from these examples that possessive constructions exclude the reflexive pronoun, unlike bare reflexive constructions: bare reflexive constructions allow further reflexivization.

Reinhart and Siloni (2005) already showed that reflexivization is very productive in syntax languages: "any transitive verb whose external argument is an agent, an experiencer, or even a cause can reflexivize" (p. 410). Their conclusion is compatible with Junker and Martineau's (1987) analysis. These studies are relevant for Gungbe as well. In this language, almost all verbs allow bare reflexive constructions. In appropriate contexts, these constructions can be doubled with an additional reflexive pronoun as further indicated in (47).

(47) a. *Dótù xwlé àtán ná é-ɖé.*
   Dotu shave beard PREP 3SG-self
   'Dotu shaved (by himself).'
 b. *Dótù fún nùkúmɛ̀ ná é-ɖé.*
   Dotu wash face PREP 3SG-self
   'Dotu washed his face (by himself).'

The productive nature of bare reflexive constructions in Gungbe suggests that this is a syntax language in terms of Reinhart and Siloni (2005). We postulate that these constructions actually involve a silent reflexive pronoun. This view corroborates with the fact that the sentences in (46b) and (47) include an additional reflexive pronoun which yields an emphatic meaning: there is some relevance in the fact that the agent carried out the action by herself on herself. The emphatic nature of these constructions suggests that they should be analyzed as instances of doubling (cf. Ghomeshi, Jackendoff, Rosen, and Russell 2004, Aboh and Dyakonova 2009, Aboh, Smith, and Zribi-Hertz 2012). Similar emphatic constructions are possible in French by adding the complex form *lui-même*.

5.3 Analyzing the Gungbe bare reflexives

Keeping to the rationale of our analysis for French and German, we propose that in Gungbe bare reflexives, the bare noun phrase realizes the internal argument and is licensed for accusative case. We further suggest that the reflexive meaning arises because these constructions involve a silent reflexive pronoun that merges in Voice, similarly to French *se*. This silent argument receives dative case. Bundling, on the other hand, targets the unassigned benefactive role and bundles it together with the agent, thus yielding the reflexive meaning. Accordingly, Gungbe bare reflexive constructions can be represented as in (48), which stands for the underlying structure of example (38b).

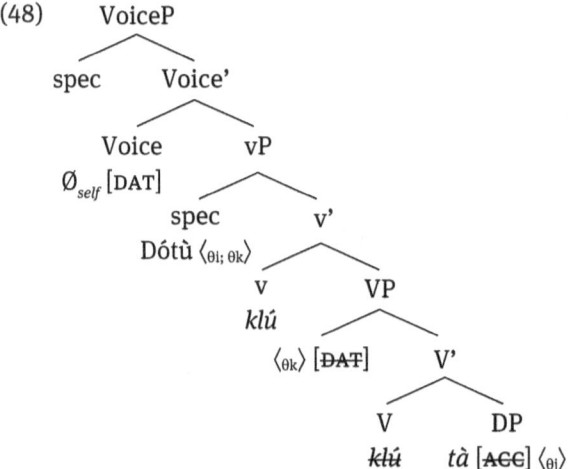

It appears from this analysis that French, German, and Gungbe share the same underlying structure even though these languages express this structure differently. While French and Gungbe realize Voice with the clitic *se* or null reflexive pronoun, respectively, German expresses [Spec VoiceP] which hosts the strong pronoun *sich*.

6 Conclusion

In this paper we propose an analysis that accounts for reflexives with an additional direct object in French and German, building on Reinhart and Siloni (2005) and Sportiche (2014). Our analysis considers the following main ideas: (i) A functional projection VoiceP is merged, which selects vP. The so-called reflexive pronoun is merged in this functional projection, as its head (the French clitic *se* or Gungbe null reflexive pronoun) or in its specifier (the German strong pronoun *sich*). (ii) Bundling targets the Agent and benefactive theta-roles. This complex theta-role is mapped onto the subject position. (iii) The reflexive pronoun absorbs the closest unlicensed case (left behind by the bundled internal argument). After these operations have taken place, further movement operations can proceed to derive the sentence's surface structure.

The proposed analysis extends to bare reflexive constructions in Gungbe. In terms of Reinhart and Siloni's (2005) Lexicon-Syntax Parameter, it can be concluded that Gungbe, which does not seem to have any morphological means to allow arity operations in the lexicon, should be considered a syntax language.

References

Aboh, Enoch Oladé. 2004. *The morphosyntax of complement-head sequences.* New York: Oxford University Press.
Aboh, Enoch Oladé & Michel DeGraff. 2014. Some notes on bare noun phrases in Haitian Creole and in Gungbe: A transatlantic sprachbund perspective. In Tor, A. Åfarli & Brit Mæhlum (eds.), *The sociolinguistics of grammar,* 203–236. Amsterdam: John Benjamins.
Aboh, Enoch Oladé & Marina Dyakonova. 2009. Predicate doubling and parallel chains. *Lingua* 119(7). 1035–1065.
Aboh, Enoch Oladé, Norval Smith & Anne Zribi-Hertz. 2012. *The morphosyntax of reiteration in Creole and non-Creole languages.* Amsterdam & Philadelphia: John Benjamins.
de Alencar, Leonel F & Carmen Kelling. 2005. Are reflexive constructions transitive or intransitive? Evidence from German and Romance. In Miriam Butt & Tracy Holloway King (eds.), *Proceedings of the LFG05 Conference,* 1–20. Stanford: CSLI Publications.
Awóyalé, Yiwola. 1986. Reflexivization in Kwa languages. In Dimmendaal, Gerrit (ed.), *Current Approaches to African Linguistics* 3. 1–14. Dordrecht: Foris.
Benedicto, Elena & Diane Brentari. 2004. Where did All the arguments go? Argument-changing properties of classifiers in ASL. *Natural Language & Linguistic Theory* 22(4). 743–810.
Cardinaletti, Anna & Michal Starke. 1996. Deficient pronouns: A view from Germanic. In Höskuldur Thráinsson, Samuel David Epstein & Steve Peter (eds.), *Studies in comparative Germanic syntax volume II,* 21–65. Dordrecht: Kluwer.
Déchaine, Rose-Marie & Martina Wiltschko. 2002. Decomposing pronouns. *Linguistic Inquiry* 33. 409–442.

Ghomeishi, Jila, Ray Jackendoff, Nicole Rosen & Kevin Russell. 2004. Contrastive focus reduplication in English. *Natural Language & Linguistic Theory* 22. 307–357.

Junker, Marie-Odile & France Martineau. 1987. Les possessions inaliénables dans les constructions objet. *Revue Romane* 22(2). 194–209.

Kayne, Richard. 1975. *French syntax. The transformational cycle.* Cambridge MA.: The MIT Press.

Kayne, Richard. 2000. Person morphemes and reflexives in Italian, French and related languages. In Richard Kayne (ed.), *Parameters and universals*, 131–152. Oxford: Oxford University Press.

Koeneman, Olaf & Ad Neeleman. 2001. Predication, verb movement and the distribution of expletives. *Lingua* 111(3). 189–233.

Labelle, Marie. 2008. The French reflexive and reciprocal se. *Natural Language & Linguistic Theory* 833–876.

Osam, Kweku E. 2002. Reflexive marking and related functions in Akan. *Journal of Asian and African Studies* 64. 141–151.

Oya, Toshiaki. 2010. Three types of reflexive verbs in German. *Linguistics* 48(1). 227–257.

Postma, Gertjan. 1997. Logical entailment and the possessive nature of reflexive pronouns. In Hans Bennis, Pierre Pica & Johan Rooryck (eds.), *Atomism and binding*, 295–322. Dordrecht: Foris.

Reinhart, Tanya & Tal Siloni. 2005. The lexicon-syntax parameter. Reflexivization and other arity operations. *Linguistic Inquiry* 36(3). 389–436.

Sportiche, Dominique. 2014. French reflexive *se*: Binding and merge locality. In Enoch Oladé Aboh, Maria Teresa Guasti & Ian Roberts (eds.), *Locality*, 104–137. Oxford: Oxford University Press.

Virginia Hill
A micro-parameter for allocutive agreement

1 Introduction

One of the main debates in current studies of generative grammar concerns the interface between conversational pragmatics and syntax: is it or is it not the case that at least some of the pragmatic features involved in direct addresses arise as functional features computed in narrow syntax? The arguments range from admissibility (e.g., starting with Speas & Tenny 2003) to denial (e.g., DeCat 2013). The syntactization thesis gains increasing attention as linguists detect further empirical evidence to support it (e.g., the systematic distribution and syntactic behavior of particles of direct address, as in Haegeman 2014 or Miyagawa 2012), while also benefiting from new theoretical tools, especially in cartography (e.g., such as initiated in Cinque 1999; Rizzi 1997), that allow for a finer-grained representation of the left periphery of clauses.

Having these considerations in the background, the present paper brings a new piece of evidence to support the syntactic computation of the hearer/addressee pragmatic role. More precisely, it is argued that the syntactic mapping of speech acts at the left periphery of clauses allows us to detect the presence of allocutive agreement in some varieties of imperative clauses in Romanian and Albanian, in contexts which have been so far treated as "mysterious" in both traditional and formal approaches. Furthermore, the paper points out that this analysis is very informative for typology, since the allocutive agreement parameter discussed here may increase the inventory of Balkan Sprachbund properties.

2 Data, questions and hypothesis

Several studies of Romanian dialectology and historical linguistics point out and discuss the variation of morpheme ordering in imperative clauses, as shown in (1).

(1) a. *Duceți-vă*   în   cel   sătcel   **Default**
       go.2PL=REFL.2PL in   that hamlet
       'Go into that hamlet' (NT {26v}; mid17[th] c.)
    b. *Duce-vă-ți*   de   la   mine   **Marked**
       go.REFL.2PL=2PL from at   me
       'Go away from me' (Antim {354}; mid18[th] c.)

In (1a), the imperative verb displays the ending -*ți* for 2nd person plural, and is followed by the reflexive clitic *vă*, which is also in the 2nd person plural. This is the default morpheme ordering in Romanian imperative clauses, in both modern standard and colloquial registers, as well as in Old Romanian. However, the reverse morpheme ordering in (1b) is also possible in Old Romanian and in regional varieties of Modern Romanian. In this version, the reflexive clitic *vă* seems to be able to intervene between the verb stem and the person ending -*ți*. This is a marked option occurring since the 18th century texts (Frâncu 1981). For example, we see it in Eustatievici's grammar, as in (2). This morpheme ordering is preserved in certain regional varieties, and was included in *ALR I* with examples as in (3).

(2) *alege-vă-ț*   *voi*
  choose.IMP=REFL.2PL=2PL you
  'choose yourselves' (Eustatievici {57}; mid 18th c.)

(3) *întoarce-vă-ți*   *până* *mai* *e* *vreme*
  return.IMP.=REFL.2PL=2PL until still is time
  'return while you still have time' (from Mării 1969: 258/4; 20th c.)

Studies in dialectology and historical linguistics attribute the variation between (1a) and (1b) to metathesis in morphophonology, which would have arisen due to analogy with other inflectional forms that contain both *vă* and *ți*. The relevant inflectional forms differ from one study to another (Byck 1935; Morariu 1921; Istrătescu 1937; Mării 1969; Frâncu 1981). The same studies point out that a similar variation of morpheme ordering occurs in Albanian, in the same context (i.e., imperative clauses). Since the accounts these studies propose rely on the morphophonological properties of Romanian, they cannot be extended to Albanian, as the morphophonological rules are different for the two languages. Also, there is no historical context for albano-romanian bilingualism, so the crosslinguistic similarity remains unexplained.

As an alternative to the previous studies, this paper argues that a syntactic approach is more successful than the morphophonological ones for explaining and predicting the variation in (1a) and (1b), but only on the condition that such an approach makes use of the theoretical apparatus allowing for the encoding of speech acts features at the left periphery of clauses. In particular, the foregoing analysis capitalizes on the fact that imperative clauses encode a direct address, according to the distinctions in Svennung (1958). This has been discussed in several recent studies that point out the presence of a functional feature in these contexts, which encodes the pragmatic role of *addressee*.

Technically, keeping in mind that the clause hierarchy projects on the axis vP > TP > CP, the encoding of the *addressee* takes place above C. The relevant projection is labelled differently in different studies (e.g., SAP in Speas & Tenny 2003; JussiveP in Zanuttini 2008, Zanuttini et al 2012; SeP in Isac 2013), but here I will adopt the SAP label, which has been used more frequently (e.g., Miyagawa 2012; Haegeman & Hill 2014; Hill 2014). The resulting hierarchy is then vP > TP > CP > SAP.

On the basis of this theoretical framework, the hypothesis for the ongoing analysis is that -*ti* in (1b) encodes the *addressee* (i.e., it stands for the allocutive agreement), not the grammatical person, and that morphologically, this -*ti* is a clitic, not a suffix. The justification for this analysis concerns the interpretation: the switch from (1a) to (1b) triggers a change of interpretation at the pragmatic level, especially with respect to the identification of the addressee and his/her relation to the speaker. The restrictions on the occurrence of the allocutive agreement and on the word order further entail that the clausal derivation involves a higher functional field that encodes the speaker's point of view.

3 Defining *allocutive agreement*

The concept of allocutive agreement was introduced in the studies on Basque language (e.g., Trask 1997). The following definition ensues from the Basque data:

(4) Allocutive agreement = the morphosyntactic encoding of a physical property of the addressee, optionally clustered with the specification of (non)plurality and of the type of interpersonal relation with the speaker.

In Basque, all these properties are spelled out through one ending. For example, the clause 'I am Amalia' may display three different endings on the verb, as in (5), according to the pragmatic interpretation intended by the speaker: a formal address does not use the allocutive agreement (5a), whereas an informal address does. For the latter, the ending differs according to whether the addressee is a woman (5b) or a man (5c).

(5) a. *Amaia n-a-iz*   **Formal**
      Amaia ABS.1SG-PRES-be
 b. *Amaia n-a-u-**n***   **Informal** (feminine)
      Amaia ABS.1SG-PRES-have-2SG.FEM
 c. *Amaia n-a-u-**k***   **Informal** (masculine)
      Amaia ABS.1SG-PRES-have-2SG.MASC
      (https://en.wikipedia.org/wiki/Allocutive_agreement)

In (5), the endings -*n* or -*k* indicate not only the physical gender of the addressee, but also the number (singular) and the familiar interpersonal relation with the speaker.[1]

4 Clues for allocutive agreement in Romanian

There are several clues that indicate the allocutive agreement status of -*ți* in (1b): First, speakers of any registers and regional varieties can use the unmarked version in (1a), which gives no specifications about the addressee. However, as Mării (1969) points out, in certain regional varieties some speakers opt for the morpheme ordering in (1a) when they address women, but for (1b) when they address men. In some other regiolects, speakers opt for (1a) when they address adults but for (1b) when they address children. Hence, these speakers use the contrast in morpheme ordering to encode properties of the addressee, such as gender, or the nature of the relation between speaker and addressee.

The second clue comes from utterances as in (6).

(6) *duceți-vă-ți*
 go. IMP.2PL=REFL.2PL=2PL
 'Go!'

These forms arise regionally around the 20th century and indicate the possibility of repeating the morpheme -*ți*. In Romanian, no other inflected verb form accepts the reduplication of the person ending. So one of the two -*ți* is likely to encode something else than the grammatical person of the subject.

Finally, utterances as in (7) indicate the dissociation between -*ți* and the subject agreement.

(7) *mărturisește-te-ți*   *la biserică*[2]
 confess. IMP.2SG=REFL.2SG=ALLOC.2PL   in church

The old women in the rural area around Alexandria use (7) when they address their grandchildren. Since in (7) the grammatical person is in singular, marking the

---

[1] Oyharçabal (1993) notices that the Basque allocutive agreement is excluded from imperatives. This has to do with the mutual exclusion between the ending for T-phi 2nd person and the ending for the addressee agreement. The languages discussed in this paper show the systematic opposite option: the allocutive agreement occurs mainly in imperatives, and the morpheme is identical to that for T-phi 2nd person. This is an interesting typological contrast to be accounted for in some other paper. Note that there is independent evidence for the allocutive agreement versus grammatical agreement status of Rom. *ți* and Albanian *ni*, since the former may arguably occur sometimes on gerunds and the latter as attached to DPs and PPs – data provided in this paper.
[2] I thank Monica Irimia for pointing out this regional variation.

subject-verb agreement, it means that final -*ţi*, usually associated with 2nd person plural, does not encode the person of the subject, but some other feature having to do with the age of the addressee and their familiar relation with the speaker.

5 Analysis

5.1 Theoretical framework

The starting point for the analysis is the structure of the unmarked version of an imperative clause, such as (1a). Recent studies on the syntax of imperatives argue for the representation of a speech act projection at the left periphery of these clauses in order to better grasp the possible variation in the type of subjects that may arise in these constructions. The basic configuration is given in (8), following the general idea in Speas & Tenny (2003).

(8)
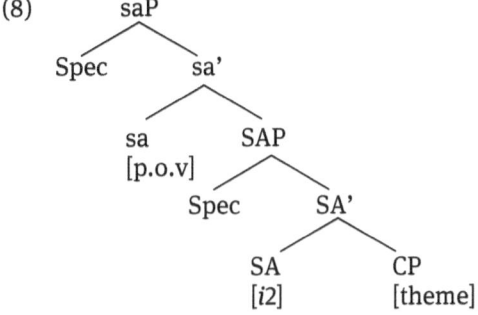

In this model, SA has the same properties as V, that is, it projects upwards while computing the pragmatic roles of addressee, speaker and sentience (the topic of conversation), in a way that parallels the computation of thematic roles as subject, indirect object and direct object. The pragmatic roles are encoded as the functional features of [point of view], [2nd person] and [theme].

The relevant advantage of (8) over the CP capped analyses of imperative clauses is that it provides two positions for encoding phi-features (i.e., SA and C/T lower in the hierarchy), so imperatives clauses where the addressee is different from the grammatical subject can be accounted for; for example: "Sargent, nobody leave this room!" (Zanuttini 2008). The feature that encodes the addressee role is an interpretable 2nd person, since it is clear that there is an addressee. However, further indications about this addressee may need to be encoded, depending on language register. In regional varieties, some physical properties of the addressee are also encoded, and/or his/her social status in relation to the speaker. These are mapped as uninterpretable features that need valuation. Crucially, the allocutive agreement feature is different from the phi-feature in T, which is uninterpretable (i.e., it can be 1st, 2nd, 3rd) and unvalued.

5.2 Implementation

In Romanian, a default imperative clause allows for the word order in (9).

(9) [Mariei]_{TOPIC} [flori]_{FOCUS} **du-i** mâine, nu bomboane.
    Maria.DAT flowers give.IMP.2SG=to.her tomorrow not candy
    'As for Maria, give her some flowers tomorrow, not candies.'

In (9), the clitic pronoun *-i* is in the TP field (Dobrovie-Sorin 1994; Alboiu 2002 a.o.), let's say in a CliticP (KLP). The verb precedes it, indicating V-to-C above T/KL, which is the standard approach to most Romance and Balkan languages (Rivero & Terzi 1995; Zanuttini 1997 a.o.). Furthermore, considering the articulated hierarchy of the CP (i.e., as in Rizzi 1997), the word order in (9) indicates that the verb moves to Fin, since it is above T/KL but lower than Topic > Focus constituents.³ Accordingly, the underlying configuration for (1a) is as in (10).

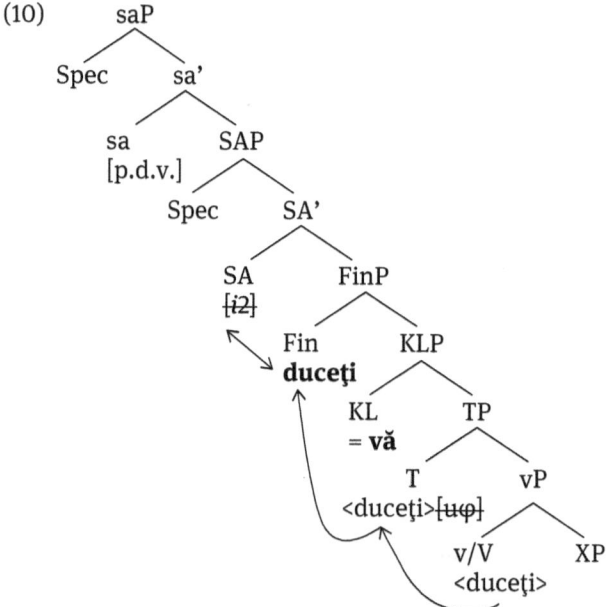

In this configuration, the verb checks the phi-feature of T by V/v-to-T, and moves to Fin, to check the deontic modality feature inherent to imperative CPs (Isac 2013). The phi-feature [*i*2] in SA is checked by long distance Agree between SA and Fin. This configuration imposes identity between the addressee and the subject. The

---

3 Rizzi's (1997) hierarchy is as follows: [_{CP} Force > Top > Focus > Fin] > TP.

word order in (9) and the identification of Fin as the landing site for V movement is important only insofar as it prevents an analysis where V would move up to SA. In the rest of the paper, I use Fin interchangeably with C.

Now we can consider the structure of (1b) according to the same pattern.

Before proceeding to the clause structure, it is important to take into account Frâncu's (1981) observation that the rise of the morpheme ordering in (1b) has been preceded by the ordering in (11), which can be seen in texts that predate (1b) by a hundred years.

(11) a. ***Întoarce-vă***   de   asupra mea,   că   eu am făcut   rău
    turn.IMP=REFL.2PL from above me   that I   have.1=done damage
    'Turn from me, because I've damaged and wronged...'
                                                    (NB 165/15 apud Frâncu 1981: 84)
 b. ***Mărturisi-vă***   Lui   şi   lăudaţi   numele   lui
    confess.IMP=REFL.2PL to.him and glorify.IMP.2PL name.the his
    'Confess to Him and glorify his name' (NB 125/25,39 apud Frâncu 1981: 84)
 c. ***Întoarce-vă***   către   mine
    turn.IMP=REFL.2PL   towards   Me
    'Return towards me' (NB 10,211/10 apud Frâncu 1981: 84)

In (11), *vă* has the double task of spelling out the reflexive pronoun and the ending for subject-verb agreement, since, although -*ţi* is absent, the interpretation is that of 2nd person for both the reflexive and the person ending.[4] As (11b) indicates, -*ţi* is present in the author's grammar, since it occurs on imperative verbs with active voice (e.g., *lăudaţi* 'glorify'), but is eliminated when the imperative is in reflexive voice, where *vă* takes over the function of spelling out the subject-verb agreement as well as the reflexivity.

The implication of (11) is that, on the one hand, the clitic *vă* is reanalysed as a suffix, which is always the status of the grammatical person marker in Romanian; and on the other hand, -*ţi* is available for reanalysis somewhere else. Crucially, the attestation of such constructions about a century before the variation in (1a)/(1b) arises indicates a time of instability in the classification of post-verbal morphemes, when one and the same item may be treated either as a clitic or as an affix. Thus, the underlying configuration for (11) is given in (12), where the clause structure is similar to the one in (10), the only difference being the spelling of the subject-verb agreement as -*vă* instead of -*ţi*.

---

4 As an anonymous reviewer noticed, another possibility is to say that T-phi is realized as a morpheme zero. The main point is that T-phi is valued as 2nd plural here, although the verb stem is also used for 2nd singular. However, the singular reading is blocked by the presence of *vă*. So, the result is the same: *vă* is the key for number valuation on T, which plausibly entails *vă* in T.

(12) = (10)

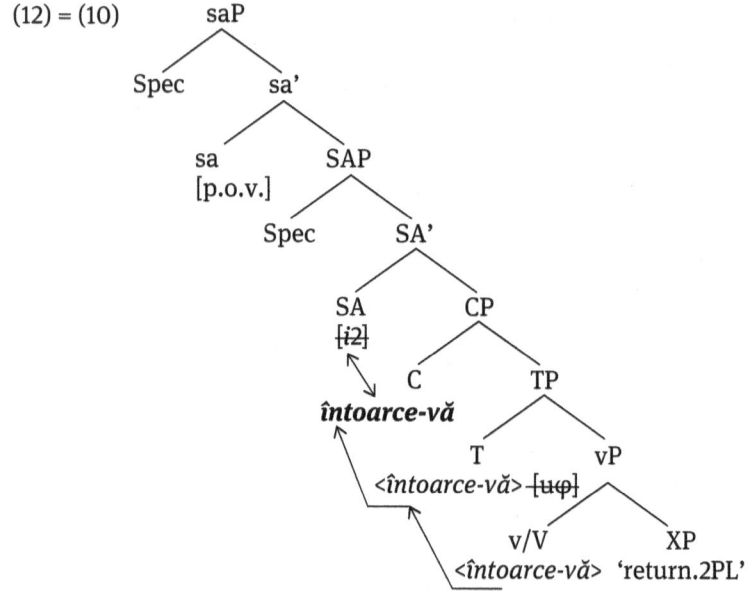

The unstable status of morphemes, as proposed for (11), can explain the reanalysis of -*ți* upwards in the hierarchy (as in Roberts & Roussou 2003) from T to SA, that is, as the allocutive agreement marker that spells out the higher phi-feature, where the association with the 2nd person is maintained. Thus, [*i*2] in SA is checked through the direct merge of -*ți*, as in (13).

(13)

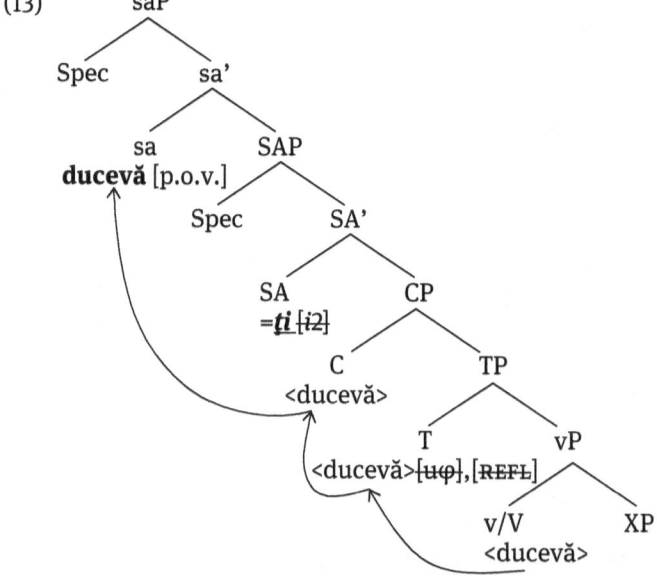

The visibility of SA in (13) (versus its non-spelling in 10–12) is justifiable through the speaker's marking of his/her point of view: the speaker intends to indicate their position of authority in relation to the addressee. In this context, [p.o.v] acts as a probe, triggering head-to-head movement of the verb for feature checking and valuation. The outcome is V/T/C-to-sa in (13). Note that in (13) *vă* has the affixal status, as in (12), so it raises with the verb. Also, the direct merge of *-ți* in SA checks and deletes the feature associated with this head, so SA is not visible to verb movement, in the same way KL allows for verb movement to C without intervention.

The analysis proposed so far can be summarized as follows: at the time when the status of post-verbal morphemes was unstable (between affixal or clitic), (1a) arises when *-ți* counts as affixal and *vă* as clitic; on the other hand, (1b) arises from the opposite analysis, with *vă* affixal and *-ți* clitic. Information regarding the clitic versus affixal status of allocutive *-ți* comes from two sources: (i) it may rarely occur on gerund verbs (e.g., *bucurându-vă-ți* 'enjoying yourselves'), and there is no justification for agreement affix on gerunds; and (ii) its Albanian equivalent is clearly a clitic, since it attaches to DPs and PPs, see (17)–(18) below. Importantly, the alternation of ordering between *vă* and *ți* takes place in syntax, since it affects the interpretation, and more precisely, the pragmatic values it involves.[5] Thus, the relevant syntactic computation takes place in the area where the pragmatic features relevant to speech acts are mapped to syntax as functional features.

As mentioned for (13), the [p.o.v] feature is the essential ingredient for deriving an imperative with allocutive agreement. As any uninterpretable feature, it can probe either a head or a XP, and (13) illustrates the head-to-head movement option. However, Mării (1969) and Frâncu (1981) point out that by the 19th century utterances as in (14) start to appear, where the verb is in active, not in reflexive voice. These versions of imperative clauses are rare and geographically limited.

(14) *Împleți-vă-ți*   muzeul   de   săpături,   inscripții
     fill.IMP.2PL=DAT.2PL=2PL museum.the of diggings   inscriptions
     'Fill your museum with diggings and inscriptions' (Bolliac apud Frâncu 1981: 87)

In (14), *-ți* is used twice, once for spelling out the subject-verb agreement, and once for allocutive agreement. At that time, the two uses of this morpheme were stabilized; that is, the allocutive agreement analysis of *-ți* ceased to depend on the affixal status of the reflexive *vă*.

The consequence of this stabilization is that the reflexive *vă* has also a stable clitic status, and as such, it can be replaced by other clitic pronouns, as in (15).

---

5 I assume that interpretation cannot be altered at PF, so the cases of mesoclisis discussed here cannot be considered as purely PF phenomena, as they are in Arregi (2015).

(15) *cătați-le-ți*
search.IMP.2PL=them=ALLOC.2PL
'search for them' (Frâncu 1981: 87)

Therefore, (14) and (15) follow a similar derivational pattern, detailed in (16), where the clitic pronouns are located in KLP, in the inflectional field, and [p.o.v] probes a constituent instead of the verb. That is, vP moves above CP after being vacated of lexical items. CP is then moved to Spec, saP.

(16)

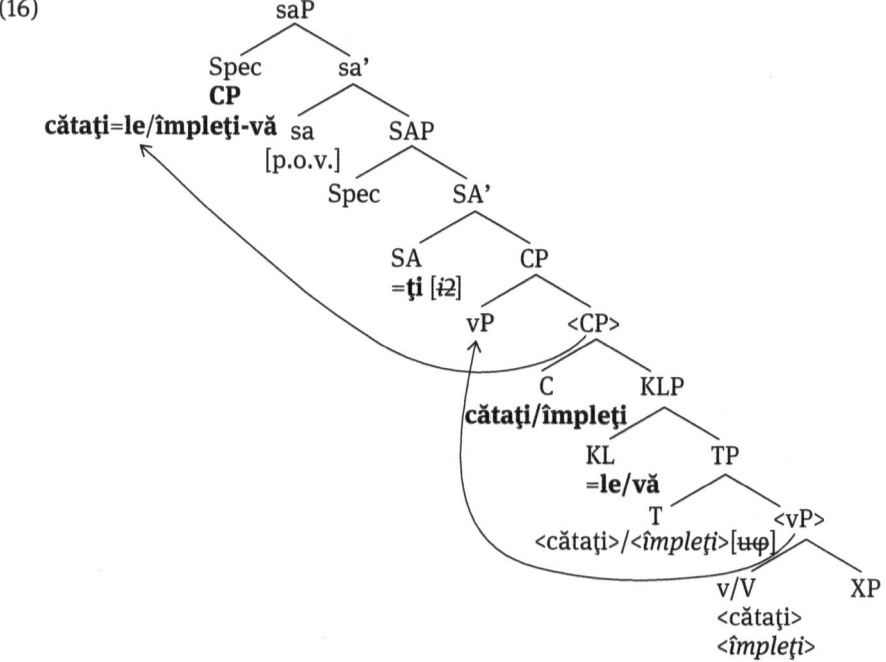

To conclude, the allocutive agreement takes place in syntax in Romanian imperative clauses, and the underlying derivation consists of two options: (i) head-to-head movement to sa, as in (13), or (ii) phrasal movement, through CP to Spec, saP, as in (16). Diachronically, (13) precedes (16), and the emergence of (16) is motivated by the stabilisation of the morphological status of the morphemes *vă* and *ți*.

6 Albanian

The syntactic analysis proposed so far has the advantage of capturing the variation between (1a) and (1b) not only for Romanian, but for any other language where such variation is related to interpretation. Albanian is a case in order.

In this language, the particle *ni* appears on formulae of direct address as a mark of politeness and plurality, as shown in (17) (data from Joseph 2010).

(17) a. *mirëdita**ni***
good.day.ni.PL
'Good day!'
b. *o   burra**ni**!*
PRT oameni.ni.PL
'hey folks,...'
c. *tungjatjeta**ni**!*
hello. ni.PL

In (17), *ni* attaches to phrasal constituents, so it may only be a clitic and, pragmatically, an indicator of allocutive agreement.

Albanian *ni* is also used as a verb suffix that spells out the subject-verb agreement for 2nd person plural. Thus, Albanian imperative clauses have the possibility of reverting the morpheme ordering in the same way Romanian does in (1b) versus (1a). This is illustrated in (18) (data from Kallulli 1995).

(18) a. *Hap-**ni**-e   dritaren!*
open-2PL-it.ACC   window
'Open the window!'
b. *Hap-e-**ni**   dritaren!*
open-it-2PL   window
'Open the window!'

In (18), the morpheme *ni* is a suffix spelling out the subject verb agreement in (18a), but a clitic used for allocutive agreement in (18b).

Let us start again by considering the underlying structure of a default imperative clause, this time in Albanian. According to Kallulli (1995), the respective configuration involves V-to-C, as in (19).

(19)   Albanian: default imperative clause

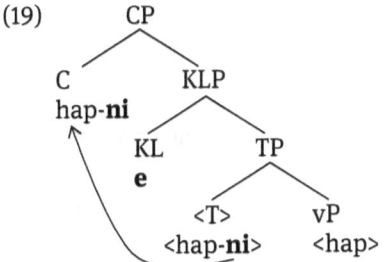

Predictably, the configuration in (19), which is responsible for the derivation of (18a), is identical to the structure of a default imperative clause in Romanian, as given in (10).

On the other hand, the marked morpheme ordering in (18b) follows the pattern in (16), with phrasal movement, given that any clitic pronoun may intervene between the verb stem and *ni*. Hence, the configuration in (16) is repeated as (20) for Albanian.

(20) Albanian: marked imperative clause

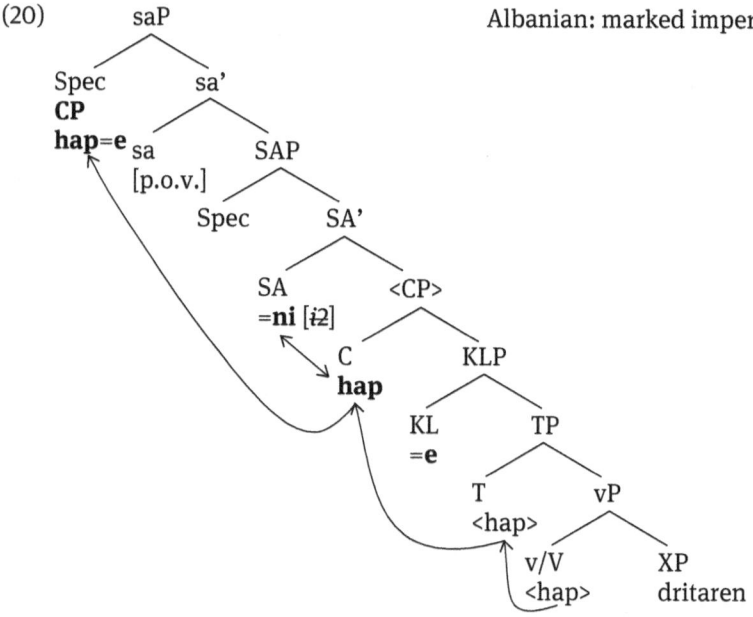

In sum, Albanian assigns a double morphological status to *-ni* in the same way *-ţi* is treated in Romanian: it is an affix when it spells out the grammatical person ending, but a clitic when it spells out the allocutive agreement. Unlike Romanian, Albanian does not display the option for head-to-head movement under probing from [p.o.v] in sa, but only the phrasal movement option. This is predictable under the observation that no reflexive pronoun is reanalysed as a person suffix in Albanian, the way *-vă* is in Romanian (see example 11).

The main point is that the syntactic analysis proposed here provides a systematic account with crosslinguistic applicability, without the need of language contact justification. It follows that anytime a language has post-verbal elements with unstable or dual morphological status, morpheme reordering may arise, and this reordering may be used for varying the interpretation.

In Albanian and Romanian, the variation in interpretation has to do with the allocutive agreement, an option that may have deep roots in diachrony: according to Rasmussen (1985), *ni* is an Indo-European deictic adverb that was reanalyzed as a bound morpheme for encoding the 2nd person or the addressee in general. This element also occurs in Old Romanian texts, as an attention drawer at the beginning of a direct address (no relation to verb syntax), and is still preserved as such in regional varieties. The point is that Balkan languages inherited the tendency of encoding the addressee in more complex ways (e.g., through dedicated vocative particles, reversed vocatives, use of the definite article for signalling the interpersonal relations), and this is also reflected in the morpheme reordering in imperative clauses, which are prototypical formulae of direct address. Historical linguists (e.g., Francu 1981; Joseph 2010) claim that the same mechanism is used for the same purpose in other Balkan languages (i.e., Serbian, Thessalian Greek, South Italian dialects), genetically unrelated to Albanian or Romanian. Hence, one may make an argument for the marking of allocutive agreement as a Balkan Sprachbund property, on a par with clitic doubling, subjunctive versus infinitive etc.

7 Conclusions

This paper focused on the variation of morpheme ordering shown in (1a, b) for Romanian and in (18a, b) for Albanian, and argued that it does not allow for free alternation, but it involves a switch in the interpretation. Since the LF interface receives indications for interpretation from syntax, the morpheme (re)ordering in Romanian and Albanian is implemented in syntax, not at a later point, at the PF interface (e.g., see Arregi 2015 for Spanish).

More precisely, the analysis established that the switch in interpretation has to do with the (non)marking of the allocutive agreement in imperative clauses. This context is sensitive to the encoding of the addressee since the imperative is inherently a form of address, on a par with the vocative.[6] Furthermore, since the imperative involves V-to-C, all the morphemes are post-verbal and facilitate instability in the speaker's analysis of their morphological status, as suffixes or clitics. The exploitation of this dual morphological status, together with upward reanalysis in the syntactic hierarchy and the options for feature checking mechanisms (e.g., direct merge or head-to-head or phrasal movement) led to intra and crosslinguistic variation in the derivational output which, relies, however, on a stable and uniform underlying pattern.

The uniform underlying pattern for these constructions was shown to include a speech acts field at the left periphery of clauses. Without this field,

---

[6] Empirical evidence for the inherent relation between imperatives and vocatives is provided in various studies, consisting mainly in the occurrence of vocative endings on imperative verbs or phonological truncations and merging with vocative particles (Schadeberg 1990; Floricic & Molinu 2012; Hill 2014: ch. 7). This type of feature copying and phonological processing do not occur with other verbs in the presence of vocatives.

the syntactic encoding of the allocutive agreement cannot be fully accounted for (see also Miyagawa 2012). For example, without a saP field, the morpheme reordering in (15) and (18b) needs either a purely phonological approach (which is inappropriate when changes in readings occur), or resort to stipulations such as verb excorporation, where the person ending/suffix is left in T (Kallulli 1995). Furthermore, there would be no way of distinguishing between the mechanism deriving (1b), that is, head-to-head movement, from the mechanism deriving (15), that is phrasal movement, which would lead to wrong predictions with respect to pronoun alternation, which, for Romanian, is restricted with head-to-head movement but free with phrasal movement.

Acknowledgements: I take this opportunity to extend an official "thank you" to Liliane, who taught me generative grammar and continued to provide moral support, advice and collaboration over the years.

Sources

ALR I	Pop, Sever & Emil Petrovici (eds). 1942. *Atlasul lingvistic român* (ALR I), vol. II. [The Romanian linguistic atlas]. Sibiu-Leipzig Publishers.
Antim	Ştrempel, Gabriel (ed). 1972. *Antim Ivireanu. Opere*. [Writings by Antim Ivireanu]. Bucureşti: Editura Minerva.
CEV	Puşcariu, Sextil & Alexie Procopovici (eds.). 1914. *Coresi, Carte cu învăţătură (1581)*. [Catechism book printed by Coresi in 1581]. Bucureşti: Atelierele Grafice Socec & Co.
Eustat	Ursu, Nicolae (ed.). 1969. *Eustatievici Braşoveanul. Gramatica rumânească*. [Romanian grammar by Eustatievich of Brashov]. Bucureşti: Editura Ştiinţifică.
NB	Moisil, Florica & Dan Zamfirescu (eds.). 1970. *Învăţăturile lui Neagoe Basarab către fiul său Theodosie*. [Neagoe Basarab's teachings to Theodosie, his son]. Bucureşti: Editura Minerva.
Neculce	Iordan, Iorgu. 1955. *Ion Neculce, Letopiseţul Ţării Moldovei*. [The chronicle of the Moldavian Principality by Ion Neculce]. Bucureşti: Editura de Stat.
NT	Anonymous editor. 1988. *Simion Ştefan. Noul Testament (1648)*. [The New Testament edited by Simion Stefan in 1648]. Alba Iulia: Editura Episcopiei Ortodoxe Române.

References

Arregi, Karlos. 2015. How to sell a melon: Post-syntactic mesoclisis in Spanish imperatives. Paper presented at the Linguistic Symposium on Romance Languages 45, University of Campinas, May 6–9.

Byck, Jacques. 1935. Sur l'impératif en roumain. *Bulletin Linguistique* III. 54–64.

Floricic, Frank & Lucia Molinu. 2012. Romance monosyllabic imperatives and markedness. In Stolz T., Nau N & Stroh C. (eds.), *Monosyllables: from phonology to typology*, 149–172. Berlin: Akademie-Verlag.

Frâncu, Constantin. 1981/82.Vechimea unei particularități dialectale dacoromâne cu corespondent în albaneză. *Anuar de lingvistică și istorie literară* XXVIII, 81–90.

Haegeman, Liliane & Virginia Hill. 2013. The syntacticization of discourse. In Raffaella Folli, Robert Truswell & Christina Sevdali (eds.), *Syntax and its limits*, 370–390. Oxford: Oxford University Press.

Hill, Virginia. 2014. *Vocatives: How syntax meets with pragmatics*. Leiden: Brill.

Isac, Daniela. 2013. What's in an imperative. Concordia University manuscript.

Isac, Dana & Edith Jakab. 2004. Mood and force features in the languages of the Balkans. In Olga Mišeska-Tomić (ed.), *Balkan syntax and semantics*, 315–338. Amsterdam: John Benjamins.

Joseph, Brian. 2010. Revisiting the origin of the Albanian 2nd plural verbal ending –*ni*. In Ronald Kim, Norbert Oettinger, Elisabeth Rieken & Michael Weiss (eds.), *Ex Anatiolia Lux*, 180–183. New York: Beech Stave Press.

Kallulli, Dalina. 1995. *Clitics in Albanian*. Trondheim: University of Trondheim dissertation.

Mării, Ion. 1969. Însemnări despre imperativele regionale. [Notes on regional imperatives]. *Cercetări de lingvistică* 14. 255–263.

Morariu, Leca. 1921. *Morfologia verbului predicativ românesc*. [The morphology of the Romanian full verb]. Cluj: University of Cluj dissertation.

Oyharçabal, B. 1993. Verb agreement with non-arguments: On allocutive agreement. In Hualde J. I & Ortiz de Urbina J. (eds), *Generative studies in Basque linguistics*, 89–114. Amsterdam: John Benjamins.

Rasmussen, Jens E. 1985. Miscellaneous morphological problems in Indo-European languages. *Lingua Posnaniensis* 28. 27–62.

Rizzi, Luigi. 1997. The fine structure of the left periphery. In Liliane Haegeman (ed.), *Elements of grammar*, 281–339. Dordrecht: Kluwer.

Schadeberg, T.C. 1990. *A sketch of Umbundu*. Köln: Rudiger Koppe Verlag.

Speas, Peggy & Carol Tenny. 2003. Configurational properties of point of view roles. In Anne-Marie Di Sciullo (ed.), *Asymmetry in grammar*, 315–344. Amsterdam: John Benjamins.

Svennung, J. 1958. *Anredeformen Vergleichende Forschungen*. Uppsala: Almqvist & Wiksell Boktryckeri AB.

Trask, Larry. 1997. *The history of Basque*. London: Routledge.

Zanuttini, Raffaella. 2008. Encoding the addressee in the syntax: Evidence from English imperative subjects. *Natural Language and Linguistic Theory* 26(1). 185–218.

Zanuttini, Raffaella, Pak M & Portner P. (2012). A syntactic analysis of interpretive restrictions on imperative, promissive and exhortative subjects. *Natural Language and Linguistic Theory*, 30(4). 1231–1274.

Kathleen M. O'Connor
Apposition in English and French

1 Introduction

Both English and French allow structures such as those in (1), where a non-restrictive non-finite element follows and modifies a noun phrase (DP).

(1) a. *John, my best friend, is a doctor.*
    b. *John, in hospital with flu, isn't coming to the meeting.*
    c. *John, happy about his course schedule, called up Bill for a drink.*

The non-restrictive modifier in (1a) appears to be a DP as well, while in (1b) it is a prepositional phrase and in (1c) an adjective phrase.

These three types do not always receive a unified analysis. The DP-DP types such as in (1a) are often treated differently from the types in (1b) and (1c) under the heading of apposition (e.g. Heringa 2011), whereas other researchers (Doron 1992; O'Connor 2008) treat all three types as a single category.

These disparities arise in large part because the category of apposition is itself ill-defined, giving rise to widespread disagreement about what apposition is and what characterizes apposition. For example, Burton-Roberts (1975) claims that the two parts of the apposition should be interchangeable (2a), which clearly rules out non-nominal types (2b), (2c).

(2) a. *My best friend, John, is a doctor.*
    b. **In hospital with flu, John, isn't coming to the meeting.*
    c. **Happy about his course schedule, John, called up Bill for a drink.*

Other analyses (e.g. Quirk et al. 1985) treat apposition as lying along a continuum, such that some structures would be more fully appositional than others.

Apposition is widely recognized as sharing certain characteristics in common with other structures such as non-restrictive relative clauses (3a) and absolute constructions (3b).

(3) a. John, who is in hospital with flu, isn't coming to the meeting.
    b. (Being) in hospital with flu, John isn't coming to the meeting.

The resemblance to non-restrictive relatives has inspired many researchers to propose that appositives are derived from non-restrictive relatives and vice versa (e.g. deVries 2006; see O'Connor (2008) for a summary), though it is not clear that all appositives are interchangeable with a non-restrictive relative. The examples in section 2, in which the appositive contains a complementiser, illustrate this fact.

As for absolutes, it may be that the two structures overlap to some extent, but an absolute, unlike an appositive, can be found before the DP that it modifies (O'Connor 2008) and often indicates a causal relationship between the two parts. For example, the appositive in (1a) cannot be fronted as an absolute (4) because there is no cause-effect relationship between the fact that John is my best friend and the fact that he is a doctor.

(4)   *My best friend, John is a doctor.

While there is clearly much work remaining to be done on the differences and overlap between these various structures, space constraints do not allow us to fully explore all of the parameters here. We will focus on DP, PP and AP types that follow a DP and are set off from the rest of the clause by punctuation indicating non-restrictiveness, i.e. a comma, a hyphen, parentheses, etc.

These may in fact constitute a subset of a wider category, which Griffiths (2015) refers to as attributions and Cardoso and deVries (2010) call attributive appositions (see also Heringa (2011) for a semantic typology of appositives). Griffiths (2015) takes the view that different types of appositives are derived syntactically from different underlying syntactic sources. It would be impossible here to do justice to this larger discussion of the external syntax of apposition, i.e. the relationship between the appositive and the host clause. O'Connor (2008) provides an initial summary of the approaches to the syntactic derivation of apposition and Griffiths (2015) also gives a complete discussion of the different alternatives. The reader is urged to consult these references for a complete discussion.

Under approaches that treat the DP, AP and PP types as belonging to the same category, efforts are concentrated on showing that all three types share much in common and should thus be seen as different examples of the same structure. Such approaches are less concerned with the relationship between the two parts of the apposition and more interested in the internal structure of the non-restrictive modifier itself. This is the approach that we will adopt here. We will revisit the internal structure of the second part of the apposition (henceforth, the appositive) in English and French in order to show that, in fact, all three types do indeed form a unified class in both languages. We will further argue that appositives should be more properly understood as non-finite clauses, rather than as single constituents.

In section 2, we examine the CP level of appositives and show that they are capable of hosting complementisers. In section 3, based on a study of adverbs, we show that appositives contain a large amount of functional structure. We turn in section 4 to the interaction of adverb positions with DP positions and reveal that appositives contain a certain number of DP projections. Section 5 contains a conclusion.

2 CP level of appositives

One of the clearest indicators that appositives consist of more than just a single constituent comes from the fact that appositives appear to contain a CP-level as evidenced by the presence of complementisers. This can be seen in the examples in (5).

(5) a. The road, <u>though no longer an officially designated route</u>, has been celebrated in books ('The Grapes of Wrath'), song ('Get Your Kicks on Route 66') and a TV series ('Route 66'). (*Los Angeles Times*, 26/12/02, page B2, col. 1)

b. *Près   de   vingt-cinq   ans   plus   tard,   le   sticker,   <u>quoiqu'un</u>*
near   of   twenty-five   years   more   late   the   sticker   though-a
<u>*peu   défraichi,*</u>   *orne   toujours   le   vieil   instrument*
little   faded   decorates   still   the   old   instrument
'Nearly twenty-five years later, the sticker, though a little faded, still decorates the old instrument.' (*Le monde online*, "Le retour de M. Clash", 24/12/14)

We adopt here the Split-CP hypothesis as proposed in Rizzi (1997) in which the CP is made up of several projections, including ForceP, TopP, FocP and FinP. ForceP hosts conjunctions and instantiates the illocutionary force of a proposition. TopP and FocP host topic-comment and focus-presupposition structures respectively, while FinP is the site of features relating to the finiteness of the proposition.

Haegeman (2004), in her study of central and peripheral adverbials in English, proposes that ForceP must be further broken down into two projections, SubP and ForceP, since some adverbial clauses, namely so-called central adverbial clauses, contain a conjunction, but have no independent illocutionary force. Furthermore, central adverbial clauses fail to authorize the topicalization or focalization of arguments, leading Haegeman (2004) to propose that the projection ForceP must be present to authorize the projection of TopP and FocP. Thus, a clause maximally contains the following projections[1]:

(6) SubP > ForceP > TopP > FocP > FinP

---

[1] Haegeman (2004) proposes an additional TopP lower than FocP that licenses topics in clitic left disclocation in Romance and that depends on the presence of FinP. We will not consider this topic position here, since clitic left dislocation would not be possible in the French examples given the absence of a verb in the appositives.

The presence of conjunctions indicates that the CP of appositives contains the projection SubP. Moreover, they may contain the conjunctions found in peripheral adverbial clauses, as seen in (5), which indicates that they have a ForceP projection and thus an illocutionary force independent of that of the host clause. This is confirmed by the fact that appositives may contain the high modal adverbs (evaluative, epistemic, evidential, see below), providing further evidence of independent illocutionary force, since these modal adverbs are typically associated with assertive force (Hooper and Thompson 1973; Haegeman 2008).

The presence of ForceP leads to questions about the possibility of topicalization or focalization within an appositive, following Haegeman's early (2003, 2006) hypothesis that ForceP authorizes the TopP and FocP projections. This prediction is not borne out in the case of appositives, as the examples in (7) and (8) show.

(7) a. His boss, *though happy with his efforts*, did not give him a raise.
　　b. *His boss, *though with his efforts happy*, did not give him a raise.
　　c. *His boss, *with his efforts though happy*, did not give him a raise.

(8) a. Son　　patron,　*quoique　content　de　ses　efforts,*　ne　lui　　a
　　　　his　　boss　　　though　　happy　　of　his　efforts　　neg　to-him　has
　　　　pas　　donné　　d'augmentation.
　　　　not　　given　　of raise
　　　　'His boss, though happy with his efforts, did not give him a raise.'
　　b. *Son patron, *quoique de ses efforts content*, ne lui a pas donné d'augmentation.
　　c. *Son patron, *de ses efforts quoique content*, ne lui a pas donné d'augmentation.

The failure to license topicalisation or focalization in appositives may be due to one of two factors. First, for whatever reason, other non-finite structures, such as infinitival clauses, fail to license a topic or a focus (Culicover and Levine 2001; Hooper and Thompson 1973), so it is possible that the non-finite nature of appositives is responsible for the lack of topicalization or focus.

Second, following Haegeman (2007, 2008) the absence of fronted arguments can be interpreted as the result of an intervention effect. This means that the same intervention effects that rule out a topic or a focus in a non-restrictive relative clause are at work. Under this assumption, a topic or focus in a non-restrictive relative blocks the movement of a relative element to SubP. Such a solution presupposes that appositives contain the relativization of a null element, which is blocked by a topic or focus, as in (9) and (10). (Note that (10) is the French version of (9a) and (9b)). This scenario is supported by Heringa (2011), who shows that appositives do indeed contain an E-type pronoun consistent with a relative clause analysis.

(9) a. *His boss, <u>who was appreciative of his efforts</u>, gave him a sizeable rise.*
b. **His boss, <u>who of his efforts was appreciative</u>, gave him a sizeable rise.*
c. **His boss, <u>who his efforts was appreciative of</u>, gave him a sizeable rise.*

(10) a. *Son patron, <u>qui était content de ses efforts</u>, lui a donné une grosse augmentation.*
b. **Son patron, <u>qui de ses efforts était content</u>, lui a donné une grosse augmentation.*

In sum, then, appositives appear to contain a CP consisting of a SubP and a Force P. SubP hosts the various complementisers allowed in appositives, and ForceP allows appositives to have an illocutionary force separate from that of the main clause, as evidenced by the presence of conjunctions that introduce peripheral adverbials. The absence of topicalisation and focalization indicates that the TopP and FocP projections appear to be absent. As for FinP, it is not clear whether this projection is present in the absence of a [+finite] feature, but it could be assumed that non-finite structures contain a FinP projection with a [-finite] feature.

3 Functional structure in appositives

3.1 Tests for functional structure

Several tests have been identified for detecting the presence of functional structure. Alexiadou, Haegeman, and Stavrou (2007) identify semantic, syntactic and morphological arguments that can be used to argue for the presence of functional structure. One semantic argument centers around the verb as the semantic nucleus of the clause that expresses information about tense. As for the DP, it may contain information about reference, including the number of the noun, and may even indicate whether the noun is an argument or a predicate by the presence or optional absence of a definite determiner.

Morphological arguments are based on the fact that, in many languages, inflectional morphemes surface on lexical heads and are seen as evidence of functional heads. For example, verbs can be inflected for tense, aspect, modality and voice, whereas a DP can be inflected for gender and number.

In terms of syntax, the distribution of phrases and lexical heads can indicate the presence of functional structure. For example, consider the position of adverbs in English compared to French, as in (11), where the adverb *always / toujours* is found between the subject and the verb *eat* in English, but after the verb *mange* in French (Alexiadou, Haegeman, and Stavrou 2007: 26).

(11) a. *Nelson always eats biscuits.*
   b. *Nelson mange toujours des croquettes.*

Assuming that the verb in English remains in its base position, while the verb in French moves to a position higher than the adverb, we must posit the existence of a functional projection that can host the verb (Pollock 1989). In English, though the verb does not raise as high as it does in French, some movement is allowed, since an adverb can appear in more than one position with respect to the auxiliary, as in (12) from Alexiadou, Haegeman, and Stavrou (2007: 27).

(12) a. *Nelson will have already eaten the biscuits.*
   b. *Nelson has already eaten the biscuits.*

Another piece of syntactic evidence relates to adverbs. It has been proposed that adverbs are related to the presence of functional projections in the clause, either because the adverb is adjoined to particular functional projections (Ernst 2002) or because the adverb is located in the specifier of dedicated functional heads (Alexiadou 1997; Cinque 1999; Laenzlinger 1998).

3.2 Applying the tests to appositives

It is difficult to apply many of these tests to appositives given their non-finite nature. In the absence of a verb, evidence for functional projections related to tense, aspect, mood and voice on the verb is naturally absent as well. Despite this issue, there is evidence that appositives can contain functional structure beyond what we have already shown in section 2, i.e. that appositives contain at least two functional projections belonging to the CP level.

On the semantic level, there are indications that appositives are or can contain predicates (Burton-Roberts 2006; Doron 1992). Two pieces of evidence support this argument. First, as shown in (1), appositives can belong to categories typically associated with predicates, such as a DP, PP or AP. Second, as pointed out by Doron (1992), the definite article is not obligatory on a singular DP in an appositive, which is a characteristic of predicate DPs. Examples are given in (13).

(13) a. *"Amy has worked with Brett Gorvy and she knows exactly how he operates," said Morgan Long, director of investment at the Fine Art Fund Group in London.* (*New York Times* online, "With acquisition, Sotheby's shifts strategy", 25/01/16)

b. *Thibaud Simphal,* <u>directeur général d'Uber en France,</u>
   Thibaud Simphal   director   general   of-Uber   in   France
   appelle   les   taxis   à   rejoindre   sa   plateforme   de   réservation
   calls   the   taxis   to   to-join   his   platform   of   reservation
   'Thibaud Simphal, managing director of Uber in France, is calling on taxis to join his reservation platform.' (*Le monde* online, "Les chauffeurs de taxis partent en guerre contre les VTC", 25/01/16)

Given these facts, an appositive can be said to contain functional structure related to predicates, for example a PredicateP (Bowers 1993), vP (Grimshaw 1991) or a RelatorP (den Dikken 2006).

In terms of syntax, it is clear that a DP in an appositive can indicate number, and, in French, gender. The absence of a verb makes it difficult to identify functional structure related to tense, aspect, mood and voice on the verb. However, it is possible to use the presence of adverbs to examine functional structure. Appositives can contain adverbs, as seen in (14). We examine this test in further detail in section 3.3.

(14) a. *Mr. Bertarelli,* <u>often the navigator on the boat his team races</u>, *has sailed competitively since his 20s.* (*New York Times* online, "Billionaires' yacht rivalry spills into courtroom", 30/08/08)

   b. *...aucune   marge   de   manoeuvre   n'est   ici   laissé   au*
      no   margin   of   maneuver   neg-is here left   to-the
      joueur,   qui   n'est   finalement   là   que   pour   assister
      player   who   neg-is finally   there that   for   to-attend
      au   déroulé   de   scènes,   certes   souvent   bouleversantes
      to-the   unrolling of   scenes   certainly often   upsetting
      'No room to maneuver is given to the player here, who is in the end there only to witness the unfolding of the scenes, certainly often upsetting.' (*Le monde* online, "'That dragon cancer', le jeu vidéo qui nous met face à la maladie d'un enfant de 5 ans", 18/01/16)

3.3 Adverbs and functional structure

Broadly speaking, two different approaches to adverb position can be distinguished in the literature: an approach based on adjunction and an approached based on functional projections. Under the adjunction approach, exemplified by Ernst (2002), adverbs are assumed to be adjoined to different projections of the clause as a function of what elements in the clause they modify. For example, manner adverbs are adjoined to the PredicateP or to the VP, which accounts for their interpretation as modifying the action of the verb itself independent of the subject. In terms of functional structure, the presence of an adverb in an appositive is evidence for the presence of the projection that the adverb is adjoined to, which may or may not be a functional projection.

In the functional specifier approach, typified by Cinque (1999) as part of the cartographic approach to clause structure, adverbs are found in the specifiers of dedicated functional projections that account for the interpretation of the adverb. As a function of the language, the heads of these projections may be empty or may contain markers of tense, aspect, modality, etc. These projections are organized into a fixed hierarchy located in the IP level of the clause above the VP projection (or whatever projections compose it). The assumption is that adverbs themselves do not generally move, which means that the different positions available to an adverb relative to other elements in the clause must be the result of the movement of these other elements. Cinque (1999) further proposes that this sequence of functional projections is universal, such that all languages contain the same set of functional projections ordered in the same way. Thus, the presence of an adverb is evidence for the presence of the functional projection in whose specifier it is found.

Both of these approaches allow for the detection of functional structure (O'Connor 2009). We will adopt the functional specifier approach as presented by Cinque for the purposes of this paper. This account provides for a far more detailed comparison of functional structure and also allows for a more fine-grained analysis of DP positions, as we will see in section 4.

Cinque (1999) thus proposes a highly articulated functional structure for the IP domain of the clause with a large number of functional projections. This hierarchy is shown in (15), from the highest adverb domain to the lowest. The English and French adverbs are given for each projection, given in the subscript. See also Laenzlinger (2002) on the French hierarchy. Note that there may be more than one adverb associated with each projection; the adverbs given here are representative of their class.

(15) *frankly / franchement*$_{\text{MoodSpeechAct}}$ > *fortunately / heureusement*$_{\text{MoodEvaluative}}$ > *allegedly / apparemment*$_{\text{MoodEvidential}}$ > *probably / probablement*$_{\text{ModEpistemic}}$ > *once / une fois / autrefois*$_{\text{T(Past)}}$ > *then / ensuite*$_{\text{T(Future)}}$ > *perhaps / peut-être*$_{\text{MoodIrrealis}}$ > *necessarily / nécessairement*$_{\text{ModNecessity}}$ > *possibly*$_{\text{ModPossibility}}$ > *willingly / intentionnellement*$_{\text{ModVolitional}}$ > *inevitably / inévitablement*$_{\text{ModObligation}}$ > *cleverly / intelligemment*$_{\text{ModAbility/Permission}}$ > *usually / habituellement*$_{\text{AspHabitual}}$ > *again / de nouveau*$_{\text{AspRepetitive(I)}}$ > *often / souvent*$_{\text{AspFrequentative(I)}}$ > *quickly / rapidement*$_{\text{AspCelerative(I)}}$ > *already /*

déjà~T(Anterior)~ > *no longer / (ne) plus*~AspTerminative~ > *still / encore*~AspContinuative~ > *always / toujours*~AspPerfect~ > *just / juste*~AspRetrospective~ > *soon / bientôt*~AspProximative~ > *briefly / brièvement*~AspDurative~ > *characteristically / typiquement*~AspGeneric / Progressive~ > *almost / presque*~AspProspective~ > *completely / entièrement* ~AspSgCompletive(I)~ > *tout*~AspPlCompletive~ > *well / bien*~Voice~ > *fast/early / vite* ~AspCelerative(II)~ > *again / de nouveau*~AspRepetitive(II)~ > *often / souvent* ~AspFrequentative(II)~ > *completely / complètement*~AspSgCompletive(II)~

It should be noted that the adverb *tout* for AspectPluralCompletive does not have an equivalent in English. Similarly, the adverb *possibly* in English does not have a good French equivalent. Such cases are not necessarily indicative of different adverb hierarchies in the two languages but can be seen as an indicator that the specifiers are not obligatorily filled. Furthermore, some adverbs occur twice in the hierarchy, which is linked to the fact that some adverbs can have two interpretations. For example, *again* can have the meaning of "do something a second, third, etc. time" or it can have a restitutive meaning, as in "put the book on the shelf again". The idea is that there are in fact two adverbs *again*, each one associated with a different projection, which accounts for the two meanings.

Based on this account, the presence of any of these adverbs in an apposition indicates the presence of the corresponding functional projection. Rather than go through each of the 30 adverbs for each language to show that they can be present in appositives, we will use a selection of adverbs. In fact, adverbs are often seen as divided into distinct classes (e.g. Ernst, 2002; Jackendoff 1972; Laenzlinger 2002; Tenny 2000). Tenny (2000) for example proposes that Cinque's (1999) should be grouped into six groups according to their semantic properties in order to reduce the number of projections and to make the classes less arbitrary.

Tenny (2000) proposes the classes given in (16) along with their corresponding adverbs:

(16) a. Point of view adverbs: frankly, fortunately, allegedly, probably
b. Deictic time adverbs: once, then
c. Truth value adverbs: perhaps, necessarily, possibly
d. Subject-oriented adverbs: willingly, inevitably, cleverly
e. Middle aspect adverbs: usually, again, often, quickly, already, no longer, still, always, just, soon, briefly, characteristically, almost
f. Core event adverbs: completely, well, fast/early, again, often, completely

Thus, if we combine Cinque's (1999) hierarchy with Tenny's (2000) proposal, we can assume that the presence of one adverb from each class within an appositive indicates the presence of the corresponding functional projection.

The sentences in (17) give representative examples of appositions containing adverbs from the classes in (16) for English, and (18) provides examples for French.

(17) a. Point of view adverbs: *Tyrie said someone, probably Bailey, head of the BoE's Prudential Regulation Authority supervisory arm, needed to take "a leadership role"...* (*New York Times* online, "Senior lawmaker urges UK banks to invest in IT to prevent failures, 23/01/16)[2]
  b. Deictic time adverbs: *His clubhouse, first on Pitkin avenue and then in a brownstone on Eastern Parkway, doled out tons of coal, Passover food baskets and other largess.* (*New York Times* online, "An old-time king-maker and his political legacy", 24/08/08)
  c. Truth value adverbs: *Somewhere, a child, perhaps a girl, will be born to mark this threshold event.* (http://www.rotarydoctorbank.org /99i/db_99_3b.htm)
  d. Subject-oriented adverbs: *Seemingly still in shock from his ordeal, Mr. Confortola gave a sketchy recollection of the events, inevitably full of questions about what happened and what went wrong.* (*New York Times* online, "Tragic toll after chaos on mountain", 06/08/08)
  e. Middle aspect adverbs: *Fill out the form provided by your state's health department, usually available from your doctor or local hospital.* (*New York Times* online, "Personal health; Name a proxy early to prepare for the unexpected", 18/11/03)
  f. Core event adverbs: *...Douglas Brinkley writes, "My hope is that this history, fast out of the gates, may serve as an opening effort in Katrina scholarship."* (*New York Times* online, "Hell and high water", 09/07/06)

(18) a. Point of view adverbs: Le premier ministre turc Ahmet Davutoglu
        the first minister Turkish Ahmet Davutoglu
        a convoqué mardi une réunion de crise après la
        has summoned Tuesday a meeting of crisis after the
        violente explosion, probablement un attentat, qui a
        violent explosion probably an attack that has
        tué au moins dix personnes dans le coeur
        killed to-the less ten people in the heart
        historique d'Istanbul
        historical of-Istanbul

---

[2] Note that example (17a) contains stacked appositives. We are not able to provide an analysis here of how this works, but speculate that in some cases the two appositives share a single anchor, while in others the anchor for the second appositive is contained in the first. See O'Connor and Patin (2015) for a prosody-syntax interface analysis of stacked apposition.

'The Turkish prime minister Ahmet Davutoglu summoned Tuesday an emergency meeting in Ankara after the violent explosion, probably an attack, which killed at least ten people in the historic center of Istanbul.' (*Le Figaro* online, "Explosion à Istanbul : réunion de crise à Ankara", 12/01/16)

b. Deictic time adverbs: *Le tribunal correctionnel de Montpellier*
the court criminal of Montpellier
a condamné, mardi 4 mars à un an de prison
has sentenced Tuesday 4 March to one year of prison
dont, six mois ferme, un homme qui avait
of-which six months firm a man who had
laissé conduire un ami ivre, auteur ensuite d'un
let to-drive a friend drunk author then of-a
accident mortel
accident fatal

'The Montpellier criminal court sentenced Tuesday 4 March to one year of prison, including a six-month mandatory sentence, a man who had let his friend, later the cause of a fatal accident, drive drunk.' (*L'Obs* online, "Il laisse un ami ivre prendre le volant : 6 mois ferme", 05/03/14)

c. Truth value adverbs: *On voit aujourd'hui de plus en plus de*
one sees today of more in more of
très jeunes femmes investir dans de très belles pièces –
very young women to-invest in of very beautiful pieces
pas nécessairement des robes.
not necessarily of-the dresses

'We see today more and more very young women investing in very beautiful pieces – not necessarily dresses.' (*L'Obs* online, "Maria Grazi Chiuri et Pierpaolo Piccioli: on a rencontré le duo derrière Valentino", 07/09/15)

d. Subject-oriented adverbs: *Pour raccourcir mon séjour –*
for to-shorten my stay
inévitablement dangereux au Revier – et faire en
inevitably dangerous to-the infirmary and to-do in
sorte que je ne sois pas obligé d'attendre longtemps
sort that I neg be not obliged of-to-attend long
avant d'être opéré, il avait mis de la crème
before of-to-be operated he had put of the cream

'In order to shorten my stay – inevitably dangerous at the infirmary – and to ensure that I wouldn't be obliged to wait long before being operated, he had put cream...' (*Survivant d'Auschwitz*, Thomas Geve, 2011, Jean-Claude Gawsewitch éditeur)

e. Middle aspect verbs: *Les chansons de Trenet – souvent des*
   the songs of Trenet often of-the
   standards – le permettent.
   standards it permit
   'Trenet's songs – often standards – permit it.' (*L'Obs*, "Benjamin Biolay: Juger l'attitude des gens pendant l'Occupation est obscène", 15/6/15)

f. Core event adverbs: *D'autant plus que le film, complètement*
   of-much more that the film completely
   con, est tiré d'un roman de L. Ron Hubbard.
   stupid is drawn of-a novel of L. Ron Hubbard
   'All the more so as the film, completely stupid, is based on a novel by L. Ron Hubbard.' (*L'Obs*, "Plaidoyer pour la science fiction", 11/1/16)

As the above examples show, appositives can indeed include a large number of functional projections. Alongside the facts about complementisers from section 2, we see that in both French and English, appositives have both a CP- and an IP-level and are thus more akin to clauses than to single constituents. In the next section, we will further explore the IP domain with a look at DP positions.

4 DP positions in appositives

4.1 Relationship between adverbs and DP positions

As part of his study on adverbs, Cinque (1999) proposes that there are a number of DP projections available in the clause distributed among the adverb projections. Given that the adverbs appear in a fixed order and do not move, except under certain circumstances, the fact that a DP can appear in two distinct positions with respect to a single adverb shows that there must be more than one position available to host a DP. For example, if we take the examples in (19), the position of *George* with respect to *probably* indicates at least three different DP positions in the clause, since *probably* always occupies the same position (Cinque 1999: 109).

(19) a. *Probably George will have read the book.*
   b. *George probably will have read the book.*
   c. *George will probably have read the book.*

Cinque's (1999) proposal makes clear predictions about positions. If a DP can appear to the left of a particular adverb class, it should be able to appear to the left of all adverbs that are lower in the hierarchy. Furthermore, Cinque (1999) notes that the subject in a finite clause must appear to the left of, or higher than, a particular adverb in the hierarchy and that this adverb is somewhat arbitrarily chosen. In English, the adverb is *already* and in French it is the equivalent adverb *déjà*. This means that in English and French finite clauses, it should be impossible to find *already/déjà* and any adverbs below them in a higher position than the subject.³ Though Cinque (1999) does not offer a full explanation as to why different languages should designate different adverbs as defining the lower limit of the subject positions, he suggests that the lowest subject position, i.e. immediately above *already/déjà*, is where nominative case is assigned.

With regard to apposition, the positions of adverbs relative to DPs provide an idea of the available DP positions in appositives. It has been noted elsewhere that appositives can contain different types of quantifiers associated with DP positions (Doron 1992, O'Connor 2008, 2012). These include floating quantifiers (FQs) and what O'Connor terms simple (non-floating) quantifiers such as *many* and complex quantifiers such as *many of them*.

In the present paper, we will focus on floating quantifiers.

4.2 Floating quantifiers and adverbs

Cinque (1999) bases his analysis of FQs on the positions that they can occupy relative to adverbs and negation. Following Sportiche (1988), he assumes that an FQ that is separated from the DP it quantifies has been stranded in a position through which the DP has passed. Cinque (1999) tries to determine different DP positions that can host FQs by examining where the FQs can be found relative to

---

3 This is somewhat simplified. Both *already* and *déjà* can be found before a subject:
(i) *Already its distinctive copper-coloured windows have gone.* (*Guardian*, 10/03/02, page 7, col. 7)
(ii) Alors déjà ils ne parlent pas de meneurs...
 so already they neg talk not of leaders
 'So already they are not talking about leaders.' (http://www.lequipe.fr/Basket/Actualites/Ils-ont-la-passe-dans-le-sang/615504)
In these cases, however, *already* means something like 'sooner than expected' as opposed to 'before now'. It is with the sense of 'before now' that *already* must be lower than the subject. See O'Connor (2008, Chapter 4, footnote 8) for a fuller explanation.

the adverbs and negation found around the verb. For French, he examines the elements in (20):

(20) *pas > déjà > plus > toujours > complètement > tout > bien*

By examining where FQs can and cannot be found with respect to these adverbs, he comes up with the result in (21), where the highest FQ appears between the negative *pas* and the adverb *déjà*.

(21) *pas > FQ > déjà > plus > FQ > toujours > FQ > complètement > tout > bien*

This is then confirmed for English, giving the equivalent schema in (22):

(22) *not > FQ > already > no longer > FQ > always > FQ > completely > well*

For the appositives, we can distinguish two scenarios with respect to FQs and adverbs. If FQs are found among the higher adverbs, e.g. above *already / déjà*, then this means that the FQ is located in one of the DP positions that can host a subject. On the other hand, if an FQ can be found in a position among the lower adverbs, then the FQ is located in a lower DP position, but one that cannot host a subject. We will examine the two predictions below.

4.3 FQs in subject DP positions

In both English and French, FQs can be found to the left of adverbs higher than *already / déjà*. This indicates that the FQ is located in a position that could potentially host a subject. Some examples are given in (23) and (24).

(23) a. *Three "Messiah" presentations were at Episcopal parishes, all evidently with affluent memberships.* (*New York Times* online, "Critic's notebook; 'Messiah' around in its many permutations", 26/12/92)
   b. *To analyze the paint strata on a canvas, conservators remove tiny paint samples, each perhaps the size of a pinhead.* (*New York Times* online, "An enigma sometimes wrapped in a fake", 01/10/95)
   c. *The experiment brings Macari abreast of Channing Daughters, in Bridgehampton, which produces two sauvignon blancs, both usually first-rate.* (*New York Times* online, "Second style in Sauvignon", 09/11/08)

(24) a. *Plus   de   20 métabolites   ont   été   identifiés,   tous*
       more   of   20 metabolites   have   been   identified   all
       probablement   moins   actifs   que   la   nicotine.
       probably   less   active   that   the   nicotine

'More than 20 metabolites have been identified, all probably less active than nicotine.' (*Le Figaro* online, http://sante.lefigaro.fr/medicaments/3640906-nicotinell-1mg-cpr-sucer-menthe-96/10-proprietes-pharmacologiques)

b. Dans   les   11 étages   il   y   aura   39 appartements,   <u>tous</u>
   in   the   11 floors   it   there will-have   39 apartments   all
   <u>évidemment</u>   <u>extrêmement</u>   <u>luxueux</u>...
   evidently   extremely   luxurious
   'On the 11 floors there will be 39 apartments, all evidently extremely luxurious.' (http://thecreatorsproject.vice.com/fr/blog/zaha-hadid-is-building-a-sculpture-you-can-live-in)

c. *Elle   a   un   seul   nom   mais   éventuellement   plusieurs*
   It   has   one   single   name   but   potentially   several
   sites,   <u>tous</u>   <u>nécessairement</u>   <u>dans</u>   <u>le</u>   <u>même</u>   <u>pays</u>.
   sites   all   necessarily   in   the   same   country
   'It has only one name but potentially several sites, all necessarily in the same country.' (http://users.polytech.unice.fr/~hugues/BDR/Harmo/TD1harmo/td1.html)

As the above examples reveal, appositives contain DP positions among the adverb projections. However, though these may be positions that can host a subject, the result does not necessarily mean that the FQ is the subject of the appositive. In fact, the position is consistent with that of subject or FQ in a finite clause, as shown in (25), where (25a) and (25c) show the FQ in a lower position with a DP subject and (25b) and (25d) show the FQ in the subject position.

(25) a. *The two sauvignon blancs are both usually first rate.*
     b. *Both are usually first rate.*
     c. *Les 39 appartements sont tous évidemment luxueux.*
     d. *Tous sont évidemment luxueux.*

To summarize, then, the appositives in English and French appear to contain DP positions among the higher adverbs, but it is not clear that the FQs in such examples actually serve as subjects.

4.4 FQs in lower DP positions

The next question is whether or not the appositives contain DP positions among the lower adverbs. In this case, the FQ would not be located in a subject position. Examples are given in (26) and (27).

(26) a. *These girls, <u>already both mightily aware of and spooked by their new sexuality</u>, have to listen to a sex-ed lecture on HPV delivered with a stunning lack of empathy.* (*New York Times* online, "When mysterious symptoms strike a small town", 18/06/14)
   b. *The scheduled equipping of the second and third divisions, <u>still both in the United States</u>, has been deferred.* (*New York Times* online, "Army buys armor the marines use", 23/08/52)

(27) a.
...le	Centre-Gauche PCS		a	annoncé	les	candidatures	de
the	Center-Left PCS		has	announced	the	candidacy	of

Vital Studer,	Benoît Rey,	Danièle Mayer Aldana,	Claude Chassot	et
Vital Studer	Benoît Rey	Danièle Mayer Aldana	Claude Chassot	and

du	secrétaire	de	la	section	fribourgeoise	Diego Frieden,
of-the	secretary	of	the	section	Fribourgois	Diego Frieden

déjà	tous	en	lice	lors	des	précédentes	élections
already	all	in	arena	during	of-the	preceding	elections

fédérales	en	2011
federal	in	2011

'The center-left PCS has announced the candidatures of BR, DMA, CC and of Fribourg section secretary DF, already all in the running during the last federal elections in 2011.' (http://www.rts.ch/info/dossiers/2015/elections-federales/fribourg/6909610-le-centre-gauche-pcs-fribourg-dans-la-course-aux-federales.html)

   b.
Ca	veut	pas	dire	qu'on	aime	plus	tous
that	wants	not	to-say	that-one	likes	no-longer	all

nos	vieux	morceaux	(toujours	tous	disponibles	sur
our	old	pieces	still	all	available	on

www.lifeisnotdead.ch)	même	si	on	les	joue	plus
www.lifeisnotdead.ch	even	if	one	them	plays	no-longer

'That doesn't mean that we no longer like all our old songs (still all available on www.lifeisdead.ch) even if we don't play them anymore.' (http://forum.fribourg-est-independant.org/viewtopic.php?id=822)

As shown by these examples, appositives in both French and English contain DP positions among the lower, post-subject adverbs. Since FQs in such positions are often viewed as the result of stranding by the subject as it passes through the DP position, one could reasonably conclude that appositives do indeed contain a subject of some type. Due to space limitations, we cannot fully explore this idea here, but such an analysis is proposed in O'Connor (2008) based on the behavior of non-floating quantifiers and the presence of reflexive pronouns, among other evidence.

5 Conclusion

The data from apposition in French and English reveal that appositives do not consist of a single constituent, but rather have a larger structure that is similar to that of a clause. More precisely, the presence of complementisers reveals that appositives have a (truncated) CP level. Moving down the clause structure, the study of adverbs reveals that appositives have an extensive IP structure including functional structure relating to adverb projections and a series of DP projections capable of hosting floating quantifiers.

This predicts then, that any differences between French and English clauses should also be evident in appositives. Though is it difficult to test these with the non-verbal appositives studied here, similar structures containing a non-finite verb do display such difference. In (28), we see that the French present participle appears before the negative particle *pas* whereas the English participle in the gloss occurs after the negation, reflecting the well-known fact that French verbs can occur in a higher position than English verbs (Pollock 1989).

(28) *Mais imaginez une minute qu'un salarié de notre*
but imagine a minute that-a employee of our
premier exemple (ne travaillant pas le mercredi) veuille
first example neg working not the Wednesday wants
poser uniquement ses mardis en congés payés.
to-place only his Tuesdays in leave paid
'But imagine for a moment that an employee from our first example (not working on Wednesdays) wants to ask for his Tuesdays only as paid leave.'
(https://nereo.com/blog/p/comment-decompter-les-conges-payes-pour-les-salaries-a-temps-partiel.html)

Naturally, many questions are left unexplored. With respect to apposition, we leave aside other questions relating to the internal syntax, including the representation of the predication inside an appositive and the nature of the presumed subject. We also leave aside the (rather large) question of the external syntax of appositives – how the appositive is linked to the clause that surrounds it (but see O'Connor (2008) and Heringa (2011) and references therein).

Given the similarity of apposition in French and English, we might also wonder whether apposition in other languages shares the same characteristics. A recent comparison of apposition in English and the Bantu language of Shingazidja (O'Connor and Patin 2015) reveals that apposition in these two languages, though typologically quite different, do in fact share many of the same features explored here for French and English.

Finally, such work also raises questions about the status of apposition itself. Should it be considered a function in its own right? How should it be defined? Through a greater exploration of apposition across languages, we can arrive at the answers to some of these questions.

Acknowledgements: I am grateful to the editors and to two anonymous reviewers for helpful comments on earlier versions of this chapter. Warm thanks as always to Liliane Haegeman, without whom this work would not have been possible.

References

Alexiadou, Artemis. 1997. *Adverb placement: A case study in antisymmetric syntax.* Amsterdam: John Benjamins.
Alexiadou, Artemis, Liliane Haegeman & Melita Stavrou. 2007. *Noun phrase in the generative perspective.* Berlin: Mouton de Gruyter.
Bowers, John. 1993. The syntax of predication. *Linguistic Inquiry* 24. 591–656.
Burton-Roberts, Noel. 1975. Nominal apposition. *Foundations of Language* 13. 391–419.
Burton-Roberts, Noel. 2006. Parentheticals. In Keith Brown (ed.), *Encyclopaedia of language and linguistics*, 2nd edition, vol. 9, 179–182. Amsterdam: Elsevier.
Cardoso, Adriana & Mark deVries. 2010. Internal and external heads in appositive constructions. University of Lisbon and University of Groningen, unpublished manuscript.
Cinque, Guglielmo. 1999. *Adverbs and functional heads: A cross-linguistic perspective.* Oxford: Oxford University Press.
Culicover, Peter W & Robert D. Levine. 2001. Stylistic inversion in English: A reconsideration. *Natural Language & Linguistic Theory* 19. 283–310.
Dikken, Marcel den. 2006. *Relators and linkers: The syntax of predication, predicate inversion and copulas.* Cambridge, MA: The MIT Press.
Doron, Edit. 1992. Appositive predicates. *Belgian Journal of Linguistics* 7. 23–33.
Ernst, Thomas. 2002. *The syntax of adjuncts.* Cambridge: Cambridge University Press.
Griffiths, Robert. 2015. *On appositives.* Utrecht: Lot.
Grimshaw, Jane. 1991. Extended projections. Brandeis University, unpublished manuscript.
Haegeman, Liliane. 2003. Notes on long adverbial fronting in English and the left periphery. *Linguistic Inquiry* 34, 640–649.
Haegeman, Liliane. 2004. Topicalization, CLLD and the left periphery. In Benjamin Shaer, Werner Frey & Claudia Maienborn (eds.), *Proceedings of the dislocated elements workshop,* vol. 2, 157–192. Berlin: Zentrum für Allgemeine Sprachwissenschaft.
Haegeman, Liliane. 2006. Argument fronting in English, Romance CLLD and the left periphery. In Raffaella Zanuttini, Héctor Campos, Elena Herburger & Paul H. Portner (eds.), *Cross-linguistic research in syntax and semantics: Negation, tense and clausal architecture,* 27–52. Washington, DC: Georgetown University Press.
Haegeman, Liliane. 2008. The syntax of adverbial clauses. In *Pragmatic functions and syntactic theory. In view of Japanese main clauses* (Report: Grant-in-Aid for Scientific Research (B) # 19320063), 175–211. Tokyo: Graduate School of Language Sciences, Kanda University of International Studies.

Heringa, Herman. 2011. *Appositional constructions*. Utrecht: Lot.
Hooper, Joan & Sandra Thompson. 1973. On the applicability of root transformations. *Linguistic Inquiry* 4. 465–497.
Jackendoff, Ray. 1972. *Semantic interpretation in generative grammar*. Cambridge, MA: The MIT Press.
Laenzlinger, Christopher. 1998. *Comparative studies in word order variation*. Amsterdam: John Benjamins.
Laenzlinger, Christopher. 2002. A feature-based theory of adverb syntax. *Generative grammar in Geneva* 3. 67–105.
O'Connor, Kathleen M. 2008. *Aspects de la syntaxe et de l'interprétation de l'apposition à antécédent nominal*. Lille, France: Université Charles-de-Gaulle – Lille 3 dissertation.
O'Connor, Kathleen M. 2009. Adverbs as evidence for higher syntactic structure in appositives. Paper presented at the International Conference on the Linguistics of Contemporary English, University of London, 14–17 July.
O'Connor, Kathleen M. 2012. On the position of subjects and floating quantifiers in appositives. In Joanna Błaszczak, Bozena Rozwadowska & Wojciech Witkowski (eds.), *Current issues in generative linguistics: Syntax, semantics and phonology*, 76–89. Wroclaw: Center for General and Comparative Linguistics at the University of Wroclaw.
O'Connor, Kathleen M & Cédric Patin. 2015. The syntax and prosody of apposition in Shingazidja. *Phonology* 32. 111–145.
Pollock, Jean-Yves. 1989. Verb movement, universal grammar and the structure of IP. *Linguistic Inquiry* 20. 365–424.
Quirk, Randolph, Sidney Greenbaum, Geoffrey Leech & Jan Svartvik. 1985. *A comprehensive grammar of the English language*. London: Longman.
Rizzi, Luigi. 1997. The fine structure of the left periphery. In Liliane Haegeman (ed.), *Elements of grammar*, 281–337. Dordrecht: Kluwer.
Sportiche, Dominique. 1988. A theory of floating quantifiers and its corollaries for constituent structure. *Linguistic Inquiry* 19. 425–449.
Tenny, Carol L. 2000. Core events and adverbial modification. In Carol Tenny & James Pustejovsky (eds.), *Events as grammatical objects*, 285–334. Stanford, CA: CSLI Publications.
Vries, Mark de. 2006. The syntax of appositive relativisation: On specifying coordination, false free relatives and promotion. *Linguistic Inquiry* 37. 229–270.

Luigi Rizzi
Locality and the functional sequence in the left periphery

1 "Further explanation" of the properties of the sequence: The role of interface and locality principles

Cartographic studies have focused on the sequences of functional elements which characterize the fine structure of the different zones of clauses and phrases. Such functional sequences have well-defined properties, which have been the target of extensive study in recent year: properties of ordering, of dependencies and mutual incompatibilities between positions, of freezing induced by certain functional elements and the like. These discoveries have substantially enriched the empirical coverage of theoretical and comparative syntax.

Why is it that we typically find certain properties of ordering and co-occurrence restrictions, rather than others? As pointed out in Cinque and Rizzi (2010) it is unlikely that the functional hierarchy may be an absolute syntactic primitive, unrelated to other requirements or constraints: why should natural language syntax have evolved to express such a complex and apparently unmotivated primitive? It is more plausible that the functional hierarchy and its properties (to the extent to which they are universal) may be rooted elsewhere.

So, properties of the functional sequence should be amenable to "further explanations" in terms of deductive interactions involving basic ingredients and fundamental principles of linguistic computations. The search for such further explanations should be considered an integral part of the cartographic endeavor (Rizzi 2013). What could be possible sources of "further explanation" for the properties of functional sequences? Two broadly defined candidates come to mind:
1. Certain properties could derive from requirements of the interface systems. For instance, it could be that functional head B may necessarily occur under functional head A (thus giving the linear order AB in head initial languages and BA in head-final languages) because the opposite hierarchical order would yield a structure not properly interpretable. Ordering of aspect below tense may be a case in point, as well as other cases of the strict orders between functional elements in the IP spine systematically mapped in Cinque (1999)

and much subsequent work inspired by this seminal reference. A special case of the impact of interface requirements may be the ordering properties that follow from selectional requirements, e.g., the fact that the Force head in embedded clauses must be high enough to be accessible to higher selectors, which want to know if their complement is a declarative or a question, for instance (Rizzi 1997).

2. When the functional heads occurring in specific orders trigger movement, the ordering may be a consequence of locality requirements. For instance, Abels (2012) has argued that almost all the ordering effects observed in the Italian left periphery may follow from the theory of locality based on a version of featural Relativized Minimality, along the lines developed in Starke (2001), Rizzi (2004): if A is a stronger island-creating element than B, then B will not be extractable from the domain of A, neither long-distance, nor locally. So, if A and B can co-occur in the same left periphery, the only possible local order will be A B, as B A would violate locality. In the same vein, Haegeman (2012) has argued that the theory of locality may capture certain cross-linguistically variable restrictions on the occurrence of left peripheral constructions in some kinds of adverbial clauses. I will come back later on to her analysis of the contrast between English and Italian (and French) concerning the possible occurrence of topics in adverbial clauses. Other properties of the layers appearing in the sequence, e.g., the "halting problems" for wh-movement and related phenomena, may be derivable from other computational ingredients, such as the labeling algorithm (Chomsky 2013, 2015, Rizzi 2015a, 2015b, 2016 and the papers published in Boskovic 2016).

In this paper I will focus on the role of interface and locality principles in constraining the functional sequences in many ways.

2 On the possible relevance of locality: Constraints in the English left periphery

English and Italian express topic – comment configurations with two constructions which differ in important ways. Italian uses the Clitic Left Dislocation construction, in which a direct object topic is obligatorily resumed by a clitic. Omission of the clitic renders the structure ungrammatical:

(1) *Il tuo libro, *(lo) voglio leggere.*
 'Your book, I (it) want to read.'

Cinque (1990) argued that the impossibility of simply preposing a topic, without clitic resumption, follows from the fact that the clause-internal gap in (2) should be interpreted as a variable, and the topic is not an operator, so that a variable would remain unbound in (1), plausibly a violation of Full Interpretation (Chomsky 1986) and/or of Koopman and Sportiche's (1982) Bijection Principle:

(2)   * *Il tuo libro, voglio leggere___.*
       'Your book, I want to read ___.'

In this respect, Italian/Romance ClLD has opposite syntactic requirements with respect to corrective focus movement to the left periphery, a construction which sharply differs from topic – comment in prosodic contour and pragmatic conditions for felicitous use (on the typology of focus in Romance see Belletti 2009, Cruschina 2012, Bianchi, Bocci, Cruschina 2016, Rizzi and Bocci 2016 for recent discussion). Focus movement allows and requires a clause internal gap:

(3)   *IL TUO LIBRO voglio leggere___, non il suo.*
       'YOUR BOOK I want to read, not his.'

In terms of Cinque's approach, this is expected if a correctively focused element is characterized by an operator feature, an assumption which is supported by the observation that focus gives rise to Weak Cross-over effects, the hallmark of certain prototypical operators (e.g., question and negative operators: Rizzi 1997). It should be noticed that the operator status seems to be a necessary, not a sufficient property for giving rise to Weak-Crossover effects, as certain operators, e.g, relative operators in appositive relative clauses, do not give rise to the effect, so, only a proper subset of the operators give rise to Weak-Crossover; for our purposes the implication "if Weak Cross-over then operator" is sufficient to establish the operator nature of focus, in line with much work on the logical form of focal structures.

English topicalization differs from Romance topicalization in permitting a gap, as the grammaticality of the gloss of (2) shows. Cinque (1990), updating the classical approach to topicalization in Chomsky (1977), proposes that English resorts to a null operator mediating between the gap and the topic. The representation then is something like the following:

(4)   *Your book Op I want to read___.*

That null operators are an option made available by UG is suggested by many constructions which use this device: relatives (under the matching analysis), *easy to please* constructions, parasitic gaps, etc. The rationale here is that, as English lacks clitics, it resorts to the null operator as a functional equivalent of the clitic, to solve the problem of connecting the topic to a gap. The plausibility of the null operator analysis is enhanced by the observation that some closely related languages, like Dutch, can use an overt (relative-like) operator in topicalization, alternating with the null variant:

(5) Die man (die) ken ik.   (Dutch: Koster 1978)
 'That man, I know.'

Italian and other Romance languages also resort to null operators in certain constructions, including appositive relatives, *easy to please* and parasitic gaps. Presumably, the use of the null operator in the topic construction is blocked by the availability of the clitic in the language (English also permits pronominal resumption in Ross' (1967) Left Dislocation, *Your book, I will read it*; this option may not block the null operator if Left Dislocation and Topicalization differ to some extent at the interpretive level, as suggested in Rodman 1974).

Assuming Cinque's analysis, Haegeman (2012) traces to the same explanatory scheme other distributional differences between English and Italian topicalization. In Italian a topic structure is possible in various kinds of adverbial environments which disallow the construction in English, e.g., in temporal adverbial clauses:

(6) *Quando gli esami di primo anno li hai superati __, ti puoi iscrivere al secondo anno.*
 'When the first year exams you them have passed, you can register for the second year.'

(7) **When the first year exams you have passed __, you can register for the second year.*

Under Cinque's analysis, the presence of a topic requires a null operator in (7). Then, Haegeman argues, if the subordinator *when* is moved from an IP internal position, it necessarily crosses the null operator; as *when* itself plausibly belongs to the class of operators, the derived configuration violates featural Relativized Minimality:

(8) **When$_{Op}$ the first year exams Op you __ have passed __ you can register for the second year.*

As the Italian topicalization construction involves no null operator, but only a topic (crucially, not a member of the operator class), no violation of locality arises in (6). So, under Haegeman's (2012) analysis, an apparently unrelated distributional difference between the two languages can be deductively connected to the fundamental difference between English and Italian topicalization, the involvement of a null operator in the former by not in the latter.

3 The incompatibility of two topics in English vs. the proliferation of topics in Romance

There are other systematic differences between the topic constructions in the two languages. An important one is that Italian allows as many topics as there are topicalizable elements, whereas English fundamentally requires a unique topic. This is particularly clear when we restrict our attention to DP topics, whereas certain PP's with topic-like interpretation may enjoy more freedom (see below). Take the case in which both the main and the embedded (infinitival) clause have a direct object: both can be Cl left-dislocated, in any order:

(9) a. *Ho convinto Gianni a comprare il tuo libro.*
    'I convinced Gianni to buy your book.'
  b. *Gianni, lo ho convinto a comprare il tuo libro.*
    'Gianni, I convinced him to buy your book.'
  c. *Il tuo libro, ho convinto Gianni a comprarlo.*
    'Your book, I convinced Gianni to buy it.'
  d. *Gianni, il tuo libro, lo ho convinto a comprarlo.*
    'Gianni, your book, I convinced him to buy it.'
  e. *Il tuo libro, Gianni, lo ho convinto a comprarlo.*
    'Your book, Gianni, I convinced him to buy it.'

On the contrary, in English the two objects can be topicalized independently, but cannot co-occur in the left periphery:

(10) a. *I convinced John to buy your book.*
   b. *John, I convinced __ to buy your book.*
   c. *Your book, I convinced John to buy __.*
   d. **John, your book, I convinced __ to buy __.*
   e. **Your book, John, I convinced __ to buy _ .*

Again, the hypothesis that a topic DP always involves a null operator in English immediately captures the ill-formedness of (10d-e). The relevant representation would be something like the following:

(11) **John Op, your book Op, I convinced ___ to buy ___.*

In this representation, one null operator would inevitably cross over the other, giving rise to a violation of featural Relativized Minimality. In Italian, on the other hand, the representations of (9d-e) do not involve null operators, so that no violation of fRM is produced.[1]

Another significant difference between the two languages is that in English a topic and a focus cannot naturally co-occur, whereas in Italian the configuration is fine:

(12) ??*John, YOUR BOOK I convinced __ to buy __ (not Bill's book).*

(13) *Gianni, IL TUO LIBRO lo ho convinto a comprare __ (non quello di Piero).*
 'Gianni, YOUR BOOK I convinced him to buy __ (not Piero's)'

In English a corrective focus may also involve a null operator; or perhaps, as in Italian, the focalized constituent inherently counts as an operator, hence it can directly bind its gap. Whatever analysis turns out to be correct, we still have a member of the operator class, Op, crossing over another member of the operator class, the focalized element, which gives rise to a violation. As Italian does not use Op, topic and focus belong to distinct featural classes, and therefore no violation arises in (13).

Going back to the incompatibility of two topics in English, it should be noticed that clear cases illustrating it involve two DP's: on the contrary, a DP can co-occur with a PP with topic-like interpretation in certain cases, as in the following example provided by Ian Roberts (p.c.):

(14) *Words like that, in front of my mother, I would never say __ __.*

Apparently, a topic-like PP (at least in certain cases) has an additional structural option w.r.t. a DP topic, one which does not involve Op: one plausible possibility is that this kind of PP can also target the Mod(ification) position postulated in Rizzi (2004), a position which is involved in the attraction of highlighted adverbials of various kinds. So, if the representation of (14) is (15),

(15) *Words like that Op, in front of my mother Mod, I would never say __ __.*

---

[1] If the topic is moved to the left periphery in the Romance ClLD construction (as proposed in Cinque 1977 on the basis of island sensitivity; a movement analysis is also supported by the existence of reconstruction effects: Cecchetto 2000), the question arises of why movement of a +Top element across another +Top element does not give rise to a violation of fRM. In Rizzi (2004) I suggested that the topic feature may be excluded from the computation of fRM; or that multiple topics may give rise to an "equidistance" situation (Chomsky 1995) voiding the locality effect. Other options come to mind, which I will not discuss here.

we expect the structure to be possible, as it does not violate fRM: Mod belongs to a featural class distinct from the operator class (Rizzi 2004).

That such PP's can target Mod is also shown by the contrast between such preposed elements and topic DP's in anti-adjacency environments. *That*-trace effects, as in (16a), can be alleviated by a preposed adverbial, as in (16b), but not by a genuine topic (16)c. This is the antiadjacency effect, or adverb effect (Bresnan 1977, Culicover 1993, Browning 1996, Rizzi 1997):

(16) a. *This is the man who Peter said that __ will sell his house next year.
  b. This is the man who Peter said that next year, __ will sell his house __.
  c. *This is the man who Peter said that his house, __ will sell __ next year.

In a nutshell, the interpolation of a Mod layer has a beneficial effect on the *that*-trace environment, whereas the interpolation of a topic does not change things (see Rizzi 2014 for a possible analysis of the alleviating effect crucially relying on the Mod layer). Now, PP's like the one in (15) have a similar ameliorating effect:

(17) This is a man who I think that, in front of my mother, ___ would never say words like that.

This supports the view that the PP in (15), (17) indeed targets the Mod layer, whence the lack of intervention effect in (15) (under fRM), and the alleviating effect in (17), on a par with (16b).²

4 The incompatibility of two left-peripheral foci in Italian

Whereas two (or more) topics and a topic and a focus can co-occur in the Italian left periphery, co-occurrence of two foci is sharply excluded:

(18) a. *GIANNI ho convinto __ a comprare il libro, non Piero.*
  'GIANNI I convinced to buy the book, not Piero.'

---

2 Aboh (2004) observes that topics are unique in Gungbe. This state of affairs interestingly contrasts with the one found in Abiji (Hager-Mboua 2014), which permits a multiplicity of topics, each one followed by an overt topic marker. The contrast could not be attributed to locality (in the terms developed in this section), as both languages involve pronominal resumption of topics. So, a primitive parametric difference may be involved here, or interface factors may be at play: it could be that Gungbe may only allow topics with interpretive properties requiring uniqueness (some kinds of topics are unique in the typology of Frascarelli and Hinterhoelzl 2007, Bianchi and Frascarelli 2010, whereas others permit recursion). I will leave this issue open here.

b. *IL LIBRO ho convinto Gianni a comprare __, non il disco.*[3]
   'THE BOOK I convinced Gianni to buy__, not the record'
c. **GIANNI IL LIBRO ho convinto __ a comprare __, non Piero, il disco.*
   'GIANNI THE BOOK I convinced __ to buy __, not Piero, the record'

The uniqueness of focus seems to hold generally for left-peripheral focus, also in languages permitting multiple topics, such as Italian or Abidji (Hager-Mboua 2014); and a similar incompatibility has been observed in Finno-ugric (Puskas 2000), other African languages (Aboh 2004), Creole languages (Durrleman 2008). A principled explanation thus seems to be in order.

An early attempt to provide a further explanation of this uniqueness requirement was made in Rizzi (1997). Uniqueness of focus, it was proposed, may follow from the interface properties of the Focus – Presupposition configuration. Assume (19) to be the interpretive routine triggered by the focal head in the left periphery:

(19) [   ] Foc [   ]
     "Focus"   "Presupposition"

I.e., something like "interpret my Spec as the Focus (of the appropriate kind, here corrective focus), and my complement as the presupposed part". Now, if a Foc2 head was recursively embedded as the complement of a higher Foc1 head, we would have that a focal element, the Spec of Foc2, would be contained in the complement of the higher Foc1 (underscored in (20)), a presupposed part according to (19). But something cannot be at the same time presupposed and focalized, two conflicting requirements. Therefore Foc recursion in a given left peripheral system is barred by the functioning of the interpretive system at the interface:

(20) *[GIANNI] **Foc1** [[IL LIBRO] **Foc2** [ho convinto __ a comprare __
     'GIANNI   THE BOOK   I convinced __ to buy __'

Liliane Haegeman (p.c.) points out that, under the analysis proposed for (11) on the ban of double topicalization in English, (18c) is also ruled out by locality: the higher focus necessarily moves across the lower focus in (18c), thus triggering a violation of fRM, with the focalized element, an operator, crossing the other focalized element, also an operator. So, do we still need an interface account to (redundantly) exclude such examples?

---

[3] (18b) sounds slightly unnatural, presumably because the direct object of *convincere* is in the presupposed part, and the natural way to express a presupposed object is through an object clitic. Anyway, (18c) is severely ill-formed, in sharp contrasts with both (18a-b).

I think we need the interface account for independent reasons. Certain cases of double focalization are not captured by locality, and still they are ill-formed. In order to see that, we need cases in which a left peripheral element is externally merged directly in the left periphery, and not moved from a clause internal position. A case in point may be provided by "scene-setting" adverbial expressions (Reinhart 1981, Benincà and Poletto 2004). The fact that scene setting elements may be externally merged in the left periphery is shown by the fact that they do not give rise to reconstruction effects. Consider the famous contrast discussed by Reinhart (1981) between (21a) and (21b):

(21) a. *In this picture of John$_i$, he$_i$ looks sick.*
 b. **In this picture of John$_i$, he$_i$ found a scratch.*
 b'. **In this picture of John$_i$, he$_i$ found a scratch <in this picture of John$_i$>*

Example (21b), involving the preposing of a locative expression from the IP, gives rise to condition C effects under reconstruction. In terms of the copy-theory of traces, the representation is (21b'), where principle C is violated. The well-formedness of (21a) thus suggests that here the adverbial simply "sets the scene" for the event reported in the following clause, and it is not derived from a clause-internal position. If there is no movement, and no trace, the lack of reconstruction is correctly expected.

Let us now see what happens in constructions with scene-setting adverbials in case of corrective focalization. Double corrective focalization of the scene setting adverbial and of a clause-internal element is still excluded:

(22) a. *NELLA FOTO, Gianni sembra il più alto, non nel ritratto.*
 'IN THE PICTURE Gianni looks the tallest one, not in the portrait.'
 b. *Nella foto, GIANNI sembra il più alto, non Piero.*
 'In the picture, GIANNI looks the tallest one, not Piero.'
 c. **NELLA FOTO GIANNI sembra il più alto, non nel ritratto, Piero.*
 'IN THE PICTURE GIANNI looks the tallest one, not in the portrait, Piero.'

So, given a statement like (23a), if the interlocutor disagrees both on who looks the tallest and in what image this is visible, s/he will have to express his/her disagreement through two clauses, as in (23)B, while a single clause with two corrective foci, as in (22)c, is impossible:

(23) A: *Nel ritratto, Piero sembra il più alto...*
 'In the portrait, Piero seems the tallest one...'
 B: *No, GIANNI sembra il più alto, non Piero; e NELLA FOTO si ha questa impressione, non nel ritratto.*
 'No, GIANNI seems the tallest one, not Piero; and IN THE PICTURE one has this impression, not in the portrait'

The ill-formedness of (22c) is not captured by locality, if no movement of the scene-setting adverbial from a clause internal position is involved here. If more than one Foc head could occur in a left periphery, the scene setting adverbial could be moved to the Spec of a higher focus (say Foc1 in (22)c') from the left-peripheral position dedicated to such adverbials (Beninca' and Poletto 2004), and another element could be moved to the Spec of a lower focus (Foc2), in which case the two paths would not cross, and there would be no violation of fRM:

(22) c'. *NELLA FOTO   Foc1 __ ... GIANNI Foc2 ... __   sembra il più alto, non nel ritratto, Piero.
    'IN THE PICTURE   GIANNI   looks the tallest, not in the portrait, Piero.'

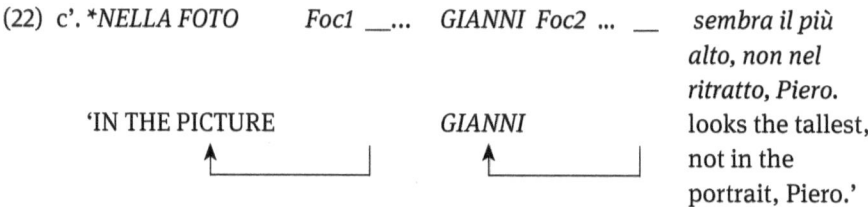

On the contrary, the ill-formedness of (22c) immediately follows from the interface analysis, as GIANNI would be in the presupposed part of the higher focus Foc1, which would give rise to the interpretive clash. It thus appears that, even if fRM excludes most cases of double left peripheral corrective focalization, we also need the interface account to cover all the cases.

Italian provides an even more straightforward piece of evidence supporting the view that the interface account must be maintained. In Italian a constituent can be correctively focused by movement to the main left periphery, or to an embedded left periphery, but not simultaneously in main and embedded domains:

(24) a. *A GIANNI ho detto __ che dovrebbe leggere il tuo libro, non a Piero.*
       'TO GIANNI I said   that he should read your book, not to Piero.'
    b. *Ho detto a Gianni che IL TUO LIBRO dovrebbe leggere __, non quello di Antonio*
       'I said to Gianni that YOUR BOOK he should read, not Antonio's.'
    c. **A GIANNI ho detto __ che IL TUO LIBRO dovrebbe leggere __, non a Piero, quello di Antonio.*
       'TO GIANNI I said __ that YOUR BOOK he should read __, not to Piero, Antonio's.'

Again, locality cannot rule out (24c) because the two foci never cross each other in their movements to the respective left peripheries. On the other hand, the interface account captures the ill-formedness of (24c), under the assumption that the presupposed part includes not just the simple clause complement of Foc, but the whole complex clause: so, the presupposition of the main clause Foc1 in (24c) is the whole complex clausal constituent underscored in the following:

(24) c'. *A GIANNI Foc1 <u>ho detto ___ che IL TUO LIBRO Foc2 dovrebbe leggere ___</u>, non a Piero, quello di Antonio.*
'TO GIANNI Foc1 <u>I said ___ that YOUR BOOK Foc 2 he should read ___</u>, not to Piero, Antonio's.'

In (24c') the presupposed part of Foc1 includes a corrective focus, the Spec of Foc2, hence the interpretive clash arises here. In conclusion, the impossibility of co-occurrence of two left-peripheral focus positions appears to be more general than what would be expected simply on the basis of a locality account.

We may now ask the reciprocal to Haegeman's question: could an interface analysis be proposed as an alternative to the locality analysis to bar double topic constructions in English such as (11), repeated here for convenience:

(11) **John Op, your book Op, I convinced ___ to buy ___*

The answer seems to be negative: the only interpretive requirement that a comment must have seems to be that it should contain some new information (and perhaps even that is not strictly needed if a topic – comment structure is used to confirm the information expressed by the interlocutor, so that the whole utterance is given information). In any event, nothing in the interpretation of a comment precludes the possibility that it may have in turn a topic-comment structure, as is shown by the possibility of Top recursion in Italian. Therefore, (11) is uniquely excluded by locality.

In conclusion, both the locality analysis and the interface analysis appear to be needed to ban multiple occurrences of operator-like elements in the left periphery.[4]

Aboh (2004) observes that, while Gungbe disallows Foc recursion in the same left periphery, cases of activation of the left-peripheral focus in distinct clauses akin to (24) are possible. Under the interface analysis proposed here, this state of affairs suggests that the calculation of what counts as presupposition is submitted to parametric variation: apparently, in Gungbe only the simple clause complement of Foc is interpreted as presupposed, whereas this property extends in Italian to the whole complex structure which is complement of Foc, including embedded clausal domains. I will leave open here the question whether this

---

[4] I will not address here the phenomenon of multiple wh-movement, permitted in certain languages; see Krapova and Cinque (2008) for an analysis of how a violation of fRM is alleviated in such cases.

is a primitive parametric choice, or a consequence of independent differences between the two languages.[5]

5 Constraints on lower Top in Italian

In addition to the higher Top position, robustly attested across languages, Italian permits a Top position lower than Foc:

(25) a. *Alla riunione, QUESTO, a Gianni, gli avresti dovuto dire, non quello che hai detto.*
'At the meeting, THIS, to Gianni, you should have said to him, not what you said.'
b. *A Gianni, QUESTO, alla riunione, gli avresti dovuto dire, non quello che hai detto.*
'To Gianni, THIS, at the meeting, you should have said to him, not what you said'

In Rizzi (1997) this position is treated as identical to the higher Top position, and in fact in many cases the two topics surrounding Foc seem interchangeable, as in (25).

Nevertheless, Frascarelli and Hinterhoelzl (2006), Bianchi and Frascarelli (2010) have observed that distinct topic positions may differ in interpretive properties, while sharing a common core of topical interpretation.

---

5 An anonymous reviewer raises the issue of the proper analysis of contrastive topics, which, according to Wagner (2008) would be cases of nested focus (focus within focus). As a contrastive topic typically cooccurs with an independent focus, this analysis does not seem to be immediately compatible with the account of the ban against multiple foci proposed here (see, in particular the next section, in which several well-formed examples of a left-peripheral contrastive topic immediately followed by a corrective focus are discussed).
In fact, the Romance languages provide clear syntactic evidence to distinguish contrastive topic and focus: the former requires clitic resumption (like other kinds of topics):
(i) Q: *Hai deciso che cosa fare del libro? E del disco?*
'Did you decide what to do of the book? And of the record?'
A: *Il libro *(lo) darò a Maria, e il disco, a Francesca*
'The book, I will give *(it) to Maria, and the book, to Francesca'
whereas a left-peripheral focus is not clitic-resumed (Rizzi 1997). So, I will continue to assume that a contrastive topic is a particular kind of topic, structurally and interpretively distinct from focus, as in Frascarelli and Hinterhoelzl (2006), Bianchi and Frascarelli (2010). See also section 5.

One salient difference between topic positions preceding and following focus is that the higher Top field can host a contrastive topic (a topic explicitly contrasted with another topic salient in discourse), whereas the lower topic disallows the contrastive interpretation. This can be made clear if appropriate contexts are built. In a dialogue introduced by (26A), in replies like (26B) and (26B'), the topic is not contrasted with any other salient referent, and both Top Foc and Foc Top orders are possible:

(26) A: *So che vorrebbero regalare un disco a Mario per il suo compleanno...*
  'I know that they would want to give a record to Mario on his birthday...'
  B: *No, a Mario, UN LIBRO gli vorrebbero regalare, non un disco.*
  'No, to Mario, A BOOK they would want to give, not a record.'
  B': *No, UN LIBRO, a Mario, gli vorrebbero regalare, non un disco.*
  'No, A BOOK, to Mario, they would want to give, not a record'

On the other hand, in (27) the topic is contrastive, as Mario is contrasted with another salient referent, Gianni, mentioned in the immediate discourse context. Here the order Top Foc is possible, but the order Foc Top is not:

(27) A: *So che vorrebbero regalare un disco a Mario e un libro a Gianni...*
  'I know that they would want to give a record to Mario and a book to Gianni...'
  B: *No, a Mario UN LIBRO gli vorrebbero regalare, e a Gianni UN DISCO.*
  'No, to Mario, A BOOK they would want to give, and to Gianni A RECORD'
  B': **No, UN LIBRO a Mario gli vorrebbero regalare, e UN DISCO a Gianni.*
  'No, A BOOK to Mario they would want to give, and A RECORD to Gianni'

The following is another case illustrating the same point, with a dative focus and an accusative topic:

(28) A: *Darò il libro di linguistica al professore, e quello di fantascienza allo studente...*
  'I will give the book about linguistics to the professor, and the one about science fiction to the student...'
  B: *No, il libro di fantascienza, AL PROFESSORE lo dovresti dare, e quello di linguistica ALLO STUDENTE.*
  'No, the book about science fiction, TO THE PROFESSOR you should give, and the one about linguistics, TO THE STUDENT.'
  B': **No, AL PROFESSORE, il libro di fantascienza, lo dovresti dare, e ALLO STUDENTE quello di linguistica.*
  'No, TO THE PROFESSOR, the book about science fiction, you should give, and TO THE STUDENT the one about linguistics.'

So, the pattern we obtain is the following:

(29) a. OK   Top ...   Foc ...   (as in 27B, 28B)
             [+contr]
     b. *   Foc ...   Top ...   (as in 27B', 28B')
                        [+contr]
     c. OK   Foc ...   Top ...   (as in (26B'))
                        [−contr]

The preceding discussion of the role of locality in constraining left peripheral orders immediately suggests a possible analysis. Suppose that contrastive topics are marked by the feature [+contrast], whose relevance for intervention has been highlighted by Neeleman and van de Koot (2010). In our terms, the natural assumption is that +contrast is a feature belonging to the operator class. If it is so, (29b) is excluded by fRM: an element marked by an Op feature, the focal element, is moved across an element which is also marked by an Op feature, the contrastive topic, and this yields a violation of fRM. (27B'), (28B') are thus excluded. On the other hand, (29c) is fine because a focus is extracted from the domain of a "pure" (non-contrastive) topic, hence across an element which is disjoint in relevant features for the computation of locality. Therefore, the order Foc – Top (non contrastive) is possible, as in (26B').

What about the well-formedness of (29a)? Here the contrastive topic is extracted from the domain of a focus, hence an element carrying an operator feature is moved across another such element. Why doesn't this induce a minimality violation? This is in fact an instance of a large class of cases in which weak island effects are alleviated. By and large, the logic of the approach to fRM in Starke (2001), Rizzi (2004) and developed in Friedmann, Belletti and Rizzi (2009) in the context of acquisition studies, is that when a featurally richer element is extracted from the domain of a featurally more impoverished element, the locality violation is alleviated. A straightforward sense in which in (27)B the extracted topic is more complex than the focus defining the extraction domain is that the topic is specified both by a topic feature and by an operator feature (+contrast), whereas the focus is solely characterized by an operator feature (+focus):

(27) B: *No,   a Mario   UN LIBRO   gli vorrebbero regalare, e a Gianni UN DISCO.*
        'No,   to Mario, A BOOK   they would want to give, and to Gianni A RECORD'
               [+Top, +contr]   [+Foc]

We are, therefore, in an inclusion configuration, one which in the system proposed by Friedmann, Belletti and Rizzi (2009) is tolerated by the adult system (whereas it appears to raise insurmountable problems for children: see the reference quoted and much related work).

6 Degrees of acceptability

The full acceptability of the inclusion configuration in (29)a raises an issue in relation to the gradation of judgments in the domain which originally motivated the fRM approach: extractions from Weak Islands. Both bare and lexically restricted wh-elements are freely extractable with declaratives, giving rise to fully acceptable structures:

(30) a. Which book do you think that John read __ ?
   [+Q, +NP]
   b. What do you think that John read __ ?
   [+Q]

In extraction from indirect questions, though, we get a contrast. Lexically restricted wh-elements are marginal, whereas bare wh-elements are more severely degraded:

(31) a. ??Which book do you wonder if John read __ ?
   [+Q, +NP]   [+Q]
   b. *What do you wonder if John read __ ?
   [+Q]   [+Q]

The amelioration of (31a) over (31b) has been taken as the paradigmatic case supporting the view that an element with a more complex featural specification is more easily extractable from a WI environment than a simpler element. Here I am assuming that the relevant features are +Q and +NP, the latter characterizing lexically restricted wh-elements, as in Friedmann et al. (op cit.).[6]

If this approach is combined with the analysis of the distribution of contrastive topics just presented, the question which arises is the following. (31a) shows that when the featural specification of the target properly includes the specification of the intervener, the intervention configuration gives rise to marginality. This case contrasts with both the identity relation, giving rise to stronger deviance (as in (31b), and with disjunction, which, all other things being equal, gives rise to full acceptability, as in (30a-b). Along the lines of the proposed analysis, (27B) would also be a case of proper inclusion, with the contrastive topic, specified as +Top and +contrast (the latter an operator feature) extracted across a focalized element, which also is characterized by an Op feature (+Foc). But (27B)

---

[6] Other proposals have assumed that the additional specification of *which book* is D-linking, or topicality: see Rizzi (2011) for discussion; I will not addressed these alternatives here, which leave the core of the issue unchanged.

is perceived as fully acceptable. So, why is it not degraded, in contrast with (31a) (or the Italian equivalent, also degraded to some extent)?

In order to capture this discrepancy between two cases of proper inclusion, I would like to adopt the approach proposed in Villata, Franck, Rizzi (2015), according to which not all features entering into the computation of locality have the same weight. In particular, the Top, Foc and Q features are criterial features, in the sense of Rizzi (1997) and much subsequent work, i.e., features which (among other properties) are able to trigger movement on their own. On the other hand, such features as +NP, +Contrast are non-criterial: they have the role of finely modulating the landing site and interpretation of the moved element, so they somehow operate in tandem with the criterial features, but do not have the capacity of triggering A'-movement on their own. So, it appears that while criterial inclusion (i.e., inclusion in which the feature in common between X and Z is the criterial feature) determines a degradation in acceptability, non-criterial inclusion (a case of inclusion in which the feature in common between Y and Z is non-criterial) does not affect acceptability. Then, (27B), a case of non-criterial inclusion (because +Contrast is a non-criterial operator feature), is fully acceptable, much as a lexically restricted object question or relative crossing a lexically restricted subject:

(32) a. *Which politician   did   the journalist   attack __?*
         [+Q, +NP]   [+NP]
     b. *Here is   the politician   that   the journalist   attacked __.*
                            [+R. +NP]   [+NP]

(where +R is the criterial feature characterizing the relative head). (32a-b), both cases of non-criterial inclusion (with non-criterial feature +NP in common between X and Z), are fully acceptable, on a par with (27B). Non-criterial inclusion has an impact on locality which is visible elsewhere (i.e., in the acquisition of these complex constructions, according to the analysis in Friedmann, Belletti and Rizzi 2009, and, possibly, on adult processing: Belletti and Rizzi 2013), but it does not affect acceptability.

7 Selection and the delimiting positions of Force and Fin

An independent element which may contribute to determine the order of elements in functional sequences is selection. Selectional requirements may demand that certain specifications be structurally adjacent to selectors, thus enforcing certain orders. An early reference to selection as a property determining order is in Rizzi (1997)'s discussion of Force and Fin as the delimiting heads of the complementizer space. Force, it is argued, expresses a property that external selectors want to know about, the clausal type (if a clause is a declarative, or a question, or an exclamative, etc., Cheng 1991), therefore it must be the most prominent head of the left periphery. Fin selects an IP agreeing in finiteness with it (for instance, complementizer *di* in Italian selects an infinitival IP), hence it must be structurally adjacent to the IP. This follows from a strict theory of selection:

(33) *Local selection: Selection is strictly local, in that a head can only select a structurally adjacent head.*

I.e., in the following configuration, H1 can select H2 and H2 can select H3, but H1 cannot directly select H3:

(34) *H1 [$_\alpha$ H2 [$_\beta$ H3 ...*

Problems for this simple and restrictive approach to selection are raised by certain cartographic discoveries. Consider, for instance, the observation that an indirect yes-no question in Italian can be introduced by a topic preceding the interrogative marker *se* (if):

(35) *Non so   a Gianni   se   gli potremo parlare*
     'I don't know   to Gianni   if   we could speak to him.'

Clearly, the embedded clause cannot be a TopP: the higher verb selects for an indirect question, not a clause introduced by a topic. The nature of the clause as an indirect question is expressed by the question particle *se* (if) which is in a lower position (the position Int of Rizzi 2001 and subsequent work) so that, under (33), the main verb cannot directly select for Int. Assuming (33) it must be the case that the embedded clause is introduced by a Force marker expressing interrogative force, as is suggested by the representation in (36).

(36) *Non so*   [Force   [*a Gianni* Top   [Op   *se*$_{+Int}$ *gli potremo parlare*]]]
     'I don't   to Gianni   if   we could speak to him.'
     know

Similar problems arise for indirect wh-questions, in which the wh-element fills the lower Foc position, (and possibly an even lower wh-position: see Rizzi and Bocci 2016 for discussion):

(36') *Non so*   [Force   [*a Gianni* Top   [*che cosa* Foc   *gli potremo dire __*]]]
      'I don't know   to Gianni   what   we could tell him.'

If we stick to the restrictive theory of selection based on (33), in (36), (36') Force must carry the specification +Int, accessible to the higher selector. Clearly, Force$_{+Int}$ must be connected to Int, headed by the interrogative marker *se*, and possibly hosting a yes-no null operator akin to English *whether* in (36); and, analogously, Force$_{+Int}$ must be connected to the lower position hosting the wh-phrase in (36') and other wh-questions. A natural way to ensure this connection is to assume a (Probe-Goal) Agree relation, which is local but not as strictly local as (33). As all probe-goal relations, it is constrained by Relativized Minimality, which blocks the relation only if the intervener has certain featural characteristics in common with the elements involved in the relation; an intervening Top layer does not interfere in the relation between Force$_{+Int}$ and Int, so a representation like (37) is well-formed:

(37) *Non so*   [*Force*$_{+Int}$ [*a Gianni* Top   [Op   *se*$_{+Int}$ ... *gli potremo parlare* ...]]]
    'I don't know   to Gianni   if we could speak to him.'

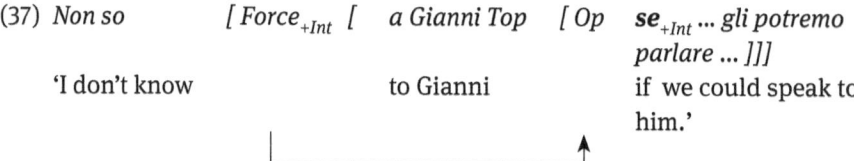

(Whether the Agree relation targets the yes-no (or wh-) operator, as the arrow in (37) suggests, or the Int head, is not crucial for our discussion here).

The necessity of separating a higher Force marker and the position(s) of the interrogative operator is straightforwardly supported by the Spanish reported question construction (Plann 1982, Suner 1994, McCloskey 1992, Saito 2012, Rizzi 2013). If I hear María ask the question "Are there newspapers on Monday?", I can report this speech event by uttering the following (examples due to Maria Lluisa Hernanz, discussed in Rizzi 2013):

(38) *María preguntó*   **que**   *el lunes*   **si** *había periódicos*
     Maria asked   that   the Monday   if there were newspapers

Que overtly realizes the Force head abstractly postulated in (37), which here expresses both the reported character of the clause (as complementizer *to* in Saito's 2012 analysis of the Japanese equivalent), and its interrogative force; the latter specification agrees with *si* in the Int position across the topicalized adverbial:

(39) *María preguntó*   **que**$_{+Rep+Int}$ *el lunes*   Op   **si**$_{+Int}$ *había periódicos*
     Maria asked   that   the Monday   if there were newspapers

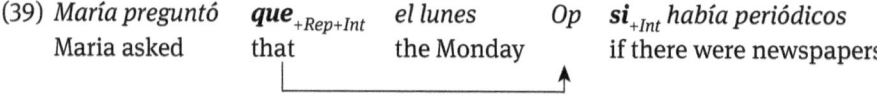

The construction is dependent on the nature of the main verb: it can be selected by main verbs like *ask*, compatible with both reports and questions, but not by main verbs which are not verbs of saying, like *remember/forget*, which are only compatible with ordinary (non-reported) questions.

In wh-questions which are also interpreted as reported questions, the wh-element presumably is in the lower Foc position (or in an even lower position adjacent to Fin: see Rizzi and Bocci 2016 on Italian), and *que* enters into an Agree relation with this position (across an intervening topic, in cases like (40)):

(40) *Le pregunté [que*+Rep+Int [*Juan* Top [**cómo** Foc+Int ... *cocinaba]]]*
     Maria asked   that   Juan   how   he cooked

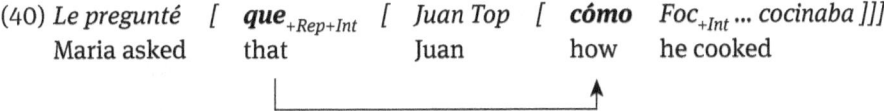

This kind of overtly complex structure of the CP system, specialized for reported questions in Spanish, is generalized to all indirect questions in Hungarian (whether yes-no or wh, reported or not). In this language, all embedded questions are introduced by complementizer *hogy* (that); yes-no questions are marked by the enclitic particle *–e*, attached to the verb, as in (41), while wh-questions have the wh-element in focus position, as in (42), (43). In the spirit of what we just proposed, in all these cases we assume an Agree relation between *hogy* and the position marking the clause as a yes-no or wh-question:

(41) *Kiváncsi vagyok,   hogy*+Int   *elmentek-e*+Int   *a vendégek.*
     curious   be-PRES-1SG that   PART-left-3PL-E the guests-NOM
     'I wonder if the guests have left.'

(42) *Kiváncsi vagyok,   hogy*+Int   *kit*   Foc+Int   *keresett   Zeta.*
     curious   be-PRES-1SG that   who-ACC   looked-for Zeta-NOM
     'I wonder whom Zeta looked for.'

(43) *Kiváncsi vagyok,   hogy*+Int *Zeta*   Top *kit*   Foc+Int *keresett*
     curious   be-PRES-1SG that   Zeta-NOM   who-ACC   looked-for
     'I wonder whom Zeta looked for.'   Puskas (2000:226)

Example (43) shows that the Agree relation can hold across a Topic, as is expected under fRM. The relevant representation is:

(43') *Kiváncsi vagyok,   hogy*+Int *Zeta*   Top *kit*   Foc+Int *keresett*
     curious   be-PRES-1SG that   Zeta-NOM   who-ACC   looked-for

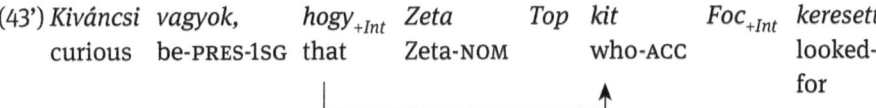

Hungarian straightforwardly shows that Int (for yes-no questions) or the wh-element (for wh-questions) are not hosted in the highest C position in all kinds of embedded questions; under the restrictive theory of selection we are assuming this requires an Agree approach connecting Force and the criterial position.

8 Some theoretical speculations

Apparently, the following property holds in Italian, Spanish, and, very straightforwardly, in Hungarian:

(44) **Force** *(the typing position selected for)* and the **criterial position** *(the position which hosts the interrogative operator) are distinct positions in the C-sequence.*

Why should this separation hold? Wouldn't it be simpler for natural languages to always unify the typing position and the criterial position, which share the same featural content, rather than duplicating the relevant feature on two positions?

I would like to speculate that the separation may be connected to the way in which Phase Theory works. In standard Phase Theory, the C head defines the full clausal phase. If one combines cartographic representations and Phase Theory, C is split into finer components, hence the important question arises of what left peripheral head, or heads, define(s) the clausal phase. A plausible candidate is, of course, the Force head, which manifests the properties of autonomy at the interfaces that are expected from phase heads (Chomsky 2001). Things could of course be more complex and there could be more than one left peripheral head defining a phase, but certainly Force is the first and most immediately plausible candidate that comes to mind.

If this is correct, why couldn't the Force layer also play the role of the criterial layer, hosting the criterial operator in its Spec, and avoiding the necessity of having an independent criterial layer in a lower position, as in statement (44)? Remember that according to Phase Theory the escape hatch for extracting something from a phase is the specifier of the phase edge, the phrasal position which is not sent to Spell-out at the end of the phase. Then, if the Force layer and the criterial layer coincided, the Spec of the Force head would systematically be filled by the criterial operator, hence the structure would not have an escape hatch available for extraction, and would always be a strong island. So, the separation of the Force layer and of the criterial layer may be seen as a device to provide a possible escape hatch, and make extraction from an embedded clause possible.

An additional question that arises has to do with the generality of (44): languages like Italian, Spanish, Hungarian, etc., which freely permit elements like topics to occur in a LP position higher than the criterial position, clearly require the dissociation of Force and the criterial position; does this requirement hold in general? A language with Force = Criterial position would have the relevant constructions (indirect questions, in particular) always functioning as strong islands, because the Spec providing an escape hatch from the clause would be systematically unavailable for extraction in such languages. This could offer a device to address a rather elusive element of variation, the fact that extractions from indirect questions appear to be more acceptable in some languages than in other languages, an issue on the research agenda ever since the late 1970's (see Rizzi 1978, 1982, Chomsky 1981). I will not try to develop this possible path in this paper.

A separate question is raised by the assumed system to satisfy selection in clausal complements. The strictly local approach to selection that we have adopted enforces a two-steps selection procedure, a strictly local selection of a clause headed by Force with the appropriate specifications, and a somewhat less local Agree relation connecting Force to the criterial position. I.e., going back to (37), we would have:

(37') *Non so*   [*Force*$_{+Int}$ [*a Gianni* Top   [*Op*   *se*$_{+Int}$ ... *gli potremo parlare* ... *]]]*
     'I don't know'   to Gianni   if we could speak to him.'

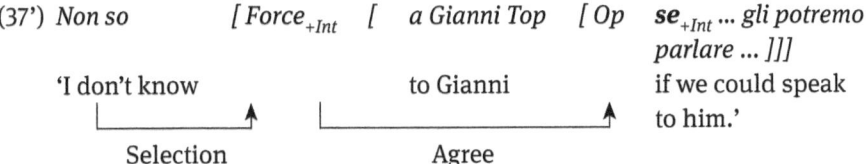

         Selection   Agree

But couldn't one assume that the system is simpler, and selection from the higher verb in (35), (36), (37), (38), (39), (41)-(43) is directly satisfied through an Agree relation from the higher verb, connecting it directly to the criterial layer and bypassing the Force layer? I.e., couldn't selection work as in (37")?

(37") *Non so*   [*Force*$_{+Int}$ [*a Gianni* Top   [*Op*   *se*$_{+Int}$ ... *gli potremo parlare* ... *]]]*
     'I don't know'   to Gianni   if we could speak to him.'

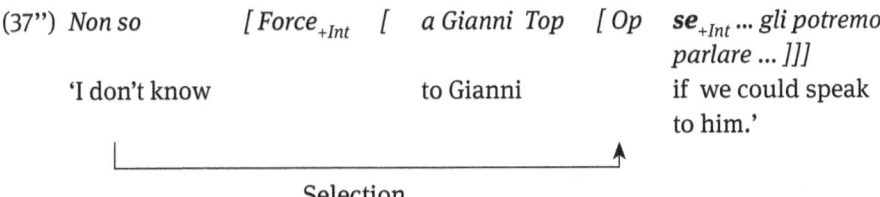

                 Selection

The assumption that selection may be satisfied by Agree certainly creates problems elsewhere. For instance, it would permit selection of a complement to be possible "at a distance", across intervening material provided that the interveners do not affect the Agree relation. This does not seem to be correct. E.g., if a verb could directly select a direct object across adverbial material via Agree, all languages would be expected to have this option, and the important results connecting V Adv O orders to verb movement (in French and other languages: Emonds 1978, Pollock 1989, Belletti 1990) would be lost.

The facts that we have reviewed in this section are very naturally captured by the two steps analysis of selection expressed in (37'). The point is that the Force head is spelled out in language particular ways, depending both on the selectional properties of the main verb and the presence or absence of a lower criterial layer. In Italian and English, Force is realized as zero both in reported questions and simple embedded questions, and as *che/that* in embedded declaratives. In Spanish and Japanese the cake is cut differently, and Force is realized as *que/to* in declaratives and reported questions, whereas simple embedded questions have zero realization in Force (Int is realized in a lower head, giving rise to the *que si, ka to* sequences, respectively; again, see Saito 2012, Rizzi 2013 for discussion). Hungarian shows no variation at all, the Force head being invariably realized as *hogy* in declaratives, reported questions, and simple indirect questions:

(45)

	$Force_{Decl}$	$Force_{Int+Rep}$	$Force_{Int}$
Italian	che	Ø	Ø
English	that	Ø	Ø
Spanish	que	que	Ø
Japanese	to	to	Ø
Hungarian	hogy	hogy	hogy

This double dependency determining the spell-out of Force is naturally expressed by the two steps analysis, which connects the main verb to Force via selection, and the latter to the criterial position via Agree, as in (37').

If selection cannot be satisfied by Agree, and is strictly local, so that a two-step analysis of (37) is enforced, the question arises of why it is so.

Suppose that selection is a precondition for external merge; i.e., A and B can be externally merged only if a selectional relation holds, i.e., A selects B or B selects A. Then, a very straightforward way of capturing the strictly local nature of selection would be to assume that external merge can only see the label of the elements which are merged, and cannot look inside such elements and their internal structure at all. Let us reconsider (34):

(34) $H1\ [_\alpha H2\ [_\beta H3\ ...$

When H1 is merged with α, the operation can only see the label of α, which is determined by H2 (in fact the label of α is H2, under bare phrase structure and restrictive labeling algorithms, as in Chomsky 2013, 2015, Rizzi 2014, 2015); so the operation cannot be sensitive to properties of H3, an element internal to α.

Another way of stating this conclusion may be the following: selection is not to be assimilated to feature checking, which is formally implemented by the Agree operation. Selection and Agree differ in the locality conditions they must obey: Agree respects featural Relativized Minimality, whereas selection respects a stricter condition like (33), structural adjacency. In fact, this follows from the way in which computation proceeds: if selection is a prerequisite for external merge, the system only sees the labels of the elements A and B to be merged. An Agree relation between A and an element internal to B cannot be defined because Agree requires c-command, and c-command cannot be defined here because A and B are not (yet) connected in a tree structure; so the only properties visible to the external merge operation are the labels of A and B, whence the strict locality of selection.

The analysis of the preceding paragraph presupposes the idea that selection is a prerequisite of external merge. This is plausible, but not obvious. E.g., Chomsky (2004) has argued that selection is checked post-syntactically, at the end of a phase, in which case selection could not be a prerequisite for merge. If this is correct, the strict locality of selection could not be derived by the way of functioning of external merge, as suggested in the previous paragraph. An alternative to consider could be that Agree is a formal operation available in the syntactic box, but not in the systems at the interface with syntax (much as merge itself, in fact). So presumably interface systems can interpret positions which are syntactically marked as agreeing in syntax, but do not have the power to establish such relations on their own. If selection is an interface property, then it cannot establish Agree relations, and can only see strict adjacency. The different ideas mentioned in this speculative section have significant ramifications and consequences elsewhere, which I will not try to address in this paper.

9 The interplay of selection and locality

The theory of locality may have an important role in the "further explanation" of properties of functional sequences, as was underscored by Abels (2012), Haegeman (2012), Rizzi (2013), and in previous sections of the present article. Consider, for instance, the following asymmetry between topic and focus: a topic can both precede and follow Int, as is shown in Italian (46), but a focus can only follow Int, as shown in (47):

(46) a. *Mi domando se il tuo libro, lo abbiano già letto.*
    'I wonder if your book, they have already read it.'
  b. *Mi domando, il tuo libro, se lo abbiano già letto.*
    'I wonder, your book, if they have already read it'

(47) a. *Mi domando se PROPRIO QUESTO volessero dire (e non qualcos'altro).*
    'I wonder if PRECISELY THIS they wanted to say (and not something else).'
  b. **Mi domando PROPRIO QUESTO se volessero dire (e non qualcos'altro).*
    'I wonder EXACTLY THIS if they wanted to say (and not something else).'

Here, as Abels (2012) points out for similar cases, a plausible candidate is locality, and more specifically Relativized Minimality (Rizzi 1990) in its featural version (Starke 2001, Rizzi 2004). The representations of (47) are given in (48):

(48) a. *Mi domando Op se PROPRIO QUESTO volessero dire* ___
                                                              (e non qualcos'altro)
     'I wonder   if   EXACTLY THIS   they wanted to say
                                                         (and not something else).'

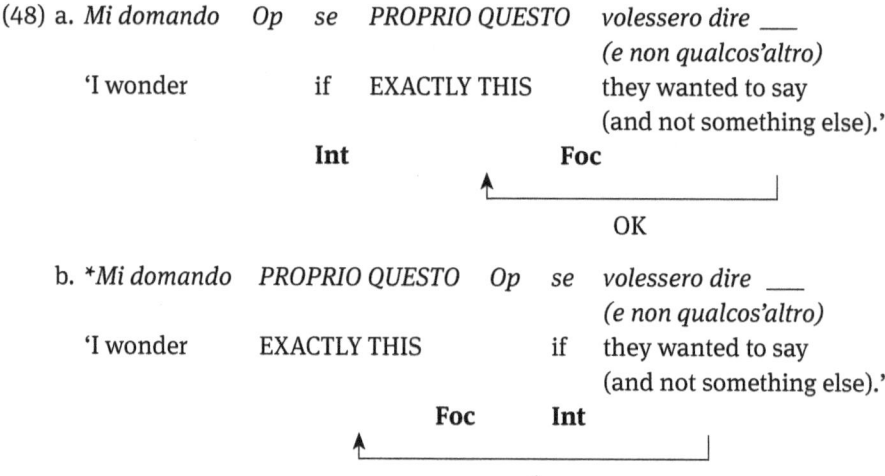

b. **Mi domando PROPRIO QUESTO Op se volessero dire* ___
                                                      (e non qualcos'altro)
   'I wonder   EXACTLY THIS   if   they wanted to say
                                                         (and not something else).'

If the Int position hosts a yes-no operator Op in its Spec, an element bearing the +Foc feature, which also is a member of the operator class, cannot jump across it in (48b). When the focal element remains lower than Int, there is no crossing of another operator, and the structure is fine, as in (48a). A Topic, not bearing an operator feature (nor involving a null Op in Romance), can move across Int without any problem, as in (46b).

All this is pretty straightforward, but Cinque and Krapova (2013), Callegari (2014) have noticed problems for a locality approach to similar cases of ordering in the sequence. One general problem is this. All other things being equal, if a given ordering *A-B is excluded in the sequence as a locality effect (A cannot be moved across B), one would predict equal status for any movement of A across B, including long-distance extraction. But this prediction is not met in some cases.

For instance, in the case of (48b), long-distance focus extraction from an *if* clause and local ordering Foc – Int should be on a par under a locality approach, but long distance extraction from an *if* clause is distinctly more acceptable than local movement of Focus across *if*. Compare (48b) with the corresponding case of long distance extraction:

(49) ?*PROPRIO QUESTO* Foc *mi domando* Op *se*$_{+Int}$ *volessero dire* ___
                                                            (e non qualcos'altro)
     'EXACTLY THIS   I wonder   if   they wanted to say
                                                            (and not something else).'

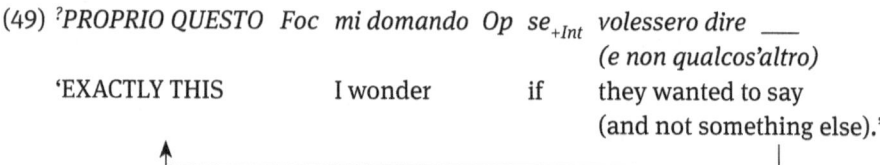

Clearly, a more severe violation is involved in local ordering ... Foc – Int ... then in long distance extraction Foc ..... Int .... Why is it so?

We can now capitalize on the two-step approach to selection introduced in the previous section to tackle this problem. Remember that the critical ingredient was the Agree relation which must be established between Force and the criterial position. A more complete representation of (48b), also expressing this Agree relation, would be the following:

(48) b'. *Mi domando   Force$_{+Int}$ PROPRIO   Foc   Op   se$_{+Int}$ volessero
                                         QUESTO   dire ___ ...
         'I wonder   EXACTLY   if   they wanted
                                         THIS   to say ...'
                                                    Foc   Int

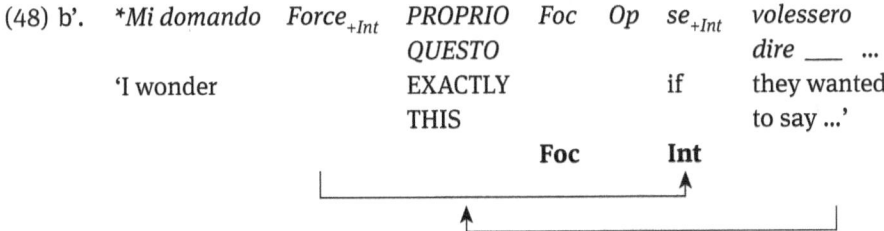

Here we have a double violation of RM, indicated by the two arrows in (48b'): the yes-no Op intervenes between the focal operator *PROPRIO QUESTO* and its trace, thus disrupting the antecedent-trace relation, and the focal operator intervenes between Force$_{+Int}$ and Int, thus disrupting the required Agree relation. We thus have two violations of Relativized Minimality here. On the other hand, there is only a single violation of RM in (49), with the yes-no operator intervening between the focal operator, extracted from the embedded clause, and its trace (moreover here the effect may also be weakened by whatever property makes violations with argumental operators weaker than with non-argumental operators). Moreover there is no violation of RM at all when we have the order Int Foc in embedded questions, as in (48a), with the following more complete representation:

(48) a'.   Mi domando   Force$_{+Int}$ Op   se$_{+Int}$ PROPRIO   Foc   volessero
                                                             QUESTO   dire ___ ...
           'I wonder   EXACTLY   they wanted
                                                             THIS   to say ....'
                        Force   Int   Foc

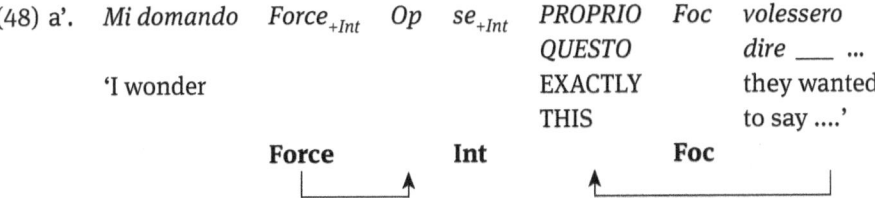

Here focus movement stops at a position lower than Int: therefore it does not cross another operator position; moreover, the focus position does not interfere with the Agree relation connecting Force and the yes-no operator.

So, we have

(50) – 0 violations of RM in (48a).
     – 1 violation of RM in (49).
     – 2 violations of RM in (48b).

This captures the gradation of acceptability pretty accurately. Notice that this presupposes that violations of RM are cumulative, but this is entirely in the spirit of the featural approach, which is precisely intended to capture graded judgments. In the classical cases the severity of the violation depends on the featural overlap between target and intervener, whereas in (50) the gradation depends on the number of violations. We may look at these ideas as addressing distinct dimensions of the same general issue of graded judgments, providing independent but consistent tools for a quantitative approach to degrees of acceptability.[7]

10 Conclusion

The empirical discoveries of cartographic research raise issues of further explanation: why do structural maps have the properties of ordering and distribution that we observe? How do such properties relate to fundamental ingredients of linguistic computations? These issues directly connect cartographic work to fundamental theoretical research, and nourish the theoretical reflection with novel empirical materials. Two broad factors may be involved in forms of further explanation. Interface systems may demand that syntactic elements be organized in certain ways; and formal principles constraining syntactic computations, such as locality, may determine certain properties of functional sequences.

That intervention effects, captured in terms of featural Relativized Minimality, may determine certain orderings and other distributional constraints in functional sequences has been shown in Abels (2012), Haegeman (2012) and much related work. In this paper I have used this mode of explanation to capture the uniqueness of topics in English, as opposed to the possible proliferation of topics in Romance. This cross-linguistic difference has been made to follow from the

---

[7] In Rizzi (1997: 330, fn. 18, ex. (ii)a) I had observed that a focalized indirect object can be marginally moved locally across a wh-element in an indirect question. The example is reproduce here:
(i)   ?Mi domando A GIANNI che cosa abbiano detto (, non a Piero)
       'I wonder TO GIANNI what they said (, not to Piero)'
This marginal possibility is not expected given the analysis in the text, as a double violation of fRM should be produced here. It should be noticed that if a direct object is locally focus moved across a wh-element, a more severe violation is produced, more in line with (47)b:
(ii)   *Mi domando QUESTO a chi abbiano detto (, non qualcos'altro)
       'I wonder THIS to whom they said (, not something else)'
I will leave open here what determines the amelioration of (i). Puskas (2000: 272, fn. 33) has observed that a similar option holds in Hungarian.

theory of locality, in interaction with an independent difference between the topic constructions in the two types of languages: clitic resumption in Romance, as opposed to the use of a null operator in English.

The relevance of interface factors has been illustrated by the uniqueness of left-peripheral (corrective) focus, which has been traced back to the properties of the interface routine for the interpretation of configurations involving clause-initial focus. The interface explanation and the locality effect overlap in part in this case, but one cannot be reduced to the other, as the uniqueness of focus also holds in structures which would not involve intervention configurations.

Another plausible interface factor is selection, which straightforwardly determines the delimiting positions of Force and Fin in the left periphery (Rizzi 1997). Combined with a strictly local theory of selection, this factor implies a two-step analysis of the selectional properties of indirect questions in which the Force position and the criterial position are clearly distinct: the Force position is selected by the external selector, and agrees in interrogative features with the criterial position. I used the two-step approach to also capture certain fine grained judgments concerning focus movement across Int locally and long distance: local focus movement across Int violates fRM twice, which accounts for the particularly severe nature of the violation.

Acknowledgements: I would like to thank Adriana Belletti, Valentina Bianchi, Giuliano Bocci, Genoveva Puskas, Ian Roberts, Ur Shlonsky, and an anonymous reviewer for helpful comments. This research was supported in part by the ERC Advanced Grant 340297 SynCart.

References

Abels, Klaus. 2012. The Italian left periphery: A view from locality. *Linguistic inquiry* 43. 229–254.
Aboh, Enoch Olade. 2004. *The morphosyntax of complement-head sequences: Clause structure and word order patterns in Kwa*. New York: Oxford University Press.
Belletti, Adriana. 1990. *Generalized verb movement: Aspects of verb syntax*. Torino: Rosenberg et Sellier.
Belletti, Adriana. 2004. Aspects of the low IP area. In Luigi Rizzi (ed.), *The structure of CP and IP. The cartography of syntactic structure*, Vol. 2, 16–51. New York: Oxford University Press.
Belletti, Adriana. 2009. *Structures and strategies*. London and New York: Routledge.
Belletti, Adriana & Luigi Rizzi. 2013. Intervention in grammar and processing. In Ivano Caponigro & C. Cecchetto (eds.), *From grammar to meaning*, 294–311. Cambridge: Cambridge University Press.

Benincà, Paola & Cecilia Poletto. 2004. Topic, focus and V2: Defining the CP sublayers. In Luigi Rizzi (ed.), *The structure of CP and IP. The cartography of syntactic structure*, Vol. 2, 52–75. New York: Oxford University Press.

Bianchi, Valentina & Mara Frascarelli. 2010. Is topic a root phenomenon? *Iberia* 2. 43–48.

Bianchi Valentina, Giuliano Bocci & Silvio Cruschina. 2016. Focus fronting, unexpectedness, and evaluative implicatures. *Semantics and Pragmatics* 9.3. 1–54.

Bošković, Željko (ed.). 2016. On labels. Special issue, *The Linguistic Review* 33.1.

Bresnan, Joan W. 1977. Variables in the theory of transformations. In Peter Culicover, Thomas Wasow & Adrian Akmajian (eds.), *Formal syntax*, 157–196. New York: Academic Press.

Browning, Maggie A. 1996. CP Recursion and that-t Effects. *Linguistic Inquiry* 27. 237–255.

Callegari, Elena. 2014. Why locality-based accounts of the left periphery are unfit to account for its variation. Paper presented at *Variation in C: Macro- and micro-comparative approaches to complementizers and the CP phase*, University of Venice, 21–22 October.

Cecchetto, Carlo. 2000. Doubling structures and reconstruction. *Probus* 12. 93–126.

Cheng, Lisa Lai-Shen. 1991. On the typology of Wh questions. Cambridge, MA: MIT dissertation.

Chomsky, Noam. 1977. On Wh-movement. In Peter Culicover, Thomas Wasow & Adrian Akmajian (eds.), *Formal syntax*, 71–132. New York: Academic Press.

Chomsky, Noam. 1981. *Lectures on government and binding*. Dordrecht: Foris Publications.

Chomsky, Noam. 1995. *The minimalist program*. Cambridge, MA: The MIT Press.

Chomsky, Noam. 2004. Beyond explanatory adequacy. In Adriana Belletti (ed.), *Structures and beyond. The cartography of syntactic structure*, Vol. 3, 104–131. New York: Oxford University Press.

Chomsky, Noam. 2013. Problems of projection. *Lingua* 130. 33–49.

Chomsky, Noam. 2015. Problems of projection. Extensions. In Elisa Di Domenico, Cornelia Hamann & Simona Matteini (eds.), *Structures, strategies and beyond: Studies in honour of Adriana Belletti*, 1–16. Amsterdam: Benjamins.

Cinque, Guglielmo. 1977. The movement nature of left dislocation. *Linguistic inquiry*. 397–412.

Cinque, Guglielmo. 1990. *Types of A' dependencies*. Cambridge, MA: The MIT Press.

Cinque, Guglielmo. 1999. *Adverbs and functional heads: A cross-linguistic perspective*. New York: Oxford University Press.

Cinque, Guglielmo & Krapova, Iliyana. 2013. DP and CP: A Relativized Minimality approach to one of their non parallelisms. Paper presented at *Congrès International des Linguistes*, University of Geneva, 21–27 July.

Cinque, Guglielmo & Luigi Rizzi. 2010. The cartography of syntactic structures. In Bernd Heine & Heiko Narrog (eds.), *The Oxford handbook of linguistic analysis*, 51–66. New York: Oxford University Press.

Cruschina, Silvio. 2012. *Discourse-related features and functional projections*. New York: Oxford University Press.

Culicover, Peter. 1993. The adverb effect: Evidence against ECP accounts of the that-t effect. *Proceedings of NELS* 23. 97–110.

Durrleman, Stephanie. 2008. *The syntax of Jamaican Creole*. Amsterdam: Benjamins.

Emonds, Joseph. 1978. The verbal complex V'-V in French. *Linguistic Inquiry* 9. 151–175.

Frascarelli, Mara & Roland Hinterhölzl. 2007. Types of topics in German and Italian. In Susanne Winkler & Kerstin Schwabe (eds.), *On information structure, meaning and form*, 87–116. Amsterdam: John Benjamins.

Friedmann, Naama, Adriana Belletti & Luigi Rizzi. 2009. Relativized relatives: Types of intervention in the acquisition of A'dependencies. *Lingua* 119. 67–88.

Haegeman, Liliane. 2012. *Adverbial clauses, main clause phenomena, and the composition of the left periphery. The Cartography of Syntactic Structures*, Vol. 8. Oxford University Press.

Hager M'Boua, Clarisse. 2014. Structure de la phrase en Abidji. Geneva: University of Geneva dissertation.

Koopman, Hilda & Dominique Sportiche. 1982. Variables and the Bijection Principle. *The Linguistic Review* 2. 139–160.

Koster, Jan. 1978. *Locality principles in syntax*. Dordrecht: Foris Publications.

Krapova, Ilyana & Guglielmo Cinque. 2008. On the order of wh-phrases in Bulgarian multiple wh-fronting. In Gerhild Zybatow, Luka Szucsich, Uwe Junghanns & Roland Meyer (eds.), *Formal Description of Slavic Languages: The Fifth Conference, Leipzig 2003*. 318–336. Frankfurt am Main: Peter Lang.

McCloskey, James. 1992. Adjunction, selection and embedded Verb Second. *Working Paper LRC-92-07*. University of California, Santa Cruz: Linguistics Research Center.

Neeleman, Ad & Hans Van De Koot. 2008. Dutch scrambling and the nature of discourse templates. *The Journal of Comparative Germanic Linguistics* 11. 137–189.

Plann, Susan. 1982. Indirect questions in Spanish. *Linguistic Inquiry* 13. 297–312.

Pollock, Jean-Yves. 1989. Verb movement, Universal Grammar, and the structure of IP. *Linguistic Inquiry* 20. 365–424.

Puskás, Genoveva. 2000. *Word order in Hungarian: The syntax of Ā-positions*. Amsterdam: Benjamins.

Reinhart, Tanya. 1981. Pragmatics and linguistics: An analysis of sentence topics. *Philosophica* 27. 53–94.

Rizzi, Luigi. 1978. Violations of the Wh Island Constraint in Italian and the Subjacency Condition. *Montreal Working Papers in Linguistics* 11. 155–190.

Rizzi, Luigi. 1982. *Issues in Italian syntax*. Dordrecht: Foris.

Rizzi, Luigi. 1990. *Relativized Minimality*. Cambridge, MA: The MIT Press.

Rizzi, Luigi. 1997. The fine structure of the left periphery. In Liliane Haegeman (ed.), *Elements of grammar: A handbook of generative syntax*, 281–337. Dordrecht: Kluwer.

Rizzi, Luigi. 2001. On the position "int(errogative)" in the left periphery of the clause. In Guglielmo Cinque & Giampaolo Salvi (eds.), *Current studies in Italian syntax: Essays offered to Lorenzo Renzi*, 267–296. Amsterdam: Elsevier.

Rizzi, Luigi. 2004. Locality and left periphery. In Adriana Belletti (ed.), *Structures and beyond. The cartography of syntactic structure*, Vol. 3, 223–251. New York: Oxford University Press.

Rizzi, Luigi. 2011. Minimality. In Cedric Boeckx (ed.), *A handbook of minimalism*, 220–238. New York: Oxford University Press.

Rizzi, Luigi. 2013. Notes on cartography and further explanation. *Probus* 25. 197–226.

Rizzi, Luigi. 2014. Some consequences of criterial freezing. In Peter Svenonius (ed.), *Functional structure from top to toe. The cartography of syntactic structure*, Vol. 9, 19–45. New York: Oxford University Press.

Rizzi, Luigi. 2015a. Cartography, criteria, and labeling. In Ur Shlonsky (ed.). *Beyond functional sequence. The cartography of syntactic structure*, Vol. 10, 314–338. New York: Oxford University Press.

Rizzi, Luigi. 2015b. Notes on labeling and subject positions. In Elisa Di Domenico, Cornelia Hamann & Simona Matteini (eds.), *Structures, strategies and beyond – Studies in honour of Adriana Belletti*, 17–46. Amsterdam: Benjamins.

Rizzi, Luigi. 2016. Labeling, maximality, and the head – phrase distinction. *The Linguistic Review* 33. 103–127.

Rizzi, Luigi & Giuliano Bocci. 2016. The left periphery of the clause – Primarily illustrated for Italian. To appear in *The Blackwell companion to syntax*, 2nd edition.
Rodman, Robert. 1974. On Left Dislocation. *Papers in Linguistics* 7. 437–466.
Ross, John Robert. 1967. *Constraints on variables in syntax*. Cambridge, MA: MIT dissertation.
Saito, Mamoru. 2012. *Sentence types and the Japanese Right Periphery*. Nagoya:Nanzan University manuscript.
Starke, Michal. 2001. Move dissolves into merge: A theory of locality. Geneva: University of Geneva dissertation.
Suñer, Margarita. 1994. V-Movement and the licensing of argumental Wh-phrases in Spanish. *Natural Language & Linguistic Theory* 12. 335–372.
Villata, Sandra, Luigi Rizzi & Julie Franck. 2016. Intervention effects and Relativized Minimality: New experimental evidence from graded judgments. *Lingua* 179. 76–96.
Wagner, Michael 2008. A compositional analysis of contrastive topics. *Proceedings* of NELS 38. 1–14.

Ur Shlonsky
Wh in situ and criterial freezing

1 Introduction: Subject extraction in the criterial approach

The more stringent constraints delimiting subject movement as compared with object movement are attributed by Rizzi and Shlonsky (2007) and related work to criterial freezing, (1).

(1)   Criterial Freezing: A phrase moved to a position dedicated to some scope-discourse interpretive property, a criterial position, is frozen in place.

Following Rizzi (2006), it is assumed that the classical EPP, the requirement that clauses have subjects, can be restated as a criterial requirement, namely the Subject Criterion, which is formally akin to the Topic Criterion, the Focus Criterion, the Q or Wh Criterion, etc.

Thematic subjects are attracted to Spec/Subj, see Cardinaletti (2004), where they satisfy the Subject Criterion. In accordance with (1), they become frozen and cannot move further. Movement of objects and other complements is not similarly constrained since there is no Object Criterion, parallel to the Subject Criterion.

The familiar subject-object asymmetry in long movement from an embedded clause – the *that-trace* effect – is effectively reduced, in this approach, to a violation of criterial freezing. The subject in (2a) is frozen in Spec/Subj but object wh movement in (2b) is unperturbed.

(2)   a. *[Which boy] do you think that <which boy> saw this movie?
      b. [Which movie] do you think that this boy saw <which movie>?

The goal of this contribution – based on an oral presentation at the 2012 Complementizer Agreement workshop organized by Liliane Haegeman in Ghent – is to explore the relevance of the subject criterion for covert movement, in particular that of subject wh in situ.

DOI 10.1515/9781501504037-013

2 Wh in situ in French

The main target language of this study is French, in which wh in situ is an option, illustrated in (3), alongside wh ex situ in (4).

(3) In situ wh
    a. *Tu   as   vu   qui?*
       You have seen who
       'Who did you see?'
    b. *Tu   es   parti   quand?*
       You are left   when
       'When did you leave?'
    c. *Tu   as   fait   ça   comment ?*
       You have done that how
       'How did you do that?'

(4) Ex situ wh
    a. *qui   tu   as   vu   <qui>?*
       who you have seen who
    b. *Quand tu   es   parti   <quand>?*
       when you are left when
    c. *Comment tu   as   fait   ça   <comment>?*
       how you have done that how

What is the position of the *wh* subject in (5)? Is *qui* 'who' in situ – in the canonical subject position Spec/Subj – or ex situ, namely in the left peripheral domain, in Spec/Foc, as per Rizzi (1997)?

(5) *Qui a   fait   ça?*
    who has done that
    'Who did that?'

(5) provides no indication as to whether *qui* is in situ and not moved to Spec/Foc or whether it is string-vacuously moved to this position. The following paragraphs provide several arguments to the effect that subject wh words are *not* in situ and can only occur ex situ.[1]

---

[1] To the best of my knowledge, the claim that subject wh in French is not in situ was first defended in Koopman (1983; 1984). Koopman showed that in both Vata and French, wh in situ alternates with *wh* movement except in subject position, a fact she attributed to a violation of the Empty category Principle (ECP), induced by the unavailability of proper government from C.

2.1 The *que/quoi* alternation

Consider the distribution of the *que/quoi* 'what'. *Quoi* is grammatical in situ in (6a) but not ex situ in (6b), while *que* is the moved variant, as in the contrast in (7).

(6) a. *Jean   a   fait   quoi?*
       John has   done   what
       'What has John done?'
    b. **Quoi* a   fait   Jean?*
       what   has   done   John
       'What has John done?'
(7) a. **Jean   a   fait   que?*
       John has   done   what
       'What has John done?'
    b. *Qu'   a   fait   Jean?*
       what has done   John
       'What has John done?'

In subject position, neither *que* nor *quoi* are possible, (see Plunkett 2000, a.o.)

(8) a. **Que   flotte   dans l'eau?*
       what   floats   in the-water
       'What is floating in the water?'
    b. **Quoi   flotte   dans l'eau?*
       what   floats   in the-water
       'What is floating in the water?'

Friedemann (1997) argues that *que* – but not *quoi* – is a clitic and requires a verbal host in C. Movement of T to C (known as *subject clitic inversion*) provides *que* with a host in (9). In subject *wh* questions such as (8a), however, T does not move to C (Rizzi 1996), and *que* is bereft of a host. Consequently, (8a) is ungrammatical.

(9) *Qu'   as-tu   vu*
    what   have-you   see
    'What have you seen?'

This leaves us with the ungrammaticality of (8b), with *quoi*. Note, first, that *quoi* is not inherently incompatible with subjects or with nominative Case (pace Goldsmith (1978)). Plunkett (2000: 514) cites (10), a non-echo interpretation. The marginal acceptability of this example, as compared with the sharp ungrammaticality of (11), is quite probably due to the ameliorating effect of a third *wh* (*où* 'where') in (10), as Kayne (1983) discusses with respect to the examples in (12).

(10) (?)Qui   a   dit   que   quoi   traînait   où?
     who   has   said   that   what   lay around   where
     'Who said that what was lying around where?'

(11) *Qui   a   dit   que   quoi   traînait   dans   le couloir?
     who   has   said   that   what   lay round   in   the corridor
     'Who said that what was lying around in the corridor?'

(12) a. ?We're trying to find out which man said that which woman was in love with which boy.

    3 wh phrases

    b. *We're trying to find out which man said that which woman was in love with him.

    2 wh phrases

Whatever the explanation for the "third *wh* effect" may be (see Kayne (1983) and, more recently, Pesetsky (2000)), (10) demonstrates that *quoi* is not incompatible with (nominative) subjects as such. If it were, then a nominative *quoi* would be uniformly unacceptable, independently of the putative "third *wh* effect". But if *quoi* can be a nominative form, what rules out (8b)? If French does not allow *wh* subjects in situ, as hypothesized here, then (8b) must instantiate ex situ wh and since *quoi* is ruled out ex situ, as the contrasts in (6) and (7) clearly demonstrate, (8b) has no grammatical derivation.

2.2 The D-linking particle *ça*

The discourse particle *ça* can attach to bare (not lexically restricted) wh elements, inducing a D-linked interpretation of the wh expression. Cheng and Rooryck (2000) briefly discuss this particle, noting that it is only compatible with wh in situ, as shown by the contrast in (13) (see also Baunaz (2011: 30)).

(13) a. T'as   vu   qui ça?   wh in situ
        you've   seen   who ça
     b. *Qui ça   t'as   vu?   wh ex situ
        who ça   you've   seen
        'Who did you see?'

Relevant to the status of subject *wh* is the fact that wh+*ça* is unacceptable in subject position:

(14) *Qui ça est parti?

If *qui ça* in (14) were in-situ in subject position, it should be grammatical, on a par with (13a). The fact that is ungrammatical indicates that it cannot be in situ.

2.3 Subject object asymmetries in Bantu wh in situ

The French pattern of optional wh in situ for non-subjects and only ex-situ (cleft) for subjects is apparently not uncommon in Niger-Congo (nor in Austronesian: Potsdam (2006), Sabel (2005)). This asymmetry between subjects and non-subjects in Vata (Kru) was discussed by Koopman (1983) and has since been described in detail for many languages, particularly in Bantu. Some illustrative examples are discussed in the following paragraphs.

In Northern Sotho non-subjects can be either in situ or appear clause-initially in what is characterized as a "cleft construction" (Zerbian 2006), which we can understand as an instantiation of a relative clause-like structure in which the wh word is external to the clause with which it is associated. These two options are illustrated with a direct object in (15) (the *wh*-phrase appears in bold type).[2]

(15) a. *Mo-kgalabje   o   nyaka   **ma:ng?***
       CL1-old man   SC1   look.for who
    b. *Ké   **mang**   o   mo-kgalabje   a   mo*
       COP who   RPRN.CL1   CL1-old.man   SC1   OC1
       'It is who that the old man is looking for?'

Subject wh interrogatives, however, must exploit the cleft strategy.

(16) a. ***Mang**   o   nyaka   ngaka?*
       who   SC1   look.for   CL9.doctor
       'Who is looking for the doctor?'
    b. *Ké   **mang**   (yo)   a   nyaka-ng   nga:ka?*
       COP who   RPRN.CL1   SC1   look.for-REL   CL9.doctor

Similarly, in Zulu (Nguni: Bantu; Sabel and Zeller (2006)), a non-subject *wh* can either appear in situ or fronted, in which case it is clefted and prefixed with the auxiliary *y-*.

(17) a. *U-bona   **(i)ni?***
       2ndSG-see   what9
       'What do you see?'
    b. ***Y-ini**   o-yi-bona-yo?*
       COP-what9   RC2ndSG-OC9-see-RS
       'What is it that you see?'

---

2 The abbreviations used in the glosses are the following:
CL = noun class; COP = copula; DEM = demonstrative pronoun; EXPL = expletive prefix; PASS = passive; RC = relative concord; REL = relative tense; RPRN= relative pronoun; SC = subject concord.

A preverbal subject *wh*-phrase, however, cannot appear in the subject position, as (18) shows for active as well as passivized subjects.

(18) a. *****Ubani** u-banga   lowo   msindo?
         who.1a SP1a-cause   DEM3   noise3
         'Who is making that noise?'
    b. *****Ubani** u-ya-shay-wa?
         Who.1a SP1a-FOC-beat-PASS
         'Who is beaten?'

(19) illustrates that the *wh*-ex situ variants of both sentences are possible:

(19) a. Ng-***ubani***   o-banga   lowo   msindo?
         COP-who1a   RC1a-cause   DEM3   noise3
         'Who is it that is making that noise?'
    b. Ng-***ubani***   o-shay-wa-yo?
         COP-who1a   RC1a-beat-PASS-RS
         'Who is it that is beaten?'

Muriungi also reaches the conclusion that subjects cannot be questioned in situ, on the basis of detailed studies of Kitharaka (Muriungi 2003) and Gichuka (Muriungi, Mutegi and Karuri 2014).[3]

2.4 Wh in situ and clitic placement in European Portuguese

Moving closer to home, consider European Portuguese which, like French, has *wh* both in situ and ex situ, (Ambar and Veloso 2001; Cheng and Rooryck 2002).

(20) a. *O João   comprou   que livro?*
         the João bought   which book
    b. *Que livro   comprou   o João?*
         which book bought   the João
       'Which book did João buy?'

Wh-movement in European Portuguese interacts with clitic placement in the following way: Object clitics appear as enclitics on the verb in (affirmative) declarative sentences but as proclitics in other contexts, among them when wh movement

---

[3] Potsdam (2006) and Sabel and Zeller (2006) account for the subject-non subject asymmetry in different terms, as a reviewer points out.

applies in the clause, Madeira (1993) a.o, (see e.g., Shlonsky (2004) for a general discussion of this phenomenon).

(21) a. O Pedro   encontrou-a   no cinema.   [*a encontrou]
       the Pedro   met-her$_{cl}$ in-the cinema
       'Pedro met her at the cinema.'
   b. Onde   a encontrou   o Pedro?   [*encontrou-a]
       where her$_{cl}$ met the Pedro
       'Where did Pedro meet her?'

When wh takes the in-situ option, enclisis is manifested, as in declaratives. Madeira (1993) cites (22).

(22) O Pedro   encontrou-a   onde?   [*a encontrou]
     the Pedro met-her$_{cl}$ where
     'Where did Pedro meet her?'

What happens to subject *wh*? Raposo and Uriagereka (2005) cite (23), which shows that subject *wh* is incompatible with enclisis, just like moved non-subjects. Since the canonical position of subjects in European Portuguese, as in French, is in Spec/Subj, word order considerations cannot determine whether *quem* 'who' in (23) is in situ or ex situ. The fact that proclisis is forced in the sentence strongly suggests that subject wh must be ex situ.

(23) Quem   a viu   ontem?   [*viu-a]
     who   her$_{cl}$-saw yesterday
     'Who saw her yesterday?'

2.5 French wh in situ in embedded subject position

In root interrogatives such as (5), word order provides no indication as to whether *wh* is in situ or ex situ, since *wh* movement is string-vacuous. Section 2 presented indirect evidence from French and more direct evidence from other languages to the effect that the in situ option is not available to subject wh.

Embedded clauses, however, provide a structurally unambiguous environment to test the grammaticality of subject wh in situ in French. This is so because when the subject wh is in an embedded clause, following the complementizer, it must be in situ.

The sentences in (24), adapted from Aoun et al. (1987: 559), are revealing in this context, as they illustrate a subject-object asymmetry: Subject *qui* in situ is sharply degraded as compared with object *qui* in situ.

(24) a. *Jean pense [que quoi t'intéresse]?
    John thinks that what you-interests
    'What does John thinks that interests you?'
  b. Jean pense [que tu aimes quoi]?
    John thinks that you like what?
    'What does John think that you like?'

Obenauer (1994) provides almost identical judgements.[4]

(25) a. Il a dit que Marie devait parler à qui?
    he has said that M. should speak to who?
    'Who did he say that Mary should speak to?'
  b. ??Il a dit que qui devait parler à Marie?
    he said that who should speak to M.
    'Who did he say that should speak to Mary?'

---

4 The data is (perhaps unsurprisingly) more complex and requires further study. Thus, F. Berthelot (pers. comm.) senses a D-linking effect with embedded in situ wh subjects. The examples in (i) feature a lexically-restricted embedded wh subject and are judged acceptable.
(i) a. Tu penses que quel joueur gagnera le match?
    you think that which player will win the match
    'Which player do you think will win the match?'
  b. Tu penses que quel boxeur sera exclu en premier?
    you think that which boxer will be eliminated first
    'Which boxer do you think will be eliminated first?'
(ii) contrasts a lexically-unrestricted wh subject but one which calls for an answer from a given set of possisble answers with one which doesn't.
(ii) a. Tu voudrais que qui s'occupe de la partie administrative (Paul ou Laura)?
    you would like that who take care of the part administrative (Paul or Laura)
    'Who would you like to take care of the administrative part (Paul or Laura)'
  b. ??Tu voudrais que qui nous invite à dîner?
    you would like that who us invite to dinner
    'Who would you like to invite us for dinner?'
Finally, the wh in situ in B's answer in (iii) is ungrammatical since the question in A is accompanied by the presupposition that neither speaker nor hearer have any clue of the possible set of answers.
(iii) A: Il y a eu une prise d'otages à l'UBS Cornavin.
    There has been a taking of hostages at the UBS Cornavin
    'Hostages were taken at the UBS Cornavin.'
  B: ??Ah bon! Tu penses que qui a fait le coup?
    Ah, really! You think that who made the hit
    'Ah, really! Who do you think made the hit?'
The fact that D-linked wh escapes conditions which constrain non D-linked wh (e.g. Superiority) was discovered by Pesetsky (1987) but remains elusive (see Pesetsky 1987, 2000 for possible explanations).

Obenauer perceives an even sharper subject-object asymmetry with wh in situ in strong islands (op. cit, p. 297). (See Shlonsky (2012) for an analysis that applies Richards' (2000) insights on the distribution of wh in situ in Japanese to Obenauer's treatment of wh in situ in strong islands in terms of LF pied piping of the island.)

(26) a. *Il a construit une machine qui sert à (faire) quoi?*
    He has built a machine that serves (to do) what
  b. **?*Il a construit une machine que qui va utiliser?*
    He has built a machine that who is going to use

The preceding survey demonstrates that the ban on subject wh in situ is a substantive empirical generalization. We now turn to accounting for it.

3 An account of the ban on subject wh in situ

3.1 The difficulties faced by ECP-based accounts

The subject-object asymmetry characteristic of wh in situ in embedded subject position was discovered in English by Aoun et al. (1981) and Kayne (1981). It figured prominently in the 1980s literature on the conditions governing empty categories. English allows (non-echo) wh in situ only in multiple questions.[5] Kayne (1981) proposed that the ungrammaticality of (27a), (as compared with the near-grammaticality of (27b)) should be attributed to a violation of the ECP, which bans traces from ungoverned positions such as the subject position in (28).[6]

---

5 Chomsky's (1986) proposal that wh in subject position remains in Spec/T – a consequence of the ban against vacuous movement – is belied by much of the data presented in this contribution. For a critical evaluation of Chomsky's hypothesis with respect to English, see Agbayani (2006), a.o.
6 Kayne's judgements in (27) (adopted also by Chomsky (1981)) are challenged by Lasnik and Saito (1992: 116–117), who note a substantial contrast between overt wh-movement of an embedded subject and wh in situ. They cite:
(i)   **Who do you think that left?*
(ii) *?Who thinks that who left?*
(iii) *?Who wonders whether who left?*
Hegarty's (1992 §4.6) judgements accord with those of Lasnik and Saito. He argues that English wh in situ in a multiple wh question can be more easily D-linked in embedded clauses than in root clauses and, following Pesetsky (1987), does not undergo LF raising but is unselectively-bound by a matrix Q. The English data are clearly in need of further study.

(27) a. *We're trying to find out who said that who was in love with him.
    b. ?We're trying to find out who said that she was in love with who.

(28) *Who$_i$ does he think that t_i is in love with him?

Kayne's proposal was that the ECP holds not only of overt movement, but of covert movement as well. The idea is that wh in situ undergoes covert movement in LF, leaving behind an ungoverned trace in subject position.

This proposal (or more contemporary incarnations of the ECP as a locality condition on chains, eschewing reference to empty categories as such) provides a principled explanation for the violation incurred by long subject extraction in e.g., (28) and (27a) and hence accounts for the unavailability of subject wh in situ. The proposal, as well as other ECP-based approaches, falls short of accounting for the impossibility of root (as opposed to embedded) subject wh in situ. Kayne's (1983) assimilation of the violation incurred by (27a) to that of (28) does not carry over to the pair in (29): Here, overt movement is grammatical but in situ wh is not, yet covert movement of *qui* in (29b) renders it structurally identical to (29a).

(29) a. [$_{CP}$ Qui$_i$ [$_{TP}$ t_i flotte dans l'eau]]?
    b. *[$_{TP}$ Qui flotte dans l'eau]?
       who floats in the-water
       'Who is floating in the water?

This shortcoming led Koopman (1983) to adapt Aoun et al's (1981) "Comp indexing rule" to these cases and encode the difference between (29a) and (29b) in terms of a restriction of this rule to apply prior to LF-movement (at S-structure, in her terms). While this device *expresses* the difference between (29a) and (29b) it does not *explain* it: Neither the specific Comp indexing rule nor the limitation of syntactic operations to intermediate levels of syntactic representation are statable in the theoretical frameworks that are generally assumed nowadays. One is led to seek an alternative explanation.

3.2 Criterial Freezing

Rizzi (2006) proposes that the preverbal subject position is a criterial position, that is, a position with a particular scope/discourse property, like the positions of peripheral wh, focus and topic. A nominal moved into that position cannot be further moved; it is subject to Criterial Freezing, introduced in (1) and repeated in (30).

(30) Criterial Freezing: A phrase moved to a position dedicated to some
     scope-discourse interpretive property, a criterial position, is frozen in place.

Rizzi follows Cardinaletti (2004) in assuming that preverbal subjects are specifiers of a dedicated head Subj⁰, and satisfy the Subject Criterion in a Spec-head configuration. (30) has the consequence of banning further movement from Spec/Subj.

(31) [$_{SubjP}$ DP [Subj XP]]

Since there is no object criterion similar to the Subject Criterion, the subject-object asymmetry in wh-movement, illustrated in (2a) and (2b), can be expressed in the criterial approach without reference to particular constraints on empty categories.

However, since languages do have ways of questioning the subject, the computational system engineers various devices to circumvent the freezing problem. Among the strategies of subject extraction discussed in Rizzi and Shlonsky (2006; 2007) and Shlonsky (2014) are the following: (a) Truncation of the embedded clause down to and including SubjP, (32), which accounts for the *that/*trace effect in (2a) and (28); (b) an expletive use of a Fin⁰ with nominal features to satisfy the Subject Criterion – spelled out as *qui* in French – which absolves the subject nominal from movement to Spec/Subj and allows it to extract directly from a lower position, (33).

(32) **Truncation (non-merge) of sections of the clausal anatomy (here, down to and including the embedded SubjP):**
Who do you think [$_{CP}$ that [$_{SubjP}$ [$_{TP}$ <who> talked to Mary]]]?

(33) **An expletive use of FIN to satisfy the Subject Criterion coupled with extraction of the subject from a post-verbal position:**
Quel garçon   crois-tu   [... FIN$_{NOM}$ SUBJ   <quel garçon>   gagnera ?
which boy   think-you   qui   will win
'Which boy do you think is going to win?'

Short wh-movement, in this approach, also exploits the expletive FIN strategy of (33) coupled with extraction of *quel garçon* 'which boy' from a lower position. (5) is represented as (34) (see Rizzi and Shlonsky 2007 for details).

(34) ...   [$_{FocP}$ *Quel garçon*   FOC   ...   [$_{FinP}$ FIN$_{NOM}$ [$_{SubjP}$ SUBJ
                    which boy
       a   [$_{vP}$ *<quel garçon>   fait   ça]]]?*
       has   done   that
       'Which boy has done that?'

The criterial approach allows us to express Kayne's insight that the violation incurred by (27) is of the same nature as that in (28). The wh subject in situ is in

Spec/Subj and criterial freezing rules out covert movement of a wh subject in LF just as it blocks overt movement.

A subject wh in situ can survive in situ if it is not in Spec/Subj but in a lower (postverbal) position. French makes only limited use of phrasal expletives, but can mobilize a nominal Fin head to satisfy the Subject Criterion, as in (34), allowing the subject phrase to overtly move to the left periphery from a lower position. Zulu differs from French in deploying a nominal expletive in this context. Consider Sabel and Zeller's (2006) examples in (35) (wh in situ in bold). In (35a), the thematic subject is in Spec/Subj, where it becomes criterially-frozen: Covert movement to Spec/Foc is blocked and the Wh Criterion is consequently violated. In (35b), the expletive *ku* sits in Spec/Subj, where it satisfies the Subject Criterion, allowing the thematic subject to remain in a lower, non-criterial position. Covert movement can then apply to the subject phrase without incurring a violation of criterial freezing.

(35) a. *[$_{CP}$ *U-cabanga* [$_{CP}$ *ukuthi* [$_{TP}$ **ubani** *u-sebenzile* [$_{vP}$___]]]]?
    2ndSG-think   that   who1a   SP1a-worked
b. [$_{CP}$ *U-cabanga* [$_{CP}$ *ukuthi* [$_{TP}$ *ku-sebenze* [$_{vP}$ **bani**]]]]?
    2ndSG-think   that   EXPL-worked   who1a
'Who do you think worked?'
Sabel and Zeller (2006, ex. (13))

European Portuguese wh in situ in embedded clauses cannot appear in a preverbal position, but only post-verbally, in either a VOS or VSO order, as Cheng and Rooryck (2002) show. Presumably, Spec/Subj here is filled with an expletive pro, an option available in null subject languages.

(36) a. *O João   pensa   que   **quem**   viu   a Maria?
        the João thinks that who   saw   the Maria
b. O João   pensa   que   viu   a Maria   **quem**?
        the João thinks that saw   the Maria who
c. O João   pensa   que   viu   **quem**   a Maria?
        the João thinks that saw   who   the Maria
'Who does João think saw Maria?'

I have tried to show that the ban on the occurrence of wh in situ in Spec/Subj in the languages discussed in this section – French, European Portuguese and some Bantu – follows from Criterial Freezing: If the subject moved to Spec/Subj it would be criterially frozen and blocked from covertly moving to the canonical wh position in the left periphery, Spec/Foc, incurring a violation of the Wh Criterion.

The characteristic feature of these languages is that wh in situ is optional, as Sabel (2005) and Sabel and Zeller (2006) have observed. In languages in which wh in situ does not alternate with wh movement, (e.g., Chinese, Japanese,) a ban on subject wh in situ has not been observed, as far as I know. It is conceivable that in such languages, a subject wh in situ does not have to covertly move to Spec/Foc. If the Wh Criterion can be satisfied by agreement without movement or semantically, by choice functions (see e.g., Tsai (1994)), Criterial Freezing in Spec/Subj – which crucially bans further *movement* but not other operations targeting the subject – would have no impact on the wellformedness of subject wh questions at the interface.

3.3 French wh in situ: What moves covertly?

Among the numerous theoretical and empirical challenges to the idea that covert movement is covert *phrasal* movement of the wh phrase, I would like to consider the following, which has figured prominently, though not uncontroversially, in recent discussions of wh in situ in French.

Mathieu (1999), a.o, argues that the sensitivity of wh in situ arguments (e.g., direct objects,) to weak islands and interveners resembles the sensitivity to islands and intervention of overtly moved non-arguments. The following paradigms illustrate this observation. In each of the sets in (38)–(40), wh in situ is judged on par with adjunct extraction and not with argument extraction. This is, prima facie, surprising, since the wh in situ is itself an argument in the three sets.

(37) *Tu te demandes comment aider Marie.*   Baseline
      you wonder how to help Marie
      'You wonder how to help Marie.'

(38) a. **Tu te demandes comment aider qui?*   Argument wh in situ
        you wonder how to help who(m)   in a wh island
        'Who(m) do you wonder how to help?'
     b. *?Qui te demandes-tu comment aider?*   Overtly-moved
        who(m) you wonder how to help   argument out of a wh
        'Who(m) do you wonder how to help?'   island
     c. **Comment te demandes-tu qui aider?*   Overtly-moved
        how 2refl ask-you who help   adjunct out of a wh
        'How do you wonder who to help?'   island

(39) a. **Seulement JEAN arrive à faire quoi?*   Argument wh in situ
        only JOHN is able to do what   under a focus
        'What is only John able to do?'

    b. *Comment seulement JEAN arrive à faire cela?   Overtly-moved
       how only JOHN is able to do that   adjunct over a focus
       'How is only John able to do that?'
    c. *Qu'est-ce que seulement JEAN arrive à faire?*   Overtly-moved
       What only JOHN is able to do   argument over a focus
       'What is only John able to do?'

(40) a. *Tu crois qu'elle (n')a pas rencontré qui?*   Argument wh in situ
       you think that she has not met who   under negation
       'Who do you think she hasn't met?'
    b. *Comment crois-tu qu'elle (n')a pas réparé la voiture?*   Overtly-moved
       how think-you that she has not fixed the car   adjunct over
       'How do you think she didn't fix the car?'   negation
    c. *Qui crois-tu qu'elle (n')a pas rencontré?*   Overtly-moved
       who think-you that she has not met   argument over
       'Who do you think she hasn't met?'   negation

Mathieu's (1999) point, which builds on proposals by Watanabe (1992) and Hagstrom (1998) for other wh in situ languages, is that covert movement of wh in situ does not effect the entire constituent and is thus not the invisible parallel to overt movement, but rather targets a phonologically-null wh operator, a sub-constituent of the wh phrase in situ. This accounts for the non-argument-like behavior of wh in situ under Rizzi's (1990) characterization, since the moved operator is a sub-constituent of an argument and not an argument itself.[7]

4 Subextraction and criterial freezing

As stated, criterial freezing of a subject correctly blocks movement of the subject from Spec/Subj, but it does not block movement of a subconstituent of the subject. In a criterial configuration such as (41), for example, the DP in Spec/Subj satisfies the Subject Criterion and is blocked from further movement by Criterial Freezing, (30). But X, a subconstituent of the subject nominal, is not constrained by (30).

---

[7] Matters are a bit trickier in relation to Rizzi's (2001) characterization of the class of elements which are unaffected by Relativized Minimality, i.e., DPs, because it isn't obvious that the null operator diagnosed by Mathieu is or must be a non-DP.

(41)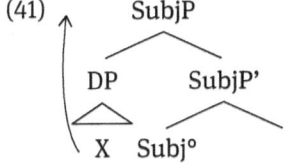

The problem of subextraction from within a criterially-frozen subject phrase arises also in (Italian) focus movement, which resembles wh movement in many respects. A well-known property of subjects in Italian is that they are compatible with *ne* cliticization (of the nominal restriction of a quantificational DP) when they occur in postverbal position, (42a), but not when they occur in preverbal position, (42b).

(42) a. Ne   sono venuti [cinque <ne>]
of-them have arrived five
'Five of them have arrived.'
b. *[cinque <ne>]   ne sono venuti
five   of them have arrived

The *ne*-cliticization test was used by Rizzi (1982) as a diagnostic criterion to locate the extraction site of wh subjects. The conclusion that he drew from the grammaticality of *ne* cliticization in (43) was that the launching site of wh movement is the postverbal position (as in (42a)) and not the preverbal one (as in (42b)). Note that *ne* is obligatory in (43), which should be interpreted to mean that the subject *must* be extracted from the postverbal position.[8]

(43) *Quante ne sono venuti?*
how many of them have arrived

Bocci (2013:81) extends Rizzi's reasoning to focalization and provides the examples in (44). He reasons that if the subject could be focalized in situ, then we would not expect *ne* cliticization to be obligatory. The fact that it is shows that focalization of the subject patterns like wh movement of the subject, involving obligatory movement to the left periphery from a postverbal position.

---

[8] An outstanding problem that needs to be addressed is why *ne* cannot be extracted from a postverbal DP prior to raising of the subject from its VP-internal position. Such a derivation would incorrectly yield (42b).

(44) a. *No, QUATTRO sono arrivate, non dieci!
'No, FOUR have arrived, not ten!'
b. No, QUATTRO ne sono arrivate, non dieci!
'No, FOUR of them have arrived, not ten!'

Bocci attributes the ungrammaticality of (44a) to a violation of Criterial Freezing but, as pointed out above, in relation to subject wh movement, the formulation of Criterial Freezing in (30) falls short of deriving the ungrammaticality of this sentence. Leaving the focalized subject phrase in situ and moving only the focus feature within it should remain a valid option. Note that objects in Italian may be focalized either by movement to the left periphery or in situ, as in (45).[9] The fact that subjects cannot exploit the in situ option suggests that criterial freezing is at work, but the suggestion can become an explanation only if the principle of criterial freezing is sharpened so that it blocks movement of a wh or a focus *feature* or subconstituent from inside a phrase in a criterial position.

(45) a. No, sto leggendo il GIORNALE, non il libro!
no, am reading the paper, not the book
'No, I am reading the PAPER, not the book!'
b. No, il GIORNALE sto leggendo, non il libro!
No. the paper am reading, not the book
'No, (it's) the paper I am reading, not the book!'

One possible sharpening consists of banning all subextraction from a phrase in a criterial position. If Criterial Freezing had the consequence of rendering an element inaccessible to further syntactic operations, impenetrable, as it were, then a probe could not target any feature within it and subextraction would be impossible.

This, however, is too strong, as noted by Rizzi (2007), referring to observations due to Lasnik and Saito (1992). Rizzi cites (46), which exemplifies a focalized phrase – DI GIANNI – moved out of a wh constituent in a criterial position.

(46) DI GIANNI non sapevo quale libro avessi scelto, (non di Piero)
'BY GIANNI I didn't know which book you had selected, (not by Piero)'

The same point can be illustrated by wh subextraction of a PP from a subject, although for reasons unclear, the status of such subextraction is quite variable across speakers, languages and within these, among verb classes, a topic which

---

[9] Italian lacks wh in situ and, conversely, French lacks Italian-like focus fronting. Thus, the parallel between wh in situ and focus in situ only comes to light by putting together patterns from the two languages.

has sparked lively research in recent years, see e.g. Polinsky et al. (2013) and references cited therein. Starke (2001: 36–37) cites the pair in (47), noting that subextraction from the subject phrase in (47b) is only very slightly degraded for some speakers, as compared with subextraction from the object phrase in (47a).

(47) a. *[De quel film]$_i$ est-ce que tu as raté [la première partie t$_i$]?*
 of which film did you miss the first part of?
 b. #*[De quel film]$_i$ est-ce que tu crois que [la première partie t$_i$] va créer un scandale?*
 of which film do you think that the first part will cause a scandal

From the perspective of criterial freezing, there is an important difference between licit cases of sub-extraction such as (46) and (47b) and the cases of illicit extraction from subjects discussed throughout this chapter. In the former, the subextracted element is an independent constituent within the subject phrase, whereas in the latter, it is inscribed in the morphology of the noun or, in cases of lexically-restricted wh phrases like *quel film* 'what/which film', of the determiner. In (46), the subextracted focused element is a constituent. In (44a), focus is a feature on the subject itself, not a subconstituent thereof.

Let us think of the wh or Q feature on the subject (or the focus feature in the Italian examples in (44) and (45)) as an indissoluble component of its label. The subject nominal thus bears the label <Subj, wh/Q>. When it is merged with Subj (SubjP or Subj' in the traditional X' system), labeling of the node produced by this merge is successful, since both the subject phrase and the phrase it is merged with share the label Subj, as in the schema in (48).

(48)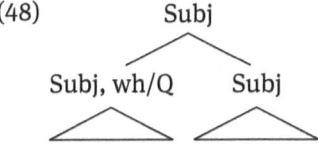

In (48), only the highest occurrence of Subj is maximal. Maximality of the label is the essential ingredient of Rizzi's (2015a; 2015b) implementation of Criterial Freezing in terms of Chomsky's (2013; 2015) labeling algorithm. He argues

(49) a. that only labeled maximal objects can be moved, and
 b. that in a criterial configuration, the criterial goal (the specifier of the criterial head) ceases to be maximal.

The criterial freezing of the subject phrase (and that of wh phrases, focus phrases, etc.) is effectively derived from this implementation of the labeling algorithm. Since wh/Q in (48) is part of the label of the subject nominal, which is not maximal, further movement is blocked. If the subject phrase remains in its base position and does not merge with Subj, it can be attracted to the wh/Q head in the left periphery, where a criterial configuration can be licitly established and labeling can be successful:

(50)

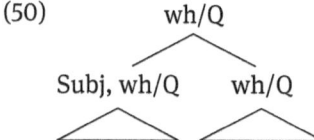

In sentences such as (46), the highest occurrence of wh/Q is maximal. The focalized PP *di Gianni* 'of Gianni' – labeled P in (51) – is also maximal, so moving it does not violate (49a) – the maximality constraint on movement.

(51)

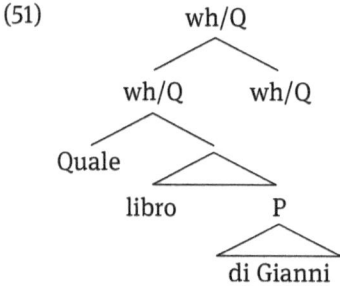

5 Conclusion

Many languages with optional wh in situ observe a subject-non subject asymmetry whereby wh in situ is only possible in non-subject position. This asymmetry seems to also characterize multiple wh constructions in English. Adopting the view that wh in situ involves featural as opposed to phrasal movement, this paper has attempted to reduce the subject-non subject asymmetry to the workings of the Criterial Freezing constraint implemented in such a way so as to freeze features included within a criterially-frozen subject.

References

Agbayani, Peter. 2006. Pied-piping, feature movement and wh-subjects. In Lisa Lai-Shen Cheng & Norbert Corver (eds.), *Wh movement moving on*, 71–94. Cambridge, MA: The MIT Press.

Ambar, Manuela & Rita Veloso. 2001. On the nature of wh-phrases - Word order and wh-in-situ. In Yves D'hulst, Johan Rooryck & Jan Schroten (eds.), *Romance languages and linguistic theory 1999*, 1–37. Amsterdam: John Benjamins.

Aoun, Joseph, Norbert Hornstein, David Lightfoot & Amy Weinberg. 1987. Two types of locality. *Linguistic inquiry* 537–577.
Aoun, Joseph, Norbert Hornstein & Dominique Sportiche. 1981. Some aspects of wide scope quantification. *Journal of Linguistic Research* 1(3). 69–95.
Baunaz, Lena. 2011. *The grammar of French quantification*. Dordrecht: Springer.
Bocci, Giuliano. 2013. *The syntax-prosody interface*. Amsterdam: John Benjamins.
Cardinaletti, Anna. 2004. Towards a cartography of subject positions. In Luigi Rizzi (ed.), *The cartography of syntactic structures. Vol 2, The structure of CP and IP*, 115–165. New York: Oxford University Press.
Cheng, Lisa Lai-Shen & Johan Rooryck. 2000. Licensing WH-in-situ. *Syntax* 3. 1–18.
Cheng, Lisa Lai-Shen & Johan Rooryck. 2002. Types of wh-in-situ. Leiden University manuscript.
Chomsky, Noam. 1981. *Lectures on government and binding*. Dordrecht: Foris.
Chomsky, Noam. 1986. *Barriers*. Cambridge, MA: MIT Press.
Chomsky, Noam. 2013. Problems of projection. *Lingua* 130. 33–49.
Chomsky, Noam. 2015. Problems of projection: Extensions. In Elisa Di Domenico, Cornelia Hamann & Simona Matteini (eds.), *Structures, strategies and beyond: Studies in honour of Adriana Belletti*, 1–16. Amsterdam: John Benjamins.
Friedemann, Marc-Ariel. 1997. *Sujets syntaxiques*. Bern: Peter Lang.
Goldsmith, John. 1978. Que, c'est quoi? Que, c'est QUOI. *Recherches linguistiques à Montréal* 11. 1–13.
Hagstrom, Paul. 1998. Decomposing questions. Cambridge, MA: MIT dissertation.
Hegarty, Michael. 1992. Adjunct extraction and chain configurations. Cambridge, MA: MIT dissertation.
Kayne, Richard. 1981. Two notes on the NIC. In Adriana Belletti, Luciana Brandi & Luigi Rizzi (eds.), *Theory of markedness in generative grammar. Proceedings of the 1979 GLOW Conference*, 317–346. Pisa: Scuola Normale Superiore.
Kayne, Richard S. 1983. Connectedness. *Linguistic Inquiry* 14(2). 223–249.
Koopman, Hilda. 1983. Control from Comp and comparative syntax. *The Linguistic Review* 2(4). (12 October 2012).
Koopman, Hilda. 1984. *The syntax of verbs: From verb movement rules in the Kru languages to Universal Grammar*. Dordrecht: Foris. http://www.getcited.org/pub/102598300 (accessed 14 December 2012).
Lasnik, Howard & Mamoru Saito. 1992. *Move alpha: Conditions on its application and output*. Cambridge, MA: The MIT Press.
Madeira, Ana. 1993. Clitic-second in European Portuguese. *Probus* 5(1–2). 155–174.
Mathieu, Eric. 1999. WH in situ and the intervention effect. In Corinne Iten & Ad Neeleman (eds.), *UCL Working Papers in Linguistics*, 441–472. London: University College.
Muriungi, Peter Kinyua. 2003. Wh-questions in Kitharaka. http://mobile.wiredspace.wits.ac.za/handle/10539/15701 (accessed 4 September 2015).
Muriungi, Peter Kinyua, Miriam Kathomi Mutegi & Mary Karuri. 2014. The Syntax of Wh-Questions in Gichuka. *Open Journal of Modern Linguistics* 4(1). 182–204.
Obenauer, Hans-Georg. 1994. Aspects de la syntaxe A-barre. Paris : Université de Paris VIII dissertation.
Pesetsky, David. 1987. Wh-in-situ: Movement and unselective binding. In Eric Reuland & Alice G.B. ter Meulen (eds.), *The representation of (in)definiteness*, 98–129. Cambridge MA: MIT Press.
Pesetsky, David. 2000. *Phrasal movement and its kin*. Cambridge MA: The MIT Press.

Plunkett, Bernadette. 2000. What's what in French questions. *Journal of Linguistics* 36(3). 511–530.
Polinsky, Maria, Carlos Gómez Gallo, Peter Graff, Ekaterina Kravtchenko, Adam Milton Morgan & Anne Sturgeon. 2013. Subject islands are different. In Jon Sprouse & Norbert Hornstein (eds.), *Experimental syntax and Island effects*, 286–309. Cambridge: Cambridge University Press.
Potsdam, Eric. 2006. The cleft structure of Malagasy wh-questions. In Hans-Martin Gärtner, Paul S. Law & Joachim Sabel (eds.), *Clause structure and adjuncts in Austronesian languages*, 195–232. (Studies in Generative Grammar 87). Berlin, New York: Mouton de Gruyter.
Raposo, Eduardo P. & Juan Uriagereka. 2005. Clitic placement in Western Iberian: A minimalist view. In Guglielmo Cinque & Richard S. Kayne (eds.), *The Oxford handbook of comparative syntax*, 639–697. Oxford: Oxford University Press.
Richards, Norvin. 2000. An island effect in Japanese. *Journal of East Asian Linguistics* 9(2). 187–205.
Rizzi, Luigi. 1982. *Issues in Italian syntax*. Dordrecht: Foris.
Rizzi, Luigi. 1990. *Relativized Minimality*. Cambridge, MA: The MIT Press.
Rizzi, Luigi. 1996. Residual verb second and the Wh-Criterion. In Adriana Belletti & Luigi Rizzi (eds.), *Parameters and functional heads*, 63–90. New York: Oxford University Press.
Rizzi, Luigi. 2001. Relativized minimality effects. In Mark Baltin & Chris Collins (eds.), *The handbook of contemporary syntactic theory*, 89–110. Oxford: Blackwell.
Rizzi, Luigi. 2007. On some properties of criterial freezing. In Vincenzo Moscati (ed.), *Studies in linguistics*, 145–158. CISCL Working Papers in Language and Cognition 1. Cambridge, MA: MIT, MIT Working Papers in Linguistics. http://www.ciscl.unisi.it/doc/doc_pub/STiL-2007-vol1.pdf.
Rizzi, Luigi. 2015a. Cartography, criteria and labeling. In Ur Shlonsky (ed.), *Beyond functional sequence*, 314–338. New York: Oxford University Press.
Rizzi, Luigi. 2015b. Labeling, maximality and the head – phrase distinction. *The Linguistic Review* 33(0). http://www.degruyter.com/view/j/tlir.ahead-of-print/tlr-2015-0016/tlr-2015-0016.xml (accessed 23 December 2015).
Rizzi, Luigi & Ur Shlonsky. 2006. Satisfying the subject criterion by a non subject: English locative inversion and heavy NP shift. In Mara Frascarelli (ed.), *Phases of interpretation*, 341–361. Berlin: Mouton de Gruyter.
Rizzi, Luigi & Ur Shlonsky. 2007. Strategies of subject extraction. In Hans Martin Gärtner & Uli Sauerland (eds.), *Interfaces + Recursion = Language? Chomsky's Minimalism and the view from syntax-semantics*, 115–160. Berlin: Mouton de Gruyter.
Sabel, Joachim. 2005. Wh-questions and extractions asymmetries in Malagasy. In Andrea Rakowksi & Norvin Richards (eds.), *Proceedings of AFLA VIII: The eighth meeting of the Austronesian Formal Linguistics Association. MIT Working Papers in Linguistics #44.*, 304–319. Cambridge, MA: MIT.
Sabel, Joachim & Jochen Zeller. 2006. Wh-question formation in Nguni. In John Mugane, John P. Hutchison & Dee A. Worman (eds.), *Selected Proceedings of the 35th annual conference on African Linguistics*, 271–283. Somerville, MA: Cascadilla Proceedings Project.
Shlonsky, Ur. 2004. Enclisis and proclisis. In Luigi Rizzi (ed.), *The structure of CP and IP*, 329–353. New York: Oxford University Press.

Shlonsky, Ur. 2012. Notes on wh in situ in French. In Laura Brugé, Anna Cardinaletti, Giuliana Giusti, Nicola Munaro & Cecilia Poletto (eds.), *Functional heads. The cartography of syntactic structures*, vol. 7, 242–252. New York: Oxford University Press.

Shlonsky, Ur. 2014. Subject positions, subject extraction, EPP and the subject criterion. In Enoch O. Aboh, Maria Teresa Guasti & Ian Roberts (eds.), *Locality*, 58–86. New York: Oxford University Press.

Starke, Michal. 2001. Move dissolves into merge: a theory of locality. Geneva: Université de Genève dissertation.

Tsai, Wei-Tien Dylan. 1994. On economizing the theory of A-bar dependencies. Cambridge, MA: MIT dissertation.

Watanabe, Akira. 1992. Subjacency and S-structure movement of wh-in-situ. *Journal of East Asian Linguistics* 1(3). 255–291.

Zerbian, Sabine. 2006. Questions in Northern Sotho. *ZAS Papers in Linguistics* 43. 257–280.

Sten Vikner
Germanic verb particle variation

1 Introduction

This paper has two closely related goals. The more "global" one is to present an overview of the variation concerning verb particles across the Germanic languages (see e.g. den Dikken 1995; Haiden 2005; McIntyre 2007 and many others), and the more "local" one is to use some of this variation data to argue for Yiddish being an SOV-language like German and Dutch rather than an SVO-language like English and the Scandinavian languages.

I will start out from the assumption that prepositions and (separable) particles have the same structure, as suggested in e.g. Taraldsen (1983: 245), Haegeman and Guéron (1999: 250–258), and Koopman (2000: 238):

(1)

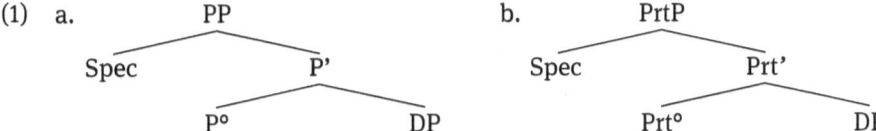

where the difference is that prepositions assign case, whereas particles do not. Therefore the complement DP (e.g. *the book* in *throw out the book*) will not be assigned a case. This problem has two potential solutions, namely either that the particle is incorporated into the verb (i.e. into V*), in which case V* (maybe via the trace in Prt°) may now assign case to the "object" (result: *He threw out the book*), or that the DP may move to PrtP-spec, where it can be assigned case directly by V° (as in ECM-constructions) (result: *He threw the book out*).

The picture can be extended to the Germanic SOV-languages, assuming that what differs between SVO and SOV is the ordering inside V' and inside V* (i.e. *syntactic* ordering, which concerns separable particles, e.g. *go under*), but crucially not inside V° (i.e. *morphological* ordering, which concerns non-separable particles, e.g. *undergo*).

This will be shown to capture why the Mainland Scandinavian languages – which otherwise show relatively little variation – display this particular kind of word order variation concerning particles (*throw the book out* vs. *throw out the book*, cf. e.g. Hulthén 1947: 159–168; Herslund 1984; Vikner 1987; Engels and Vikner 2013, 2014; Aa 2015), whereas the Germanic SOV-languages (German,

Dutch, Frisian, Low German, ...) – which otherwise show quite a lot of variation, do not have this kind of variation.

I will also argue that the view that Yiddish is an SOV-language like German and Dutch, not an SVO-language like English or Danish, is supported by facts concerning verb particles. I shall argue against Diesing's (1997: 383) claim that particles may not form the basis of an argument for the underlying order of Yiddish being SOV.

The point is that if Yiddish is an SOV-language like German and Dutch, not an SVO-language like English or Danish, then we can explain why Yiddish is like German and unlike Scandinavian in allowing even such particles to occur preverbally in non-V2 constructions that do not incorporate, as seen by their not moving along with the finite verb during V2.

2 Separable particles

All the Germanic languages, including English, have both separable and non-separable verb particles:

(2) En. a. *The patient* **under**went an operation.　　non-separable
　　　b. *The ship* went **under** after colliding with　separable
　　　　　　　　　　　　　　　　　 an iceberg.

(3) Da. a. *Kontrakten* **ud**løb i 2013.　　　　　　　 non-separable
　　　　　 contract-the out-ran in 2013
　　　b. *Vandet* løb **ud** på gulvet.　　　　　　　　 separable
　　　　 water-the ran out on floor-the

(4) Ge. a. *Das Auto* **um**fährt den Pfosten.　　　　 non-separable
　　　　 the car around-drives the stake
　　　　 'The car drives around the stake.'
　　　b. *Das Auto fährt den Pfosten* **um**.　　　　　separable
　　　　 the car drives the stake around
　　　　 'The car overturns the stake.'

(Schäfer 2016: 244–245, [17b], [16b])

The terminology used in the literature may be confusing: Sometimes the distinction is made between separable and non-separable particles, sometimes between separable and non-separable prefixes, and sometimes between particles (which are taken to be separable) and prefixes (which are taken to be non-separable). I shall refer to separable and non-separable particles, and I shall also refer to particle verbs, by which I mean the complex verb which is formed by a verb and a particle, e.g. *undergo* in (2a) and *go under* in (2b).

In this section, I will give a somewhat simplified overview of the differences between prepositions and separable particles, whereas in section 3, I will come back to the differences between separable and non-separable particles.

2.1 The differences between prepositions and (separable) particles

One of the most basic differences between prepositions (P°) and (separable) particles (Prt°) in English is that prepositions have to precede their DP-complement, whereas the particle may either precede or follow the object DP (cf. also Fraser 1976):

(5) En. a. *I accidentally stepped **on** the radio.* P°
     b. **I accidentally stepped the radio **on**.*

(6) En. a. *I accidentally switched **on** the radio.* Prt°
     b. *I accidentally switched the radio **on**.*

Haegeman and Guéron (1999: 250–254) mention the following other differences, most of which date back to Fraser (1976):

Whereas [P°+DP] may undergo *wh*-movement, this is not possible for [Prt°+DP]:

(7) En. a. ***In** which hotel did the Beatles stay ___?* P°
     b. *****In** which door did the Stones kick ___?* Prt°

Whereas [P°+DP] may undergo clefting, this is not possible for [Prt°+DP]:

(8) En. a. *It was **in** this hotel that the Beatles stayed ___.* P°
     b. **It was **in** this door that the Stones kicked ___.* Prt°

Whereas [P°+DP] may be coordinated with another [P°+DP], [Prt°+DP] may not be coordinated with another [Prt°+DP]:

(9) En. a. *He looked **up** the chimney and **down** the stairwell.* P°
     b. **She switched **off** the TV and **on** the light.* Prt°

Whereas [P°+DP] may be modified, e.g. by *right* or *straight*, this is not possible for [Prt°+DP]:

(10) En. a. The Beatles stayed **right** in this hotel. P°
     b. *The Stones kicked **right** in this door. Prt°

Consider finally ellipsis, i.e. leaving out a constituent that has already occurred in the discourse. Elision of the verb itself is only possible in the preposition case, not in the particle case:

(11) En. a. He looked up the chimney and she looked down the stairwell. P°
     b. He looked up the chimney and she _____ down the stairwell.

(12) En. a. He switched off the TV and she switched on the light. Prt°
     b. *He switched off the TV and she _____ on the light.

On the other hand, the sequence V°+Prt° may undergo elision, whereas this is not possible for the sequence V°+P°:

(13) En. a. He looked up the chimney and she looked up the stairwell. P°
     b. *He looked up the chimney and she _____ the stairwell.

(14) En. a. He switched off the TV and she switched off the light. Prt°
     b. He switched off the TV and she _____ the light.

2.2 Verbs and particles in the Germanic SVO-languages

The analysis of the examples with prepositions is relatively uncontroversial, as in (15a):

(15)

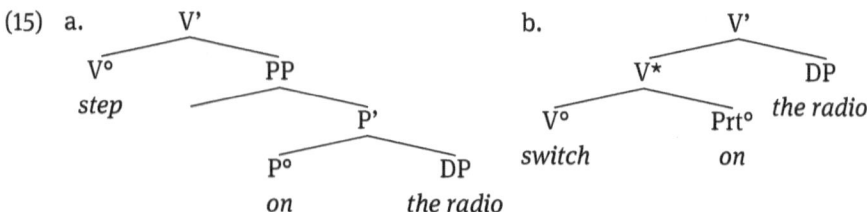

The analysis of the particle examples, however, is not uncontroversial. Consider the "single verb hypothesis", as in (15b) above. The difference between (15a) and (15b) could explain the following:

In (15a), [P°+DP] make up a constituent, namely PP, which would account for why [P°+DP] may undergo *wh*-movement, (7a), clefting, (8a), coordination, (9a), and modification, (10a). The verb may undergo gapping on its own, (11b), as it is a constituent, but the verb and the preposition may not undergo gapping together, (13b), as they do not form a constituent.

In (15b), [Prt°+DP] do not make up a constituent, which would account for why [Prt°+DP] may not undergo *wh*-movement, (7b), clefting, (8b), or coordination, (9b). The impossibility of the modification in (10b) is caused by the impossibility of interrupting V*. The verb and the particle may undergo gapping together, (14b), as they form a constituent.

The reason why the verb may not undergo gapping on its own, (12b), might be that it is not possible to gap part of a verb, and according to (15b), the verb *switched* in (12b) constitutes part of the complex verb *switched on*.

However, under closer scrutiny, "the single verb hypothesis" in (15b) (as defended e.g. in McIntyre 2013) has at least three problems:

The first problem with "the single verb hypothesis" is that if [V°+Prt°] constitute a verb, then we would not expect that the particle could be moved to CP-spec, but this is possible in both Swedish and Danish (actually, all Danish examples with both particles and objects would be problematic, because the object occurs between V° and Prt°, see e.g. (23) below):

(16) a. Sw. **Ut** kastade dom mej inte, bara ned för trappan.
(Holmberg 1999: 17)
    b. Da. **Ud** smed de mig ikke, kun ned ad trappen.
            out threw they me not, just down of stairs-the

(17) Da. *Herstedvester har ladet Magnus sidde på bænken efter*
         Herstedvester has let Magnus sit on bench-the after
         *det gule kort, og ... ... **ind** har de sat Emre.*
         the yellow card, and ... in have they put Emre.
         http://ekstrabladet.dk/skolefodbold/nyheder/sjaellandmidt/
         article4596398.ece

The second problem with "the single verb hypothesis" is that if [V°+Prt°] constitute a verb, then we would expect the inflectional endings to be attached to the right edge of this verb. This is not the case, however, as these endings occur in the middle of this "verb":

(18) En. a. *He [switch-onned] the radio this morning.
      b. He [switched on] the radio this morning.

(19) En. a. *He [switch-ons] the radio every morning.
　　 b. He [switches on] the radio every morning.

The third problem with "the single verb hypothesis" is that if [V°+Prt°] constitute a complex morphological unit, then we would expect this complex element to have the same category (etc.) as its daughter on the right, as is the case in other compounds: *dark-room* is a noun like *room* (its daughter on the right), not an adjective like *dark*, whereas *tax-free* is an adjective like *free* (its daughter on the right), not a noun like *tax*. *To switch on* however is not a particle like its right hand daughter *on*, but a verb, just like its daughter on the left, *switch*. In other words, it violates Williams' (1981: 248) "Right Hand Head Rule".

Therefore Taraldsen (1983: 245), Haegeman and Guéron (1999: 257–258), and Koopman (2000: 238) assume that the basic structure of particle constructions is parallel to the examples with prepositions, as in (20a). In other words, separable particles and prepositions are different variants of the same word class, which might also be supported by the fact that many prepositions and particles are identical in form.

(20)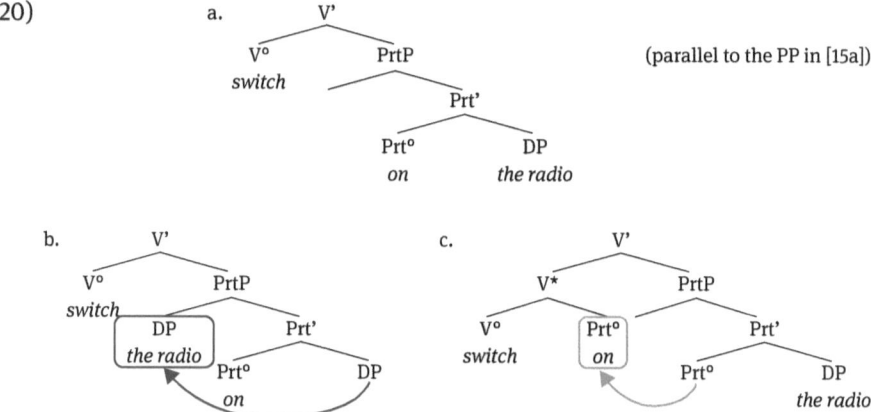

The idea is that (20a) is the basic structure, which however will never make it to the surface. Prt° is unable to assign case, and therefore the DP would not be assigned a case.

There are two ways out of this problem (as also suggested e.g. in Engels and Vikner 2013: 227):

One solution is that the DP moves to the specifier position of PrtP, (20b), where it may be assigned case directly from the verb, in a configuration very reminiscent of ECM (exceptional case marking, as e.g. discussed for English in Chomsky 1981: 98 and Haegeman and Guéron 1999: 231–234 and for Danish in Vikner 2014). This option accounts for the possibility of the DP-Prt° order in e.g. (6b) above.

The other solution is that the particle is incorporated into the verb, (20c), forming a complex verb V*, which is a new intermediate level, i.e. larger than a V° but smaller than a V', as suggested by e.g. Haegeman and Guéron (1999: 254) and Vikner (2005: 92), but see also section 3.2 below and the references there). The (complex) verb can now assign case to the DP (maybe via the trace of the particle in Prt°). This option accounts for the possibility of the DP-Prt° order in e.g. (6a) above.

The availability of both (20b) and (20c) is still compatible with the properties discussed above:

In neither (20b) nor (20c) is Prt° part of the V°, and therefore this analysis predicts e.g. *switch on* to attach its verbal inflection to *switch* rather than to *switch on*, (18) and (19), and the analysis is also compatible with *switch on* not being a particle like *on*.

In neither (20b) nor (20c) is there a constituent [Prt°+DP], and this fact accounts for why [Prt°+DP] may not undergo *wh*-movement, (7b), clefting, (8b), or coordination, (9b). The impossibility of the modification in (10b) is caused by the impossibility of interrupting V*. The verb and the particle may undergo gapping together, (14b), as they form a constituent, V* in (13b).

English and Norwegian allow both (20b) and (20c), whereas Danish (and Faroese) only allows (20b) and Swedish only allows (20c) (see e.g. Hulthén 1947: 159–168; Herslund 1984; Vikner 1987):[1]

(21) En. a. *Peter threw out the carpet.* both (20b)
     b. *Peter threw the carpet out.* and (20c)

(22) No. a. *Petter kastet bort teppet.* and (20c)
     b. *Petter kastet teppet bort.*

(23) Da. a. **Peter smed ud tæppet.* only (20b)
     b. *Peter smed tæppet ud.*

(24) Sw. a. *Peter kastade bort mattan.* only (20c)
     b. **Peter kastade mattan bort.*

---

[1] Although English (and Norwegian) allow both (20b) and (20c), this is only true for full DPs like *the radio* in (6a,b). If the DP is a pronoun, this is not so, only (20c) is possible:
(i) En. a. **While jumping, he accidentally switched on it.* = (20b)
    b. *While jumping, he accidentally switched it on.* = (20c)
See Aa (2015) for a much more detailed discussion of the difference (22a) vs. (22b), ultimately arguing that they have different semantics.

As also shown in Vikner (1987, 2007), Engels and Vikner (2013, 2014), among others, the pattern in (22)–(24) is exactly the same as the pattern with verbs embedded under causative *let*:

(25) No. a. *Petter* lot *støvsuge* *teppet*. } both (20b) and (20c)
　　　 b. *Petter* lot **teppet** *støvsuge*.

(26) Da. a. **Peter* lod *støvsuge* *tæppet*. } only (20b)
　　　 b. *Peter* lod **tæppet** *støvsuge*.

(27) Sw. a. *Peter* lät ***dammsuga*** ***mattan***. } only (20c)
　　　 b. **Peter* lät *mattan* *dammsuga*.
　　　　　 Peter let carpet-the vacuum-clean carpet-the
　　　　　 (i.e. [20b, c] with VP instead of PrtP and with V° instead of Prt°)

As I take it that Danish/Norwegian/Swedish are SVO-languages, (25b) and (26b) must involve movement of the DP – the unacceptable alternative is that (25a) and (27a) involve movement of the infinitive, which in turn would require Norwegian and Swedish to be SOV-languages.

The parallels between (22)–(24) and (25)–(27) therefore lead me to assume that also (22b) and (23b) involve movement of the DP rather than assume that (22b) and (23b) show that particles are head-final in Danish (which would not be compatible with assuming particles and prepositions to have the same basic structure, as in [15a] and [20a]).

2.3 Verbs and particles in the Germanic SOV-languages

If we assume the analysis of particle verbs in the SVO-languages in (20) above, the question now is to which extent it also applies to particle verbs in the SOV-languages. I would like to suggest that only those orders differ between the SVO- and the SOV-languages which are linked to V° and its complement (i.e. V°/V* follows PrtP in e.g. German rather than precede PrtP as in e.g. English and Danish). All other orders are the same in the SVO- and the SOV-languages (i.e. P°/ Prt° precedes DP in both German and English/Danish).[2]

---

[2] See van Riemsdijk (1978: 129) and Zwart (2011: 339–341) and references there for arguments that what might seem to be postpositions in Dutch may be analysed as prepositional.

(28) a. Ge. *Peter   wird   das   Radio   anmachen.*
     b. Du. *Pieter   zal   de   radio   aanzetten.*
     c. Af. *Pieter   sal   die   radio   aanskakel.*
            Peter   will   the   radio   on-switch

(29) a.

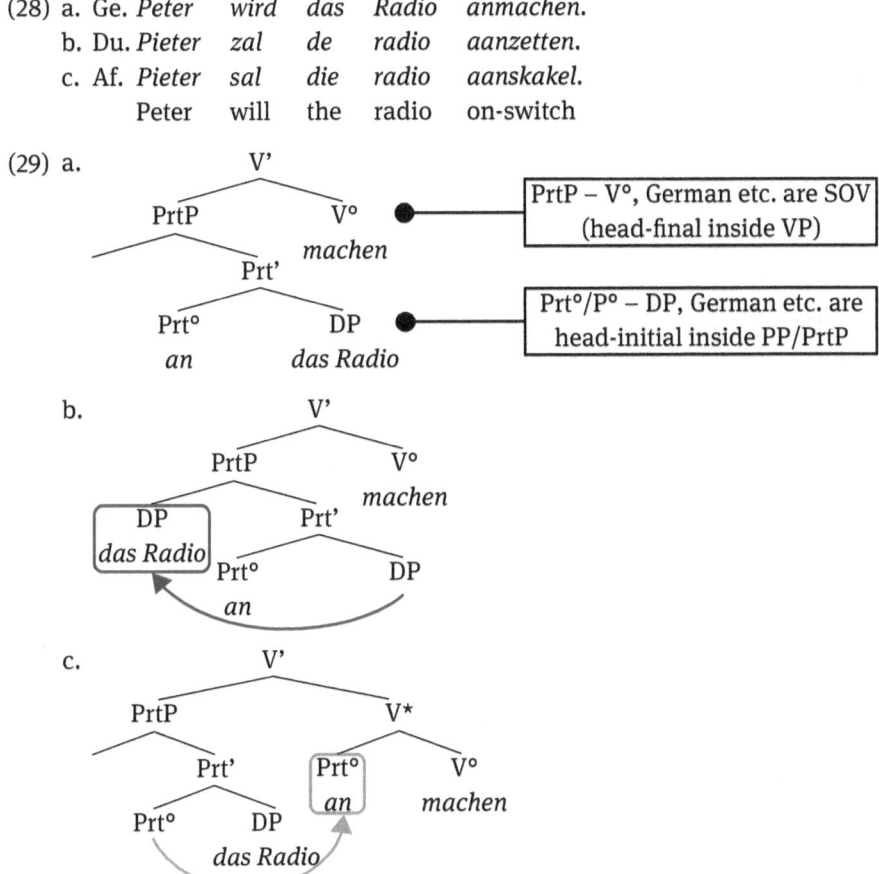

In other words, the ordering differences and similarities concerning particle incorporation between SVO-languages, (20), and SOV-languages, (29), are:

The position of the separable particle (regardless of whether it is the head of its own phrase, PrtP, (20b) and (29b), or it is a sister of V° and a daughter of V*, (20c) and (29c) is to the left of the verb in the SOV-languages, (29), Ge. *anmachen*, but to the right of the verb in the SVO-languages, (20), En. *switch on*. It should be admitted that although such a strict correlation between V°-DP and Prt°-DP versus DP-V° and DP-Prt° is the null hypothesis, and also generally assumed in the literature, not all linguists agree, cf. e.g. Elenbaas and van Kemenade (2014).

This is a syntactic property (the separable particle is never part of V°), and it therefore depends on the sequence between a verb and its complement in the language in question (in other words, it depends on the SOV/SVO-difference, Ge. *Ich habe das Buch gelesen* vs. Da. *Jeg har læst bogen* and En. *I have read the book*).

On the other hand, the position of the non-separable particle (which is always both a sister of V° and a daughter of V°), is to the left of the verb both in the SOV-languages, Ge. *verstehen*, and in the SVO-languages, Da. *forstå*, En. *understand*.

This is a morphological property (the non-separable particle is always part of V°), and it therefore does not co-vary with the SOV/SVO-difference. This is just like the position of the verbal inflectional morphemes, which is also a morphological property, and which also does not vary across the Germanic SOV/SVO-languages. (Non-separable particles will be discussed in more detail in section 3 below).

As was the case with (20b, c), (29b, c) illustrate two different ways of case being assigned to the complement DP of the (separable) particle, see also the English and Scandinavian variation as to DP-Prt° or Prt°-DP order, (21)–(24) above.[3,4]

The question why there is no variation in the SOV-languages comparable to (21)–(24) may now be answered: Whether an SOV-language employs only (29b), only (29c), or both, would not make any difference, as both (29b, c) will yield the same ordering predictions (as opposed to [20b, c], which yield different predictions). As pointed out by an anonymous reviewer, all that can be shown is thus that each SOV-language uses (29b) or (29c) or both, but not which one of these three options is used in a given language.

This is because (29c) is the same as in SVO, i.e. movement to the left, whereas (29b) is different from SVO, movement to the right (if V° is to the right of PrtP, then quasi-incorporation of Prt° into the V* is necessarily movement to the right). In the SOV-languages, the two movements thus have "identical" results (i.e. as far as the sequence is concerned).[5]

---

3 It might seem feasible to allow only (29b), where there is no incorporation of the particle into V*, as an analysis of separable particles in the SOV-languages. However, we know from Swedish that this will not work, given that although Swedish only employs option (20c) with separable particles, these nevertheless remain separable, cf. (16a) and (24a).

4 It might seem that if the DP would adjoin to PrtP rather than move into PrtP-spec, movement of particles to CP-spec would receive a better analysis under (29b), i.e. then PrtP could move to CP-spec. However, also in Swedish, particles may move to CP-spec, and Swedish only allows (20c). For a possible analysis of particles in CP-spec, see the analysis of remnant VP-topicalisation in Engels and Vikner (2013, 2014), which predicts that if the particle has a DP-complement, the particle can only end up in CP-spec on its own if the DP-complement has undergone object shift, as does *mej/mig* in (16).

5 A potential problem is that in some German cases, the particle might seem to be the case assigner, e.g. *Sie ist dem Bankräuber nachgefahren* 'She is the bank robber after-driven', i.e. she followed the bank robber by car. Here the DP has dative case, which is exactly what *nach* assigns when it is a preposition. Furthermore, the verb *fahren*, 'drive', can only have the perfect auxiliary *sein*, 'be', here, although it would normally have *haben*, 'have' when it assigns a case. See e.g. McIntyre (2007: 359) for discussion and references.

In other words, by assuming that prepositions and particles are different variants of the same word class, (20) and (29), we not only reduce the number of word classes, but we also obtain a promising account of why this particular kind of word order variation concerning particles found in Mainland Scandinavian is not found in the Germanic SOV-languages.

In section 3 below, I will argue that if Yiddish is assumed to be SOV, such an account will also be able to account for why Yiddish particles and particle verbs behave so very differently from English/Scandinavian ones and so much like German/Dutch/Afrikaans ones.

2.4 Passives with particles and prepositions

As the DP is assigned case from the verb in either version of the particle construction, it is not surprising that both versions of this construction may be passivised:

(30) En. a. [The radio]$_1$ was accidentally switched t$_1$ on t$_1$.
 b. [The radio]$_1$ was accidentally [switched on$_2$] t$_2$ t$_1$.

It is more surprising that also the prepositional construction may be passivised ("pseudo-passive"):

(31) En. Peter$_1$ will be laughed at t$_1$.

What is peculiar about the prepositional passive is that passivisation prevents not the verb *laugh* but the preposition *at* from assigning case, even though passivisation affects the morphology of the verb and not that of the preposition.

One possible analysis is to say that the reason why the passivisation of the verb *laugh* prevents the preposition *at* from assigning case is that the preposition in some sense 'forms part' of the verb. If we assume that also a preposition may form a V* together with a verb, just like the particle did in (20c), we can now account for the passivisation in (31)/(32). If the preposition is incorporated into the verb in a passive construction, the DP which is left without case will have to move to find (nominative) case in the subject position, cf. (32).[6]

---

[6] If the preposition were to be incorporated into the verb in an active construction, the DP which would be left without case, would have nowhere to find a case, and so the construction would be impossible for independent reasons.

(32)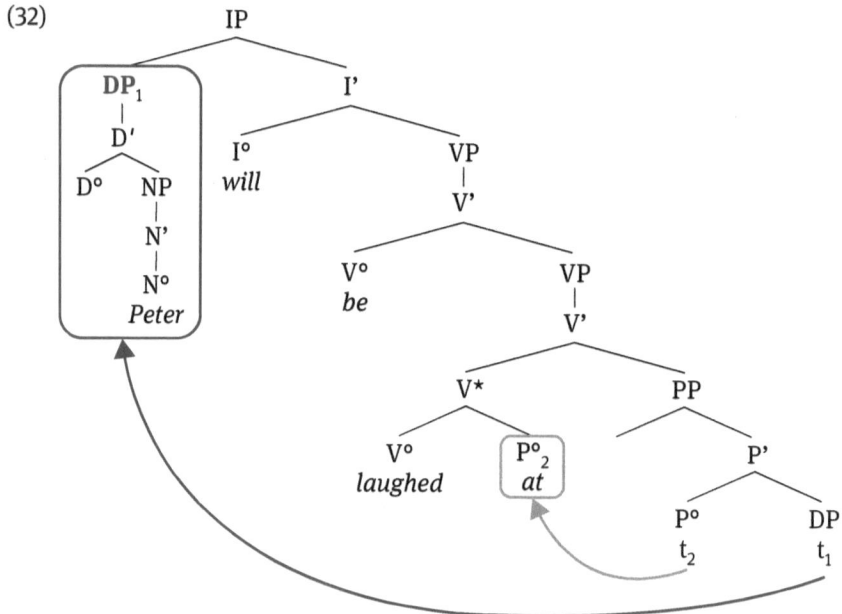

This analysis results in a cross-linguistic prediction: Only one of the SVO-languages mentioned above (namely Danish) did not allow incorporation into the V* of the particle, and so we would expect that only Danish would not allow examples like (31)/(32) which involve a parallel kind of incorporation. This prediction would seem to hold, at least approximately:[7]

(33) En. *He was laughed at.*

(34) No. *Han ble ledd av.*
 he was laughed at (Vinje 1987: 140)

---

[7] As in Vikner (1995: 246), I here follow Herslund (1984: 70, footnote 7) in the assumption that Danish does not allow prepositional passives ("pseudo-passives"), although I admit that this is not fully supported by the data. Laanemets and Engdahl (2015: 232) thus find several examples of prepositional passive in Danish (in 0,8% of their examples with the *s*-passive and in 5,0% of their examples with the *blive*-passive). These figures, however, are clearly smaller than in both Norwegian (3,8% and 7,8% respectively) and Swedish (4,3% and 13,3% respectively). My analysis in this section thus may offer the beginning of an account for why the share of passives that consists of prepositional passives is much smaller in Danish than in Norwegian and Swedish, but the analysis has no explanation for why prepositional passives occur in Danish at all.

It should also be said that Engdahl and Laanemets (2015: 300) compute prepositional passive to be more or less equally frequent in Danish and Swedish in respect to the total number of running words in their corpora (because passive in general is less frequent in Swedish than in Danish), but here I assume that it is the difference in frequency of prepositional passives in relation to the total number of passives that is relevant.

(35) Sw. *Skandalen   skrattades   åt.*
        scandal-the was-laughed   at   (Platzack 1998: 122)

(36) Da. a. ??*Han   blev   grinet   af.*
       b. ??*Skandalen   blev   grinet   af.*
          he/scandal-the was   laughed   at

(37) Da. a. *Ham   blev   der   grinet   af.*
       b. *Skandalen   blev   der   grinet   af.*
         him/scandal-the was   there laughed at

In this section, the focus was mainly on separable particles. This is where the verb particle variation is, both between different types of SVO-languages and between SVO-languages and SOV-languages, and it was suggested that what differs between SVO and SOV is the ordering inside V' and inside V* (i.e. syntactic ordering, which concerns separable particles), but crucially not inside V° (i.e. morphological ordering, which concerns non-separable particles).

We are now ready to have a more detailed look at both separable and non-separable verb particles, in particular with a view to the status of Yiddish as an SVO-language or an SOV-language.

3 Separable vs. non-separable particles

In this section, I will try to show that the view that Yiddish is an SOV-language like German and Dutch (as advocated in e.g. Hall 1979; Geilfuß 1991; Haider and Rosengren 1998: 78–81; Sadock 1998; Vikner 2001a, 2001b, 2003), not an SVO-language like English or Danish, is supported by the facts concerning verb particles.

3.1 Yiddish: SVO or SOV?

Many linguists agree with Diesing (1997) that Yiddish syntactically is very much like e.g. German, but with the essential difference that Yiddish is SVO where German is SOV. I disagree with this view, as will be argued below. In fact, I think that if we are looking for an SVO-language which has a great many properties in common with German, then Danish is a very good candidate, whereas Yiddish is not.[8]

---

[8] I still consider German and Yiddish to be much closer to each other than German and Danish, it is just that SOV vs. SVO is a basic difference between German and Danish, whereas I do not think that it is a difference between German and Yiddish at all.

It is not as simple as one might think to establish whether Yiddish is SVO (like English and Danish) or SOV (like German and Dutch), because in Yiddish, both SVO or SOV are possible as surface orders:

(38) Yi. a. *Ikh   hob   gezen   **Moyshn**.*
     b. *Ikh   hob   **Moyshn**   gezen.*
     I   have   (Moyshe)   seen   (Moyshe)
                    (den Besten and Moed-van Walraven 1986: 125, [43])

If the basic order in Yiddish is SVO, then the SVO-order in e.g. (38a) would not require any object movement at all, and the SOV-order in e.g. (38b) could be derived by means of scrambling:

(39) Yi. a. *Ikh   hob   gezen   **Moyshn**.*   no movement, = (38a)
     b. *Ikh   hob   **Moyshn**   gezen   _____.*   scrambling, = (38b)
     I   have   (Moyshe)   seen   (Moyshe)

If, on the other hand, the basic order in Yiddish is SOV, then the SOV-order in e.g. (38b) would not require any object movement at all, and the SVO-order in e.g. (38a) could be derived by means of extraposition:

(40) Yi. a. *Ikh   hob   _____   gezen   **Moyshn**.*   extraposition, = (38a)
     b. *Ikh   hob   **Moyshn**   gezen.*   no movement, = (38b)
     I   have   (Moyshe)   seen   (Moyshe)

The problem is that it can be independently shown that Yiddish actually has both extraposition and scrambling, which again means that we have to look elsewhere (e.g. to the behaviour of verb particles) in order to find out what the base order in Yiddish really is.

Let me briefly review the evidence for extraposition, which is particularly relevant here because the existence of extraposition in Yiddish is what allows me to claim that Yiddish is an SOV-language and still allow for Yiddish SVO-examples like (58b), (59b) below.

Santorini (1993: 231, 243) argues that regardless of whether Yiddish is SOV or SVO, examples like the following three all show that Yiddish has extraposition:

(41) Yi. a. *Geveyntlekh   hot   ongehoybn   esn   **der   balebos**.*
          normally   has   begun   eat   the   host
          'Normally, the host would be the one who took the first bite.'

b. *Durkh*   *a*   *kleyn*   *shtetl*   *hot*   *gedarft*   *durkhforn*   **der**
through   a   small   town   has   must   through-drive   the
keyser.
emperor
'The emperor had to drive through a small town'
c. *Hot*   *men*   *derlangt*   *oyfn*   *tish*   **fish**.
has   one   served   on-the   table   fish
'Fish was put on the table'   (Santorini 1993: 231, [1a], [2a,b])

The point is that the subject would normally have occurred immediately after *hot* 'has' in both (41a, b). As it here occurs in the sentence-final position, it must have undergone extraposition (irrespective of whether Yiddish is SOV or SVO). As for (41c), the object *fish* would normally have occurred immediately before *derlangt* 'put' if Yiddish was SOV, and immediately after *derlangt* if Yiddish was SVO, so in either case it would have to have undergone extraposition to get to its actual position, the sentence-final position.

Furthermore, as shown in Vikner (1995), Yiddish does not require extraposed constituents to be particularly heavy, (44b), as opposed to English and Scandinavian, exemplified by Icelandic in (44a):

(42) a. Ic. ...   *að*   *það*   *hefur*   **einhver**   *borðað*   *epli*.
   b. Yi. ...   *as*   *es*   *hot*   **emetser**   *gegesn*   *an*   *epl*.
   ... that   there   has   someone   eaten   an   apple
                                      (Vikner 1995: 189, [43b, c])

(43) a. Ic. ...   *að*   *það*   *hefur*   *borðað*   *þetta*   *epli*   **einhver**
   ... that   there   has   eaten   this   apple   some
strákur   *frá*   **Danmörku**.
boy   from   Denmark
   b. Yi. ...   *az*   *es*   *hot*   *gegesn*   *an*   *epl*   *a*   **yingl**   *fun*
   ... that   there   has   eaten   an   apple   a   boy   from
Danmark.
Denmark   (Vikner 1995: 200, [76], [77])

(44) a. Ic. *...   *að*   *það*   *hefur*   *borðað*   *epli*   **einhver**.
   b. Yi. ...   *az*   *es*   *hot*   *gegesn*   *an*   *epl*   **emetser**.
   ... that   there   has   eaten   an   apple   someone
                                      (Vikner 1995: 200, [75b, c])

(42) shows that both Icelandic and Yiddish allow transitive expletives, (43) shows that both allow extraposition of a heavy subject in such a construction, and finally (44) shows that only Yiddish allows extraposition of a subject which is not heavy.

In other words, as far as the word order data is concerned, it would seem that Yiddish is compatible both with an SVO base and with an SOV base.[9]

3.2 Different types of incorporation: V° and V*

In this subsection I repeat what I take to be the basic difference between separable and non-separable particle verbs, namely that only the non-separable ones form a X°-constituent (i.e. a V°) in the syntax. Separable particle verbs never form a V°, but they may form a constituent of a higher projection level, the one which was labelled V* in (20c)/(29c) above.

As already hinted at above, I would like to suggest that separable particles are not incorporated into the verb to the same extent that non-separable particles are. If we assume that a non-separable particle and its verb (*understand*) constitute a V°, then a separable particle and its verb (*send off*) do not form a V°.

This does not mean that verb and separable particle may not somehow form a constituent, it only means that they do not together constitute a V°. I take it that the closest they may get to each other is to form a syntactic constituent which is not quite as small as V°, even if it may be smaller than V', given that they are taken to form almost a head but not quite by e.g. Booij (1990) where they constitute a V* (which is more than V° but less than V'). For further discussion, see e.g. Haegeman and Guéron (1999: 254), Zeller (2001: 58–69), Haiden (2005), and also Booij (2008: 9, 2009: 8) on "pseudo-incorporation"/"quasi-incorporation" where V* is analysed as [$_{V'}$ V N], i.e. a VP where the object does not project any XP. See also sections 2.2 and 2.3 above on whether a given language uses the option of incorporating separable particles into V*. In other words, a separable particle is either the head of its own phrase, PrtP, or it is a sister of V° and a

---

9 It has been pointed out to me that there might be more than just the two commonly assumed types of Germanic languages (SOV: German/Dutch/Afrikaans/Frisian/Low German and SVO: English and the five Scandinavian languages), namely a third language type which is variable as to the SOV/SVO-distinction. As was the case with the number of word classes earlier, I think that the assumption of additional types/elements (here: the assumption of a further type of Germanic language) should be seen as an absolute last resort (cf. Occam's razor). Given the clear and independent evidence for both scrambling and extraposition in Yiddish, the assumption of an additional type of language is a last resort that we do not have to make use of.

I do not think that the discussion in this paper has any bearing on the position of I° (or T°), but to answer a question asked by an anonymous reviewer, I believe I° to be medial (to the left of VP) in all of the languages discussed here, cf. Vikner (2005), where I argued that no Germanic SOV-language has V°-to- I° movement.

daughter of V*, whereas a non-separable particle is always both a sister of V° and a daughter of V°.[10]

I will (continue to) use the notation V*, but I will take it only to indicate a constituent which is larger than a V°, i.e. I have nothing to say about whether V* is as big as V' or not (cf. Zeller's 2001: 162 formulation Vn, n>0). (45) illustrates the analyses of the verbs used in the rest of this article.

This follows Haiden (1997: 105), Wurmbrand (1998: 271), and many others, in taking verb and separable particle to form a lexical unit but not necessarily also a syntactic X°-constituent.

(45)

	Morphology	Syntax	
	non-separable	separable (in SOV-languages)	separable (in SVO-languages)
a.	V° [Prt° V°]	V* [Prt° V°]	V* [V° Prt°]
b.	Yi. *farshteyn* Ge. *verstehen* Da. *forstå* En. *understand*		
c.		Yi. *avekshikn* Ge. *abschicken*	Da. *sende afsted* En. *send off*

Verb and separable particle would have this (i.e. lexical unity without syntactic unity) in common with many other combinations of a verb plus (part of) its complement, e.g. idiomatic expressions like English *to spill the beans* (i.e. 'to reveal a secret'), Danish *stille træskoene* (literally 'to put down the wooden shoes', i.e. 'to die'), German *jemandem einen Korb geben* (literally 'to give somebody a basket', i.e. 'to say no to an offer'), and Yiddish *hakn a tshaynik* (literally 'to beat a teapot', i.e. 'to talk nonsense'). Because such expressions have a non-compositional semantics, i.e. their meaning cannot be inferred from the meaning of their parts, the entire expression, e.g. *spill the beans*, has to be listed as a separate lexical entry. However, although they thus form one lexical unit, they do not form a syntactic one, as shown e.g. by Müller (2000), see also O'Grady (1998) and Nunberg, Sag, and Wasow (1994): Syntactic operations,

---

[10] Ackema and Neeleman (2004: 71) suggest for particle verbs that the separable particle (syntactic compounding) is the unmarked option, and that the non-separable particles (morphological compounding) are the ones that have to be marked in the lexicon.

e.g. passivisation or V2, can affect part of such expressions while leaving other parts unaffected, so that the different parts of the lexical unit can end up rather far apart in the syntax:

(46) En. **The beans** were finally **spilled** by John.

(47) Da. *I 1980 **stillede** han desværre **træskoene**.*
in 1980 put-down he unfortunately wooden-shoes-the
'In 1980, he unfortunately died.'

(48) Ge. *Warum **gab** sie ihm gestern **einen Korb**?*
why gave she him yesterday a basket
'Why did she turn him down yesterday?'

(49) Yi. *Far vos **hakt** er shtendik **a tshaynik**?*
why beats he constantly a teapot
'Why does he always talk nonsense?'

This is clearly parallel to those verbs with separable particles that do not have a compositional semantics, e.g. German *aufhören*, Yiddish *oyfhern*, and Danish *høre op*, literally 'to up-hear' i.e. 'to stop'. The meaning of the particle verb cannot be computed from the meaning of its constituent parts, i.e. *hear* and *up*. Although *hear* and *up* have to be listed independently in the lexicon, the lexicon therefore also has to contain separate entries for *aufhören*, *oyfhern*, and *høre op*.[11]

3.3 Lexical differences between German, Yiddish, and Danish

Across the three languages almost all possible combinatorial possibilities exist, i.e. not only are there particle verbs which are separable in all three languages, (50), and others which are non-separable in all three languages, (57), but there are also particle verbs which are separable in one language and non-separable in the other two or vice versa, (51), (54)–(56). Only two combinations are not found, (52) and (53): There would seem to be no particle verbs which are separable in German and non-separable in Yiddish. The particle verbs which are non-separable in German and separable in Yiddish, (54) and (55), involve

---

[11] Gold (1998: 192–194) in fact argues that it follows from *oyfhern* forming a lexical unit that it must form a syntactic X°-constituent. I disagree with this conclusion, because of the data from idiomatic expressions cited above.

only five prepositions/particles (*durch/durkh* 'through', *hinter* 'behind', *über/iber* 'above', *um/arum* 'around', and *unter* 'below', see e.g. Olsen 1997: 11–16; Zifonun, Hoffmann, and Strecker 1997: 2088 on their special properties).

The following table only includes one example of each particle in each of the groups, and it only contains particle verbs which are clearly semantically parallel across the three languages. "+" indicates a separable particle, whereas "–" indicates a non-separable particle:[12, 13]

(50)   German: +   Yiddish: +   Danish: +
  a. **ab**brennen   **op**brenen   brænde **af**   burn down
  b. **ab**schicken   **avek**shikn   sende **afsted**   send off
  c. **auf**wachsen   **oyf**vaksn   vokse **op**   grow up
  d. **aus**halten   **oys**haltn   holde **ud**   endure, stand
  e. **ein**kaufen   **ayn**koyfn   købe **ind**   buy, shop
  f. **herein**kommen   **arayn**kumen   komme **ind**   come in, enter
  g. **(hin)aus**gehen   **aroys**geyn   gå **ud**   go out
  h. **nach**geben   **nokh**gebn   give **efter**   give in, indulge
  i. sich **um**sehen   **um**kukn zikh   se sig **om**   look around
  j. **zu**nageln   **tsu**noglen   sømme **til**   nail shut
  k. **zurück**ziehen   **tsurik**tsien   trække **tilbage**   retract
  l. **zusammen**stoßen   **tsunoyf**shtoysn støde **sammen**   clash, collide

(51)   German: +   Yiddish: +   Danish: –
  a. **ab**weichen   **op**vaikhn   **af**vige   deviate
  b. **an**kommen   **on**kumen   **an**komme   arrive

---

12 Some, but not all, of the Danish particle verbs that I have classified here as separable also occur as non-separable particle verbs in very formal or technical usage but not in colloquial Danish (see e.g. Lundskær-Nielsen and Holmes 2011: 134–135).

This tendency can also be observed in different examples where both the separable and non-separable variants are well-established forms. Consider German *auslaufen*, Yiddish *oysloyfn* 'run out, leak, expire'. In Danish, the corresponding particle verb is separable in a more concrete sense, but non-separable in a more figurative or technical sense:
(i) Da. a. *Vandet   løb   ud   på gulvet.*
        b. **Vandet   udløb   på gulvet.*
           water-the (out)ran (out) on floor-the
(ii) Da. a. ??*Kontrakten   løb   ud   i 2013.*
         b.   Kontrakten   **udløb**   i 2013.
              contract-the (out)ran (out) in 2013
13 As pointed out by a reviewer, many simplifications are made in the table in (50)–(57), e.g. in assuming parallels between Ge./Yi. *ziehen/tsien* and Da. *trække*, Ge./Yi. *schicken/shikn* and Da. *sende*, etc.

c.	**auf**suchen	**oyf**zukhn	**op**søge	look up (a person)
d.	**bei**legen	**bay**leygn	**ved**lægge	append (e.g. to a letter)
e.	**durch**führen	**durkh**firn	**gennem**føre	carry out
f.	**ein**wenden	**ayn**vendn	**ind**vende	object
g.	**um**stoßen	**um**shtoysn	**om**støde	reverse (e.g. a decision)
h.	**zu**lassen	**tsu**lozn	**til**lade	allow

(52) German: +   Yiddish: −   Danish: +
---

(53) German: +   Yiddish: −   Danish: −
---

(54) German: −   Yiddish: +   Danish: +
  überspringen   **iber**hipn   springe **over**   skip, pass over

(55) German: −   Yiddish: +   Danish: −
  a. **durch**löchern   **durkh**lekhern   **gennem**hulle   make holes in
  b. **um**ringen   **arum**ringen   **om**ringe   surround, encircle
  c. **über**reden   **iber**redn   **over**tale   persuade
  d. **unter**drücken   **unter**drikn   **under**trykke   suppress

(56) German: −   Yiddish: −   Danish: +
  zerschlagen   **tses**hlogn   slå **itu**   smash to pieces

(57) German: −   Yiddish: −   Danish: −
  a. **be**merken   **ba**merkn   **be**mærke   notice
  b. **ent**schuldigen   **ant**shuldikn   **und**skylde   apologise
  c. **er**kennen   **der**kenen   **er**kende   recognise
  d. **ver**stehen   **far**shteyn   **for**stå   understand

3.4 Syntactic differences between German, Yiddish, and Danish

German, Yiddish and Danish are all V2, which means that in declarative main clauses, the finite verb must be in the second position, irrespective of whether the first position is occupied by the subject, (58), or by some other constituent, (59):

(58) a. Ge. [Der Junge] **wird** auf dem Weg   eine Katze   sehen. V2
     b. Yi. [Dos yingl] **vet** oyfn   veg zen a   kats.   V2
     c. Da. [Drengen] **vil**   se   en kat på vejen.   V2
          the boy   will (on the way) (see) a   cat (on way-the) (see)

(59) a. Ge. [Auf dem Weg] **wird** der Junge eine Katze sehen. V2
    b. Yi. [Oyfn veg] **vet** dos yingl zen a kats. V2
    c. Da. [På vejen] **vil** drengen se en kat. (see) V2
         on the way will the boy (see) a cat (see)

If the finite verb is e.g. in the third position, the main clause is not well-formed:

(60) a. Ge. *[Auf dem Weg] [der Junge] **wird** eine Katze sehen. *V3
    b. Yi. *[Oyfn veg] [dos yingl] **vet** zen a kats. *V3
    c. Da. *[På vejen] [drengen] **vil** se en kat. *V3
         on the way the boy will (see) a cat (see)
         ([58b], [59a, b], [60a, b] are from Santorini 1992: 596–597, [1], [4])

As (59) shows, in main clauses, the finite verb moves out of the clause to a position in front of the subject position, whereas non-finite verbs do not undergo this movement, and this difference will be exploited below.

In Danish, the distinction between separable and non-separable particles can be seen both when the verb undergoes V2 and when it does not. In non-V2-contexts, the separable particle occurs after the verb, whereas the non-separable particle before the verb:

(61) a. Da. Brevet vil han sende **afsted**. separable: right of V
    b. Da. *Brevet vil han **afsted**sende.
         letter-the will he (off)send (off)

(62) a. Da. *Brevet vil han ikke stå **for**.
    b. Da. Brevet vil han ikke **for**stå. non-separable: left of V
         letter-the will he not (under)stand (under)

In V2-contexts, the separable particle is left behind when the verb moves, whereas the non-separable particle moves as part of the verb (this is, of course, the defining property for separability):

(63) a. Da. Brevet sender han **afsted**. separable: stays behind
    b. Da. *Brevet **afsted**sender han.
         letter-the (off)sends he (off)

(64) a. Da. *Brevet står han ikke **for**.
    b. Da. Brevet **for**står han ikke. non-separable: moves along
         letter-the (under)stands he not (under)

In parallel examples in German and Yiddish, on the other hand, the distinction between separable and non-separable particles can only be seen when the verb undergoes movement, e.g. V2. In non-V2-contexts, both the separable particle and the non-separable particle occur before the verb:

(65) a. Ge. *Den Brief wird er schicken **ab**.
     b. Yi. ??Dem briv vet er shikn **avek**.
     c. Ge. Den Brief wird er **ab**schicken.   separable: left of V
     d. Yi. Dem briv vet er **avek**shikn.   separable: left of V
             the letter will he (off)send (off)

(66) a. Ge. *Den Brief wird er nicht stehen **ver**.
     b. Yi. *Dem briv vet er nisht shteyn **far**.
     c. Ge. Den Brief wird er nicht **ver**stehen.   non-separable: left of V
     d. Yi. Dem briv vet er nisht **far**shteyn.   non-separable: left of V
             the letter will he not (under)stand (under)

In V2-contexts, the separable particle is left behind when the verb moves, whereas the non-separable particle moves as part of the verb:

(67) a. Ge. Den Brief schickt er **ab**.   separable: stays behind
     b. Yi. Dem briv shikt er **avek**.   separable: stays behind
     c. Ge. *Den Brief **ab**schickt er.
     d. Yi. *Dem briv **avek**shikt er.
             the letter (off)sends he (off)
             ([67b] is from den Besten and Moed-van Walraven 1986: 119, [20b])

(68) a. Ge. *Den Brief steht er nicht **ver**.
     b. Yi. *Dem briv shteyt er nisht **far**.
     c. Ge. Den Brief **ver**steht er nicht.   non-separable: moves along
     d. Yi. Dem briv **far**shteyt er nisht.   non-separable: moves along
             the letter (under)stands he not (under)

This pattern is exactly as expected under the assumptions made in section 2.3 above, namely that the position of the separable particle is a syntactic property, and therefore depends on the syntactic sequence of a verb and its complement in the language in question (viz. the SOV/SVO-difference: The separable particle occurs after the verb in English/Danish, and before the verb in German), whereas the position of the non-separable particle is a morphological property, and thus does not co-vary with the syntactic sequence of a verb and its complement (the non-separable particle occurs before the verb in both Danish and German).

The fact that Yiddish behaves like German and differently from Danish is expected if Yiddish is an SOV-language, but it is highly unexpected if Yiddish was SVO.[14]

---

[14] For more parallels between German and Yiddish as far as verb particles are concerned, see Vikner (2001b: 40–47).

4 Conclusion

I started out from the suggestion that prepositions and (separable) particles have the same structure:

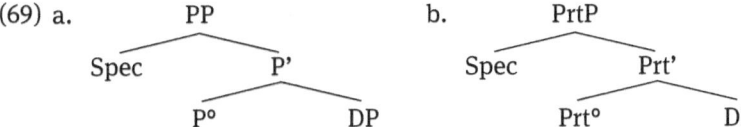

(69) a. PP
         Spec   P'
                P°   DP

b. PrtP
    Spec   Prt'
            Prt°   DP

the difference being that prepositions assign case, whereas particles do not. Therefore the complement DP (e.g. *the book* in *throw out the book*) will not be assigned case. This problem had the two potential solutions that either the particle is incorporated into the verb (i.e. into V*), in which case V* (maybe via the trace in Prt°) may now assign case to the "object", resulting in *He threw out the book*, or that the DP may move to PrtP-spec, where it can be assigned case directly by V° (as in ECM-constructions), resulting in *He threw the book out*.

The SVO-languages vary as to which strategy they allow, leading to variation in particle constructions across the SVO-languages (and similar variation in prepositional passives). The same strategies were then shown to have non-distinct results for the SOV-languages, explaining why the SOV-languages do not have any variation in particle constructions with separable particles similar to the one found among the SVO-languages. In other words, what varies between SVO and SOV is only the sequence between a verb and a separable particle (i.e. the syntactic sequence, English/Danish ≠ German, e.g. *to send off ~ at sende afsted ~ abzuschicken*), but not the sequence between a verb and a non-separable particle (i.e. the morphological sequence, English/Danish = German, e.g. *to understand ~ at forstå ~ zu verstehen*).

This was used to account for why the particular kind of word order variation concerning particles found in Mainland Scandinavian (Hulthén 1947: 159–168; Herslund 1984; Vikner 1987; Engels and Vikner 2013, 2014; Aa 2015, and very many others) is not found in the Germanic SOV-languages.

In Section 3, the discussion was extended to the difference between separable and non-separable particles, and I argued that even when separable particles incorporate into the verb (which they never do in Danish, and only sometimes in English and Norwegian), they do not incorporate to the same extent as non-separable particles, in that only the latter incorporate into V°.

These properties were discussed and tested with reference to whether the particle could be left behind when its verb moves (only possible with separable particles), and special attention was paid to particles in Yiddish, comparing them to Danish and German, with the following conclusion: If Yiddish is an SOV-language like German and Dutch, not an SVO-language like English or Danish, then we can account for why Yiddish is like German and unlike Scandinavian in allowing even those particles to occur preverbally in non-V2 constructions that do not incorporate (as seen by their not moving along with the finite verb during V2).

Acknowledgments: This paper is only a small token of my gratitude to Liliane Haegeman for making my career in linguistics possible in the first place (by employing me as her assistant in 1984 and by being my PhD supervisor) and for setting such a good example, both as a researcher and as a teacher. Thanks are also due to a number of anonymous reviewers, to Maia Andréasson, Theresa Biberauer, Ken Ramshøj Christensen, Elisabet Engdahl, Eva Engels, Eric Haeberli, Lars Heltoft, Shin-Sook Kim, Vilma Symanczyk Joppe, Henrik Jørgensen, Robert Külpmann, Gereon Müller, Bjarne Ørsnes, Vieri Samek-Lodovici, Peter Sells, Manuela Schönenberger, Michelle Sheehan, Carl Vikner, Johanna Wood, and to the audiences at various talks at the universities of Aalborg, Aarhus, Berlin (Humboldt, ZAS), Cambridge, Edinburgh, Gothenburg, Konstanz, Leipzig, London (UCL), Lund, Marburg, Newcastle, Salzburg, Stuttgart, and York. This work was carried out as part of two research projects at Aarhus University financed by "Forskningsrådet for Kultur og Kommunikation" (Danish Research Council for Culture and Communication): Object Positions – Comparative Syntax in a Cross-Theoretical Perspective and Similarities and Differences between Clauses and Nominals.

References

Aa, Leiv Inge. 2015. *The grammar of verb-particle constructions in spoken Norwegian.* Trondheim: Norwegian University of Science and Technology dissertation.
Ackema, Peter & Ad Neeleman. 2004. *Beyond morphology – Interface conditions on word formation.* Oxford: Oxford University Press.
Besten, Hans den & Corretje Moed-van Walraven. 1986. The syntax of verbs in Yiddish. In Hubert Haider & Martin Prinzhorn (eds.), *Verb second phenomena in Germanic languages*, 111–135. Dordrecht: Foris.
Booij, Geert. 1990. The boundary between morphology and syntax: Separable complex verbs in Dutch. In Geert Booij & Jaap van Marle (eds.), *Yearbook of morphology 1990*, 45–63. Dordrecht: Foris.
Booij, Geert. 2008. Pseudo-incorporation in Dutch. *Groninger Arbeiten zur Germanistischen Linguistik* 46. 3–26.
Booij, Geert. 2009. A constructional analysis of quasi-incorporation in Dutch. *Gengo Kenkyu* 135. 5–37.

Chomsky, Noam. 1981. *Lectures on government and binding*. Dordrecht: Foris.
Diesing, Molly. 1997. Yiddish VP order and the typology of object movement in Germanic. *Natural Language and Linguistic Theory* 15. 369–427.
Dikken, Marcel den. 1995. *Particles – On the syntax of verb particle, triadic, and causative constructions*. Oxford: Oxford University Press.
Elenbaas, Marion & Ans van Kemenade. 2014. Verb particles and OV/VO in the history of English. *Studia Linguistica* 68. 140–167.
Engels, Eva & Sten Vikner. 2013. Scandinavian object shift, remnant VP-topicalisation, verb particles and causatives. *Nordic Journal of Linguistics* 36. 219–244.
Engels, Eva & Sten Vikner. 2014. *Scandinavian object shift and Optimality Theory*. Basingstoke: Palgrave Macmillan.
Fraser, Bruce. 1976. *The verb-particle combination in English*. New York: Academic Press.
Geilfuß, Jochen. 1991. Jiddisch als SOV-Sprache. *Zeitschrift für Sprachwissenschaft* 9. 170–183.
Gold, Elaine. 1998. *Aspect, tense and the lexicon: Expression of time in Yiddish*. Toronto: University of Toronto dissertation.
Hall, Beatrice. 1979. Accounting for Yiddish word order or what's a nice NP like you doing in a place like this. In Jürgen Meisel & Martin Pam (eds.), *Linear order and generative theory*, 253–287. Amsterdam: John Benjamins.
Haegeman, Liliane & Jacqueline Guéron. 1999. *English grammar – a generative perspective*. Oxford: Blackwell.
Haiden, Martin. 1997. Verbal inflection and the structure of IP in German. *Groninger Arbeiten zur Germanistischen Linguistik* 41. 77–106.
Haiden, Martin. 2005. Verb particle constructions. In Henk van Riemsdijk & Martin Everaert (eds.), *The syntax companion*, vol. 5, 344–375. Oxford: Blackwell.
Haider, Hubert & Inger Rosengren. 1998. Scrambling. *Sprache und Pragmatik* 49. 1–104.
Herslund, Michael. 1984. Particles, prefixes, and preposition stranding. In Finn Sørensen & Lars Heltoft (eds.), *Topics in Danish syntax* (Nydanske Studier og Almen Kommunikationsteori, NyS 14), 34–71. Copenhagen: Akademisk Forlag.
Holmberg, Anders. 1999. Remarks on Holmberg's generalization. *Studia Linguistica* 53. 1–39.
Hulthén, Lage. 1947. *Studier i jämförande nunordisk syntax* [Studies in comparative contemporary Scandinavian syntax], part II (Göteborg Högskolas Årsskrift 53.4). Gothenburg: Elanders Bogtryckeri.
Koopman, Hilda. 2000. *The syntax of specifiers and heads*. London: Routledge
Laanemets, Anu & Elisabet Engdahl. 2015. Findes der præpositionspassiv i dansk? [Do prepositional passives exist in Danish?] In Inger Schoonderbeek Hansen & TinaThode Hougaard (eds.), *15. Møde om Udforskningen af Dansk Sprog (MUDS 15)* [15th conference on the research into the Danish language], 219–236. http://muds.dk/rapporter/MUDS_15.pdf (accessed 28 November 2016).
Lundskær-Nielsen, Tom & Philip Holmes. 2011. *Danish - An essential grammar*. London: Routledge.
McIntyre, Andrew. 2007. Particle verbs and argument structure. *Language and Linguistics Compass* 1. 350–367.
McIntyre, Andrew. 2013. English particle verbs are complex heads: Evidence from nominalization. In Holden Härtl (ed.), *Interfaces of morphology*, 41–57. Berlin: De Gruyter Mouton.
Müller, Gereon. 2000. On idioms, pronouns and proper alignment in syntax, hand-out from a talk at the GGS conference, University of Potsdam, June 2000.
Nunberg, Geoffrey, Ivan A. Sag & Thomas Wasow. 1994. Idioms. *Language* 70. 491–538.

O'Grady, William. 1998. The syntax of idioms. *Natural Language and Linguistic Theory* 16. 279–312.
Olsen, Susan. 1997. Zur Kategorie Verbpartikel. *Beiträge zur Geschichte der Deutschen Sprache und Literatur* 119. 1–32.
Platzack, Christer. 1998. *Svenskans inre grammatik – det minimalistiska programmet* [The internal grammar of Swedish – the minimalist programme]. Lund: Studentlitteratur.
Riemsdijk, Henk van. 1978. *A case study in syntactic markedness: The binding nature of prepositional phrases*. Dordrecht: Foris.
Sadock, Jerrold. 1998. A vestige of verb final syntax in Yiddish. *Monatshefte für deutschsprachige Literatur und Kultur* 90. 220–226
Santorini, Beatrice. 1992. Variation and change in Yiddish subordinate clause word order. *Natural Language and Linguistic Theory* 10. 595–640.
Santorini, Beatrice. 1993. Jiddisch als gemischte OV/VO-Sprache. In Werner Abraham & Josef Bayer (eds.), *Dialektsyntax*, 230–245 (Sonderheft 5, *Linguistische Berichte*). Opladen: Westdeutscher Verlag.
Schäfer, Roland. 2016. *Einführung in die grammatische Beschreibung des Deutschen*. 2nd and revised edn. Berlin: Language Science Press.
http://langsci-press.org/catalog/book/101 (accessed 28 November 2016).
Taraldsen, Tarald. 1983. *Parametric variation in Phrase Structure: A case study*. Tromsø: University of Tromsø dissertation.
Vikner, Sten. 1987. Case assignment differences between Danish and Swedish. In Robin Allan & Michael Barnes (eds.), *Proceedings of the Seventh Conference of Scandinavian Studies in Great Britain*, 262–281. London: University College London. www.hum.au.dk/engelsk/engsv/papers/vikn87a.pdf (accessed 28 November 2016).
Vikner, Sten. 1995. *Verb movement and expletive subjects in the Germanic languages*. Oxford: Oxford University Press.
Vikner, Sten. 2001a. Predicative adjective agreement. In Kirsten Adamzik & Helen Christen (eds.), *Sprachkontakt, Sprachvergleich, Sprachvariation: Festschrift für Gottfried Kolde*, 399–414. Tübingen: Niemeyer. www.hum.au.dk/engelsk/engsv/papers/vikn01b.pdf (accessed 28 November 2016).
Vikner, Sten. 2001b. *Verb movement variation in Germanic and Optimality Theory*. Tübingen: University of Tübingen Habilitationsschrift. www.hum.au.dk/engelsk/engsv/papers/viknhabi.pdf (accessed 28 Nov. 2016).
Vikner, Sten. 2003. Null objects under coordination in Yiddish and Scandinavian. In Lars-Olof Delsing, Cecilia Falk, Gunlög Josefsson & Halldór Ármann Sigurðsson (eds.), *Grammar in focus: Festschrift for Christer Platzack*, vol. II, 365–375. Lund: Dept. of Scandinavian Languages, University of Lund. www.hum.au.dk/engelsk/engsv/papers/vikn03a.pdf (accessed 28 November 2016).
Vikner, Sten. 2005. Immobile complex verbs in Germanic. *Journal of Comparative Germanic Linguistics* 8. 83–115. www.hum.au.dk/engelsk/engsv/papers/vikn05b.pdf (accessed 28 November 2016).
Vikner, Sten. 2007. Teoretisk og komparativ syntaks [Theoretical and comparative syntax]. In Henrik Jørgensen & Peter Widell (eds.), *Det bedre argument – Festskrift til Ole Togeby, 7. marts 2007* [The better argument - festschrift for Ole Togeby, March 7, 2007], 469–480. Aarhus: Wessel & Huitfeld. www.hum.au.dk/engelsk/engsv/papers/vikn07a.pdf (accessed 28 November 2016).

Vikner, Sten. 2014. Kan en konstituent være både subjekt og objekt på samme tid? – om indlejrede infinitivsætninger på dansk [Can a constituent be both a subject and an object at the same time? - on embedded infinitival clauses in Danish]. In Ole Togeby, Sten Vikner & Henrik Jørgensen (eds.): *Problemer og perspektiver i dansk syntaks – med Kristian Mikkelsen som anledning* [Problems and Perspectives in Danish Syntax - on the occasion of the 100th anniversary of *Dansk Ordföjningslære* (Danish syntax) by Kristian Mikkelsen], 171–191. Odense: Universitets-Jubilæets danske Samfund/Syddansk Universitetsforlag. www.hum.au.dk/engelsk/engsv/papers/vikn14a.pdf (accessed 28 November 2016).

Vinje, Finn-Erik. 1987. *Moderne Norsk – Råd og regler for praktisk språkbruk* [Modern Norwegian – advice and rules for the practical use of the language]. Oslo: Universitetsforlaget.

Williams, Edwin. 1981. On the notions lexically related and head of a word. *Linguistic Inquiry* 12(2). 245–274.

Wurmbrand, Susi. 1998. Heads or Phrases? Particles in particular. In Wolfgang Kehrein & Richard Wiese (eds.), *Phonology and morphology of the Germanic languages*, 267–295. Tübingen: Niemeyer.

Zeller, Jochen. 2001. *Particle verbs and local domains*. Amsterdam: John Benjamins.

Zifonun, Gisela, Ludger Hoffmann & Bruno Strecker (eds.). 1997. *Grammatik der Deutschen Sprache*. Berlin: Mouton de Gruyter.

Zwart, Jan-Wouter. 2011. *The syntax of Dutch*. Cambridge: Cambridge University Press.

Part III: **Comparative syntax: Language acquisition and change**

Lieven Danckaert
The loss of Latin OV: Steps towards an analysis

1 Introduction: Diagnosing object placement in Latin

This paper is concerned with the alternation between the word orders OV and VO in Latin. As is well known, in the Romance languages only the latter variant survives, but at this point little is known about why the OV-order was lost. As a starting point I will take the discussion of object placement in Latin offered in Danckaert (2017: chapter 3). As shown there, direct object noun phrases can appear in various positions in the Latin clause.[1] One can make a basic distinction between VP-internal and VP-external objects. Importantly, whether or not a given object appears VP-internally can only be diagnosed in clauses with an auxiliary and a non-finite verb, i.e. monoclausal environments in which the auxiliary lexicalizes some projection in the T-domain, and where the (non-finite) lexical verb occupies a lower position, plausibly one inside the (articulated) VP-layer.[2] In contrast, object placement in clauses with a single verb form are always (multiple ways) ambiguous. Consider why this is so.

Following among others Embick (2000) I will assume that the phrase structure of the minimal pair in (1) is not fundamentally different, in that both tokens involve a monoclausal domain with an equal amount of functional structure. In the a-example we see an OV-clause with the synthetic verb form *obtinuit* '(he) obtained', whereas the quasi-synonymous example in (1b) contains an analytic form of the deponent predicate *adipiscor* 'obtain', consisting of a (transitive) past participle and a finite BE-auxiliary:

(1) a. *imperi-um   obtin-u-it*
       supreme.authority-ACC obtain-PRF-3SG
       'He obtained authority.' (Liv. 9.34.1)

---

[1] In this paper I will not be concerned with direct objects that are unambiguously left-peripheral (on which, see Danckaert 2012), focusing only on those objects that appear in the TP or VP-layer.
[2] Throughout this paper I will informally use the term "verb phrase" (VP) as shorthand for a more complex structure involving more than one projection (see for instance the trees in (2) and (3)). Similarly, the labels "TP" and "CP" also refer to more elaborate structures (the inflectional layer and articulated left periphery respectively).

DOI 10.1515/9781501504037-015

b. *imperi-um*   *adept-us*   *est*
supreme.authority-ACC   obtained-NOM   be.PRS.3SG
'He obtained the empire.' (Tac. Ann. 2.42.3)

A first approximation of a structural representation of (1a) is given in (2a): I will further refine this analysis in section 3. The structure in (2a) features an articulated verb phrase consisting of three layers, with an a-categorial root at the bottom of the extended projection, a verbalizing head *v* right on top of that, and thirdly a Voice head which determines whether a given clause is transitive or not. In the case of transitive clauses, an agentive, external argument is present in SpecVoiceP. As can be observed, I take it that synthetic lexical verbs like *obtinuit* evacuate the verb phrase through repeated application of head movement, to end up in T°. The direct object *imperium* sits in its base position, which I take to be the complement position of the lexical root. Note that for reasons of space, here and in the remainder of this paper I do not represent bar levels of projections which do not have an overtly filled specifier: for instance, in (2a) (in which overt terminals are marked in boldface) VoiceP is represented as a leftward complement of T°, and this pair of nodes is immediately dominated by TP:[3]

(2) a.

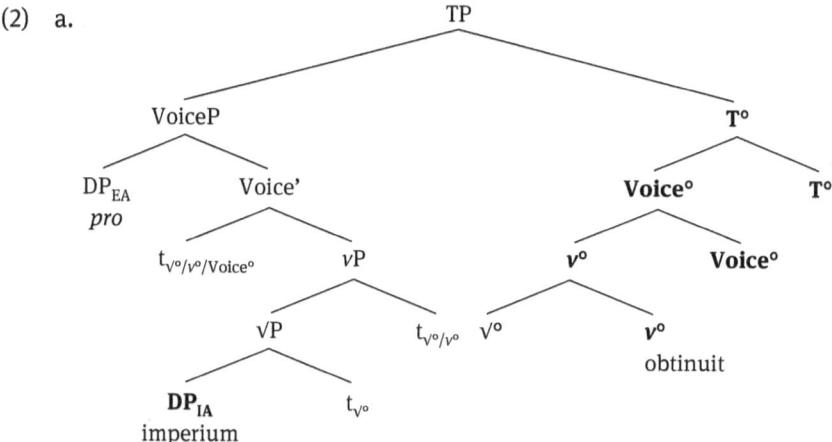

In contrast, in a clause with an analytic deponent verb, the T-node is lexicalized by a base generated auxiliary, and the lexical verb appears much lower

---

[3] For the sake of simplicity, here and elsewhere in this paper I represent complement-head sequences as base-generated as such rather than being derived through movement (which would be in line with the antisymmetric programme laid out in Kayne (1994)). Nothing crucially hinges on this.

in the structure. Again following Danckaert (2017), I assume that in the case of non-finite verbs the root head moves to *v* (but not to Voice). The structure of a clause like (1b) can thus be detailed as in (2b):

b.
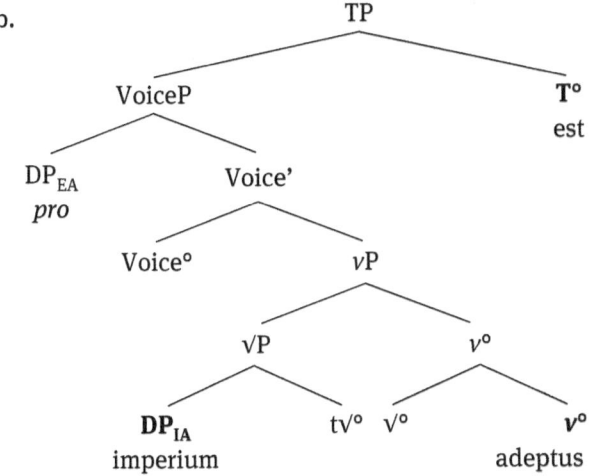

In other words, the synthetic/analytic alternation illustrated in (1) is not associated with a difference *qua* phrase structure, but rather, it involves two different lexicalization patterns of the same syntactic structure.

Consider now why monoclausal domains with more than one verb form provide us with more accurate information about object placement than clauses with a single verb. Imagine for instance that the structure of (1a) did not involve a head-final *v*P (as in (2a)), but rather a head-initial one, as in (3a), where T° is shorthand for an internally complex verbal head (cf. (2a)):

(3) a.
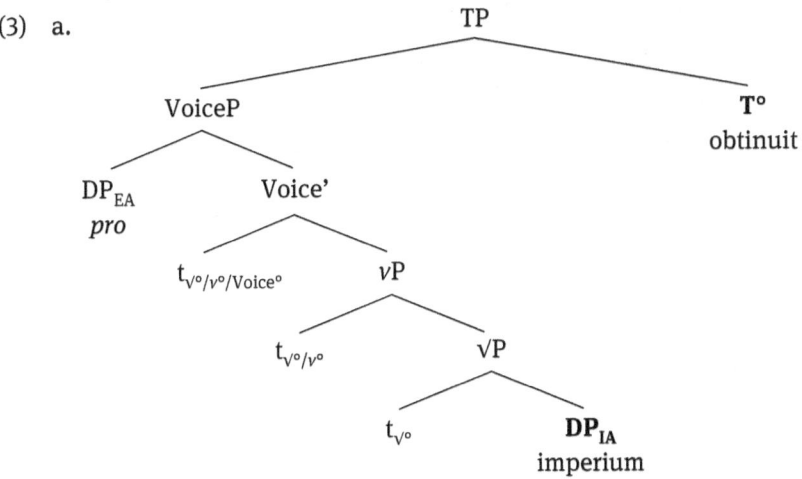

Importantly, although there is a clear structural difference between (2a) and (3a) (head-final *v*P vs. head-initial *v*P), this difference is not reflected in the linear string. However, in the case of clauses with an analytic deponent verb, changing the headedness of *v*P does in fact translate into a different surface word order. More specifically, a structure like (3b) yields the order VOAux rather than OVAux (2b):

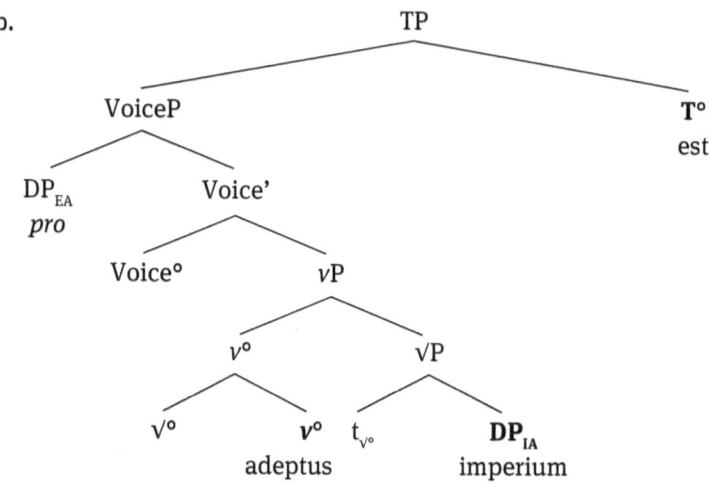

In other words, in the absence of a second verb form, it is impossible to tell apart VP-internal OV from VP-internal VO. Therefore, I will only take into account data from clauses with a direct object, an auxiliary and a non-finite verb. Crucially, it is important to make sure that a given selection of clauses with an auxiliary only contains monoclausal domains which only differ in the number of overtly lexicalized verb forms they feature, and not in the number of possible object positions. As argued at length in Danckaert (2017), two such environments are available in Latin, namely (i) clauses with an analytic deponent verb of the type exemplified in (1b), and (ii) clauses with a modal verb (*possum* 'be able' or *debeo* 'have to') (on the monoclausal status of the latter environment, see Danckaert 2017: 140–173).

Again as a first approximation, I will consider clauses featuring the orders OVAux and AuxOV to exemplify VP-internal OV, whereas the orders VOAux and AuxVO can be taken to involve VP-internal VO. I will refer to the grammar that generates VP-internal OV as the OV grammar, and to the one that gives rise to VP-internal VO as the VO grammar. I will adopt the "competing grammars" approach to language variation and change (Kroch 1989, 1994), which assumes that the language learner can acquire full competence in two or more grammars whose output is perhaps functionally, but not truth-conditionally distinct. As will be discussed in more detail in section 4, each competing grammar is associated with a different probability of usage. In the case at hand, we can safely assume that both the OV and the VO grammar were available to speakers of Latin throughout the entire period under investigation (viz. 200 BC – 600 AD).

Importantly, in clauses with more than one verb form we can also distinguish two types of VP-external objects. In VAuxO-clauses, we see a type of VP-external VO which I will call "extraposition". On the other hand, in clauses featuring the order OAuxV, the object can be said to have undergone leftward movement to a position outside the verb phrase, yielding a non-local type of OV which I will refer to as "object shift". Note that in many cases, two of the word order patterns that I classified earlier as VP-internal are actually structurally ambiguous, in that they could also involve a VP-external object. More particularly, OVAux-clauses are ambiguous between an [[OV]Aux] (VP-internal OV) and an [O [[t_O V]Aux] (VP-external OV) parse, and AuxVO-clauses can either be analysed as [Aux[VO]] (VP-internal VO), or as [Aux[V t_O]] O] (VP-external VO). I will come back to this particular issue in section 5.

In the following section, I will give a descriptive overview of the most important developments concerning object placement in the history of Latin, starting with VP-internal objects.

2 Object placement in the history of Latin: A descriptive overview

2.1 VP-internal OV and VO

The data to be presented in this and the following subsection are drawn from a corpus study of 38 Latin text samples (3.604.912 words) dating from ca. 200 BC to 600 AD.[4] From this corpus, I collected a sample of 6.365 clauses with an auxiliary (BE, *possum* or *debeo*), a transitive lexical verb, and an overt, non-left-peripheral direct object. I only included direct objects realized as a noun phrase or as a demonstrative pronoun (and thus excluding all personal pronouns functioning as a direct object, as well as all clausal objects). The full dataset as well as the R-code used to produce all graphs, tables and statistical tests are available at the following URL: https://opendata.uit.no/dataset.xhtml?persistentId=doi:10.18710/VWDJ1Y.

In Graph 1, I have plotted the diachronic development of VP-internal VO. More specifically, what is shown is the average frequency (in percentages) of the

---

[4] This is the same sample as the one used in Danckaert (2017), modulo the fact that the Vulgate was left out of account, as object placement in this text is quite different than in any other Late Latin text. I hope to address the topic of object placement in Biblical Latin in future work. Also, note that in Danckaert (2017) no pronominal objects (i.e. not even demonstratives) were taken into account.

word order patterns AuxVO and VOAux (as compared to the combined frequencies of the orders AuxOV and OVAux). In order to make sure that the estimated values are as accurate as possible, I excluded all data points which do not contain at least 20 clauses with an auxiliary and a VP-internal object.

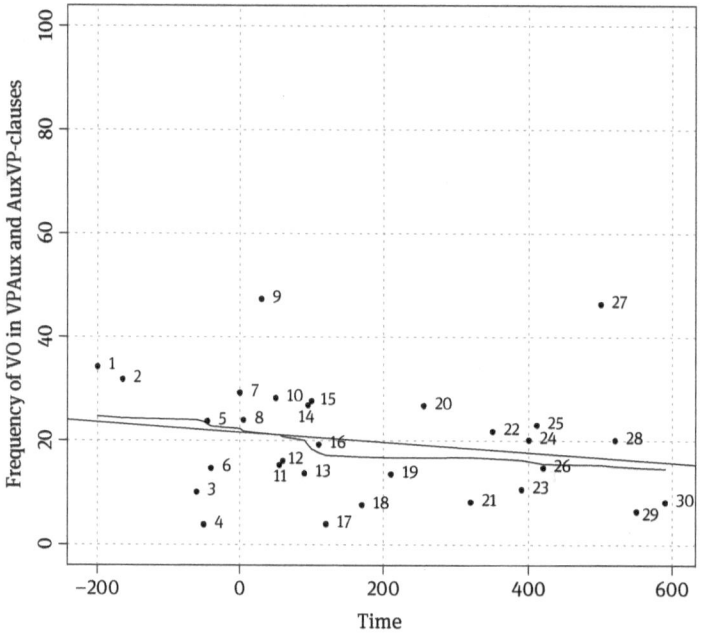

Graph 1: Frequency (in %) of the order VO in clauses with an auxiliary (BE or modal), unambiguously VP-external objects excluded, ca. 200 BC – 600 AD. Case labels: 1 = Plautus, 2 = Terence, 3 = Cicero, 4 = Caesar, 5 = Varro, 6 = Sallust, 7 = Vitruvius, 8 = Livy, 9 = Celsus, 10 = Seneca, 11 = Columella, 12 = Petronius, 13 = Frontinus, 14 = Quintilian, 15 = Pliny the Younger, 16 = Tacitus, 17 = Suetonius, 18 = Gaius, 19 = Tertullian, 20 = Cyprian, 21 = *Historia Augusta*, 22 = Palladius, 23 = Jerome, 24 = Augustine, 25 = *Gesta Conlationis Carthaginiensis*, 26 = Vegetius, 27 = Pompeius Maurus, 28 = Caesarius of Arles, 29 = Iordanes, 30 = Gregory.

Let me briefly comment upon what can be observed in this data set. First of all, recall that some of the tokens in this sample of VP-internal objects are actually structurally ambiguous: more particularly, some of the AuxVO-examples might well involve object extraposition, but as we will see below, there are reasons to assume that the amount of noise that this complicating factor adds to the data remains fairly constant over time. Second, throughout the entire period we see a fair amount of synchronic variation (spread above and below the regression lines), whose exact nature is at this point not well understood. In all likelihood, at a synchronic level the distribution of object noun phrases is to a large extent sensitive to the referentiality/information status of the object, as well as to for instance its syntactic category (full noun phrase vs. demonstrative pronoun), and related to this, its prosodic weight and internal complexity. Third, as suggested by both the straight and the smoothed regression lines, there does not seem to be any major diachronic development with respect to the frequency of the order VO, which remains constant at about 20%. If anything, the data reveal a minor decrease of the head-initial order.[5]

However, when we have a closer look at the data, it appears that this diachronic stability is only apparent. In particular, as shown in Graph 2, the development of the VO pattern is very different in VPAux and in AuxVP-clauses. The most important observation is that in Late Latin, the order VO is highly dispreferred in VPAux-clauses, whereas it readily occurs in Late Latin AuxVP-clauses:[6]

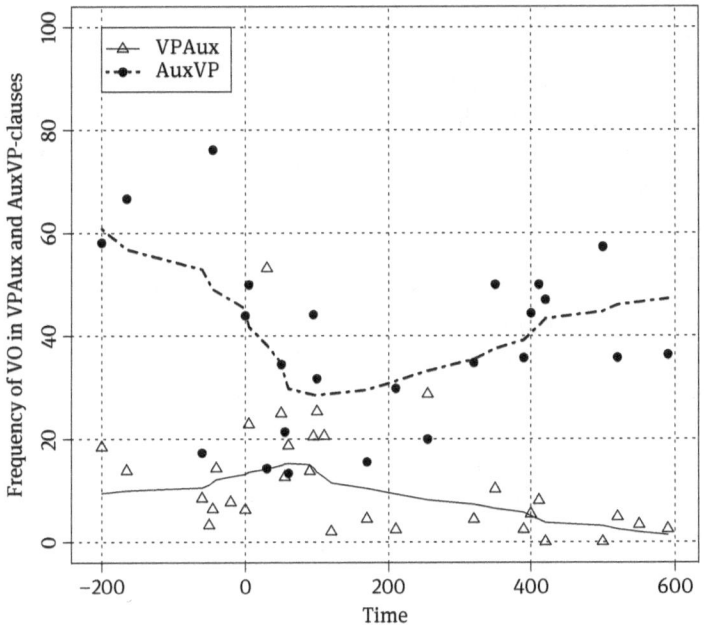

Graph 2: Frequency (in %) of the order VO in clauses with an auxiliary (BE or modal), VP-external objects excluded, ca. 200 BC – 600 AD. VPAux and AuxVP-clauses compared.

---

5 It is unlikely that this diachronic trend is significant: if we split up the data set in Graph 1 into two subsets, an earlier one with all the data points from before 200 AD, and a later one with the samples from after that date, and if we compare the average rates of VO in these two periods, it turns out that a slight difference in absolute terms (21.00% vs. 18.36%) is not statistically significant (independent samples t-test, p = .5324).
6 In Graph 2 I only included authors/texts for which my corpus contains a sufficient amount of clauses featuring an auxiliary, a transitive V and a (pro)nominal direct object in both AuxVP and VPAux-clauses (viz. a minimum of 12 tokens per type of clause).

As can be observed, in the case of VPAux-clauses the VO-order is the minority variant in all but one of the subsamples (viz. Celsus at 30 AD), and the only period in which the order VOAux is more or less productive is around the 1st century AD. Importantly, this pattern is strongly dispreferred by all authors after Cyprian (ca. 250 AD). The development of the VO pattern in AuxVP-clauses is more difficult to evaluate (partly because I only have information from four samples dating from before 0 AD). On the one hand, we observe very high values for three (very) early authors (viz. Plautus at 200 BC, Terence at 165 BC and Varro at 45 BC). On the other hand, if we were to abstract away from these data points, in the remainder of the texts there seems to be some upward trend. I leave it for future research to investigate whether taking into account a number of synchronic variables (see my earlier remarks) can help us to assess with more confidence if it is indeed the case that the factor Time is a good predictor to model the OV/VO alternation in AuxVP-clauses.

In any event, it seems clear that there is a marked contrast between the left-hand half of Graph 2 and the right-hand one. The most plausible way to interpret these facts would be to assume that the observed contrast is a reflex of a major shift from one grammatical system to another. In what follows, I will refer to these two systems as Grammar A and Grammar B, which I take to be in competition with one another in the same way as the OV and the VO grammar. As will be elaborated on in section 3, we can assume that Grammar A was more prevalent in the early stages of the period documented in my corpus, and that Grammar B is more strongly represented in later times. The transition from A to B has no doubt been a gradual process, but given the fairly sharp contrast between the first and the last four centuries in Graph 2, it seems to be the case that the spread of Grammar B (and the concomitant demise of Grammar A) accelerated quite fast at some point before 200 AD. One can hypothesize that Grammar B was available (but perhaps used at very low frequencies) from the earliest texts onwards, but as ever, it is impossible to tell when exactly this new grammar was first actuated.

2.2 VP-external OV and VO

I now turn to two types of VP-external object placement, namely object extraposition (which results in a linear VO-sequence) and object shift (a type of non-local OV). As mentioned, a given OV or VO-sequence is often structurally ambiguous between a VP-internal and a VP-external parse, which is why I will pay special attention to the way in which object extraposition and object shift can be distinguished from structures involving a VP-internal object.

2.2.1 Object extraposition

I will start by discussing object extraposition, which for now I will informally define as the occurrence of a direct object DP in a clause-final position, without this DP being located inside the VP, a characterization that I will further refine in section 5.1.2. Roughly speaking, there are two families of analyses of XP extraposition, one involving right adjunction to TP (or to some other maximal projection in the articulated middle field, or even in the left periphery), and one involving leftward movement of the "extraposed" constituent, followed by remnant movement of some portion of the extended verb phrase (as in Kayne 1994). Here I will not take a stance as to which analysis is on the right track.

As mentioned, in Latin object extraposition can only be observed in VPAux-clauses: whenever we find the order VAuxO, we can be sure that the object has been extraposed. In contrast, in AuxVP-clauses it is much more difficult to diagnose extraposition, as many AuxVO patterns are (at least) two-ways ambiguous: I will return to this point in section 5.

Importantly for the study of the OV/VO alternation, in VAuxO-clauses it is impossible to determine the headedness of *v*P, and as a result this type of clause does not inform the language learner about the genuine competition between the OV and the VO grammar (as defined above). As shown in (4) (a representation of (5a), in which for the sake of simplicity a rightward movement analysis of extraposition is assumed), it is not clear whether the base position of the direct object *reum* is to the left or to the right of the lexical verb:

(4)
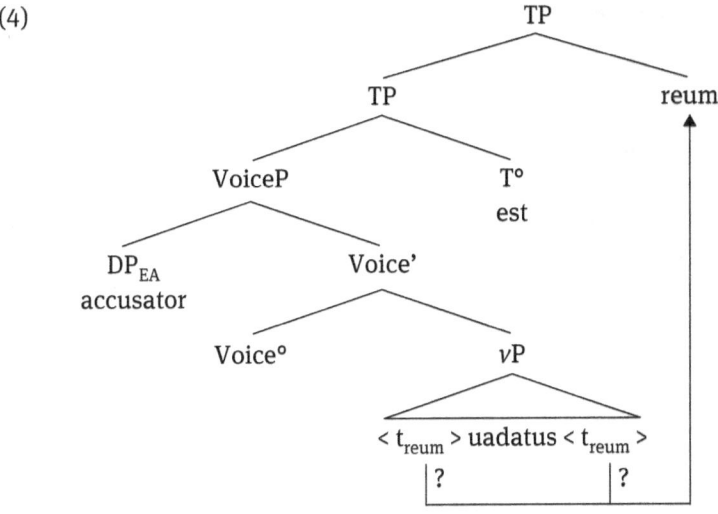

Given our current state of knowledge, there is close to nothing we know about the synchronic determinants of object extraposition. For one thing, it is not clear whether an extraposed object DP is systematically associated with a particular information status (old or new information, afterthought,…). In any event, it does not seem to be the case that only prosodically heavy constituents can be extraposed (still assuming an informal characterization of this phenomenon). Consider for instance the two examples in (5). Although longer DPs, such as the (bracketed) modified direct object in (5b), are perhaps more likely to be extraposed, a short bare noun such as *reum* '(the) accused' can also occur to the right of a VAux-sequence (5a):

(5) a. *Tot   uad-ibus   accusator   uadat-us*
       so.many   guarantees-ABL   prosecutor.NOM   admitted.to.bail-NOM.M.SG
       est   re-um.
       be.PRS.3SG   accused-ACC
       'With so many guarantees the prosecutor admitted the accused to bail.'
       (Liv. 3.13.8)

   b. *Complex-us   es   [funest-um   illud   animal*
       embraced-NOM.M.SG be.PRS.2SG deadly-ACC   this.ACC.N.SG animal.ACC
       ex   nefari-is   stupr-is,   ex   civil-i   cruor-e,
       out.of horrible-ABL sexual.misconduct-ABL out.of civil-ABL blood-ABL
       ex   omn-i   sceler-um   inportunitat-e   concret-um].
       out.of all-ABL   crimes-GEN   relentlessness-ABL   composed-ACC
       'You embraced this deadly monster, composed of horrible misconduct, civil bloodshed, and all sorts of perverse crimes.' (Cic. Pis. 21)

I will return to this last point in section 5.1.2 below, where I will suggest that the two examples in (5) represent two fundamentally different types of object extraposition, which are presumably associated with different semantic and/or pragmatic properties.

Let us now have a look at the diachronic development of object extraposition in Latin. Graph 3 shows the relative frequency of this pattern over time, compared to the (combined) incidence of the orders OVAux and VOAux (all averages calculated on the basis of samples consisting of at least 21 clauses):

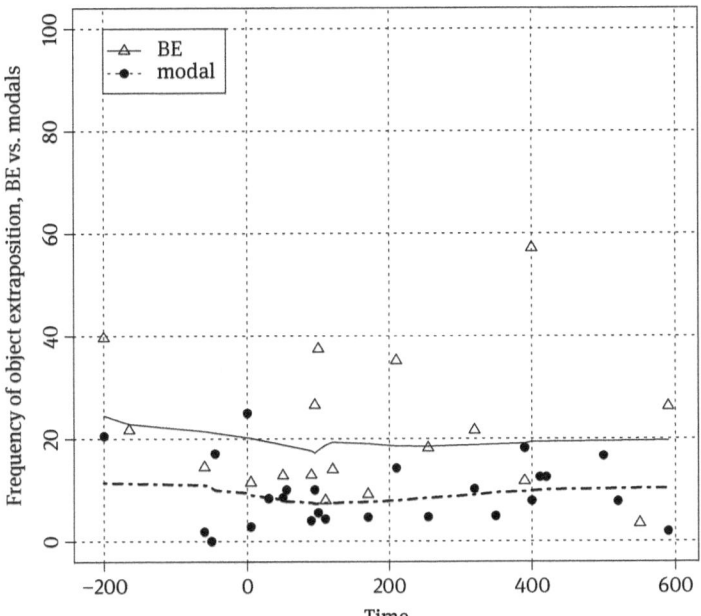

Graph 3: Frequency (in %) of the order VAuxO, ca. 200 BC – 600 AD. Clauses with a BE-auxiliary and a modal compared.

As can be observed, I have plotted the data for clauses with a BE-auxiliary and with a modal separately, as the two conditions do not exactly pattern alike, the rate of object extraposition being on average about twice as high in clauses with a transitive deponent predicate. In any event, there does not seem to be any major diachronic development with respect to the availability of noun phrase extraposition, in either condition. When we compare the incidence of extraposition in the earlier period (all texts until 200 AD) with the corresponding data for the later period, we see that the phenomenon is slightly more frequent in the second period (a mean frequency 12.87% in the earlier period, compared to 15.88% in the later one), but as can be expected, this difference is not statistically significant (independent samples t-test, p = .3916).[7] The two boxplots in Graph 4 visualize this comparison perhaps more clearly, where the horizontal lines inside the boxes represent the median (rather than the mean) of each group:

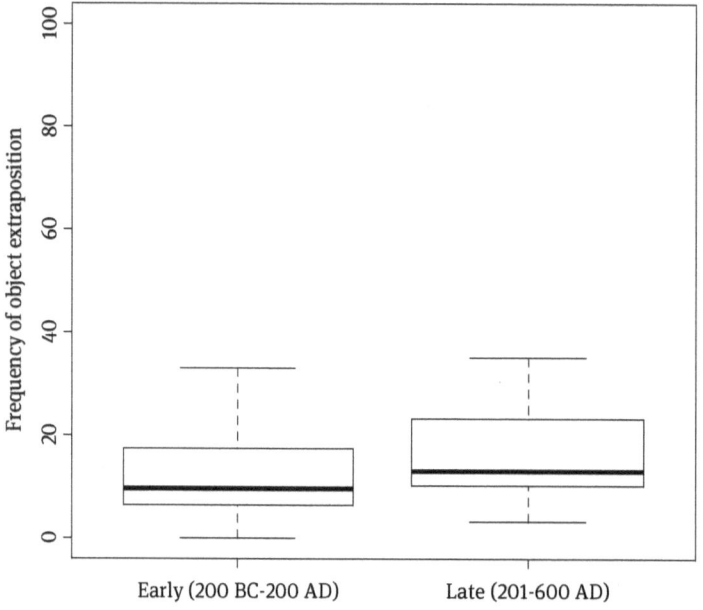

Graph 4: Frequency (in %) of the order VAuxO, early and late period compared.

On the basis of the data reviewed in the past section, we can conclude that it is unlikely that the phenomenon of object extraposition is in any crucial way related to the eventual decline of the OV-order. For a similar observation on extraposition in the history of Yiddish, see Santorini (1993). I will now proceed to show that the facts pertaining to the diachrony of object shift are perhaps more interesting.

2.2.2 Object shift

The second pattern of VP-external object placement is a type of non-local OV, which can be diagnosed unambiguously whenever we find the order OAuxV. I will refer to this pattern as "object shift", without prejudging anything about the

---

[7] Note that I am lumping together the data for the two auxiliary types.

discourse interpretation of the phenomenon (I could alternatively have called it "scrambling"), and without implying that the analysis of the Latin data is to be assimilated to comparable middle field phenomena in present day Germanic languages. An example is given in (6), and a (simplified) structure of this word order pattern involving left adjunction to TP is given in (7):[8]

(6) Denique ex   bellic-a   uictori-a   non fere   quemquam
    then   from military-ABL victory-ABL not almost   anyone.ACC
    est   inuidi-a   ciu-ium   consecut-a.
    be.PRS.3SG jealousy-NOM citizens-GEN followed-NOM.F.SG
    'Almost nobody has incurred the hatred of fellow citizens after a victory in war.' (Cic. Sest. 51)

(7)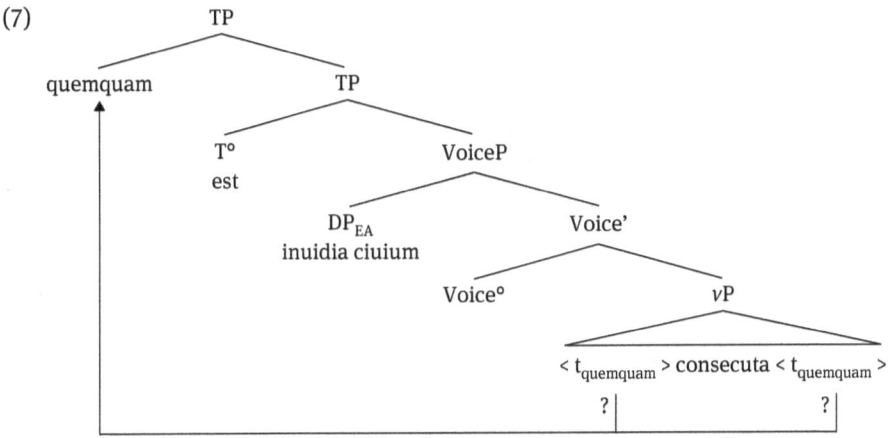

Before I turn to the diachronic development of this word order pattern, a few comments are in order concerning Late Latin BE-auxiliaries. As pointed out in Danckaert (2016, 2017: chapter 6), in Late Latin periphrastic verb forms consisting of a form of *esse* 'be' and a (passive or deponent) past participle show a very strong – and unexpected – preference for appearing in the head-final order PaPa-Aux. As a result, data about object placement in AuxVP-clauses with an analytic deponent verb in Late Latin are scarce, and therefore difficult to interpret. More particularly, for the entire last 400 years in the corpus, I only found 74 AuxVP-clauses with a nominal direct object in clauses with a BE-auxiliary, compared to

---

8 Alternatively, one could of course assume a structure with movement to the specifier of a dedicated functional projection. In the present context nothing hinges on this. For discussion of an additional type of object movement which targets a position below T (and I which I will refer to as short-distance object scrambling), see sections 5.1.1 and 5.1.2.3.

289 tokens in the first four centuries. In contrast, in clauses with a modal verb, no such "small sample size issue" arises at all:

Tab. 1: Object placement in AuxVP-clauses with a BE-auxiliary and a modal (absolute frequencies)

	Early (200 BC – 200 AD)		Late (201 – 600 AD)	
	BE	modal	BE	modal
AuxVO	28	185	11	251
AuxOV	24	412	5	349
OAuxV	237	309	58	487
Totals:	289	906	74	1087

For this reason, I will illustrate the diachronic development of object shift on the basis of data from clauses with a modal verb. The basic picture is given in Graph 5, which shows the relative frequency of the order OAuxV (as compared to the combined frequencies of the orders AuxOV and AuxVO) in 23 data points in my corpus with a least 20 clauses with a modal verb, a transitive V and a (pro)nominal direct object:

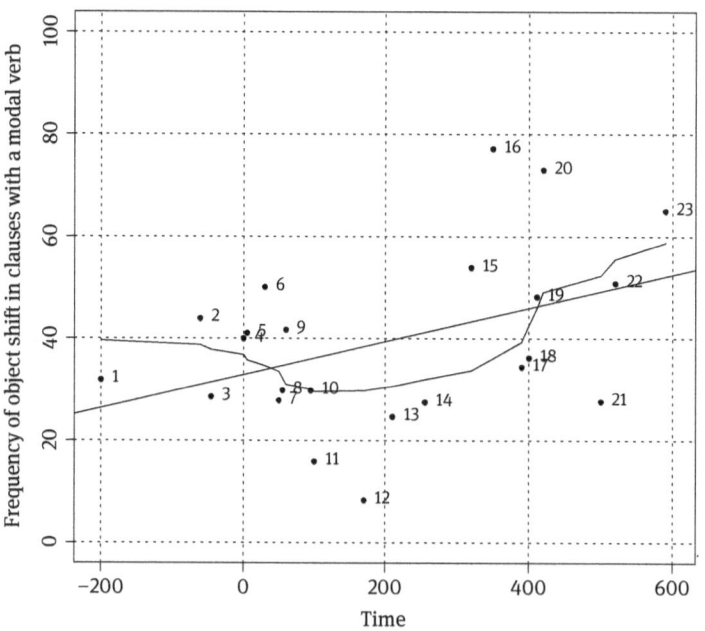

Graph 5: Frequency (in %) of the order OAuxV in clauses with a modal verb, ca. 200 BC – 600 AD. Case labels: 1 = Plautus, 2 = Cicero, 3 = Varro, 4 = Vitruvius, 5 = Livy, 6 = Celsus, 7 = Seneca, 8 = Columella, 9 = Petronius, 10 = Quintilian, 11 = Pliny the Younger, 12 = Gaius, 13 = Tertullian, 14 = Cyprian, 15 = *Historia Augusta*, 16 = Palladius, 17 = Jerome, 18 = Augustine, 19 = *Gesta Conlationis Carthaginiensis*, 20 = Vegetius, 21 = Pompeius Maurus, 22 = Caesarius of Arles, 23 = Gregory.

As suggested by the discrepancy between the trajectories of the smoothed and the straight regression lines, the diachronic trend in this data set is partly obscured by a great amount of synchronic variation, but it seems clear enough that the incidence of object shift does not remain constant over time. Rather, object shift appears to be more frequent in the later centuries.

This is confirmed when we adopt a cruder time measure and simply compare the average rate of object shift in the earlier period with the corresponding value for the later period:

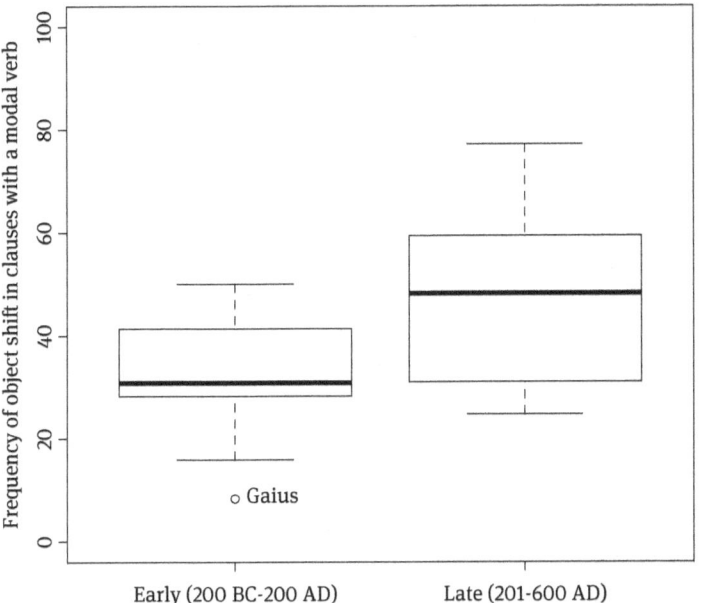

Graph 6: Frequency (in %) of the order OAuxV, early and late period compared.

In the first period, the mean rate of application of object shift is 32.40%, compared to 47.13% in the later one. This difference can be shown to be statistically significant (independent samples t-test, p = .03977).

2.3 Interim summary

To sum up this descriptive section, we can say that despite the fact that the overall rate of VO does not increase during the lifespan of the Latin language, there is good evidence that syntax of object placement does not remain constant throughout the 800 years studied. First, in Late Latin the availability of the order VO clearly becomes sensitive to the headedness of the T-node (or whatever functional projection BE-auxiliaries and modal verbs are located in) (cf. Graph 2). Second, we have also seen that there is a change concerning one particular pattern of VP-external object placement, viz. the OAuxV-order which I referred to as "object shift" (Graphs 5 and 6). On the other hand, the rate of object extraposition cannot be shown to change over time (Graphs 3 and 4).

In the remainder of this paper, I would like to explore the idea that the object shift data – despite leading to higher frequencies of surface OV – can shed light on the eventual loss of VP-internal OV: both phenomena can be thought to follow from a more general reorganization of the structure of the Latin clause. In section 3, I will start by elaborating on the properties of Grammar A and Grammar B, and I will show how these two systems differ with respect to possible patterns of object placement. Next, in section 4 I will introduce Yang's (2000, 2002) model of language change, which makes crucial reference to the notion of competing grammars mentioned earlier. Finally, in sections 5 and 6 I will apply this model to the diachrony of Latin object placement. I will argue that the conditions under which the OV grammar can be cued are very different in Classical and in Late Latin, and that it is ultimately the shift from Grammar A to Grammar B that caused the VO grammar to prevail. I will also propose that the increased frequency of object shift is to be understood as a side effect of this same change in clause structure.

3 Latin clause structure in diachrony

In this section I provide an overview of the main properties of Grammar A and Grammar B, i.e. the older and the more innovative grammatical system that I distinguished on the basis of visual inspection of Graph 2. The discussion is entirely based on Danckaert (2017), to which the reader is referred for further details and references.

3.1 Grammar A

The core idea is that the parametric difference between Grammar A and Grammar B is related to the way in which the EPP requirement is satisfied. As a starting point I will adopt the idea that there is a functional head in the articulated T-field which bears an EPP-feature. Simply put, the syntax has to insert an element endowed with φ-features in that particular locus of the clause. Following among others Alexiadou and Anagnostopoulou (1998), Biberauer (2003) and Biberauer and Roberts (2005) I will assume that there are multiple syntactic mechanisms available to satisfy a clause's EPP requirement. In a nutshell, the relevant requirement can either be satisfied by means of V-movement, DP-movement, or expletive insertion. In addition, moving verbs or DPs can also pied-pipe other phrasal material, leading to a derivation in which an entire VP is displaced, much along the lines of Haegeman (2000).[9] Finally, EPP-checking through V-movement (without pied-piping) goes hand in hand with optional (discourse-driven) subject movement. The reader is referred to the references mentioned as well as to Danckaert (2017) for further discussion.

Against the backdrop of this parametric system, it was proposed in Danckaert (2017) that Grammar A employs the mechanism of VP movement to satisfy the clause's EPP requirement. To be more precise, what is probed for is the hierarchically highest nominal argument in the extended verb phrase, and when undergoing movement this element pied-pipes the entire verb phrase. The basic structure of such a derivation looks like in (8), which is a more accurate representation of a Classical Latin INFL-final clause than the one given earlier in (2a). In this structure, EPP-driven VP movement effectively derives the VPAux order characteristic of especially Early and Classical Latin.

(8)

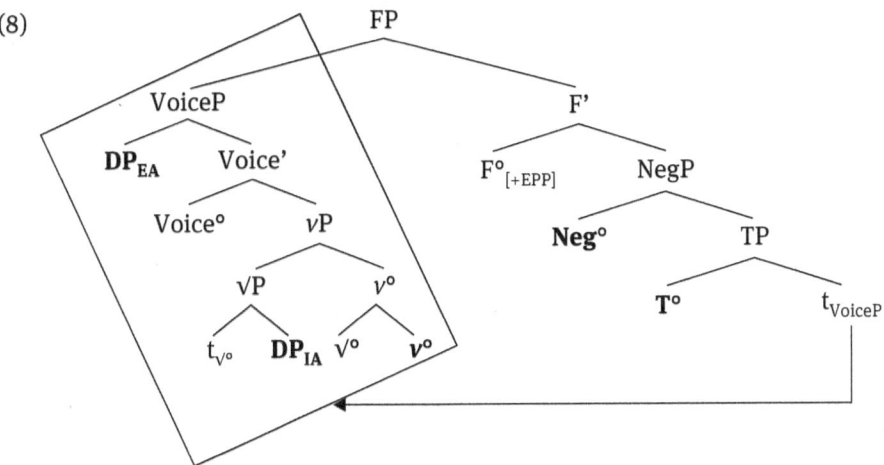

---

9 For a very comparable proposal on Latin, see also Mackenzie & van der Wurff (2012).

As can be observed, I am assuming that an EPP feature is located in a projection that I labelled "FP", without further committing myself to the exact nature of this functional head. In any event, one has to assume that the relevant instance of VP movement is not strictly local, as there clearly is functional structure present between the launching and the landing site of the moved VP (at least T and Neg, witness the availability of VP-Neg-Aux orders). Note also that under this analysis, subject DPs do not undergo A-movement, but remain in their base position (unless of course they are A'-moved at a later stage of the derivation, cf. section 5.1.1). Importantly, to the best of my knowledge there is no positive evidence for there being more than one non-left-peripheral position for (preverbal) subjects in Grammar A.[10] In other words, in this grammar all unambiguously non-left-peripheral preverbal subjects should be located inside the verb phrase. I will come back to this in section 3.3.

One important consequence of this analysis is that the structure derived through EPP-driven movement is not subject to the Final-Over-Final-Constraint (FOFC) as defined by Biberauer, Holmberg, and Roberts (2014), which rules out all (and only) structures in which a head-final projection dominates one or more head-initial projections (in the same extended projection). Now recall that up until the beginning of the second century AD, VO-orders in VPAux-clauses are attested at fairly high frequencies in Latin (cf. Graph 2), which suggests that the VOAux-orders thus created do not involve a VP which is dominated by (the highest node of) TP. Rather, if we assume that VPAux-orders in Grammar A do indeed involve non-local displacement, it follows that the external syntax of the VP has no influence on the availability of OV and VO-orders.

Before moving on to discussing the properties of Grammar B, let me briefly comment on early occurrences of the order Aux-V. Given the assumed universal character of the EPP requirement, and given the lack of alternative mechanisms to satisfy the EPP in the context of Grammar A, it would follow that in this grammar, the verb phrase is moved past T in every single clause, yielding only V(P)-Aux orders. This conclusion is potentially at odds with the well-known fact that AuxVP-clauses are attested from the earliest texts onwards. However, as argued in Danckaert (2017: 238–240), there is evidence that at least some of these early AuxVP-orders are in fact derived by means of VP movement and subsequent auxiliary fronting. Such a structure would look like (9):

---

10 One way to further test whether this is indeed the case would be to look at placement of subjects with respect to adverbs (in VOAux-clauses, generated by Grammar A). Note that there is good evidence that in Classical Latin external arguments can appear below VP adjuncts (Danckaert 2017: 234–235).

(9)
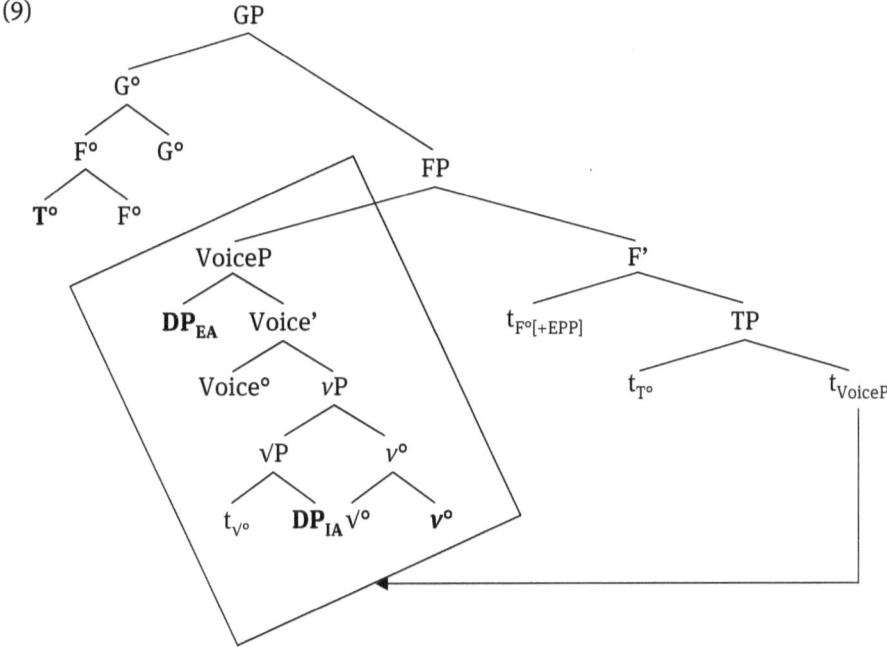

As we will see below, such a structure is often very difficult to distinguish from the output of Grammar B (in which AuxVP-orders can be base-generated), and in actual practice it is impossible to decide on a case to case basis whether a given AuxVP-clause was generated by Grammar A or by Grammar B. Suffice it to say that both grammars could produce similar surface orders, but we can expect auxiliary fronting to be used more often in earlier times.

3.2 Grammar B

In order to account for the data summarized in Graph 2 ("loss of VOAux"), it was proposed in Danckaert (2017) that the VPAux output of Grammar A was reanalysed as a (string identical) structure in which the verb phrase and the T-node hosting auxiliaries and synthetic finite verbs are in a more local configuration. More particularly, the details of the proposed reanalysis can be summarized as in (10):[11]

(10) a. [$_{FP}$ [$_{VoiceP}$ S O V] [$_{F,[EPP]}$ [$_{TP}$ Aux t$_{VoiceP}$]]] Grammar A
 b. [$_{SubjP}$ <S> [$_{Subj,}$ [$_{FP}$ [$_{TP}$ [$_{VoiceP}$ <S> O V] t$_{Aux}$] Aux]]] Grammar B

---

11 Clauses with only one verb were of course reanalysed in a similar fashion.

A more detailed structure of a VPAux-clause in Grammar B is given in (11). As indicated, the main difference between Grammar A and Grammar B concerns the way in which the EPP requirement is satisfied: in the new grammar, it is the hierarchically highest verb which head moves to F°.

(11)
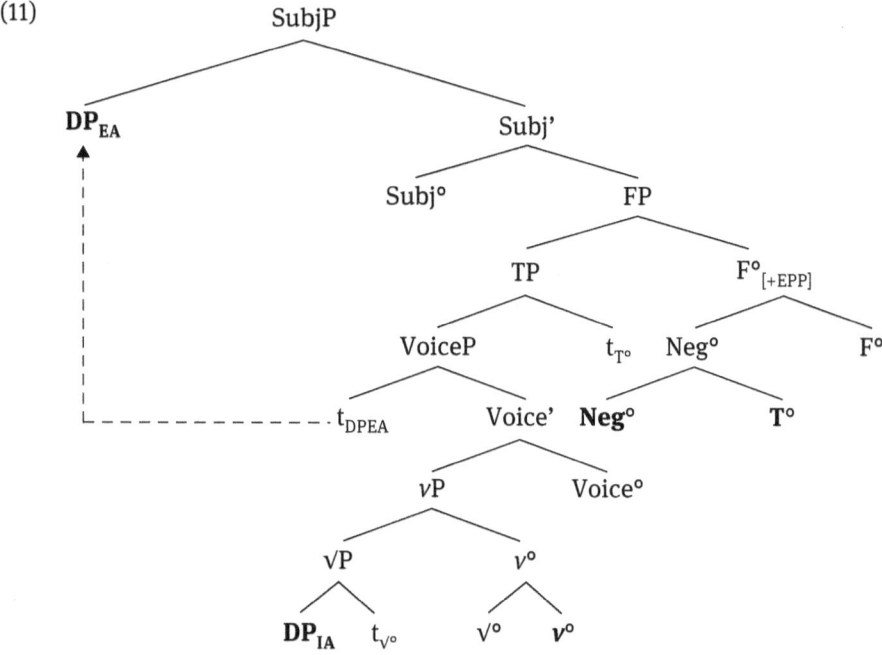

As argued in Danckaert (2017), the ultimate cause of the reanalysis is related to the diachronic development of the preverbal negator. As can be seen in (11), the F°-node is occupied by a complex head consisting of T and a proclitic negator. The reader is referred to Danckaert (2017: 248–252) for additional discussion of the role of negation in bringing about the shift from Grammar A to Grammar B.

Importantly, note that I assume that it is possible for the subject DP (the external argument in a transitive clause) to evacuate the verb phrase and move to a dedicated subject position in the high TP (but lower than the left periphery). I assume that this projection can be equated to Cardinaletti's (2004) SubjP (see also Rizzi 2006). I will come back to the reasons that prompt me to postulate the availability of this additional A-position in Grammar B in section 3.3. In any event, note that in this new grammar all VPAux-orders (abstracting away from left-peripheral VP movement) involve a structure in which VP is dominated by TP (and where TP is dominated by FP). Importantly, such a structure is correctly predicted to be subject to FOFC, and we thus correctly derive the quasi-absence of VOAux-orders in Late Latin (i.e. at the stage in which Grammar B is the dominant grammar).

Given that in Grammar B VP movement is no longer required to arrive at a well-formed syntactic structure, we also expect AuxVP-orders to be available much more freely than in Grammar A. In terms of sheer frequency of occurrence, this does indeed seem to be the case: for instance, in clauses with a modal verb and an infinitive we clearly see that the order "modal-infinitive" becomes more frequent as time goes by (Danckaert 2016, 2017).[12] One can then think that in Grammar B, the structure of an AuxVP-clause is essentially the same as the one of a VPAux-clause like (11), modulo the headedness of a number of projections in the lower part of the clause (or alternatively, the presence vs. absence of roll-up movement):

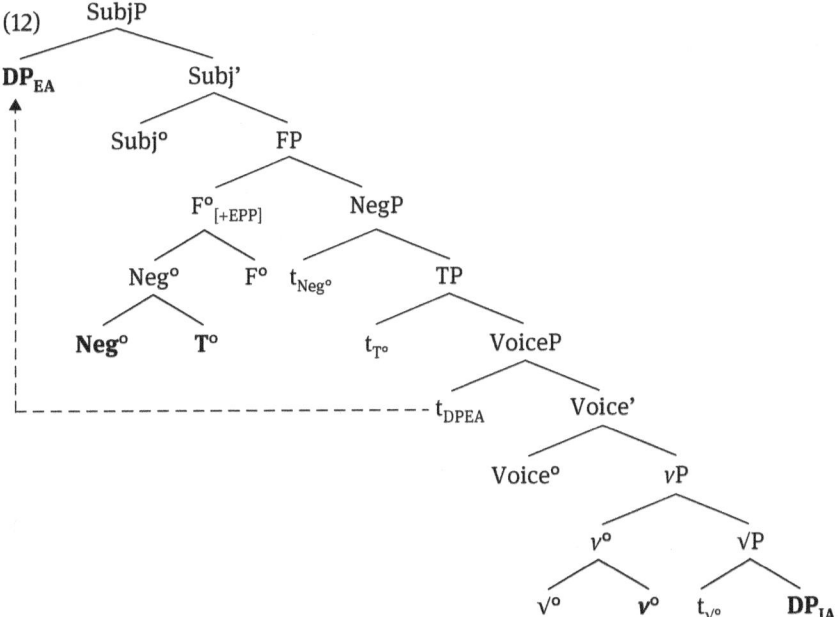

---

[12] But as documented in Danckaert (2017: chapter 6), no such increase in AuxVP-orders can be observed in the case of (passive and deponent) BE-periphrases.

Here too I assume that subjects can optionally undergo A-movement, much in the spirit of Alexiadou and Anagnostopoulou's (1998) proposals about present day Romance. In the case of Late Latin, there can be little doubt about the non-left-peripheral character of this subject position, given the fact that a preverbal subject typically appears to the right of subordinating conjunctions, which according to Danckaert (2012) can be considered a reliable diagnostic to distinguish left-peripheral from TP-internal material (see also section 5.1.1 on this last point).

As the proposed difference between Grammar A and Grammar B concerning the availability of TP-internal subject positions will play a crucial role in the upcoming discussion, I will now present some evidence in support of this proposal.

3.3 The distribution of internal arguments in Grammar A and Grammar B

One interesting contrast between early and later Latin concerns the distribution of internal arguments in active and passive clauses (see also Danckaert 2014). Assuming this contrast to be a reflex of the fact that Grammar A is being replaced by Grammar B, we can hypothesize that the observed contrast is related to the availability of (optional) A-movement for subjects in Grammar B (and the absence thereof in Grammar A).

The basic facts are summarized in Graph 7. The two boxplots on the left show data on placement of direct objects in AuxVP-clauses, which as we have seen is the only environment in which VP-internal (Aux-IA-V) and VP-external (IA-Aux-V) internal arguments can be told apart. The two boxes on the right summarize the corresponding data for internal arguments in passive clauses, i.e. derived subjects.[13] What is measured is the average rate of the order "IA-Aux-V", as opposed to the incidence of AuxVP-clauses in which the internal argument appears lower than the auxiliary (i.e. all clauses exhibiting the orders "Aux-IA-V" and "Aux-V-IA"):

---

13 For reasons spelled out in section 2.2.2, especially in Late Latin it is difficult to obtain reliable results for clauses with a BE-auxiliary, which is why I only consider clauses with a modal verb. For both active and passive clauses I only took into account samples with at least 20 AuxVP-clauses with an overt passive subject.

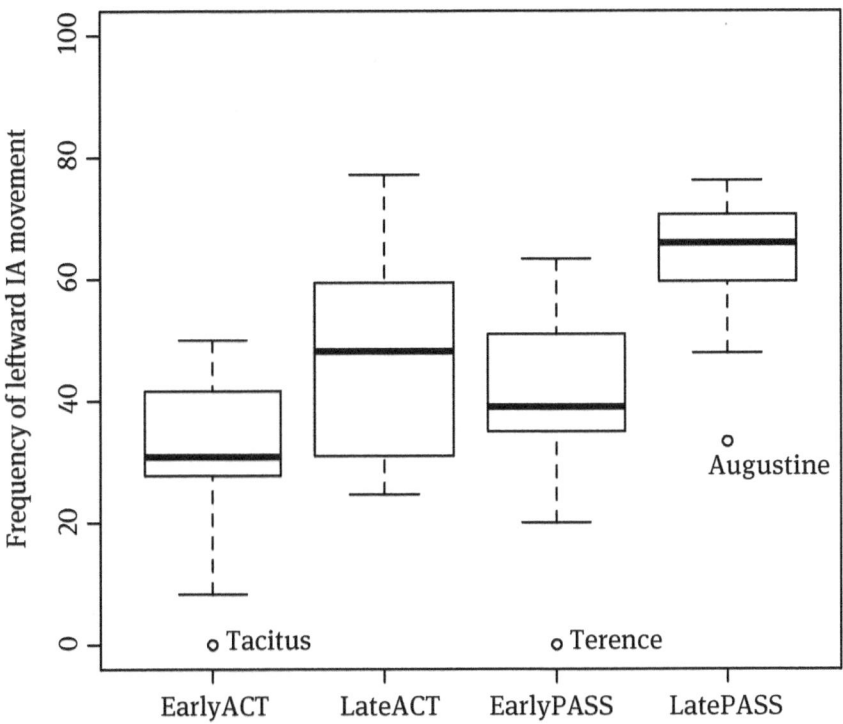

Graph 7: Frequency (in %) of leftward movement of internal arguments in active and passive clauses.

As we saw earlier, the rate of object shift (OAuxV) increases over time. In Graph 7 we now also see that a similar effect obtains for passive subjects, but apparently a bit more strongly so: whereas there is substantial overlap between the space covered by the two left-hand boxes, no such overlap can be observed for passive subjects, suggesting that in Grammar B subjects evacuate the verb phrase more often than direct objects. The results of a logistic regression corroborate this conclusion. In a model predicting leftward movement of internal arguments in AuxVP-clauses, in which I included Time, Voice (active vs. passive), Type of auxiliary (*possum* vs. *debeo*), Type of clause (main vs. embedded) and Type of internal argument (full noun phrases vs. bare demonstrative pronouns) as independent variables, an interaction term between the predictors Time and Voice comes out as significant. The results of the relevant model are summarized in Tab. 2:

Tab. 2: Summary of a logistic model predicting leftward movement of internal arguments in clauses with a modal verb (200 BC – 590 AD)

Coefficients:	Estimate (log odds)	Standard error	Significant? (p-value)
(Intercept)	−0.4946488	0.1595408	0.001932 (**)
Time	0.0007365	0.0002026	0.000279 (***)
Voice:Passive	0.7272785	0.2209584	0.000997 (***)
Auxiliary:*possum*	0.1011143	0.1610798	0.530182
Clausetype:Main	0.1118976	0.1686109	0.506918
IAtype:pronoun	0.7562841	0.1263615	2.16e-09 (***)
Time*Voice:Passive	0.0009404	0.0004226	0.026073 (*)
Voice:passive*Auxiliary:*possum*	−0.4737445	0.2189870	0.030515 (*)
Auxiliary:*possum**Clausetype:Main	−0.9570590	0.1925929	6.72e-07 (***)
Significance codes: '***': < 0.001; '**': < 0.01; '*': < 0.05; '.': < 0.1; ' ': > 01.			

As can be observed, passive clauses have a higher baseline probability of exhibiting leftward movement of internal arguments. In addition, the overall probability for internal arguments to evacuate the VP increases over time (cf. the positive log odds for the predictor Time). The crucial information can be found in the shaded row, where it is shown that the relative strength of the factor Voice increases over time, in such a way that it gradually favours subject movement more strongly than object movement.

This diachronic effect falls out naturally if we assume that subjects in Grammar B have an additional A-position at their disposal (viz. SubjP), which is not accessible for objects. Note however that this does not yet explain why the rate of object shift increases too: I will come back to this point at the end of section 5.

Before I return to the competition between the OV and VO grammar, I will first provide some additional details on the particular approach to language change that I will assume, namely the variational acquisition model proposed in Yang (2000, 2002).

4 Yang's variational acquisition model of language change

As mentioned in the beginning of this paper, I am assuming a grammar competition approach to language variation and change (Kroch 1989, 1995; Pintzuk 1999, 2003). In the case at hand, this approach entails that – presumably at all documented stages of the Latin language – both the OV and the VO grammar, and probably also both Grammar A and Grammar B were part of speakers' linguistic competence. Variation resides in the frequencies at which these two pairs of competing grammars were employed. In addition, it is conceivable that these different grammars were associated with different conditions of usage, although at present very little is known about this type of synchronic variation in Latin.

Yang (2000, 2002) provides a probabilistic algorithm to model the dynamics of two or more competing grammars, and to determine how successful a grammar is in parsing the data a language acquiring child is exposed to.[14] A crucial ingredient of his approach is the (among generative linguists very common) assumption that language change is essentially a discontinuous process, whereby a language acquiring child reanalyses (part of) the data that she is exposed to during the critical period, in the sense that she assigns a phrase structure analysis to a given surface string in the Primary Linguistic Data (PLD) which is different from the representation assumed by the speaker producing the relevant utterance (see Lightfoot 1979 and subsequent literature). In Yang (2000, 2002), each grammar G that a child has access to is taken to be associated with a probabilistic weight, which can be defined as the probability that the child will use G and not one of G's competitors to produce and parse utterances of a given language. More precisely, each time a child chooses grammar G_1 and successfully parses a sentence from the PLD, the weight of G_1 increases, and concomitantly, the weight of the competing grammar G_2 decreases. I refer to Yang (2000, 2002) for the mathematical details of this proposal.

Assuming a two-way competition between a grammar G_1 and a grammar G_2, we can distinguish three types of clauses in the PLD: (i) clauses that can only be generated by G_1, (ii) clauses that can only be generated by G_2 and (iii) clauses that are structurally ambiguous in that both grammars G_1 and G_2 can generate them. Yang (2000, 2002) then defines the "fitness" of a grammar G_1 as the proportion of clauses in the PLD that can only be generated by grammar G_1. It should be clear that it is data from structurally unambiguous clauses that determine the fitness of a pair of competing grammars.

Finally, we can characterize the "advantage" of a grammar G_1 over its competitor G_2 as the fitness of G_1 minus the fitness of G_2. Yang's approach predicts that in the long run, the fittest grammar will win out, unless independent factors bring about a change through which the fitness of G_1 and G_2 is recalibrated. The author emphasizes that the eventual success of a given grammar

---

14 For a recent application of this approach to language change (as well as a very clear exposition of its basic tenets), see Heycock & Wallenberg (2013).

does not crucially depend on the initial probabilistic weight of this grammar (say the frequency at which this grammar is used by speakers of a previous generation). Instead, even if a grammar starts out as a very small minority, from the moment that it generates a higher proportion of *unambiguous* clauses than any of its competitors, it is predicted to stand a good chance to eventually take over from the other grammar.

In what follows, I will apply this system to the competition between the Latin OV and VO grammars introduced in the opening sections of this paper.

5 Unambiguous evidence for VP-internal object placement

In order to estimate the fitness of the OV and the VO grammar at various stages of the Latin language, we first have to determine under which conditions both grammars were cued unambiguously. Importantly, these conditions differ quite strongly in the context of Grammar A and Grammar B, which I will therefore treat separately.

Before starting the discussion, let me add the disclaimer that given the remarkable degree of word order flexibility characteristic of Latin (for a brief demonstration, see Danckaert 2017: 3–9), the best one can do is try to control for structural ambiguity as much as possible. For some of the cases that I will take to involve "unambiguous OV" or "unambiguous VO" one could in principle imagine an alternative derivation involving (multiple instances of) remnant movement, but I take it that the criteria that I will use are restrictive enough to arrive at close enough an approximation of the actual rates of unambiguously VP-internal OV and VO.

5.1 Cueing object placement in Grammar A

5.1.1 The OV grammar

I will start by looking at unambiguous evidence for the OV grammar in a Grammar A setting. Recall that the basic structure for a transitive clause was proposed to look like (13), with EPP-driven VP movement to SpecFP, leaving all the verb's arguments *in situ* (that is, whenever these arguments do not further move to a specialized scope-discourse position above FP).

(13)
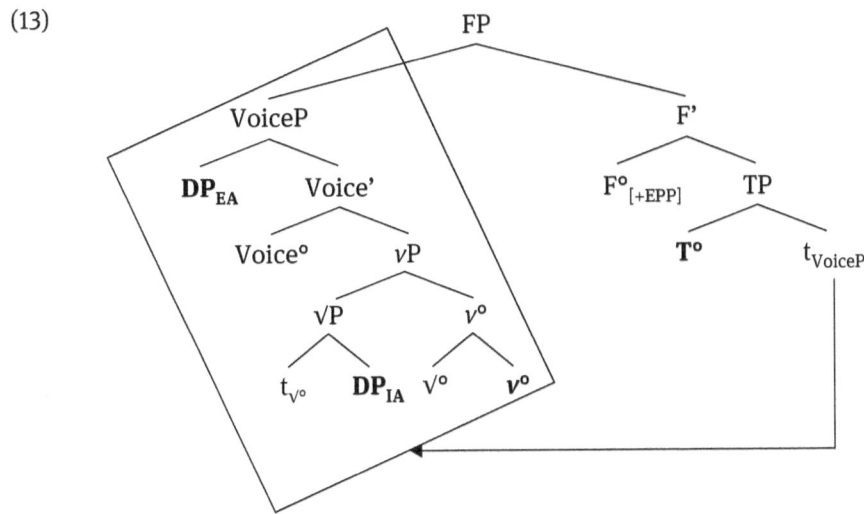

So under which conditions could the language learner be confident that a given OV-sequence was generated by the OV grammar? First of all, note that it is not necessary for there to be strict linear adjacency between O and V: depending on certain details concerning the articulation of the inner layers of the verb phrase, and in particular the way in which the various elements in a complex verb phrase are linearized, it is conceivable that for instance an indirect object DP or a PP argument ends up in between O and V. However, in order for a given direct object to be VP-internal, no material should intervene between O and V which we can be sure to be first merged higher than vP: such an element would indicate that the direct object has evacuated the thematic domain.

Let us first of all assume that external arguments are always first merged higher than internal arguments (given some version of UTAH). If so, the presence of a(n overt) preverbal external argument in an OVAux-clause could in principle serve as a diagnostic to signal the upper boundary of the thematic domain, and by this token it could constitute evidence for the VP-internal position of a given direct object. Needless to say, this can only be possible if the subject itself sits in its base position. In other words, what we need is the presence of an unambiguously non-left-peripheral preverbal subject to the left of O in an OV-clause. There are two diagnostics to further determine the exact location of a given subject argument (in the CP, TP or VP-layer), namely (i) subordinating conjunctions and question words in root interrogatives and (ii) (finite) auxiliaries.

As to the first, *wh*-words and conjunctions like *cum* 'when' and *si* 'if' can be taken to be located at the lower edge of the left periphery (FinP according to Danckaert 2012). By this token, any subject DP appearing to the left of such an element, such as *Caesar* 'Caesar' in (14), must be located in the left periphery (cf. (15)).[15] Given the islandhood of (tensed) adverbial clauses, we can be confident that the fronted element does indeed sit inside the embedded clause, and not in the superordinate domain.

(14) [*Caesar*   [*cum*   *ab*   *host-e*   *non*   *ampl-ius*   *passu-um*
      Caesar   when   from   enemy-ABL   not   far-COMP.ADV   steps-GEN
      XII   *mil-ibus*   *abes-se-t]]   *ut*   *era-t*
      twelve   thousands-ABL   be.away-IPFV.SBJV-3SG   as   be.IPFV-3SG
      constitut-um   *ad*   *eum*   *legat-i*   *reuert-untur*.
      decided-NOM.N.SG   to   him.ACC   ambassadors-NOM   return-PRS.3PL
      'When Caesar was less than twelve miles away from the enemy, the ambassadors returned to him, as had been determined.' (Caes. Gal. 4.11)

(15)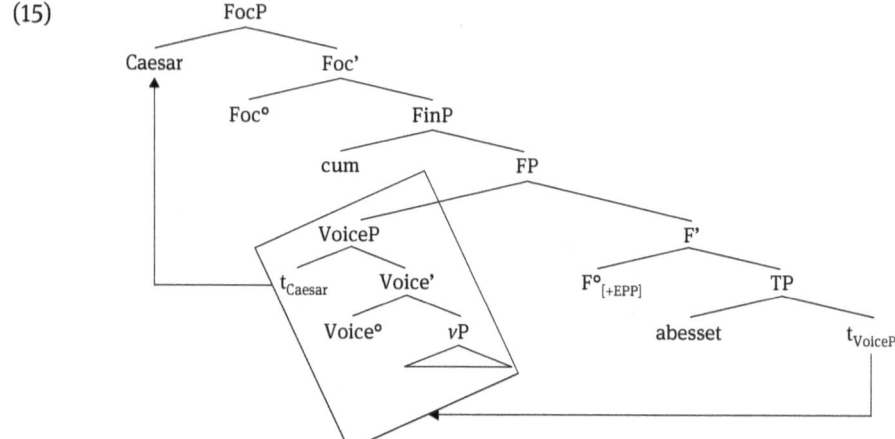

On the other hand, all subjects appearing lower than a clause-introducing element must be non-left-peripheral. Moreover, given that Grammar A does not have A-movement for subjects (i.e. movement targeting a position somewhere in the articulated T-field), all non-left-peripheral subjects should be VP-internal, and should therefore be a reliable diagnostic to identify VP-internal objects. For instance, for the specific case of an embedded OV-sequence like (16), in which the external argument intervenes between O and V, we can be sure that the direct object must have been displaced to a position higher than VoiceP:

---

15 Observe that the structure in (15) involves subextraction from a subject (complex specifier). As shown in Haegeman, Jiménez-Fernández & Radford (2014), although restricted under certain conditions, this operation is not categorically banned.

(16) sed si=ue fund-um locuple-s mercat-us est OSVAux
    but if=or farm-ACC rich-NOM.M.SG bought-NOM.M.SG be.PRS.3SG
    'but if a rich man has bought a farm' (Col. 1.praef.12)

A possible representation of such a clause is given in (17), where the shifted direct object *fundum* 'farm' appears in the specifier of a projection that I've simply labelled ObjP (for want of a better label). Importantly, it is impossible to decide whether the input structure of this derivation involves a right-headed or a left-headed *v*P, and therefore such examples are uninformative for the language learner when it comes to assessing the fitness of the OV and the VO grammar.

(17)

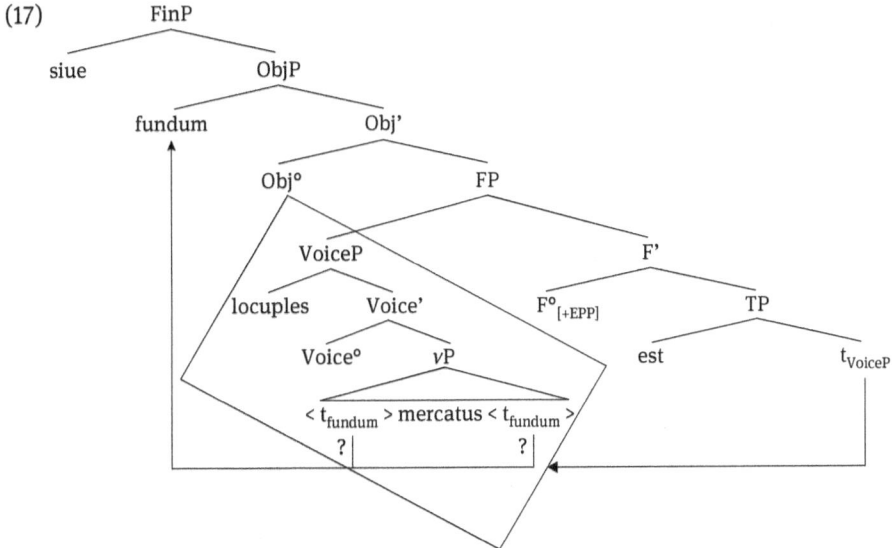

The second diagnostic which can identify a non-left-peripheral subject as such is a pre-VP auxiliary. This is so because the hierarchically highest verb (usually the finite verb) of a clause can never appear in the left periphery of the clause (Danckaert 2012: 275).[16] From this it follows that any subject DP to the right of an auxiliary should itself be non-left-peripheral too, and in a Grammar A setting, it would then be VP-internal.[17] In AuxVP-clauses of the Grammar A type, all AuxSOV-sequences

---

[16] As clauses with more than one element that one could reasonably describe as "auxiliaries" are increasingly rare in Latin (basically restricted to clauses in which the two modals *debeo* and *possum* (always in this order) co-occur, and combinations of an epistemic modal and an infinitival BE-periphrasis), an auxiliary will almost always be the hierarchically highest verb in the clause in which it appears.

[17] Given the present analysis, all CSAuxVP-clauses, i.e. clauses in which a non-left-peripheral subject has unambiguously evacuated the VP, must have been generated by Grammar B, constituting a case in which AuxVP-clauses are not ambiguous between a Grammar A and a Grammar B parse.

would then constitute unambiguous evidence for the OV grammar. In contrast, AuxOSV-clauses such as (18) would involve object movement of the same type as in (17) (with subsequent auxiliary fronting, as in (9)). As a result, AuxOSV-clauses too would not provide the language learner with any unambiguous evidence in favour of the OV or the VO grammar.[18]

(18) *Non,   inquam,   iudic-es,   es-se-t   [ull-am   part-em   **AuxOSV**
       not   say.IPFV.1SG   judges-VOC   be-IPFV.SBJV-3SG any-ACC   part-ACC
       ist-ius   nequiti-ae]   [fugitiu-orum   insolenti-a]
       that-GEN.M.SG   depravity-GEN   fugitives-GEN   insolence-NOM
       consecut-a.
       obtained-NOM.F.SG*
       'As I said, gentlemen, the insolent fugitives would not have committed a fraction of this man's crimes.' (Cic. Ver. 3.66)

To sum up, in Grammar A the strings CSOVAux and AuxSOV should constitute environments in which the language learner can be confident that an OV-sequence is generated by the OV grammar (or put differently, that the direct object is VP-internal). All other linear OV-orders are either ambiguous, or unambiguously involve a VP-external object.

5.1.2 The VO grammar

Let us then consider under which conditions the VO grammar could be cued in a Grammar A setting. Whereas matters are fairly straightforward in VPAux-clauses, the correct analysis of object placement in AuxVP-clauses is far more problematic.

5.1.2.1 VOAux

Unambiguous instances of VP-internal VO can first of all be found in clauses in which a VO chunk appears to the left of the auxiliary, which instantiate the type of apparent violation of FOFC which is only possible in Grammar A, as discussed earlier. I shall take it that various types of VOAux-clauses unambiguously cue the VO grammar, regardless of whether the three elements involved are string adjacent or

---

18 Observe that the type of object movement which is at work in an example like (18) is different from the type of object shift found in OAuxV-clauses which was discussed in section 2.2.2 (landing site below or above T). In section 5.1.2.3 I will return to the syntax of various types of (non-left-peripheral) object movement.

not. For instance, alongside SVOAux (and VOAuxS-sequences), clauses with the order VOSAux (which arguably involve movement of *v*P to some position past VoiceP prior to movement of VoiceP to SpecFP) would also provide the language learner with sufficient evidence to postulate that a given token was generated by the VO grammar.

As mentioned, the analysis of clauses in which the direct object follows the auxiliary is less straightforward. As I will argue in the following sections, post-Aux direct objects can either involve (i) genuine VP-internal VO, (ii) extraposition (in a sense to be made more precise) or (iii) short-distance scrambling followed by remnant movement.

5.1.2.2 Two different VAuxO patterns

As a starting point earlier in this paper (section 2.2.1), I took it that VAuxO-clauses involve object extraposition, and that clauses featuring the order AuxVO are in principle ambiguous between a structure with a VP-internal object and one in which the object is extraposed. As I will now proceed to show, one has to make a further distinction between (at least) two different types of non-local VO. I will illustrate this point by looking at VPAux-clauses, as in this environment we can most easily tell apart local from non-local VO patterns, but both types of non-local VO are available in AuxVP-clauses too.

In the informal characterization of extraposition offered earlier, it was mentioned that only those direct objects that occur in an absolute clause-final position can in principle qualify as extraposed. However, it is certainly not the case that in all AuxVO-clauses no additional (clausemate) XP occurs to the right of the object. For instance, whenever we find the linear sequence VAuxO, a post-Aux subject (in boldface) can either immediately precede (19) or follow (20) the direct object:

(19) *Ita ut censu-era-t Quincti-us fec-erunt,*
thus as recommend-PLPRF.3SG Quinctius-NOM do-PRF.3PL
nec aspernat-us est **consul** *legation-em.*
and.not scorned-NOM.M.SG be.PRS.3SG consul.NOM delegation-ACC
'They acted as Quinctius had recommended, and the consul did not reject the delegation.' (Liv. 36.35.6)

(20) *Ergo in ill-o secut-a est honest-am*
PRT in this-ABL.M.SG followed-NOM.F.SG be.PRS.3SG honest-ACC
caus-am **non** *honest-a uictori-a.*
cause-ACC not honest-NOM victory-NOM
'So in his (Sulla's ld) case an ill-deserved victory has followed a just cause.' (Cic. Off. 2.27)

The problem with examples like (20) is that it is on the one hand certain that the object *honestam causam* 'a just cause' does not sit inside the verb phrase, but on the other hand, it also doesn't occur in a clause-final position. If we are to maintain that extraposed constituents obligatorily occur in an absolute clause-final position (an assumption that would also imply that per clause only one constituent can be extraposed), it would follow that not all objects in VAuxO-clauses are extraposed. But can we really make a strong case for the claim that extraposed objects should appear at the very end of a clause?

5.1.2.3 The syntax of postposed objects

In order to answer this last question, it is first of all important to note that what I have informally been calling "extraposition" in fact corresponds to a number of distinct syntactic phenomena. On the one hand, there are certain types of extraposition which can be iterated, and therefore do not qualify as processes that invariably put a given constituent at the absolute end of a clause. Such is the case with extraposition of relative clauses, as well as with extraposition of PPs associated with a nominal constituent.[19] For instance, in both English (21a) and Dutch (21b) it is possible for more than one extraposed relative clause to be associated with a single antecedent (examples from Keller (1995: 302) and de Vries (1999, his (14a)); see also Guéron and May (1984: 28)):

(21) a. *A paper just came out [which talks about extraposition] [which you might be interested in].*
  b. *Ik   heb   de   man   gesignaleerd   [die   je   beschreef],*
     I   have the   man   noticed   who   you   described
     [die   een   rode   koffer   draagt].
      who   a   red   suitcase carries
     'I have noticed the man who you described, who carries a red suitcase.'

In addition, in (my own variety of) Dutch multiple PPs can be extraposed from one single noun phrase (cf. (22d)). (22b-c) show that the two PPs are indeed two separate constituents):

(22) a. *Ik   heb   [een   man   [uit   Rusland]   [met   vier   gouden*
      I   have a   man   from   Russia   with   four   golden
      tanden]]   gezien.
      teeth   seen
      'I saw a man from Russia with four golden teeth.'

---

19 Note that extraposition of relative clauses and extraposition of PPs are themselves two distinct syntactic phenomena (Fox & Nissenbaum 1999; Sheehan 2010).

b. *? Ik heb [een man [met vier gouden tanden]] gezien [uit Rusland].*
c. *Ik heb [een man uit Rusland] gezien [met vier gouden tanden].*
d. *Ik heb [een man] gezien [uit Rusland] [met vier gouden tanden].*

These data clearly show that there is no requirement for extraposed relative clauses and PPs to appear at the very right edge of a clause (in whatever way these structures are to be analysed).

On the other hand, the syntax of extraposed (right-peripheral) subjects and objects seems to be very different.[20] As is well known, in contrast with extraposed relative clauses and PPs, postposed argument DPs are typically prosodically heavy (and/or internally complex), and usually also focalized. The most famous member of this family of phenomena is no doubt Heavy Noun Phrase Shift (HNPS) in English, which has a clear tendency to appear at the very end of a clause.[21] For instance, as argued by Svenonius (1992), objects that have undergone HNPS obligatorily follow all other VP-internal material, and thus differ from non-heavy objects which are separated from the lexical verb only by a particle (examples from den Dikken 1995: 87, his (131)). As den Dikken points out, an example like (23c), in which a direct object appears at the end of the clause and to the right of a post-verbal adjunct, only becomes acceptable if the direct object is sufficiently heavy.

(23) a. *They set the bomb off [with a transmitter].*
b. *They set off the bomb [with a transmitter].*
c. **They set off [with a transmitter] the bomb.*

But then what about the relative position of a shifted heavy object and two postverbal adjuncts?[22] As it turns out, speakers have a preference for the shifted object to appear at the very end of the clause, as in (24):

(24) *I met [$_{PP}$ on the street] [$_{DP}$ last Monday] [$_{DP}$ my rich uncle from New York].*

To the extent that any adjunct can appear after a heavy shifted object (some of the speakers that I consulted reject this pattern, but see footnote 22), the additional adjunct is always destressed, whereas it is the object that receives focal stress.

---

20 Compare also the discussion in Pintzuk and Kroch (1989).
21 In their discussion of a number of postposition phenomena, Huddleston and Pullum (2002: 1382) note that "[a]n element is said to be postposed when it appears to the right of its basic position, at the end of the clause (save perhaps from one or more adjuncts)". They do not given any examples in which 'one or more adjuncts' follows for instance an object that has undergone HNPS, but see the discussion of (24) and (25) below.
22 At least in English, it does not seem possible to test whether HNPS is compatible with extraposition (of PPs and relative clauses) from nominal constituents, given that these operations are generally blocked by the presence of a (fully referential) direct object (on this effect with PP extraposition, see Guéron 1980: 663–664).

For instance, (25) can only be (marginally) acceptable when *last Monday* is delivered with flat intonation, which plausibly indicates that the clause-final adjunct is not properly integrated in the same clause as the heavy object, but rather right-dislocated.

(25) % I met [*_PP_* on the street] [*_DP_* my rich uncle from New York] [*_DP_* last Monday].

Assuming a coordination analysis to (backgrounding) right-dislocation, as in Ott and de Vries (2016),[23] it would be possible to maintain that a HNPS constituent always appears in an absolute clause-final position.

Facts similar to the ones concerning HNPS in English also hold for one particular type of VS-orders in French, which Lahousse (2006) calls "focus inversion" (26). This type of inversion is distinct from "genuine" subject-verb inversion, where the subject remains in its base position. As the author shows, in cases of French focus inversion a postverbal subject cannot be followed by for instance a PP, witness the ungrammaticality of (26b) (examples from Lahousse (2006: 426, 453), based on Kampers-Manhe, Marandin, Drijkoningen, Doetjes, and Hulk (2004)):

(26) a. *Pass-er-a*   [*_PP_* devant   le   conseil   de   discipline]
        go-FUT-3SG   before   the   committee   of   discipline
        [*_DP_* tout   élève   de   l'   établissement   au
              every   pupil   of   the   institution   with.the
        comportement   incivil].
        behaviour   inappropriate.
        'Every pupil of the school with inappropriate behaviour will appear before the disciplinary committee.'

   b. **Passera [*_DP_* tout élève de l'établissement au comportement incivil] [*_PP_* devant le conseil de discipline].*

Here I will not further analyse the syntax of these two types of argument extraposition: the reader is referred to Lahousse (2006) and Wallenberg (2015) for more detailed discussion.

5.1.2.4 Two types of VP-external VO configurations in Latin

Given this more fine-grained typology of extraposition phenomena, we can now try to analyse the contrast between the Latin data in (20) (clause-final vs. non-clause-final object in VAuxO-clauses). What I would like to propose is that one

---

[23] As pointed out in Ott & de Vries (2016), backgrounding right dislocation can affect XPs of various categories, including adverbs, in which case no co-indexed correlate is needed in the preceding clause.

has to distinguish two types of VAuxO-clauses, one involving extraposition akin to English HNPS, and one involving (short-distance) object scrambling followed by (EPP-driven) movement of a remnant VP (a series of operations which typically yields the same surface order as application of HNPS). The former is predicted to typically feature heavy and/or focalized direct objects, whereas no such weight effect is expected in the latter case.

One advantage of this proposal is that it allows us to make sense of the observation that not all direct objects in VAuxO-clauses are prosodically heavy (however the notion of prosodic weight is exactly operationalized). Recall from section 2.2.1 that direct objects that follow a VAux-sequence can either be short or long. Two examples are repeated here for convenience:

(27) a. *Tot   uad-ibus   accusator   uadat-us*
       so.many   guarantees-ABL   prosecutor.NOM   admitted.to.bail-NOM.M.SG
       est   re-um.
       be.PRS.3SG   accused-ACC
       'With so many guarantees the prosecutor admitted the accused to bail.'
       (Liv. 3.13.8)

   b. *Complex-us   es   [funest-um   illud   animal*
       embraced-NOM.M.SG   be.PRS.2SG deadly-ACC   this.ACC.N.SG   animal.ACC
       ex   nefari-is   stupr-is,   ex   civil-i   cruor-e,
       out.of   horrible-ABL   sexual.misconduct-ABL   out.of   civil-ABL   blood-ABL
       ex   omn-i   sceler-um   inportunitat-e   concret-um].
       out.of   all-ABL   crimes-GEN   relentlessness-ABL   composed-ACC
       'You embraced this deadly monster, composed of horrible misconduct, civil bloodshed, and all sorts of perverse crimes.' (Cic. Pis. 21)

In the second example, the clause-final direct object is clearly very long, and internally complex: this seems like a good candidate to instantiate genuine object extraposition, of the type that favours prosodically heavy constituents, and requires the extraposed element to appear in an absolute clause-final position.

In contrast, (27a) can be assumed to have a very different syntax. Given that the direct object *reum* 'the accused' in this example is clearly very short, and given that this element refers to a well established discourse referent (viz. the murderer Caeso), whose vicissitudes have been under discussion for quite a while at the point where (27a) is added to the discourse, it seems reasonable to assume that this direct object has been scrambled out of the verb phrase, to a fairly low position just above the thematic nucleus of the clause, before the remnant VP moves to SpecFP. The relevant structure would look as in (28), where the landing site of the object is called "ScrP", to borrow a label from Devine and Stephens (2006):

(28) [$_{FP}$ [$_{VoiceP}$ S t$_O$ V] [$_{F,[EPP]}$ [$_{TP}$ Aux [$_{ScrP}$ O [$_{Scr,}$ t$_{VoiceP}$]]]]]

Let us at this point take stock. Recall that we are ultimately concerned with AuxVO-clauses, and that we want to know under which conditions the language learner could be confident that these involve a VP-internal rather than a VP-external object. We have also seen that there are two types of VP-external VO, one involving HNPS ("extraposition") and one involving short scrambling. Note first of all that the only type of derivation in which this last operation could give rise to the order Aux(S)VO involves short object movement, followed by remnant VoiceP movement and finally an additional step of auxiliary raising (plausibly of the type detailed in (9)). Given the complexity of this derivation, we can assume that this pattern should be rare. On the other hand, a HNPS analysis of AuxVO-clauses seems more likely, even if the object is followed by an additional (right-dislocated) XP. In a Grammar A setting the string AuxVOXP would then be three-ways ambiguous between (i) a structure in which a heavy shifted object is followed by a right-dislocated XP, (ii) one involving a VP-internal object followed by a right-dislocated XP and (iii) one with a VP-internal object followed by a clausemate XP. Needless to say, telling apart these three possible structures is not at all a trivial task.

In order to maximally ensure that I correctly distinguish VP-internal objects from cases that can in principle involve a VP-external object (and which are therefore not informative about the OV/VO alternation proper), I first of all decided to classify as "ambiguous" all VO-clauses in which the object appears at the very right edge of the clause. Of the remaining AuxVOXP-clauses, I classified as "unambiguous" only those cases in which the object is relatively short, that is, if it is either (i) a one-word expression (33 tokens in my corpus), (ii) a noun modified by a single adjective or genitive (12 tokens), or (iii) a pair of two coordinated (single word) noun phrases (1 token). In addition, I excluded all cases where there can be reasonable doubt that the XP following the direct object is part of the same clause as the VO-sequence: for instance, I left aside all cases where the only element after a VO string is an adverbial clause, which might very well not be fully syntactically integrated in the clause to its left.

5.1.2.5 Summary

I conclude this section with an overview of possible patterns of linear VO orderings (Tab. 3, where the #-sign stands for the right edge of a clause). I take it that only the two patterns in the shaded row (VO in VPAux-clauses, and one type of VO in AuxVP-clauses) constitute unambiguous evidence for the VO grammar in a Grammar A setting.

Tab. 3: VO patterns in Grammar A

Word order pattern	Possible parses	Type of object placement
VAuxO#	2	– short scrambling + remnant movement – HNPS (extraposition)
AuxVO#	2 (3?)	– VP-internal VO – HNPS (extraposition) (– short scrambling + remnant movement + Aux raising?)
AuxVOshortXP# (where XP is not an adverbial clause)	1	– VP-internal VO
VOAux	1	– VP-internal VO

5.2 Cueing object placement in Grammar B

5.2.1 The VO grammar

Let us then consider how the OV and the VO grammar can be cued in Grammar B. As to the latter, given that neither the syntax of VP-internal VO (a head-initial vP) nor the syntax of HNPS/extraposition (whatever its exact nature) are in principle affected by the shift from Grammar A to Grammar B, nothing changes with respect to the way in which the VO grammar is cued in AuxVP-clauses. However, given that VPAux-clauses no longer involve non-local VP movement, but rather a structure which is subject to FOFC (namely one whereby the top segment of the T-projection dominates the entire verb phrase), in Grammar B it is no longer possible to generate VP-internal VO whenever the T-node is head-final. Put differently, it must be the case that all cases of VOAux found in Late Latin texts were generated by the declining Grammar A.

5.2.2 The OV grammar

On the other hand, given the major change that took place with respect to the syntax of preverbal subjects, the conditions under which the language acquirer can be confident that a given OV string was generated by the OV grammar are very different in Grammar A and Grammar B. However, here too the differences are confined to VPAux-clauses.

Consider first the structure of an AuxVP-clause with an overt subject and object as generated by Grammar B. (29) shows the derivation of a negated clause, where the finite verb (with a proclitic negator attached to it) winds up in F°:

(29)

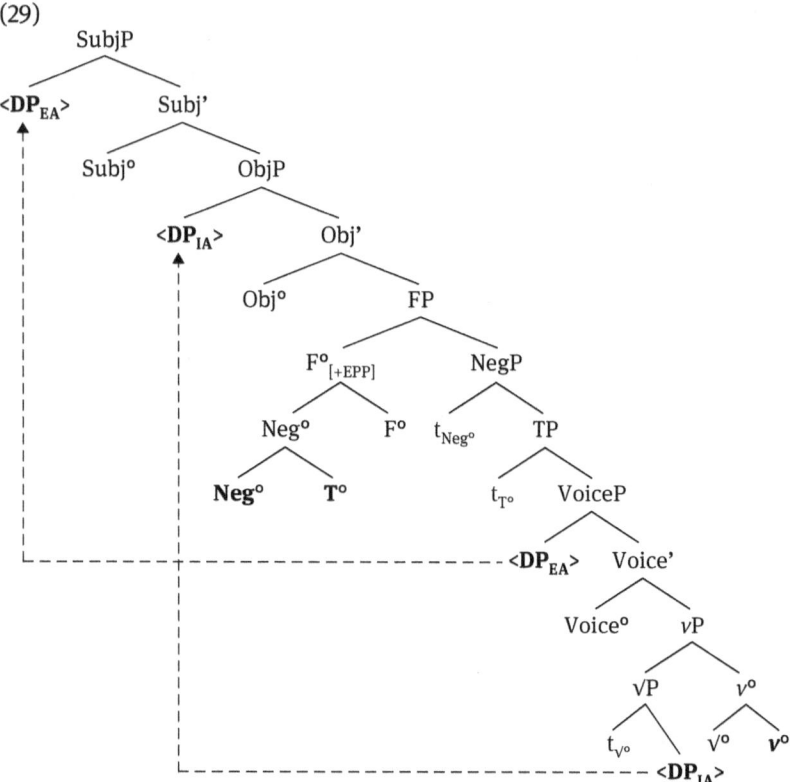

(29) represents the structure of an AuxVP-clause with a transitive predicate, and two possible positions for the direct object[24], as well as two possible positions for the subject.[25] As to the former, both the VP-internal pattern of object placement and the pattern of object shift were available in Grammar A too: I assume that Grammar B behaves exactly the same in this respect. What is new is the possibility for subjects to undergo A-movement (by assumption to SpecSubjP). As mentioned, the conditions under which VP-internal OV can be cued are the same as in Grammar A (modulo the different positions for the auxiliary in Grammars A

---

24 Note that I am abstracting away from the short-distance object scrambling pattern (which in an AuxVP-clause would yield the order AuxO(S)V) discussed above.

25 As a reviewer points out, in order for it to be possible for the subject to move across a shifted object, one would have to assume that the latter does not count as an intervener for the former. Although it remains to be seen how exactly the relevant facts are to be accounted for 'locality-wise', it seems to be the default case that whenever two of a verb's arguments simultaneously evacuate the VP to move to the TP-layer, the argument with the higher base position also targets the higher TP-internal position. For early discussion of such 'order preservation' effects in the middle field, see Haegeman (1993a,b).

and B): whenever neither the auxiliary nor the subject intervenes between O and V, and whenever the subject remains in its base position (i.e. surfaces to the right of the auxiliary but to the left of V), the child is presented with sufficient evidence to postulate that the a given OV string involves a VP-internal direct object. Put differently, the word order AuxSOV serves as a cue for the OV grammar.[26]

Crucially, the situation is very different in VPAux-clauses. A basic structure for this type of clause in Grammar B is given in (30), where again two possible positions for direct objects (*in situ* or shifted) are indicated, as well as two positions for the subject (*in situ* or A-moved):

(30)
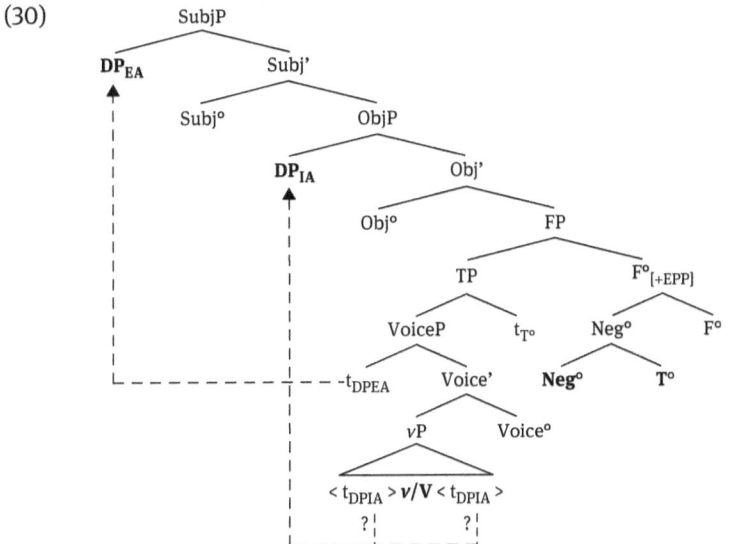

The crucial observation is that whenever the subject moves to SpecSubjP, application of object shift (or of short-distance scrambling, for that matter) becomes string vacuous, and as usual, whenever a parse involving object shift is available, it is impossible to tell whether the structure involves a left or a right-headed *v*P. As a result, even if a given preverbal subject in an SOVAux-clause appears lower than a subordinating conjunction or *wh*-word (which excludes an analysis involving a left-peripheral subject), it is still impossible for the language learner to determine whether the subject is in SubjP or in VoiceP, and by this token, the status of the direct object (*in situ* or shifted) also becomes ambiguous. As we will see in the final part of this paper, this state of affairs has major consequences for the fitness of the OV grammar in Grammar B.

---

[26] "Note however that this - perhaps not innocuously - presupposes that in Grammar B there is no auxiliary fronting past SubjP (and possibly a subject in SpecSubjP): if such an operation could be shown to exist, then AuxSOV-clauses would in fact not unambiguously cue the OV grammar."

5.3 Object shift revisited

The main results of section 5 are summarized in Tab. 4. As can be seen, in Grammar B, both the OV and the VO grammar can be cued unambiguously in fewer environments (cf. the underscored word order patterns in the Grammar A column).

Tab. 4: Cues for the OV and the VO grammar: summary

	Grammar A (roughly early period, 200 BC – 200 AD)	Grammar B (roughly late period, 201 – 600 AD)
OV grammar	CSOVAux, AuxSOV	AuxSOV
VO grammar	VOAux, AuxVOXP (where XP is not an adverbial clause)	AuxVOXP (where XP is not an adverbial clause)
Ambiguous	all other word orders	all other word orders

What I will suggest in section 6 is that it was the fact that the string CSOVAux at a certain point became structurally ambiguous which dealt the fatal blow to the OV grammar. More particularly, despite having a fairly high token frequency (see below), in Grammar B this type of clause does not provide the language learner with any reliable clues to determine the exact structural position of subjects and objects.

Interestingly, this hypothesis might help us to understand the observation made earlier concerning the diachronic development of object shift, and more particularly the increasing frequencies of the order OAuxV (cf. section 2.2.2). Recall from section 3.2 that the transition from Grammar A to Grammar B was argued to involve reanalysis of VPAux-clauses like (31a) as the structure in (31b). Note however that as things stand, this simple scenario does not explain why the rate of object shift increases over time.

(31) a. $[_{FP} [_{VoiceP}$ S O V] $[_{F,[EPP]} [_{TP}$ Aux t_{VoiceP}]]]   Grammar A, OV
    b. $[_{SubjP}$ <S> $[_{Subj,} [_{FP} [_{TP} [_{VoiceP}$ <S> O V] t_{Aux}] Aux]]]   Grammar B, OV

Given that in Grammar B, there is no longer one single non-left-peripheral position for preverbal subjects, we can speculate that the output of Grammar A (OVAux and VOAux) was not simply reanalysed as (31b), which contains only one object position. More precisely, in the context of Grammar B there does not seem to be robust enough evidence to postulate one single "default" position for preverbal direct objects, as (31b) suggests. Instead, we can assume the following structure to be the target of reanalysis:

(31) c. $[_{SubjP}$ <S> $[_{Subj,} [_{ObjP}$ <O> $[_{Obj,} [_{FP} [_{TP} [_{VoiceP}$ <S> <O> V] t_{Aux}] Aux]]]]]   Grammar B, OS

As can be seen, this structure not only contains two subject positions, but also two object positions (viz. one inside VP and one above TP which hosts shifted objects), both of which are also available in Grammar A.[27] The idea would be that VP-internal direct objects in OVAux and VOAux strings generated by Grammar A were reanalysed either as shifted or as VP-internal (but always preverbal). The more liberal distribution of preverbal objects would itself be the result of the increased positional flexibility of preverbal subjects. The obvious advantage of this approach is that it readily provides us with an analysis of why the rate of object shift increases over time, a fact that remains otherwise unexplained. We can also speculate that in Late Latin object shift was information-structurally less marked than in Classical Latin, but needless to say, further research is needed to check whether this is correct.

This being said, we can now move on to apply the system from Yang (2000, 2002) to the Latin corpus data.

6 Assessing the fitness of the OV and the VO grammar

6.1 Periodization

Recall that my initial hypothesis concerning the existence of Grammar A and Grammar B was based on the data summarized in Graph 2, which show that at around 200 AD (or perhaps a bit earlier), the headedness of the verb phrase (*v*P) ceases to be independent from the headedness of TP, witness the rather sudden decrease in productivity of the order VOAux. This observation, as well as the data on the distribution of internal arguments discussed in section 3.3, prompted me to the conclusion that Grammar A is more frequently used in the period from 200 BC until 200 AD, and that Grammar B is the dominant one in the following four centuries.

Recall also that in many cases it is impossible to tell whether a given clause was generated by Grammar A or by Grammar B, as both can produce VPAux and AuxVP-orders alike. What I will do to deal with this problem is make a simple binary distinction between the earlier and the later period in my corpus (first four centuries vs. last four centuries), and assume that in the former we see Grammar A at work, and in the latter Grammar B. The sharp contrast observed in Graph 2 (which I interpret to mean that somewhere before 200 AD the frequency of usage of Grammar

---

27 I wish to remain agnostic as to whether the pragmatic correlates of object shift (say its conditions of usage) change over time or rather remain stable.

B rises sharply) suggests that this idealization is not too far off the mark, but it should be obvious that it is at least to some extent a simplification of the actual situation, as there can be no doubt that some of the clauses in the earlier period are the output of Grammar B, and some in the later period of Grammar A. In any event, as I will now proceed to show, even given this approximation, a fairly clear contrast between the two periods emerges, which might help us to understand why the OV grammar eventually lost out.

6.2 The results

The below results are based on the analysis of a sample of 6309 clauses drawn from the corpus mentioned at the beginning of section 2.1, which all contain an auxiliary (BE or a modal), a transitive lexical verb and a non-discontinuous direct object. 2158 clauses also feature an overt, non-discontinuous subject (which can be nominal, pronominal or clausal (free relative)). The sample for the early period is slightly bigger than the one for the later period (3911 vs. 2398 clauses).

In order to calculate how fit the OV and the VO grammar are in terms of Yang's variational acquisition model, we have to look at the proportion of unambiguous OV and VO-clauses in our sample. The results are summarized in Tab. 5 (absolute frequencies):

Tab. 5: Frequency of ambiguous and unambiguous OV and VO patterns

	Early period (200 BC – 200 AD, Grammar A)			Late period (201 – 600 AD, Grammar B)		
	Environment	N	Total	Environment	N	Total
Unambiguous OV	AuxSOV	65	487	AuxSOV	23	23
	CSOVAux	422		(CSOVAux)	(48)	(71)
Unambiguous VO	AuxVOXP	16	420	AuxVOXP	30	30
	VOAux	404		(VOAux)	(66)	(96)
Ambiguous		3004			2279 (2183)	
Total # of clauses		3911			2332	

Let us have a closer look at these results. First, observe that for the sake of completeness, in the rightmost column I added how frequently the two patterns that only in a Grammar A setting constitute unambiguous evidence for either the OV or the VO grammar are attested. However, note that these two types of clauses do not quite have the same status: as we have seen, the CSOVAux pattern becomes ambiguous, but VOAux-orders in principle still provide unambiguous evidence for the VO grammar, even in times when the grammar that is needed to generate them (Grammar A) was on its way out. Below, I will not take into account the evidence from Late Latin VOAux-clauses when calculating the fitness of the VO grammar in the context of Grammar B. It is important to bear in mind that this follows from my decision to treat all tokens from the early period as Grammar A clauses, and all tokens from the later period as the output of Grammar B. As mentioned, from a practical point of view assuming this type of idealization seems the only feasible option, but it is of course a simplification. In any event, the fact that I leave aside all Late Latin VOAux-clauses implies that my estimate of the fitness of the VO grammar in this period is probably overly conservative.

Second, it is very striking that the proportion of unambiguous OV and VO-clauses is much higher in Grammar A than in Grammar B. Note that this is not just a result of the fact that the these two grammars are cued in fewer environments in Grammar B: even if CSOVAux and VOAux-clauses were to be taken into account, the total of unambiguous OV and VO-clauses would still be relatively low (as compared to the figures obtained for the first four centuries).

Let us then look at the estimated fitness of the OV and the VO grammar in both periods. The results are summarized in Tab. 6:

Tab. 6: Fitness of the OV and VO grammar over time

	Early period (200 BC – 200 AD, Grammar A)	Late period (201 – 600 AD, Grammar B)
OV grammar	487/3004 = .162	23/2279 = .010
VO grammar	420/3004 = .140	30/2279 = .013

Overall, the variational acquisition model seems to perform very well. On the one hand, it correctly captures the fact that in the earlier centuries the OV grammar is clearly the predominant one, with an estimated advantage over the VO grammar of 2.2%.[28] On the other hand, in the later period it gives a narrow advantage of the VO grammar over its competitor, despite the fact that in absolute terms, the fitness of the VO grammar (as well as of the OV grammar) decreases quite dramatically. This result is not only compatible with the observation that in the Late Latin period we do not witness any strong increase of the VO-order, but also with the fact that the VO grammar eventually turned out to be extremely successful, an observation that has for a long time resisted a satisfactory explanation. However, it needs to be added that in the late period the difference between the two grammars is very small, and indeed not statistically significant at the .05 level (i.e. we cannot exclude that the fact that we observe 30 VO tokens out of a total of 53 unambiguous clauses is not due to chance, Pearson's chi-squared test,

---

28 The probability of obtaining 487 OV-clauses out of a total of 907 unambiguous tokens is statistically significant (Pearson's chi-squared test, p = .0022).

p = 0.0692). This state of affairs might very well be related to the fact that the sample of unambiguous clauses is very small (only 53 for a period of 400 years). In any event, we can hope that a follow-up study that looks at a larger corpus of Late Latin might provide us with more conclusive evidence that the VO grammar was indeed fitter in a Grammar B context than its competitor.

7 Conclusion

In this paper I have offered a first attempt to analyse the loss of OV word orders in Latin/Romance. Assuming Yang's (2000, 2002) variational acquisition model of language change, I have suggested that the eventual decline of the OV grammar can be traced back to an independent change in the grammar of Latin, namely one concerning the way in which the clausal EPP requirement is satisfied (Danckaert 2017). The crucial Late Latin innovation was argued to be the development of optional A-movement for subjects: as an indirect result of this, in the Late Latin period the VO grammar is more robustly cued than the OV grammar, despite the fact that the overall frequency of the order VO remains more or less constant over time (and in certain environments even decreases). Given this result, Yang's model correctly predicts the VO-order to oust the competing OV pattern. I have also shown that the rate of object extraposition (which yields linear VO-sequences) remains fairly stable during the lifespan of the Latin language, which suggests that this phenomenon is unrelated to the spread of the VO-order. Finally, the rate of object shift (i.e. a non-local type of OV) can in fact be shown to increase over time. This development too was suggested to be related to the new setting of the EPP parameter and the novel patterns of subject placement that follow from it.

Acknowledgements: It is my great pleasure to dedicate this paper to my supervisor, mentor, occasional co-author and good friend Liliane Haegeman, whose work on word order in Flemish/Dutch has always been a major source of inspiration for my own work on Latin. Non-standard abbreviations used are the following: FOFC = Final-Over-Final Constraint; HNPS = Heavy Noun Phrase Shift; ObjP = Object Phrase; PLD = Primary Linguistic Data; SubjP: Subject Phrase. In the glosses, abbreviations not mentioned in the Leipzig Glossing Rules are COMP for "comparative", PLPRF for "pluperfect" and PRT for "particle". In references to Latin examples, the same abbreviations are used as in the Oxford Latin Dictionary. The research reported on in this paper was funded by a postdoctoral grant of the Research Foundation – Flanders, grant nr. FWO13/PDO/024.

References

Alexiadou, Artemis & Elena Anagnostopoulou. 1998. Parametrizing AGR: Word order, movement and EPP-checking. *Natural Language and Linguistic Theory* 16. 491–539.

Biberauer, Theresa. 2003. *Verb second (V2) in Afrikaans: A minimalist investigation of word order variation.* Cambridge: University of Cambridge dissertation.

Biberauer, Theresa & Ian Roberts. 2005. Changing EPP parameters in the history of English: Accounting for variation and change. *English Language and Linguistics* 9. 5–46.

Biberauer, Theresa, Anders Holmberg & Ian Roberts. 2014. A syntactic universal and its consequences. *Linguistic Inquiry* 45. 169–225.

Cardinaletti, Anna. 2004. Towards a cartography of subject positions. In Luigi Rizzi (ed.), *The Structure of CP and IP*, 115–165. Oxford: Oxford University Press.

Danckaert, Lieven. 2011. *On the left periphery of Latin embedded clauses.* Gent: Ghent University dissertation.

Danckaert, Lieven. 2012. *Latin embedded clauses: The left periphery.* Amsterdam: John Benjamins.

Danckaert, Lieven. 2014. The derivation of Classical Latin Aux-final clauses: Implications for the internal structure of the verb phrase. In Karen Lahousse & Stefania Marzo (eds.), *Romance languages and linguistic theory 2012*, 141–159. Amsterdam: John Benjamins.

Danckaert, Lieven. 2016. Variation and change in Latin BE-periphrases: Empirical and methodological considerations. In James N. Adams & Nigel Vincent (eds.), *Early and Late Latin: Continuity or change?*, 132–162. Cambridge: Cambridge University Press.

Danckaert, Lieven. 2017. *The development of Latin clause structure: A study of the extended verb phrase.* Oxford: Oxford University Press.

Devine, Andrew & Laurence Stephens. 2006. *Latin word order: Structured meaning and information.* Oxford: Oxford University Press.

de Vries, Mark. 1999. Extraposition of relative clauses as specifying coordination. In Tina Cambier-Langeveld, Anikó Lipták, Michael Redford & Eric Jan van der Torre (eds.), *Proceedings of ConSole VII*, 293–309. Leiden: Student Organisation of Linguistics in Europe.

Embick, David. 2000. Features, syntax and categories in the Latin perfect. *Linguistic Inquiry* 31. 185–230.

Fox, Danny & Jon Nissenbaum. 1999. Extraposition and scope: A case for overt QR. In Sonya Bird, Andrew Carnie, Jason D. Haugen, and Peter Norquest, *Proceedings of the 18th West Coast Conference on Formal Linguistics*, 132–144. Somerville, MA: Cascadilla Press.

Guéron, Jacqueline. 1980. On the syntax and semantics of PP extraposition. *Linguistic Inquiry* 11. 637–678.

Guéron, Jacqueline & Robert May. 1984. Extraposition and logical form. *Linguistic Inquiry* 15. 1–31.

Haegeman, Liliane. 1993a. Some speculations on argument shift, clitics and crossing in West Flemish. In Werner Abraham & Josef Bayer (eds.), *Dialektsyntax*, 131–160. Opladen: Westdeutscher Verlag.

Haegeman, Liliane. 1993b. The morphology and distribution of object clitics in West Flemish. *Studia Linguistica* 47. 57–94.

Haegeman, Liliane. 2000. Remnant movement and OV order. In Peter Svenonius (ed.), *The derivation of OV and VO*, 69–96. Amsterdam: John Benjamins.

Haegeman, Liliane, Ángel Jiménez-Fernández & Andrew Radford. 2014. Deconstructing the Subject Condition in terms of cumulative constraint violation. *The Linguistic Review* 31. 73–150.

Heycock, Caroline & Joel Wallenberg. 2013. How variational acquisition drives syntactic change: The loss of verb movement in Scandinavian. *Journal of Comparative Germanic Linguistics* 16. 127–157.

Huddleston, Rodney & Geoffrey Pullum. 2002. *The Cambridge grammar of the English language*. Cambridge: Cambridge University Press.

Kampers-Manhe, Brigitte, Jean-Marie Marandin, Frank Drijkoningen, Jenny Doetjes & Aafke Hulk. 2004. Subject NP inversion. In Francis Corblin & Henriëtte de Swart (eds.), *Handbook of French semantics*, 553–579. Stanford, CA: Center for the Study of Language and Information.

Kayne, Richard. 1994. *The antisymmetry of syntax*. Cambridge, MA: The MIT Press.

Keller, Frank. 1995. Towards an account of extraposition in HPSG. In Steven Abney & Erhard Hinrichs (eds.), *Proceedings of the Seventh Conference of the European Chapter of the Association for Computational Linguistics*, 301–306. Dublin: Association for Computational Linguistics.

Kroch, Anthony. 1989. Reflexes of grammar in patterns of language change. *Language Variation and Change* 1. 199–244.

Kroch, Anthony. 1994. Morphosyntactic variation. In Katherine Beals, Jeannette Denton, Robert Knippen, Lynette Melnar, Hisami Suzuki & Erica Zeinfeld (eds.), *Papers from the Thirtieth Regional Meeting of the Chicago Linguistics Society, volume 2: The Parasession on variation in linguistic theory*, 180–201. Chicago: Chicago Linguistics Society.

Lightfoot, David. 1979. *Principles of diachronic syntax*. Cambridge: Cambridge University Press.

Mackenzie, Ian & Wim van der Wurff. 2012. Relic syntax in Middle English and Medieval Spanish: Parameter interaction in language change. *Language* 88. 846–876.

Pintzuk, Susan. 1999. *Phrase structures in competition: Variation and change in Old English word order*. New York: Garland.

Pintzuk, Susan. 2003. Variationist approaches to syntactic change. In Brian D. Joseph & Richard D. Janda (eds.), *The handbook of historical linguistics*, 509–528. Oxford: Blackwell.

Pintzuk, Susan & Anthony Kroch. 1989. The rightward movement of complements and adjuncts in the Old English of *Beowulf*. *Language Variation and Change* 1. 115–143.

Ott, Dennis & Mark de Vries. 2016. Right-dislocation as deletion. *Natural Language and Linguistic Theory* 34. 641–690.

Rizzi, Luigi. 2006. On the form of chains: Criterial positions and ECP effects. In Lisa Cheng & Norbert Corver (eds.), *Wh-movement: Moving on*, 97–133. Cambridge, MA: The MIT Press.

Santorini, Beatrice. 1993. The rate of phrase structure change in the history of Yiddish. *Language Variation and Change* 5. 257–283.

Sheehan, Michelle. 2010. Extraposition and antisymmetry. *Linguistic Variation Yearbook* 10. 203–254.

Svenonius, Peter. 1992. Movement of P° in the English verb-particle construction. In H. Andrew Black & James McCloskey (eds.), *Syntax at Santa Cruz 1*, 93–113. Santa Cruz, CA: Syntax Research Center of the University of California at Santa Cruz.

Yang, Charles. 2000. Internal and external forces in language change. *Language Variation and Change* 12. 231–250.

Yang, Charles. 2002. *Knowledge and learning in natural language*. Oxford: Oxford University Press.

Wallenberg, Joel. 2015. Antisymmetry and Heavy NP Shift across Germanic. In Theresa Biberauer & George Walkden (eds.), *Syntax over time: Lexical, morphological and information-structural interactions*, 336–349. Oxford: Oxford University Press.

Eric Haeberli
Medial NP-adjuncts in English: A diachronic perspective

1 Introduction

In Present-Day English, adjuncts can occur in three main areas of the clause: clause-initially (before the subject), clause-finally (after the main verb) or clause-medially (between the subject and the main verb). The focus of this paper will be the latter domain, which corresponds to the area between the subject and the finite main verb or, if the finite verbal element is an auxiliary, the area between the subject and the non-finite main verb either to the left or to the right of the finite auxiliary. In the literature, it is sometimes claimed that this clause-medial adjunct position is restricted to adverbs. However, as has regularly been shown (cf. e.g. Haegeman 1983, 2002; De Clerq, Haegeman, and Lohndal 2012), medial NP- and PP-adjuncts are not entirely ruled out and they can be found in corpus data. This is illustrated in (1).

(1) a. ... he **yesterday** published his version of last week's events...
(Haegeman 2002: 79)
b. The Government will **this week** announce a pay rise ...
(Haegeman 1983: 74)
c. ... Thompson **in one letter** talks of his relationship with a girl...
(Haegeman 2002: 83)
d. The actor was **at that time** living in London.   (De Clerq et al. 2012: 7)

Although medial NP- and PP-adjuncts are not entirely banned in Present-Day English, it is nevertheless the case that speakers often do not accept such word orders. Furthermore, their frequency of occurrence in corpora is very low and their use seems to be subject to register variation, with journalistic prose being a favourable context for the use of medial NP- and PP-adjuncts.

The main question these observations raise is why an adjunct position that is commonly occupied by adverbs is so restrictive with respect to hosting other types of adjuncts. The aim of this paper is to try to shed some light on this issue by examining the diachronic development of the syntax of medial NP-adjuncts in the history of English. In Old English, the occurrence of adverbs as well as NP-adjuncts in a surface position between the subject and the main verb is very common, as Old English has head-final properties and the main verb, in particular in subordinate clauses, frequently occurs towards the end of a clause. What is therefore of interest from a diachronic point of view is the question how the distinctive properties of adverbs on the one hand and NP-adjuncts on the other with respect to medial placement emerged in the history of English. To address this issue, I will examine the development of NP-adjuncts in the currently available parsed historical corpora covering approximately 1000 years of history from Old to Late Modern English. These data will then be set against comparable data related to the placement of adverbs. The aim will be to identify the way in which the two types of elements developed the different distributional properties that characterize them today and to examine to what extent the diachronic evidence can contribute to an account of clause-medial adjunct placement in Present-Day English.

The paper is structured as follows. Section 2 provides an overview of observations made in the literature with respect to the status of clause-medial placement of NP-adjuncts and of accounts of the constraints on this word order option that have been proposed in earlier work. In section 3, the diachronic development of medial placement of NP-adjuncts with finite main verbs and its theoretical analysis will be discussed. Section 4 explores some additional issues that are raised by clauses with finite auxiliaries and non-finite main verbs. Finally, section 5 concludes the paper.

2 Medial NP-adjuncts in Present-Day English

This section presents some observations and analyses found in the earlier literature with respect to clause-medial nominal constituents in Present-Day English. My discussion relies heavily on Haegeman (2002), who refers to elements such as *tomorrow*, *yesterday*, *last week*, *one day*, or *next year* as NP-adjuncts, a label that I will adopt here without wanting to make any claims as to the exact internal structure of these items (cf. also Haegeman 2002: 105, note 3). Haegeman observes that, while a temporal adverb like *recently* can occur in any area of the clause, the situation is more complex for NP-adjuncts due to the status of clause-medial placement. This contrast is illustrated in examples (2) and (3) (Haegeman 2002: 81, examples 3 and 5).

(2)   a. **Recently** he left for London.
       b. He **recently** left for London.
       c. He left for London **recently**.

(3) a. ***Tomorrow*** *he leaves for London.*
    b. *(*) He **tomorrow** leaves for London.*
    c. *He leaves for London **tomorrow**.*

The diacritic used in (3b) reflects somewhat conflicting observations made in the literature, with several authors ruling this word order explicitly out (cf. Haegeman 2002: 81–83). These judgments include clauses with finite verbs as in (3b) but also clauses with finite auxiliaries as shown in (4) (examples from McCawley 1988: 201).[1]

(4) a. **John will **tomorrow** finish his assignment.*
    b. **Nancy must **last Friday** have gone to Florida.*

As Haegeman points out, the restriction on the use of NP-adjuncts in medial position is sometimes also explicitly mentioned in pedagogical grammars.

Contrasting with these observations based on grammaticality judgments, corpus data discussed in the literature show that medial NP-adjuncts are by no means unattested. In particular journalistic prose is regularly mentioned as favouring the use of this word order option. The following two examples illustrate this register (Haegeman 2002: 79/80).

(5) a. *A judge **last week** held that a civilian clerk for the city of London police, Esther Thomas, could sue the paper under the Protection against harassment act.* (Guardian, *March 2001, p. 2, col. 3*)
    b. *Frustrated rail passengers will **today** still face chaos and delays on large parts of the network after the holiday break amid increasing anger among the 25 train-operating companies that Railtrack is failing to deliver its recovery programme.* (Guardian, *2 January 2001, p. 1, col. 1*)

In a quantitative analysis of a corpus of newspapers and other prose work, Jacobson (1964: 148), cited by Haegeman (1983: 73), found that clause-medial placement of NP-adjuncts like *today* or *yesterday* is far more frequent in journalistic prose (19%)

---

[1] That clauses with auxiliaries should be treated on a par with those containing a finite main verb is commonly accepted. Thus, for example Quirk et al. (1985: 491) start their discussion of medial placement of adverbials with examples like (i).
(i) *The driver **suddenly** started the engine.*
But they then observe that "[i]n the following variants of [(i)], any native speaker would feel that the adverbials are still in the same position", where "the following variants" refers to examples like (ii), where the adverbial occurs between the auxiliary and the non-finite main verb.
(ii) *The driver has **suddenly** started the engine.*

than in other prose texts (3%).² These data also show, however, that the medial word order option cannot simply be reduced to a single register as it can be found elsewhere albeit at a very low frequency.

Although mid-position NP-adjuncts can be found in language production, the fact that, with the possible exception of journalistic prose, they are rare and that native speakers tend to be reluctant to accept examples of this type suggests that clause-medial placement of NP-adjuncts is strongly constrained. This observation raises two main questions. First, why is medial placement constrained with NP-adjuncts whereas adverbs freely occur in this position? Second, why does register play a role in the use of mid-position NP-adjuncts?

With respect to the first question, one factor that could be argued to play an important role is the length of the constituent occurring in medial position. Hasselgård (2010: 101) observes that there is "a great dominance of adjuncts realised by one word in [...] medial position", and she supports this claim by quantitative evidence according to which 79% of all cases with an adjunct in medial position in her corpus contain a one-word adjunct, 16% a two- to four-word adjunct, and 5% an adjunct that is five words or longer.³ Hasselgård (2010: 102) suggests that this preference for one-word adjuncts could be related to the kind of principles of processing efficiency proposed in Hawkins' work. According to Hawkins (2004), the human processor prefers to minimize the domains in which essential relations between linguistic items are established (Minimize Domains, MiD). If we assume that one of these essential relations is the thematic relation between the subject and its predicate, the occurrence of an adjunct between the two increases the domain in which this relation is established and with each additional word contained in this adjunct the domain is further increased. This effect could be argued to be reinforced if we assume that agreement between the subject and the finite verb is also a relation that is relevant for the purposes of MiD.

---

2 Jacobson's figure for journalistic prose happens to be nearly identical to what Haegeman (2002: 85) found in a small-scale study of NP-adjuncts in the first six pages of *The Guardian* of 5 June 2001 (20.4% in a sample of 49 clauses containing an NP-adjunct).

3 Given Hasselgård's discussion elsewhere, my understanding is that these data include clear parentheticals (i.e. adjuncts typographically set apart by commas or dashes). If such examples were left aside, the predominance of one-word adjuncts in medial position would undoubtedly be even more striking.

Note also that Hasselgård defines the medial domain somewhat differently from what I assume here. Her data for medial placement include cases in which an adjunct occurs between the main verb and its complement as she refers to the area between the subject and the verb's complement as the medial position. Such clauses of the type V-adjunct-O will be treated as involving clause-final placement here.

Thus, from the point of view of MiD, if medial adjunct placement is chosen, a one-word adjunct is preferred because it violates MiD only minimally whereas longer adjuncts lead to more important violations of MiD and are therefore less likely to be used.[4]

Although an approach along these lines may provide a promising account of the length constraints on clause-medial adjunct placement, it is not immediately clear whether it is sufficient to explain the properties of NP-adjuncts in this way. It is certainly the case that many NP-adjuncts contain more than one word (e.g. *this week* in [1b], *last week* in [5a]). But others such as *yesterday* (1a) or *tomorrow* (3b) consist of a single word and would therefore be expected to behave like the numerous one-word adjuncts like *recently* in (2b) that regularly occur in medial position. The fact that the one-word NP-adjuncts are etymologically complex (*yesterday, to-morrow, to-night, to-day*) should not be relevant for these purposes since certain other one-word adjuncts that could be decomposed (e.g. *some-times*) are perfectly acceptable in mid-position (*Miss Marple sometimes reads crime novels*).

These observations suggest that a simple word-length distinction cannot account for the behaviour of NP-adjuncts. The way NP-adjuncts could be distinguished from typical medial adjuncts, however, is by taking structural properties into account. Typical mid-position adjuncts are structurally very simple as they "are for the most part rather short adverb phrases, especially solitary adverbs" (Quirk et al. 1985: 493). As for NP-adjuncts, some are straightforwardly more complex as for example *this week*, which, apart from the N-head *week*, must involve a second head, say D, hosting the demonstrative. By analogy, one-word NP-adjuncts such as *tomorrow* could be argued to be DPs as well, but simply with an empty D-head. Further structural complexity could be assumed if we follow McCawley (1988: 202) (cited by Haegeman 2002: 83) in analysing temporal NP-adjuncts as PPs with a zero preposition. Thus, whereas typical clause-medial adjuncts consist of a single projection headed by an adverb, one-word NP-adjuncts can be argued to contain (at least) one or two additional structural layers. This contrast could then be related to Hawkins' MiD principle provided that empty heads have the same status with respect to MiD as overt ones in that they count for the purposes of counting the size of a domain. For the purposes of our discussion later in this paper, I will assume that this is the case. However,

---

[4] Hasselgård (2010: 101) cites Biber et al. (1999: 808) for a very similar intuition. According to these authors, adjuncts in medial position "interrupt the flow of obligatory components of the clause. For example, they may separate the subject from the verb, the auxiliary verb from the main verb, or the verb from its complement. It is thus not surprising that these positions have a strong preference for one-word adverbials".

given that the structures Hawkins uses in his analyses are very surface-oriented and generally lack empty elements, it would remain to be seen in more detail whether such a hypothesis could easily be integrated into the general system that Hawkins outlines.

Structural differences also play an important role in Ernst's (2002) analysis of adjunct placement. The fact that "[t]here may be restrictions on relatively heavy adjuncts in VO languages between the subject and the verb" (2002: 449) is crucially related by Ernst to a theory of weight in which weight is determined by (a) category membership and (b) stress/focus. With respect to category membership the following hierarchy is proposed: CP > PP > DP > AP > AdvP with complement > AdvP without complement > Adv. This hierarchy is then argued to have an impact on adjunct placement, with the light adjuncts at the very bottom of this hierarchy favouring preverbal placement. However, while in a Hawkins-type analysis the observed restrictions on medial placement can be argued to follow from independently motivated processing constraints, the effect that weight and the related structural hierarchy have in Ernst's analysis seems to be of a more stipulative nature.

Another factor that could potentially have an influence on the status of word orders with medial adjuncts is the way in which they are structurally derived. In principle, the minimal assumption would be that medial NP-adjuncts occur in the same structural position(s) as medial adverbs, i.e. in the inflectional domain between the subject and the main verb either in dedicated specifier positions (as postulated e.g. by Alexiadou 1997 and Cinque 1999 for adverbs) or in adjoined positions (cf. e.g. Ernst 2002). The restrictions on medial placement of NP-adjuncts would then be entirely due to the kind of constraints discussed in the previous paragraphs. An alternative to such an approach would be that word orders with medial NP-adjuncts are not derived in the same way as those with medial adverbs, and that this difference has an impact on their use. An approach in which medial NP-adjuncts and adverbs are treated as syntactically distinct is proposed by Haegeman (2002). Following work by Benincà and Poletto (2004) and Cardinaletti (2004), Haegeman (2002) assumes that NP-adjuncts occupy an IP-edge position whereas adverbs occur IP-internally. For NP-adjuncts to be able to occupy an initial and a medial position, a subject position above the IP-edge and one below must be postulated. Following Cardinaletti, Haegeman assumes that the higher subject position, labelled Spec,SubjP, hosts the "subject of predication" and that "[s]uch a subject is the prominent argument that the sentence is about" (2002: 103). Medial NP-adjuncts can only be derived if the subject occurs in this higher subject position and thus qualifies as a subject of predication, whereas medial adverbs are possible independently of subject placement. It could be argued then that this derivational difference is the source of the more restricted use of medial NP-adjuncts as compared to medial adverbs. However, it is difficult to see how this hypothesis would be sufficient to fully explain the marginal status of medial NP-adjuncts in Present-Day English as they would in principle be expected to be entirely acceptable provided that the subject qualifies as a subject of predication. Some further structural assumptions or factors of the type discussed earlier may therefore be needed.

Before turning to the diachronic development of medial placement of adjunct NPs, let us briefly consider the register issues and, more specifically, the question as to why, as mentioned earlier, journalistic prose seems to be a particularly favourable context for this phenomenon in Present-Day English. Ernst (2002) mentions the register effect in connection with the following pair of examples involving adjunct PPs (2002: 173).

(6) a. *Maureen (*for several years) walked (for several years).*
    b. *The relief officials have for several days tried to move tons of supplies into the devastated valley.*

Ernst observes that cases like (6b) are "typical of more formal and journalistic prose" (2002: 173). After adding several additional examples of this type, he concludes that what they show is that "acceptability in [the medial] position climbs as the length of the string of postverbal material increases". Thus, the lightness of an adjunct in principle favours medial placement, but the heavier the rest of the clause is the heavier a medial adjunct can be: "[I]t is relative (not absolute) heaviness that is at stake" (Ernst 2002: 173). Ernst does not make this fully explicit, but given that he mentions relative heaviness in connection with register differences, his hypothesis would have to be that medial NP-adjuncts occur more frequently in formal and journalistic prose because the postverbal domain is heavier in these registers than in others. However, this hypothesis remains to be evaluated on the basis of a detailed corpus study involving different types of registers.

An alternative account of the register effects with medial adjuncts is provided by Hasselgård (2010: 102–105), who invokes information-structural factors. Hasselgård starts by pointing out that "medial position is not associated with any kind of focus, in contrast to initial and end position which involve thematic and end focus respectively" (2010: 102). The relatively frequent occurrence of medial NP-adjuncts in journalistic prose could then be related to the fact that "news articles, typically reporting what happened the day before the newspaper is distributed, often have relatively self-evident adverbials such as *now, last night, yesterday* etc. in medial position" (2010: 105). Such adverbials are not focus-worthy, and the medial position allows the speaker/writer to background them informationally. In terms of this account, other genres would differ from journalistic prose in that adjuncts of this type play a more important information-structural role.[5]

In the following sections, I will present data tracing the historical development of medial NP-adjuncts, and I will examine how it can be integrated into the analyses of the situation in Present-Day English as presented above.

3 Medial NP-adjuncts in clauses with finite main verbs in the history of English

For this study of the development of medial NP-adjuncts in the history of English, data were collected from the currently available parsed historical corpora of English, covering a wide range of prose texts from the 9th century up to 1914: *The York-Toronto-Helsinki Parsed Corpus of Old English Prose* (Taylor, Warner, Pintzuk, and Beths 2003; 9th to 11th centuries), the *Penn-Helsinki Parsed Corpus of Middle English 2* (PPCME2; Kroch and Taylor 2000a; 1150–1500), the *Penn-Helsinki Parsed Corpus of Early Modern English* (PPCEME; Kroch, Santorini, and Delfs 2004; 1500–1710), *The Parsed Corpus of Early English Correspondence* (PCEEC; Taylor et al. 2006; 1410–1695), the *Penn Parsed Corpus of Modern British English 2* (PPCMBE2; Kroch, Santorini, and Diertani 2016; 1700–1914). Given that the NPs in medial position that are cited in the literature are generally of the temporal kind, I retrieved all affirmative clauses containing a constituent labelled as NP-TMP in the parsed corpora.[6] Some of these clauses were then manually removed: (a) clauses containing an adjunct that patterns with adverbs like *recently* in (2) and that is entirely unproblematic in medial position in Present-Day English (*sometimes, once* or *twice* and spelling variants thereof); (b) *oftentimes* and spelling variants thereof on the grounds that the initial part of the compound regularly occurs in medial position in Present-Day English;

---

[5] A proposal along these lines can also be found in Jacobson (1964: 148): "The reason for the higher percentage of [medial placement] in news-columns must be that these nearly always report what has happened during the day or the day before and that therefore the adverbs *to-day* and *yesterday* are rather unimportant in the context".

[6] The parsed corpora also distinguish other non-argumental NPs: NP-ADV (a relatively restricted class including adverbial free relatives (e.g. *come what may*), adverbial genitives (e.g. *needs, thanks to...*) or certain set phrases (e.g. *face to face*)), NP-DIR (e.g. *that way, southwards*), NP-LOC (e.g. *home*), NP-MSR (e.g. *a long time*), and NP-ADT (described in the corpus manual as a catch-all category that covers any remaining cases of adjunct NPs). Since the NPs included under these labels generally do not occur in medial position, I did not include them in my searches.

As for the focus on affirmative clauses, the aim is to avoid any potential issues of scope that could have an influence on the distribution of the NP-adjunct in negative clauses.

(c) parenthetical adjuncts that are typographically set off by a comma before and/ or after the adjunct since the distribution of parentheticals is known to be less constrained.[7] Based on the remaining data, I examined the distribution of temporal NP-adjuncts in all main and subordinate clauses with an overt subject and a finite main verb (not including copula *be*) from Old to Late Modern English.[8]

3.1 Data

As (7) shows with clauses from different periods, temporal NP-adjuncts in medial position can be found throughout the history of English.[9]

(7) a. *for þat þe   he   **þis dai**   aros   of deaðe.*   (CMTRINIT,97.1303; 1225)
    because he   this day   arose   of death
    'because this day he arose from death'
   b. *Myn   Maister Markham   **yesterday**   rode owte   of London be-tymes.*
                                                    (PASTON,II,142.319.8721; 1456)
    my   Master Markham   yesterday   rode out   of London early
    'My Master Markham rode out of London yesterday at an early hour'
   c. *One of my Fellow Prisoners **last night** receiv'd a letter from his wife ...*
                                                    (PHENRY-E3-H,341.46; 1685)
   d. *If the head mistress **each week** looks over the mark-book in the presence of the class and the teacher ...*   (BEALE-1898-2,31.460; 1898)

In addition to clauses with medial NP-adjuncts as in (7), the data collected also include all clauses with the corresponding elements in pre-subject position and in postverbal position. Any number of additional elements may occur in these clauses. In order to trace the diachronic development of medial NP-adjuncts throughout the history of English, the frequency of medial placement was measured (a) against the

---

7 This method based to the presence of commas does of course not allow us to identify all adjuncts that would have been prosodically marked as parenthetical in spoken language as it is unlikely that commas were consistently used in this context by all authors throughout the history of English. The aim here is therefore simply to reduce the influence of parenthetical intonation on our data to a minimum.
8 Substantial clause type differences can only be found in Old English and Early Middle English (1150–1250), with medial adjunct placement being more frequent in subordinate clauses than in main clauses. Given that for most periods this variable does not make a difference, I leave it aside for the purposes of Tab. 1.
9 Historical examples are followed by the reference as used in the corpora and, at the end, the year of composition of the text.

total of all clauses with an NP-adjunct and (b) against the total of all clauses with an NP-adjunct following the subject (only medial or postverbal). The latter method was used for Tab. 1 as this allows us to compare the data for NP-adjuncts with those for adverbs reported in Haeberli and Ihsane (2016). The figures in the final column of Tab. 1 are taken from that source.[10]

Tab. 1: The distribution of NP-adjuncts and finite main verbs as compared to adverbs from Old to Late Modern English

Periods	$SX_{NP}V$	SVX_{NP}	Total (X = NP)	% $SX_{NP}V$	Total (X = Adv)	% $SX_{Adv}V$
Old English	296	522	818	36.2%	13410	70.2%
1150–1250	12	44	56	21.4%	782	38.2%
1250–1350	0	16	16	0.0%	185	13.5%
1350–1420	4	90	94	4.3%	1650	9.9%
1420–1475	11	173	184	6.0%	1905	8.5%
1475–1500	3	86	89	3.4%	745	16.5%
1500–1525	7	69	76	9.2%	566	37.3%
1525–1570	8	182	190	4.2%	2336	34.3%
1570–1640	22	600	622	3.5%	2917	37.7%
1640–1710	20	504	524	3.8%	4048	42.6%
1710–1770	10	264	274	3.6%	1049	54.4%
1770–1840	16	330	346	4.6%	1172	56.5%
1840–1914	11	395	406	2.7%	930	54.2%

---

10 The periodization in Tab. 1 follows to a large extent the divisions used in the Penn corpora. The only exception is the period 1420–1570, which is divided into four subperiods here rather than the two in the Penn corpora. This is because the time around 1500 is a period of major change in the verbal syntax of English and a more fine-grained division has turned out to be useful for the adverb data examined by Haeberli and Ihsane (2016).

Note also that, after 1570, the periods adopted for the NP-adjunct data in Tab. 1 and those used by Haeberli and Ihsane differ slightly in some cases (1570–1640 is matched in Tab. 1 with the adverb data for 1575–1625 in Haeberli and Ihsane; 1640–1710 is compared to 1625–1700 for adverbs; 1710–1770 is compared to 1700–1770). These minor differences are unlikely to have affected the general picture that emerges from the comparative data in Tab. 1.

Finally, it should also be pointed out that the percentages obtained for adverbs and NP-adjuncts in Tab. 1 and Tab. 3 below for the three periods after 1710 are not based on exactly the same datasets. For adverbs as examined in Haeberli and Ihsane's work, the first version of the PPCMBE was used, whereas for the present study of NP-adjuncts the PPCMBE2 is used. The PPCMBE2 is an expanded version of the PPCMBE1 with an overall size that is multiplied approximately by three. For a relatively rare phenomenon like medial placement of NP-adjuncts, it seemed appropriate to use the bigger corpus even if this meant that the comparisons with adverbs are not based on exactly the same material. But once again, it is unlikely that this difference has a substantial influence on the overall picture we obtain for the situation in Late Modern English.

The frequencies in Tab. 1 show that, while medial NP-adjuncts are common in Old English, their frequency declines rapidly thereafter. The Early Middle English period 1150–1250 is a transitional period during which the rate of medial placement of NP-adjuncts remains non-negligible. But from 1250 onwards this word order becomes a highly marginal phenomenon with frequencies mainly ranging around 3%–4%. The occasional peaks at 6.0% or 9.2% do not differ in statistically significant ways from the surrounding periods.[11]

As the final column in Tab. 1 shows, this development is strikingly different from what is found with adverbs. In Old English, preverbal adverb placement is nearly twice as common as preverbal NP-adjunct placement. The same ratio can also be observed for the Early Middle English period 1150–1250. The decline then proceeds with both orders, and in the periods 1350–1420 and 1420–1475 the difference between the two is no longer statistically significant (chi-square = 3.3, p = 0.07 for 1350–1420; chi-square = 1.36, p = 0.24 for 1420–1475). But from 1475 onwards, the two diachronic trajectories separate, with SAdvV increasing rapidly. The contrast between the two contexts is statistically significant from 1475 onwards (chi-square = 10.7, p = 0.001 for 1475–1500). The increase in preverbal adverb placement occurs in two main steps (the first one around 1500, the second one around 1700), with this word order becoming the majority option in Late Modern English. In contrast, medial NP-adjunct placement remains stable at a very low frequency throughout Early and Late Modern English. Fig. 1 summarizes these quantitative findings.

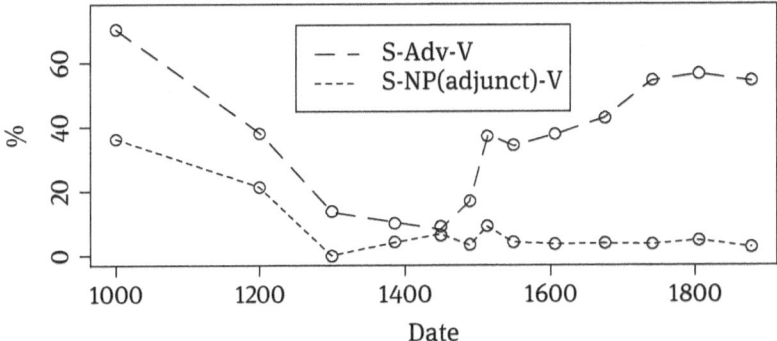

Fig. 1: Medial placement of adverbs and NP-adjuncts from Old to Late Modern English

---

11 Measuring the frequency of medial NP-adjuncts against the total number of NP-adjuncts (i.e. including clause-initial NP-adjuncts) does not lead to a fundamentally different picture. We start with a frequency of 27.1% of medial NP-adjuncts in Old English, followed by a first decline to 17.6% in the period 1150–1250. Then from 1250 onwards, the frequencies are low, generally around 1% to 2.5% with a single peak in the period 1420–1475 at 4.0%.

3.2 Analysis

In this subsection, I will take Haeberli and Ihsane's (2016) analysis of adverb placement as a starting point to explore the question as to why NP-adjuncts do not undergo the same diachronic development. As Fig. 1 illustrates, there are two main differences to be accounted for: (a) Initially, the diachronic development is identical, but medial adverb placement is much more frequent; (b) From around 1500 onwards, medial placement of adverbs increases rapidly while there is stagnation at a low level with NP-adjuncts.

Let us start by considering the first issue, and more specifically the situation in Old English. Haeberli and Ihsane relate the high frequency of preverbal adverb placement in Old English to two factors. First, following Pintzuk (1999) and much subsequent work, it is assumed that Old English shows variation with respect to directionality: The finite verb can occupy a head position (T in Haeberli and Ihsane's analysis) that takes its complement to the left or to the right.[12] The former option derives verb-final or verb-late clauses in which even elements like objects or particles precede the verb. In such clauses, adverbs also occur in a position before the verb. However, Haeberli and Ihsane argue that, although a head-final analysis may account for a large part of the SAdvV orders in Old English, it cannot be maintained for all of them. As has been shown (cf. e.g. Pintzuk 1999, 2005; Pintzuk and Haeberli 2008), clauses involving certain postverbal elements such as pronouns and particles are not compatible with a head-final structure since these elements cannot undergo rightward movement past a verb. Instead, their occurrence in postverbal position must be due to a head-initial structure. But even in such clauses, adverbs can occur between the subject and the finite main verb, and they do so with a non-negligible frequency (28.7% (n = 345); cf. Haeberli and Ihsane 2016: 506). Interestingly, a large majority of these cases (more than 70%) involve the adverb 'then' (þa, þonne), which has been argued to have the status of a discourse particle (van Kemande and Los 2006). Adopting a proposal made by van Kemenade (2011), Haeberli and Ihsane therefore assume that medial adverb placement with head-initial structure may initially have involved a discourse particle position (Spec,PrtP) occurring between TP (hosting the verb in its head) and a higher subject position. Haeberli and Ihsane situate this subject position above the Fin head but do not attribute a more specific label to it. This

---

[12] For simplicity's sake, I will refer to variation in directionality here rather than to the presence or absence of different leftward movements that would have to be assumed within a purely head-initial clause structure. The main points to be made below should not be affected by this choice in any substantial way.

subject position is distinguished from a lower one in Spec,TP. A partial clause structure based on these proposals is given in (8), which also includes elements of Haeberli and Ihsane's structural analysis below TP that will be relevant for our later discussion.

(8) SU1 ... Fin [$_{PrtP}$ **þa, þonne** [$_{TP}$ SU2 [$_T$V] ... Adv ... [$_{Asp}$ ¥] [$_{VP}$ ¥]]]

Given that adverbs other than 'then' can be found in this position (e.g. *eac* 'also', *nu* 'now', *sona* 'soon', *swa* 'so'), albeit at low frequencies, it must be assumed that the use of PrtP in Old English is being extended to other adverbs that do not have the status of discourse particles. I will represent this extension in (9) by labelling the projection above TP as an unspecified functional projection FP.

(9) SU1 ... Fin [$_{FP}$ **Prt/Adv** [$_{TP}$ SU2 [$_T$V] ... Adv ... [$_{Asp}$ ¥] [$_{VP}$ ¥]]]

As for NP-adjuncts, head-final structure can also be invoked as a source for medial placement. But is the second derivational option, which involves head-initial structure, also available for NP-adjuncts? In order to address this question, we have to identify clauses that are clearly head-initial (i.e. clauses that have a non-extraposable element like a pronoun or a particle to the right of the verb) and that contain an NP-adjunct. Unfortunately, there are only 26 clauses of this type in our corpus. But in none of these does the NP-adjunct occur in medial position. This finding may suggest that the medial position is not available for NP-adjuncts in head-initial structures in Old English. Due to the small amount of data, this conclusion has to remain somewhat speculative, but in terms of the analysis of adverbs outlined in the previous paragraph, such a restriction would not be entirely surprising. As pointed out, the medial position with head-initial structure is primarily used by the discourse particle *þa/þonne* in Old English (Spec,PrtP). This element is structurally and prosodically light. It would be plausible to assume then that, although the discourse particle position starts hosting other elements as well, they remain similar in nature. This would be the case for other adverbs, but not for the more complex NP-adjuncts.

If these hypotheses are on the right track, the frequency differences with respect to medial placement with different types of adjuncts in Old English could be accounted for in terms of the options that are available to derive this word order: both head-initial and head-final structure with adverbs, only head-final structure with NP-adjuncts.

After the Old English period, head-final structure declines. There is some evidence for residues of head-final structure in the functional domain in the earliest Middle English period 1150–1250 (cf. e.g. Haeberli and Ingham 2007: 18, Kroch and Taylor 2000b: 138–142) but after that English can to a large extent be considered as purely head-initial in the functional domain. Given the importance of head-final structure for deriving SXV order in Old English, it is not surprising that this order rapidly declines in Early Middle English both with adverbs and with NP-adjuncts. Haeberli and Ihsane (2016: 508–510) identify two further developments in this period that are of relevance for our purposes. First, the distinction between the two subject positions SU1 and SU2 in (8) and (9) becomes blurred, and the language moves towards a system, shown in (10), where the subject and the finite verb occur in a specifier-head relation in TP.

(10) ... Fin [$_{FP}$ **Prt/Adv** [$_{TP}$ SU [$_T$V] ... **Adv** ... [$_{Asp}$ ∀] [VP ∀]]]

If we assume that T'-adjunction of adjuncts is ruled out, the likelihood for an adjunct to occur between the subject and the verb is thus further reduced. Second, to account for remaining SAdvV orders up to the middle of the 15th century, Haeberli and Ihsane propose that high subject placement marginally persists until then, and that SAdvV continues being derived as in (9) above. Since *þa/þonne* lose their status as discourse particles in Middle English (cf. van Kemenade and Los 2006: 244), the position between the high subject and the verb extends its role more and more and hosts any type of adverb. What we may assume then is that NP-adjuncts start occurring in this position as well. Hence, SXV is derived identically with adverbs and NP-adjuncts at this point, as shown in (11). But due to the decline of the higher subject position and the rise of the structure in (10), SXV as derived in (11) has the status of a marginal word order option with both elements.

(11) **SU1** ... Fin [$_{FP}$ **Adv/NP**$_{adjunct}$ [$_{TP}$ SU2 [$_T$V] ... **Adv** ... [$_{Asp}$ ∀] [$_{VP}$ ∀]]]

After 1475, this situation changes rapidly. The frequency of SAdvV order is multiplied nearly by five within 50 years whereas no significant development can be observed with NP-adjuncts. With respect to adverbs, Haeberli and Ihsane (2016: 514–520) conclude that the rise of SAdvV is the result of the loss of verb movement past adverbs. More precisely, they propose that verb movement to a high inflectional head (T) is lost and replaced by verb movement to a lower inflectional head (Asp) around 1500.[13] This is illustrated in (12).

(12) ... Fin [$_{FP}$ Adv/NP$_{adjunct}$ [$_{TP}$ **SU** ... **Adv** ... [$_{Asp}$ V] [$_{VP}$ ∀]]]

The question that remains then is why the identical word order pattern with NP-adjuncts does not undergo the same diachronic development. There are two

---

[13] The hypothesis that verb movement to T is replaced by verb movement to Asp rather than by complete absence of verb movement is based on the fact that the word order V-*not* remains very strong in the 16th century and beyond. Cases of V-*not* are analysed by Haeberli and Ihsane as involving verb movement to Asp past negation occurring in a NegP between AspP and VP.

main possibilities to account for this contrast. First, it could be argued that NP-adjuncts are banned from the medial position(s) occupied by adverbs between T and Asp in (12), and clauses with a medial NP-adjunct must therefore be derived in a different way. The alternative, shown in (13), is that the grammar does not distinguish between the two types of adjuncts and they can in principle be merged in the same structural positions.

(13) ... Fin $[_{FP}$ Adv/NP$_{adjunct}$ $[_{TP}$ **SU** ... **Adv/NP**$_{adjunct}$ ... $[_{Asp}$ **V** $]$ $[_{VP}$ ∀ $]]]$

Independent factors of the type described in section 2 above would then have to account for the restrictions on medial placement of NP-adjuncts, e.g. processing constraints (Hawkins), relative heaviness/lightness (Ernst), or information structure (Hasselgård).

The first scenario is potentially plausible given Haegeman's (2002) approach to medial NP-adjuncts in Present-Day English. As discussed in section 2, Haegeman proposes that NP-adjuncts do not occur in the inflectional domain but at the IP-edge and that clause-medial placement of an NP-adjunct involves subject movement beyond the IP-edge. The structure I proposed in (11) above for medial NP-adjuncts in Late Middle English (1350–1475), corresponds very much to Haegeman's hypotheses: NP-adjuncts occupy a position above TP (i.e. Haegeman's IP-edge) and the subject is in an even higher position (Haegeman's Spec,SubjP). Thus, we could assume that the way in which clauses with medial NP-adjuncts are derived has been stable since the Late Middle English period. The loss of verb movement to T therefore had an effect on the distribution of adverbs only but not on that of NP-adjuncts.

Although this convergence of two independently proposed analyses is encouraging, I will argue in the next section on the basis of evidence from clauses with a finite auxiliary and a non-finite main verb that the historical development of NP-adjuncts is somewhat more complex than suggested by the data examined so far.

4 Medial NP-adjuncts in clauses with a finite auxiliary and a non-finite main verb

4.1 Data

In clauses with a finite auxiliary, two medial positions between the subject and the main verb have to be distinguished: (a) Position M1 between the subject and the auxiliary; (b) Position M2 between the auxiliary and the non-finite main verb.[14] Temporal NP-adjuncts can be found in both positions throughout the history of English. Example (14) below illustrates option M1, whereas placement in M2 is shown in (15).

(14) a. *and þe Kyng Eldrede and his broþer Alurede* **þat day** *were descomfited*
(CMBRUT3,108.3257; c1400)
and the king Æthelred and his brother Alfred that day were beaten
'and king Æthelred and his brother Alfred were beaten that day.'
b. *The souldgerors* **that night** *were kept in whiles it was tenne of the clok*
(GARDIN,153.007.677; 1545)
the soldiers that night were kept in until it was ten o' clock
'The soldiers were kept in that night until it was ten o'clock.'
c. *if we* **this day** *are examined concerning a good deed done to an impotent man*
(ERV-NEW-1881-2,4,1A.869; 1881)

(15) a. *And for a long tyme aftur he was* **eche day** *techyng in þe temple*
(CMWYCSER,261.650; c1400)
and for a long time after he was each day teaching in the temple
'And for a long time after, he taught in the temple every day'
b. *And the Quene of Hungarye hath* **this night** *invited me to suppe with her tomorowe at night*
(GARDIN, 191.013.1054; 1545)
And the Queen of Hungary has this night invited me to sup with her tomorrow at night
'And the Queen of Hungary invited me tonight to sup with her tomorrow'
c. *she has* **this morning** *eaten the greatest part of this Trout;*
(WALTON-E3-H,210.23; 1676)
d. *They will* **every day and hour** *be stronger*
(SOUTHEY-1813-1,178.88, *Life of Nelson*; 1813)
e. *Ah, my sweet friend, we were* **this moment** *speaking of you*
(COYNE-1855-2,18.782; 1855)

---

14 To be precise, an additional distinction could be made here for cases where the finite auxiliary is followed by a non-finite auxiliary (or possibly even two) and then the main verb. However, such cases do not occur very frequently, and a separate quantitative analysis would not seem to be of much relevance for our purposes. M2 therefore includes word orders of the type $SAux_{finite}X_{NP}Aux_{non-finite}V$ as well as $SAux_{finite}Aux_{non-finite}X_{NP}V$.

For the quantitative analysis of medial placement of NP-adjuncts with auxiliaries, the same corpora and the same methods were used as for clauses with finite main verbs in section 3, the only difference being that three distributional options are distinguished rather than two. The results are presented in Tab. 2, with percentages given for the options that are of interest to us, i.e. M1 and M2.

Tab. 2: The distribution of NP-adjuncts, finite auxiliaries and non-finite main verbs from Old to Late Modern English

Periods	M1 $SX_{NP}AuxV$	M2 $SAuxX_{NP}V$	$SAuxVX_{NP}$	Total
Old English	33 (20.5%)	52 (32.3%)	76	161
1150–1250	2 (13.3%)	6 (40.0%)	7	15
1250–1350	0 (0.0%)	2 (25.0%)	6	8
1350–1420	4 (6.1%)	15 (22.7%)	47	66
1420–1475	2 (0.9%)	27 (11.6%)	204	233
1475–1500	1 (1.5%)	5 (7.7%)	59	65
1500–1525	1 (2.0%)	12 (24.0%)	37	50
1525–1570	12 (7.4%)	38 (23.3%)	113	163
1570–1640	7 (1.4%)	96 (18.6%)	414	517
1640–1710	9 (2.3%)	84 (21.1%)	305	398
1710–1770	1 (0.5%)	32 (17.2%)	153	186
1770–1840	1 (0.4%)	34 (12.5%)	238	273
1840–1914	1 (0.4%)	10 (3.7%)	261	272

The word order option M1 is most frequent in Old English. Once again, this can be related to the head-final properties of Old English as SXAuxV can be analysed as the occurrence of the auxiliary in a head-final projection and rightward movement of the main verb (Verb (Projection) Raising, cf. van Kemenade 1987; Haeberli and Pintzuk 2012). The frequency of M1 then declines with the loss of head-final structure. From 1250 onwards, SXAuxV order is extremely rare throughout the history of English with frequencies generally not reaching more than 2%.

Word order option M2 is also more frequent in Old English than in most of the later periods. However, the difference is less substantial here. The reason for this is that SAuxXV can be straightforwardly derived by a head-initial grammar, and the decline of head-final structure does therefore not affect option M2 in as important a way. Only cases where SAuxXV is derived through head-final structure with Verb Projection Raising are no longer available after the Old English period. Despite this limited influence of the loss of head-final structure, we can observe a downward trend for M2 that persists throughout the Middle English period and reaches a low point at the end of the 15th century with 7.7% of M2. After that, the frequency goes back to the level of the 14th century around 20% and remains relatively stable until 1770. A second decline can then be observed in the Late Modern English period, with the decline in the period 1840–1914 being particularly significant (chi-square 14.15, p < 0.001).

As was done in Tab. 1 for main verbs, I will now compare clauses with NP-adjuncts on the one hand and clauses with an adverb of any type on the other. Columns 2 and 3 repeat the frequencies for NP-adjuncts from Tab. 2 whereas columns 5 and 6 present corresponding figures for the distribution of one-word AdvPs (based on Haeberli and Ihsane in preparation). The total number of clauses on which the percentages are based (i.e. M1 + M2 + SAuxVX) are listed in columns 4 and 7.

Tab. 3: Medial NP-adjuncts and adverbs in clauses with finite auxiliaries

Periods	M1 $SX_{NP}AuxV$	M2 $SAuxX_{NP}V$	Total (X = NP)	M1 $SX_{Adv}AuxV$	M2 $SAuxX_{Adv}V$	Total (X = Adv)
Old English	20.5%	32.3%	161	23.1%	64.4%	3463
1150–1250	13.3%	40.0%	15	10.6%	59.2%	407
1250–1350	0.0%	25.0%	8	3.6%	56.5%	168
1350–1420	6.1%	22.7%	66	3.9%	51.3%	1196
1420–1475	0.9%	11.6%	233	1.4%	50.1%	1659
1475–1500	1.5%	7.7%	65	2.6%	52.2%	699
1500–1525	2.0%	24.0%	50	2.9%	63.0%	622
1525–1570	7.4%	23.3%	163	3.2%	59.8%	3262
1570–1640	1.4%	18.6%	517	2.0%	65.7%	4045
1640–1710	2.3%	21.1%	398	1.6%	67.4%	6438
1710–1770	0.5%	17.2%	186	2.8%	74.3%	1186
1770–1840	0.4%	12.5%	273	2.9%	75.1%	1575
1840–1914	0.4%	3.7%	272	3.9%	70.2%	1245

If we first consider the status of the M1 position, we can observe that the diachronic developments with the two types of adjuncts are very similar. SXAuxV occurs with a frequency of around 20% in Old English, then the rate declines and remains at very low levels from 1250 onwards. Although adverbs tend to occur in pre-auxiliary position somewhat more frequently, the differences are minor in terms of percentage points as well as proportionally, with the exception of the Late Modern English period (1710–1914) where M1 is between 5 to 10 times more frequent with adverbs.

The situation is different with M2. Already in Old English, M2 order is over 30% more frequent with adverbs than with NP-adjuncts, and a substantial difference in the range of 30% to 40% then persists throughout the history of English. Proportionally, the frequencies are generally about twice to three times as high with adverbs compared to NP-adjuncts. At two points, in the 15th century and after 1710, the frequency differences are even increased due to a decline in SAuxXV order with NP-adjuncts. The development is particularly striking in the second one of these periods, as the decline with NP-adjuncts goes together with a certain increase with adverbs. The result of this is a very strong contrast between the two contexts in the final period examined, with the frequency difference reaching 66.5% and M2 being nearly twenty times more frequent with adverbs.

The auxiliary data thus confirm the finding in section 3 that medial placement is considerably less common with NP-adjuncts than with adverbs throughout the entire history of English. One issue that remains to be considered now is what the status of medial NP-adjunct placement is in the different contexts presented in Tabs. 1 and 2, i.e. in clauses with finite main verbs as opposed to clauses with finite auxiliaries. Before repeating the relevant data, a preliminary point is necessary, however. As often observed in the literature (cf. Lightfoot 1979, 2006 among many others), auxiliaries behave syntactically like regular main verbs in Old and Middle English whereas, after the Middle English period, the two verbal elements start having distinctive properties. This contrast is generally analysed structurally in terms of the decline of verb movement with finite main verbs, and the absence of such a decline with auxiliaries. Thus, from a structural point of view, data involving finite main verbs and finite auxiliaries can be compared in a straightforward manner up to around 1500 as the two elements occupy identical positions. With the reanalysis of auxiliaries, however, such a parallelism no longer holds and comparisons have to take the distinct structural distribution of auxiliaries and main verbs into account. This development is illustrated for adverbs in (16).[15]

(16) a. *Before 1500: SU (Adv) [$_T$ V$_{+fin}$/Aux$_{+fin}$] ... (Adv) ... [$_{VP}$ ...]*
 b. *After 1500: SU (Adv) [$_T$ Aux$_{+fin}$] ... (Adv) ... [$_{Asp}$ V$_{+fin}$] [$_{VP}$ ...]*

Table 4 compares the figures for medial placement of NP-adjuncts with auxiliaries from Tab. 2 and with main verbs from Tab. 1.

---

15 As pointed out in footnote 13 above, V-to-Asp as represented in (16b) is then lost by the 18th century as well, and the finite verb remains within the VP.

Tab. 4: Medial NP-adjuncts in clauses with finite auxiliaries and in clauses with finite main verbs

Periods	M1 SX$_{NP}$AuxV	M2 SAuxX$_{NP}$V	SX$_{NP}$V
Old English	20.5%	32.3%	36.2%
1150–1250	13.3%	40.0%	21.4%
1250–1350	0.0%	25.0%	0.0%
1350–1420	6.1%	22.7%	4.3%
1420–1475	0.9%	11.6%	6.0%
1475–1500	1.5%	7.7%	3.4%
1500–1525	2.0%	24.0%	9.2%
1525–1570	7.4%	23.3%	4.2%
1570–1640	1.4%	18.6%	3.5%
1640–1710	2.3%	21.1%	3.8%
1710–1770	0.5%	17.2%	3.6%
1770–1840	0.4%	12.5%	4.6%
1840–1914	0.4%	3.7%	2.7%

Let us start by considering the data up to 1500. As discussed in section 3.2, SXV orders are best analysed in this period as involving verb movement to T. Given the observations made in the previous paragraph, the same assumption can be made for auxiliaries. Thus, the data for SXV order can be directly compared with those for SXAuxV order (M1) in Tab. 4, and we can indeed observe that the two contexts have very similar properties. Although SXV is generally somewhat more frequent than SXAuxV, the overall diachronic development is identical and the occurrences of SXV/SXAuxV have a very marginal status from 1250 onwards. As for the M2 order with auxiliaries, it shows that NP-adjuncts can occur in the domain between T and the VP occupied by the main verb and that they do so with considerable frequencies although a certain decrease can be observed in the 15th century.

After 1500, main verbs no longer move to T whereas auxiliaries can still be assumed to occupy this position. This means that SXV order now has to be compared with M1 and M2 combined, since adjuncts occupying the equivalent of the M2 position in clauses without an auxiliary precede the finite main verb once verb movement past adverbs has been lost. When we compare the frequencies for M1+M2 with the frequencies for SXV in Tab. 4 after 1500, we can observe that there is a substantial contrast between auxiliaries and main verbs. Whereas the auxiliary data suggest that medial placement of NP-adjuncts is common (around 20%, with the exception of the final decline), the figures involving finite main verbs show a very different picture (low frequencies around 4%, with the exception of a statistically not significant peak at 9.2% at the beginning). The consistently low rates observed in main verb contexts even after the loss of verb movement past adverbs is now all the more surprising given the relatively high frequencies found in auxiliary contexts.

One final point to be made with respect to Tab. 4 is that the contrast between auxiliaries and main verbs disappears in the last period (1840–1914). The frequency of medial placement with auxiliaries remains somewhat higher (4.1% for M1+M2, 2.7% for SXV), but the contrast is not statistically significant (chi-square 0.92, p = 0.34). In the preceding period (1770–1840), we still find a highly significant difference between the two contexts (12.9% vs. 4.5%; chi-square 13.56, p < 0.001).

4.2 Analysis

With these additional findings in mind, we can return to the question raised in section 3.2 as to how the unexpected quantitative stability of SXV order with NP-adjuncts after 1500 can be explained. Two possibilities were suggested in section 3.2. Either NP-adjuncts are blocked from the positions occupied by medial adverbs throughout the history of English and clauses with medial NP-adjuncts are derived in a different way (as proposed e.g. in Haegeman's 2002 account of Present-Day English); (ii) NP-adjuncts and adverbs can be merged in the same positions but the use of the medial positions is restricted by factors that are external to the grammar as such (e.g. processing constraints and/or information structure). According to this option, NP-adjuncts could be inserted in the Adv positions in structure (16).

The data in Tab. 4 now provide some evidence against option (i). The non-negligible frequencies with which NP-adjuncts occur in the medial position M2 with auxiliaries at least up to the 19th century are most easily accounted for if we assume that placement of NP-adjuncts in a structural position between T and the VP is not ruled out. If it were, the quantitative distribution of the two options M1 and M2 would be highly surprising given a structural analysis along the lines proposed by Haegeman (2002). As Haegeman points out (2002: 107, fn. 26), in terms of her analysis, the word order SAuxX$_{NP}$V would presumably have to be analysed as being the result of insertion of the NP-adjunct at the IP-edge, movement of the subject to SubjP and, in addition, auxiliary movement to the head of SubjP. Without the last step, we would obtain the order SX$_{NP}$AuxV. This would imply that throughout the history of English a word order option (M2) that is derivationally more complex is strongly favoured over one (M1) that is simpler. Given the role economy considerations play in generative theory, this would be an unexpected conclusion.

In sum, an account of the diachronic developments immediately after 1500 in terms of different structural analyses for adverbs and NP-adjuncts seems to be problematic. Let us therefore adopt what would be the minimal assumption, namely that NP-adjuncts can, in principle, be merged in the same positions as adverbs at this point in the history of English. In terms of this hypothesis, we have to explain why medial placement of NP-adjuncts occurs much more frequently in clauses with a finite auxiliary than in clauses with a finite main verb. A possible account of this could be based on Hawkins' (2004) Minimize Domains (MiD) approach. As pointed out in section 2, according to this approach, the human processor prefers to minimize the domains in which essential relations between linguistic items are established. If we assume that both the thematic relation between a verb and its subject and the agreement relation between a finite verbal element and the subject are part of these essential relations, we immediately get the desired result for the quantitative contrasts shown in Tab. 4.[16] In a clause with a finite auxiliary and the word order SAuxXV (M2), X only affects the size of the domain for one of these two relations, the thematic relation. The agreement relation is established optimally under adjacency between the subject and the auxiliary. With finite main verbs, however, the domains for both the thematic relation and the agreement relation are affected by the presence of an adjunct in the order SXV. Thus, medial placement of an adjunct in the position M2 with an auxiliary is preferred over medial placement with a finite main verb because the negative effects of the adjunct on MiD are smaller with the former than with the latter. As a consequence, SAuxXV order is used more frequently than SXV order. The same frequency contrasts between auxiliaries and main verbs would then also be expected with adverbs. A comparison of the frequencies for SXV order with adverbs in Tab. 1 (rise from 8.5% in the 15th century to over 50% in Late Modern English) and SAuxXV with adverbs in Tab. 3 (frequencies between 50% and over 75%) shows that this expectation is borne out. Furthermore, as pointed out earlier, the frequencies with adverbs are systematically higher in both contexts compared to NP-adjuncts, which, as observed in section 2, could be related to the richer structure of NP-adjuncts as compared to one-word AdvPs.

---

16 Hawkins (2004) does not explicitly consider the role of subject-verb agreement in a language like English. However, the assumptions made here would be in line with some of the general points made by Hawkins. For example, he suggests that the MiD "predicts that *all* syntactic and semantic relations between categories will prefer minimal domains for processing" (emphasis his) and that "[t]he more syntactic and semantic relations linking two categories, and the more minimal their domains can be in the processing of each, the more adjacent or proximate these categories should be" (2004: 33).

If a processing account of the contrast between auxiliaries and main verbs with respect to medial placement of adjuncts is on the right track, there is one aspect of the data presented in Tabs. 1 to 4 that remains unexpected. The minimal assumption would be that processing constraints remain stable over time. In our case, this means that the advantage of clauses with auxiliaries over those with main verbs with respect to medial placement of NP-adjuncts should lead to substantially higher frequencies with auxiliaries throughout the history of English. This is to a large extent the case, but as pointed out in the discussion of Tab. 4 already, there is one clear exception to this generalization occurring in the period 1840–1914.[17]

Although somewhat speculative, the following scenario could account for this development. When we consider the proportion of NP-adjuncts among all medial adjuncts, we can observe that it gradually declines from 1500 onwards. This is shown in Tab. 5, which compares the numbers of medial NP-adjuncts and other medial adjuncts in Late Middle English, Early Modern English and Late Modern English: one-word AdvPs (X = Adv; data based on Haeberli and Ihsane 2016), AdvPs containing more than one word (X = AdvP [>1]), adjunct PPs,[18] and other adjuncts that were excluded from the counts for NP- and PP-adjuncts.[19,20]

---

[17] A second significant contrast is found in the period 1475–1500. Although medial placement with auxiliaries is more frequent in this period than with main verbs (9.2% for M1+M2, 3.4% for SXV; cf. Tab. 4), the difference is not statistically significant (Fisher's Exact Test, p = 0.17). However, the amount of evidence for this period is very limited, and I will have to leave it open here how this contrast may best be accounted for.

[18] For this column, all clauses with a constituent in medial position that are labelled as PP in the parsed corpora were examined. I excluded the following elements from the counts: clear cases of PP-arguments; elements of the type X+P such as *therefore* or *thereby*; two-word PPs that regularly occur in medial position in Present-Day English such as *at last, at least, indeed, in fact* or *of course*; parentheticals marked with a comma before and/or after the PP. Future research will have to investigate in more detail the diachronic development of PP-adjuncts in the history of English and the way this development can be integrated into the account of NP-adjuncts outlined in this paper.

[19] This group mainly includes adjuncts that are labelled as NP-TMP or PP in the parsed corpora but are entirely productive in medial position in Present-Day English such as *sometimes, once* or *twice* for NPs and the elements mentioned in fn. 18 above for PPs. Parenthetical elements that are preceded and/or followed by a comma in the corpora are not included in this table.

[20] As pointed out in fn. 10, the tables in this paper are generally based on a larger version of the Late Modern English corpus (PPCMBE2) than Haeberli and Ihsane's work. In order to make the data from the different studies comparable, I have based the figures in Tab. 5 only on text files that occur in the first version of the PPCMBE. Hence, the numbers for NP-adjuncts in this table are lower than the totals for the periods 1710–1770, 1770–1840 and 1840–1914 in Tabs. 1 and 2.

Tab. 5: NP-adjuncts and other adjuncts in medial position

Period	NP	Adv	AdvP (>1)	PP	Other	Total	%NP
1350–1500: SXV	19	448	32	230	46	775	2.5%
1500–1710: SXV	57	3373	208	643	209	4490	1.3%
1710–1914: SXV	13	1773	95	77	286	2244	0.6%
1350–1500: M1+M2	54	1897	190	430	63	2634	2.1%
1500–1710: M1+M2	259	8319	1275	2438	925	13216	2.0%
1710–1914: M1+M2	26	3065	293	779	757	4920	0.5%

The data in Tab. 5 show that, in the texts examined, the number of medial NP-adjuncts has always been rather low compared to that of other adjuncts in the same position. But the relative frequency of medial NP-adjuncts is reduced even further in Early and Late Modern English. Statistically significant decreases can be observed with finite main verbs (SXV) from Late Middle to Early Modern English (chi-square = 6.49, p = 0.01) and from Early to Late Modern English (chi-square = 6.93, p < 0.01), and with auxiliaries (M1+M2) from Early to Late Modern English (chi-square = 47.48, p < 0.001). What could be argued then is that, once the frequency of medial NP-adjuncts falls below a certain threshold, the adjunct positions in the inflectional domain are reanalysed by language learners as categorially restricted and no longer available to NP-adjuncts. As a consequence of this, the rare remaining medial NP-adjuncts have to be given a different structural analysis. Here, an approach along the lines proposed by Haegeman (2002) with NP-adjuncts merged at the IP-edge would now be conceivable. What this would suggest then is that the distinctive structure for NP-adjuncts proposed for Present-Day English by Haegeman emerged only in the Late Modern English period.

However, these observations do not allow us to answer our initial question yet, i.e. why by the end of the Late Modern English period medial NP-adjuncts stop being more frequent with auxiliaries as compared to main verbs. In terms of the processing factors (MiD) discussed earlier, the order $SAuxX_{NP}V$ (M2) should be favoured over $SX_{NP}V$ regardless of the structural position in which the adjunct occurs. What the diachronic development may suggest is that the processing advantage of medial NP-adjuncts in M2 is offset by negative effects of the structural change occurring in Late Modern English. In terms of Haegeman's (2002) analysis, this is indeed what can be argued to happen. As discussed earlier, the hypothesis that NP-adjuncts are merged at the IP-edge implies that with the orders $SX_{NP}V$ and $SX_{NP}AuxV$ (M1) the subject moves past the adjunct to a high subject position in SubjP. But to derive $SAuxX_{NP}V$ (M2), a further derivational step is necessary besides subject movement: Movement of the auxiliary to the head of

SubjP. Thus, from the point of view of derivational economy, $SX_{NP}V$ and M1 are favoured over M2 because they involve fewer derivational steps, whereas, from the point of view of processing, M2 is favoured over $SX_{NP}V$ and M1 due to MiD. It could be argued then that, on balance, M2 no longer has a privileged status once NP-adjuncts are reanalysed as occurring at the IP-edge, and that the loss of the frequency contrasts observed earlier is a consequence of this structural change. Such a conclusion must remain somewhat speculative at this point, however. First, although the analysis proposed gives the desired result, it raises the potential problem of attributing a cumulative effect on usage frequencies to factors that are of a fundamentally distinct nature, i.e. processing constraints and economy constraints on structural derivations. It remains to be seen whether such a hypothesis is legitimate and finds independent support in other contexts. Secondly, being based on Haegeman's analysis of Present-Day English, the above proposals imply that the quantitative pattern observed for the period 1840–1914 has remained stable since then. Future research will have to determine whether this is indeed the case. Finally, the proposals made above have further consequences as for example for the analysis of PP-adjuncts, an issue that I will have to leave for future research.

The aim of the analysis so far in terms of processing and structural change has been to explain the lower frequencies of medial NP-adjuncts as compared to adverbs and the frequency differences between main verb and auxiliary contexts. What these proposals cannot account for so far is the register variation that has been observed for Present-Day English. Preferences due to processing advantages would be expected to hold across registers. Similarly, the fact that we assign a distinctive structure to medial NP-adjuncts would not explain why this option is more common in journalistic prose than elsewhere. An additional factor is therefore likely to play a role here. As discussed in section 2, Hasselgård (2010) proposes that the relevant factor is information structure. More precisely, she notes that medial adjuncts tend to lack focus and have low informational content, and that this may frequently be true of NP-adjuncts in journalistic prose but much less so in other registers. Hasselgård's hypothesis could now be integrated into our account. As observed in section 3.2, the earliest occurrences of medial adverb placement in head-initial structure as found in Old English mostly involve the elements *þa* and *þonne* ('then'). These have been analysed as discourse particles and have a very low informational content. The information-structural constraints on the medial adjunct position in head-initial contexts could therefore be argued to have its origin in Old English and thus to have been in place throughout the history of English. If this is correct, it is not only preferences due to processing advantages but also information-structural preferences that contribute to the higher frequencies of medial placement with adverbs as compared to NP-adjuncts in the history of English.[21] However, this additional factor is unlikely to be relevant for the contrast between main verb and auxiliary contexts discussed in the previous paragraphs, as the information-structural properties of NP-adjuncts would not be expected to be affected substantially by the presence or absence of an auxiliary.

5 Conclusion

Present-Day English shows a surprising contrast with respect to adjunct placement between the subject and the main verb. Whereas adverbs productively occupy this medial area of the clause, the occurrence of NP-adjuncts is very constrained. Although medial NP-adjuncts can be found in corpora, they are infrequent and tend to be judged as marginal or ungrammatical by speakers. Furthermore, they seem to be subject to register variation, with journalistic prose regularly being identified as a context that favours the use of medial NP-adjuncts. The aim of this paper was to shed new light on this distributional contrast between adverbs and NP-adjuncts by exploring the diachronic development of adjunct placement from Old to Late Modern English.

A quantitative overview of the placement of adverbs and NP-adjuncts throughout the history of English led to two main findings. First, ever since the decline of head-final structure in early English, the frequency of medial placement of NP-adjuncts in clauses with finite main verbs has been very low. This is in contrast to adverbs, which, after a low-frequency phase in Late Middle English, become more and more common in medial position as a consequence of the decline of

---

21 Given these proposals, it may be unexpected now that, as observed earlier, there are no statistically significant contrasts between NP-adjuncts and adverbs in clauses with finite main verbs in two Late Middle English periods (1350–1420, 1420–1475). Several observations can be made in this respect. First, even though statistical significance is not reached, the rates of medial placement remain higher with adverbs in these periods than with NPs. Second, the contrast is very close to significance in the first period (p = 0.07). Third, more than half of the examples of $SX_{NP}V$ in the period 1420–1475 come from two authors only (6 out of 11). Furthermore, this is one of only two periods after 1150 with a rate of $SX_{NP}V$ above 5%. These two observations may suggest that our sample is not necessarily representative. Finally, I proposed earlier that SAdvV is a word order option that is on its way out of the language in this period and that it is generally derivationally complex (adverb placement above TP and subject in a high position). This marked status may have led to a reduction of the rate of SAdvV to a level that is comparable to $SX_{NP}V$ despite the processing and information-structural advantages. Overall, it seems to me that the Late Middle English data do not provide sufficiently robust evidence against the hypothesis that processing and information-structural properties affect medial adjunct placement throughout the history of English.

verb movement around 1500. Second, data involving clauses with a finite auxiliary and a non-finite main verb show that, although a clear contrast between adverbs and NP-adjuncts remains, medial placement of the latter is considerably more frequent in this context than with finite main verbs. In particular, word orders with the NP-adjunct between the auxiliary and the non-finite main verb are fairly common. It is only in the Late Modern English period that medial NP-adjuncts decline with auxiliaries. In the final period examined (1840–1914), they are rare in both types of clauses (2.7% with main verbs, 4.1% with auxiliaries) and the contrast is no longer statistically significant.

In order to account for these quantitative patterns, I proposed that, from Old English to the 19th century, NP-adjuncts are similar to adverbs with respect to where they are merged in the clause structure. More precisely, NP-adjuncts, like adverbs, can occupy a position in the domain between TP and VP. This accounts for why NP-adjuncts regularly occur between a finite auxiliary and a non-finite main verb throughout most of the history of English. As for the fact that medial placement is substantially less frequent with NP-adjuncts than with adverbs, I followed proposals made in the literature for Present-Day English, assuming that processing constraints (cf. Hawkins's 2004 MiD) and information-structural properties (cf. Hasselgård 2010) disfavour the use of NP-adjuncts in a medial position compared to adverbs. These hypotheses also allow us to account for frequency differences between clauses with finite main verbs and clauses with finite auxiliaries (MiD), and for register variation (information structure). Finally, with respect to the decrease of NP-medial adjuncts in clauses with auxiliaries in Late Modern English, I suggested that it may be due to a structural reanalysis that removed the advantage auxiliaries had over main verbs with respect to medial placement of NP-adjuncts. As for the cause of this structural reanalysis, I related it to a decline of the proportion of NPs among all medial adjuncts in the modern period. This decline can be argued to have led language learners to reanalyze the adjunct positions in the inflectional domain as categorially constrained and unavailable for NPs. Remaining instances of medial NP-adjuncts would then have been reanalyzed as involving a different structure, one involving the IP-edge as proposed for Present-Day English by Haegeman (2002).

Acknowledgements: It is a pleasure for me to dedicate this paper to Liliane Haegeman, without whom neither this nor any of my earlier papers would ever have been written. I would like to thank Liliane for having made me discover and enjoy syntax and, from then onwards, for providing inspiration and support, and for being a great friend. I am grateful to two anonymous reviewers for their comments and suggestions. The research reported here was supported by Swiss National Science Foundation grants no. 124619 and 143302.

References

Alexiadou, Artemis. 1997. *Adverb placement: A case study in antisymmetric syntax*. Amsterdam: John Benjamins.

Benincà, Paola & Cecilia Poletto. 2004. Topic, focus and V2: Defining the CP sublayers. In Luigi Rizzi (ed.), *The structure of CP and IP*, 52–75. Oxford: Oxford University Press.

Biber, Douglas, Stig Johansson, Geoffrey Leech, Susan Conrad & Edward Finegan. 1999. *Longman grammar of spoken and written English*. Harlow: Pearson Education.

Cardinaletti, Anna. 2004. Towards a cartography of subject positions. In Luigi Rizzi (ed.), *The structure of CP and IP*, 115–165. Oxford: Oxford University Press.

Cinque, Guglielmo. 1999. *Adverbs and functional heads. A cross-linguistic perspective*. Oxford: Oxford University Press.

De Clerq, Karen, Liliane Haegeman & Terje Lohndal. 2012. Medial adjunct PPs in English: Implications for the syntax of sentential negation. *Nordic Journal of Linguistics* 35. 5–26.

Ernst, Thomas. 2002. *The syntax of adjuncts*. Cambridge: Cambridge University Press.

Haeberli, Eric & Tabea Ihsane. 2016. Revisiting the loss of verb movement in the history of English. *Natural Language and Linguistic Theory* 34. 497–542.

Haeberli, Eric & Tabea Ihsane. In preparation. Pre-auxiliary placement of adverbs in the history of English. University of Geneva manuscript.

Haeberli, Eric & Richard Ingham. 2007. The position of negation and adverbs in Early Middle English. *Lingua* 117. 1–25.

Haeberli, Eric & Susan Pintzuk. 2012. Revisiting verb (projection) raising in Old English. In Diane Jonas, John Whitman & Andrew Garrett (eds.), *Grammatical change: Origins, nature, outcomes*, 219–238. Oxford: Oxford University Press.

Haegeman, Liliane. 1983. Mid-position of time adverbials in journalistic prose: An attempt at an explanation. *Studia Anglica Posnaniensia* 15. 73–76.

Haegeman, Liliane. 2002. Sentence-medial NP-adjuncts in English. *Nordic Journal of Linguistics* 25. 79–108.

Hasselgård, Hilde. 2010. *Adjunct adverbials in English*. Cambridge: Cambridge University Press.

Hawkins, John. 2004. *Efficiency and complexity in grammars*. Oxford: Oxford University Press.

Jacobson, Sven. 1964. Adverbial positions in English. Stockholm: AB Studentbok.

Kemenade, Ans van. 1987. *Syntactic case and morphological case in the history of English*. Dordrecht: Foris.

Kemenade, Ans van. 2011. Secondary negation and information structure organisation in the history of English. In Pierre Larrivée & Richard Ingham (eds.), *The evolution of negation: Beyond the Jespersen cycle*, 77–114. Berlin: Mouton de Gruyter.

Kemenade, Ans van and Bettelou Los. 2006. Discourse adverbs and clausal syntax in Old and Middle English. In Ans van Kemenade & Bettelou Los (eds.), *The handbook of the history of English*, 224–248. Oxford: Blackwell.

Kroch, Anthony, Beatrice Santorini & Lauren Delfs. 2004. *Penn-Helsinki parsed corpus of Early Modern English*. Department of Linguistics, University of Pennsylvania. http://www.ling.upenn.edu/hist-corpora/PPCEME-RELEASE-3/index.html.

Kroch, Anthony, Beatrice Santorini & Ariel Diertani. 2016. *Penn parsed corpus of Modern British English*. 2nd edn. Department of Linguistics, University of Pennsylvania. http://www.ling.upenn.edu/hist-corpora/PPCMBE2-RELEASE-1/index.html.

Kroch, Anthony & Ann Taylor. 2000a. *Penn-Helsinki parsed corpus of Middle English*. 2nd edn. Department of Linguistics, University of Pennsylvania. http://www.ling.upenn.edu/hist-corpora/PPCME2-RELEASE-4/index.html.

Kroch, Anthony & Ann Taylor. 2000b. Verb object order in Early Middle English. In Susan Pintzuk, George Tsoulas & Anthony Warner (eds.), *Diachronic syntax: Models and mechanisms*, 132–163. Oxford: Oxford University Press.

Lightfoot, David. 1979. *Diachronic syntax*. Cambridge: Cambridge University Press.

Lightfoot, David. 2006. Cuing a new grammar. In Ans van Kemenade & Bettelou Los (eds.), *The handbook of the history of English*, 24–44. Oxford: Blackwell.

McCawley, James. 1988. *The syntactic phenomena of English*. Vol. 1. Chicago: Chicago University Press.

Pintzuk, Susan. 1999. *Phrase structures in competition: Variation and change in Old English word order*. New York: Garland.

Pintzuk, Susan. 2005. Arguments against a universal base: Evidence from Old English. *English Language and Linguistics* 9. 115–138.

Pintzuk, Susan & Eric Haeberli. 2008. Structural variation in Old English root clauses. *Language Variation and Change* 20. 367–407.

Quirk, Randolph, Sidney Greenbaum, Geoffrey Leech & Jan Svartvik. 1985. *A comprehensive grammar of the English language*. London: Longman.

Taylor, Ann, Arja Nurmi, Anthony Warner, Susan Pintzuk & Terttu Nevalainen. 2006. *The parsed corpus of early English correspondence*. York: University of York and Helsinki: University of Helsinki. http://www-users.york.ac.uk/~lang22/PCEEC-manual/index.htm.

Taylor, Ann, Anthony Warner, Susan Pintzuk & Frank Beths. 2003. *The York-Toronto-Helsinki parsed corpus of Old English*. York: University of York. http://www-users.york.ac.uk/~lang22/YCOE/YcoeHome.htm.

Eric Lander
Gothic *sai* and the Proto-Germanic verb-based discourse particle **se*

1 Introduction

Discourse particles are often derived from (imperative) verbs (e.g. Derolez and Simon-Vandenbergen 1988, Haegeman and Hill 2011[1], Haegeman 2014). Indeed, one available etymology of the Northwest Germanic (NWGmc) reinforcer particle **-si*, which was appended to the neutral demonstrative in Northwest Germanic to form the so-called reinforced demonstrative (cf. Runic Norse F.NOM.SG **susi**, M.NOM.SG **sasi**, N.NOM/ACC.SG **þatsi**; Old Norse F.NOM.SG *þessi*, M.NOM.SG *þessi*, N.NOM/ACC.SG *þetta*; Old English F.NOM.SG *þēos*, M.NOM.SG *þēs*, N.NOM/ACC.SG *þis*; Old Frisian F.NOM.SG *thius*, M.NOM.SG *this*, N.NOM/ACC.SG *thit*; Old Saxon F.NOM.SG *thius*, M.NOM.SG **these*, N.NOM/ACC.SG *thit(t)*; Old High German F.NOM.SG *dësiu*, M.NOM.SG *dësēr*, N.NOM/ACC.SG *diz*), is that it derives from the imperative 'see! look!'. As mentioned by Haegeman and Hill (2011: 5), though Gothic (East Germanic) did not develop such a reinforced demonstrative, it nevertheless has a particle *sai* which potentially has a verbal etymology (cf. imperative *saiƕ* 'see! look!') and may thus be cognate with Northwest Germanic **-si*. In this paper I show that in the case of Northwest Germanic **-si* and Gothic *sai*, the 'see'-based (verbal) etymology is superior to the non-verbal (pronominal) etymologies that have been proposed. By establishing a verbal, 'see'-based discourse particle in all three Germanic branches, we can securely reconstruct a Proto-Germanic discourse particle **se* < **seh^w* 'see! look!'. The paper includes an exhaustive corpus study of Gothic *sai* and *saiƕ*, along with some discussion of the grammaticalization cline involved.

2 The Northwest Germanic reinforced demonstrative

The reinforced demonstrative 'this' is a morphological innovation which is shared by the North and West branches of the Germanic language family. Some examples are given in (1).

---

[1] See also Haegeman and Hill (2013), though this version does not include discussion of Gothic *sai*.

DOI 10.1515/9781501504037-017

(1) a. Old Norse F/M.NOM.SG *þessi*, F.ACC.SG *þessa*, M.NOM.PL *þessir*
   b. Old English M.ACC.SG *þisne*, F.GEN/DAT.SG *þis-re* > *þisse*, M/N.DAT.SG / DAT.PL *þis(s)um*
   c. Old Frisian M.ACC.SG *thissen*, M/N.GEN.SG *thisses*, F/M/N.NOM/ACC.PL *thisse*
   d. Old Saxon F.ACC.SG *thesa*, M.ACC.SG *thesan*, GEN.PL *thesaro*
   e. Old High German F.NOM.SG *dësiu*, M.NOM.SG *dësēr*, DAT.PL *dësēm*

For the full paradigms, see Gordon ([1927] 1956: 295) for Old Norse; Lass (1994: 145) and Campbell ([1959] 2003: 291) for Old English; Bremmer (2009: 55) and Markey (1981: 136) for Old Frisian; Rauch (1992: 196), Cathey (2000: 37), Galleé (1910: 240) for Old Saxon (see Nielsen 2000: 158 for *thitt*); and Braune and Reiffenstein ([1886] 2004: 250) and Wright ([1888] 1906: 67) for Old High German.

Gothic (East Germanic) never developed such a reinforced demonstrative, but as we will see below, it still had the right ingredients, as it were, to do so. Lander (2015) discusses in detail the word-internal syntax of the reinforced demonstrative and the structure of these paradigms in the Old Northwest Germanic languages. In this paper, I focus on one aspect of the prehistory of these forms, namely the origins of the all-important reinforcer *-si* which gave rise to the reinforced demonstrative. It turns out that Gothic, despite its lack of a reinforced demonstrative per se, can teach us about the origins of NWGmc *-si*.

The reinforced demonstrative was originally formed in (Proto-)Northwest Germanic by the addition of the reinforcer *-si*, which I will refer to as the *sigmatic reinforcer*, to the neutral demonstrative (cf. OED, P-Z: 3295). Interestingly, this archaic stage of Northwest Germanic is preserved in some Runic Norse (RN) inscriptions, as seen in (2) (where the NWGmc forms are mostly based on Nielsen's 2000: 230–235 reconstruction of the Early Runic neutral demonstrative paradigm).[2]

---

[2] Following standard convention, runic forms are transliterated into boldface Roman letters and transcribed into Old Norse orthography. The *Samnordisk runtextdatabas* of Uppsala University has been consulted for the runic. The specific inscriptions referred to in (2) are: (2a) DR 229; (2b) Ög 10, Ög 157, Ög 162, Ög 212, Sm 17, Sm 80, Sö 101, U 69, U 126, U 345; (2c) Sö 137, Sö 340 / DR 189; (2d) Sö 158 / extremely prevalent, e.g. DR 40, Ög 44; (2e) Sö 47 / Sö 46; (2f) Öl 1; (2g) Sö 40; (2h) Sö 346; (2i) DR 4, DR 42, DR 133, DR 143, DR 209, DR 277, DR 293, DR 294, Nä 3, Ög Fv1970; 310, Sö 173, Sö 296, Vg 67, Vg 115.

(2) a. F.NOM.SG **susi** (súsi)   <   NWGmc *sōsi
    b. F.ACC.SG **þasi** (þási)   <   NWGmc *þō-si
    c. M.NOM.SG **saʀ:si** (saʀsi)
       M.NOM.SG **sasi** (sási)   <   NWGmc *sa-si
    d. M.ACC.SG þan:si (þansi)
       M.ACC.SG þansi (þansi)   <   NWGmc *þan-si
    e. N.ACC.SG þat:si (þatsi)
       N.ACC.SG þatsi (þatsi)   <   NWGmc *þat-si
    f. M.DAT.SG þaimsi (þæimsi)   <   NWGmc *þaim-si
    g. F.ACC.PL **þaʀsi** (þársi)   <   NWGmc *þōz-si
    h. M.NOM.PL **þiʀsi** (þeirsi)   <   NWGmc *þai(z)-si
    i. N.NOM/ACC.PL þausi (þausi)   <   NWGmc *þō-si

The combination of neutral demonstrative plus sigmatic reinforcer will henceforth be referred to as a 'Dem-*si*' form.

Dem-*si* forms display what may be called 'internal inflection' (*Binnenflexion*). For instance, the M.DAT.SG inflectional component (K) in þæi-*m*-si is to the left of the reinforcer component (R), making it word-internal, as seen in (3).

(3) Internal inflection in Runic Norse
    þæi-   -m   -si
    D   K   R

Roughly speaking, the next step in the historical development of the reinforced demonstrative involved the absorption of the sibilant in *-*si* into the D component *þa-. This D component, moreover, does not retain the original vowel quality, typically shifting from the low vowel *a* to the front/mid *e* or front/high *i* by different language-specific mechanisms. The result of these developments is a new stem which looks something like þes- or þis- (the reinforced demonstrative stems being ON þess-, OE þis(s)-, OF thiss-, OS thes-, OHG dës(s)-, which can all be seen in (1)). Furthermore, this new reinforced demonstrative stem is usually inflected with strong adjective endings rather than the pronominal endings of the older Dem-*si* stage (see Haugen 1982: 100–101, EWAhd II: 611, 613).

The coalition between þe- and the sigmatic reinforcer -s (< *-*si*) to form a new reinforced demonstrative stem results in a shift in the position of the inflectional component. As seen in (2) and (3), in the Dem-*si* stage K appears to the left of R (e.g. *þæi-m-si, þa-t-si, þa-n-si*). When the new reinforced demonstrative stem arises, however, R shifts to a position immediately adjacent to the D element, giving *þe-s-* or *þi-s-*. This stem is then inflected with strong adjectival K, meaning that K ends up to the right of R. Such a configuration may be referred to as 'external inflection' (*Endflexion*). This is illustrated for Old Norse in (4), where *-um* is the M.DAT.SG (and DAT.PL) strong adjective ending.

(4)   External inflection in Old Norse

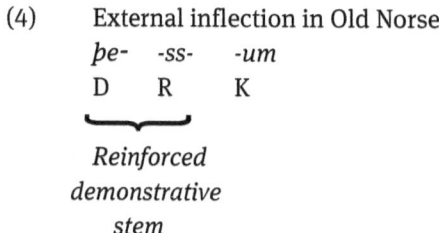

In sum, the old sigmatic reinforcer *-*si* played an absolutely central role in the development of the Northwest Germanic reinforced demonstrative paradigms. In the rest of this paper I will zoom in on the etymology and history of the sigmatic reinforcer *-*si* and what Gothic – which, recall, did not develop a reinforced demonstrative – can teach us about it.

3 Two etymologies for the sigmatic reinforcer and the centrality of Gothic *sai* in both

In this section I discuss two hypotheses about the etymological history of the sigmatic reinforcer. It will be seen that the Gothic particle *sai* 'lo, behold' is of central importance to both hypotheses; therefore the two hypotheses compete, so to speak, for the right to claim this particle.

The first hypothesis for the etymology of *-*si* is that it should be identified with the imperative verb **se*/**si* 'see! look!' (OED, P-Z: 3295; Feist [1923] 1939: 403 attributes the verbal etymology ultimately to J. Grimm). Informally speaking, the idea is that a structure like *that-see* 'look at that!' developed into *this*, where the

-s is cognate with the verb see. The detailed development of *-si according to the verbal hypothesis is illustrated in Fig. 1.

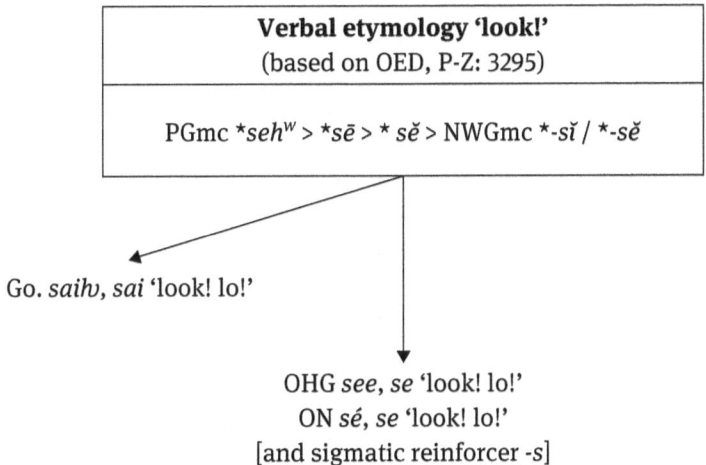

Fig. 1: Verbal etymology of the sigmatic reinforcer

The infinitive of the verb 'see' in Proto-Germanic (PGmc) was *seh^w-an. Taking the stem of this, *seh^w, gives us the imperative singular form 'see!', which is the starting point for the etymology in Fig. 1. From here the idea is that the imperative *seh^w grammaticalized into a discourse particle. Part of this grammaticalization involved phonological reduction, whereby the final labiovelar consonant h^w was lost. This deletion led to compensatory lengthening of the vowel, giving *sē. As the grammaticalization process continued, this vowel was reduced as well, giving *se. By the time we reach the Northwest Germanic stage, the particle has become a clitic *-se. The unstressed vowel system in the early history of North Germanic was reduced to a three-way contrast between *i, *a, and *u (Haugen 1982: 29), so unstressed *e in *se shifted to *i, giving NGmc *-si. In West Germanic, both *-se and *-si existed (probably partly due to borrowing, cf. Nielsen 2000: 212).

Evidence for this development – from imperative verb to discourse particle – can be found in all three branches of Germanic. Though Gothic (East Germanic) never fully followed through by developing a reinforced demonstrative of its own, it still shows the full imperative form saiƕ (<ai> = ɛ before h^w) 'see!', as well as (according to the verbal hypothesis) a reduced discourse particle *sai* [sɛ].³ The same pair of full and reduced versions of 'see!' can be seen in Old High German (West Germanic) and Old Norse (North Germanic), in addition, of course, to the sigmatic reinforcer -*s* (< *-*si*) which is an integral part of the reinforced demonstrative paradigms of both North and West Germanic.

In other words, according to Fig. 1 we have a pan-Germanic element **se(hʷ)*: all three branches of Germanic show evidence for an imperative 'see!' and a reduced discourse particle grammaticalized from the full imperative. Indeed, the grammaticalization of imperative verbs into interjections or discourse particles is a very common phenomenon crosslinguistically speaking. See Haegeman and Hill (2011) for contemporary West Flemish and Romanian examples, as well as Haegeman (2014) on West Flemish. Consult Derolez and Simon-Vandenbergen (1988) for more on West Flemish, as well as notes on verbal interjections in Old English, Italian, Swiss German, Latin, and Greek. Feist (1939: 403) also provides examples from Finnish, Lithuanian/Latvian, and Icelandic. See also Tanghe and Jansegers (2014) for a study of Spanish and Italian discourse markers derived from verbs of perception.

The second hypothesis is that *-*si* has its origins in a locative-pronominal element with a meaning like 'there' or 'here' (see the EWAhd II: 608–17; also Feist 1939: 403, citing proposals by Meyer 1869 and Osthoff 1901). The detailed development of *-*si* according to the locative-pronominal hypothesis is illustrated in Fig. 2.

---

3 There would appear to be some potential problems for the verbal etymology here, since the apocope of *hv* (the Gothic grapheme for *hʷ*) is not part of any known regular sound change (though a reviewer suggests that haplology may be at least partially responsible, so that when the final -*hv* of *saihv* appears before word-initial *hv*-, as in (6b), (7), and (11), there is deletion of word-final -*hv*) and the short(ened) vowel ε is not expected word-finally (it should only appear before *h*, *hv*, or *r*). Derolez and Simon-Vandenbergen (1988: 102) point out, however, that interjections are known to be a diverse group of items with unexpected phonological properties. Though they are content to call the vowel quantity "unsystemic" (Derolez and Simon-Vandenbergen 1988: 101) and leave it at that – "If we can agree, then, that interjections are not subject to the phonological constraints of the language..." (Derolez and Simon-Vandenbergen 1988: 103) – thinking in terms of grammaticalization might be more insightful. In the case of *sai*, the irregular phonology would be due to its having been targeted by grammaticalization. See also Van Bergen (2013) for the grammaticalization of the Old English adhortative interjection *uton* 'let us' for another relevant case of irregular phonological changes occurring during the grammaticalization process.

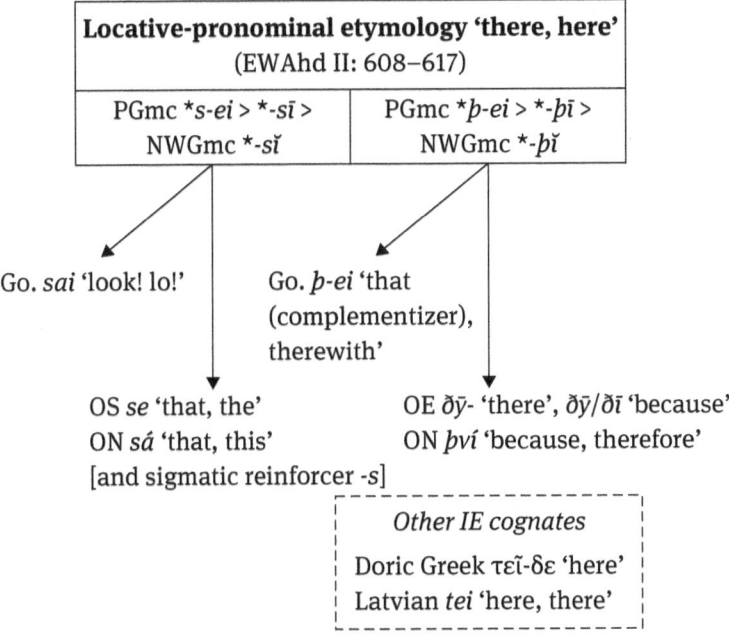

Fig. 2: Locative-pronominal etymology of the sigmatic reinforcer

According to the locative-pronominal etymology, there was a locatival component *-ei in Proto-Germanic which could combine with the pronominal roots *s- (M/F.SG) and *þ- (other/oblique). Thus our starting points here are the items *s-ei and *þ-ei. From here the Proto-Germanic diphthong *ei changed to a long *ī in late Proto-Germanic (Antonsen 2002: 28), yielding *sī and *þī. Eventually, due to grammaticalization and cliticization of the *sī and *þī particles, the vowel is shortened. The result is *-si and *-þi.

Evidence for this development appears to be found in all three branches of Germanic. For the item *þei, the EWAhd II provides Go. þei 'that, therewith' for East Germanic, OE ðȳ- 'there' and ðȳ/ðī 'because' for West Germanic, and ON því 'because, therefore' for North Germanic, in addition to some relevant non-Germanic cognates from Doric Greek and Latvian. For the item *sei, however, the evidence is scantier. For this component of the locative-pronominal hypothesis, the EWAhd II provides the M.NOM.SG demonstratives se from Old Saxon (and Old English) and sá from Old Norse. While there is no doubt that these derive from a Proto-Indo-European pronominal root *s-, the claim here is, more precisely, that OS/OE se and ON sá support the reconstruction of a supposed locatival *sei. This leap is not very well grounded, since se and sá do not derive from *sei but rather from PGmc M.NOM.SG *sa.[4] This casts doubt on the EWAhd's etymology in Fig. 2. Notice what happens when OS *se* and ON *sá* are removed from the locative-pronominal etymology, as illustrated in Fig. 3.

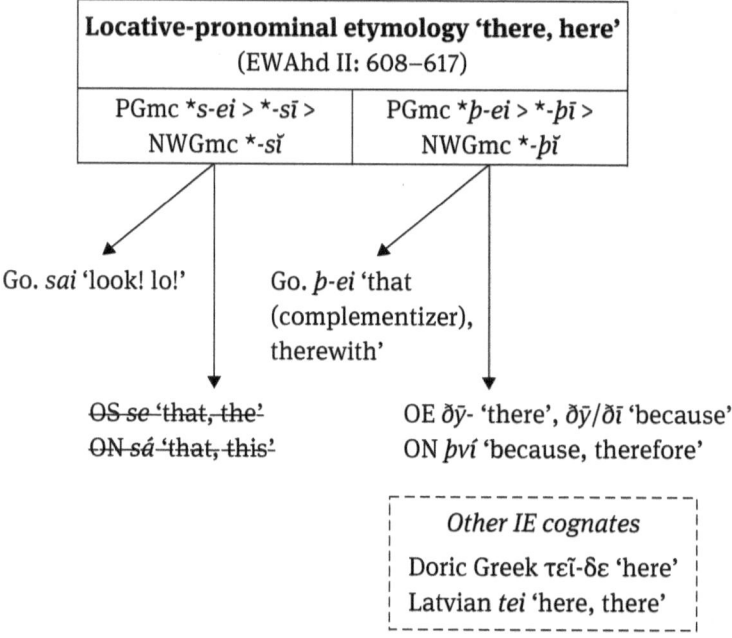

Fig. 3: Locative-pronominal etymology of the sigmatic reinforcer without OS *se* and ON *sá*

In Fig. 3 we see that Go. *sai* is the only item left over to support the reconstruction of a Proto-Germanic locative **sei*, which is the item that supposedly gives **-si* in Northwest Germanic.

When all is said and done, the identity of Go. *sai* is the keystone for both the verbal hypothesis and the locative-pronominal hypothesis. The verbal etymology considers *sai* an attestation of a discourse particle derived from the imperative *saiƕ*, while the locative-pronominal etymology presses *sai* into service as the

---

[4] As for NGmc, ON *sá* clearly comes from **sa* (more precisely, the addition of a pleonastic M.NOM.SG marker **-R* gave **sa-R* and then compensatory lengthening resulting from subsequent loss of this marker gave ON *sá*, with a long vowel). In WGmc, OS/OE *sĕ* could on the basis of its front vowel come from a variant of **sa*, namely **sai* (Klingenschmitt 1987: 182). The point is that there is a perfectly reasonable proto-form for these forms in the non-locative **sa(i)*, whereas deriving the forms from the locative proto-form **sei* requires an extra set of assumptions.

continuation of a Proto-Germanic locative with the pronominal root *s-. Since both hypotheses are vying for the support of *sai*, it is critically important to investigate the identity of Go. *sai* in order to see which hypothesis it actually supports. The losing hypothesis will have to forfeit *sai*, which deals a serious blow to its credibility. For the verbal etymology, the forfeiture of *sai* means the loss of a verb-based discourse particle in East Germanic, meaning that only two – rather than all three – branches of Germanic support the reconstructed grammaticalization process from imperative to particle. For the locative-pronominal etymology, the forfeiture of *sai* means the loss of the sole evidence for an *s-based locative in Proto-Germanic (since OS *se* and ON *sá* do not make the cut).

4 The true identity of Gothic *sai*

In this section I present a number of reasons to believe that Go. *sai* is a verbal particle/interjection rather than a continuation of a Proto-Germanic locative *sei*. My view is therefore that *sai* supports the verbal hypothesis and not the locative-pronominal hypothesis.

Gothic did not innovate a (*si-based[5]) reinforced demonstrative. The language does, however, have the neutral demonstrative *sa, sô, þata* (Tab. 1) and also the items *saiƕ* and *sai*.

Tab. 1: Gothic Dem (Braune 1905: 69)

	M.SG	F.SG	N.SG	M.PL	F.PL	N.PL
NOM	sa	sô	þata	þai	þôs	þô
ACC	þana	þô	þata	þans	þôs	þô
GEN	þis	þizôs	þis	þizê	þizô	þizê
DAT	þamma	þizai	þamma	þaim	þaim	þaim

While *saiƕ* is obviously the imperative form of *saiƕan*, as we have seen there is some debate about the identity of *sai*, which is actually much more frequently attested than *saiƕ* in the corpus of Gothic.

First, it is certainly a weak point in the locative-pronominal hypothesis that the locative was for the most part lost very early on, already in Proto-Germanic.

---

5 There is evidence for a "defective" proximal demonstrative in Gothic, namely the forms *himma, hina, hita,* based on Gmc *hi-* (Braune 1905: 70).

One remnant in Gothic which survived was *þei* 'that (complementizer), therewith' (cf. Figures 2 and 3). Importantly, however, this form shows the oblique root *þ-* instead of the root *s-*. This does little to support the proposed etymology of *sai* – in fact the existence of *þei* highlights how unlikely it is that a second locative, based on the highly restricted *s*-root no less, survived into Gothic as well.

Second, the question arises why the proposed Gothic locative would show up as *sai* [sɛ] (or perhaps [saɪ]; see below) and not *sei* [siː], on a par with *þei* [þiː]. The '*e*-flavored' locatival morpheme (PGmc *-ei*) is required for the rest of the Germanic cognates given in Figures 2 and 3, and even for the Gothic form *þei*. This would make locative *sai* an odd outlier in both Gothic and Germanic as a whole. In fact, the EWAhd (II: 612) must offer a slight variation on the main hypothesis in order to account for the vocalism: M.LOC.SG pre-Gmc **soī* > PGmc **saī* > Go. *sai*.

Third, it should be noted that the locative-pronominal view of Go. *sai* is similar to an older hypothesis from Meyer (1869), cited in Feist (1939: 403). Meyer's idea is that *sai* is a Gothic-internal innovation whereby the M.NOM.SG pronoun *sa* is suffixed by a deictic particle *-i* (cf. Gk. *νυν-í* 'now', *οὑτοσ-í* 'this here'), giving *sai*. Meyer's hypothesis implies that *sai* (i.e. *sa-i*) should have a diphthong [aɪ]. Indeed, this is also what the EWAhd (II: 612) predicts with its proposed development of pre-Gmc **soī* > PGmc **saī* > Go. *sai*. Now, while the Gothic digraph <ai> usually represents the monophthong [ɛ], it could also be used to represent a diphthong [aɪ]. However, in such cases a trema < ¨ > (indicating diaeresis/hiatus) was available in order to avoid ambiguity. Had *sai* had a diphthongal pronunciation, then Wulfila would very likely have written <saï>, but this spelling is *never* found in the original text (Luc de Grauwe, p.c.). This means *sai* should be read [sɛ] and that the Meyer/EWAhd prediction is not borne out.[6,7]

Finally, and perhaps most convincingly, there is plenty of positive evidence in favor of the verbal etymology (as opposed to just negative evidence against the locative-pronominal etymology).

---

[6] Meyer's hypothesis also predicts that other forms in the demonstrative paradigm of Gothic should, like *sa-i*, be able to display deictic appendages, as in F.NOM.SG **so-i*, N.NOM/ACC.SG **þata-i*, M/N.DAT.SG **þamma-i*, M.ACC.PL **þans-i*, etc. Such forms are not attested in Gothic.

[7] Yet another hypothesis for Go. *sai* cited in Feist (1939: 403) is Osthoff (1901), who proposes that *sai* is the M.NOM.SG demonstrative pronoun *sa* plus the N.NOM/ACC.SG pronoun *ita*, on a par with Skt. *sḗd* < *sá-íd*. This hypothesis is incoherent, however. In Sanskrit the *í* of the neuter pronoun is conflated with the preceding *á* according to regular sandhi rules and the dental of the neuter pronoun remains completely intact (*sá-íd* > *sḗd*). In Gothic, on the other hand, one would need to claim that the dental and the following vowel are completely deleted, leaving only the initial *i* (*sa-ita* > *sa-i*). These two processes are scarcely on a par.

In the rest of this section I present an exhaustive corpus study of Go. *sai*. In connection with this, some methodological notes are at this point in order. First, I have consulted both *Project Wulfila* and Streitberg (2000) for the Gothic, and Streitberg (2000) for the Greek (a common enough practice, though various issues remain with Streitberg's view of Wulfila's Greek *Vorlage*). Second, I have made special note of cases which are in some significant way *not* direct word-for-word translations from the Greek (see below for examples), as it is generally agreed that such cases give us the best glimpse into native Gothic syntax. Seventeen cases of *sai* are of interest in this way, by my classification (17/96 = 17.7%), and they are marked by an asterisk at the end (...*). Third, my figure of 96 excludes 13 occurrences of *sai*, two of which are editorial additions by Streitberg and 11 of which are duplicates (due to the fact that Codex Ambrosianus A and B overlap to a great extent).

To begin with, Derolez and Simon-Vandenbergen (1988) point out that *sai*'s most common usage is as a translation for the Greek imperative singular ἰδού or the interjection ἴδε, both of which can be translated as 'see! lo!'. I have found that out of a total of 96 instances of *sai* in the Gothic corpus, 82 of them correspond to Greek ἰδού, ἴδε, or the imperative plural ἴδετε (as for the rest of the instances of *sai*, see below). The distribution of these 82 cases is shown in Tab. 2. Relevant examples are provided in (5), (6), and (7).

Tab. 2: Translation of *sai*

Greek	*sai*
ἰδού	63/82
ἴδε	18/82
ἴδετε	1/82

(5) **ἰδού**

a. *jah   sai   mans   bairandans   ana   ligra   mannan*
    and   SAI   men   carrying   on   bed.DAT   man.ACC
    καὶ   ἰδοὺ ἄνδρες φέροντες   ἐπὶ   κλίνης   ἄνθρωπον
    and   IDOU men   carrying   on   bed.GEN   man.ACC
    'And behold, men brought in a man on a bed' (Luke 5:18)

b. *gaggiþ,   sai   ik   insandja   izwis   swe   lamba*
    go.2PL   SAI   I   send.forth   you.PL   as   lambs
    in   midumai   wulfe.
    in   middle.DAT   wolves.GEN
    ὑπάγετε: ἰδοὺ   ἀποστέλλω   ὑμᾶς   ὡς   ἄρνας
    go.away.2PL   IDOU   send.forth.1SG   you.PL   as   lambs

```
                ἐν    μέσῳ          λύκων.
                in    middle.DAT    wolves.GEN
```
'Go your ways: behold, I send you forth as lambs among wolves.' (Luke 10:3)

(6) **ἴδε**

```
a. jah    sai,   andaugiba    rodeiþ        jah    waiht       du    imma
   and    SAI    boldly       speaks.3SG    and    anything    to    him
   ni     qiþand
   not    say.3PL
   καὶ    ἴδε    παρρησίᾳ        λαλεῖ          καὶ    οὐδὲν       αὐτῷ
   and    IDE    boldness.DAT    speaks.3SG     and    nothing     him.DAT
   λέγουσιν
   say.3PL
```
'But lo, he speaks boldly and they say nothing to him' (John 7:26)

```
b. sai,   hvan   filu              ana        þuk     weitwodjand.
   SAI    how    many.things       against    thee    witness.3PL
   ἴδε    πόσα                     σου                καταμαρτυροῦσιν
   IDE    how.many.things          you.GEN            against.witness.3PL
```
'Behold how many things they witness against thee.' (Mark 15:4)

(7) **ἴδετε**

```
sai,       hvileikaim    bokom     gamelida      izwis
SAI        what          letter    wrote.1SG     you.DAT.PL
meinai     handau.*
my.DAT     hand.DAT
ἴδετε      πηλίκοις      ὑμῖν          γράμμασιν     ἔγραψα        τῇ
IDE.2PL    how.great     you.DAT.PL    letter(s)     wrote.1SG     the.DAT
ἐμῇ        χειρί.
my.DAT     hand.DAT
```
'See what a letter I wrote to you with my own hand.' (Galatians 6:11)

Let us now compare the distribution of the particle *sai* which was just discussed with the distribution of the morphologically transparent imperative forms *saihv* 'see.SG!', *saihviþ* 'see.PL!', and *saihvats* 'see.DU!'. As for *saihv* 'see.SG!', there are six attested cases in the Gothic corpus. In half of these cases, the Greek counterpart is ἴδε or ἰδού, and for the other half the counterpart is ὅρα 'see.SG!' or βλέπε 'see.SG!', both imperative singulars of 'see' verbs.[8] The Greek forms which *saihv* is used to translate are shown in Tab. 3.

---

[8] ὁράω and βλέπω can also mean 'take heed, beware'.

Tab. 3: Translation of Greek forms by *saiƕ*

Greek	*saiƕ*
ἰδού (Cor. II 7:11)	1/6
ἴδε (John 7:52, 11:34)	2/6
ὅρα (Matt. 8:4, Mark 1:44)	2/6
βλέπε (Col. 4:17)	1/6

Next, the item *saiƕiþ* 'see.PL!' has 11 attested instances in the Gothic corpus, all of which are translations for either Gk. ὁρᾶτε 'see.PL!' or βλέπετε 'see.PL!'. This is shown in Tab. 4.

Tab. 4: Translation of Greek forms by *saiƕiþ*

Greek	*saiƕiþ*
ὁρᾶτε (Thess.I 5:15)	1/11
βλέπετε (Luke 8:18, Mark 4:24, 8:15, 12:38, Cor.I 10:18, 16:10, Gal. 5:15, Phil. 3:2 (3x))	10/11

There is also a single case of *saiƕats* 'see.DU!' (Matt. 9:30), which corresponds to Gk. ὁρᾶτε 'see.PL!'.

These translation data show that there is a direct link between *sai* and the morphologically transparent imperative forms of the verb *saiƕan*. As seen in Tab. 5, Wulfila used the particle *sai* very much like the imperative *saiƕ* in that both were used to translate ἰδού and ἴδε (though only the morphological imperative *saiƕ/saiƕiþ/saiƕats* could be used for ὁράω and βλέπω, since presumably *sai* was too 'impoverished' to do so).

Tab. 5: Wulfila's use of *sai* in relation to imperative verb forms of *saiƕan*

sai	*saiƕ* 'see.SG!'	*saiƕiþ* 'see.PL!'
ἰδού	ἰδού	
ἴδε	ἴδε	
	ὅρα	ὁρᾶτε
	βλέπε	βλέπετε

The data from Wulfila's Greek-to-Gothic translations, then, support the view that *sai* is simply a derivative of *saiƕ*. This is further evidence for the verbal nature of the particle *sai*, since *saiƕ* is without a doubt verbal.

Next let us turn to some particularly interesting cases, including some attestations of *sai* which do not have direct counterparts in the Greek. Consider first the Gothic phrase *sai nu* 'lo now' in the examples in (8). This phrase is clearly cognate with OHG *sē-nu* and ON *sé nu*, both of which are more obviously verbal.[9]

(8)[10] a. *sai   nu   ju   ni   sijuþ   gasteis   jah   aljakonjai**
       SAI   now   ye   not   are   strangers and   foreigners
       ἄρα   οὖν   οὐκέτι ἐστὲ   ξένοι   καὶ   πάροικοι
       so   then   no.longer are   strangers   and   foreigners
    'Behold now, ye are no more strangers and foreigners' (Ephesians 2:19)

   b. *sai   nu   selein   jah   ƕassein   [garaihta]   gudis**
       SAI   now   goodness and   severity   [righteous] god.GEN
       ἴδε   οὖν   χρηστότητα καὶ   ἀποτομίαν   θεοῦ
       IDE   then   goodness   and   severity   god.GEN
    'Behold now the goodness and severity of god' (Romans 11:22)

Here Wulfila has chosen to translate the Greek connective particle οὖν (cooccurring with ἴδε in (8b) but not in (8a)) as *sai nu*. The clear link between the 'native' Gothic phrase *sai nu* and the West Germanic and North Germanic items mentioned adds yet more credibility to the verbal analysis of *sai*.

For further evidence, consider the example in (9), also pointed out by Derolez and Simon-Vandenbergen (1988: 97), where *sai* takes an accusative object. This suggests that *sai* is a verb selecting accusative case, especially considering that in Greek the object of the sentence (ὁ τόπος) is in the nominative singular.

(9) *sai   þana   staþ   þarei   galagidedun   ina**
   SAI   the.ACC   place.ACC   where   laid.3PL   him
   ἴδε   ὁ   τόπος   ὅπου   ἔθηκαν   αὐτόν
   IDE   the.NOM   place.NOM   where   laid.3PL   him
   'Behold the place where they laid him' (Mark 16:6)

---

9 Though a reviewer notes that at least OHG *sēnu* seems to be semantically quite bleached, in that it does not always straightforwardly instruct someone to look at something.
10 Non-italicized *jah* in (8a) means that the original Gothic text is not perfectly legible, and bracketed *garaihta* in (8b) and (10) is an editorial deletion on the part of Streitberg.

An additional example of *sai* selecting accusative is (8b), repeated here as (10). Note, though, that the Greek also has accusative objects here (i.e. χρηστότητα and ἀποτομίαν).

(10) sai   nu   selein   jah   ƕassein   [garaihta]   gudis*
     SAI   now   goodness   and   severity   [righteous]   god.GEN
     ἴδε   οὖν   χρηστότητα καὶ   ἀποτομίαν   θεοῦ
     IDE   then goodness   and   severity   god.GEN
     'Behold now the goodness and severity of god' (Romans 11:22)

There is also some evidence for *sai* being associated with interjective force. Consider (11), where *sai* is inserted, without a direct Greek counterpart, to support an exclamative.

(11) sai,   ƕaiwa   agluba   þai   faiho   gahabandans   in
     SAI   how   difficultly they   riches   having   into
     þiudangardja   gudis   galeiþand*
     kingdom.ACC   god.GEN   enter
     πῶς   δυσκόλως   οἱ   τὰ   χρήματα   ἔχοντες   εἰς
     how   difficultly they   the   riches   having   into
     τὴν   βασιλείαν   τοῦ   θεοῦ   εἰσελεύσονται
     the.ACC   kingdom.ACC   the.GEN   god.GEN   will.go.into
     'How difficult it is for the rich to enter into the kingdom of god!' (Mark 10:23)

If we take interrogatives to be like exclamatives in having a focus feature of some kind, a similar thing may be happening in (12). Here *sai* is inserted, again without a Greek counterpart, to support a question (note the interrogative particle *jau*).[11]

(12) sai,   jau   ainshun   þize   reike   galaubidedi   imma
     SAI   Q   anyone   these.GEN   rulers.GEN   believed   him
     aiþþau   Fareisaie?*
     or   Pharisees.GEN
     μή   τις   ἐκ   τῶν   ἀρχόντων   ἐπίστευσεν   εἰς   αὐτὸν
     Q   anyone from   the.GEN   rulers.GEN   believed   into   him
     ἢ   ἐκ   τῶν   Φαρισαίων;
     or   from   the.GEN Pharisees.GEN
     'Has any one of these rulers or Pharisees believed him?' (John 7:48)

---

11 (11) and (12) happen to be cited together by Derolez and Simon-Vandenbergen (1988: 98–99) as well, but only in order to point out that there are no direct counterparts in the Greek. There is no mention of illocutionary force, even though this would support their claim that *sai* is an interjection.

The sentences in (11) and (12), then, place *sai* even more firmly in the verbal or clausal domain.

With the identity of Go. *sai* as a verbal interjective particle secured, we have lent strong support to the verbal etymology summarized above in Fig. 1 – and simultaneously undermined the locative-pronominal etymology in Fig. 2 – of the Northwest Germanic sigmatic reinforcer *-si*. It is reasonable, furthermore, to reconstruct all the way back to Proto-Germanic both a full imperative *seh^w and also a reduced imperative/interjection *se, since all three branches of Germanic show straightforward evidence for these items.[12]

5 The grammaticalization of *sai*

In their discussion of verbal particles in West Flemish and Romanian, Haegeman and Hill (2011: 6) propose that a highly grammaticalized particle like West Flemish *zè* (< *zie* 'see!') is still merged in the clausal structure due to having a [V] feature. Nonetheless, this item can eventually lose this [V] feature as part of the grammaticalization process, at which point it is formally nominal and thus able to incorporate into a nominal XP. Their hypothesis is sketched in (13).

(13) Adapted from Haegeman and Hill (2011: 5–6)
    a. *[Dienen boek]$_i$ zè moe-j t$_i$ lezen.*
        this book zÈ must-you read
        'This book you gotta read.'
    b. $[_{FP}$ $[_F$ zè $[_{CP}$ ... XP]]]
    c. $[_{FP}$ XP $[_F$ zè $[_{CP}$ ... XP]]]
    d. $[_{FP}$ XP-zè $[_F$ Ø $[_{CP}$ ... XP-zè]]]

As Haegeman and Hill (2011: 5) write, "for a discourse particle to have become part and parcel of a demonstrative pronoun, as has arguably happened with Gothic *sai* 'see', there must have been a 'point of entry' through the syntax. If the particle were completely outside the clausal syntax, then such a development would be unexpected."

In (13c), the particle *zè* has moved as far left as it can in the clausal hierarchy (cf. Roberts and Roussou 2003), so the only option for further grammaticalization

---

12 The fact remains, of course, that reinforcers very often do derive from some type of pronoun crosslinguistically (already in Germanic we have Swedish *den/det där* 'that', *den/det här* 'this', Afrikaans *daar-die* 'that', *hier-die* 'this', etc.). The point is that in the specific case of *se, we must assign a verbal rather than a pronominal etymology.

is to 'move into' the dislocated XP, as shown in (13d). Now, zooming in on (13d), it could be proposed that *zè* has become reanalyzed as the head of a nominal topic or focus phrase (cf. Aboh 2004). This idea is illustrated in (14), where the particle *zè* is a head in the extended nominal projection and has therefore become "part and parcel" of the XP *dienen boek* 'this book'.

(14) [*dienen boek*]-*zè* < [$_{FocP}$ [*dienen boek*] [$_{Foc}$ *zè* [...[$_{DemP}$ ~~*dienen boek*~~]]]]

Though it has not (yet) happened in West Flemish, from here the particle could in theory continue its leftward journey, for instance by becoming even more phonologically reduced (*zè* > -*z*) and attaching to the demonstrative specifically, so that [*dienen boek*]-*zè* becomes (the hypothetical) [*dienen-z*] *boek*.

(15) *dienen-z* < [$_{FocP}$ *dienen* [$_{Foc}$ -*z* [...[$_{DemP}$ ~~*dienen*~~ [$_{NP}$ *boek*]]]]]

As indicated in (15), this would yield a newly reinforced demonstrative like *dienen-z* (= *dienen-s* with final obstruent devoicing).

As for Go. *sai*, in terms of grammaticalization we can say that it was still at quite an early stage. On the other hand, NWGmc *-s(i)* (which is also attested later than Gothic) is at a much later stage of development, namely the stage at which it has become a demonstrative-internal element.

(16) imperative   >   discourse marker   >   Dem-internal reinforcer

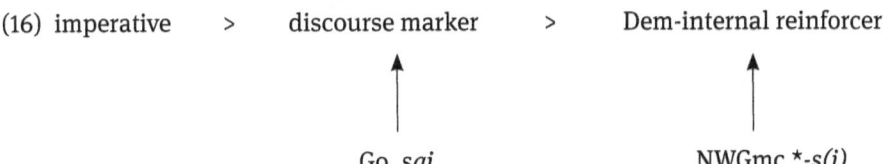

                                Go. *sai*   NWGmc *-s(i)*

We could speculate that Go. *sai* had actually begun to weaken prosodically and was perhaps developing in the direction of a word-internal morpheme much like the Northwest Germanic sigmatic reinforcer -*s(i)*. There are some suggestive attestations of *sai* which seem to fit into each of the stages in the grammaticalization cline given in (17).[13]

(17) *seh*^{w} >   *sē*   >   *sĕ*   >   -*sĕ*

The first stage, namely [*seh*^{w}], is obviously represented by the full imperative *saiƕ*, which as mentioned above has 6 attestations, one of which can be seen in (18).

---

[13] This can be thought of in terms of Cardinaletti and Starke (1999), according to whom prosodic independence, among other things, is linked to how much underlying structure is present: strong pronouns correspond to the full structure [C [Σ [I [Lexical category]]]], weak pronouns to the smaller structure [Σ [I [Lexical category]]], and clitic pronouns to the even smaller structure [I [Lexical category]].

(18) *ussokei jah saiƕ þatei praufetus us Galeilaia ni urreisiþ.*
    search and look for prophet out.of Galilee not arises
    'Search and look: for out of Galilee arises no prophet.' (John 7:52)

As for the next two stages, the North Germanic and West Germanic 'see'-forms could be either long-voweled [sē] or short-voweled [sĕ] when preceding an adverb like *nu* 'now' (or in Old Norse the pronoun *þu* 'thou'). This is shown in (19).

(19) a. Long-voweled [sē]
     ON *sé, sé(ð) nú* 'see now', *sé hér nú* 'see here now', *sé þú / séðú* 'see thou' (Cleasby and Vigfússon 1874: 533)
     OHG *see* (Derolez and Simon-Vandenbergen 1988: 99–100), *sēnu, sī-nu* (Feist 1939: 403), *see hear nu* (Wauchope 1992: 59)
   b. Short-voweled [sĕ]
     ON *se, se þu* (see Derolez and Simon-Vandenbergen 1988: 101–102)
     OHG *sënu, sinu* (Sievers [1872] 1892: 419, who suggests these forms may be "verkürzt" versions of *sênu*)

Even though we cannot be absolutely certain on the basis of spelling, it is possible that Go. *sai* was like ON and OHG in having either the value [sē] or [sĕ] when it preceded an adverb like *nu* 'now'.

(20) *sai nu ju ni sijuþ gasteis jah aljakonjai**
    SAI now ye not are strangers and foreigners
    'Behold now, ye are no more strangers and foreigners' (Ephesians 2:19)

Finally, when *sai* appears to the right of first-constituent adverbs like *suns* 'immediately' and *nu* 'now', it can tentatively be taken to be in a Wackernagel (1892) position. In other words, when ADV > *sai*, then *sai* has the value [sĕ], as in the examples in (21).

(21) a. *iþ nu sai, ufkunnandans guþ...**
       but now SAI knowing god
       'But now, after you have known god...' (Galatians 4:9)
    b. *iþ nu sai, jah taujan ustiuhaiþ...**
       but now SAI and do perform.2PL.OPT
       'But now, perform the doing of it...' (Corinthians II 8:11)
    c. *jah suns sai, ahma ina ustauh in auþida.**
       and immediately SAI spirit him drives in wilderness.ACC
       'And immediately the spirit drives him into the wilderness.' (Mark 1:12)

On this view, a sequence like *þar-uh sai* 'there-and SAI' (Luke 7:12*, 7:37*) would actually be a 'clitic chain' (see Fortson 2004: §15.43), where *sai* has the value [-sĕ], that is, the fourth stage in (17). The expected next stage, however, in which the clitic -*sĕ* is further reduced to -*s*, is not attested in Gothic.

To sum up, the variable placement of *sai* in relation to adverbs suggests that it may have been somewhat prosodically promiscuous and participating in the grammaticalization cline in (16) and (17).

6 Conclusion

The Northwest Germanic sigmatic reinforcer *-si* played a crucial role in the development of the reinforced demonstrative (ON *þessi*, *þessi*, *þetta*; OE *þēs*, *þēos*, *þis*; OF *thius*, *this*, *thit*; OS *thius*, **these*, *thit(t)*; OHG *dësiu*, *dësēr*, *diz*). The etymological history of this reinforcer turns out to hinge quite crucially on the exact identity of the Gothic particle *sai*. If *sai* is a verbal item (derived from the full imperative *saiƕ* 'see! look!', then it is very likely that Northwest Germanic *-si* has a verbal 'see'-based etymology as well, but if *sai* is a locative-pronominal item (on a par with OE *ðȳ-* 'there', for instance), then a pronominal etymology for Northwest Germanic *-si* gains significant support. On the basis of an exhaustive corpus study of the particle *sai*, I have shown in this paper that the verbal etymology of Go. *sai* (and therefore also of Northwest Germanic *-si*) is superior to the non-verbal (pronominal) etymologies which have been proposed. By establishing a verbal 'see'-based discourse particle in all three branches of the Germanic family, we can securely reconstruct a Proto-Germanic discourse particle **se*, derived from the full form **seh^w* 'see! look!'.

Acknowledgements: Above all, my deepest thanks to Liliane Haegeman for the initial suggestion to investigate Go. *sai* and the many inspiring conversations on this topic that followed. This paper is based on a section of my dissertation (Lander 2015: §1.4.1), for which Liliane served as supervisor. I am also indebted to Michal Starke for many lengthy and productive discussions. Thanks also to Katrín Axelsdóttir, Anne Breitbarth, Luc de Grauwe, Sverre Stausland Johnsen, Hans Frede Nielsen, the members of GIST, and audiences at IGG 39, SCL 25, and GLOW 37. I am also grateful to two anonymous reviewers for helpful comments and suggestions.

References

Aboh, Enoch. 2004. Topic and focus within D. *Linguistics in the Netherlands 2004* 21. 1–12.
Antonsen, Elmer H. 2002. *Runes and Germanic linguistics*. New York: Mouton de Gruyter.
Braune, Wilhelm. 1905. *Gotische Grammatik*. Halle: Max Niemeyer.
Braune, Wilhelm with Ingo Reiffenstein (ed.). 2004 [1886]. *Althochdeutsche Grammatik I* (15th edn.). Tübingen: Max Niemeyer Verlag.
Bremmer, Rolf H. Jr. 2009. *An introduction to Old Frisian: History, grammar, reader, glossary*. Amsterdam: John Benjamins.
Campbell, Alistair. 2003 [1959]. *Old English grammar*. New York: Oxford University Press.
Cardinaletti, Anna & Michal Starke. 1999. The typology of structural deficiency: A case study of the three classes of pronouns. In Henk van Riemsdijk (ed.), *Clitics in the languages of Europe*, 145–233. Berlin: Mouton de Gruyter.
Cathey, James E. 2000. *Old Saxon*. Munich: LINCOM Publishers.
Cleasby, Richard & Guðbrandur Vigfússon. 1874. *An Icelandic-English dictionary*. www.ling.upenn.edu/~kurisuto/germanic/oi_cleasbyvigfusson_about.html
Craigie, William, James Murray & John Simpson (eds.). 1971. *The compact edition of the Oxford English Dictionary: Volume II, P-Z*. Oxford University Press.
Derolez, René & Anne-Marie Simon-Vandenbergen. 1988. Gothic *saihw* and *sai*, with some notes on imperative interjections in Germanic. In Mohammad Ali Jazayery, Edgar C. Polomé, Werner Winter (eds.), *Languages and cultures: Studies in honor of Edgar C. Polomé*, 97–110. Berlin: Mouton de Gruyter.
EWAhd II = Lloyd et al. (1998)
Feist, Sigmund. 1939 [1923]. *Vergleichendes Wörterbuch der Gotischen Sprache* (3rd edn.). Leiden: E. J. Brill.
Fortson, Benjamin W. IV. 2004. *Indo-European language and culture: An introduction*. Malden: Blackwell Publishing.
Galleé, Johan Hendrik. 1910. *Altsächsische Grammatik*. Halle: Max Niemeyer.
Gordon, E. V. with A. R. Taylor (ed.). 1956 [1927]. *An introduction to Old Norse* (2nd edn.). Oxford: Oxford University Press.
Haegeman, Liliane. 2014. West Flemish verb-based discourse markers and the articulation of the Speech Act layer. *Studia Linguistica* 68(1). 116–139.
Haegeman, Liliane & Virginia Hill. 2011. The syntacticization of discourse. Paper presented at OnLI II University of Ulster, 2–4 December 2010. http://www.gist.ugent.be/members/lilianehaegeman.
Haegeman, Liliane & Virginia Hill. 2013. The syntacticization of discourse. In Raffaella Folli, Christina Sevdali & Robert Truswell (eds.), *Syntax and its limits*, 370–390. Oxford: Oxford University Press.
Haugen, Einar. 1982. *Scandinavian language structures*. Minneapolis: University of Minnesota Press.
Klingenschmitt, Gert. 1987. Erbe und Neuerung beim germanischen Demonstrativpronomen. In Herbert Kolb, Klaus Matzel & Karl Stackmann; Rolf Bergmann, Heinrich Tiefenbach & Lothar Voetz (eds.), *Althochdeutsch, Band I: Grammatik. Glossen und Texte*, 169–189. Heidelberg: Carl Winter Universitätsverlag.
Lander, Eric. 2015. *The nanosyntax of the Northwest Germanic reinforced demonstrative*. Ghent: Ghent University dissertation.

Lass, Roger. 1994. *Old English: A historical linguistic companion*. Cambridge: Cambridge University Press.
Lloyd, Albert Larry, Otto Springer & Rosemarie Lühr (eds.). 1998. *Etymologisches Wörterbuch des Althochdeutschen: Band II, bî-ezzo*. Göttingen: Vandenhoeck & Ruprecht.
Markey, Thomas L. 1981. *Frisian*. The Hague: Mouton de Gruyter.
Nielsen, Hans Frede. 2000. *The Early Runic language of Scandinavia*. Heidelberg: Carl Winter Universitätsverlag.
OED, P-Z = Craigie et al. (1971)
Project Wulfila. www.wulfila.be. Antwerp University.
Rauch, Irmengard. 1992. *The Old Saxon language: Grammar, epic narrative, linguistic interference* (Berkeley Models of Grammars, Vol. 1). New York: Peter Lang.
Roberts, Ian & Anna Roussou. 2003. *Syntactic change: A Minimalist approach to grammaticalization*. Cambridge: Cambridge University Press.
Samnordisk runtextdatabas. www.nordiska.uu.se/forskn/samnord.htm. Uppsala University. Accessed 13 February, 2013.
Sievers, Eduard. 1892 [1872]. *Tatian: Lateinisch und altdeutsch mit ausführlichem Glossar* (2nd edn.). Paderborn: Ferdinand Schöningh.
Streitberg, Wilhelm. 2000 [1910]. *Die Gotische Bibel* (2 volumes). Heidelberg: Carl Winter Universitätsverlag.
Tanghe, Sanne & Marlies Jansegers. 2014. Marcadores del discurso derivados de los verbos de percepción: Un análisis comparativo entre el español y el italiano. *Revue Romane* 49(1). 1–31.
Van Bergen, Linda. 2013. Let's talk about *uton*. In A. H. Jucker, D. Landert, A. Seiler & N. Studer-Joho (eds.), *Meaning in the history of English: Words and texts in context*, 1–27. Amsterdam: John Benjamins.
Wackernagel, Jacob. 1892. Über ein Gesetz der indogermanischen Wortstellung. *Indogermanische Forschungen* 1. 333–436.
Wauchope, Mary Michele. 1992. Old High German *nu*. In Rosina L. Lippi-Green (ed.), *Recent developments in Germanic linguistics*, 57–68. Amsterdam: John Benjamins.
Wright, Joseph. 1906 [1888]. *An Old High German primer, with grammar, notes, and glossary* (2nd edn.). Oxford: Clarendon Press.

Terje Lohndal and Rosalind Thornton
The 3SGS morpheme in child and adult English: A formal analysis

1 Introduction

For decades, formal linguists have struggled with how to analyze the position of the verb in a sentence. Various mechanisms and analyses have been implemented ranging from specific morphological operations to mechanisms that are part of the syntactic derivation and representation. Since Chomsky (1957), the position of the verb has been related to the interaction between a verbal root and its inflectional morpheme (the position is labeled T in this paper).[1] That is, researchers have asked whether the verb should be decomposed into smaller units, and if so, how these units combine across languages. For the past 30 years, the verb has been considered to occupy one of three main positions: the C head, the T head, and the V head (Stowell 1981; Chomsky 1986); cf. (1).[2]

(1)
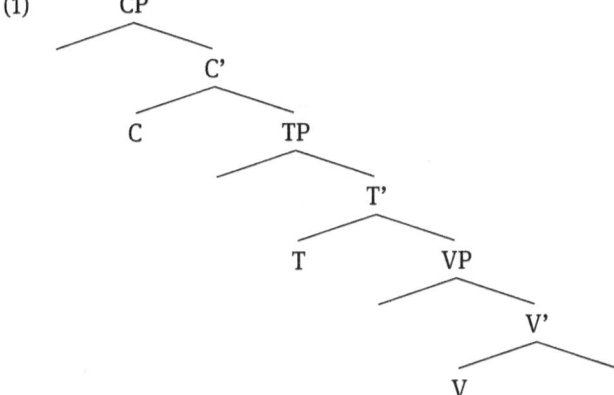

---
[1] See Lasnik (2000) and Freidin (2004) for comprehensive reviews and discussion.
[2] Here we have decided to use TP and not IP for the inflectional position, following what has become the main convention in the field.

DOI 10.1515/9781501504037-018

V has been assumed to be the base position, where a verb that does not move remains. A verb that moves would either move to T or further onwards to C. Since the early 1990s, the structure has expanded and now contains a rich inventory of possible head positions (Chomsky 1995; Rizzi 1997; Cinque 1999, etc.). In this paper, we will assume a fairly traditional structure, mainly for expository convenience.

Despite the considerable number of research papers that have investigated the dependency between the root and the inflectional morpheme, there is still no agreed-upon analysis. There are various reasons why this is the case.

One reason is that there is a lot of variation between languages and an agreed-upon analysis should be able to account for this variation. In some languages, all verbs in main clauses are moved (e.g., Scandinavian languages; Holmberg and Platzack 1995), whereas others are like English in not moving main verbs but auxiliaries. Languages like French move their main verbs to T but not to C, and so on and so forth. The variation clearly demonstrates that children acquiring the syntactic patterns of their local language need to pay close attention to the position of the verb in the structure.

Another issue concerns the locus of verb movement. A range of different proposals have been advanced, ranging from purely syntactic mechanisms (Emonds 1978; den Besten 1983; Koopman 1984; Travis 1984; Baker 1985; 1988, Larson 1988; Vikner 1995; Julien 2002, 2007; Freidin 2004; Lechner 2005; Roberts 2010, 2013) to the claim that verb movement and head movement more generally is purely a PF phenomenon (see Chomsky 2001; Boeckx and Stjepanović 2001; Flagg 2002; Sauerland and Elbourne 2002). Some scholars have also advocated a mixed approach that combines aspects of syntax, morphology and phonology (e.g., Bobaljik 1995, 2003; Embick and Noyer 2001; Zwart 2001; Adger 2003; Harley 2004, 2011, 2013; Matushansky 2006), and yet others have eliminated head movement altogether by incorporating its effects under remnant movement (Koopman and Szabolcsi 2000; Mahajan 2000, 2003; Nilsen 2003; Müller 2004; Svenonius 2007). For useful overview articles, see Roberts (2001, 2011) and Barrie and Mathieu (2014). As is obvious, our understanding of verb movement still appears fairly inadequate, but the present situation underscores the need for continued work on head movement and verbal morphology in order to hopefully one day better understand the phenomena.

In this paper, we look at the issue through the lens of child language acquisition. We discuss data from a production experiment designed to uncover children's knowledge of verbal inflection. These data will lend support to one specific view of head movement, namely what we labeled the mixed approach above. Specifically, we will argue that head movement is syntactic, and that there is variation across varieties when it comes to which member of a chain of related heads is spelled out (Zwart 2001; Adger 2003).

The outline is as follows. Section 2 provides an empirical overview by focusing on production data from child English compared with the standard adult language. In section 3, we present the approach to head movement that we will rely on in this paper. Section 4 analyzes the data from section 2. In section 5, we make a few concluding remarks.

2 Empirical overview: Child English

It has been useful to formalize cross-linguistic differences in verb movement as parameters (see e.g., Pollock 1989; White 1990/1991). Thus, children acquiring any language must appeal to their linguistic experience to decide whether their language raises the verb to C, to T, or whether it remains in situ.[3] These word order parameters have been proposed to be set very early in the course of acquisition. According to Wexler (1998), the main word order parameters are set by the time the child enters the two-word stage, roughly around 18 months of age or possibly even earlier. These parameters include VO versus OV (Swedish versus German); V to T, V2 and the null subject parameter. Although word order parameters are mastered early, until about 3 years of age, children often use the infinitive form of the verb in main clauses. For this reason, children are said to be in the 'Optional Infinitive Stage'. However, it is also the case that when children do raise the verb, they raise it appropriately for their language, and in verb raising languages, provide appropriate inflection. This has been found for child Dutch (de Haan 1986; Jordens 1990; Haegeman 1995b), child German (Meisel and Müller 1992; Jordens 1990; Poeppel and Wexler 1993; Weissenborn 1990), child French (Pierce 1992; Verrips and Weissenborn 1992) among others. See also Wexler (1994) and Phillips (2010) for a review.

In contrast to many Romance and Germanic languages, main verbs in English do not raise, and indeed, English-speaking children are not observed to produce verb raising. English-speaking children have not been observed to raise the verb higher than negation to produce utterances like *Tigger fits not*, for example. Since English does not have a special morphological form for the stem, there is no clear morphological test for whether or not they use infinitive forms in main clauses. However, Wexler (1994) argues that English-speaking children do produce infinitive

---

[3] Arguably a more fine-grained typology is needed, viz. the variation among Norwegian dialects where children are clearly distinguishing between fine-grained syntactic properties that sometimes are contingent on information structure as well (see Westergaard 2009, 2013 inter alia).

verb forms in main clauses. His claim is that children's omissions of inflection, such as the 3rd person *s* (hence '3SGS') from the verb indicate that children are producing the infinitival form of the verb, not just the verb stem. Thus children's optional production of the 3SGS morpheme and other tense-related morphemes such as auxiliary verbs is taken to characterize the Optional Infinitive stage in English. Wexler (1994) goes on to argue that the overall distribution of child data in negative sentences should provide strong support for an Optional Infinitive stage in English. Our data support such a stage, but show that the data from spontaneous production on which conclusions have been drawn do not reveal the full picture. We will provide data from elicited production experiments that show not only omissions of the 3SGS in negative sentences, but its presence in non-target positions. These data lead us to a different perspective on the nature of the Optional Infinitive grammar and what children need to acquire to produce adult-like sentential negation. We turn next to a review of the English child data.

2.1 Inflection in child English

In adult English the 3SGS inflectional morpheme is realized in different positions in affirmative and negative sentences. In affirmative sentences, it is affixed to the main verb, as in (2a), while in negative sentences it is realized on the auxiliary verb *do*, as shown in (2b, 2c). Note that the 3SGS morpheme is realized on *do* whether the negation is the free standing form of negation *not* or the form *n't* which is incorporated into the more colloquial *doesn't*.

(2) a. *Tigger fits*
 b. *Tigger doesn't fit*
 c. *Tigger does not fit*

Children acquiring English do not converge immediately on consistent use of the range of adult sentences in (2). We will fill out the developmental picture, taking Bellugi's (1967) seminal dissertation on sentential negation in the 'Harvard' children Adam, Eve and Sarah (Brown 1973) as a starting point. We review subsequent research from Harris and Wexler (1996) and Schütze (2010) and also incorporate empirical findings from elicited production studies. We review data from a longitudinal study of four 2-year-old children reported in Thornton and Tesan (2013) and an elicited production study with 25 children aged from 2;05 to 3;04 (mean age of 2;11) by Thornton and Rombough (2015) to complete the developmental picture.

It is now well documented that English-speaking children in the Optional Infinitive stage, that is, children roughly up to about age 3 years, do not use tense-related morphemes, including the 3SGS morpheme consistently (Rizzi 1994;

Schütze and Wexler 1996; Wexler 1994, 1998; Phillips 2010). Spontaneous speech transcripts reveal that children's non-target productions largely feature omissions of the tense-related morphemes. Sporadic uses of the 3SGS used 'high' rather than affixed to the verb, have been observed. For example, Aran and Warren from the Manchester corpus produce the affirmative sentences shown in (3) (Theakston, Lieven, and Tomasello 2003). Such errant uses of the 3SGS morpheme have largely been relegated to performance errors or analyzed as lexically-specific rote-learned items (e.g. Wilson 2003).

(3) a. *That one's go up there* (Warren, file 10a, ll 529)
   b. *That one's go in* (Warren file 11b, ll 48)
   c. *Teddy's do wiggle wiggle wiggle* (Warren file 15a, ll 40)
   d. *That's go in the holes* (Aran file 18b, ll 614)

Similar examples appear in experimental contexts in some children's productions. In an experiment eliciting negative sentences with 2- to 3-year-old children, Thornton and Rombough (2015) report a child (pseudonym Jade) who produced the 3SGS in non-target positions quite consistently when testing a selection of boxes to see if they open. The child's succession of affirmative and negative utterances stating that some boxes open while others do not are given in (4). Of the 27 negative productions produced by this child in the experimental session, 21 realized inflection before the main verb, either as a contracted form on the subject NP or as the copula, and of the 42 positive productions, 19 featured preverbal inflection. The non-target inflection appears to be too frequent to result from performance considerations. The alternative is that the 'misplaced' 3SGS is likely to be a reflection of this child's grammar at this stage of her grammatical development.

(4) *It's not working, This one opens, This one's opens, It's not open, Not open, That's open* (x2), *That is open, This opens, It's not, This is open* (x2)

As can be seen from the range of productions in (4), this child often puts the 3SGS morpheme in a 'high' position, presumably T.[4] It is of interest that in examples like *That is open* (assuming the intended meaning 'That opens') the 3SGS sometimes

---

[4] Another possible alternative to the proposal that children sometimes use the 3SGS morpheme in the T position would be to propose that children are simply using rote-learned high frequency combinations such as *that's* and *it's* and inserting them as unanalyzed wholes into the subject position (cf. Wilson 2003). Such a proposal is unlikely, given that such subject NPs do not occur with modals, sentences where a 3SGS morpheme is not required. That is, children have not been observed to produce utterances such as #*It's can open* or #*This one's won't open* in the longitudinal sample reported in Thornton and Tesan (2007, 2013) or in the data collected from 25 children in Thornton and Rombough (2015).

emerges as a stand-alone form of *be*; this may occur in those cases when the subject NP already ends in a sibilant.[5]

Before we simply assume that the *s* in utterances like (3) and (4) (other than the ones with *is*) is the 3SGS in a 'high' position, it is worth considering the alternative that the *s* could be an auxiliary form of *be*, and that the child has simply omitted the aspectual *-ing* morpheme in her productions. That is, utterances like *It's not open* or *It's not work* could, potentially, be intended as *It's not opening* or *It's not working*. First, omission of the *-ing* morpheme is not generally considered to be a characteristic property of the Optional Infinitive stage, given that this morpheme concerns aspect and not tense. At least for slightly older 3 year-old children, Rice and Wexler (1996) report that the accuracy rates differ greatly for tense/agreement and aspect, with 55% omission for 3SGS but only 10% for the aspectual *-ing* morpheme. Therefore, it is unlikely that children like Jade are simply omitting the aspectual suffix in productions like (3) and (4). Furthermore, if such omissions were a property of the Optional Infinitive stage, we would expect them to be more widespread across the population of children, and not confined to particular children. A second reason to doubt the alternative explanation is that the form with preverbal inflection also shows up with verbs like *fit* (Jade produces *It's fits*), which do not lend themselves to the aspectual form (**It's fitting*). Assuming that children have the knowledge that lexical verbs such as *fit* are not used in the present progressive form, productions such as *It's fit* would be unanticipated on the alternative explanation. Therefore, from this point forward, we will assume that in productions such as *It's fit*, the *s* is the 3SGS morpheme, positioned 'high', in T.

2.2 Negation in the optional infinitive stage

The classic study of negation is Bellugi's (1967) dissertation and the related paper by Klima and Bellugi (1966). Bellugi (1967) proposed that two stages precede the adult stage at which children can produce sentential negation using a negative auxiliary verb; at the first stage negation appeared either initially or finally in a phrase or utterance, and at the second stage, it could be viewed as internal to the sentence and expressed by *not* or *no*. For literature that reports on children's early acquisition of negation see Déprez and Pierce (1993); Drozd (1995); Cameron-Faulkner, Lieven, and Theakston (2007); Harris and Wexler (1996) among others.

---

[5] Such utterances also occur with other verbs. For example, Jade also produces *This is drive* and *This is jumps*.

As Bellugi (1967) noted almost 50 years ago, 2-year-old children in the Optional Infinitive stage frequently omit the 3SGS morpheme and produce sentential negation with *not*, as in (5a). Bellugi reported that soon after sentences like (5a) with *not* (or *no*) emerge, children use *can't* and *don't* as in (5b, 5c). These forms did not occur with progressive verbs, as in (5d). At the time *don't* and *can't* appeared, the children did not use the auxiliary verb system productively.

A similar progression was seen in the longitudinal development of a child (Brian) documented by Cameron-Faulkner, Lieven, and Theakston (2007). These data document Brian's 'multiword' negation, which includes both sentential negation and anaphoric negation. Brian's data are investigated from 2;3 to 3;3 years of age. It is worth reviewing his pattern of development, because the data are also compared with the parental input. At 2;3 his predominant form of negation is *no*, which accounted for 97% of the sample. There is no information concerning whether these uses of *no* are sentential negation or other uses. By 2;6, use of *no* has decreased to 60%, and *not* is used in 40% of utterances. The first negative auxiliaries are *don't* and *can't*, and are reported to be used productively by 2;9. By 3;3 *don't* accounts for over half of Brian's negative utterances, and *not* decreases, accounting for only 17% of negated utterances at 3;3. In the final sample at 3;3, negative auxiliaries *didn't* and *won't* emerge, but no cases of *doesn't* are documented. As part of the study, the parental input from 10 files was analyzed, 5 files from each of two time periods. There is little difference between the two samples, so for brevity, the parental input when Brian is 2;8 is reported. In these files, *no* accounts for 30% of the multiword negation. Since *no* is not used for sentential negation in English, these uses are likely to be anaphoric negation, modifying DPs and so on. The negative marker *not* is used 21%, *don't* appears in 19% of the productions, *can't* 10%, *won't* 6% and other negative auxiliary verbs account for 13%. In other words, putting aside the 30% irrelevant uses of *no*, *not* accounts for 21% and negative auxiliary verbs account for the other 49% of the input data. The important point to take away from these data is that the parental input contains many negative auxiliary verbs, while they are absent from children's early productions.

In fact since the only negative auxiliary verbs used by the children early in acquisition were *can't* and *don't*, Bellugi concluded that these lexical items were unanalyzed 'chunks,' or what she termed "lexical representatives of the negative element" (Bellugi 1967: 59). For Bellugi, the only true negative marker in the children's grammars at this stage of development was *not* (or possibly *no*).

(5) a. *Tigger not fit*
 b. *Tigger can't fit*
 c. *Tigger don't fit*
 d. #*Tigger don't/can't sleeping*

As Schütze (2010) notes, other researchers, such as Bloom (1970) and Hyams (1986) have made similar proposals arguing that *can't* and *don't* are unanalyzed forms and are potential substitutes for *not*. Schütze argues that such proposals do not account for the empirical facts. For one thing, Schütze argues that *can't* and *don't* are not always the first negative-looking auxiliaries in children's grammars as Bellugi had proposed. Second, he claims that distributional facts argue against such proposals. For example, if the distribution of *don't* and *can't* were identical with *not*, examples such as the following would be anticipated (Schütze 2010: 238):

(6)   a. *He('s) don't happy*
     b. *He might don't laugh*
     c. *He did don't laugh*
     d. *He('s) don't singing*

In a search of 5 children from the CHILDES database, he concludes that errors in the use of *don't*, *doesn't*, and *didn't* total less than 5% of the productions collected for the children he investigated.[6] Thus Schütze concludes "The fact that *not* and *don't* are used correctly the vast majority of the time makes it unlikely that children are confusing them" (Schütze 2010: 244). However, since non-adult agreement occurs quite frequently for *don't*, Schütze recognizes that the form *don't* is a grammatical option for some children. As a consequence, he offers a different account for children's uses of non-agreeing *don't*. (See Guasti and Rizzi 2002 for a further alternative account.)

In order to explain Schütze's account, we first need to outline his theoretical assumptions. First, as in Schütze and Wexler (1996), Schütze assumes that what characterizes the Optional Infinitive stage is that the Tense and/or Agreement features may be underspecified in the sentence representation. Underspecification of features in the IP can result in omission of the 3SGS, yielding utterances like *Tigger not fit*. A further assumption is that a Mood projection, that signifies indicative mood, is generated above the IP projection. The head of the Mood projection hosts *do*, but can also be spelled out as null. It will be null in those cases when Infl affixes to a verb to its right. Turning to negation, Schütze assumes that *n't* is the contracted form of *not* and that both forms of negation are heads. Following Harris and Wexler (1996), Schütze assumes that children may have a preference for *n't* over *not* in their productions, irrespective of the features that are realized in Infl. With these assumptions in place, children's productions of *don't* can be explained. The proposal is that if children underspecify Infl and it spells out as

---

[6] Schütze (2010) investigated data from Abe (2;05–3;03), Adam (2;03–4;10), Sarah (2;09–5;0), Nina (2;00–3;03) and Ross (2;06–5;02).

null, then their preferred form of negation, *n't* has no host. In this case, use of *do* is triggered by "the need for an adjacent morphologically dependent element to have a host word" (Schütze 2010: 251). Therefore *do* steps in to provide a host for *n't*. The syntax for an utterance like *He don't cry* is summarized in (7).

(7) He M$_{\text{Indic}}$ [$_\text{I}$ 0] n't [$_{\text{VP}}$ cry]

In the study by Harris and Wexler (1996) on sentential negation in the Optional Infinitive stage, the focus is on the range of sentence types that should and should not occur, given the assumption that Tense is expressed 'optionally' during this stage of development (Wexler 1994).[7] Since children can fail to realize a morpheme for Tense, children are expected to produce utterances with *not*, as Bellugi (1967) had observed. For Harris and Wexler (1996), use of *do* is taken to indicate that a projection for Tense is present in the phrase structure representation. Therefore, even though (8b) is missing the 3SGS morpheme, it is still taken to express Tense, and thus, (8a) is expected to appear optionally alongside (8b, 8c) in children's productions.

(8) a. *Tigger not fit*
    b. *Tigger don't fit*
    c. *Tigger doesn't fit*
    d. **Tigger not fits*

A further prediction followed from the assumption that *not* is a head. Harris and Wexler predicted that children would not produce utterances such as *Tigger not fits*, as in (8d), with inflection realized on the main verb, since such productions would violate the Head Movement Constraint (Travis 1984). Harris and Wexler conducted a search of 10 children's data in the CHILDES database which yielded results largely compatible with their proposal. There were some instances of inflected main verbs like (8d) but these were taken to be performance errors given that they did not exceed 10% (5/54 of *not-V* examples) in the children's data.

2.3 Data on negation from elicited production

It is important to point out that both Schütze's (2010) study and the earlier study by Harris and Wexler (1996) test their predictions using spontaneous production data from transcripts available in the CHILDES database (MacWhinney 2000).

---

[7] Harris and Wexler (1996) only assume that Tense is expressed optionally. In their paper, it is not assumed that Agreement is also optional.

As Snyder (2007) has argued, children tend to be 'grammatically conservative' in their spontaneous productions. Experimental techniques encourage children to attempt structures that they might otherwise avoid. Given that spontaneous production data do not yield an abundance of sentential negation, elicited production is an appropriate methodology to probe children's grammatical hypotheses.

In a longitudinal study of the development of inflection and negation in 4 children from age 2 to 3 years of age Thornton and Tesan (2007, 2013)[8] analyzed data that were evoked using elicited production techniques together with children's spontaneous productions. Thornton and Tesan's findings did not replicate Harris and Wexler's predicted pattern of utterances in (8). In their corpus of 497 examples of sentential negation elicited from the 4 children, Thornton and Tesan (2007, 2013) observed that medial negation sentences like *Tigger not fit* co-existed with alternatives in which a 3SGS morpheme was present in the utterance, but did not occupy its target position inside the lexical item *doesn't*. These non-target forms were eventually replaced by *doesn't*, but this form was not present in the early sessions with these children.

Table 1 summarizes the breakdown of the data from children's productions of sentential negation in the corpus. It can be seen from the rightmost column in the table that at least 3 of the 4 children produced all of the non-target versions of sentential negation.

To verify these findings in a larger sample of children, Thornton and Rombough (2015) conducted a study eliciting sentential negation from 25 2- to 3-year-old children (mean age 2;11). The context used to elicit sentential negation had children test groups of items for a variety of properties. They tested whether toy characters fit in a bus, whether dog toys squeak, whether items stick on a magnetic board, and

Tab. 1: Breakdown of sentential negation for children as reported in Appendix C in Thornton and Tesan (2013) (*N* = 4)

Negative Sentence Type		Raw No. (% of corpus)	No. of Children
NP not V	(*Tigger not fit*)	101/497 (20%)	4
NP don't V	(*Tigger don't fit*)	80/497 (16%)	4
NP's not V	(*Tigger's not fit*)	30/497 (6%)	3
NP not V-s	(*Tigger not fits*)	77/497 (15%)	3
NP don't V-s	(*Tigger don't fits*)	22/497 (4%)	3
NP doesn't V	(*Tigger doesn't fit*)	187/497 (38%)	4

---

[8] The children participated in the study at the following ages: Child 1 (Caitlyn) 1;9.4–2;8.29; Child 2 (Kristen) 2;0.12–3;0.8; Child 3 (Georgia) 1;10.23–2;8.20; Child 4 (Curtis) 2;1.9–3;8.03.

so on. Children were handed the items one at a time to test. In the 'fit' scenario, for example, children successfully got two toy characters to fit through the door of a toy bus, but the third character was too tall, and in this context a negative sentence was anticipated. In this context, a negative sentence like *Tigger doesn't fit* is natural for adults. Each child was exposed to at least 5 scenarios eliciting different verbs, though the actual number of opportunities each child had to produce negative sentences varied, depending on how successful they were, and their enjoyment of the task. Such differences are inevitable with young children. Using this protocol, 585 full sentence productions were elicited. Once the productions with modals, past tense *didn't*, progressive *-ing* etc. were excluded, there were 442 productions remaining for analysis. These productions were all produced in a context in which adults would use *doesn't*. The breakdown of children's productions is given in Tab. 2 (and individual subject data are also detailed below in Tabs. 3 and 4).

The study by Thornton and Rombough (2015) also evoked many negative sentences that were non-adult in form, as can be seen in Tab. 2.[9] As observed in the earlier study, children produced sentential negation with just a bare verb, and with inflection in preverbal position as well as on the inflected main verb. The

Tab. 2: Children's full sentence productions excluding productions with modals, past tense and progressive *-ing* (*N* = 25). Table 2 combines Tabs. 3 and 4 in Thornton and Rombough (2015).

Negative Sentence Type	Raw No. (%)
NP not V (*Tigger not fit*)	46/442 (10.4%)
No Subject V (*No it fit*)	8/442 (1.8%)
NP don't V (*Tigger don't fit*)	39/442 (8.8%)
NP's not V (*Tigger's not fit*)	19/442 (4.3%)
NP not V-s (*Tigger not fits*)	50/442 (11.3%)
NP don't V-s (*Tigger don't fits*)	22/442 (5%)
No Subj V-s (*No it fits*)	8/442 (1.8%)
*NP didn't V-s (*Tigger didn't fits*)	2/442 (0.5%)
NP's not V-s (*Tigger's not fits*)	4/442 (1%)
NP doesn't V (*Tigger doesn't fit*)	232/442 (52.5%)
NP's doesn't V-s (*Tigger's doesn't fits*)	12/442 (2.7%)

*Included because it has a non-target *s*

---

[9] The 4 children whose data were reported in Thornton and Tesan (2013) did not produce what has sometimes been termed 'external negation' because the negation is first in the string. There were 2 children in the Thornton and Rombough (2015) study who produced such utterances, and these are incorporated in Tab. 2. The syntax of these utterances falls outside the scope of this paper, but see Thornton and Rombough (2015) for discussion.

group data obscure the fact that children divided easily into 2 groups, those children whose negative sentences were adult-like and negated with *doesn't*, and those children who used the non-adult forms. Taking as a criterion for placement in an 'Advanced' group 5 or more productions of *doesn't* during the experimental session, Thornton and Rombough classified 13 children as 'Advanced' while the other 12 were categorized as 'Less Advanced'. Of the 288 full sentence productions (including modals etc.) elicited from the Advanced group, 228 were productions of *doesn't*. This stands in contrast to the Less Advanced group. This group of children produced a total of 290 full sentence productions, but only 4 were productions of *doesn't*. This means that most of the non-adult forms reported in Tab. 2 were produced by this Less Advanced group of children. As we will see shortly, Thornton and Tesan (2013) propose that *doesn't* is a likely trigger for grammatical change from the 'Less Advanced' grammar that licenses the 3SGS in non-target positions to 'Advanced' status.

The elicited production data are not compatible with Schütze's account for non-agreeing *don't*. As it stands, Schütze's theory accounts nicely for non-agreeing *don't*, but it is unable to account for the negative sentence variants in which there is a non-target 3SGS in some other position in the sentence. Recall that, according to Schütze, *do* is spelled-out in Mood only when there is an adjacent morphological element needing a host. Usually this is an affix for tense, but when Infl is underspecified, *do* can serve as the host for *n't*. Such a theory cannot

Tab. 3: Negative sentences of children in the Advanced Group (*N* = 13) in Thornton and Rombough (2015)

Advanced Group				
	It doesn't V	It don't V	It can't V	Other
Aaron	10	1		It doesn't Vs (1)
Jack	23			It doesn't Vs (2)
Ella	25		1	
Eliza	23	5	1	It didn't V (1)
Lauren	13	1	22	
Eva	14	3	6	It didn't V (2)
Heidi	22			It doesn't Vs (2)
Tyler	6			
Braxton	23		1	
Chelsea	17		6	
Jacob	12		3	
Summer	13		1	
Leah	27	1		
Total	228	11	41	8

Tab. 4: Negative sentences of children in the Less Advanced Group (N = 12) from Thornton and Rombough (2015)

Less Advanced Group

Name; Age	It doesn't V	It not V	It not Vs	It don't V	It don't Vs	It's not V	No it V	No it Vs	Other
Lara 2;07		10	9						It can't V (1)
Sienna 2;11		32	20			2			It didn't V (13)
									It didn't Vs (2)
									It can't V (4)
									It's not V-ing (1)
Jamie 2;10	1	3	21		2			1	It's not Vs (4)
Eddie 2;10							3	7	
Tahlia 2;09	1						5		It can't V (1)
									It won't V (1)
Jade 2;08						5			It's not V-ing (12)
Sarah 3;0		1				12			It's not V-ing (8)
Sean 3;03				16	1				
Lachlan 3;01				12	19				It didn't V (1)
									It doesn't Vs (7)
Lucy 3;04	2								It can't V (28)
Adam 2;05									It didn't V (14)
Thomas 3;02									It can't V (15)
Totals	4	46	50	28	22	19	8	8	105

explain instances of the 3SGS in non-target positions (e.g. *Tigger's not fit*, *Tigger don't fits* etc.). Non-agreeing *don't* should only appear when Infl is underspecified and *do* is a host for *n't*, so the appearance of the 3SGS on the main verb is unanticipated. Children's productions in which sentential negation is produced with an inflected main verb, in particular, led Thornton and Tesan to an alternative proposal. They propose that in early child grammars, the negative marker *not* is initially an adverb, not a head, as assumed by Harris and Wexler (1996) and Schütze (2010).

2.4 Thornton and Tesan (2013)

Drawing on Zeijlstra's (2004, 2008) theory of negation and learnability, Thornton and Tesan (2013) give a new interpretation to Bellugi's observation that children initially only use *not*, and do not use negative auxiliary verbs. Zeijlstra (2004) proposes a Negative Concord parameter. Basically, on one value, the negative marker is an adverb (Dutch, German etc.), while on the other value, negation is a head (Italian, Czech etc.). According to Zeijlstra (2008), children in the early stages of acquisition build maximally efficient phrase structure representations, incorporating only those functional categories instantiated in the linguistic input.[10] The proposal is that the default value of the parameter is that the negative marker is an adverb since this does not require the child to build a NegP functional projection to incorporate a negative head. If the positive input makes available a negative head, the child can change the value of the parameter. English is more complex, if *not* is assumed to be an adverb, and *n't* to be a head. In this case, at least on one learning scenario, English must retain its negative adverb and a negative head must be added to the possible options on the basis of positive input. Applying Zeijlstra's proposal to child English, Thornton and Tesan (2013) propose that children initially only use *not* as an adverb, in keeping with the default value of the Negative Concord parameter.

In the absence of experience, children apparently hypothesize that *not*, like the negative adverb *never*, permits inflection to appear on the main verb. This gives rise to the productions like *Tigger not fits* observed in young children's productions. As Tabs. 1 and 2 revealed, children also produce *Tigger don't fits*. These

---

[10] This assumption has a long history in generative linguistics. For discussion, see Fukui (1986, 1995, 2006); Lebeaux (1988); Radford (1990, 1996, 2000); van Gelderen (1993); Thráinsson (1996, 2003); Bobaljik and Thráinsson (1998); Vangsnes (1999); Fukui and Sakai (2003).

productions can be explained if we adopt Bellugi's proposal that *don't* is a 'lexical representative' of the negative element. On the present proposal, it is a lexical representative of some kind of transitional adverb, not a head as Schütze (2010) took Bellugi to be claiming. The proposal now explains children's production of negative sentences that appeared to violate the Head Movement Constraint (cf. Harris and Wexler 1996).

This proposal means that it is worth returning to check Schütze's other reasons for rejecting Bellugi's proposal that *don't* and *can't* are initially unanalyzed lexical items. Schütze (2010) makes the point that these two items do not behave uniformly in children's grammars, with some children acquiring other negative auxiliary verbs first in their grammar. This is most likely correct. The data reported in Thornton and Tesan (2013) and Thornton and Rombough (2015) do not show that the modal *can't* is used with inflected main verbs. But, in principle, it appears that children could take any form of *do* to initially be an unanalyzed form. As Tab. 2 shows, one child used *didn't* with inflected main verbs, suggesting for this child, *didn't* is unanalyzed (e.g. *Tigger didn't fits*). The last reason Schütze (2010) gives for rejecting Bellugi's proposal is that *don't* doesn't distribute like *not*, since the predicted sentences in (6) are not found in children's transcripts. This is true, though perhaps not surprising, given that even simple sentential negation is relatively infrequent in the transcripts when children are in the Optional Infinitive stage, as the scant data set in Harris and Wexler (1996) makes clear.

For reasons that are not clear, children acquiring English appear to have some difficulty recognizing that negative auxiliary verbs such as *can't*, *don't*, *isn't* and so forth are multimorphemic. This is problematic as this is an important step in recognizing that *n't* is a head form of negation. This step brings Thornton and Tesan (2007, 2013) to propose that the most informative lexical item to trigger this change is the form *doesn't*. Given that in this item, the 3SGS morpheme is internal, it may provide more salient information that *n't* is a negative head. Furthermore, if *doesn't* is the negative auxiliary verb that signals that children have analyzed *n't* as a head form of negation, and progressed to the adult grammar, then non-target doubling with *doesn't* is not predicted to occur. A few such productions were observed (*It doesn't fits*) as shown in Tab. 2 (12/442). Five of these were from children in the Advanced Group and the other 7 came from one child in the Less Advanced Group. In addition to 7 instances of utterances like *It doesn't fits*, this child produced 12 examples of *It don't V* and 19 examples of *It don't V-s*. The data suggest that for this child, the form *doesn't* has not been sufficiently salient to trigger morphological analysis and thus change.

In summary, the data from these investigations showing the interaction of the 3SGS morpheme and negative markers suggest that English-speaking children start with a default adverbial form of negation *not*, and add the head form of negation *n't* later, once they have interpreted the linguistic evidence. Thornton and Tesan (2007) left the status of *not* in the adult grammar as an open question. What they observed is that once children acquire the head form of negation, *n't*, the negative marker *not* disappears from children's grammars (for the time period studied). This could suggest that children temporarily refrain from using *not* because they are not sure if it is an adverbial (or a maximal projection in SpecNeg) or a head. It is important to note, though, that Thornton and Tesan were only investigating lexical main verbs. It could be that children might have continued to use *not* with *be*, where it is very natural (e.g. *He's not a student*) but these forms were not investigated. At any rate, no claims are made about the status of *not* once children acquire negative auxiliaries such as *doesn't*.

At this point, we do not have a good understanding of the syntax of children's non-target negative sentences. Why is it that they use the 3SGS morpheme on its own at first, and how can these facts be explained using current linguistic theory? And, why is it that once children acquire *do*, the non-target forms with the 3SGS magically disappear? In this paper, we aim to answer these perplexing questions.

3 Theoretical assumptions

We will develop an analysis along the lines of Zwart (2001) and Adger (2003). In both of these publications, verb movement is a question of spelling out the verb and its inflectional markers in the right position. Verb movement is syntactic in the sense that syntactic mechanisms underlie the Spell-Out mechanism they both propose, but the actual determination of which members of a chain to spell out occurs on the PF side. We will first review Zwart's (2001) approach, then Adger's (2003), before turning to our own analysis in section 4.

3.1 Zwart (2001)

Zwart (2001) develops an analysis of verb movement which starts out with the assumption that there are lexical and functional features, henceforth LEX-features and F-features. He follows Chomsky (1995) in assuming that movement is a function of a requirement of feature valuation. Zwart's specific proposal builds on the definitions in (9) and (10).

(9) α and β are *F-related* if α is involved in a feature valuation operation involving F, where F is a formal feature of β. (Zwart 2001: 37)
(10) Let γ be a chain of F-related elements (α, ..., β), where α c-commands β. Then α must contain LEX-features, and β is spelled out in the highest position of γ containing the LEX-features of β. (Zwart 2001: 38)

Assuming that LEX-movement is a last resort mechanism, (10) predicts two possibilities: Either there is no movement (β is spelled out in β) because α has LEX features, or α has no LEX-features and thus the LEX-features of β have to move to α (β is spelled out in α). The last resort nature of the operation is triggered by "phonological requirements having to do with the spell-out procedure" (Zwart 2001: 38). These "phonological" requirements are to a large extent morphological, as the verb can either be pronounced at the tail or head of the chain, cf. (9).[11] That is, either the inflection combines with the root/stem in the base position of the latter or in the base position of the former.

Zwart illustrates how this view of verb movement successfully accounts for a range of examples. For reasons of space, we will not discuss these here, but instead move to a similar account on which we will build our own analysis.

3.2 Adger (2003)

Adger (2003: 170) develops an analysis where verbal inflection in English is the realization of inflectional features on a low head (*v* for Adger). The dependency between features is encoded via Agree (Chomsky 2000), and an important assumption here is that the tense feature on the verb is uninterpretable, it is only the tense feature on T which has a semantic meaning, thus the latter is an interpretable feature. The unvalued features are deleted prior to semantic interpretation.

Adger encodes the fact that auxiliaries always move past negation as a property of feature strength (cf. Chomsky 1995): A strong feature triggers movement, a weak feature does not. A strong feature must be local to the feature

---

[11] Zwart (2001) also discusses syntactically triggered verb movement which is not observable. In this paper, we will only focus on observable instances of verb movement.

it checks or is checked by (Adger 2003: 179), which entails that the verb has to move to T whenever T is strong. The strong/weak distinction also enables Adger to articulate cross-linguistic differences, e.g., between English and French (cf. Pollock 1989).

When it comes to *do*-support, after discarding several other possibilities Adger develops a pronunciation approach based on chains. He suggests the rule in (11), which arguably is specific to English (and other languages that behave like English).

(11) *Pronouncing Tense Rule (PTR)*
In a chain (T[tense], *v*[uInfl:tense]), pronounce the tense features on *v* only if *v* is the head of T's sister (Adger 2003: 192)

This makes Adger's proposal similar to Bobaljik's (1995, 2003) proposal, which argues that adjacency is crucial for morphological realization. However, (11) is problematic in several ways, not least of which is that most proposals argue for a range of functional projections between T and *v*. However, we agree with the core intuition behind both Adger's proposal and Zwart's (2001) proposal, namely that the relationship between tense/agreement and the verb root/stem is one which should be given a PF analysis in terms of chains. In the next section, we will offer such an analysis, which also provides an analysis of the data from child language acquisition.

4 Analysis: Movement as spell-out

An analysis of negation and inflection in children acquiring English needs to respect the following assumptions outlined and argued for in section 2.

(12) a. Children start out assuming that *not* is an adverb.
b. During the stage when *not* is an adverb, children provide a range of non-target structures with the inflectional morpheme in the wrong position.
c. Children do not move main verbs, in line with their target grammar.
d. When children acquire the head form of negation, *n't* and *do*, their productions become target consistent and the inflectional morphemes in the wrong position disappear.

The data in section 2 also illustrate that the inflectional morpheme cannot appear just anywhere. It either occurs on the main verb or it occurs cliticized to the subject. It does not occur on adverbs or on negation prior to *do* being acquired.

Standard English is presumably the target grammar for the children in question. For that reason, we will first present our analysis of standard English before we turn to the child data.

Consider the structure in (13b) for the sentence in (13a).

(13) a. *Sue eats cookies.*
  b.

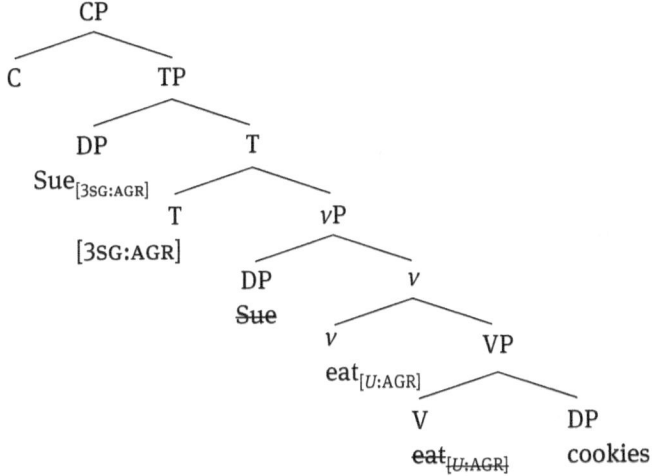

We assume that there is a v-layer that introduces the external argument, although we are not committed to its label: it could be either *v* (Chomsky 1995; Harley 1995) or Voice (Kratzer 1996); see Alexiadou, Anagnostopolou, and Schäfer (2015) for extensive discussion of the syntax of external arguments. We furthermore follow Larson (1988), Chomsky (1995) and others in assuming that the verbal root or stem moves to *v*. There is an Agree relationship between *v* and T where the root/stem carries an unvalued agreement feature, AGR. AGR encodes both tense and subject-verb agreement; we are simply using one feature for ease of presentation and because any finer decomposition does not matter for present purposes. The AGR feature on T is valued by the external argument, and T and *v* enter into an Agree relation whereby T values the features on *v*. This requires a 'downward' Agree relation, which we assume is independently justified (e.g., Adger 2003; Baker 2008; Haegeman and Lohndal 2010; Zeijlstra 2012). Once Agree has valued the feature on *v*, both T and *v* share the same feature value. Whether the feature bundle is spelled out on T or *v* is a question of variation. In English, it is spelled out on *v* for main verbs.[12] We can state this as the following language-specific PF condition which clearly has to be acquired.

---

[12] The condition needs to be so specific since the verb moves to *v* in double object constructions, viz. *Mary gave John a book* and not **Mary John gave a book*.

(14) *Pronunciation Rule*
Given an Agree chain involving verbal AGR,
a. pronounce *v* iff the head of the chain is T and no other overt head intervenes between T and *v*
b. elsewhere, pronounce the head of the chain.

Note that this assumes that the PF component has access to chain memberships, and that PF cares about adjacency, much like in Bobaljik (1995, 2003) and much other work in Distributed Morphology.

The Pronunciation Rule (14b) entails that if the structure has an auxiliary or modal verb, AGR will be pronounced on T. The structure looks as follows, where we assume that the auxiliary is merged directly in T.[13]

(15) a. *Sue will eat cookies.*
b.

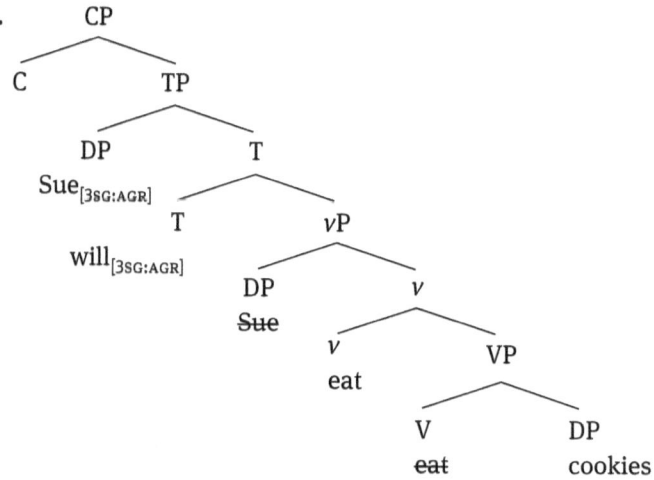

For a sentence involving negation, we assume the following representation, where negation is assumed to be a head (Adger 2003, among others).

---

13 Nothing hinges on this specific assumption. Furthermore, we set aside how the verbal morphology is realized on other verbs, e.g., the difference between *Sue will eat cookies* and *Sue has eaten cookies*.

(16) a. *Sue does not/doesn't eat cookies.*
   b.
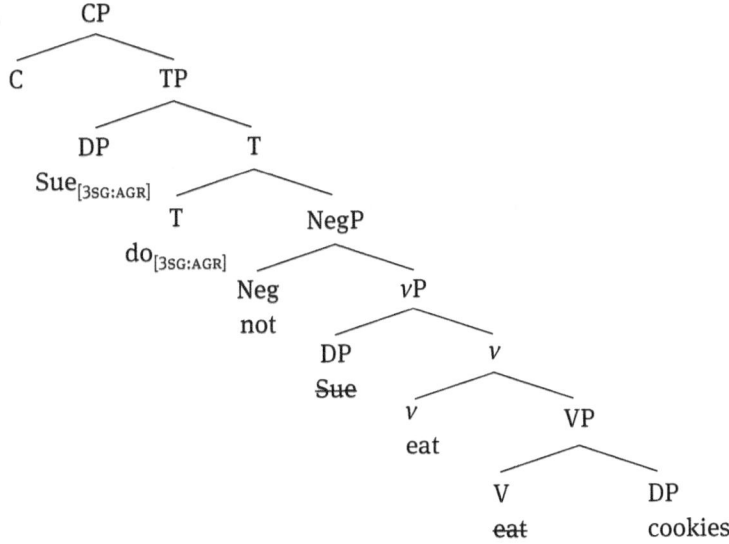

Our analysis will take as its starting point the standard analysis of *do*-insertion, outlined as follows by Roberts (2013: 560).

> *Do* is a dummy auxiliary, inserted exactly when the usual relation between Agr/T and V is blocked (e.g. by negation, emphasis or interrogation).

In a textbook, Lasnik (2000: 201) says that:

> I have not talked much about how *Do*-Support fits into the latest versions of the theory. I think this also works much the way it does in *Syntactic Structures*: a stranded affixal I is spelled out as the relevant form of *do*. That seems the simplest theory, just as it did 40 years ago.

This view is a last resort view of *do*-support, where a form of *do* is inserted in order to yield a convergent derivation. The present analysis will incorporate this last resort view of *do*-support. Importantly, recall that although negation triggers *do*-support, adverbs do not:

(17) a. *Sue never eats cookies.*
   b. *Sue often eats cookies.*

Thus, there is clearly a difference between heads, such as negation, and phrases, like adverbs. We assume that *not* blocks the Agree relation between T and v, requiring *do*-support to apply. Similarly, when C is involved by virtue of T moving to C, (14a) no longer applies, meaning that the head of the chain is pronounced.

(18) a. *Sue eats cookies.*
 b. *What does Sue eat?*

The rule in (14) is thereby able to accommodate the main aspects of the target grammar of English as far as the relationship between the verbal root/stem and the inflectional morpheme is concerned.

We would like to add that we do not regard (14) as a deep property. It is a highly descriptive PF account that does justice to the data. It may be objected that (14) is an unnatural or complicated condition. From our point of view, the important part is that (14) is language-specific and involves an aspect of grammar which has to be acquired, namely morphophonology. We assume that the grammar does not license stranded affixes in general (cf. Lasnik's (1981) Stranded Affix Filter).

Given this analysis of the target grammar, we now turn to the child data. Focusing on the non-contracted forms, we will analyze the cases in (19). That is, we will only focus on instances where the 3SGS morpheme is or should be overtly expressed.

(19) a. *Tigger not fit.*
 b. *Tigger's not fit.*
 c. *Tigger not fits.*
 d. *Tigger's not fits.*

The key ingredients of our analysis are: (i) children start out assuming that *not* is an adverbial, (ii) children have not acquired *do* in the early grammar, and (iii) children can either pronounce the 3SGS morpheme on v or T. That is, children have not yet mastered the specific pronunciation rules for English but instead assume a version of (14) as in (20).

(20) *Pronunciation Rule*
 Given an Agree chain involving verbal AGR,
 a. pronounce v or T iff the head of the chain is T and no other overt head intervenes between T and v
 b. elsewhere, pronounce the head of the chain.

Put differently, children have not yet mastered the specific conditions governing English verbal morphology. In what follows, we will argue that (20) provides an analysis of the child stage together with the two other assumptions just mentioned, and we will speculate on the transition from the child grammar to the target grammar.

In examples like *Tigger not fit* (19a), inflection is absent. This can be seen as the manifestation of an Optional Infinitive stage in the relevant children, and the analysis in Wexler (1994, 1998) would be compatible with the perspective taken in the present paper. Children also say *Tigger don't fit*, in which case we argue that *don't* is an unanalyzed unit. This means that the syntactic representation for this sentence is the same as the one for (19a): There is no inflection and *don't* presumably occupies the same structural position as *not*, which is to be adjoined to *v*P as an adverbial.

The example *Tigger's not fit* in (19b) has a 3SGS morpheme but it is attached to the subject and not to *do* as we would expect based on the target grammar. Assuming that *not* is an adverbial, it will be adjoined to *v*P. The adult Pronunciation Rule in (14) dictates that the 3SGS morpheme should be pronounced on *v* and not on T. However, children who have not yet mastered (14) may spell-out inflection in T according to (20). Since the child obeys the Stranded Affix Filter, the 3SGS cannot be left in T without a host. Given that the child has not acquired *do* at this point in time, some children instead choose to attach the 3SG morpheme to the subject, which matches in phi-features. As we noted in section 2, children also sometimes pronounce the head of the chain, even in affirmative sentences (see [3] and [4]). The attachment to the NP at the head of the chain is possible due to a match in phi-features, which also explains why 3SGS cannot attach to negation in English. Thus the imagined case in (21) does not occur in either corpora or the reported elicited production experiments in section 2.

(21) **Tigger nots fit.*

The child version of the Pronunciation Rule in (20) also allows the 3SGS to be pronounced on the verb, which is the case in (19c). Here, the 3SGS morpheme is pronounced on the verb in its base position. The structure will be as in (22).

(22)
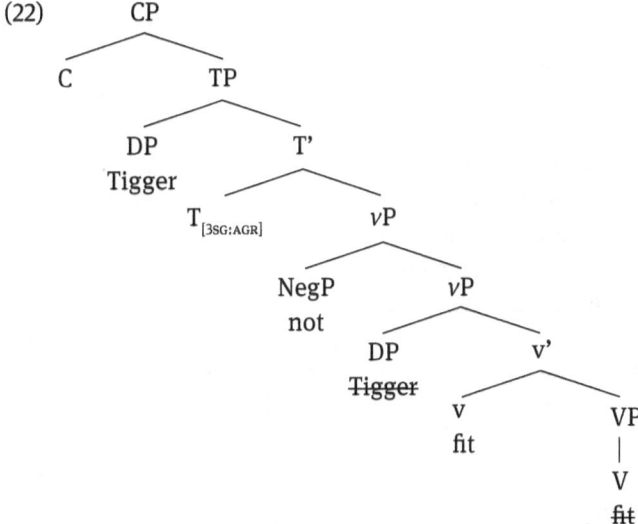

Since *not* is analyzed as an adverb, there is no overt head intervening between T and *v*. Some children choose to take up this option. Note that some children also produce *Tigger don't fits*, where we assume that *don't* is an unanalyzed unit on a par with *Tiger don't fit*. The difference is that there is inflection in this case, pronounced on the main verb, which is possible according to (20a) since *don't* is an adverbial adjoined to *v*P.

The fact that both (19b) and (19c) are possible demonstrates that in the child's early grammar, (14) has not been completely mastered but is rather assumed to be as in (20). The child seems to be exploiting the two possibilities: pronouncing the head of the chain or *v* while waiting for relevant input to decide which option is correct.

Examples like (19d), *Tigger's not fits*, show that children are also capable of pronouncing both members of the chain. These examples are not very frequent, which may be related to proposals arguing that only one member of a chain can be pronounced (cf. Nunes 2004). However, the example supports our claim that children have not initially acquired the adult version of (20), i.e., (14), a language-specific rule of their target grammar of English.

Let us assume that at some point, children take on board the positive evidence from adult simple affirmative sentences and that positive evidence, combined with indirect negative evidence from negative sentences, brings them to the conclusion that they do not have the option of producing the head of the chain. Such indirect negative evidence would be the absence of sentences like *Tigger's not fit*, compared to the presence of *Tigger doesn't fit*. The linguistic evidence brings them to the adult version (14). This means that from this point on children will not pronounce inflection in its 'high' position. Since this requires indirect negative evidence, it may account for why some children take a while to acquire the adult pronunciation rules. Examples like (19b) and (19d) will no longer occur, as children know that inflection needs a verbal host and since negation now counts as an intervener, thus inflection cannot appear on *v*.

The next question is how do children drive out the non-adult uses of the 3SGS morpheme on the main verb in negative sentences, that is, sentences as in (19d)? There are three changes that need to occur in the child's grammar before the 3SGS is eliminated from the 'low' position. First, children need to acquire the head form of negation, *n't*. As noted in section 2.4., negative auxiliaries should provide the positive evidence for the child to successfully acquire this property. Second, they need to acquire *do* so that they can negate lexical main verbs with the negative auxiliary *doesn't*. Third, triggered by the acquisition of the negative head *n't*, we propose that children reanalyze *not* as a head form of negation, realizing that *n't* is the reduced form of *not*. As we noted, Thornton and Tesan (2007) left open the question of whether the adverb *not* undergoes reanalysis to a head, but it is critical to the explanation of how children converge on the adult grammar that we present in this paper.

With these three changes in place, the non-target use of the 3SGS morpheme in (19c) and (19d) can no longer be generated. The 3SGS morpheme cannot be pronounced on *v* since the Neg head disrupts the chain so that the pronunciation rule cannot apply. Children have acquired *do*, so they can pronounce the inflectional features on *do*, in T. And, assuming that *do* is a better host than the subject constituent, children now use *do* as the host. At that point, the target grammar is in place.

In summary, the important ingredients of the analysis are (i) children start out assuming that *not* is an adverbial, (ii) children have not acquired *do* in the early grammar and (iii) they reanalyze *not* as a head. Together with the uncontroversial assumption that children have not yet internalized the input they are exposed to and start with a more permissive version of (14), we are then able to account for the stage where they produce the 3SGS morpheme in positions which the target grammar does not license.

5 Conclusion

This paper has provided an analysis of children's non-target production of the 3SGS morpheme in English and their transition to a target-like grammar. We have argued that children who grow up learning English start out with a pronunciation rule that does not specify whether the head or the tail of the chain should be pronounced. This means that the 3SGS morpheme can either appear high or low in the structure, viz. on *v* or on T. Part of this involves the starting assumption that *not* is initially an adverbial in children's grammars. Children also have not acquired the paradigm for *do*. When they acquire the latter, two additional changes also happen in tandem: the head form of negation *n't* is acquired alongside a reanalysis of *not* as the head of a NegP. Lastly they acquire the correct pronunciation rule for English, in which 3SGS is pronounced on *v* if the affix is not stranded.

The paper demonstrates the relevance of incorporating data from acquisition when investigating questions concerning grammatical architecture. We have argued that the data from child language support a specific analysis of head movement, one in which head movement is both syntactic and phonological. The developmental data have also shown that any kind of analysis of head movement needs to be able to accommodate children's stages of acquisition. The data we have presented show that children do not converge immediately on the adult grammar. Children take some time to master the morphophonological part of head movement, which coupled with the fact that negation is not initially analysed as a head, gives rise to non-adult productions of sentential negation. In time, children recover, and recategorize negation as a head which triggers convergence on the adult grammar.

Acknowledgements: This chapter is dedicated to Liliane Haegeman, whose work has always impressed and inspired us. We are grateful to two reviewers for helpful comments on a quite different earlier version of this paper. Their feedback definitely contributed to making the paper better. This research was funded, in part, by the Australian Research Council Centre of Excellence in Cognition and its Disorders (CE110001021) www.ccd.edu.au.

References

Adger, David. 2003. *Core syntax*. Oxford: Oxford University Press.
Alexiadou, Artemis, Elena Anagnostopoulou & Florian Schäfer. 2015. *External arguments in transitivity alternations: A layering approach*. Oxford: Oxford University Press.
Baker, Mark. 1985. The Mirror Principle and morphosyntactic explanation. *Linguistic Inquiry* 16. 373–416.
Baker, Mark. 1988. *Incorporation: A theory of grammatical function changing*. Chicago: University of Chicago Press.
Baker, Mark. 2008. *The syntax of agreement and concord*. Cambridge: Cambridge University Press.
Barrie, Michael & Éric Mathieu. 2014. Head movement. In Andrew Carnie, Yosuke Sato & Daniel Siddiqi (eds.), *The Routledge handbook of syntax*, 133–149. London & New York: Routledge.
Bellugi, Ursula. 1967. *The acquisition of the system of negation in children's speech*. Cambridge, MA: Harvard University dissertation.
Bloom, Lois. 1970. *Language development: Form and function in emerging grammars*. Cambridge, MA: The MIT Press.
Bobaljik, Jonathan D. 1995. *Morphosyntax: The syntax of verbal inflection*. Cambridge, MA: MIT dissertation.
Bobaljik, Jonathan D. 2003. Realizing Germanic inflection: Why morphology does not drive syntax. *Journal of Comparative Germanic Linguistics* 6. 129–167.
Bobaljik, Jonathan D & Höskuldur Thráinsson. 1998. Two heads aren't always better than one. *Syntax* 1. 37–71.
Boeckx, Cedric & Sandra Stjepanović. 2001. Head-ing toward PF. *Linguistic Inquiry* 32. 345–355.
Brown, Roger. 1973. *A first language: The early stages*. Cambridge, MA: Harvard University Press.
Cameron-Faulkner, Theo, Elena Lieven & Anna Theakston. 2007. What part of no do children not understand? A usage-based account of multiword negation. *Journal of Child Language* 34(2). 251–282.
Chomsky, Noam. 1957. *Syntactic structures*. The Hague: Mouton.
Chomsky, Noam. 1986. *Barriers*. Cambridge, MA: The MIT Press.
Chomsky, Noam. 1995. *The Minimalist Program*. Cambridge, MA: The MIT Press.
Chomsky, Noam. 2000. Minimalist inquiries: The framework. In Roger Martin, David Michaels, & Juan Uriagereka (eds.), *Step by step: Essays on Minimalist Syntax in honor of Howard Lasnik*, 89–155. Cambridge, MA: The MIT Press.

Chomsky, Noam. 2001. Derivation by Phase. In Michael Kenstowicz (ed.), *Ken Hale: A life in language*, 1–52. Cambridge, MA: The MIT Press.

Cinque, Guglielmo. 1999. *Adverbs and functional heads: A cross-linguistic perspective*. Oxford: Oxford University Press.

Déprez, Viviane & Amy Pierce. Negation and functional projects in early grammar. *Linguistic Inquiry* 24(1). 25–67.

Besten, Hans den. 1983. On the interaction of root transformations and lexical deletive rules. In Werner Abraham (ed.), *On the formal syntax of the Westgermania*, 47–131. Amsterdam: John Benjamins.

Haan, Ger de. 1986. A theory-bound approach to the acquisition of verb-placement in Dutch. In Ger de Hann & Wim Zonneveld (eds.), *Formal parameters of generative grammar*, 15–30. Dordrecht: Foris.

Drozd, Kenneth. Child English: Pre-sentential negation as metalinguistic exclamatory sentence negation. *Journal of Child Language* 22(3). 583–610.

Embick, David & Rolf Noyer. 2001. Movement operations after syntax. *Linguistic Inquiry* 32. 555–598.

Emonds, Joseph. 1978. The verbal complex V' – V in French. *Linguistic Inquiry* 9. 151–175.

Flagg, Elissa. 2002. *Interface issues in the English imperative*. Cambridge, MA: MIT dissertation.

Freidin, Robert. 2004. Syntactic structures redux. *Syntax* 7. 101–127.

Fukui, Naoki. 1986. *A theory of category projection and its applications*. Cambridge, MA: MIT dissertation.

Fukui, Naoki. 1995. *Theory of projection in syntax*. Stanford, CA: CSLI Publications.

Fukui, Naoki. 2006. *Theoretical comparative syntax: Studies in macroparameters*. London: Routledge.

Fukui, Naoki & Hiromu Sakai. 2003. The visibility guideline for functional categories: Verb-raising in Japanese and related issues. *Lingua* 113. 321–375.

Gelderen, Elly van. 1993. *The rise of functional categories*. Amsterdam: John Benjamins.

Guasti, Maria Teresa & Luigi Rizzi. 2002. Agreement and tense as distinct syntactic positions: Evidence from acquisition. In Guglielmo Cinque (ed.), *Functional structure in DP and IP: The cartography of syntactic structures*, vol. 1, 167–194. New York: Oxford University Press.

Haegeman, Liliane. 1995. *The syntax of negation*. Cambridge: Cambridge University Press.

Haegeman, Liliane. 1995b. Root infinitives, tense and truncated structures in Dutch. *Language Acquisition* 4. 205–255.

Haegeman, Liliane & Terje Lohndal. 2010. Negative concord and (multiple) Agree: A case study of West Flemish. *Linguistic Inquiry* 41. 181–211.

Harley, Heidi. 1995. *Subjects, events, and licensing*. Cambridge, MA: MIT dissertation.

Harley, Heidi. 2004. Merge, conflation, and head movement: The First Sister Principle revisited. In Keir Moulton & Matthew Wolf (eds.), *NELS (North East Linguistic Society)* 34. 239–254. Amherst: University of Massachusetts, GLSA.

Harley, Heidi. 2011. Affixation and the Mirror Principle. In Raffaella Folli & Christiane Ulbrich (eds.), *Interfaces in linguistics: New research perspectives*, 166–186. Oxford: Oxford University Press.

Harley, Heidi. 2013. Getting morphemes in order: Merger, affixation, and head movement. In Lisa Lai-Shen Cheng & Norbert Corver (eds.), *Diagnosing syntax*, 112–119. Oxford: Oxford University Press.

Harris, Anthony & Ken Wexler. 1996. The Optional-Infinitive stage in child language: Evidence from negation. In Harald Clahsen (ed.), *Generative perspectives on language acquisition*, 1–42. Amsterdam: John Benjamins.

Holmberg, Anders & Christer Platzack. 1995. *The role of inflection in Scandinavian syntax.* Oxford: Oxford University Press.

Hyams, Nina. 1986. *Language acquisition and the theory of parameters.* Dordrecht: Reidel.

Jordens, Peter. 1990. The acquisition of verb placement in Dutch and German. *Linguistics* 28. 1407–1448.

Julien, Marit. 2002. *Syntactic heads and word formation.* New York: Oxford University Press.

Julien, Marit. 2007. On the relation between morphology and syntax. In Charles Reiss & Gillian Ramchand (eds.), *The Oxford handbook of linguistic interfaces*, 209–238. Oxford: Oxford University Press.

Klima, Edward & Ursula Bellugi. 1966. Syntactic regularities in the speech of children. In John Lyons & Roger Wales (eds.), *Psycholinguistics papers*, 183–208. Ediburgh: Edinburgh University Press.

Koopman, Hilda. 1984. *The syntax of verbs.* Dordrecht: Foris.

Koopman, Hilda & Anna Szabolcsi. 2000. *Verbal complexes.* Cambridge, MA: The MIT Press.

Kratzer, Angelika. 1996. Severing the external argument from the verb. In Johan Rooryck & Laurie Zaring (eds.), *Phrase structure and the lexicon*, 109–137. Dordrecht: Kluwer.

Larson, Richard K. 1988. On the double object construction. *Linguistic Inquiry* 19. 381–405.

Lasnik, Howard. 1981. Restricting the theory of transformations. In Norbert Hornstein & David Lightfoot (eds.), *Explanation in linguistics*, 152–173. London: Longmans.

Lasnik, Howard. 2000. *Syntactic structures revisited.* Cambridge, MA: The MIT Press.

Lebeaux, David S. 1988. *Language acquisition and the form of the grammar.* Amherst MA: University of Massachusetts dissertation.

Lechner, Winfried. 2005. Interpretive effects of head movement. Universität Tübingen manuscript.

MacWhinney, Brian. 2000. *The CHILDES project: Tools for analyzing talk.* Mahwah, NJ: Lawrence Erlbaum.

Mahajan, Anoop. 2000. Eliminating head movement. *GLOW (Generative Linguistics in the Old World) Newsletter* 44. 44–45.

Mahajan, Anoop. 2003. Word order and (remnant) VP movement. In Simin Karimi (ed.), *Word order and scrambling*, 217–237. Oxford: Blackwell.

Matushansky, Ora. 2006. Head movement in linguistic theory. *Linguistic Inquiry* 37. 69–109.

Meisel, Juergen & Natascha Müller. 1992. Finiteness and verb placement in early child grammars: Evidence from simultaneous acquisition of French and German in bilinguals. In Jürgen Meisel (ed.), *The acquisition of verb placement*, 109–138. Dordrecht: Kluwer.

Müller, Gereon. 2004. Verb-second as vP-first. *Journal of Comparative Germanic Linguistics* 7. 179–234.

Nilsen, Øystein. 2003. *Eliminating positions.* Utrecht: Utrecht University dissertation.

Nunes, Jairo. 2004. *Linearization of chains and sideward movement.* Cambridge, MA: MIT Press.

Phillips, Colin. 2010. Syntax at age two: Cross-linguistic differences. *Language Acquisition* 17. 70–120.

Pierce, Amy. 1992. *Language acquisition and linguistic theory: A comparative analysis of French and English child grammars.* Dordrecht & London: Kluwer Academic Publishers.

Poeppel, David & Ken Wexler. 1993. The Full Competence hypothesis of clause structure. *Language* 69. 1–33.

Pollock, Jean-Yves. 1989. Verb movement, Universal Grammar, and the structure of IP. *Linguistic Inquiry* 20. 365–424.
Radford, Andrew. 1990. *Syntactic theory and the acquisition of English syntax*. Oxford: Blackwell.
Radford, Andrew. 1996. Towards a structure-building model of acquisition. In Harald Clahsen (ed.), *Generative perspectives on language acquisition*, 43–89. Amsterdam: John Benjamins.
Radford, Andrew. 2000. Children in search of perfection: Towards a minimalist model of acquisition. *Essex Research Reports in Linguistics* 34.
Rice, Mabel & Ken Wexler. 1996. Towards tense as a clinical marker of specific language impairment in English-speaking children. *Journal of Speech and Hearing Research* 39. 1239–1257.
Rizzi, Luigi. 1994. Some notes on linguistic theory and language development: The case of Root Infinitives. *Language Acquisition* 3. 371–393.
Rizzi, Luigi. 1997. The fine structure of the left periphery. In Liliane Haegeman (ed.), *Elements of grammar*, 281–337. Dordrecht: Kluwer.
Roberts, Ian. 2001. Head movement. In Mark Baltin & Chris Collins (eds.), *The handbook of contemporary syntactic theory*, 113–147. Malden: Blackwell.
Roberts, Ian. 2010. *Agreement and head movement. Clitics, incorporation, and defective goals*. Cambridge, MA: The MIT Press.
Roberts, Ian. 2011. Head movement and the Minimalist Program. In Cedric Boeckx (ed.), *The Oxford handbook of linguistic minimalism*, 195–219. Oxford: Oxford University Press.
Roberts, Ian. 2013. Comments on Grimshaw. *Mind & Language* 28. 560–572.
Sauerland, Uli & Paul Elbourne. 2002. Total reconstruction, PF movement, and derivational order. *Linguistic Inquiry* 33. 283–319.
Schütze, Carson. 2010. The status of non-agreeing *don't* and theories of Root Infinitives. *Language Acquisition* 17. 235–271.
Schütze, Carson & Kenneth Wexler. 1996. Subject case licensing and English Root Infinitives. *Boston University Conference on Child Language Development (BUCLD)* 20. 670–681.
Snyder, William. 2007. *Child language: The parametric approach*. Oxford: Oxford University Press.
Svenonius, Peter. 2007. 1 . 3-2. In Charles Reiss & Gillian Ramchand (eds.), *The Oxford handbook of linguistic interfaces*, 239–288. Oxford: Oxford University Press.
Stowell, Tim. 1981. *Origins of phrase structure*. Cambridge, MA: MIT dissertation.
Theakston, Anna, Elena Lieven & Michael Tomasello. 2003. The role of input in the acquisition of third person singular verbs in English. *Journal of Speech, Language, and Hearing Research* 46. 863–877.
Thornton, Rosalind & Graciela Tesan. 2007. Categorical acquisition: Parameter setting in Universal Grammar. *Biolinguistics* 1. 49–98.
Thornton, Rosalind & Graciela Tesan. 2013. Sentential negation in early child English. *Journal of Linguistics* 49. 367–411. DOI: 10.1017/S0022226712000382
Thornton, Rosalind & Kelly Rombough. 2015. The syntax-PF interface in children's negative sentences. *Language Acquisition* 22. 132–157.
Thráinsson, Höskuldur. 1996. On the (non-)universality of functional categories. In Werner Abraham, Samuel David Epstein, Höskuldur Thráinsson & C. Jan-Wouter Zwart (eds.), *Minimal ideas: Syntactic studies in the Minimalist framework*, 252–281. Amsterdam: John Benjamins.

Thráinsson, Höskuldur. 2003. Syntactic variation, historical development and Minimalism. In Randall Hendrick (ed.), *Minimalist syntax*, 152–191. Malden: Blackwell.
Travis, Lisa. 1984. *Parameters and effects of word order variation*. Cambridge, MA: MIT dissertation.
Vangsnes, Øystein Alexander. 1999. *The identification of functional architecture*. Bergen: University of Bergen dissertation.
Verrips, Maaike & Jürgen Weissenborn. 1992. Routes to verb placement in early German and French: The independence of finiteness and agreement. In Jürgen Meisel (ed.), *The acquisition of verb placement*. Dordrecht: Kluwer.
Vikner, Sten. 1995. *Verb movement and expletive subjects in the Germanic languages*. Oxford: Oxford University Press.
Weissenborn, Jürgen. 1990. Functional categories and verb movement: The acquisition of German syntax reconsidered. In Monika Rothweiler (ed.), *Spracherwerb und Grammatik: Linguistische Untersuchungen zum Erwerb von Syntax und Morphologie*. [Special Issue] *Linguistische Berichte* 3. 190–224.
Westergaard, Marit. 2009. *The acquisition of word order: Micro-cues, information structure, and economy*. Amsterdam: John Benjamins.
Westergaard, Marit. 2013. The acquisition of linguistic variation: Parameters vs. micro-cues. In Terje Lohndal (ed.), *In search of Universal Grammar*, 275–298. Amsterdam: John Benjamins.
Wexler, Kenneth. 1994. Optional Infinitives, head movement, and the economy of derivation in child language. In David Lightfoot & Norbert Hornstein (eds.), *Verb movement*, 288–315. Cambridge: Cambridge University Press.
Wexler, Kenneth. 1998. Very early parameter setting and the unique checking constraint: A new explanation of the Optional Infinitive stage. *Lingua* 106. 23–79.
White, Lydia. 1990/1991. The verb-movement parameter in second language acquisition. *Language Acquisition* 4. 337–360.
Wilson, Stephen. 2003. Lexically specific constructions in the acquisition of inflection in English. *Journal of Child Language* 30. 75–115.
Zeijlstra, Hedde. 2004. *Sentential negation and Negative Concord*. Amsterdam: University of Amsterdam dissertation.
Zeijlstra, Hedde. 2008. On the syntactic flexibility of formal features. In Theresa Biberauer (ed.), *The limits of syntactic variation*, 143–174. Amsterdam: John Benjamins.
Zeijlstra, Hedde. 2012. There is only one way to Agree. *The Linguistic Review* 29. 491–539.
Zwart, C. Jan-Wouter. 2001. Syntactic and phonological verb-movement. *Syntax* 4. 34–62.

Index

Afrikaans 381, 386 fn. 9, 492 fn. 12
A-movement 109 fn. 4, 119, 131, 422, 428, 438, 444
absolute construction 299, 300
adjective 58, 64–65, 76 fn. 13, 77–80, 272, 276–77
adverb 5, 7, 9, 50, 54, 57–97, 99–100, 102 fn. 1, 104, 179, 194 fn. 4, 225, 233 fn. 18, 248, 294, 301–315, 325, 418 fn. 10, 434 fn. 23, 447–461, 464–468, 472, 473, 494, 495, 512, 513, 516, 519, 522
adverb classes 60 fn. 1, 68
adverbial clauses 57, 58, 94, 100, 191 fn. 2, 301, 302, 320, 322, 428, 436, 437, 440
Agree 15–17, 20–21, 28, 33 fn. 18, 59, 68, 87, 90, 114–115, 134, 236, 288, 336–343, 361, 515–520
Albanian 2, 7, 284, 286 fn. 1, 291, 292, 293, 294, 295
Alemannic 185, 186, 188, 192, 213
allocutive agreement 7, 251, 283–287, 290–295
Ancient Greek 62, 482, 483, 484, 487–491
appositive 7, 299–315, 321, 322
aspect 61–65, 70–73, 77, 85, 87–89, 174 fn. 25, 307, 319, 504
auxiliary (see also negative auxiliary) 9, 36 fn. 21, 41, 60, 62, 84, 89, 264 fn. 3, 304, 380 fn. 5, 401–443, 447–449, 461–472, 502–506, 518
avertive 5, 153, 166, 169, 170

Bantu 8, 251 fn. 30, 315, 353–354, 360
bare reflexive constructions 275–281
Basque 251, 285, 286 fn. 1
Bavarian 185, 186, 188, 189, 196 fn. 6, 213
Belfast English 185
bundling 264, 270, 274–75, 281

cartography, cartographic approach 5, 7, 22, 59, 86, 87, 90, 143, 283, 306, 319, 335, 338, 344
causative 4, 13–43, 60, 83, 87, 262, 271, 378

chain (see also chain-uniformity, clitic chain, T-chain) 9, 21, 30, 358, 500, 514–523
chain-uniformity 191
Chinese 361
ci-sentences 6, 243–246
clitic chain 495
cliticization 3, 36, 122, 192, 193, 196, 216, 263, 363
competing grammars, see grammar competition
complementizer 3, 5, 6, 58, 107, 110–113, 115, 116, 123, 133, 153–166, 169–170, 173–180, 185, 190–196, 335–337, 355, 483, 484, 486
complex verb 143, 373, 375, 377
construal 57–67, 75–78, 83, 85–91, 93, 169 fn. 19
control 51–53, 83, 139–140
criterion, criterial 23, 24, 25 fn. 11, 32, 33, 34, 37, 38, 43, 334, 337–340, 343, 345, 359
– criterial freezing 8, 32, 33, 37, 38, 39, 42, 349, 358–366
– criterial head 4, 13, 31, 32, 37, 365
– Subject Criterion 8, 23, 349, 359, 360, 362
– Wh Criterion 8, 349, 360, 361
Czech 264, 512

D-linking 188, 333 fn. 6, 352, 356 fn. 4
Danish 8, 375–378, 382, 383, 387–394
discourse particle 9, 221, 250, 352, 458, 459, 460, 471, 477–497
do-support 516, 519
doubly-filled COMP 6, 185
DP projection 300, 310, 315
Dutch 194, 195, 265, 322, 371, 372, 378 fn. 2, 381, 383, 384, 386 fn. 9, 394, 432, 501, 512

Early Modern English 469, 470
ecco 6, 221–255
ECM 26–29, 371, 376, 393
economy 58, 190, 191, 467, 471
ECP 350 fn. 1, 357–58

ellipsis 99–143, 374
English (see also Belfast English, Early Modern English, Irish English, Middle English, Late Modern English, Old English) 1–5, 7–9, 13, 25 fn. 11, 26, 27, 29–32, 39, 42, 47–54, 61–93, 101, 102, 104, 106, 114, 117, 118, 119, 124, 125, 131, 141 fn. 21, 157, 158, 166, 185, 222, 223 fn. 5, 234, 237, 249, 265, 269, 272, 275, 276, 299–315, 320–324, 326, 329, 336, 339, 340, 344, 345, 357, 366, 371–387, 393, 394, 432–435, 447–454, 461, 469 fn. 18/19, 470–473, 500, 512, 515–523
EPP/Extended Projection Principle 8, 103, 194 fn. 4, 349, 416–420, 426, 435, 444
extended projection 103, 106, 110, 122, 127, 136, 143
extraposition 384–385, 405–412, 416, 431–435, 437

fare-*a* 15, 16, 19, 20, 24, 32
fare-*da* 15, 18, 19, 20, 32
Faroese 377
feature
– agreement 59, 195, 517
– aspect 62, 64
– cause 31
– checking 291, 295, 340
– clause-typing 163
– criterial 24, 334
– EPP 416, 418
– finiteness 301, 303, 523
– focus 334, 342, 364, 365, 491
– formal 59, 75
– interrogative (wh, Q) 190, 333, 334, 345, 365
– LEX 514, 515
– locative 231, 241, 249
– modal 155, 166, 288
– negative 107, 112, 114–116, 123, 155
– number 51, 62, 73
– operator 321, 332–334, 342
– phi 236, 288, 290, 417, 521
– speech act 284
– tense 5, 57, 59, 61–63, 93, 516
– topic 324 fn. 1, 332, 334

– verbal 232, 241, 242 fn. 26, 492
– other 6, 109 fn. 4, 138 fn. 19, 154, 159, 165, 167, 223, 226, 235, 248, 283, 284, 287, 301, 359, 366
Final-Over-Final Constraint (FOFC) 418
Finnish 124 fn. 10, 482
floating quantifier, see quantifier float
focus 5, 8, 59, 69, 76, 78, 86, 88, 119–125, 142–143, 163, 171–172, 173 fn. 23, 174–176, 190, 202–203, 214, 245, 278, 288, 301–302, 321, 324–332, 341–345, 349, 350, 358, 361–365, 434, 452, 453, 491–492
free indirect discourse 234, 235, 240, 248
French 6, 7, 8, 13, 14, 26, 35–38, 50, 54 fn. 9, 62, 79, 83, 85 fn. 19, 157, 158, 166, 192, 222, 231 fn. 10, 232 fn. 16, 249, 250–252, 259–281, 299–315, 320, 339, 350–362, 364 fn. 9, 434, 500, 501, 516
Frisian (see also Old Frisian) 372, 386 fn. 9
functional head 5, 15, 17, 20, 27, 58, 86, 116, 119, 126, 138, 139, 143, 223, 231, 233, 235, 240, 241, 267, 303, 304, 319, 320, 416, 418
functional projection 5, 7, 58, 59, 178, 268, 269, 281, 304–307, 310, 413 fn. 8, 416, 459, 512, 516
functional structure 13, 16, 17, 26, 27, 31, 40, 300, 303–306, 315, 401, 418

German (see also Alemannic, Bavarian, Hessian, Old High German, Swiss German) 6, 8, 85 fn. 19, 121, 141 fn. 21, 185, 191, 194 fn. 4, 195, 196, 200, 214, 216 fn. 14, 217, 249, 259–282, 371, 372, 378–394, 501, 512
Germanic (see also Proto-Germanic) 2, 8, 9, 194, 196, 206, 371, 372, 374, 378, 380, 386 fn. 9, 393, 413, 477–486, 490–495, 501
Gothic 9, 477–495
grammar competition 404, 408, 409, 416, 424–426, 443, 444
grammaticalization 3, 193, 477, 481, 482, 483, 485, 492, 493, 495
Greek (see also Ancient Greek) 265, 295
Gungbe 260, 261, 274–281, 325 fn. 2, 329

Index — 531

head movement 100, 103, 114, 116, 122, 126–127, 131–132, 141–143, 291, 292, 294, 295, 402, 500, 507, 513, 523
heaviness (see also weight) 453, 461
Hebrew 90, 114, 127–130, 142, 143, 222 fn. 2, 227 fn. 7, 265
Hessian 194
Hungarian 2, 5, 118 fn. 6, 124 fn. 10, 142, 153–181, 265, 337, 338, 340, 344 fn. 7

Icelandic 385, 482
imperative 7, 9, 130, 155, 156, 163, 173, 174 fn. 24, 179, 180, 230 fn. 9, 232 fn. 14/16, 242 fn. 26, 249, 283–295, 477, 480–489, 492, 493, 495
indexical 6, 221, 233–236, 239, 240, 248
information structure 76, 86, 461, 471, 473, 501 fn. 3
interface 3, 7, 22–25, 31, 57, 58, 61, 71, 75, 80, 92, 217, 283, 295, 319, 320, 326–329, 338, 341, 344, 345, 361
Irish English 101
Italian 4, 6, 7, 13–42, 90, 192, 222–251, 295, 320–332, 334–343, 363–365, 482, 512

Japanese 129 fn. 13, 130, 336, 340, 357, 361

Late Modern English 9, 448, 455, 456, 457, 463, 464, 468, 469, 470, 473
labeling 4, 13–46, 320, 340, 365, 366
latent C-feature 188–191, 201
Latin 8, 9, 222 fn. 2, 223 fn. 6, 232 fn. 16, 249, 401–444, 482
Latvian 482, 483, 484
left periphery 3, 7, 22, 27, 69, 88, 163, 189, 221–224, 231, 235, 240, 248–252, 283, 284, 287, 295, 319–329, 335, 360–364, 366, 409, 427–429
locality 7, 13, 21, 22, 26, 30, 39, 40, 49, 109 fn. 4, 170, 319–334, 340–344, 358
locative 6, 81, 83, 92, 221–249, 482–486, 492, 495
Low German 372, 386 fn. 9
ly-adverbs 57–94

Middle English 455 fn. 8, 457, 459, 460, 461, 464, 465, 469, 472

Minimize Domains (MiD) 450, 451, 468, 470, 471
modal 5, 57, 58, 60, 69, 73, 82–83, 87–89, 91, 126, 154–156, 160–161, 165–166, 174, 180, 302, 404, 414–416, 421, 509, 513, 518
monosyllabic wh-constituent 6, 185–188, 192 fn. 3, 197–206, 209–217

n-insertion, n-intrusion 192–194, 214–216
narrative 78–79, 81, 86, 94 fn. 21, 234, 235, 240, 242 fn. 27
negation 3, 5, 6, 60, 73 fn. 9, 87, 89, 106–117, 119, 126, 153–181, 311, 315, 362, 420, 460 fn. 13, 501–523
negative auxiliary 504, 505, 512–514, 522
Negative Concord 512
non-restrictive relative clause 7, 299, 302
Norwegian 377, 378, 382 fn. 7, 393, 501 fn. 3
NP-adjunct 9, 447–475

object shift 405–408, 412–415, 416, 423–424, 438–441
Old English 9, 447, 455 fn. 8, 456–460, 463–466, 471, 473, 477–484, 495
Old Frisian 477–479, 495
Old High German 477–479, 482, 490, 494, 495
Old Norse 477–485, 490, 494, 495
Old Romanian 284, 294
Old Saxon 477–479, 483–485
Optional Infinitive stage 9, 501, 502, 504, 506, 513, 520
OV/VO alternation 401–444

passive 14, 15, 17, 19, 22, 28, 29, 32, 33, 35–38, 39–42, 269, 381–383, 393, 413, 421 fn. 12, 422–424
PF, Phonological Form 9, 194 fn. 4, 217, 291 fn. 5, 295, 500, 514, 516–518, 520
polarity 5, 108 fn. 3, 109 fn. 4, 114–127, 134, 138 fn. 19, 143, 177
Portuguese 8, 26, 42 fn. 26, 128, 142, 354, 355, 360
predicate inversion 4, 47–49, 50 fn. 5, 51
predication 4, 23, 48, 49, 54, 65, 82, 134, 135, 139, 452

preposition 8, 15, 19, 61, 191 fn. 2, 232 fn. 13, 262, 271, 371–394, 451
prepositional passive 381, 382
presentative 6, 221–251
PRO 51–54, 140, 236
pro 51–54, 360
processing 9, 295 fn. 6, 334, 450, 452, 461, 467–473
pronoun
– clitic (pronoun) 7, 17, 18, 20, 25 fn. 11, 36, 37, 90, 122, 188, 190–196, 203–216, 222, 231, 232, 240–250, 262, 267, 285–295, 322, 326 fn. 3, 351, 354, 363, 481, 493 fn. 13, 495
– clitic-left-dislocation 301 fn. 1, 320
– demonstrative 205, 405, 407, 423, 486 fn. 7, 492,
– null 7
– possessive 192 fn. 3, 275, 277
– reflexive (clitic) 6, 41, 259–281, 284, 289, 291, 314
– resumptive 136, 321, 330 fn. 5, 345
– silent 51
– strong 190, 203, 231, 267, 278, 280, 493 fn. 13
– weak 190, 203, 204, 267, 493 fn. 13
– other 53, 120, 122, 123, 192 fn. 3, 194–196, 203–205, 214–217, 236, 296, 302, 377 fn. 1, 424, 458, 459, 486 fn. 7, 494
Pronunciation Rule 9, 518, 520–523
prosody 6, 185, 187, 188, 199, 213, 216, 217, 308 fn. 2
Proto-Germanic 9, 477, 478, 481, 483–485, 492, 495
purposive 155–57, 161, 165–170, 174 fn. 24, 175, 178

quantifier float 3, 4, 47–54, 311–315

reanalysis 9, 160 fn. 7, 191 fn. 2, 193, 289, 290, 294, 295, 419, 420, 440, 465, 470, 471, 473, 493, 522, 523
reflexivization 260, 264, 269–270, 279
register 3, 137, 284, 286, 287, 447, 449, 450, 453, 471–473
reinforced demonstrative 9, 477–482, 485, 493, 495

relative clause (see also non-restrictive relative clause) 48 fn. 3, 100, 321, 353, 432, 433
Relativized Minimality (featural) 21, 320, 322, 324, 336, 340–342, 343–344, 362 fn. 7
Romance 2, 4, 13, 14, 22, 23, 25, 26, 27, 29, 39–42, 61, 62, 64, 195, 223 fn. 6, 232 fn. 13, 264, 267, 288, 301 fn. 1, 321, 322, 324 fn. 1, 330 fn. 5, 342, 344, 345, 401, 422, 444, 501
Romanian (see also Old Romanian) 7, 242 fn. 26, 249 fn. 28, 250, 283, 284, 286, 288, 289, 292–296, 482, 492

scope 60, 69, 74, 83, 89, 91–92, 113, 118–119, 162, 163, 165–166, 169, 175–176, 349, 358, 426
selection 59, 71, 109, 115, 134, 162, 166, 169–170, 179, 320, 334–345
separable particle 8, 371–393
Serbian 222, 295
Serbo-Croatian 249, 265
silent noun 51, 53–54
smuggling 4, 13, 14, 16, 18, 21, 22, 39–42
SOV 8, 271, 371, 372, 378–381, 383–386, 387, 393, 394
Spanish 295, 336–338, 340, 482
speech act 7, 68, 88, 231 fn. 12, 242 fn. 26, 283, 284, 287, 291, 295
structural ambiguity 405, 406, 408, 409, 425, 426, 431, 436, 439, 440, 442
subextraction 362–365, 428 fn. 15
subject extraction 358, 359
subject-object asymmetry 349, 355, 357, 359
subjunctive 154–162, 165, 168 fn. 17, 180, 295
subordinator 153–154, 160, 161, 162, 164–166, 169, 170, 178, 180, 322
successive cyclicity 49, 50
SVO 8, 371, 372, 374–378, 379, 380, 382, 383–386, 387, 393, 394
Swedish 375, 377, 378, 380 fn. 3 and fn. 4, 382 fn. 7, 492 fn. 12, 501
Swiss German 6, 185–218, 482

T-chain (Tense chain) 5, 57, 61–64, 65 fn. 4, 67, 74, 75, 85, 87, 90, 92, 93

temporal element 221–223, 226, 233
tense 5, 62–64, 73, 75–76, 80, 87, 89, 91, 93, 103, 112, 130, 132–141, 232, 235, 241, 248, 303, 305, 319, 502–504, 506, 507, 509, 510, 515–517
Tense chain (see T-chain)
topic 64, 86, 88, 109 fn. 4, 163, 171–173, 179, 230, 235, 246, 247, 301–303, 320–344, 349, 358, 493
trochaic foot 188, 200, 206, 210–217
Turkish 222
type 114, 126, 143, 153, 162–164, 169, 174

underspecification 506
underspecified 191, 506, 510, 512
unstressed 195, 199, 201, 204–207, 210, 212, 214, 217, 481

verb initial order 99–143
verb movement 5, 156, 174, 231 fn. 11, 289, 291, 339, 417, 460, 461, 465–467, 473, 500, 501, 514, 515
verb particle 8, 371, 372, 383, 384, 392 fn. 14
verb raising 89, 104, 117, 128, 131, 134, 501

verbal chunk 17 fn. 5, 23–25, 29, 30, 33 fn. 18, 34, 37, 39
verbal identity condition 128–132, 141–143
verum focus 5, 121–123, 214
voice head (see also passive) 6, 7, 105, 120 fn. 7, 269–271, 280–281, 402–404, 431, 436, 517
– causative 4, 13, 16, 17, 19, 20, 23–43

voici 222 fn. 2, 232 fn. 16, 249

Wackernagel 193, 195, 494
weight (see also heaviness) 207, 212, 216, 334, 407, 425, 426, 435, 452
West Flemish 3, 185, 194, 195, 221, 250, 482, 492, 493
wh in situ 349–366
wh-element, wh-item, wh-word 154, 160, 185, 188–193, 196–199, 201, 202, 215, 333, 335, 337, 344 fn. 7, 350, 352, 353, 427, 439

Yiddish 8, 371, 372, 381, 383–386, 387–394, 412